INTERNATIONAL HUMAN RESOURCE MANAGEMENT

SEVENTH EDITION

**PETER J. DOWLING
MARION FESTING
ALLEN D. ENGLE, SR.**

CENGAGE
Learning

Australia • Brazil • Mexico • Singapore • United Kingdom • United States

CENGAGE
Learning®

International Human Resource Management, 7th Edition
Peter J. Dowling, Marion Festing and Allen D. Engle, Sr.

Publisher: Andrew Ashwin

Development Editor: Jennifer Grene

Content Project Manager:
Phillipa Davidson-Blake

Manufacturing Buyer: Eyvett Davis

Marketing Manager: Vicky Pavlicic

Typesetter: Lumina Datamatics, Inc.

Cover design: Cyan Design

Cover image: Baloncici/Shutterstock Inc.

For product information and technology assistance,
contact **emea.info@cengage.com**.

For permission to use material from this text or product,
and for permission queries,
email **emea.permissions@cengage.com**.

British Library Cataloguing-in-Publication Data

A catalogue record for this book is available from the British Library.

ISBN: 978-1-4737-1902-6

Cengage Learning EMEA
Cheriton House, North Way, Andover, Hampshire, SP10 5BE, United Kingdom

Cengage Learning products are represented in Canada by Nelson Education Ltd

For your lifelong learning solutions, visit **www.cengage.co.uk**

Purchase your next print book or e-book at **www.cengagebrain.com**

Printed in Singapore by Seng Lee Press
Print Number 03   Print Year 2020

BRIEF CONTENTS

CONTENTS

PREFACE

In writing the Preface for the 7th Edition of *International Human Resource Management* two important published documents illustrate the context for HRM in International Business in the first quarter of the 21st Century. One is the Internet document *Decent Work and the 2030 Agenda for Sustainable Development* published by the International Labour Organization (ILO) which states that "over 600 million new jobs need to be created by 2030, just to keep pace with the growth of the working-age population. That is around 40 million per year. We also need to improve conditions for the 780 million women and men who are working but not earning enough to lift themselves and their families out of US\$2-a-day poverty". In addition, we observe the demographic challenges of low birth rates in many industrialized countries and a lack of qualified talent.

A second document is the *Special Report on Companies* published by *The Economist* (17 Sept. 2016) titled *The rise of the superstars*. This report notes that "a small group of giant companies (some old, some new) are once again dominating the global economy" and asks the question "Is that a good or a bad thing?". There is also a chart which lists the world's ten largest listed companies by market capitalization in billions of US dollars in 2006 and 2016. The 2016 companies are Apple, Alphabet, Microsoft, Berkshire Hathaway, Exxon Mobil, Amazon, Facebook, Johnson & Johnson, General Electric and China Mobile. Of this list only Microsoft, Exxon Mobil and General Electric were on the 2006 list, indicating the extent of change in what *The Economist* describes as "a virtually new world" (page 5).

We also acknowledge the so-called megatrends highlighted by many authors, mainly from consulting firms. An important issue they address is the complex and ongoing effect of demographic shifts on global business practices. In part, many countries are characterized by higher life expectancies and lower birth rates. This is not only a challenge for the social welfare systems[1] but also for companies and their human resource management.

According to this and other studies other challenges include the rise of the individual, the enabling technology and digitalization, the interconnected global economy, new market and global responsibilities as well as a rise in entrepreneurship[2]. In preparing the 7th Edition the authors have attempted to pay considerable care and attention to this new world of international business.

The world of global business is very different than it was in 1990 when the first edition of this text was introduced. Our task remains to capture key human issues, those complexities, challenges, and choices faced by individuals and organizations engaged in global business and exchange. This world remains as compelling and critical as it was some 27 years ago.

The more significant changes to the Seventh Edition include the following:

Several of the IHRM in Action cases embedded throughout the chapters have been significantly updated. These changes will help students grasp the principles and models in the chapter and better apply these ideas to a range of settings or contexts.

A new case, written particularly for this edition, has been added in the area of career development and repatriation. The nine in-depth cases at the end of the text have been written by the co-authors or solicited from global experts to provide a range of in-depth applications for all of the major functional areas of IHRM. Extensive teaching notes are provided for adopters of the text. Long time users of the text will find a more systematic and extensive set of cases, but hopefully our loyal adopters will still find some of their favorite cases remain as well. Our feedback on these end-of-text cases was outstandingly positive in the 6th edition and we feel this new edition builds on that strength.

As in previous editions, the challenge of this Seventh Edition has been to organize the complexities particular to HRM activities in MNEs in such a way that provides teachers (of both undergraduate and graduate students) real choice as to how they will present the material. We have tried to find a balance that is meaningful and appropriate to the varying cultures represented by potential adopters and readers, and across educational traditions, institutions, and forms, while accurately capturing the compelling realities facing HRM professionals in MNEs. As always, we welcome your comments and suggestions for improvement in this task.

The author team remains an excellent example of collaborative work (across a significant number of time zones) in the 21st century with tri-continental representation from the Asia Pacific, Europe, and North America.

ENDNOTES

1. www.kpmg.com/Global/en/IssuesAndInsights/ ArticlesPublications/future-state-government/Documents/ future-state-2030-v3.pdf

2. see also www.rolandberger.com/gallery/ trend-compendium/tc2030/content/assets/ trendcompendium2030.pdf; www.ey.com/Publication/ vwLUAssets/ey-megatrends-report-2015/$FILE/ey-megatrends-report-2015.pdf

ACKNOWLEDGMENTS

First we would like to thank the scores of academics and practitioners who have come up to us at conferences and workshops, as well as communicated by emails sent over the last four years, sharing with us their comments and suggestions. Many of the improvements to this new edition of the book outlined above are the direct result of these conversations. The tricky task of balancing the need for continuity and meeting expectations for an enduring and highly successful title with the need to update and revise materials in what is still a very young and dynamic academic area of study is made easier by the support of our peers and colleagues around the world. We thank you for your patience, ongoing interest in and commitment to our book.

As with previous editions, we have received a great deal of assistance from numerous colleagues in various educational institutions and organizations across the globe. Particular thanks go to the following colleagues for their assistance with this edition of the book:

Ruth Alas; Estonian Business School

John Boudreau; University of Southern California

Helen De Cieri; Monash University

Barry Gerhart; University of Wisconsin-Madison

Wolfgang Mayrhofer; Vienna University of Economics and Business

Mark Mendenhall; University of Tennessee-Chattanooga

Molly Pepper; Gonzaga University

József Poór; Szent István University Gödöllö, Hungary

Susanne Royer; University of Flensburg

Hugh Scullion; National University of Ireland, Galway

Günter Stahl; Vienna University of Economics and Business

Shuming Zhao; Nanjing University

Cherrie Zhu; Monash University

Particular thanks go to Maike Andresen, Claudia Fischer, Manfred Froehlecke, Martine Cardel Gertsen, Yvonne McNulty, Ihar Sahakiants, and Mette Zølner for their case contributions.

We also gratefully acknowledge the support of the following institutions:

LA TROBE UNIVERSITY

Peter Dowling thanks Tim Majoribanks, Associate Head of the School of Business and his HRM and International Business colleagues for providing a supportive academic environment.

ESCP EUROPE, BERLIN CAMPUS

Marion Festing thanks the Dean of ESCP Europe, Professor Frank Bournois and her colleagues for providing a supportive environment for writing and research. Special thanks go to the team of the Chair of Human Resource Management and Intercultural Leadership for outstanding support.

EASTERN KENTUCKY UNIVERSITY

Allen Engle thanks the EKU Foundation Board, Harold Glenn Campbell as well as Lana Carnes, Chair of the Department of Management, Marketing and International Business in the College of Business and Technology for their ongoing financial support of research and travel. He would also like to acknowledge the longstanding technical and creative help of Ron Yoder and Florencia Tosiani.

The assistance from staff at Cengage Learning UK has been greatly appreciated. In particular, we thank our Publisher, Annabel Ainscow, for her ongoing assistance and advice with this edition and Jenny Grene for all of her work on the production of the book.

The Publisher would like to thank the following academics who supplied feedback on this and the previous edition:

Mark Williams; University of Surrey

Rachel Williams; Cardiff University

Elaine Farndale; Penn State University

Rosmini Omar; University Teknologi Malaysia

Nancy Long; San Jose State University

Peter Mclean; University of Wollongong NSW

Jay Leighton; Curtin University of Technology

Anne-Marie Francesco; Hong Kong Baptist University

Alan Burton-Jones; Bond University

Finally, our personal thanks to the following individuals for their understanding, support, and encouragement throughout the process of completing this Seventh Edition:

Fiona Dowling

Christian Daubenspeck, Janik and Annika

Elizabeth Hoffman Engle, Kathryn, Caroline and Allen Engle

Peter J. Dowling,
Melbourne

Marion Festing,
Berlin

Allen D. Engle, Sr.,
Richmond, Kentucky

ABOUT THE AUTHORS

PETER J. DOWLING (PhD, Flinders University) is Professor of International Management and Strategy at La Trobe University, Melbourne, Australia. Previous academic appointments include the University of Melbourne, Monash University, the University of Tasmania and Victoria University of Wellington. He has also held visiting appointments in the USA at Cornell University and Michigan State University and in Germany at the University of Paderborn and the University of Bayreuth. He has co-authored a number of books including *Strategic Management: Competitiveness and Globalization* (Pacific Rim, 3rd ed.) and *Human Resource Management in Australia* (2nd ed.) and written or co-authored over 70 journal articles and book chapters. He was Founding Editor of *Asia Pacific Journal of Human Resources* (1987–1996); one of three Editors-in-Chief of the *International Journal of Human Resource Management* (2012–2015); and serves on the editorial boards of *Asia Pacific Journal of Human Resources*; *International Studies of Management & Organization*; *Management International Review*; *Thunderbird International*; and *ZfP-German Journal of Human Resource Research*.

Peter is currently President of the Australia and New Zealand International Business Academy, a Life Fellow of the Australian Human Resources Institute and a Life Fellow of the Australian and New Zealand Academy of Management. Former roles include past President of the Australian and New Zealand Academy of Management and past President of the International Federation of Scholarly Associations of Management.

MARION FESTING (PhD, University of Paderborn) is Professor of Human Resource Management and Intercultural Leadership at ESCP Europe, and Rector of the Berlin Campus as well as the former European Dean of Research of this business school. Previous appointments include the University of Paderborn, Germany. Marion has gained educational, research and work experience in France, Australia, Tunisia, Taiwan and the USA. She has co-authored and edited a number of books, including a monograph on Strategic International Human Resource Management (*Strategisches Internationales Personalmanagement*, 2nd ed.) and a co-authored text on International Human Resource Management (*Internationales Personalmanagement*, 3rd ed.). Marion has also written or co-authored over 100 book chapters and journal articles and published in international journals such as *Academy of Management Perspectives*, *Human Resource Management*, *Human Resource Management Review*, *International Journal of Human Resource Management*, *Journal of World Business*, *Thunderbird International Business Review*, *Economic and Industrial Demography*, *European Management Journal*, *European Journal of International Management*,

Journal for East European Management Studies and *International Journal of Globalization and Small Business*. Recently, together with her colleagues she was awarded a best paper award at the Academy of Management Conference in Vancouver (2015) for her work on the impact of international business education on career success.

Marion is the Co-Editor of the German Journal of *Human Resource Management* and serves on various editorial boards. She is also the German ambassador of the HR-Division of the Academy of Management and is involved in many academic organizations. In 2012 she was the co-track chair (HRM) of the IFSAM conference in Limerick/Ireland in 2012. In 2013 she organized the 11th EIASM Workshop on International Strategy and Cross-Cultural Management at the Berlin Campus of ESCP Europe. In 2014 she organized the 3rd EIASM workshop on Talent Management, also at the Berlin Campus of ESCP Europe in the context of her responsibilities as the Academic Director of the ESCP Europe Talent Management Institute.

Her current research interests focus on transnational HRM strategies, global performance management, global careers, global talent management and global rewards and diversity and inclusion.

ALLEN D. ENGLE, SR. (DBA, University of Kentucky) is a Professor of Management in the College of Business and Technology and Foundation Professor at Eastern Kentucky University, where he holds the Harold Glenn Campbell Endowed Chair in International Business. He is a national and regional professional member of World at Work (formerly the American Compensation Association) and of the Society for Human Resource Management, and a long-time member of the US Academy of Management and the Academy of International Business. While at Eastern, he has taught courses in management (undergraduate and graduate), a number of areas within human resource administration, organizational behavior, organizational theory and international management (undergraduate and graduate). For nine years he held an appointment as Visiting Professor at ESCP Europe in Berlin. He has been Visiting Lecturer at the FHS Hochschule Für Technik, Wirtschaft und Soziale Arbeit, St Gallen in Switzerland and Visiting Professor of International Management at the University of Pécs in Hungary. Allen is a founding member of the Central and Eastern European International Research Team (CEEIRT).

His research interests are in the topic areas of compensation theory and practices, global performance management, leadership and organizational change, job analysis, managerial competencies and organizational design, particularly as they impact on multinational firms. He has published in regional, national and international academic journals, presenting academic papers on many of the topic areas presented above at conferences in the USA, Australia, Canada, the Czech Republic, Estonia, France, Germany, Hungary, Ireland, Italy, Japan, Poland, Slovenia, Spain and the UK. Allen has consulted for regional firms and presented professional seminars in the areas of performance-appraisal systems, executive team building, strategically responsive compensation systems, intercultural management issues and organizational change.

CENGAGE
Learning®

Digital Support Resources

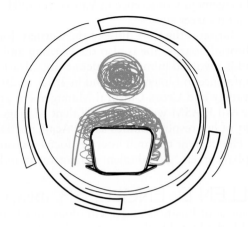

All of our Higher Education textbooks are accompanied by a range of digital support resources. Each title's resources are carefully tailored to the specific needs of the particular book's readers. Examples of the kind of resources provided include:

- A password protected area for instructors with, for example, a testbank, PowerPoint slides and an instructor's manual.

- An open-access area for students including, for example, useful weblinks and glossary terms.

Lecturers: to discover the dedicated lecturer digital support resources accompanying this textbook please register here for access: login.cengage.com.

Students: to discover the dedicated student digital support resources accompanying this textbook, please search for **International Human Resource Management** on: cengagebrain.co.uk

ENGAGED WITH YOU | **www.cengage.co.uk**

CHAPTER 1
INTRODUCTION

Chapter Objectives

In this introductory chapter, we establish the scope of the book. We:

- define key terms in **international human resource management** (IHRM) and consider several definitions of IHRM

- introduce the historically significant issue of expatriate assignment management and review the evolution of these assignments to reflect the increasing diversity with regard to what constitutes international work and the type and length of international assignments

- outline the differences between domestic and international **human resource management** (HRM) and detail a model that summarizes the variables that moderate these differences, and

- present the complexity of IHRM; the increasing potential for challenges to existing IHRM practices and current models; and the increasing awareness of a wide number of choices within IHRM practices due to increased transparency and faster and more detailed diffusion of these practices across organizational units and firms.

SCOPE OF THE BOOK

The field of IHRM has been characterized by three broad approaches.[1] The first approach[2] emphasizes cross-cultural management: examining human behavior within organizations from an international perspective. A second approach developed from the comparative industrial relations and HRM literature[3] and seeks to describe, compare, and analyze HRM systems in various countries. A third approach seeks to focus on aspects of HRM in multinational firms.[4] These approaches are depicted in Figure 1.1. In this book, we take the third approach. Our objective is to explore the implications that the process of internationalization has for the activities and policies of HRM. In particular, we are interested in how HRM is practiced in multinational enterprises.

FIGURE 1.1   Interrelationships between approaches to the field

As Figure 1.1 demonstrates, there is an inevitable overlap between the three approaches when one is attempting to provide an accurate view of the global realities of operating in the international business environment. Obviously, cross-cultural management issues are important when dealing with the cultural aspects of foreign operations. Some of these aspects will be taken up in Chapter 2, where we deal with the cultural context of HRM in the **host country** context – indicated by (a) in Figure 1.1. Chapter 9 deals with international industrial relations and the global institutional context and draws on literature from the comparative industrial relations field – (b) in the above figure. While the focus of much of this book is on the established MNE – a firm which owns or controls business activities in more than one foreign country – we recognize that small, internationalizing firms which are yet to reach multinational firm status, and family-owned firms, also face IHRM issues and many of these issues are addressed in Chapter 4.

DEFINING IHRM

Before we can offer a definition of IHRM, we should first define the general field of HRM. Typically, HRM refers to those activities undertaken by an organization to effectively utilize its **human resources (HR)**. These activities would include at least the following:

- HR planning
- staffing (recruitment, selection, placement)
- performance management
- training and development
- compensation (remuneration) and benefits
- industrial relations.

The question is, of course, which activities change when HRM goes international? An excellent early model developed by Morgan[5] is very helpful in terms of answering this question. Morgan presents IHRM in three dimensions:

1 The broad HR activities of procurement, allocation, and utilization. (These three broad activities can be easily expanded into the six HR activities listed above.)

2 The *national or country categories* involved in IHRM activities:

   ● the host-country where a subsidiary may be located

   ● the parent-country where the firm is headquartered, and

   ● *'other' countries* that may be the source of labor, finance, and other inputs.

3 The *three categories of employees of an international firm*:

   ● host-country nationals (HCNs)

   ● parent-country nationals (PCNs), and

   ● third-country nationals (TCNs).

Thus, for example, the US multinational IBM employs British citizens in its British operations (HCNs), often sends US citizens (PCNs) to Asia-Pacific countries on assignment, and may send some of its Singaporean employees on an assignment to its Chinese operations (as TCNs). The nationality of the employee is a major factor in determining the person's 'category', which in turn is frequently a major driver of the employee's compensation and employment contract.

Morgan defines IHRM as the interplay among the three dimensions of *human resource activities*, *countries of operation*, and *type of employees*. We can see that in broad terms IHRM involves the same activities as **domestic HRM** (e.g. procurement refers to HR planning and staffing). However, domestic HRM is involved with employees *within only one national boundary*. Increasingly, domestic HRM is taking on some of the flavor of IHRM as it deals more and more with a multicultural workforce. Thus, some of the current focus of domestic HRM on issues of managing workforce diversity may prove to be beneficial to the practice of IHRM. However, it must be remembered that the way in which diversity is managed within a *single national, legal, and cultural context* may not necessarily transfer to a multinational context without some modification.

What is an expatriate?

One obvious difference between domestic and IHRM is that staff are moved across national boundaries into various roles within the international firm's foreign operations – these employees have traditionally been called '**expatriates**'. An expatriate is an employee who is working and temporarily residing in a foreign country. Many firms prefer to call such employees 'international assignees'. While it is clear in the literature that PCNs are always expatriates, it is often overlooked that TCNs are also expatriates, as are HCNs who are transferred into parent-country operations outside their own home country.[6] Figure 1.2 illustrates how all three categories may become expatriates.

The term '**inpatriate**' has come into vogue to signify the transfer of subsidiary staff into the parent-country (headquarters) operations.[7] For many managers this term has added a level of confusion surrounding the definition of an expatriate. The (US) Society for Human Resource Management defines an inpatriate as a 'foreign manager in the US'. Thus, an inpatriate is also defined as an expatriate. A further indication of the confusion created by the use of the term 'inpatriate' is that some writers in international management define all HCN employees as inpatriates. HCNs only become inpatriates when they are transferred into the parent-country operations as expatriates, as illustrated in Figure 1.2.

Given the substantial amount of jargon in IHRM, it is questionable as to whether the term 'inpatriate' adds enough value to justify its use. However, some firms now use the term 'inpatriate' for all staff transferred into a country. For clarity, we will use the term 'expatriate' throughout this text to refer to employees who are transferred out of their home base/parent country into some other area of the firm's international operations. In doing so, we recognize that there is increasing diversity with regard to what constitutes international work, the type and length of international assignments, and the increasingly strategic role of the HR function in many organizations, which in turn influences the nature of some expatriate roles.

FIGURE 1.2 International assignments create expatriates

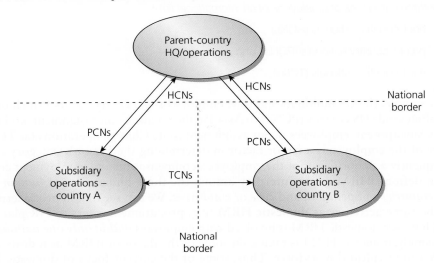

Stahl, Björkman, and Morris have recognized this expansion in the scope of the field of IHRM in their *Handbook of Research in International Human Resource Management*, where they define the field of IHRM as follows:

> *We define the field of IHRM broadly to cover all issues related to managing the global workforce and its contribution to firm outcomes. Hence, our definition of IHRM covers a wide range of HR issues facing MNEs in different parts of their organizations. Additionally we include comparative analyses of HRM in different countries.*[8]

We believe that this broad definition accurately captures the expanding scope of the IHRM field and we will use this definition in this book.

DIFFERENCES BETWEEN DOMESTIC AND INTERNATIONAL HRM

In our view, the *complexity* of operating in different countries and employing different national categories of workers is a key variable that differentiates domestic and international HRM, rather than any major differences between the HRM activities performed. Dowling[9] argues that the complexity of international HR can be attributed to six factors:

1   more HR activities

2   the need for a broader perspective

3   more involvement in employees' personal lives

4   changes in emphasis as the workforce mix of expatriates and locals varies

5   risk exposure

6   broader external influences.

Each of these factors is now discussed in detail to illustrate its characteristics.

More HR activities

To operate in an international environment, a HR department must engage in a number of activities that would not be necessary in a domestic environment. Examples of required international activities are:

● international taxation

● international relocation and orientation

● administrative services for expatriates

● host-government relations

● language translation services.

Expatriates are subject to international taxation, and often have both domestic (i.e. their home-country) and host-country tax liabilities. Therefore, **tax equalization** policies must be designed to ensure that there is no tax incentive or disincentive associated with any particular international assignment.[10] The administration of tax equalization policies is complicated by the wide variations in tax laws across host countries and by the possible time lag between the completion of an expatriate assignment and the settlement of domestic and international tax liabilities. In recognition of these difficulties, many MNEs retain the services of a major accounting firm for international taxation advice.

International relocation and orientation involves the following activities:

● arranging for pre-departure training

● providing immigration and travel details

● providing housing, shopping, medical care, recreation, and schooling information

● finalizing compensation details such as delivery of salary overseas, determination of various overseas allowances and taxation treatment.

The issues involved when expatriates return to their home-country ('repatriation') are covered in detail in Chapter 7. Many of these factors may be a source of anxiety for the expatriate and require considerable time and attention to successfully resolve potential problems – certainly much more time than would be involved in a domestic transfer/relocation such as London to Manchester, Frankfurt to Munich, New York to Dallas, Sydney to Melbourne, or Beijing to Shanghai.

An MNE also needs to provide administrative services for expatriates in the host countries in which it operates.[11] Providing these services can often be a time-consuming and complex activity because policies and procedures are not always clear-cut and may conflict with local conditions. Ethical questions can arise when a practice that is legal and accepted in the host country may be at best unethical and at worst illegal in the home country. For example, a situation may arise in which a host country requires an AIDS test for a work permit for an employee whose parent firm is headquartered in the USA, where employment-related AIDS testing remains a controversial issue. How does the corporate HR manager deal with the potential expatriate employee who refuses to meet this requirement for an AIDS test, and the overseas affiliate which needs the services of a specialist expatriate from headquarters? These issues add to the complexity of providing administrative services to expatriates.

Host-government relations represent an important activity for the HR department in a MNE, particularly in developing countries where work permits and other important certificates are often more easily obtained when a personal relationship exists between the relevant government officials and multinational managers. Maintaining such relationships helps resolve potential problems that can be caused by ambiguous eligibility and/or compliance criteria for documentation such as work permits. US-based multinationals, however, must be careful in how they deal with relevant government officials, as payment or payment-in-kind, such as dinners and gifts, may violate the US Foreign Corrupt Practices Act (FCPA).[12] Provision of language translation services for internal and external correspondence is an additional international activity for the HR department. Morgan[13] notes that if the HR department is the major user of language translation services, the role of this translation group is often expanded to provide translation services to all foreign operation departments within the MNE.

The need for a broader perspective

HR managers working in a domestic environment generally administer programs for a single national group of employees who are covered by a uniform compensation policy and taxed by one national government. Because HR managers working in an international environment face the problem of designing and administering programs for more than one national group of employees (e.g. PCN, HCN, and TCN employees who may work together in Zurich at the European regional headquarters of a US-based multinational), they need to take a broader view of issues. For example, a broader, more international perspective on expatriate benefits would endorse the view that all expatriate employees, regardless of nationality, should receive a foreign service or expatriate premium when working in a foreign location. Yet some MNEs that routinely pay such premiums to their PCN employees on overseas assignment (even if the assignments are to desirable locations) are reluctant to pay premiums to foreign nationals assigned to the home country of the firm. Such a policy confirms the traditional perception of many HCN and TCN employees that PCN employees (particularly US and European PCNs) are given preferential treatment.[14] Complex **equity** issues arise when employees of various nationalities work together and the resolution of these issues remains one of the major challenges in the IHRM field. (Equity issues with regard to compensation are discussed in Chapter 8.)

More involvement in employees' personal lives

A greater degree of involvement in employees' personal lives is necessary for the selection, training, and effective management of both PCN and TCN employees. The HR department or HR professional needs to ensure that the expatriate employee understands housing arrangements, health care, and all aspects of the compensation package provided for the assignment (cost-of-living allowances, premiums, taxes, and so on). Many MNEs have an 'International HR Services' section that co-ordinates administration of the above programs and provides services for PCNs and TCNs, such as providing advice and information on matters relating to banking, investments, home rental while on assignment, co-ordinating home visits and final repatriation.

In the domestic setting, the HR department's involvement with an employee's family is relatively limited and may not extend beyond providing employee benefits such as health insurance coverage for eligible family members and some assistance in relocating the employee and family members. In the international setting, however, the HR department must be much more involved in order to provide the level of support required and will need to know more about the employee's personal life. For example, some national governments require the presentation of a marriage certificate before granting a visa for an accompanying spouse. Thus, marital status could become an aspect of the selection process, regardless of the best intentions of the MNE to avoid using a potentially discriminatory selection criterion. In such a situation, the HR department should advise all candidates being considered for the position of the host country's visa requirements with regard to marital status and allow candidates to decide whether they wish to remain in the selection process. Apart from providing suitable housing and schooling in the assignment location, the HR department may also need to assist children placed at boarding schools in the home country – a situation that is less frequently encountered in the USA but relatively common in many other countries, particularly former British colonies such as Singapore, Hong Kong, Australia and New Zealand, and in Europe.[15] In more remote or less hospitable assignment locations, the HR department may be required to develop, and even run, recreational programs. For a domestic assignment, most of these matters either would not arise or would be seen as the responsibility of the employee rather than the HR department. In a sense the '**psychological contract**' is now between the MNE and the entire immediate family of the international assignee.[16]

Changes in emphasis as the workforce mix of PCNs and HCNs varies

As foreign operations mature, the emphasis put on various HR activities change. For example, as the need for PCNs and TCNs declines and more trained locals become available, resources previously allocated to areas such as expatriate taxation, relocation, and orientation are transferred to activities such as local staff selection, training, and management development. The latter activity may require the establishment of a program to bring high-potential local staff to corporate headquarters for developmental assignments. The need to change emphasis in HR operations as a foreign subsidiary matures is clearly a factor that would broaden the responsibilities of local HR activities such as HR planning, staffing, training and development, and compensation.

Risk exposure

Frequently the human and financial consequences of failure in the international arena are more severe than in domestic business. For example, while we discuss the topic in more detail in Chapter 5, expatriate failure (the premature return of an expatriate from an international assignment) and underperformance while on international assignment is a potentially high-cost problem for MNEs. The direct costs of failure (salary, training costs, travel costs, and relocation expenses) to the parent firm may be as high as three times the domestic salary plus relocation expenses, depending on currency exchange rates and location of assignments. Indirect costs such as loss of foreign market share and damage to key host-country relationships may also be considerable.

Another aspect of risk exposure that is relevant to IHRM is terrorism, particularly since the World Trade Center attack in New York in 2001. Most major MNEs must now consider political risk and terrorism when planning international meetings and assignments, and spending on protection against terrorism is increasing. Terrorism has also clearly had an effect on the way in which employees assess potential international assignment locations.[17] The HR department may also need to devise emergency evacuation procedures for highly volatile assignment locations subject to political or terrorist violence, or major epidemic or pandemic crises such as Zika virus, severe acute respiratory syndrome (SARS), and avian influenza.[18] For a comprehensive analysis of the impact of SARS on HRM in the Hong Kong service sector, see Lee and Warner.[19]

Broader external influences

The major external factors that influence IHRM are the type of government, the state of the economy and the generally accepted practices of doing business in each of the various host countries in which MNEs operate. A host government can, for example, dictate hiring procedures, as has been the case until recently in Malaysia. The Malaysian government during the 1970s introduced a requirement that foreign firms comply with an extensive set of affirmative action rules designed to provide additional employment opportunities for the indigenous Malay ethnic group, who constitute the majority of the population of Malaysia but tend to be under-represented in business and professional employment groups relative to Chinese Malaysians and Indian Malaysians. Various statistics showing employment levels of indigenous Malays throughout the firm (particularly at middle and senior management levels) were required to be forwarded to the relevant government department. Many foreign investors regarded these requirements as a major reason for complaints about bureaucracy and inflexibility with regard to perceived affirmative action appointments at management level in Malaysia and these complaints are one significant reason for a subsequent revision of these requirements.

In developed countries, labor is more expensive and better organized than in less-developed countries and national and/or state governments require compliance with legal requirements on issues such as labor relations, taxation, and health and safety. These factors shape the activities of the subsidiary HR manager to a considerable extent. In less-developed countries, labor tends to be cheaper, less organized, and government regulation is less pervasive, so these factors take less time. The subsidiary HR manager must spend more time, however, learning and interpreting the local ways of doing business and the general code of conduct regarding activities such as gift giving and employment of family members. It is also likely that the subsidiary HR manager will become more involved in administering benefits either provided or financed by the MNE, such as housing, education, and other facilities not readily available in the local economy.

VARIABLES THAT MODERATE DIFFERENCES BETWEEN DOMESTIC AND INTERNATIONAL HRM

Earlier in this chapter it was argued that the complexity involved in operating in different countries and employing different national categories of employees is a key variable that differentiates domestic and international HRM, rather than any major differences between the HRM activities performed. Many successful firms from advanced economies with limited experience in international business tend to significantly underestimate the complexities involved in successful international operations – particularly in emerging economies. There is considerable evidence to suggest that business failures in the international arena are often linked to poor management of HR. In addition to complexity, there are four other variables that *moderate* (that is, either diminish or accentuate) differences between domestic and IHRM. These four additional moderators are:

- the cultural environment
- the industry (or industries) with which the multinational is primarily involved
- the extent of reliance of the multinational on its home-country domestic market
- the attitudes of senior management.

Together with the complexity involved in operating in different countries, these five variables constitute a model that explains the differences between domestic and international HRM (see Figure 1.3).

FIGURE 1.3 A model of the variables that moderate differences between domestic and IHRM

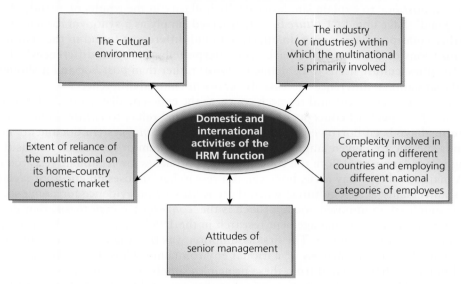

Source: P. J. Dowling 'Completing the Puzzle: Issues in the Development of the Field of International Human Resource Management', (mir) *Management International Review*, Special Issue No. 3/99 (1999), p. 31. Reproduced with kind permission from VS Verlag Für Sozialwissenschaften.

THE CULTURAL ENVIRONMENT

In Chapter 2, 'The Cultural Context of IHRM', we cover the concept of **culture** in considerable detail, so our comments in this introductory chapter are necessarily brief. There are many definitions of culture, but the term is usually used to describe a shaping process over time. This process generates relative stability, reflecting a shared knowledge structure that attenuates (i.e. reduces) variability in values, behavioral norms, and patterns of behavior.[20] An important characteristic of culture is that it is so subtle a process that one is not always conscious of its relationship to values, attitudes, and behaviors. One usually has to be confronted with a different culture in order to fully appreciate this effect. Anyone traveling abroad, either as a tourist or on business, experiences situations that demonstrate cultural differences in language, food, dress, hygiene, and attitudes to time. While the traveller can perceive these differences as novel, even enjoyable, for people required to live and work in a new country, such differences can prove difficult. They may experience **culture shock** – a phenomenon experienced by people who move across cultures. The new environment requires many adjustments in a relatively short period of time, challenging people's frames of reference to such an extent that their sense of self, especially in terms of nationality, comes into question. People, in effect, experience a shock reaction to new cultural experiences that cause psychological disorientation because they misunderstand or do not recognize important cues. Culture shock can lead to negative feelings about the host country and its people and a longing to return home.[21]

Because international business involves the interaction and movement of people across national boundaries, an appreciation of cultural differences and when these differences are important is essential. Research into these aspects has assisted in furthering our understanding of the cultural environment as an important variable that moderates differences between domestic and IHRM. However, while cross-cultural and comparative research attempts to explore and explain similarities and differences, there are problems associated with such research. A major problem is that there is little agreement on either an exact definition of culture or on the operationalization of this concept. For many researchers, culture has become an omnibus variable, representing a range of social, historic, economic, and political factors that are invoked *post hoc* to explain similarity or dissimilarity in the results of a study. As Bhagat and McQuaid[22] have noted, "*Culture* has often served simply as a synonym for *nation* without any further conceptual grounding. In effect, national differences found in the characteristics of organizations or their members have been interpreted as cultural differences". To reduce these difficulties, culture needs to be defined *a priori* rather than *post hoc* and it should not be assumed that national differences necessarily represent cultural differences.

Another issue in cross-cultural research concerns the **emic-etic** distinction.[23] '*Emic*' refers to *culture-specific* aspects of concepts or behavior, and '*etic*' refers to *culture-common* aspects. These terms have been borrowed from linguistics: a phon*emic* system documents meaningful sounds specific to a given language, and a phon*etic* system organizes all sounds that have meaning in any language.[24] Both the emic and etic approaches are legitimate research orientations. A major problem may arise, however, if a researcher imposes an etic approach (that is, assumes universality across cultures) when there is little or no evidence for doing so. A well-known example of an imposed etic approach is the '*convergence hypothesis*' that dominated much of US and European management research in the 1950s and 1960s. This approach was based on two key assumptions.[25] The first assumption was that there were principles of sound management that held regardless of national environments. Thus, the existence of local or national practices that deviated from these principles simply indicated a need to change these local practices. The second assumption was that the universality of sound management practices would lead to societies becoming more and more alike in the future. Given that the USA was the leading industrial economy at that time, the point of convergence was the US model.

To use Kuhn's[26] terminology, the convergence hypothesis became an established paradigm that many researchers found difficult to give up, despite a growing body of evidence supporting a divergence hypothesis. In an important early paper that reviewed the convergence/divergence debate, Child[27] made the point that there is evidence for both convergence and divergence. The majority of the convergence studies, however, focus on *macrolevel* variables (for example, organizational structure and technology used by MNEs across cultures) and the majority of the divergence studies focus on *microlevel* variables (for example, the behavior of people within firms). His conclusion was that, although firms in different countries are becoming more alike (an etic or convergence approach), the behavior of individuals within these firms is maintaining its *cultural specificity* (an emic or divergence approach). As noted above, both emic and etic approaches are legitimate research orientations, but methodological difficulties may arise if the distinction between these two approaches is ignored or if unwarranted universality assumptions are made.[28] The debate on assumptions of universality is not limited to the literature in international management as this issue has also become a topic of debate in the field of international relations and strategic studies where international management research is cited.[29] For an excellent review of the convergence/divergence question, see Brewster.[30]

Cultural awareness and the role of the international HR manager

Despite the methodological concerns about cross-cultural research, it is now generally recognized that culturally insensitive attitudes and behaviors stemming from ignorance or from misguided beliefs ("my way is best", or "what works at home will work here") are not only inappropriate but can all too often contribute to *international business failure*. Therefore, an awareness of cultural differences is essential for the HR manager at corporate headquarters as well as in the host location.[31] Activities such as hiring, promoting, rewarding, and dismissal will be determined by the legal context and practices of the host country and are usually based on a value system relevant to that country's culture. A firm may decide to head up a new overseas operation with an expatriate general manager but appoint a local national as the HR department manager to ensure that they have a person who is familiar with the host country's HR practices. This particular policy approach can assist in avoiding problems but may still lead to dilemmas for senior managers. For example, in a number of developing countries (Indonesia is one such example) local managers are expected (i.e. there is a perceived obligation) to employ their extended family if they are in a position to do so. This may lead to a situation where people are hired who do not possess the required technical competence or do not have sufficient experience. While this could be seen as a successful example of adapting to local expectations and customs, from a Western perspective this practice would be seen as nepotism, a negative practice which is not in the best interests of the enterprise because the best people have not been hired for the job.

Coping with cultural differences and recognizing how and when these differences are relevant are constant challenges for international firms. Helping to prepare assignees and their families for working and living in a new cultural environment has become a key activity for HR departments in those MNEs that appreciate (or have been forced, through experience, to appreciate) the impact that the cultural environment can have on staff performance and well-being.

INDUSTRY TYPE

Porter[32] suggests that the industry (or industries if the firm is a conglomerate) in which a MNE is involved is of considerable importance because patterns of international competition vary widely from one industry to another. At one end of the continuum of international competition is the multidomestic industry, one in which competition in each country is essentially independent of competition in other countries. Traditional examples include retailing, distribution, and insurance. At the other end of the continuum is the global industry, one in which a firm's competitive position in one country is significantly influenced by its position in other countries. Examples include commercial aircraft, semiconductors, and copiers. The key distinction between a multidomestic industry and a global industry is described by Porter as follows:

> The global industry is not merely a collection of domestic industries but a series of linked domestic industries in which the rivals compete against each other on a truly worldwide basis [. . .]. In a multidomestic industry, then, international strategy collapses to a series of domestic strategies. The issues that are uniquely international revolve around how to do business abroad, how to select good countries in which to compete (or assess country risk), and mechanisms to achieve the one-time transfer of know-how. These are questions that are relatively well developed in the literature. In a global industry, however, managing international activities like a portfolio will undermine the possibility of achieving competitive advantage. In a global industry, a firm must in some way integrate its activities on a worldwide basis to capture the linkages among countries.

The role of the HRM function in multidomestic and global industries can be analyzed using Porter's well-known value-chain model.[33] In Porter's model, HRM is seen as one of four support activities for the five primary activities of the firm. Since HR are involved in each of the primary and support activities, the HRM function is seen as cutting across the entire value chain of a firm. If the firm is in a multidomestic industry, the role of the HR department will most likely be more domestic in structure and orientation. At times there may be considerable demand for international services from the HRM function (for example, when a new plant or office is established in a foreign location and the need for expatriate employees arises), but these activities would not be pivotal – indeed, many of these services may be provided via consultants and/or temporary employees. The main role for the HRM function would be to support the primary activities of the firm in each domestic market to achieve a competitive advantage through either cost/efficiency or product/service differentiation.

If the multinational is in a global industry, however, the *'imperative for co-ordination'* described by Porter would require a HRM function structured to deliver the international support required by the primary activities of the MNE. The need to develop co-ordination raises complex problems for any multinational. As Laurent[34] has noted:

> *In order to build, maintain, and develop their corporate identity, multinational organizations need to strive for consistency in their ways of managing people on a worldwide basis. Yet, and in order to be effective locally, they also need to adapt those ways to the specific cultural requirements of different societies. While the global nature of the business may call for increased consistency, the variety of cultural environments may be calling for differentiation.*

Laurent proposes that a truly international conception of HRM would require the following steps:

1   An explicit recognition by the parent organization that its own peculiar ways of managing HR reflect some assumptions and values of its home culture.

2   An explicit recognition by the parent organization that its peculiar ways are neither universally better nor worse than others but are different and likely to exhibit strengths and weaknesses, particularly abroad.

3   An explicit recognition by the parent organization that its foreign subsidiaries may have other preferred ways of managing people that are neither intrinsically better nor worse but could possibly be more effective locally.

4   A willingness from headquarters to not only acknowledge cultural differences but also to take active steps in order to make them discussable and therefore usable.

5   The building of a genuine belief by all parties involved that more creative and effective ways of managing people could be developed as a result of cross-cultural learning.

In offering this proposal, Laurent acknowledges that these are difficult steps that few firms have taken:

> *They have more to do with states of mind and mindsets than with behavior. As such, these processes can only be facilitated and this may represent a primary mission for executives in charge of IHRM.*[35]

Implicit in Laurent's analysis is the idea that, by taking the steps he describes, a MNE attempting to implement a global strategy via co-ordination of activities would be better able to work through the difficulties and complex trade-offs inherent in such a strategy. Increasingly, multinationals are taking a more strategic approach to the role of HRM and are using staff transfers and training programs to assist in co-ordination of activities. We discuss these issues in more detail in subsequent chapters of this book.

EXTENT OF RELIANCE OF THE MULTINATIONAL ON ITS HOME-COUNTRY DOMESTIC MARKET

A pervasive but often ignored factor that influences the behavior of MNEs and resultant HR practices is the extent of reliance of the multinational on its home-country domestic market. When, for example, we look through lists of large firms in business magazines, it is frequently assumed that a global market perspective would be dominant in the firm's culture and thinking. However, size is not the only key variable when looking at a multinational – the extent of reliance of the multinational on its home-country domestic market may also be very important. In fact, for many firms, a small home market is one of the key drivers for seeking new international markets.

TABLE 1.1   Fortune 2016 Global 500 Top 10 ranked by US$ millions revenues

1. Walmart (USA)	$482,130
2. State Grid (China)	$329,601
3. China National Petroleum (China)	$299,271
4. Sinopec Group (China)	$294,344
5. Royal Dutch Shell (Britain and the Netherlands)	$272,156
6. Exxon Mobil (USA)	$246,204
7. Volkswagen (Germany)	$236,600
8. Toyota Motor (Japan)	$236,592
9. Apple (USA)	$233,715
10. BP (Britain)	$225,982

Source: Fortune.com accessed 30 July 2016

The only US firms in the top ten multinationals ranked by global revenues (see Table 1.1) are Walmart, Exxon Mobil, and Apple. The reason for this lower ranking of US firms in terms of impact is as obvious as it is important – *the size of the domestic market* for US firms. A very large domestic market (for US firms this is in effect the North American Free Trade Agreement [NAFTA] market) influences all aspects of how a multinational organizes its activities. For example, it will be more likely to use an international division as the way it organizes its international activities (see Chapter 3) and, even if it uses a global product structure, the importance of the domestic market may be pervasive.

A large domestic market will also influence the attitudes of senior managers towards their international activities and will generate a large number of managers with an experience base of predominantly or even exclusively domestic market experience. Thus, multinationals from small advanced economies like Switzerland (population 8 million), Ireland (5 million), Australia (24 million), and the Netherlands (17 million) and medium-sized advanced economies like Canada (36 million), the UK (65 million), and France (65 million) are in a quite different position compared to multinationals based in the USA, which is the largest advanced economy in the world with a population of 324 million. A similar point has been made by Van Den Bulke and his colleagues in their study of the role of small nations in the global economy.[36] As already noted, US multinationals also enjoy the advantage of a dominant position in the very large NAFTA market (the USA, Canada, and Mexico).

It is worth keeping in mind that the frequent criticism of US companies, US senior managers and US business schools as inward-looking and ethnocentric may perhaps be true to some extent, *but it is equally true* that a focus on domestic US sales and revenue is also an entirely rational response to the overwhelming importance of the North American market for many of these businesses. The demands of a large domestic market present a challenge to the globalization efforts of many US firms. As Cavusgil[37] has noted when commenting on internationalizing business education, the task of internationalizing business education in the USA is a large one. So too is the task facing many US firms in terms of developing global managers – an issue to which we shall return in Chapter 7.

ATTITUDES OF SENIOR MANAGEMENT TO INTERNATIONAL OPERATIONS

The point made by Laurent earlier in this chapter that some of the changes required to truly internationalize the HR function "have more to do with states of mind and mindsets than with behaviors" illustrates the importance of a final variable that may moderate differences between international and domestic HRM: the attitudes of senior management to international operations.[38] It is likely that, if senior management does not have a strong international orientation, the importance of international operations may be underemphasized (or possibly even ignored) in terms of corporate goals and objectives. In such situations, managers may tend to focus on domestic issues and minimize differences between international and domestic environments.

Not surprisingly, senior managers with little international experience (and successful careers built on domestic experience) may assume that there is a great deal of transferability between domestic and international HRM practices. This failure to recognize differences in managing HR in foreign environments – regardless of whether it is because of ethnocentrism, inadequate information or a lack of international perspective – frequently results in major difficulties in international operations. The challenge for the corporate HR manager who wishes to contribute to the internationalization of their firm is to work with top management in fostering the desired 'global mindset'. This goal requires, of course, a HR manager who is able to think globally and to formulate and implement HR policies that facilitate the development of globally oriented staff.[39]

APPLYING A STRATEGIC VIEW OF IHRM

Our discussion up to this point has suggested that a broader or more strategic view of IHRM is required to better explain the complexity and challenges of managing IHRM issues. An example of a theoretical framework that has been derived from a strategic approach using a multiple methodological approach is that of De Cieri and Dowling.[40] Their framework is depicted in Figure 1.4 and assumes that MNEs operate in the context of worldwide conditions, including the influences of industry (global or multidomestic) and regional, national, and local markets that include geopolitical, legal, socio-cultural, and economic characteristics.

In strategic management practice, the acronym 'PEST', which represents the *political, economic, sociological, and technological* acronym and analytical tool, has often been used to describe the macroenvironmental factors that may influence MNEs. Recent additions to this set of factors include *legal* and *environmental/ecological* elements (PESTLE). Although this analytical tool is popular in consulting and management practice, it appears to have received little academic research attention or usage.[41] De Cieri and Dowling suggest that exploration and adoption of the PESTLE acronym in academic work would help to bring research and practitioner approaches closer together. They propose that external factors have direct influence on both internal/organization factors and strategic human resource management (SHRM) strategy and practices, and that external factors have a direct influence on MNE performance. A large body of research has explored these relationships; of particular note is the Cranet study of European HRM practices in different national contexts.[42] There are streams of research within the international business field investigating the implications of each of the external factors for MNEs; for example, there is an extensive body of research that has explored the implications of national culture.[43] Further, research in countries undergoing significant economic transformation, such as China, indicates that the HR function has been substantially influenced by the changing external environment.[44]

FIGURE 1.4 A framework of SHRM in MNEs

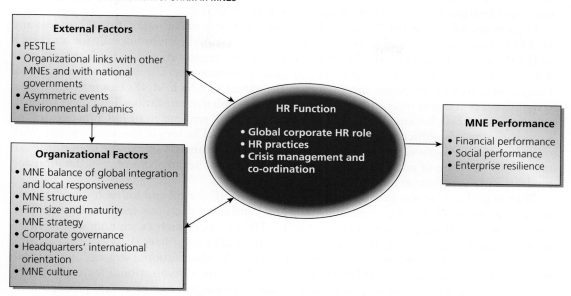

Source: De Cieri, H. & Dowling, P. J. 'Strategic human resource management in multinational enterprises: Developments and directions', in G. Stahl, I. Björkman and S. Morris (eds.) *Handbook of Research in International Human Resource Management*, 2nd ed. (Cheltenham, UK: Edward Elgar, 2012). Reproduced with permission from Helen De Cieri and Peter J. Dowling.

Other external factors include *organizational links with other MNEs and national governments, asymmetric events,* and *environmental dynamics.* Organizational networks and alliances may be complex relationship webs based upon personal relationships and may include parent-country managers and employees, host-country managers and employees, and host-country governments. Central to network management is an emphasis on HR that recognizes that knowledge, power, and perceived trustworthiness are often person-specific rather than organization-specific.

In the twenty-first century, the context for international business also reflects heightened concerns about security, risk, and volatility in global markets. In particular, terrorism has been identified by several International Business scholars as an important concern.[45] In relatively common usage since the unexpected terrorist attacks in New York in September 2001, asymmetric events have been described by Gray[46] as threats that our political, strategic, and military cultures regard as *unusual*. In terms of trying to define asymmetric events, Gray notes that they tend to be:

● unmatched in our arsenal of capabilities and plans – such events may or may not appear truly dangerous, but they will certainly look different from war as we have known it

● highly leveraged against our particular assets – military and, probably more often, civil

● designed not only to secure leverage against our assets, but also intended to work around, offset, and negate what in other contexts are our strengths

● difficult to respond to in a discriminate and proportionate manner.

Thus, asymmetric events are not only difficult to deal with when they occur, they are difficult to plan for, recognize, and respond to with specific planning processes and training.[47] The influence of external factors on MNEs involves complex environmental dynamics. As Andreadis[48]

has noted, MNEs operate in a dynamic environment and that environment should be taken into consideration when evaluating organizational effectiveness.

Organizational (or 'internal') factors have been a major focus of international business and SHRM research because these factors are suggested to hold implications not only for areas such as HRM but also for overall MNE performance. The first organizational factor listed in Figure 1.4 is *MNE balance of global integration and local responsiveness*. The act of balancing global integration and local responsiveness refers to the extent to which MNEs can maximize local responsiveness and also integrate units into a cohesive, global organization. To achieve this balance is no easy task because, as Morris *et al.*[49] have noted, replication of HR practices across subsidiaries may be difficult due to the influences of external factors in the local context. With regard to *MNE structure*, the organizational structure literature has shown the importance not only of the structure of international operations[50] but also of mechanisms of co-ordination and mode of entry into foreign markets, for HRM in MNEs.[51]

With regard to *firm size and maturity*, for both the MNE overall and for each subsidiary, the size and maturity of the organization (or unit) may influence decisions with respect to HRM. For example, staffing decisions and demand for HR practices such as training will be influenced by the skill and experience mix within the firm and/or subsidiary (Lawler *et al.*, 2011).[52] In terms of *MNE strategy*, as has been well documented, organizational strategy in the MNE has substantial implications for HRM in MNEs.[53] With the organizational factor *corporate governance*, issues related to corporate governance and incorporation of ethical principles and values into international business practice have become increasingly important for MNE managers, particularly in light of cases of corporate wrongdoing.[54] HR managers may be required to play important roles in corporate governance, such as the design, implementation, and maintenance of corporate codes of conduct.

Following on from the pioneering work of Perlmutter (see Chapter 5), the organizational factor *headquarters' international orientation* recognizes that international orientation of the MNE's headquarters will involve aspects such as the extent and diversity of experience in managing international operations.[55] These elements are well established as important factors for HRM in MNEs, as is the factor *organizational culture*, which is defined by Kidger as the "sense of common identity and purpose across the whole organization",[56] and is the final organizational factor included in the framework. For MNEs seeking a high level of global integration, this factor may facilitate the development of a global mindset and enhance firm performance.[57] Overall, the model offered by De Cieri and Dowling aims to assist in the cross-fertilization of ideas to further develop theory and empirical research in strategic HRM in multinational firms.

THE CHANGING CONTEXT OF IHRM

As Figures 1.3 and 1.4 show, international firms compete in an increasingly complex environment where the level of challenge of doing business can be highly variable. Internationalizing firms rely on having the right people to manage and operate their businesses and good IHRM practices that are appropriate to the context in which they occur. This combination of appropriate people and HR practices has been a constant critical success factor in international business ventures. For example, the following quotation is taken from a detailed case study of a large US multinational, where the authors, Desatnick and Bennett,[58] concluded:

> The primary causes of failure in multinational ventures stem from a lack of understanding of the essential differences in managing HR, at all levels, in foreign environments. Certain management philosophies and techniques have proved successful in the domestic environment: their application in a foreign environment too often leads to frustration, failure, and underachievement. These 'human' considerations are as important as the financial and marketing criteria upon which so many decisions to undertake multinational ventures depend.

This study was reported in 1978 but many international managers today would concur with the sentiments expressed in this quote. In this book we attempt to demonstrate some ways in which an appreciation of the international dimensions of HRM can assist in this process.

SUMMARY

The purpose of this chapter has been to provide an overview of the emerging field of IHRM. We did this by:

- defining key terms in IHRM and considering several definitions of IHRM

- introducing the historically significant issue of expatriate assignment management and reviewing the evolution of these assignments to reflect the increasing diversity with regard to what constitutes international work and the type and length of international assignments

- outlining the differences between domestic and IHRM by looking at six factors which differentiate international and domestic HR (more HR activities; the need for a broader perspective; more involvement in employees' personal lives; changes in emphasis as the workforce mix of expatriates and locals varies; risk exposure; and more external influences) and detailing a model which summarizes the variables that moderate these differences, and

- presenting the complexity of IHRM, the increasing potential for challenges to existing IHRM practices and current models, and an increasing awareness of the wide number of choices within IHRM practices due to increased transparency and faster and more detailed diffusion of these practices across organizational units and firms.

We concluded that the *complexity involved in operating in different countries and employing different national categories of employees* is a key variable differentiating domestic and IHRM, rather than any major differences between the HR activities performed. We also discussed four other variables that moderate differences between domestic and IHRM: the *cultural environment*; the *industry (or industries) with which the multinational is primarily involved*; the *extent of reliance of the multinational on its home-country domestic market*; and the *attitudes of senior management*. These five variables are shown in Figure 1.3. Finally, we discussed a model of SHRM in multinational enterprises (Figure 1.4), which draws together a number of external factors and organizational factors that impact on IHRM strategy and practice and, in turn, MNE goals.

In our discussion of the international dimensions of HRM in this book, we shall be drawing on the HRM literature. Subsequent chapters will examine the cultural and organizational contexts of IHRM; IHRM in cross-border mergers and acquisitions, international alliances, and Small and Medium Sized Enterprises (SMEs); staffing, recruitment, and selection; international performance management; training, development, and careers; international compensation; international industrial relations and the global institutional context; and trends and future challenges in IHRM. We will provide comparative data on HRM practices in different countries, but our major emphasis is on the international dimensions of HRM confronting MNEs, whether large or small, when facing the challenge of managing people globally.

DISCUSSION QUESTIONS

1   What are the main similarities and differences between domestic and international HRM?

2   Define these terms: IHRM, PCN, HCN, and TCN.

3   Discuss two HR activities in which a multinational firm must engage that would not be required in a domestic environment.

4   Why is a greater degree of involvement in employees' personal lives inevitable in many IHRM activities?

5   Discuss at least two of the variables that moderate differences between domestic and international HR practices.

FURTHER READING

C. Brewster and W. Mayrhofer (eds.) *Handbook of Research on Comparative Human Resource Management* (Cheltenham, UK: Edward Elgar, 2012).

J. Doh, D. Ahlstrom, B. Ambos, D. Collings, J. Cullen, A. Gaur, S. Ang, C. Schwens and L. Zander (guest eds.) Special Issue: 'The World of Global Business 1965–2015', *Journal of World Business,* Vol. 51, No. 1 (2015).

P. Dowling, E. Rose and N. Donnelly (guest eds.) Special Issue: 'The Role and Importance of International Business in Small Population Advanced Economies', *International Studies of Management & Organization* , Vol. 45, No. 2 (2013).

K. Lundby and J. Jolton (eds.) *Going Global: Practical Applications and Recommendations for HR and OD Professionals in*

the Global Workspace (San Francisco, USA: Jossey-Bass, 2010).

G. Stahl, I. Björkman and S. Morris (eds.) *Handbook of Research in International Human Resource Management*, 2nd ed. (Cheltenham, UK: Edward Elgar, 2012).

G. Wood, C. Brewster and M. Brookes (eds.) *Human Resource Management and the Institutional Perspective* (New York: Routledge, 2014).

P. Wright, S. Snell and L. Dyer (guest eds.) Special Issue: 'New models of strategic HRM in a global context', *International Journal of Human Resource Management,* 16(6) (2005).

NOTES AND REFERENCES

1.   H. De Cieri and P. Dowling 'Strategic Human Resource Management in Multinational Enterprises: Theoretical and Empirical Developments', in R. Wright *et al.* (eds.) *Research and Theory in SHRM: An agenda for the 21st century* (Greenwich, CT: JAI Press, 1999).

2.   For an example of this approach, see N. Adler and A. Gundersen *International Dimensions of Organizational Behavior,* 5th ed. (Cincinnati, OH: South-Western, 2008).

3.   See for example, J. Lamare, E. Farndale and P. Gunnigle 'Employment Relations and IHRM', in D. Collings, G. Wood and P. Caligiuri (eds.) *The Routledge Companion to International Human Resource Management* (London: Routledge), pp. 99–120.

4.   See P. Dowling and R. Schuler *International Dimensions of Human Resource Management,* 1st ed. (Boston, MA: PWS-Kent, 1990); P. Dowling, R. Schuler and D. Welch *International Dimensions of Human Resource Management,* 2nd ed. (Belmont, CA: Wadsworth, 1994); P. Dowling, D. Welch and R. Schuler *International Human Resource Management: Managing People in a Multinational Context,* 3rd ed. (Cincinnati, OH: South-Western, 1998); P. Dowling and D. Welch *International Human Resource Management: Managing People in a Multinational Context,* 4th ed. (London, UK: Thomson, 2004); P. Dowling, M. Festing and A. Engle *International Human Resource Management: Managing People in a*

Multinational Context, 5th ed. (London, UK: Thomson, 2008).

5. P. Morgan, 'International Human Resource Management: Fact or Fiction', *Personnel Administrator*, Vol. 31, No. 9 (1986), pp. 43–47.

6. See H. De Cieri, S. McGaughey and P. Dowling, 'Relocation'. in M. Warner (ed.) *International Encyclopedia of Business and Management*, Vol. 5 (London: Routledge, 1996), pp. 4300–10, for further discussion of this point. For a presentation of the significant impact international assignment research has had on IHRM and international business research, see D. Welch and I. Bjorkman ' The Place of International Human Resource Management in International Business', *Management International Review*, Vol. 55 (2015), pp. 303–322.

7. For an example of the way in which the term is being used, see M. Harvey, M. Novicevic and C. Speier 'Strategic Global Human Resource Management: The Role of Inpatriate Managers', *Human Resource Management Review*, Vol. 10, No. 2 (2000), pp. 153–175.

8. G. Stahl, I. Björkman and S. Morris (eds.) *Handbook of Research in International Human Resource Management*, 2nd ed. (Cheltenham, UK: Edward Elgar, 2012), p. 1.

9. P. Dowling 'International and Domestic Personnel/Human Resource Management: Similarities and Differences', in R. Schuler, S. Youngblood and V. Huber (eds.) *Readings in Personnel and Human Resource Management*, 3rd ed. (St. Paul, MN: West Publishing, 1988).

10. See D. Pinney 'Structuring an Expatriate Tax Reimbursement Program', *Personnel Administrator*, Vol. 27, No. 7 (1982), pp. 19–25; and M. Gajek and M. M. Sabo 'The Bottom Line: What HR Managers Need to Know About the New Expatriate Regulations', *Personnel Administrator*, Vol. 31, No. 2 (1986), pp. 87–92. Needless to say there are a large number of international consulting firms set up for assisting in this fast-changing area. CCH's longstanding publication, the *Master Tax Guide* for 2012 contains a chapter dedicated to 'taxation of foreign activities/taxpayers'. There is even a specialized bimonthly journal, *International Tax Journal*, published by CCH. Although US in focus, it does present the interaction of international tax regulations and US tax laws.

11. For a recent review of issues and trends see *Mindful Mobility – 2015 Global Mobility Trends Survey Report*, Brookfield Global Relocation Services LLC.

12. For up-to-date information on the FCPA see the US Department of Justice website: www.justice.gov/criminal/fraud/fcpa/. For an overview of corruption and culture, see Y. Akbar and V. Vujic 'Explaining Corruption: The Role of National Culture and its Implications for International Management', *Cross-Cultural Management*, Vol. 21, No. 2 (2014), pp. 191–218.

13. P. Morgan 'International Human Resource Management: Fact or Fiction'. We will deal with the complexities of the relationship between language fluency, transacting business and cross-cultural understanding in Chapter 2 and throughout this book.

14. A classic textbook such as R. D. Robinson *International Business Management: A Guide to Decision Making,* 2nd ed. (Hinsdale, IL: Dryden, 1978) provides good coverage on this point of traditional preferential treatment for US and European expatriates.

15. Although less common in the USA, the use of private boarding schools is common in countries (particularly European countries and former British colonies such as Australia) which have a colonial tradition where both colonial administrators and business people often undertake long assignments overseas and expect to leave their children at a private boarding school in their home country. This is especially true of Britain, which also has a strong cultural tradition of the middle and upper classes sending their children to private boarding schools, even if the parents are working in Britain. A curious tradition in Britain is to describe these schools as 'public' schools, even though almost all are private institutions that charge – often very substantial – fees.

16. Some evidence of how HR practitioners view and deal with how complex the personal and professional lives of MNE members can become is presented by E. Bardoel 'Work-life Management Tensions in Multinational Enterprises (MNEs)', *International Journal of Human Resource Management* (2015) (DOI: 10.1080/09585192.2015.1074089).

17. See 'Terrorism', Chapter 4 in T. Gladwin and I. Walter *Multinationals Under Fire: Lessons in the Management of Conflict* (New York: John Wiley, 1980); M. Czinkota, G. Knight, P. Liesch and J. Steen 'Terrorism and International Business: A Research Agenda', *Journal of International Business Studies*, Vol. 41, No. 5 (2010), pp. 826–843.

18. For the latest information on epidemic and pandemic crises see the World Health Organization website at: www.who.int/csr/outbreaknetwork/en and the U.S. Center for Disease Control at https://www.cdc.gov/.

19. G. Lee and M. Warner 'Epidemics, Labor Markets and Unemployment: The Impact of SARS on Human Resource Management in the Hong Kong Service Sector', *International Journal of Human Resource Management*, Vol. 16, No. 5 (2005), pp. 752–771.

20. M. Erez and P. C. Earley *Culture, Self-Identity and Work* (Oxford: Oxford University Press, 1993).

21. J. E. Harris and R. T. Moran *Managing Cultural Differences* (Houston, TX: Gulf, 1979).

22. R. S. Bhagat and S. J. McQuaid 'Role of Subjective Culture in Organizations: A Review and Directions for Future Research', *Journal of Applied Psychology*, Vol. 67 (1982), pp. 653–685.

23. See J. Berry 'Introduction to Methodology', in H. Triandis and J. Berry (eds.), *Handbook of Cross-Cultural Psychology*, Vol. 2: 'Methodology' (Boston, MA: Allyn and Bacon, 1980); H. De Cieri and P. Dowling, 'Cross-cultural Issues in Organizational Behavior', in C. Cooper and D. Rousseau (eds.) *Trends in Organizational Behavior*, Vol. 2 (Chichester: John Wiley & Sons, 1995), pp.127–145; and M. Teagarden and M. A. Von Glinow, 'Human Resource Management in Cross-cultural Contexts: Emic Practices Versus Etic Philosophies', *Management International Review*, 37 (1 – Special Issue) (1997), pp. 7–20.

24. Se P. Buckley, M. Chapman, J. Clegg and H. Gajewska-DeMattos 'A Linguistic and Philosophical Analysis of Emic and Etic and their Use in International Business Research', *Management International Review*, Vol. 54 (2015), pp. 307–324.

25. See G. Hofstede 'The Cultural Relativity of Organizational Practices and Theories', *Journal of International Business Studies*, Vol. 14, No. 2 (1983), pp. 75–89.

26. T. Kuhn *The Structure of Scientific Revolution*, 2nd ed. (Chicago, IL: University of Chicago Press, 1962).

27. J. Child 'Culture, Contingency and Capitalism in the Cross-National Study of Organizations', in L. Cummings and B. Staw (eds.), *Research in Organizational Behavior*, Vol. 3 (Greenwich, CT: JAI Publishers, 1981).

28. See D. Ricks *Blunders in International Business* (Cambridge, MA: Blackwell, 1993) for a comprehensive collection of mistakes made by MNEs that paid insufficient attention to their cultural environment in their international business operations. For further literature on this topic see the following: M. Tayeb 'Organizations and National Culture: Methodology Considered', *Organization Studies*, 15, No. 3 (1994), pp. 429–446; J. Delery and D. Doty 'Modes of Theorizing in Strategic Human Resource Management: Tests of Universalistic, Contingency, and Configurational Performance Predictions', *Academy of Management Journal*, Vol. 39 (1996), pp. 802–835; and P. Sparrow (ed.) *Handbook of International Human Resource Management* (Chichester, UK: John Wiley & Sons, 2009).

29. S. Huntington 'The West: Unique, Not Universal', *Foreign Affairs*, November/December (1996), pp. 28–46.

30. C. Brewster 'Comparing HRM Policies and Practices Across Geographical Borders', in G. Stahl and I. Björkman (eds.) *Handbook of Research in International Human Resource Management* (Cheltenham, UK: Edward Elgar, 2006), pp. 68–90.

31. R. Tung 'Managing Cross-national and Intra-national Diversity', *Human Resource Management*, Vol. 32, No. 4 (1993), pp. 461–477.

32. M. Porter 'Changing Patterns of International Competition', *California Management Review*, Vol. 28, No. 2 (1986), pp. 9–40.

33. M. Porter *Competitive Advantage: Creating and Sustaining Superior Performance* (New York: The Free Press, 1985).

34. A. Laurent 'The Cross-Cultural Puzzle of International Human Resource Management', *Human Resource Management*, Vol. 25 (1986), pp. 91–102.

35. *ibid*, p. 100.

36. D. Van Den Bulke, A. Verbeke and W. Yuan (eds.) *Handbook on Small Nations in the Global Economy: The Contribution of Multinational Enterprises to National Economic Success* (Cheltenham, UK: Edward Elgar, 2009).

37. S. Tamer Cavusgil *Internationalizing Business Education: Meeting the Challenge* (East Lansing, MI: Michigan State University Press, 1993).

38. A. Laurent, *op. cit.*, p. 100.

39. See C. Bartlett and P. Beamish *Transnational Management: Text, Cases & Readings in Cross-border Management* 7th ed. (Boston, MA: McGraw-Hill/Irwin, 2014).

40. H. De Cieri and P. Dowling 'Strategic Human Resource Management in Multinational Enterprises: Developments and Directions', in G. Stahl, I. Björkman and S. Morris (eds.) *Handbook of Research in International Human Resource Management*, 2nd ed. (Cheltenham, UK: Edward Elgar, 2012).

41. T. Hughes, N. O'Regan and D. Wornham 'The Credibility Issue: Closing the Academic/practitioner Gap', *Strategic Change*, Vol. 17, Nos. 7–8 (2008), pp. 215–233.

42. M. Brookes, R. Croucher, M. Fenton-O'Creevy and P. Gooderham 'Measuring Competing Explanations of Human Resource Management Practices Through the Cranet Survey', *Human Resource Management Review*, Vol. 21, No.1 (2011), pp. 68–79.

43. R. Tung and A. Verbeke 'Beyond Hofstede and Globe: Improving the Quality of Cross-cultural Research', *Journal of International Business Studies*, Vol. 41, No. 8 (2010), pp. 1259–1274.

44. See C. Zhu and P. Dowling 'The Impact of the Economic System Upon Human Resource Management Practices in China', *Human Resource Planning*, Vol. 17, No. 4 (1994), pp. 1–21; and C. Zhu, B. Thomson and H. De Cieri 'A Retrospective and Prospective Analysis of HRM Research in China: Implications and Directions for Future Study', *Human Resource Management*, Vol. 47, No. 1 (2008), pp. 135–158.

45. W. Henisz, E. Mansfield and M. A. Von Glinow 'Conflict, Security, and Political Risk: International Business in Challenging Times', *Journal of International Business Studies*, Vol. 41 (2010), pp. 759–764.

46. C. Gray 'Thinking Asymmetrically in Times of Terror', *Parameters*, Vol. 32, No.1 (2002), pp. 5–14.

47. See I. Colville, A. Pye and M. Carter 'Organizing to Counter Terrorism: Sensemaking Amidst Dynamic Complexity', *Human Relations*, Vol. 66, No. 9, (2013), pp. 1201–1223.

48. N. Andreadis, 'Learning and Organizational Effectiveness: A Systems Perspective', *Performance Improvement*, Vol. 48, No. 1 (2009), pp. 5–11.

49. S. Morris, P. Wright, J. Trevor, P. Stiles, G. Stahl, S. Snell, J. Paauwe and E. Farndale 'Global Challenges to Replicating HR: The Role of People, Processes, and Systems', *Human Resource Management*, Vol. 48 (2009), pp. 973–995.

50. M. Czinkota and I. Ronkainen 'Trends and Indications in International Business. Topics for Future Research', *Management International Review*, Vol. 49 (2008), pp. 249–266.

51. J. Lawler, S. Chen, P. Wu, J. Bae and B. Bai 'High performance Work Systems in Foreign Subsidiaries of American Multinationals: An Institutional Model', *Journal of International Business Studies*, Vol. 42, No. 2 (2011), pp. 202–220.

52. *Ibid*.

53. T. Crook, D. Ketchen Jr., J. Combs and S. Todd 'Strategic Resources and Performance: A Meta-analysis', *Strategic Management Journal*, Vol. 29 (2010), pp. 1141–1154.

54. M. Czinkota and I. Ronkainen, *op. cit.*

55. H. Perlmutter 'The Tortuous Evolution of the Multinational Corporation', *Columbia Journal of World Business*, Vol. 4, No. 1 (1969), pp. 9–18; A-W. Harzing 'An Empirical Analysis and Extension of the Bartlett and Ghoshal Typology of Multinational Companies', *Journal of International Business Studies*, Vol. 31, No. 1 (2000), pp. 101–120.

56. P. Kidger 'Management Structure in Multinational Enterprises', *Employee Relations*, Vol. 24, Nos. 1/2 (2002), pp. 69–85.

57. Ernst & Young 'Redrawing the Map: Globalization and the Changing World of Business' (EYGM Limited, 2010); O. Levy, S. Beechler, S. Taylor and N. Boyacigiller 'What We Talk About When We Talk About "Global Mindset": Managerial Cognition in Multinational Corporations', *Journal of International Business Studies*, Vol. 38 (2007), pp. 231–258.

58. R. Desatnick and M. Bennett *Human Resource Management in the Multinational Company* (New York: Nichols, 1978).

CHAPTER 2
THE CULTURAL
CONTEXT OF IHRM

Chapter Objectives

Chapter 1 observed that international human resource management (IHRM) differs from nationally oriented human resource management (HRM) predominantly in the complexities that result from employees of various national origins working in different countries. People who work in internationally operating companies, and customers, suppliers or representatives of government institutions in the host country, often face very different cultural and institutional environments due to various socialization experiences.

In this chapter we systematically review the environment of international HRM decisions so that the complexity of these decisions can be better understood and adequate solutions developed. The following themes are discussed:

- definitions of **culture**
- cultural concepts
- results of intercultural management studies such as Hofstede, the Global Leadership and Organizational Behavior Effectiveness (GLOBE) study, and others
- reflections on cross-cultural management research
- discussion of the development of cultures.

These concepts are highly relevant to developing a more comprehensive understanding and explanation of the complexity of IHRM.

INTRODUCTION

Consideration of the foreign environment is seen in the literature as a key problem of international management.[1] Dülfer and Jöstingmeier point out the special situation of professional employees and managers working abroad, because these individuals are exposed to influences that greatly differ from their country-of-origin environment.[2] An environmental analysis is particularly useful for identifying HR issues associated with international operations. In Europe, the discipline that primarily deals with the comparison of various cultures is called 'intercultural comparative research' and in the English-speaking world it is referred to as 'cross-cultural management'. A central role in this discussion is occupied by **cross-cultural management studies** by Hofstede[3] and the GLOBE study.[4] An overview of other studies will also be provided.

Introduction to cross-cultural management research

The first contributions to cross-cultural management research were made in the early 1960s. Engagement in this subject area was prompted by the increasing international complexity of the global economy and the resulting problems experienced by managers when dealing with employees and with customers and suppliers in various host countries. The resulting unforeseen conflicts and low performance of many foreign business enterprises began to create doubts about the assumption that management research and knowledge from the English-speaking world was readily transferrable to other countries and cultures.[5] This problem was initially the focus of research in US universities[6] and is now studied at business schools and universities around the world, which has led to the well-established broad research field of International Business.

The goals of cross-cultural management studies include:

- description of organizational behavior within countries and cultures
- comparison of organizational behavior between countries and cultures
- explanation and improvement of interaction between employees, customers, suppliers, or business partners from different countries and cultures.[7]

The common feature of cross-cultural management research is the basic assumption that there are differences between management practices in various countries and that the respective environment is of particular significance in explaining these differences. This perspective rejects the approach of researchers who assume universal transferability of management knowledge – i.e. a universalistic, culture-free approach to management.[8]

Cross-cultural studies have often been the focus of substantial debate and criticism. The rather atheoretical foundations of some cross-cultural research and methodological weaknesses in many empirical studies are problematic. These problems have frequently caused contradictory research results and led to vigorous debate in this field. Criticisms have been voiced on the nature and use of the construct of 'culture' – a collective term or residual variable that is undefined or inadequately defined and/or operationalized at the start of a research study – as an independent variable for explaining the variation in management practices between different countries. Despite numerous critical arguments, the knowledge gained from intercultural comparative research is a first step towards understanding the complexity of international management and HRM. The next section covers the possibilities of conceptualizing the concept of culture and its content.

Definition of culture

Numerous definitions and concepts of culture are discussed in relevant literature. The term originated from the Latin word *colere*, which was used in the context of tilling the soil and simply signified plant cultivation. To date, there is no predominant consensus on the exact meaning of culture.[9] As early as the 1950s, Kluckhohn and Kroeber had already put together 164 definitions of culture from the English-speaking countries and condensed them into a comprehensive, well-established and accepted definition of culture:

> *Culture consists in patterned ways of thinking, feeling, and reacting, acquired and transmitted mainly by symbols, constituting the distinctive achievements of human groups [. . .] including their embodiments in artefacts; the essential core of culture consists of traditional [. . .] ideas and especially their attached values [. . .].*[10]

This model was labeled by the well-known Dutch researcher Geert Hofstede as 'mental programming' or *Software of the Mind*, the title of his 1991 book.[11]

> *Using the analogy of the way in which computers are programmed, this book will call such patterns of thinking, feeling, and acting mental programs, or, as the subtitle goes: "software of the mind". This does not mean, of course, that people are programmed the way computers are. A person's behavior is only partially determined by her or his mental programs: (s)he has a basic ability to deviate from them, and to react in ways which are new, creative, destructive, or unexpected. The "software of the mind" [. . .] only indicates what reactions are likely and understandable, given one's past.*[12]

The approach of Hofstede and psychologists such as Triandis[13] analytically gather typical characteristics of cultures and transform them into respective instruments for handling these phenomena.[14] This brief discussion indicates that the basic understanding of culture affects the handling of the culture phenomenon and its subsequent operationalization.[15] The next section presents a well-known and recognized concept of culture.

Schein's concept of culture

Schein's[16] concept of culture was developed in the course of organizational and not national culture research. However, it can be applied to the analysis of national cultures, given awareness that these two constructs are not exact equivalents. The important contribution of this concept is that Schein considers various levels of culture: artefacts or creations, values and underlying assumptions. *Artefacts* are described as visible organization structures and processes. They can be analyzed using conventional methods of empirical social research, but their meaning is often hard to decipher. The middle level comprises the *values* of a company or society. They are found in the intermediate level of consciousness; in other words, they are partly conscious and partly unconscious. The third level is described as *underlying assumptions*, which are often presumed to be self-evident. They include convictions, perceptions, thoughts, and feelings, which are usually invisible and unconscious. Nevertheless, they are the sources of values and the actions based on them. Schein emphasizes that relationships that lead from artefacts through values to underlying assumptions are much weaker than those leading in the contrary direction, because the influence of underlying assumptions on values and artefacts is stronger than vice versa.

The basic assumptions of Schein's ideas originate in the work of Kluckhohn and Strodtbeck from 1961.[17] According to the authors, assumptions are organized independently of individual cases in typical patterns in each culture based on the human capacity to survive. Some of the underlying assumptions will be explained in more detail below, modeled according to explanations by Schein.[18] The following questions are implicit in the six underlying assumptions:[19]

1   The *nature of reality* and the *nature of truth*: what is real and what is not? Do members of a culture assume more of an experimental position, where decisions about true and false depend on experiment, or do they follow more traditional convictions?

2   The *time dimension*: how is the time dimension defined and calculated? How important is time? Do members of a culture live more in relation to the past or to the future? Are they oriented more to the long-term or the short-term?

3   The *effect of spatial proximity and distance*: how is space attributed to members of a society? What objects and locations are private and what are public? What role does spatial distance play in evaluating relationships, e.g. in regard to level of intimacy?

4   The *nature of being human*: what does it mean to be human? Is human nature marked more by good or bad intentions? Can people change and develop, even as adults?

5   The *type of human activity*: how is the relationship to the environment evaluated? Is the environment considered more compelling or overpowering? Are the members of a society more passive in their fate or do they try to actively change it?

6   The *nature of human relationships*: what ideas about criteria of social order dominate in a society (e.g. age, origins, success)? What characterizes relationships between people? Is team success or individual success important?

The diversity of definitions and concepts, only a small part of which can be presented in this chapter, underlines the need for a clear, unambiguous definition of the term 'culture' for research work in intercultural comparative research.

Cross-cultural management studies

Cross-cultural management studies aim to describe and compare working behavior in various cultures. Suggestions on improving interaction between members of various cultures can be drawn from these analyses. This section will describe important results of cross-cultural management studies. The overview starts with the historically significant study by Hofstede. The GLOBE study and results of the studies by Trompenaars and Hampden-Turner, as well as work by Hall and Hall, are also presented and discussed.[20]

Hofstede's cross-cultural management study.   The Hofstede study occupies a special place in the field of cross-cultural comparative research[21] because it was the first major study in this field. It can be positioned on the values level, the intermediate level of Schein's concept of culture. This means that it results in variables that are partly conscious and partly unconscious. This approach is different from other studies that primarily consider the artefacts level. The latter concentrates on easily measurable but hard-to-interpret variables such as economic growth of a country or its political system.[22]

In his original study, Hofstede identified four cultural dimensions based on preliminary theoretical considerations and statistical analyses, which can be used to describe cultural differences between countries.[23] This is the most comprehensive study on this subject ever conducted by means of one questionnaire. In total, the analysis was based on 116,000 questionnaires from IBM employees. The surveyed employees represented all hierarchical levels of the company and possessed various qualifications, from unskilled workers to university graduates. Employees from a total of 38 various professional groups were surveyed.[24] In addition, the study was conducted during two different periods in IBM subsidiaries (1967–1969 and 1971–1973).[25] The questionnaire was translated into 20 different languages in total.[26] Out of 150 questions, 60 were based on the convictions and values of the respondents.[27] Since the survey questioned only individuals employed at subsidiaries of the same company, there is a high probability, according to Hofstede, that the determined differences are actually the result of national differences and the 'mental program' of the employees.[28] Four underlying dimensions of country cultures were identified from the values obtained within the scope of the study. These dimensions together explained 49 per cent of the variance.[29] Hofstede named them power distance, uncertainty avoidance, **femininity** vs. **masculinity**, and **individualism** vs. **collectivism**. A later study involving participants from the Asian Pacific region included a fifth dimension, **Confucianism** or **long-term orientation**.

The *power distance* dimension represents the scale on which the members of a culture accept that power is not distributed equally in institutions. It expresses the emotional distance between employees and superiors.[30] Power inequality exists in many cultures but may be more or less pronounced from culture to culture. Societies marked by high power distance and high power inequality accept hierarchical organization structure, in which every individual can occupy their place without any need for justification. Cultures with low power distance aspire to equal power distribution and demand explanations for any instance of formalized power inequality. The important difference between societies that differ with respect to the Power Distance Index is in how power inequality is dealt with. See IHRM in Action Case 2.1. Naturally, this implies consequences for the structure of organizations.[31]

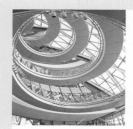

IHRM in Action Case 2.1

Establishing a branch of a family business in China

A family-owned carbon steel company from Germany has extended its business to Hong Kong. The owners bought a small traditional Chinese firm and decided to copy the successful structure they had developed at home. This structure was headed by three general managers who equally shared the responsibilities for the business activities of the firm. The consequences were as follows.

1. The Chinese employees were assigned tasks by people they had never seen before and whom they did not understand. Many misunderstandings occurred, some were quite costly.

2. The employees back in Europe were only concerned with whether the assigned tasks were completed and did not consider any other obligations to the Chinese employees, such as taking care of the relationships with the Chinese government, banks, etc.

3. Eventually, the local employees became frustrated and were ready to leave the company.

The result was that the management model was changed again and a single managing director of the subsidiary was accountable for all business activities in Hong Kong.

Discussion Questions:

1   Relate the described situation to one of the cultural dimensions identified by Hofstede. How can you explain it?

2   How does this situation compare to comparable situations in your home country? What are the limits of a cultural explanation?

Source: Based on DGFP, M. Festing, K.-P. Gempper, G. Gesche, J. Hagenmüller, U. Hann, D. Slevogt, G. Trautwein, P. Esch and S. Armutat (eds.) *Interkulturelle Managementsituation in der Praxis, Kommentierte Fallbeispiele für Führungskräfte und Personalmanager* (Bielefeld: Bertelsmann, 2004).

The cultural dimension of *uncertainty avoidance* represents the extent to which the members of a culture feel threatened by uncertain, ambiguous and/or unstructured situations and try to avoid them. Cultures with strong uncertainty avoidance are characterized by strict beliefs and behavioral codes and do not tolerate people and ideas that deviate from these. In cultures with weak uncertainty avoidance, the significance of practice exceeds the significance of principles and there is high tolerance for deviations. The major difference between countries with differing Uncertainty Avoidance Index scores is the reaction of individuals to time pressure or uncertainties in the future. People try to influence and control the future to a varying extent.[32] Just like the power distance dimension, the uncertainty avoidance dimension implies consequences for the structure of organizations. Hofstede even goes so far as to claim that countries with weaker uncertainty avoidance are more likely to bring about fundamental innovations, because they have greater tolerance for deviate thinking. See IHRM in Action Case 2.2. However, he

IHRM in Action Case 2.2

Long-term development plans of a German multinational in the USA

A German firm had developed its activities in the electrical industry in the USA for two years and the Chief Executive Officer (CEO) Peter Hansen was happy with their current performance: market share for important products had increased significantly and progress was better than expected. The number of employees had increased, including quite a few local American managers in high-level management positions – a situation which was rather unusual for a subsidiary of a German multinational in its early stage of development. The CEO's goal from the beginning was to avoid an ethnocentric approach to the American activities of his firm and to take a polycentric approach that supported recruitment of local managers.

One of these US local managers was John Miller, the marketing director of the company. During the last two years, he had been thoroughly prepared for his job. The company had sent him to various high-level training programs at top business schools and had provided him with a long-term career plan, which included short-term vertical career advancement. While Peter Hansen wanted to support the development of an American management style, he nevertheless tried to transfer some HR practices which are highly valued in Germany – particularly investing in training and taking a long-term intraorganizational career perspective. While some US firms took this approach, these ideas were not as widely accepted in the USA as in Germany. However, Peter Hansen assumed that these policies would be valued by the new US employees of the firm and would provide an important incentive for employee retention.

One morning, Peter Hansen was shocked to learn that John Miller was about to quit his job. A competitor had offered John a challenging position – in large part because he had systematically built up his knowledge and experience base, supported by his German employer. How can you interpret Peter Hansen's surprise from a cultural point of view?

Discussion Questions:

1   Relate the described situation to one of the cultural dimensions identified by Hofstede. Can you explain Peter Hansen's surprise using this theory?

2   How does this situation compare to comparable situations in your home country? What are the limits of a cultural explanation?

sees a decisive drawback for these nations in the implementation of such innovations, because detailed work and punctuality are required for implementation. An outstanding implementation of complex processes is associated with cultures with higher uncertainty avoidance. In summary, he ascertains that more Nobel Prize winners have come from Great Britain than Japan, but Japan was able to introduce more new products into the world market.[33]

The cultural dimension of *femininity vs. masculinity* identified by Hofstede is based on the assumption that values can be distinguished as more masculine or more feminine (see IHRM in Action Case 2.3). The masculine orientation comprises the pursuit of financial success, heroism, and strong performance approach; the feminine orientation contains preferences for life quality, modesty, and interpersonal relationships. Furthermore, role flexibility in the feminine-oriented cultures is more clear-cut than in more masculine cultures; in other words, the roles of the sexes can overlap.[34] The fundamental difference between the two approaches is the form of social roles attributed to gender by the relevant society.[35]

The cultural dimension of *individualism vs. collectivism* describes the extent to which individual initiative and caring for oneself and relatives is preferred by a society as opposed to, for example, public assistance or the concept of extended family. In more individualist cultures there is a more casual network of relationships between people. More collective cultures, on the contrary, have closer, more clearly defined systems of relationships. This applies both to

IHRM in Action Case 2.3
Female careers in various environments

Elisabeth Harstad was employed as a trainee at the Norwegian risk management consultancy DNV when she realized that being a woman was a barrier. Although trainees were supposed to go abroad, the company had problems finding a job for Elisabeth in a foreign subsidiary: "I wanted to go to London, Houston, or Singapore. In the end I managed to get an international assignment from Oslo to Copenhagen".

This was in the 1980s. However, Elisabeth Harstad did not give up and energetically pursued her career. She is now the manager of the research and innovation unit at DNV, and since 2006 a member of the board of directors of the large Norwegian chemical company Yara. When the new members of the board of directors were elected, for the first time it was an advantage for Elisabeth to be a woman. Since 2008, Norwegian companies are required by law to have 40 per cent female members of their board of directors. Thus, Elizabeth is part of an experiment – if women do not make it to the top on their own, politics support this process in Norway.

Discussion Questions:

1   Relate the situation in Norway to one of the cultural dimensions identified by Hofstede. How can you explain it?

2   Can the rules for quotas of female managers be applied in other countries as well? What are the advantages and disadvantages?

Source: M. Festing, P. J. Dowling, W. Weber, A. D. Engle *Internationales Personalmanagement*, 3rd ed. (Wiebaden: Gabler, 2011), based on L. Nienhaus Der neidische Blick auf die norwegische Quote (Frankfurter Allgemeine Sonntagszeitung, 2007), S. 42. Reproduced with kind permission from VS Verlag Für Sozialwissenschaften.

extended families as well as companies. A clear line is drawn between one's own group and other groups. In exchange for the care offered by their group, the group member develops a sense of loyalty to the group. The distinguishing aspect of this dimension is the predominant self-sufficiency among individuals in a society. This applies to private life and work life. See IHRM in Action Case 2.4.

With regard to professional life, collectivist companies differ from individualist companies in that the relationship between the superior and the employee in collectivist structures can be described as more informal. Furthermore, recruitment and career progression is often within the *in-group, that is the dyad composed of the supervisor and those employees that are trusted and favored by the supervisor and expected to work harder.* Management means management of groups and the reward systems are frequently group-oriented. On the contrary, individualist companies focus on individual aspects when structuring reward systems. The relationship between the superior and the employee is usually based on a relatively neutral, impersonal contractual foundation. Although the four presented dimensions were derived from data collected from employees of one multinational company, according to Hofstede they were confirmed in later studies by other researchers who worked with different methods and studied different target groups.[36]

IHRM in Action Case 2.4

Meeting on a Friday in Kenya?

Our building company had finished an important project concerning a new major road in Kenya. However, the company had not been paid for all of the completed work. The managing director of the Kenyan subsidiary of the building corporation organized a meeting with a representative of the relevant Kenyan government agency.

The meeting started and the representative was very polite and friendly. However, at the same time he also seemed to be quite nervous. Every few minutes he received a telephone call or had to initiate a telephone call himself. All telephone discussions were carried out in the local language. Despite the interruptions, I tried to explain the reason for my visit – the outstanding account balance. Of course, the government representative apologized for every interruption. However, after 15 minutes we were both very tense because the conversation had not advanced at all.

Eventually I said that I was sorry that my counterpart had so much to do and asked for another meeting next Tuesday. Instantly the government representative was relaxed again and happily confirmed the new meeting. Now he could finally concentrate on the preparation and organization of his big family meeting that weekend, which is typical for large Kenyan families.

Discussion Questions:

1   Relate the described situation to one of the cultural dimensions identified by Hofstede. How can you explain it?

2   How does this situation compare to comparable situations in your home country? What are the limits of a cultural explanation?

Source: Based on DGFP, M. Festing, K.–P. Gempper, G. Gesche, J. Hagenmüller, U. Hann, D. Slevogt, G. Trautwein, P. Esch, and S. Armutat (eds.) *Interkulturelle Managementsituation in der Praxis. Kommentierte Fallbeispiele für Führungskräfte und Personalmanager* (Bielefeld: Bertelsmann, 2004).[37]

Given the composition of the research team during Hofstede's first study, the risk that the cultural identity of researchers from Western industrial countries (Great Britain, France, Holland, Norway, USA) influenced the form of the questionnaire cannot be ruled out. There is a possibility that some questions were considered irrelevant in some cultures, while other questions relevant for these cultures were not even included. To examine possible distortion of results, a questionnaire that clearly reflects Chinese cultural identity was later designed (Chinese Value Survey). This questionnaire was translated into ten languages and used to survey 100 people from 23 countries. Only a few items in the Chinese Value Survey were transferred from the IBM questionnaire in the same form. Nevertheless, the results reflected three dimensions similar to power distance, individualism vs. collectivism, and masculinity vs. femininity. Only the uncertainty avoidance dimension could not be confirmed in this study. Instead, another dimension was discovered which could not be related to the results of the original pan-European IBM study. It was described by researchers as '**Confucianism dynamics**'. This dimension essentially reflects a basic orientation in the life of people which can be either more long-term or short-term in nature. Cultures that are described as *long-term* in this dimension are characterized by:

- endurance and/or persistence in pursuing goals
- position of ranking based on status
- adaptation of traditions to modern conditions
- respect for social and status obligations within certain limits
- high savings rates and high investment activity
- readiness to subordinate oneself to a purpose.

Short-term cultures are characterized by:

- personal candor and stability
- avoiding loss of face and respect of social and status obligations without consideration of costs
- low savings rates and low investment activity
- expectations of quick profits
- respect for traditions
- greetings, presents and courtesies based on reciprocity.

The first set of values is viewed as more future-oriented and dynamic (in particular, persistence and frugality); the second set of values is viewed as more present-oriented or past-oriented and is relatively static.[38] The name of this dimension comes from the fact that nearly all values of the short-term and long-term dimension could be drawn directly from the study of Confucianism.[39]

Country-specific results of the Hofstede study.   The results for individual countries were obtained by the evaluation of pre-determined answers, which ensured that the results could be demonstrated by point values. The point values reflect the relative rather than absolute positions of the countries.[40] The results are graphically represented with the help of co-ordinates systems, which contain a cultural dimension on the X-axis and another on the Y-axis. The representation demonstrates the extent of cultural distance between two countries with regard to these dimensions. For example, in Figure 2.1 individual countries are assigned to the co-ordinates system based on individualism vs. collectivism and power distance dimensions.

According to the Hofstede study, the US culture is characterized by individualist behavior. The same applies to the other Anglo-Saxon countries such as Australia or the UK. The extent of

FIGURE 2.1   Results of the Hofstede study (I): Power distance and individualism vs. collectivism

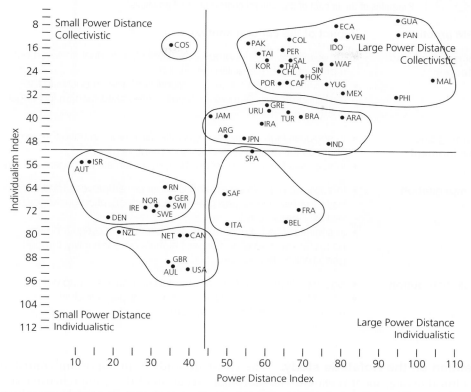

Source: Based on Geert Hofstede, Gert Jan Hofstede, Michael Minkov, "*Cultures and Organizations, Software of the Mind*", Third Revised Edition, McGraw-Hill 2010, ISBN 0-07-166418-1. Reproduced with permission.

power distance is classified as rather low for all these countries. In terms of the characteristics for both of these cultural dimensions, many South Asian countries can be described as the opposite. For example, Singapore, Hong Kong, and Taiwan (and also many South American countries) are characterized by collectivist values and a high power distance. These clusters are culturally distant from each other according to the results of the study. Countries are assigned to a cluster based on statistically established similarities among them.

Some Asian cultures tend to score high on uncertainty avoidance and high on power distance. Among them are Singapore and Hong Kong. On the contrary, the German-speaking countries such as Germany, Austria, and Switzerland build with others a cluster that can be described by a comparably strong tendency toward uncertainty avoidance and a relatively low power distance.

As a result of combining the masculinity index with the uncertainty avoidance dimension, we can identify a cluster that includes the predominantly German-speaking countries Germany, Austria, and Switzerland. All three countries are attributed more masculine values with relatively high uncertainty-avoidance tendencies. The group of predominantly German-speaking countries is the second most masculine-oriented cluster in the entire global 'geography', second only to Japan. Opposite to this is the Scandinavian cluster, including Denmark, Sweden, Norway, and Finland.

In terms of the fifth dimension, long-term vs. short-term orientation of cultures, the USA, for example, is characterized by a rather low value. Therefore, it is classified more as a short-term-oriented culture. This result is the opposite of the Asian countries, which demonstrate higher value for long-term orientation. Thus, the robust economic growth of the Four Asian Tigers – Hong Kong, Singapore, South Korea, and Taiwan – in the 1980s can be partly traced back to a strong orientation toward Confucian values.[41] Table 2.1 (overleaf) presents examples of how cultural context may affect selected HRM practices.

TABLE 2.1   Examples of the impact of the cultural context on HRM practices

HRM practices	Impact of the cultural context
Recruitment and selection	• In societies *low on 'in-group collectivism'*, individual achievements represent important selection criteria. • In societies *high on 'in-group collectivism'*, the emphasis in the recruiting process is more on team-related skills than on individual competencies.
Training and development	• In societies *high on gender egalitarianism*, women have the same chances for vertical career advancement as men. • In societies *low on gender egalitarianism*, female managers are rare.
Compensation	• In societies *high on uncertainty avoidance*, employees tend to be rather risk averse and prefer fixed compensation packages or seniority-based pay. • In societies *low on uncertainty avoidance*, employees tend to be rather risk-taking and accept high income variability through performance-based pay.
Task distribution	• Societies *high on collectivism* tend to emphasize group work. • Societies *high on individualism* rather attribute individual responsibilities in the work system.

A reflection on the Hofstede study.   The Hofstede study is an important contribution to cross-cultural management research. The thorough execution of this comprehensive study and its repetition at different points in time is very impressive. The results enable assertions about potential differences between individual cultures and could serve as guidelines for explaining behavior at least in initial orientation. However, there has been an ongoing debate and critique of Hofstede's study, aside from fundamental criticism of his concept of culture, described as determinist and universalist,[42] and his approach of trying to reduce cultures to a few dimensions instead of using more sophisticated descriptions.[43]

As noted earlier in the chapter, Hofstede's study is placed on the value level, the intermediate level of the Schein concept. However, the emerging question is to what extent the standardized questionnaire method is able to reach the unconscious and, thus, assess the deeper motives of managers' actions. Hofstede is criticized for not drawing a line between practices per se and perceived practices – in other words, a sort of wishful thinking.[44] Significant questions have been raised about the lack of separation between values and behavior[45] and the potential distortion of the 'Western outlook' of the research.[46]

Another criticism of the Hofstede study is that countries rather than cultures are delimited. The example of what was once Yugoslavia in the 1990s shows with terrible clarity that country borders by no means contain relatively homogenous cultural groups. Kaasa *et al.*[47] have compared the Hofstede data with newer data from the European Social Survey which shows that the Hofstede values should be regarded with some skepticism, especially in terms of multicultural societies like Belgium. It should be assumed that Hofstede did not adequately represent the existing ethnic groups and his study cannot classify countries with several relatively equally co-existing languages in his country clusters. Finally, it should be assumed that national cultures are not the only influencing factor of behavior.[48] This is a major reason why scholars increasingly assume a progressively lower influence of nation states on cultural identity and behavior.[49]

The following points are relevant in terms of the study's representative nature: the study was conducted in one company (IBM) only. Hofstede himself evaluates this as positive, because many conditions could be maintained constant. However, in the case of an organization that is characterized by a very strong corporate culture, such as IBM, it should be assumed that the choice of personnel is based on a similar profile of requirements around the world, which may lead to distortion of results (i.e. selected 'IBMers' were not typical national citizens). So the question is: would the results of random sampling of several companies come out differently in terms of the distinctions between individual countries or country clusters? The representative nature of data is also contested, because the IBM study sample was mainly limited to middle-class males in marketing and service positions. Kirkman *et al.*[50] acknowledge the significance of Hofstede's culture dimensions but note that future research should take the following issues into consideration:

- *Realization of intralevel studies:* along with assessing the individual level, groups, organizations, and country levels must be taken into consideration.

- *Inclusion of cross-cultural differences:* cultures should not be considered homogenous – specific intracultural variance should be taken into consideration.

- *Inclusion of theoretically relevant moderator variables:* culture should not be measured as the only influencing factor – other variables like sex, class affiliation, etc. should be taken into account.

- *Effects of interaction between culture variables:* there is a lack of empirical evidence about the interplay of individual culture variables and their interaction, which should be taken into account.

Although the historical prominence of the Hofstede study makes continuing debate of the results useful, the results must be scrutinized from today's point of view. The results of Hofstede's first study are from 1967–1973. Determining the scope of validity of these results for individual countries today certainly requires a new, comprehensive study. Although it is assumed that cultures do not change fundamentally in such a time period, certain decisive changes have occurred – for example, the reunification of Germany, which could influence average values.[51] In a recent study, Kaasa *et al.* tested Hofstede's values once again for the European sample and came to the overall conclusion that Hofstede's values are relatively stable. However, changes are seen in countries with subsequent strong economic growth (e.g. Spain, Portugal) or after significant system changes such as a country joining the European Union (EU).[52] Because of such changes it is not surprising that an index based on Hofstede's values and dimensions developed by Kogut and Singh,[53] that claims to measure cultural distance and serve as a predictor of how challenging a specific foreign location will be to a person, has been criticized as outdated, of limited validity and bound to a simplistic, static approach.[54]

The GLOBE study

The GLOBE study was a transnational project initiated by Robert J. House in 1991. The research team currently consists of 170 researchers from 62 countries.[55] GLOBE is an acronym for *Global Leadership and Organizational Behavior Effectiveness*; in other words, this project concerns the effectiveness of leadership and behavior in organizations at a global level, with special consideration given to cultural influence factors. Three research phases were planned in total. Phase I (1993/1994) consisted of the development of underlying research dimensions (new social and organizational cultural dimensions, and six leadership dimensions). The objective of Phase II (2004-2007) was to gather data on these dimensions. Phase III (2012-2013) consists of an analysis of the effects of leadership behavior on the performance and attitudes of employees.[56] The goal of the GLOBE study can be illustrated with the following questions:

- Are there leadership behaviors, attributes, and organizational practices that are generally accepted and effective across cultures?

- Are there leadership behaviors, attributes, and organizational practices that are accepted and effective in some cultures only?

- How much do leadership attributes that are traced back to social and organizational contexts affect the effectiveness of specific leadership behavior and its acceptance by subordinates?

- How much do behaviors and attributes in specific cultures influence the economic, physical, and psychological well-being of the members of societies researched in the study?

- What is the relationship between these socio-cultural variables and an international competitive capacity of the various sample societies?

The GLOBE research tries to study the complex relationships between culture, leadership behavior, organizational effectiveness, social cohabitation conditions, and the economic success of societies.[57]

Culture dimensions of the GLOBE study.   The study is to some extent based on Hofstede's dimensions: *uncertainty avoidance* and *power distance*. However, the dimensions are modified and expanded, leading to some confusion when Hofstede and GLOBE results are assessed and compared. This may be seen as somewhat ironic, given the topic area.[58] The *collectivism* dimension is divided into *social* and *group/family-based collectivism*, which describe two levels of the same dimension. The above dimensions are measured on the social and organizational level respectively. In addition, there is a distinction in the questions between practices (*as is*) and values (*should be*) of respective dimensions. Thus, the survey covers practices that are assessed as *common* in the respective societies or organizations. Furthermore, value dimensions determine what specific practices *should* be like in respective organizations or societies. Authors of the GLOBE study are purposefully trying to overcome the earlier critiques of the Hofstede study, namely that the borders between values and practices are blurred in his study and cannot be distinguished. The different dimensions are explained briefly below.

- **Institutional Collectivism** describes "the degree to which organizational and societal institutional practices encourage and reward collective distribution of resources and collective action".[59]

- **In-Group Collectivism** is "[t]he degree to which individuals express pride, loyalty, and cohesiveness in their organizations or families".[60]

- **Uncertainty Avoidance** includes "the extent to which a society, organization, or group relies on social norms, rules, and procedures to alleviate unpredictability of future events".[61]

- **Power Distance** is defined as "the degree to which members of a collective expect power to be distributed equally".[62]

- **Gender Egalitarianism** is "the degree to which a collective minimizes gender inequality".[63]

- **Assertiveness** is "[t]he degree to which individuals are assertive, confrontational, and aggressive in their relationship with others".[64]

- **Performance Orientation** is defined as "the degree to which a collective encourages and rewards group members for performance improvement and excellence".[65]

- **Humane Orientation** includes "the degree to which a collective encourages and rewards individuals for being fair, altruistic, generous, caring, and kind to others".[66]

Results of the GLOBE study.   Quantitative collection of data was conducted in 62 countries by the GLOBE study; 17,370 people from middle management, 951 organizations and three industries (finance, food, and telecommunication services) were surveyed. Based on a literature analysis by the GLOBE study authors, the analyzed countries and cultures were separated into ten land clusters and tested empirically.[67] This resulted in the following cultural regions: South Asia, Latin America, North America, the Anglo cluster, Germanic and Latin Europe, Sub-Saharan Africa, Eastern Europe, the Middle East, and Confucian Asia. These cultural regions have different characteristics within the respective cultural dimensions. Unique profiles emerge when combining cultural dimension characteristics for different cultures.

A reflection on the GLOBE study.   The GLOBE study explicitly takes into account the methodological challenges of cross-cultural comparative research, and its theoretical foundation is more comprehensive than that of the Hofstede study. The participation of 170 scholars from around the world helped to avoid a one-sided Western focus and there is a distinction between organizational cultures and national cultures.[68] Furthermore, the dimensions identified in the GLOBE study are also refined compared to other cross-cultural management studies. In view of the empirical research, for example, more branches have been included as compared to Hofstede, who has often been criticized for limiting his sample to IBM employees only. Among other differences to the Hofstede study is that managers were surveyed instead of employees.

The GLOBE study does have some limitations. Hofstede has criticized the GLOBE study, stating that the scales do not measure what they should and criticizing the further differentiation of his original five dimensions. But this criticism has been rejected by authors of the GLOBE study,[69] generating an ongoing debate.[70] In addition, it should be noted that, despite the expansion to three industries (finance, food, and telecommunications), there is limited industry focus in the GLOBE study as well – the data are not representative for other industries. Similar to the criticism of Hofstede, widespread equivalence of culture to nation can be a source of concern as well. This is yet another example of the ongoing 'level of analysis' debate in organizational studies. Although authors of the GLOBE study counteract this by taking into consideration various culture levels (individual, organizational, and social) and further distinguishing the sample in some countries (e.g. South Africa, Switzerland, and Germany), it should be noted that cultures may consist of various subcultures and that this is not sufficiently reflected in the GLOBE study at the present stage. Large population countries like China, India, and the USA are very heterogeneous and cannot really be covered by the relatively small sample of the GLOBE study.[71]

The Trompenaars and Hampden-Turner study.   Trompenaars and Hampden-Turner conducted a survey with employees of various hierarchical levels and various businesses starting in the 1980s and continuing for several decades.[72] The target group was primarily participants of cross-cultural training conducted by Trompenaars. Approximately 15,000 questionnaires were evaluated in the first study. By 2002 there were about 30,000 questionnaires from 55 countries.[73] In their book *Riding the Waves of Culture* Trompenaars and Hampden-Turner differentiated between seven dimensions, the characteristics of which mark the differences between cultures.[74] They grouped these seven dimensions by three aspects: relationships between people, concept of time and concept of nature.

Relationships between people:

- **Universalism** vs. **Particularism**: *Universalist* thought is characterized according to the authors by the following logic: "What is good and right can be defined and always applies".[75] *Particularist* cultures, on the contrary, pay more attention to individual cases, deciding what is good and correct depending on relationship and special friendship arrangements.

- **Individualism** vs. **Communitarianism**: The underlying question here is: "Do people regard themselves primarily as individuals or primarily as parts of a group?".[76] The other question is whether it is desirable that individuals primarily serve group aims or individual aims. *Individualist* cultures, similar to Hofstede's explanation, emphasize the individual, who predominantly takes care of himself.[77] Alternately, *communitarian* cultures focus on identity, responsibility and concern that focus on a larger social group.

- **Emotional** vs. **Neutral**: This dimension describes how emotions are treated and whether they are expressed or not.[78] *Neutral* cultures tend to express little emotion; business is transacted as objectively and functionally as possible. In affective cultures, an *emotional* cultural basis is accepted as a part of business life and emotions are freely expressed across many social contexts.[79]

- **Specific** vs. **diffuse**: In *diffuse* cultures a person is involved in the business relationship, whereas *specific* cultures focus more on contractually regulated aspects. Specific cultures demand precision, an objective analysis of circumstances and presentation of results, whereas diffuse cultures take other context variables into consideration.[80]

- **Ascription** vs. **Achievement**: In cultures focused on status *achievement*, people are judged based on what they have achieved; in other words, the goals they have fulfilled recently. In *ascriptive* cultures, the status is ascribed from birth by characteristics such as origin, seniority, and gender.[81]

Concept of time:

- Sequential vs. Synchronic concept of time: Cultures are differentiated by the concept of time, where they may be more past-, future- or present-oriented. The different concept of time is also demonstrated by the organization of work processes. *Sequential* behavior is behavior that occurs successively, and *synchronous* behavior is the possibility to 'multitask' and do a number of things at the same time.[82]

Concept of nature:

- **Internal** vs. **external control**: This dimension describes the concept of nature and refers to the extent to which societies try to control nature. Trompenaars and Hampden-Turner refer to the example of the Sony executive Morita, who explained the invention of the Walkman resulted from his love of classical music and a desire not to burden the world with his own music taste. This is an example of *external control*, of how people adapt heavily to the environment. In Western societies, the mindset is different; headphones are used to listen to music and ignore the environment. Another example is wearing a facemask during the cold/flu season. According to Trompenaars, in external control cultures, masks are used because one does not want to infect others, whereas in *internal control* cultures masks are used to protect one's self from outside sources of infection.[83]

An explicit rationale for the operationalization and genesis of the seven dimensions by Trompenaars and Hampden-Turner remains unclear. The authors use single aspects of other studies, like Kluckhohn and Strodtbeck, Parsons, and Hofstede – without in-depth justification for their selection – and leave out others, also with no justification. To date, Trompenaars and Hampden-Turner have not demonstrated the validity or reliability of their dimensions, or justified their classification schema. There is no empirical basis for their characterization of differences in national characteristics. Despite this lack of empirical support, this model is used extensively in executive education programs as a template to describe behavior and to draw conclusions for interaction with foreign business partners.

The cultural dimensions by Hall and Hall.   Based on their own experiences as government and corporate advisors and various qualitative studies, anthropologist Edward Hall and his wife Mildred Hall[84] have presented four dimensions that differentiate cultures. They do not claim that their model covers all possibilities, pointing out that other dimensions may also exist. The relationship between culture and communication is emphasized in particular, as one would not be possible without the other. The dimensions mainly involve cultural differences in communication forms and time and space concepts.

- **High** vs. **Low Context Communication**: Cultures differ in the way their members communicate with each other. In *high context* cultures, a more indirect form of expression is common, where the receiver must decipher the content of the message from its context, whereas in so-called *low context* cultures the players tend to communicate more to the point and verbalize all-important information. Examples of high context cultures are Japan as well as France. Germany is more of a low context culture.

- **Spatial orientation**: The focus of this dimension is on the distance between people of various cultures when communicating. Distance that is adequate for members of one culture may feel intrusive for members of another culture.

- **Monochrome** vs. **polychrome concept of time**: A *monochrome concept of time* is dominated by processes where one thing is done after the other, whereas in the *polychrome concept* these actions occur at the same time.

- **Information speed**: This dimension focuses on whether information flow in groups is high or low during communication. Thus, in the USA, people tend to exchange personal information relatively quickly, while in Europe such a rate of information exchange would require a more extended acquaintance.[85]

As already mentioned, the classification of cultural dimensions by Hall and Hall came about in an inductive way and does not claim to be complete. In addition, the dimensions are closely related and overlapping and cultural regions are represented in a macro sense, such as the USA and Europe. Intracultural differences are not touched upon, but personal differences are referred to. The works by Hall and Hall, similar to that of Trompenaars and Hampden-Turner, focus on offering a practical template, allowing individuals to perceive and handle cultural differences.

A reflection of cross-cultural management studies

Cross-cultural studies are generally subject to the problem of not doing justice to a dynamic, context-sensitive concept of culture.[86] This criticism has been widely recognized in recent years. However, intercultural interactions contain their own momentum and new aspects become more salient, which cannot be explained by existing culture dimensions. In this context, qualitative research is increasingly called on to assess these dynamic changes.[87] In addition, some authors find it important to consider culture in the context of task- or role-specific situations and not just on the values level, which is the perspective of many studies.[88]

The limits of the explanatory power of the results of cross-cultural management studies for explaining the influence of the cultural context have been very clearly outlined in an important contribution by Gerhart,[89] using the example of organizational cultures. According to Gerhart, in the GLOBE study, 23 per cent of the variance is explained by country-specific differences, however, *only 6 per cent is actually due to cultural differences*. Gerhart agrees that cultural differences are important but notes that these differences do not have as big an influence as is frequently assumed. He identifies a need for further theoretical and empirical research.[90] The static–dynamic nature of culture is increasingly discussed by practitioners and researchers alike. The next section will focus on how cultures may develop and change.

THE DEVELOPMENT OF CULTURES

So far, this chapter has primarily dealt with how culture can be defined and conceptualized and some results of cross-cultural management research have been reported. Most explanations and concepts have been based on a somewhat static outlook. We will now discuss the extent to which cultures may undergo changes over time. This discussion is closely related to the issue of whether organizations and their management practices are similar due to increasing international interconnectedness and the co-ordination of the global economy (*convergence*), or still exhibit specific cultural characteristics. For example, culture convergence between European countries is often imputed given the development of the EU and attendant harmonization of laws and regulations. Thus, increasing convergence of the cultures of individual countries within the EU is often assumed. As a result, the meaning of cultural differences may be given limited consideration. If the opposite is true and we assume a long-term stability in cultural differences (*cultural divergence*), their investigation may be a decisive success factor in international business activities for the foreseeable future. In terms of activity within the European Community, this would mean that pan-European standardization of management practices would not be easily achieved and adaptation of practices to underlying local conditions would be required.

Both of these conflicting positions on cultural convergence continue to generate controversy in the academic literature.[91] Child[92] analyzed a multitude of cross-cultural studies and discovered that there are as many researchers who came to the conclusion that cultures are similar as studies that claimed just the opposite. Upon detailed analysis he determined that studies positioned on the *macro level* (e.g. analyses of organizational structure) tended to find evidence for convergence, while studies positioned on the *micro level* (e.g. dealing with the analysis of behavior of employees) reached more divergence-oriented conclusions. As a result, it can be concluded that organizations around the world are becoming more similar in their processes and technologies, because they are embedded in institutions that are also subject to convergence,[93] but real and meaningful differences in the behavior of employees remain, and these differences are enduring.[94] This is also underlined by Schein, who assumes that the influences operating from the surface **artefact** level to the underlying assumption level are much weaker than the influence on deep assumptions on surface-level artefacts.[95]

A new combination of various cultural elements is taking place, which results in new ways of distinguishing otherness and hybridization of what were once distinct cultures.[96] Recently, transnational regions have been investigated. These are regions in which country borders are progressively superseded by cultures. Due to growing interdependence and a high flow of migration, culture is not confined to a territorially limited area. The question of how accepting a local or national majority will be to variant subcultures is a significant issue, one that will be addressed in the final chapter of the book. This issue represents new challenges for HRM, but at the same time it also offers new opportunities.

Intracultural changes must also be considered by HR managers. In this context, demographic changes are an example of where there has been considerable discussion on the extent of value shift between generations.[97] Generation Y is mentioned as an example in this context, because it is distinguished by different demands when it comes to professional relationships and employee retention.[98] Since this generation was born into an information society and grew up with the computer, these people are described as fast, self-organized learners. This generation is highly flexible when it comes to multitasking and demonstrates high potential for scrutinizing decisions due to a high level of awareness. This makes members of Generation Y attractive but somewhat self-absorbed employees with distinct preferences such as work–life balance preferences. This phenomenon will be observed beyond cultural borders. The aging of entire societies, and hence their workforces (e.g. in Japan and Italy), also represents a form of this generational phenomenon.

Finally, some researchers argue that culture is far too blunt an instrument to apply to decision processes in multinational enterprises (MNEs). Instead, they argue for an institutional focus that is better able to explain more complex and interactive forces at work. Other long time researchers in this topic area suggest that cross-cultural differences may not necessarily always have a negative impact on MNE operations and may have a positive impact on operations in MNEs.[99]

SUMMARY

In the preceding sections, we outlined how the cultural environment may influence HRM. In summary, it can be concluded that an adequate understanding of the cultural context, as it impacts the behavior of an organization's employees, is of decisive importance. Thus, results of cross-cultural comparative research may provide valuable hints to managers about how to cope with employees of foreign cultures.[100] Furthermore, these results can form the basis for the development of intercultural training measures. These results could also be of great use to HRM in an international firm because these conceptual frameworks could assist a structured analysis of the transferability of specific elements of the parent firm's existing HR policy to foreign subsidiaries. In this context, it would be conceivable to decide whether incentive systems for groups or for individuals would be effective in a specific culture.[101]

Table 2.1 summarizes these ideas about the cultural context and gives examples of environmental differences which could lead to problems when MNEs attempt to introduce worldwide standardized HRM practices.[102] Within this context, it is important to recall the discussion on the convergence and divergence of HRM and work practices, as mentioned in the first chapter.

DISCUSSION QUESTIONS

1 Define culture. How can culture be conceptualized?

2 Outline the cross-cultural management study by Hofstede and discuss it.

3 Outline the methodology and the results of the GLOBE study.

4 Compare cross-cultural management studies and list advantages and disadvantages.

5 To what extent do cultures undergo changes? Illustrate your statement with an example.

6 What do you think about the statement: "Cultures in Europe are becoming more similar?".

FURTHER READING

M. J. Adler and A. Gundersen *International Dimensions of Organizational Behavior,* 5th ed. (Mason, CA: Thomson South-Western, 2008).

S. Dolan and K. Kawamura *Cross Cultural Competence: A Field Guide for Developing Global Leaders and Managers* (Bingley, UK: Emerald Group Publishing, 2015).

G. Hofstede *Culture's Consequences: International Differences in Work Related Values*, 2nd ed. (Beverly Hills, CA: Sage, 2008).

I. Weller and B. Gerhart 'Empirical Research Issues in Comparative Human Resource Management', in C. Brewster and W. Mayrhofer (eds.) *Handbook of Research in Comparative Human Resource Management* (Cheltenham, UK: Edward Elgar, 2012).

NOTES AND REFERENCES

1. See, for example, N. J. Adler and A. Gundersen, *International Dimensions of Organizational Behavior*, 5th ed. (Cincinnati, OH: Thomson South-Western, 2008); R. M. Hodgetts, F. Luthans and J. P. Doh, *International Management: Culture, Strategy, and Behavior*, 6th ed. (New York: McGraw-Hill/Irwin, 2006).

2. See E. Dülfer and B. Jöstingmeier, *Internationales Management in unterschiedlichen Kulturbereichen*, 7th ed. (München: Oldenburg, 2008).

3. Homepage of Geert Hofstede http://www.geert-hofstede.com.

4. For more information see the website of the GLOBE Project: http://www.thunderbird.edu/-wwwfiles/ms/globe. *Organizational Behavior*, 5th ed. (Cincinnati, OH: Thomson Learning, South-Western, 2008).

5. N. J. Adler and A. Gundersen, *International Dimensions of Organizational Behavior*, 5th ed. For two recent reviews of the strengths and weakness of 'American' HRM see B. Fisher 'The Historical Development of American HRM Broadly Viewed', *Human Resource Management Review* 24 (2014), pp. 196–218 and J. Boudreau and

E. E. Lawler 'Stubborn Traditionalism in HRM: Causes and Consequences', *Human Resource Management Review*, Vol. 24 (2014), pp. 232–244.

6. See also S. A. Sackmann and M. E. Phillips, 'Contextual Influences on Culture Research: Shifting Assumptions for New Workplace Realities', *International Journal of Cross Cultural Management*, Vol. 4, No. 3 (2004), pp. 370–390.

7. N. J. Adler and A. Gundersen, *International Dimensions of Organizational Behavior*, 5th ed. For a specifc instance of how even globally accepted lean manufacturing practices can go wrong – in this case in India – see S. Mathew and R. Jones ' Toyotism and Brahminism: Employee Relations Difficulties in Establishing Lean Manufacturing in India', *Employee Relations*, Vol. 35, no. 2 (2013), pp. 200–221.

8. See the classic article by J. Child, 'Culture, Contingency and Capitalism in the Cross-National Study of Organizations', in L. L. Cummings and B. M. Staw (eds.) *Research in Organizational Behavior* (Greenwich, CT: JAI, 1981), Vol. 3, pp. 303–356.

9. For an overview about the development of new culture concepts and culture criticism see M. Fischer, M.J. 'Culture and Culture Analysis', *Theory, Culture and Society*, Vol. 23, No. 2–3 (2006), pp. 360–364. An analysis of articles in the area from 2001 to 2010 leads P. Arnold and M. Menendez to conclude that pursuing how actors enact roles in cultures and how 'cross-national learning' takes place are promising areas to move forward through the confusion. See P. Almond and M. Menendez 'Cross-National Comparative Human Resource Management and the Ideational Sphere: A Critical Review', *International Journal of Human Resource Management*, Vol. 25, no. 18 (2014), pp. 2591–2607.

10. A. L. Kroeber and C. Kluckhohn *Culture. A Critical Review of Concepts and Definitions*. (New York, NY: Random House, 1952), p. 181.

11. G. Hofstede *Culture and Organizations Software of the Mind* (London, UK: McGraw-Hill, 1991). German translation by G. Hofstede *Lokales Denken, globales Handeln Kulturen: Zusammenarbeit und Management,* 5th ed. (München: Beck, 2009).

12. G. Hofstede *Cultures and Organizations – Software of the Mind*, 4th ed. This definition is based on Hofstede's study described further on in this chapter.

13. H. C. Triandis *The Analysis of Subjective Culture* (New York: John Wiley, 1972).

14. F. Fiedler, T. Mitchell and H. C. Triandis 'The Culture Assimilator: An Approach to Cross-Cultural Training', *Journal of Applied Psychology*, Vol. 55 (1971), pp. 95–102.

15. On respective different types of culture concepts that various trends of cross-cultural management are based on, and the effects on research design and research topics, see S. A. Sackmann and M. E. Phillips 'Contextual Influences on Culture Research: Shifting Assumptions for New Workplace Realities', *International Journal of Cross Cultural Management*, Vol. 4, No. 3 (2004), pp. 370–390.

16. See E. H. Schein *Organizational Culture and Leadership*, 3rd ed. (San Francisco: Jossey-Bass, 2004).

17. F. R. Kluckhohn and F. L. Strodtbeck *Variations in Value Orientations* (Evanston, IL: Row, Peterson and Company, 1961).

18. E. H. Schein *Organizational Culture and Leadership*, 3rd ed. In addition, see also N. J. Adler and A. Gundersen *International Dimensions of Organizational Behavior*, 5th ed.

19. See also N. J. Adler and A. Gundersen *International Dimensions of Organizational Behavior*, 5th ed.

20. Other extremely important studies, like the value study by Schwartz (1999) unfortunately could not be considered here due to lack of space. The relevance of the mentioned studies is proven in an article in the *Manual of Comparative Human Resource Management* by B. S. Reiche, Y. Lee and J. Quintanilla, 'Cultural Perspectives on Comparative HRM', in C. Brewster and W. Mayrhofer (eds.) *Handbook of Research in Comparative Human Resource Management* (Cheltenham, UK: Edward Elgar, 2012), pp. 51–68.

21. B. L. Kirkman, K. B. Lowe and C. B. Gibson 'A Quarter of Century of Culture's Consequences: A Review of Empirical Research Incorporating Hofstede's Cultural Values Framework', *Journal of International Business Studies*, Vol. 37, No. 3 (2006), pp. 285–320. This article identifies those studies that apply Hofstede's cultural frames to determine how the model has impacted research in this field. However, the review is limited to articles in business and psychology journals. So it is to be assumed that Hofstede's impact is even higher in reality.

22. G. Hofstede *Culture's Consequences: International Differences in Work Related Values* (Beverly Hills: Sage, 1980). According to Hofstede, culture can be compared to an onion, which has various peels or levels. Artefacts that he subdivides into symbols, heroes and rituals are at the outer levels of the 'culture onion', according to Hofstede, whereas values are on the inner level. Changes and similarities are more probable on the outside than in the core of the culture, so measurement of values is the best approach in his opinion.

23. Remarks are supported by the following sources: G. Hofstede 'Cultural Dimensions in Management and Planning', *Asia Pacific Journal of Management*, Vol. Januar (1984a), pp. 1–22; G. Hofstede 'The Cultural Relativity of the Quality of Life Concept', *Academy of Management Review*, Vol. 9, No. 3 (1984b), pp. 389–398; G. Hofstede *Culture and Organizations – Software of the Mind* (London, UK: McGraw-Hill, 1991); G. Hofstede *Interkulturelle Zusammenarbeit. Kulturen – Organisationen – Management* (Wiesbaden: Gabler, 1993); G. Hofstede *Culture's Consequences: International Differences in Work Related Values*, 2nd ed. (Beverly Hills: Sage, 2008); G. Hofstede *Lokales Denken, globales Handeln, Kulturen, Zusammenarbeit und Management*, 5th ed. (München: Beck, 2009).

24. G. Hofstede *Culture and Organizations – Software of the Mind* (London, UK: McGraw-Hill, 1991).

25. G. Hofstede *Culture's Consequences: International Differences in Work Related Values*, 2nd ed. (Beverly Hills: Sage, 2008). The following remarks serve to explain different information about the empirical basis of studies in the literature: the first assessment involved only 40 of the 72 surveyed national subsidiaries, because no sample data that was less than 50 were to be used. The number of researched countries was later expanded by 10, while 14 other countries were combined into three country groups (East Africa, West Africa and Arabic-speaking countries), so the number went up to 53. Eight of the subsidiaries did not have enough employees from the focal country to be able to include them in the analysis. The number of entities increased later was expanded by ten countries. 14 more countries have been subsumed into three regions. G. Hofstede *Culture and Organizations – Software of the Mind* (London, UK: McGraw-Hill, 1991).

26. G. Hofstede 'Cultural Dimensions in Management and Planning', *Asia Pacific Journal of Management*, Vol. Januar (1984a), p. 3; G. Hofstede *Culture's Consequences: International Differences in Work Related Values*, 2nd ed. (Beverly Hills: Sage, 2008).

27. In general: satisfaction, perception, personal goals and preferences and demographic data. G. Hofstede *Culture's Consequences: International Differences in Work Related Values* (Beverly Hills: Sage, 1980).

28. G. Hofstede 'Cultural Dimensions in Management and Planning', *Asia Pacific Journal of Management*, Vol. Januar (1984a).

29. G. Hofstede *Culture's Consequences: International Differences in Work Related Values*, 2nd ed. (Beverly Hills: Sage, 2008).

30. G. Hofstede *Culture and Organizations – Software of the Mind* (London, UK: McGraw-Hill, 1991).

31. G. Hofstede 'Cultural Dimensions in Management and Planning', *Asia Pacific Journal of Management*, January (1984a).

32. G. Hofstede 'Cultural Dimensions in Management and Planning', *Asia Pacific Journal of Management*, January (1984a).

33. G. Hofstede *Culture and Organizations – Software of the Mind*. (London, UK: McGraw-Hill, 1991).

34. G. Hofstede *Culture and Organizations – Software of the Mind*.

35. G. Hofstede 'Cultural Dimensions in Management and Planning', *Asia Pacific Journal of Management*.

36. G. Hofstede 'Cultural Dimensions in Management and Planning', *Asia Pacific Journal of Management*, Vol. January (1984a) as well as A. Kaasa, M. Vadi and U. Varblane 'Retesting Hofstede's Cultural Dimensions of the European Sample: Some implications for Human Resource Management', in *10th International Human Resource Conference*, edited by W. Scroggins, C. Gomez, P. G. Benson, R. L. Oliver and M. J. Turner (Santa Fe, NM, USA, 2009) and B.L. Kirkman, K. B. Lowe and C. B. Gibson 'A Quarter of Century of Culture's Consequences: A Review of Empirical Research Incorporating Hofstede's Cultural Values Framework', *Journal of International Business Studies*, Vol. 37, No. 3 (2006), pp. 285–320.

37. Based on DGFP, M. Festing, K.P. Gempper, G. Gesche, J. Hagenmüller, U. Hann, D. Slevogt, G. Trautwein, P. Esch and S. Armutat (eds.) *Interkulturelle Managementsituation in der Praxis. Kommentierte Fallbeispiele für Führungskräfte und Personalmanager* (Bielefeld: Bertelsmann, 2004).

38. G. Hofstede 'Cultural Dimensions in Management and Planning', *Asia Pacific Journal of Management*.

39. G. Hofstede *Culture and Organizations – Software of the Mind* (London, UK: McGraw-Hill, 1991).

40. G. Hofstede *Culture and Organizations – Software of the Mind* (London, UK: McGraw-Hill, 1991).

41. See also G. Hofstede and M. Bond 'Confucius and Economic Growth: New Trends in Culture's Consequences', *Organizational Dynamics*, Vol. 16, No. 4 (1988), pp. 4–21.

42. B. McSweeney 'Hofstede's Model of National Cultural Differences and their Consequences: A Triumph of Faith – a Failure of Analysis', *Human Relations*, Vol. 55, No. 1 (2002).

43. On criticism see C. Early 'Leading Cultural Research in the Future: a Matter of Paradigms and Taste', *Journal of International Business Studies*, Vol. 37, No. 6 (2006), pp. 922–931; A. Kaasa, M. Vadi and U. Varblane 'Retesting Hofstede's Cultural Dimensions of the European Sample: Some implications for Human Resource Management', in *Proceedings of the 10th International Human Resource Conference*, edited by W. Scroggins, C. Gomez, P. G. Benson, R. L. Oliver and M. J. Turner (Santa Fe,

NM, USA, 2009); B. McSweeney 'Hofstede's Model of National Cultural Differences and their Consequences: A Triumph of Faith – a Failure of Analysis', *Human Relations*, Vol. 55, No. 1 (2002), pp. 89–118; W. H. Staehle *Management: Eine verhaltenswissenschaftliche Perspektive*, 8th ed. (München: Vahlen, 1999); V. Taras, J. Rowney and P. Steel 'Half a Century of Measuring Culture: A Review of Approaches, Challenges, and Limitations for Quantifying Culture', *Journal of International Management*, Vol. 15, No. 4 (2009), pp. 357–373.

44. B. McSweeney 'Hofstede's Model of National Cultural Differences and their Consequences: A Triumph of Faith – a Failure of Analysis', *Human Relations*, Vol. 55, No. 1 (2002).

45. R. J. House, N. S. Wright and R. N. Aditya 'Cross-Cultural Research on Organizational Leadership', in P. C. Earley and M. Erez (eds.), *New Perspectives on International Industrial/Organizational Psychology*, (San Francisco: Wiley, 1997), pp. 535–625.

46. G. Ailon 'Mirror, Mirror on the Wall: Culture's Consequences in a Value Test of its own Design', *Academy of Management Review*, Vol. 33, No. 4 (2008), pp. 885–904; B. McSweeney 'Hofstede's Model of National Cultural Differences and their Consequences: A Triumph of Faith – a Failure of Analysis', *Human Relations*, Vol. 55, No. 1 (2002).

47. A. Kaasa, M. Vadi and U. Varblane 'Retesting Hofstede's Cultural Dimensions of the European Sample: Some Implications for Human Resource Management', in *10th International Human Resource Conference*, edited by W. Scroggins, C. Gomez, P. G. Benson, R. L. Oliver and M. J. Turner (Santa Fe, NM, USA, 2009).

48. F. Chiang 'A Critical Examination of Hofstede's Thesis and its Application to International Reward Management', *International Journal of Human Resource Management*, Vol. 16, No. 9 (2005), pp. 1545–1563.

49. S. Hall 'The Question of Cultural Identity', in T. McGrew, S. Hall and D. Held (eds.) *Modernities and its Futures. Understanding Modern Societies* (London: Polity Press, 1992), pp. 273–326; S. Hall 'Kulturelle Identität und Globalisierung', in K.-H. Hörning and R. Winter (eds.) *Widerspenstige Kulturen. Cultural Studies als Herausforderung*, (Frankfurt/Main Suhrkamp, 1999), pp. 393–441.

50. B. L. Kirkman, K. B. Lowe and C. B. Gibson 'A Quarter of Century of Culture's Consequences: A Review of Empirical Research Incorporating Hofstede's Cultural Values Framework', *Journal of International Business Studies*, Vol. 37, No. 3 (2006).

51. W. Weber, P. J. Dowling and M. Festing 'Reducing Barriers in Management Education: Evidence from the Command Economics of Eastern Europe', in *Academy of Management* (Dallas, 1994).

52. A. Kaasa, M. Vadi and U. Varblane 'Retesting Hofstedes Cultural Dimensions of the European Sample: Some implications for Human Resource Management', in *10th International Human Resource Conference*, edited by W. Scroggins, C. Gomez, P. G. Benson, R. L. Oliver and M. J. Turner (Santa Fe, NM, USA, 2009).

53. B. Kogut and H. Singh 'The Effect of National Culture on the Choice of Entry Mode', *Journal of International Business Studies*, Vol. 19, No. 3 (1988), pp. 411–432.

54. H. Yeganeh and Z. Su 'Conceptual Foundations of Cultural Management Research', *International Journal of Cross Cultural Management*, Vol. 6, No. 3 (2006), pp. 361–376.

55. http://www.thunderbird.edu/wwwfiles/ms/globe/index.app.

56. R. J. House, P. J. Hanges, M. Javidan, P. W. Dorfman and V. Gupta (eds.) *Culture, Leadership, and Organizations: The GLOBE Study of 62 Societies* (Thousand Oaks, London, New Delhi: Sage, 2004). Detailed analyses of individual countries or cultures are based on various qualitative processes like focus group interviews, in-depth interviews and the analysis of various documents; in addition see Vol. 2 of the GLOBE Study, published by J. S. Chhokar, F. C. Brodbeck and R. J. House (eds.) *Culture and Leadership Across the World: the GLOBE Book of In-Depth Studies of 25 Societies* (Mahwah, NJ: Erlbaum, 2008). In this volume, management behavior in 25 cultures is described in depth and recommendations are made for management employees.

57. R. J. House, P. J. Hanges, M. Javidan, P. W. Dorfman and V. Gupta (ed.) *Culture, Leadership, and Organizations: The GLOBE Study of 62 Societies* (Thousand Oaks, London, New Delhi: Sage, 2004).

58. R. J. House, P. J. Hanges, M. Javidan, P. W. Dorfman and V. Gupta (ed.) *Culture, Leadership, and Organizations: The GLOBE Study of 62 Societies* (Thousand Oaks, London, New Delhi: Sage, 2004).

59. R. J. House, P. J. Hanges, M. Javidan, P. W. Dorfman and V. Gupta (ed.) *Culture, Leadership, and Organizations: The GLOBE Study of 62 Societies* (Thousand Oaks, London, New Delhi: SAGE, 2004), p. 49.

60. Ibid, p. 49.

61. Ibid, p. 49.

62. Ibid, p. 49.

63. Ibid, p. 49.

64. Ibid, p. 49.

65. Ibid, p. 49.

66. Ibid, p. 49.

67. The study integrates 59 and 62 cultural regions. Three countries are subdivided like East and West Germany, Switzerland and French-speaking Switzerland; South Africa is divided into white and black, only English-speaking Canada is considered. Ibid, p.49.

68. For detailed presentation see M. Javidan, R. J. House, P. W. Dorfman, P. J. Hanges and M. S. De Luque 'Conceptualizing and Measuring Cultures and their Consequences: a Comparative Review of GLOBE's and Hofstede's Approaches', *Journal of International Business Studies*, Vol. 37, No. 6 (2006), pp. 897–914.

69. G. Hofstede 'What did GLOBE Really Measure? Researchers' Minds Versus Respondents' Minds', *Journal of International Business Studies*, Vol. 37, No. 6 (2006), pp. 882–896.

70. On discussion between Hofstede and authors of the GLOBE study Vol. 37, No. 6 of the *Journal of International Business Studies* from 2006. For a commentary on the dispute see P. B. Smith 'When Elephants Fight, the Grass Gets Trampled: the GLOBE and Hofstede Projects', *Journal of International Business Studies*, Vol. 37, No. 6 (2006), pp. 915–921. Ongoing and forceful presentations of the differences, strengths, weaknesses and exact nature of these two very different perspectives on this topic continue unabated – see M. Minkov and G. Hofdtede (2014) 'A Replication of Hofstede's Uncertainty Avoidance Dimension Across Nationally Representative Samples From Europe', International Journal of Cross-Cultural Management, 14 (2), pp. 161–171 and S. Venaik, Y. Zhu and P. Brewer (2013) 'Looking Into the Future: Hofstede Long Term Orientation Versus GLOBE Future Orientation', Cross Cultural Management, 20 (3), pp. 360–385.

71. G. B. Graen 'In the Eye of the Beholder: Cross-Cultural Lessons in Leadership from Project GLOBE', *Academy of Management Perspectives*, Vol. 20, No. 4 (2006), pp. 95–101.

72. F. Trompenaars and C. Hampden-Turner *Riding the Waves of Culture* (London: Nicholas Brealey, 2002).

73. F. Trompenaars and C. Hampden-Turner *Riding the Waves of Culture* (London: Nicholas Brealey, 2002).

74. It should, however, be noted that these dimensions present an analytical differentiation that is hard to maintain statistically, because the value of Cronbach's alpha exceeds the minimum value of 0.7 only in five dimensions (Universalism/Particularism = 0.71; Individualism/Communitarism = 0.73; Neutral/Affective = 0.75; Ascription/Achievement = 0.71; Concept of time requires a special measurement but has a value of 0.74). The scales are not thoroughly reliable. F. Trompenaars and C. Hampden-Turner, *Riding the Waves of Culture* (London: Nicholas Brealey, 2002). Respectively, the number of dimensions varies (Ibid).

75. F. Trompenaars and C. Hampden-Turner *Riding the Waves of Culture*.

76. F. Trompenaars and C. Hampden-Turner *Riding the Waves of Culture*.

77. F. Trompenaars and C. Hampden-Turner *Riding the Waves of Culture*, Chapter 5.

78. F. Trompenaars and C. Hampden-Turner *Riding the Waves of Culture*, Chapter 4.

79. F. Trompenaars and C. Hampden-Turner *Riding the Waves of Culture*, Chapter 6.

80. F. Trompenaars and C. Hampden-Turner *Riding the Waves of Culture*, Chapter 7.

81. F. Trompenaars and C. Hampden-Turner *Riding the Waves of Culture*, Chapter 8.

82. F. Trompenaars and C. Hampden-Turner *Riding the Waves of Culture*, Chapter 9.

83. F. Trompenaars and C. Hampden-Turner *Riding the Waves of Culture*, Chapter 10.

84. E. T. Hall and M. R. Hall *Understanding Cultural Differences. Germans, Frenchs and Americans*. (Yarmouth, ME: Intercultural Press, 1990).

85. E. T. Hall and M. R. Hall *Understanding Cultural Differences. Germans, Frenchs and Americans*. (Yarmouth, ME: Intercultural Press, 1990).

86. S. A. Sackmann and M. E. Phillips 'Contextual Influences on Culture Research: Shifting Assumptions for New Workplace Realities', *International Journal of Cross Cultural Management*, Vol. 4, No. 3 (2004), pp. 370–390; A.M. Søderberg and N. Holden 'Rethinking Cross Cultural Management in a Globalizing Business World', *International Journal of Cross Cultural Management*,

Vol. 2, No. 1 (2002), pp. 103–121; H. Yeganeh and Z. Su 'Conceptual Foundations of Cultural Management Research', *International Journal of Cross Cultural Management*, Vol. 6, No. 3 (2006), pp. 361–376.

87. V. Taras, J. Rowney and P. Steel 'Half a Century of Measuring Culture: A Review of Approaches, Challenges, and Limitations for Quantifying Culture', *Journal of International Management*, Vol. 15, No. 4 (2009), pp. 357–373.

88. C. Early 'Leading Cultural Research in the Future: a Matter of Paradigms and Taste', *Journal of International Business Studies*, Vol. 37, No. 6 (2006), pp. 922–931; K.H. Hörning 'Kultur als Praxis', in F. Jaeger, B. Liebsch, J. Rüsen and J. Straub (eds.) *Handbuch der Kulturwissenschaften. Bd.1: Grundlagen und Schlüsselbegriffe* (Stuttgart: Metzler, 2004), pp. 139–151. For a presentation of the task-specific complexities of cross-cultural practices – in this case 'high performance work systems' (HPWS) – see T. Rabl, B. Gerhart, M. Jayasinghe and T. Kuhlmann 'A Meta Analysis of Country Differences in the High-Performance Work Systems – Business Performance Relationship: The Roles of National Culture and Managerial Discretion', Journal of Applied Psychology, Vol. 99, no. 6, (2014) pp. 1011–1041.

89. B. Gerhart 'How Much Does National Culture Constrain Organizational Culture?', *Management and Organization Review*, Vol. 5, No. 2 (2008), pp. 241–259. Also see B. Gerhart 'Does National Culture Constrain Organization Culture and Human Resource Strategy? The Role of Individual Mechanisms and Implications for Employee Selection', Research in Personnel and Human Resources Management, Vol. 28 (2009), pp. 1–48.

90. Also B. Gerhart and M. Fang 'National Culture and Human Resource Management: Assumptions and Evidence', *International Journal of Human Resource Management*, Vol. 16 (2005), pp. 975–990; B. L. Kirkman, K. B. Lowe and C. B. Gibson 'A Quarter of Century of Culture's Consequences: A Review of Empirical Research Incorporating Hofstede's Cultural Values Framework', *Journal of International Business Studies*, Vol. 37, No. 3 (2006), pp. 285–320; I. Weller and B. Gerhart 'Empirical Research Issues in Comparative Human Resource Management', in C. Brewster and W. Mayrhofer (eds.), *Handbook of Research in Comparative Human Resource Management* (Cheltenham, UK: Edward Elgar, Im Druck).

91. e.g. N. J. Adler and A. Gundersen *International Dimensions of Organizational Behavior*, 5th ed. (Cincinnati, OH: Thomson Learning, South-Western, 2008); J. Child 'Culture, Contingency and Capitalism in the Cross-National Study of Organizations', in L. L. Cummings and B. M. Staw (eds.) *Research in Organizational Behavior*, (Greenwich: Elsevier, 1981), Vol. 3, pp. 303–356; G. Hofstede *Culture and Organizations – Software of the Mind* (London, UK: McGraw-Hill, 1991), p. 238; D. L. Kincaid 'The Convergence Theory and Intercultural Communication', in Y. Y. Kim and W. B. Gudykunst (eds.) *Theories in Intercultural Communication* (Newbury Park, CA: Sage, 1988), pp. 280–298; J. Walls and H. Triandis 'Universal Truths: Can Universally Held Cultural Values Inform the Modern Corporation?', Cross-Cultural Management, Vol. 21, no. 3 (2014), pp. 345–356.

92. J. Child 'Culture, Contingency and Capitalism in the Cross-National Study of Organizations', in L. L. Cummings and B. M. Staw (eds.), *Research in Organizational Behavior* (Greenwich, CT: JAI, 1981), Vol. 3, pp. 303–356.

93. Like the World Polity Approach by J. W. Meyer 'The World Polity and the Authority of the Nation State', in G. M. Thomas, J. W. Meyer, F. O. Ramirez and J. Boli (eds.) *Institutional Structure. Constituting State, Society, and the Individual* (Newbury Park, CA: Sage, 1987), pp. 41–70., see J. W. Meyer 'Globalization: Theory and Trends', *International Journal of Comparative Sociology*, Vol. 48 (2007), pp. 261–273.

94. See evidence for systematic variations in job satisfaction across cultures as reported by J. Andreassi and L. Lawter 'Cultural Impact of Human Resource Practices on Job Satisfaction', *Cross-Cultural Management*, Vol. 21, no. 1 (2014), pp. 57–79; and calls for a multi-level approach to understanding the complex topic of work–life balance across cultures by A. Ollier-Malaterre, M. Valcour and L Dulk 'Theorizing National Context to Develop Comparative Work-Life Research: A Review and Research Agenda', *European Management Review*, vol. 31 (2013), pp. 433–447.

95. E. H. Schein *Organizational Culture and Leadership*, 3rd ed. (San Francisco: Jossey-Bass, 2004).

96. H. Bhabha *The Location of Culture* (New York, NY: Routledge 2005).

97. Deloitte (eds.) *Connecting across the Generations in the Workplace: What Business Leaders Need to Know to Benefit from Generational Differences* (2005). For a more complex discussion of subcultures and measurement issues in international management, see S. Venaik and D. Midgley 'Mindscapes Across Landscapes: Archtypes of Transnational and Subnational Culture', Journal of International Business Studies, Vol. 46, No. 9 (2015), pp. 1051–1079.

98. Deloitte (eds.) *Managing the Talent Crisis in Global Manufacturing. Strategies to Attract and Engage Generation Y* (2007). For a more involved and updated discussion of variations in the meaning of the work exchange across cultures and across generations, see Peter Kuchinke 'Work and its Personal, Social, and Cross-Cultural Meanings', in R. Poell, T. Rocco and G. Roth (eds.) The Routledge Companion to Human Resource Management, (London: Routledge Publishing, 2015), pp. 287–297.

99. G. Stahl and R. Tung argue to a more balanced assessment of both the positive and negative impacts that doing business across cultures actually has in MNEs. See G. Stahl and R. Tung 'Towards a More Balanced Treatment of Culture in International Business Studies: The Need For Positive Cross-Cultural Scholarship', *Journal of International Business Studies* Vol. 49, no.4, (2015) pp. 391–414.

100. On aspects of cross-cultural management particularly see D. N. Den Hartog, R. J. House, P. J. Hanges, S. A. Ruiz-Quintanilla and P. W. Dorfman 'Culture-Specific and Cross-Culturally Generalizable Implicit Leadership Theories: Are Attributes of Charismatic/Transformational Leadership Universally Endorsed?', *Leadership Quarterly*, Vol. 10, No. 2 (1999), pp. 219–256; as well as the website of the GLOBE project http://mgmt3.ucalgary

.ca/web/globe.nsf/index. In addition see information on further reading. On Global Leadership see R. J. House, N. S. Wright and R. N. Aditya 'Cross-Cultural Research on Organizational Leadership', in P. C. Earley and M. Erez (eds.) *New Perspectives on International Industrial/ Organizational Psychology* (San Francisco: Wiley, 1997), pp. 535–625; M. Mendenhall, T. Kühlmann and G. Stahl (eds.) *Developing Global Business Leaders* (Westport, CT: Quorum Books, 2001). Examples of cross-cultural behavioral situations in organizations can be found in G. Oddou and M. Mendenhall *Cases in International Organizational Behavior*, (Malden, MA: Blackwell, 2000).

101. The major empirical studies by C. B. Gibson,'Implementation of Work Teams Across Cultures: Knowledge Sources, Team Beliefs and Team Effectiveness', in Carnegie Bosch Conference on Knowledge in International Coporations (Rom, 1997); T. Kostova and L. L. Cummings 'Success of Transnational Transfer of Organizational Practices within Multinational Companies', Carnegie Bosch Institute, in Carnegie Bosch Conference on Knowledge in

International Corporations (Rom, 1997); S. H. Schwartz, 'A Theory of Cultural Values and Some Implications for Work', *Applied Psychology: An International Review*, Vol. 48, No. 1 (1999), pp. 23–47; P.C. Wu and P. R. Sparrow 'Understanding the Connections between National Value Orientations, Work Values, Commitment, and Job Satisfaction: Lessons for International HRM', in K. Macharzina, M. J. Oesterle and J. Wolf (eds.) *Global Business in the Information Age. Proceedings of the 23rd Annual EIBA Conference*, (Stuttgart: Extec, 1997), pp. 975–1012.

102. Until recently, the influence of institutional and cultural clarification approaches have frequently been analyzed separately. In the end, they are in an interdependent relationship, which has not been adequately explained until now. There is is certainly a need for future research on this – see Z. Aycan 'The Interplay between Cultural and Institutional/Structural Contingencies in Human Resource Management Practices', *International Journal of Human Resource Management*, Vol. 16, No. 7 (2005), pp. 1083–1119.

CHAPTER 3
THE ORGANIZATIONAL CONTEXT

Chapter Objectives

In this chapter, we examine how international growth places demands on management, and the factors that impact how managers of internationalizing firms respond to these challenges. We start with the premise that the human resource (HR) function does not operate in a vacuum, and that HR activities are determined by, and influence, organizational factors. We cover the following areas:

- issues of standardization and localization

- structural responses to international growth

- control and co-ordination mechanisms, including cultural control

- effect of responses on human resource management (HRM) approaches and activities.

This discussion builds upon material covered in Chapter 1 to provide a meaningful organizational context for drawing out the international dimension of HRM – the central theme of this book.

INTRODUCTION

HR practices, policies, and processes are imbedded in the strategic, structural, and technological context of the multinational enterprise (MNE).[1] This 'administrative heritage' is particularly critical for global firms, as the international organization will be called on to operate across a wide variety of competitive environments and yet somehow balance these diverse social, political, and economic contexts with the requirements of the original home context.[2] In Chapter 1, we looked at the general global environment in which firms compete. Here we focus on internal responses as firms attempt to deal with global environment challenges. Figure 3.1 illustrates the major elements encountered as a result of international growth that place demands on senior managers.

The various elements in Figure 3.1 are not mutually exclusive. For example, geographical dispersion affects firm size, creating pressure upon control mechanisms that, in turn, will influence structural change. Growth (size of the firm) will affect the flow and volume of information, which may reinforce a control response (such as which functions, systems, and processes to centralize and which to decentralize). Geographical dispersion will involve more encounters with national cultures and languages, thus affecting the flow and volume of information. The demands of the host country can influence the composition of the workforce (the mix of **parent-country nationals (PCNs)**, **host-country nationals (HCNs)**, and **third-country nationals (TCNs))**.

FIGURE 3.1 Management demands of international growth

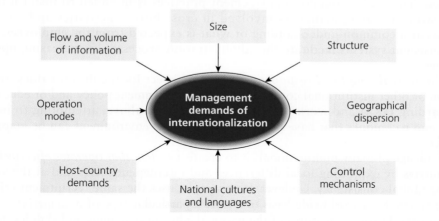

An in-depth examination of all these elements is beyond the scope of this book. Rather, the purpose of this chapter is to explore some of the managerial responses to these influences that concern HRM. Our focus remains on the connection between organizational factors, management decisions, and HR consequences. To a certain extent, how the internationalizing firm copes with the HR demands of its various foreign operations determines its ability to execute its chosen expansion strategies.[3] Indeed, early Finnish research suggests that personnel policies should lead rather than follow international operation decisions,[4] yet one could argue that most companies take the opposite approach – that is, follow market-driven strategies. We will now discuss the twin forces of standardization and localization and follow the path a domestic firm takes as it evolves into a global entity, and illustrate how the HRM function is affected by the way the internationalization process itself is managed.

STANDARDIZATION AND LOCALIZATION OF HRM PRACTICES

Controlling cross-border operations of a MNE centers around what processes, routines, procedures, and practices can and should be transferred abroad, and to what degree these require country-specific adaptation, if any, to be effectively implemented at the local level. In the processes of transferring systems and know-how, the role of people is critical. The management of people – probably the most culture-bound resource in an international context – is faced by a high level of complexity because of the diverse cultural environment of a MNE.[5]

As discussed in previous chapters, expatriates are frequently used to oversee the successful implementation of appropriate work practices. At some point, however, multinational management replaces expatriates with **local staff** with the expectation that these work practices will continue as planned. This approach is based on assumptions that appropriate behavior will have been instilled in the local workforce through training programs and hiring practices, and that the multinational's way of operating has been accepted by the local staff in the manner intended. In this way, the multinational's **corporate culture** will operate as a subtle, informal control mechanism – a substitute for direct supervision.

However, this depends on the receptivity of the local workforce to adhere to corporate norms of behavior, the effectiveness of expatriates as **agents of socialization** and whether cost considerations have led the multinational to localize management prematurely. Here, the role of appropriate HRM activities becomes crucial. The *aim of global standardization* of HRM practices is to reach the above-mentioned consistency, transparency, and an alignment of a geographically fragmented workforce around common principles and objectives.[6] The use of common management practices is intended to foster a feeling of equal treatment among managers involved in cross-border activities and, at the same time, aims at a common understanding of what is expected from the employees. Furthermore, consistent systems facilitate the administration processes by increasing operational efficiencies.[7]

The aim of *realizing local responsiveness* is to respect local cultural values, traditions, legislation or other institutional constraints such as government policy and/or education systems regarding HRM and work practices. As mentioned above, attempting to implement methods and techniques that have been successful in one environment can be inappropriate in another.[8]

The challenge of many multinationals is to create a *system that operates effectively in multiple countries* by exploiting local differences and interdependencies and at the same time sustaining global consistency. Unilever, for example, uses the same recruitment criteria and appraisal system on a worldwide basis to ensure a particular type of managerial behavior in each subsidiary. However, features of the national education systems and skill levels must be considered.[9]

This discussion has shown that the standardization–localization choice that confronts the multinational in an area of operation such as marketing, applies to the management of the global workforce as well. This is due to the fact that HRM carries out a strategic support function within the firm. However, as has been indicated above, the extent to which HRM systems are standardized or localized depends on various interdependent factors. We call this the 'HRM balance between standardization and localization'. Figure 3.2 illustrates important drivers that either foster standardization or localization.

To sum up, the exact balance of a firm's HRM standardization–localization choice is based on factors of influence such as strategy structure, firm size and maturity.[10] The strength of corporate culture plays an important role on the standardization side, while the cultural and institutional environment, including features of the local entity such as operation mode and subsidiary role, play an important role on the localization side. As Harzing[11] confirms, there exists a continuum of advantages for both standardization and localization.

A review of 16 North American- and European-based MNEs led the researchers to conclude that, between the two poles of standardization (related to what the writers call 'dependent': HRM practices that are cleared by corporate headquarters) and localization (related to what the writers call 'highly independent': HRM practices that vary at the discretion of local managers), there are intermediate strategies of standardization and localization of HR practices (referred to as 'interdependent' and 'independent' respectively).[12] Furthermore, these practices are dynamic, such that HR practices may move between these two poles in response to contextual, firm-specific strategic, environmental and regulatory developments.

FIGURE 3.2 Balancing the standardization and localization of HRM in MNEs

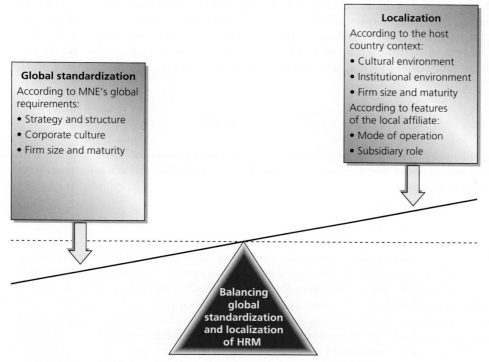

Source: This article was published in M. Festing, J. Eidems and S. Royer. 'Strategic Issues and Local Constraints in Transnational Compensation Strategies: An analysius of Cultural, Institutional and Political Influences', *European Management Journal*, Vol. 25, No 2, 2007, pp. 118–31. Copyright Elsevier 2012. Reproduced with permission.

FACTORS DRIVING STANDARDIZATION

The relationship suggested in the literature explains that a large MNE with a long international history and extensive cross-border operations:

- pursues a multinational or transnational corporate strategy[13]
- is supported by a corresponding organizational structure,[14] and that
- is reinforced by a shared worldwide corporate culture.

However, in practice, we do not always observe perfect adherence to these factors in all MNEs. For example, a worldwide corporate culture may not be shared by all employees in all subsidiaries.[15] This factor should, nonetheless, at least be the target of many firms hoping to cope with the challenges of globalization.

In such highly internationalized organizations we often find attempts to standardize HRM practices on a worldwide basis. Of course, this approach is not appropriate for the whole workforce but aims at a group of managers who are working at the cross-border boundaries of the firm in the headquarters or in foreign locations, i.e. international boundary spanners.[16] A good example of a MNE which has attempted to globally standardize compensation practices is Schering AG, a German pharmaceutical company, which introduced a global performance system for top managers worldwide.[17] Within the context of a new strategic orientation, Schering implemented a standardized bonus system for top executives that aimed at strengthening the performance culture in the company and facilitating a common orientation for all managers. The corporate element of the bonus system consisted of a standardized bonus structure. As the cultural acceptance for variable bonuses varied across Schering's subsidiaries, the proportion between the fixed and variable part of the total compensation package of managers was adapted to the country-specific conditions. The Schering example not only shows us that the implementation of global standards is possible, but at the same time it also makes it clear that local adaptations and exceptions to the standards are often needed. The factors driving the localization of HRM practices are outlined in the next section.

FACTORS DRIVING LOCALIZATION

As has been depicted in Figure 3.2, factors driving localization include the cultural and institutional environment and features of the local entity itself. We will discuss these factors in the following paragraphs.

The cultural environment

In Chapter 2 we identified national culture as a moderating variable in international human resource management (IHRM). We noted how members of a group or society who share a distinct way of life will tend to have common values, attitudes, and behaviors that are transmitted over time in a gradual, yet dynamic, process. There is evidence that culture has an important impact on work and HRM practices. Sparrow, for example, has identified cultural influences on reward behavior such as "different expectations of the manager–subordinate relationship and their influence on performance management and motivational processes".[18] Triandis[19] found that cultures where work is based on more integrated personal social 'relationships' may value a more complete balance of intrinsic and extrinsic rewards, while cultures characterized by personal independence and isolation ('individualism'), as well as rapidly changing personal and social contexts, may emphasize extrinsic rewards – given the absence of a strong and enduring social matrix that attributes meaning and power to intrinsic rewards. The examples indicate that the effectiveness of standardized practices might differ in various cultural contexts.

The institutional environment

In addition to national or regional culture, institutional settings shape the behavior and expectations of employees in subsidiaries.[20] The institutionalism perspective[21] indicates that institutional pressures may be powerful influences on HR practices.[22] According to Whitley,[23] institutional norms and values may be based on the features of a *national business system*. Elements which are relevant to HRM are, for example, the characteristics of the education system or the industrial relations system.

For example, in Germany, the dual vocational training system, which provides theoretical learning opportunities in part-time schools and practical experience in companies, is widespread. More than 60 per cent of an age group is involved in dual vocational training for more than 350 professions.[24] This kind of training represents a well-accepted qualification in Germany, whereas in other countries such as France, this system is non-existent or restricted to lower qualifications. The pervasiveness and reputation of such a training system has an impact on IHRM. More specifically, for example, the recruitment process and the selection criteria reflect the importance of these qualifications. Another example of institutional factors which can have HRM-related effects are the "scope of labor legislation and its regency of codification, [it] creates new codes of conduct through issues such as sex discrimination, equal pay for equal work, and minimum wages".[25] Thus, for legitimacy reasons, it can make sense for some organizations to offer specific benefits or advantages, for example, even if they are very expensive and normally would not be offered due to efficiency considerations.

The impact of the institutional environment on IHRM is shown in the following example, which addresses staffing decisions. A study by As-Saber, Dowling and Liesch[26] found that there was a clear preference for using HCNs in key positions by multinationals operating in India. The authors suggest that a major reason for HCN preference was the belief that an Indian would know more than an expatriate manager could learn in years on the job. Generally, localization of HR staff positions is more likely to ensure that local customs and host-government employment regulations are followed. Khilji[27] found that, although foreign multinationals in Pakistan had formulated policies, implementation was low "because managers brought up and trained in a hierarchical and *centralized* set-up resist sharing power and involving employees in decision-making". This occurred despite the host country's expectation that multinationals would transfer their best practices and act as a positive force in the introduction of what was regarded as desirable Western management styles. However, the multinationals in Khilji's study had taken a polycentric approach, with HCNs in key positions, including that of the HR manager.

Liberman and Torbiörn,[28] in their study of eight European subsidiaries of a global firm, found variation in the degree to which employees adopted corporate norms. They suggest that, at the start of a global venture, differences in management practices are attributable to cultural and institutional factors, whereas commonalities might be explained by a common corporate culture. Empirical results confirmed this. In some countries, employees were agreeable towards wearing of company clothing emblazoned with its logo, as such action did not challenge their national culture. In another focus of the study, there was great resistance to the implementation of performance assessment for non-managerial positions, as it went against existing practice in one of the subsidiaries. Taylor[29] found that Chinese employees working in Japanese plants in their home country perceived team briefings and other such forums as a new form of rhetoric, replacing the nationalist and Communist Party propaganda of the past, and this information was consequently considered of little value by workers and managers. These examples underline the importance of finding adequate solutions for the standardization–localization balance.

These above-described effects illustrate phenomena identified by the theoretical lens of institutionalism. The country-of-origin effect implies that multinationals are shaped by institutions existing in their country of origin and that they attempt to introduce these parent-country-based HRM practices in their foreign subsidiaries.[30] This is especially the case in an ethnocentric firm. The country-of-origin effects are stronger in non-restrictive local environments than in very restrictive countries. For example, US MNEs are more flexible in importing their HRM practices to British affiliates than to German units because British employment law is not as strict as that in Germany and it leaves more choices to the enterprises.[31] However, there is also evidence that MNEs tend to limit the export of practices typical for the country of origin to those that are considered to be their core competences.[32]

The host-country effect refers to the extent to which HRM practices in subsidiaries are impacted by the host-country context. For example, foreign MNEs in Germany are not free in their choice of pay levels or pay mixes. This is regulated by collective wage agreements, which are typical for the German environment and must be accepted. A similar effect exists in the headquarters. Here, HRM activities are influenced by the home-country environment.

We call these effects **home-country effects.** This differentiation reflects the discussion on home- and host-country environments, which is typical for MNEs. The home-country effect is the basis for the above-described country-of-origin effect, describing MNEs that try to transfer HRM activities shaped by their home-country environment to foreign locations.

This discussion has shown that the institutional context has an impact on HRM in several different ways. We have seen that not only can the host country's institutional context foster localization, but that forces exist from the country of origin as well. Sometimes **reverse diffusion**, i.e. the transfer of practices from foreign locations to the headquarters, can be observed. [33]For example, there is evidence that American MNEs learn from their subsidiaries in the UK.[34] Edwards *et al.*[35] have reported that a 'shared service' approach to organizing the HR function was developed in the UK and then introduced in the American headquarters. Relationships of the different effects between the institutional environment and the MNE units are delineated in Figure 3.3.

FIGURE 3.3 Institutional effects on MNEs

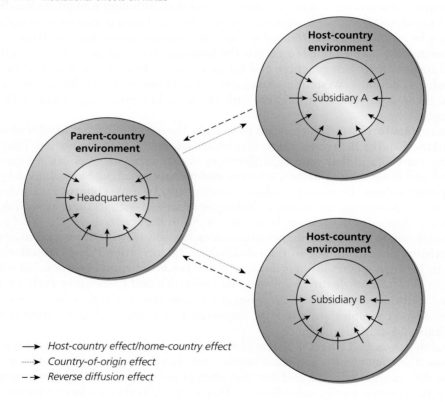

→   *Host-country effect/home-country effect*
······▸   *Country-of-origin effect*
– ▸   *Reverse diffusion effect*

Conclusions on the host-country environment

In the preceding two sections we outlined how the institutional environment may influence HRM and, in particular, attempts at global standardization and local responsiveness.[36] Table 3.1 summarizes these ideas and gives examples of environmental differences, which could lead to problems when MNEs attempt to introduce worldwide standardized HRM practices. Within this context, it is important to recall the discussion on convergence and divergence of HRM and work practices in Chapter 1.

TABLE 3.1 Examples of the impact of the cultural and institutional context on HRM practices

HRM practices	Impact of the cultural context
Recruitment and selection	*Education system* The reputation of educational institutions such as public and private universities varies in different countries. This is reflected in the recruiting processes (i.e. HR marketing) and selection criteria of the firms in those countries.
Training and development	*Education system* Education systems differ between different countries (existence of a dual vocational training system, quality, and reputation of higher education institutions). This has an effect on the training needs perceived and fulfilled by MNEs.
Compensation	*Legislation and industrial relations* Legislation such as the regulation of minimum wages or respective union agreements with respect to compensation has an impact on the firm's compensation choices with respect to pay mix and pay level.
Task distribution	*Legislation and norms* Legislations and respective norms support gender-based division of labor to a differing extent in different countries. While in some countries the percentage of female managers is relatively high, in other countries it is not common that women work at all.

Mode of operation abroad

When addressing the mode of operation, it is helpful to examine this from the level of the local affiliate. Thus, we turn to firm-endogenous factors to determine the balance between global **standardization** and **localization**. Later in the chapter we will discuss the various modes of foreign operations and their associated HRM practices. A study by Buckley *et al.*[37] provides two examples of how the mode of operation either inhibits or facilitates work standardization. In late 1978, the Chinese government announced an open-door policy and commenced economic reforms aimed at moving the country from a centrally planned to a market economy. Western firms that entered China early were more or less forced to enter into joint ventures with state-owned enterprises (SOEs), whereas those entering later have been able to establish wholly owned subsidiaries (WOSs).

One case in the Buckley *et al.* study is Shanghai Bell – a joint venture formed in 1983 between a Belgian telecommunications firm (now Alcatel Bell), the Belgian government and the Chinese Postal and Telecommunications Industries Corporation (PTIC). There was a gradual transfer of relevant technology by the Belgian firm, with a long-term reliance on Belgian expatriates. The Belgian firm had limited control over the Chinese employees in the joint venture and was constrained by its partner's expectations and differing goals.

The second case researched was much different. The US telecommunications firm Motorola established a wholly owned operation in Tianjin, China in 1992. Changing conditions in China meant that Motorola could effectively build a 'transplant factory': importing production equipment, organizational processes and practices from either the parent or other subsidiaries in its global network. This enabled Motorola to integrate the Chinese operation into the broader corporate network and to localize management. These co-ordinating and standardizing efforts have been supported by HRM initiatives such as a special management training program

(China Accelerated Management Program (CAMP)),[38] English language training and the transfer of Chinese employees into the US operations. Motorola has been able to transfer its processes and systems, such as **Six Sigma quality control**, bringing its technology, knowledge, and work practices, supported by HRM activities, into the new facilities in China relatively quickly.

Ownership and control are therefore important factors that need to be taken into consideration when multinationals attempt to standardize work and HRM practices. A firm's ability to independently implement processes and procedures is naturally higher in wholly owned subsidiaries, while the question of control in international joint ventures (IJV) remains a concern for multinational firms. Complementarities between IJV partners and the degree of interdependence between the IJV and other parts of the multinational have proven to be important influences on effective IJV operation and the transfer of work practices. For example, Yan's[39] study of 87 IJVs operating in China revealed the importance of defining a strategic objective for the IJV when determining work practices. Yan concluded that task-related influence in an IJV plays an important role in directly shaping HRM practices.

The discussion here indicates that the achievement of an acceptable balance in the standardization and localization of HRM practices is less problematic in wholly owned subsidiaries than in cross-border alliances. However, in the latter, the balance also depends on many features of a particular alliance, including ownership and control issues. As we will discuss in the next section, it is important to further differentiate wholly owned subsidiaries. We will therefore now introduce the concept of a subsidiary role.

Subsidiary role

The subsidiary role specifies the position of a particular unit in relation to the rest of the organization and defines what is expected of it in terms of contribution to the efficiency of the whole MNE. Subsidiaries can take different roles.[40] Studies have examined how subsidiary roles can differ related to subsidiary function, power and resource relationships, initiative-taking, host-country environment, predisposition of top management and the active championing of subsidiary managers.[41] Subsidiaries may be initiators as well as producers of critical competences and capabilities that contribute as specific profit centers to the competitive advantage of the whole multinational. Centers of excellence at the subsidiary level can be viewed as an indication of how some network multinationals are recognizing that levels of expertise differ across the organization and that not all innovation and 'best practice' originates from the center – that is, from headquarters. The Japanese electronics firm Hitachi's establishment of an Research and Development (R&D) center in China is an example of building up the existing R&D facility to the status of a global center for the development of air conditioners.[42]

We will now discuss the well-known typology of subsidiary roles by Gupta and Govindarajan.[43] Based on their interpretation of a MNE as a network of capital, product, and knowledge flows, they attribute the highest importance to knowledge flows. They differentiate between (1) the magnitude of knowledge flows, i.e. the intensity of the subsidiary's engagement in knowledge transfer, and (2) the directionality of transactions, which means whether subsidiaries are knowledge providers or recipients. The differentiation between knowledge inflows and outflows leads to the following typology (see Table 3.2).

Subsidiaries characterized as *global innovators* provide significant knowledge for other units and have gained importance as MNEs move towards the **transnational** model. This role is reflected in an IHRM orientation in which the parent firm develops HRM policies and practices which are then transferred to its overseas affiliates.[44]

The *integrated player* also creates knowledge but at the same time is recipient of knowledge flows. Thus, a subsidiary characterized by this role can represent an important knowledge node in the MNE network.[45] This should be supported by a highly integrated HRM orientation. Thus, the HRM practices and policies between headquarters and subsidiaries are very similar, probably characterized by a high extent of global standardization and localized elements when this is needed.

TABLE 3.2 Gupta and Govindarajan's four generic subsidiary roles

	Low outflow	High outflow
Low inflow	Local innovator	Global innovator
High inflow	Implementer	Integrated player

Source: Adapted from A. Gupta and V. Govindarajan 'Knowledge Flows and the Structure of Control within Multinational Corporations', *Academy of Management Review*, Vol. 16, No. 4 (1991), pp. 768–792.

Implementers rely heavily on knowledge from the parent or peer subsidiaries and create a relatively small amount of knowledge themselves. If the IHRM system is export-oriented – i.e. global HRM decisions are mainly made in the parent company – then the local subsidiaries are responsible for the implementation process at the local level.

In the *local innovator* role, subsidiaries engage in the creation of relevant country/region-specific knowledge in all key functional areas because they have complete local responsibility. The HRM systems in such polycentric firms only have weak ties with the headquarters. As every subsidiary operates independently from the parent company and from other subsidiaries, this independence results in a number of localized HRM policies and practices.

Harzing and Noorderhaven[46] tested this typology and found empirical support in a sample of 169 subsidiaries of MNEs headquartered in the Netherlands, France, Germany, the UK, Japan and the USA:

> In comparison to earlier studies, our results show an increasing differentiation between subsidiaries, as well as an increase in the relative importance of both knowledge and product flows between subsidiaries suggesting that MNCs [multinational corporations] are getting closer to the ideal type of the transnational company.[47]

A development towards the ideal type of the transnational corporation involves more subsidiaries engaging in high knowledge outflows, and thus taking on the role of global innovator or integrative players. The difficulties in transferring knowledge and competence with respect to management practices from the subsidiary level – whether from a designated 'center of excellence'[48] or not – to the rest of the network are similar to the difficulties that we discussed in the context of headquarters to subsidiary transfer. The 'sticky' nature of knowledge, for example, applies regardless of its origins, but the designated role of the subsidiary and the standing of its management are critical in determining the spread and adoption of subsidiary-initiated practices.

Stickiness represents one reason why some firms move towards an export-oriented approach to IHRM rather than an integrative management orientation.[49] Another major barrier to an integrative approach can be what Birkinshaw and Ridderstrâle[50] describe as "the corporate immune system". Subsidiary initiatives are often met with significant resistance. Individuals within the organization resist change or support low-risk projects, and are wary of ideas that challenge their own power base. Michailova and Husted use the terms 'knowledge-sharing hostility' and 'knowledge hoarding' to explain non-sharing behaviors identified in their study of firms operating in Russia.[51]

Increasing the mobility of managers is one way to break down these barriers and produce corporate rather than subsidiary champions who are prepared to disseminate information about subsidiary initiatives and capabilities, and recommend adoption in other parts of the organization where appropriate. Tregaskis,[52] in her study of R&D centers, reports how one firm found that personal relationships formed through visits of key staff to other units facilitated information sharing and the eventual adoption of new products by other subsidiaries. Face-to-face interactions were important in building trust and exchanges of tacit knowledge, which might be possible in the context of corporate or regional meetings. Hence, frequent personal exchanges between the MNE units via individual encounters or regional or global meetings are essential in the processes of successful identification and transfer of knowledge.[53]

This discussion has indicated how the subsidiary role and related processes of knowledge transfer may impact the balance of standardization and localization in HRM. Recalling the power and resource relationships outlined at the beginning of this section, it must be stressed that powerful subsidiaries may have a stronger position in influencing the standardization–localization balance than those affiliates active in less significant markets or with rather unspecific skills.[54] Birkinshaw and Ridderstrâle[55] define the structural power and resource-based power of subsidiaries *vis-à-vis* the corporate headquarters as two basic sources of influence within networks, and distinguish between 'core' subsidiaries and 'peripheral' subsidiaries. There is evidence that those subsidiaries controlling large market volumes and possessing strategically important, function-specific skills within the MNE network have a strong impact on the standardization–localization balance.[56]

Measures creating the HRM balance between standardization and localization

Various studies[57] have investigated co-ordination, communication, and control processes between parent organizations and subsidiaries. The analysis of these mechanisms contributes to our understanding about how the balance between globalization and localization is achieved.

Here, we will follow the distinction between structural/formal and informal/subtle co-ordination mechanisms used by Martinez and Jarillo.[58] These authors define co-ordination as "the process of integrating activities that remain dispersed across subsidiaries".[59] The essential difference between these two groups of co-ordination mechanisms is that the latter is person-oriented, whereas the former is not. Martinez and Jarillo attribute the non-person-oriented co-ordination mechanisms to simple strategies of internationalization. More complex strategies, however, require a higher co-ordination effort. A high degree of co-ordination is usually realized by using both the non-person-oriented co-ordination mechanisms and person-oriented co-ordination mechanisms.[60] In the context of corporate IHRM practices and policies, non-person-oriented co-ordination devices include, for example, written material on HRM practices such as handbooks or information leaflets either provided in print or via the intranet. However, as this is a one-way communication device, it can only supplement the complex process of balancing global and local needs. It does not meet the requirements of a complex transnational approach to IHRM. Here, person-oriented co-ordination is indispensable.

As has already been indicated in the context of knowledge transfer between subsidiaries, HR managers from the headquarters as well as from the foreign affiliates must exchange their knowledge, expectancies and experiences of the different local contexts. Therefore, meetings and common project work using a respective supporting infrastructure such as intranet platforms[61] are essential throughout the process of developing and implementing the standardization–localization balance in IHRM. Furthermore, powerful line managers acting as opinion leaders should be involved in the process as well in order to achieve broad support for the transnational HRM measures. Finally, high importance placed on the respective HRM solution by the corporate top management is essential for the success of the initiative.[62]

THE PATH TO GLOBAL STATUS

Most firms pass through several stages of organizational development as the nature and size of their international activities grow. As they go through these evolutionary stages, their organizational structures[63] change, typically due to:

- the strain imposed by growth and geographical spread

- the need for improved co-ordination and control across business units

- the constraints imposed by host-government regulations on ownership and equity.

Multinationals are not born overnight; the evolution from a domestic to a truly global organization may involve a long and somewhat tortuous process with many and diverse steps, as illustrated in Figure 3.4. Although research into internationalization has revealed a common process, it must be stressed that this process is not exactly the same for all firms.[64] As Figure 3.4 shows, some firms may use other operation modes such as licensing and subcontracting instead of, or as well as, establishing their own foreign production or service facilities.

FIGURE 3.4 Stages of internationalization

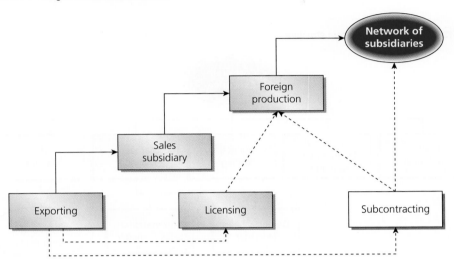

Some firms go through the various steps rapidly, while others evolve slowly over many years, although recent studies have identified a speeding up of the process. For example, some firms are able to accelerate the process through acquisitions, thus leapfrogging over intermediate steps (that is, moving directly into foreign production through the purchase of a foreign firm, rather than initial exporting followed by sales subsidiary, as per Figure 3.4 above). Nor do all firms follow the same sequence of stages as they internationalize – some firms can be driven by external factors such as host-government action (for example, a host government requirement to participate in a joint venture), or an offer to buy a company. Others are formed expressly with the international market in mind – often referred to as 'born globals'. In other words, the number of steps or stages along the path to multinational status varies from firm to firm, as does the time frame involved.[65] However, the concept of an evolutionary process is useful in illustrating the organizational adjustments required of a firm moving along the path to multinational status. As mentioned earlier, linked to this evolutionary process are structural responses, control mechanisms and HRM policies, which we will now examine.

Export

This is typically the initial stage for manufacturing firms entering international operations. As such, it rarely involves much organizational response until the level of export sales reaches a critical point. Of course, simple exporting may be difficult for service companies (such as legal firms) so that they may be forced to make an early step into foreign direct investment operations (via a branch office or joint venture).[66]

Exporting tends to be handled by an intermediary (for example, a foreign agent or distributor) as local market knowledge is deemed critical. As export sales increase, however, an export manager may be appointed to control foreign sales and actively seek new markets. This person is commonly from the domestic operations. Further growth in exporting may lead to the establishment of an export department at the same level as the domestic sales department, as the firm becomes more committed to, or more dependent upon, its foreign export sales, as Figure 3.5 (overleaf) shows.

At this stage, exporting is controlled from the domestic-based home office through a designated export manager. The role of the HR department is unclear, as indicated by the dotted arrow between these two functional areas in Figure 3.5. There is a paucity of empirical evidence about HR responses at this early internationalization stage, even though there are HR activities involved (such as the selection of export staff) and perhaps training of the foreign agency staff. As these activities are handled by the marketing department, or exporting staff, the HR department has little, if any, involvement with the development of policies and procedures surrounding the HR aspects of the firm's early international activities.[67]

FIGURE 3.5 Export department structure

Sales subsidiary

As the firm develops expertise in foreign markets, agents and distributors are often replaced by direct sales with the establishment of sales subsidiaries or branch offices in the foreign market countries. This stage may be prompted by problems with foreign agents, more confidence in the international sales activity, the desire to have greater control, and/or the decision to give greater support to the exporting activity, usually due to its increasing importance to the overall success of the organization. The export manager may be given the same authority as other functional managers, as illustrated in Figure 3.6.

FIGURE 3.6 Sales subsidiary structure

Exporting is still controlled at corporate headquarters, but the firm must make a decision regarding the co-ordination of the sales subsidiary, including staffing. If it wishes to maintain direct control, reflecting an ethnocentric attitude, it opts to staff the sales subsidiary from its headquarters through the use of PCNs. If it regards country-specific factors – such as knowledge of the foreign market, language or sensitivity to host-country needs – as important, it may staff the subsidiary with HCNs. However, it would appear that many firms use PCNs in key sales subsidiary positions.

The decision to use PCNs leads into expatriation management issues and activities. It may be that, at this point, the HR department becomes actively involved in the personnel aspects of the firm's international operations, though there is little empirical evidence as to when and how HR-designated staff become involved.

International division

For some firms, it is a short step from the establishment of a sales subsidiary to a foreign production or service facility. This step may be considered small if the firm is already assembling the product abroad to take advantage of cheap labor or to save on shipping costs or tariffs, for example. Alternatively, the firm may have a well-established export and marketing program that enables it to take advantage of host-government incentives or counter host-government controls on foreign imports by establishing a foreign production facility. For some firms, though, the transition to foreign direct investment is a large step. However, having made the decision to produce overseas, the firm may establish its own foreign production facilities, or enter into a joint venture with a local firm, or buy a local firm.[68] Regardless of the method of establishment, foreign production/service operations may trigger the creation of a separate *international division* in which all international activities are grouped, as Figure 3.7 demonstrates.

FIGURE 3.7 International division structure

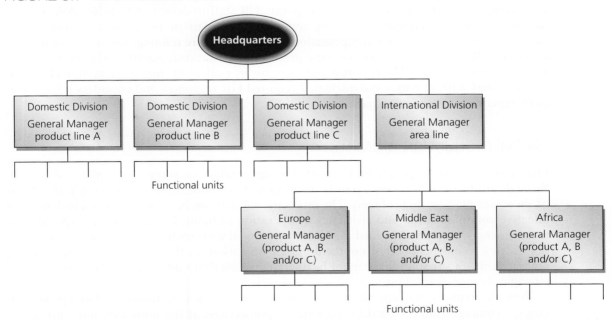

Source: Adapted from C. Hill, International Business: Competing in the Global Marketplace, 2nd edn (McGraw-Hill, Newark, 1997) copyright The McGraw-Hill Companies, Inc. Reproduced with permission.

It should be noted that the international division form of organizational structure is much more common in US firms than European firms, which often have a long history of activity in various countries that were former colonies. The two most prominent examples are Britain with long-term colonies such as Australia, Canada, India, Ceylon (now known as Sri Lanka), Hong Kong, New Zealand, South Africa, Singapore, and the West Indies; and the Netherlands with Indonesia (known as the 'Dutch East Indies'). Other former colonial powers were Portugal with Brazil, Angola, Mozambique, East Timor, and Macau; Spain with Argentina, Venezuela, Peru, Mexico, Chile, Cuba, Panama, Bolivia, and Uruguay; and France with colonies in Africa (Algeria, Morocco, Tunisia, Congo, Ivory Coast) and in Vietnam.

With the spread of international activities, typically the firm establishes what has been referred to as 'miniature replicas', as the foreign subsidiaries are structured to mirror that of the domestic organization. The subsidiary managers report to the head of the international division and there may be some informal reporting directly to the various functional heads. For example, in reference to Figure 3.7, there may be contact between the HR managers in the two country subsidiaries and the HR manager at corporate headquarters, regarding staffing issues.

Many firms at this stage of internationalization are concerned about maintaining control of the newly established subsidiary and will place PCNs in all key positions in the subsidiary. However, some firms decide that local employment conditions require local handling and place a HCN in charge of the subsidiary HR function, thus making an exception to the overall ethnocentric approach. Others may place HCNs in several key positions, including HRM, either to comply with host-government directives or to emphasize the local orientation of the subsidiary.

The role of corporate HR staff is primarily concerned with expatriate management, though there will be some monitoring of the subsidiary HR function – formally through the head of the international division. Pucik[69] has suggested that, initially, corporate HR activities are confined to supervising the selection of staff for the new international division, and expatriate managers perform a major role in: "identifying employees who can direct the daily operations of the foreign subsidiaries, supervising transfer of managerial and technical know-how, communicating corporate policies, and keeping corporate HQ informed". As the firm expands its foreign production or service facilities into other countries, increasing the size of its foreign workforce, accompanied by a growth in the number of expatriates, more formal HR policies become necessary. The capacity of corporate HR staff to design appropriate policies may depend on how institutionalized existing approaches to expatriate management concerns have become, especially policies for **compensation** and **pre-departure training**. The more isolated the corporate HR function has been from the preceding international activities, the more difficult the task is likely to be.[70] The export department (or its equivalent) may have been in charge of international staffing issues and instigated required HR responses and considers it has sufficient experience to manage expatriates.

Global product/area division

Over time, the firm moves from the early foreign production stage into a phase of growth through production, or service, standardization and diversification. Consequently, the strain of sheer size may create problems. The international division becomes overstretched, making effective communication and efficiency of operation difficult. In some cases, corporate top managers may become concerned that the international division has enjoyed too much autonomy, acting so independently from the domestic operations to the extent that it operates as a separate unit – a situation that cannot be tolerated as the firm's international activities become strategically more important.

Typically, tensions will emerge between the parent company (headquarters) and its subsidiaries, stemming from the need for national responsiveness at the subsidiary unit and global integration imperatives at the parent headquarters. The demand for national responsiveness at the subsidiary unit develops because of factors such as differences in market structures, distribution channels, customer needs, local culture, and pressure from the host government.

The need for more centralized global integration by the headquarters comes from having multinational customers, global competitors and the increasingly rapid flow of information and technology, and from the quest for large volume for economies of scale.

As a result of these various forces for change, the multinational confronts two major issues of structure:

● the extent to which key decisions are to be made at the parent-country headquarters or at the subsidiary units (*centralization* versus *decentralization*)

● the type or form of *control* exerted by the parent over the subsidiary unit.

The structural response, at this stage of internationalization, can either be a product/service-based global structure (if the growth strategy is through product or service diversification) or an area-based structure (if the growth strategy is through geographical expansion); see Figures 3.8A and 3.8B.

FIGURE 3.8A Global product division structure

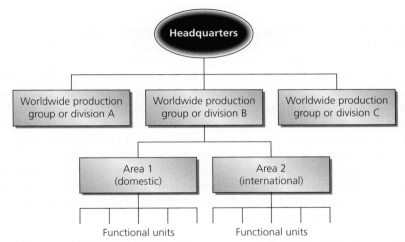

Source: Adapted from C. Hill, *International Business: Competing in the Global Marketplace*, 2nd edn (McGraw-Hill, Newark, 1997) copyright The McGraw-Hill Companies, Inc. Reproduced with permission.

FIGURE 3.8B Global area division structure

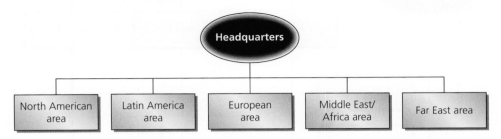

As part of the process of accommodating subsidiary concerns through decentralization, the MNE strives to adapt its HRM activities to each host country's specific requirements. This naturally impacts on the corporate HRM function. As there is an increasing devolution of responsibility for local employee decisions to each subsidiary, with corporate HR staff performing a monitoring role, intervening in local affairs occurs less frequently. This HRM monitoring role reflects management's desire for central control of strategic planning; formulating, implementing and co-ordinating strategies for its worldwide markets.[71] As well, the growth in foreign exposure combined with changes in the organizational structure of international operations results in an increase in the number of employees needed to oversee the activities between the parent firm and its foreign affiliates. Within the HRM function, the development of managers able to operate in international environments generally becomes a new imperative.[72]

As the MNE grows and the trend toward a global perspective accelerates, it increasingly confronts the 'think global, act local' paradox.[73] The increasingly complex international environment – characterized by global competitors, global customers, universal products, rapid technological change, and world-scale factories – push the multinational toward global integration while, at the same time, host governments and other stakeholders (such as customers, suppliers and employees) push for local responsiveness. To facilitate the challenge of meeting these conflicting demands, the multinational will typically need to consider a more appropriate structure and the choice appears to be between: the *matrix*; the *mixed structure*; the *heterarchy*; the *transnational*; or the *multinational network*. These options are now described and discussed.

The matrix

In the **matrix structure,** the MNE is attempting to integrate its operations across more than one dimension. As shown in Figure 3.9, the international or geographical division and the product division share joint authority. Advocates of this structural form see, as its advantages, that conflicts of interest are brought out into the open, and that each issue with priority in decision-making has an executive champion to ensure it is not neglected. In other words, the matrix is considered to bring into the management system a philosophy of matching the structure to the decision-making process. Research on the matrix structure[74] indicates that the matrix "continues to be the only organizational form which fits the strategy of simultaneous pursuit of multiple business dimensions, with each given equal priority [. . .]. [The] structural form succeeds because it fits the situation". In practice, firms that have adopted the matrix structure have met with mixed success. One reason is that it is an expensive structural form in that it requires careful implementation and commitment (and often a great deal of time) on the part of top management to be successful.

FIGURE 3.9 Global matrix structure

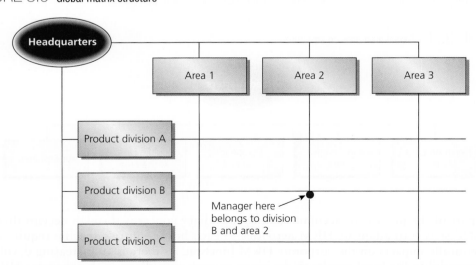

Source: Adapted from C. Hill, *International Business: Competing in the Global Marketplace*, 2nd edn (McGraw-Hill, Newark, 1997) copyright The McGraw-Hill Companies, Inc. Reproduced with permission.

In Figure 3.9, area managers are responsible for the performance of all products within the various countries that comprise their regions, while product managers are responsible for sales of their specific product ranges across the areas. For example, Product A Manager may be concerned with sales of Product A in Europe, the Americas, and in the Asia-Pacific area. Product managers typically report to a Vice President Global Products (or similar title) for matters pertaining to product and to another Vice President (perhaps a VP International) who is responsible for geographical matters. There is a similar dual reporting line for functional staff, including HR staff. Country/area HR managers may also be involved in staffing issues involving product division staff (reporting indirectly to Vice President Global Products). There may be additional reporting requirements to corporate HR at headquarters. One early and public supporter of the matrix organization was Percy Barnevik, former chief executive officer of Asea Brown Boveri (ABB), the European electrical systems and equipment manufacturer.[75] The decade-long efforts by ABB at matrix control were very influential in the popular and academic press, intriguing executives at a number of global firms.

Overall, efforts to successfully implement the matrix solution have been problematic. Bartlett and Ghoshal[76] comment that, "in practice, particularly in the international context, the matrix has proven to be all but unmanageable". They isolate four contributing factors:

1 *Dual reporting*, which leads to conflict and confusion.

2 The *proliferation of communication channels*, which creates informational logjams.

3 *Overlapping responsibilities*, which produce turf battles and a loss of accountability.

4 The *barriers of distance, language, time, and culture*, which often make it very difficult for managers to resolve conflicts and clarify confusion.

Bartlett and Ghoshal conclude that the most successful MNEs focus less on searching for the ideal structure and more on developing the abilities, behavior, and performance of individual managers. This assists in creating 'a matrix in the minds of managers', where individual capabilities are captured and the entire firm is motivated to respond co-operatively to a complicated and dynamic environment. It seems clear that, if the MNE opts for a matrix structure, particular care must be taken with staffing. As Ronen[77] notes:

It requires managers who know the business in general, who have good interpersonal skills, and who can deal with the ambiguities of responsibility and authority inherent in the matrix system. Training in such skills as planning procedures, the kinds of interpersonal skills necessary for the matrix, and the kind of analysis and orderly presentation of ideas essential to planning within a group is most important for supporting the matrix approach. Moreover, management development and HR planning are even more necessary in the volatile environment of the matrix than in traditional organizations.

Mixed structure

In an attempt to manage the growth of diverse operations, or because attempts to implement a matrix structure have been unsuccessful, some firms have opted for what can only be described as a mixed form. In an early survey conducted by Dowling[78] on this issue, more than one-third (35 per cent) of respondents indicated that they had mixed forms, and around 18 per cent had product or matrix structures. Galbraith and Kazanjian[79] also identify mixed structures that seem to have emerged in response to global pressures and trade-offs:

For example, organizations that pursued area structures kept these geographical profit centers, but added worldwide product managers. Colgate-Palmolive has always had strong country managers. But, as they doubled the funding for product research, and as Colgate Dental Cream became a universal product, product managers were added at the corporate office to direct the R&D funding and co-ordinate marketing programs worldwide. Similarly the product-divisionalized firms have been reintroducing the international division. At Motorola, the product groups had worldwide responsibility for their product lines. As they compete with the Japanese in Japan, an international group has been introduced to help co-ordinate across product lines.

Although all structural forms that result from the evolutionary development of international business are complex and difficult to manage effectively, given a MNE's developing capabilities and experience at each new stage, mixed structures appear even more complex and harder to explain and implement, as well as control. Thus, as our discussion of the matrix structure has emphasized, it is important that all employees understand the mixed framework and that attention is also given to supporting mechanisms, such as corporate identity, interpersonal relationships, management attitudes and HR systems, particularly promotion and reward policies.[80]

Beyond the matrix

Early studies of headquarter–subsidiary relationships tended to stress resources, people, and information flows from headquarters to subsidiary, examining these relationships mainly in the context of control and co-ordination. However, in the large, mature multinational, these flows are multidirectional: from headquarters to subsidiary; from subsidiary to subsidiary; and between subsidiaries.[81] The result can be a complex network of interrelated activities and relationships, and the multinational management literature identifies three descriptions of organizational structures – the **heterarchy**, the **transnational**, and the network firm. While they have been given different terms, each form recognizes that, at this stage of internationalization, the concept of a superior structure that neatly fits the corporate strategy becomes inappropriate. The proponents of these forms are in agreement that multinationals at this stage become less hierarchical. We shall take a brief look at each of these more decentralized, organic forms.

The heterarchy

This structural form was proposed by Hedlund,[82] a distinguished Swedish international management researcher, and recognizes that a MNE may have a number of different kinds of centers apart from that traditionally referred to as 'headquarters'. Hedlund argued that competitive advantage does not necessarily reside in any one country (the parent country, for example). Rather, it may be found in many, so that each subsidiary center may be simultaneously a center and a global coordinator of discrete activities, thus performing a strategic role not just for itself but for the MNE as a whole (the subsidiary labeled 'center' in Figure 3.10). For example, some multinationals may centralize R&D in a particular subsidiary. In a heterarchical MNE, control is less reliant on the top-to-bottom mechanisms of previous hierarchical modes and more reliant on normative mechanisms, such as the corporate culture and a widely shared awareness of central goals and strategies.

From a HRM perspective, the heterarchy is interesting in that its success appears to rest solely on the ability of the multinational to formulate, implement, and reinforce the required HR elements. Hedlund recognized that the heterarchy demands skillful and experienced personnel as well as sophisticated reward and punishment systems in order to develop the normative control mechanisms necessary for effective performance. The use of staff as an informal control mechanism is important, which we shall explore later in this chapter.

In a later article, Hedlund proposed a structural model he termed the 'N-form'. This model builds upon his heterarchy concept and integrates work from knowledge organization scholars. Hedlund argued that a new structural form is required to allow for knowledge management. His N-form takes away divisions, allows for temporary constellations and the use of project teams, and places stress on lateral communication and dialogue between units and individuals. The top management role was presented as that of a catalyst, architect, and protector of knowledge rather than a monitor and resource allocator.[83] The use of mechanisms such as cross-functional teams and empowerment of lower level employees was advocated to further support the N-form.

FIGURE 3.10 The networked organization

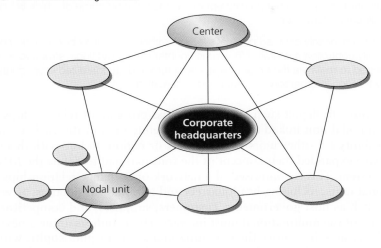

The transnational

The term 'transnational' has been coined to describe an organizational form that is characterized by an interdependence of resources and responsibilities across all business units regardless of national boundaries. The term has also become a descriptor of a particular type of multinational, one that tries to cope with the large flows of components, products, resources, people, and information among its subsidiaries, while simultaneously recognizing distributed specialized resources and capabilities. As such, the transnational demands a complex process of co-ordination and co-operation involving strong cross-unit integrating devices, a strong corporate identity, and a well-developed worldwide management perspective. In their study, Bartlett and Ghoshal[84] noted:

> Among the companies we studied, there were several that were in the process of developing such organizational capabilities. They had surpassed the classic capabilities of the multinational company that operates as **decentralized** federations of units able to sense and respond to diverse international needs and opportunities; and they had evolved beyond the abilities of the global company with its facility for managing operations on a tightly controlled worldwide basis through its centralized hub structure. They had developed what we termed transnational capabilities – the ability to manage across national boundaries, retaining local flexibility while achieving global integration. More than anything else this involved the ability to link local operations to each other and to the center in a flexible way, and in so doing, to leverage those local and central capabilities.

In fact, the matrix, the heterarchy and the transnational share a common theme regarding the HR factor. Therefore, developing transnational managers or global leaders who can think and act across national and subsidiary boundaries emerges as an important task for top management introducing these complex organizational forms. Staff transfers play a critical role in integration and co-ordination.[85]

The multinational as a network

Some scholars are advocating viewing certain large and mature internationalized firms as a network, in situations where:

- Subsidiaries have developed into significant centers for investments, activities, and influence, and can no longer be regarded as being at the periphery.[86] Interaction between headquarters and each subsidiary is likely to be dyadic, taking place between various actors at many different organizational levels and covering different exchanges, the outcome of which will be important for effective global performance.

- Such MNEs are loosely coupled political systems rather than tightly bonded, homogeneous, hierarchically controlled systems.[87] This runs counter to the traditional structure where linkages are described formally via the organization's structure and standardized procedures, and informally through interpersonal contact and socialization.[88]

Figure 3.10 attempts to depict such an intricate criss-crossing of relationships. One subsidiary may act as a nodal unit linked to a cluster of satellite organizations. Thus, one center can assume responsibility for other units in its country or region. In line with this view, Ghoshal and Bartlett[89] have expanded their concept of the transnational to define the MNE as an inter-organizational system. This is comprised of a network of exchange relationships among different organizational units, including headquarters and national subsidiaries, as well as external organizations, such as host governments, customers, suppliers, and competitors, with which the different units of the multinational must interact. These authors argue a new way of structuring is not the issue – it is more the emerging management philosophy, with its focus on management processes: "The actual configuration of the processes themselves, and the structural shell within which they are embedded, can be very different depending on the businesses and the heritage of each company".[90] Ghoshal and Bartlett cite GE, ABB, and Toyota as prime examples of companies involved in developing such processes, with Intel and Corning, Philips and Alcatel, Matsushita and Toshiba regarded as companies embarking upon a network-type configuration.

The management of a multi-centered networked organization is complex. Apart from the intraorganizational network (comprising headquarters and the numerous subsidiaries), each subsidiary also has a range of external relationships (involving local suppliers, customers, competitors, host governments, and alliance partners). The management of both the intraorganizational and interorganizational spheres, and of the total integrated network, is crucial to global corporate performance. It involves what has been termed a 'less hierarchical structure', featuring five dimensions:

1. Delegation of decision-making authority to appropriate units and levels.

2. Geographical dispersal of key functions across units in different countries.

3. Delayering of organizational levels.

4. De-bureaucratization of formal procedures.

5. Differentiation of work, responsibility, and authority across the networked subsidiaries.[91]

Research cited by Nohria and Ghoshal focuses on the capability of networking subsidiaries to package 'slack resources' (pools of capital, production or HR beyond those required for local purposes) to stimulate 'local-for-local', 'local-for-global' and 'global-for-global', innovation processes.[92] Integrated networks of these 'slack resource' pools are combined by way of interpersonal contacts, mentoring relationships, and sophisticated communications networks in order to identify and distribute new product processes and technologies.

Beyond networks

Doz, Santos and Williamson[93] have coined the term 'meta-national' to describe firms comprising three types of units. First, locally imbedded 'sensing units' are responsible for uncovering widely dispersed sources of engineering and market insights. Developing new technologies and processes can no longer be assumed to be the sole task of a conveniently located home-country headquarters R&D unit, or even a MNE-based center of excellence. Second, 'magnet' units are described as attracting these unpredictably dispersed innovative processes, creating a business plan to convert these innovations into viable services or products. Finally, a third set of units is responsible for marketing and producing adaptations of these products and services for a range of customers around the world. The meta-national system is described as:

> *a global tournament played at three levels. It is a race to identify and access new technologies and market trends ahead of the competition, a race to turn this dispersed knowledge into innovative products and services, and a race to scale and exploit these innovations in markets around the world.*[94]

The place of the HR function in structural forms

As we point out in our treatment of the various forms, there has been little direct investigation into how the HR function develops in response to structural changes as a consequence of international growth. An exception is a study of the changing role of the corporate HR function in 30 UK firms.[95] The authors, Scullion and Starkey, found three distinct groups that they describe as follows:

1   *Centralized HR* companies, characterized by large, well-resourced HR departments responsible for a wide range of activities. The key role for corporate HR was to establish and maintain control over worldwide top-level management positions, such as divisional and subsidiary managers, so that strategic staffing was under central control. Companies in this group operated within product-based or matrix structures.

2   *Decentralized HR* companies, characterized by devolving HR responsibilities to a small group who confined their role to senior management at corporate HQ. This was consistent with the decentralized approach of other functions. Companies within this group operated within product- or regional-based structures, with only one reporting using a matrix.

3   *Transition* companies, characterized by medium-sized corporate HR departments staffed by a relatively small group at corporate HQ. They operated in a decentralized, product-based structure, though one company reported using a matrix structure.

Scullion and Starkey note that the varied roles of corporate HR within these three groups impacted upon the way in which activities such as training and performance appraisal were handled, and the ability of corporate HR to plan for staff movements throughout the worldwide operations.

Different countries take different paths

The above discussion takes a generalist view of the growth of the internationalizing firm through the various stages to multinational status and the correspondent organizational structures. However, it is important to note a cultural element. If, as Stopford and Wells state, MNEs may develop global capabilities by an emphasis on product diversity, leading to worldwide product-division structures, or alternately by an emphasis on cultural responsiveness leading to regional- or area-division structures, the question arises as to what role the cultural origin of the multinational plays in the path to globalization. European firms have tended to take a different structural path than their US counterparts. An early study of 70 European multinationals revealed that European firms moved directly from a functional 'mother-daughter' structure to a global structure with worldwide product or area divisions, or to a matrix organization without the transitional stage of an international division.[96] HRM practices, changing to serve the needs of the new structure, adjusted accordingly. Swedish firms have traditionally adopted the mother-daughter structure, but Hedlund's work noted that this had changed. The Swedish multinationals in his study tended to adopt a mixture of elements of the mother-daughter structure and elements of the product division, at this stage of their internationalization process.[97] It may be that there is a preference for matrix-type structures within European firms, particularly Nordic MNEs. One could suggest that this structural form better suits the more collaborative, group-oriented work organization found within these firms.

US firms that have experimented with the matrix form appear to have met with limited success. For example, as part of a reorganization process termed 'Ford 2000', the Ford Motor Company abandoned its regional structure in 1993 and adopted a form of global matrix organization characterized by a multidisciplinary product team approach with networked plants across regions. In the process, the European regional headquarters was moved to the USA in an attempt to develop a more global decision-making perspective. In 2001, Ford announced a restructuring and plant rationalization that effectively took the company back to a regional structure. Further restructuring, particularly of its North American operations, appears to be ongoing as Ford seeks an optimal allocation of resources and operations to maintain a global competitive position.[98]

Japanese multinationals are evolving along similar lines to their US counterparts. Export divisions have become international divisions but, according to Ronen,[99] the rate of change has been slower. The characteristics of Japanese organizational culture (such as the control and reporting mechanisms and decision-making systems), the role of trading companies and the systems of management appear to contribute to the slower evolution of the international division. In some cases, despite their high degree of internationalization, Japanese firms may not adapt their structure as they become more dispersed. As mentioned previously, Ghoshal and Bartlett were able to include Japanese firms in their description of the network multinational. A 1996 study[100] of 54 companies taken from the *Fortune* 1991 list of the world's 500 largest industrial corporations revealed that the degree of internationalization differed between firms from the USA, Europe, and Japan. The study also reported that the US multinationals in the sample gave more autonomy to their international operations than did their Japanese counterparts.

We should mention that internationalizing firms from other Asian nations may also vary in structural form and growth patterns. Korean conglomerates (*chaebols*) have had a stronger preference for growth-through-acquisitions than the '**greenfield**' (building) approach taken by Japanese multinationals, and this has influenced their structural responses in terms of control and co-ordination. The so-called Chinese 'bamboo network/family firms' may face significant challenges as their international activities expand and it becomes more difficult to maintain the tight family control that characterizes overseas Chinese firms.[101]

In 1995, only three mainland Chinese firms were listed in the Fortune top 500 global companies. This number is expanding as more and more Chinese firms have international operations. A paper by Sledge notes that, by 2009, the number of Chinese firms in the Global 500 had increased to 37. This trend has continued. In the 2015 Fortune Global 500, China had a total of 100 firms listed, including three firms in the top ten (Sinopec Group #2, China National Petroleum #4, and State Grid #7). Some research has begun into the internationalization of Chinese MNEs. For example, Shen's[102] 2001 study of ten Chinese firms, mostly state-owned enterprises of various sizes and from different industries, reports an incremental approach: moving into neighboring East and South East Asia before expanding into North

America. These firms were at different stages of internationalization: four had foreign sales offices, three had sales offices and subsidiaries, and three were considered global in terms of the number of foreign subsidiaries (either wholly owned or international joint ventures). Global area divisional or global functional structures were utilized. As with China, there is a similar relative paucity of information regarding Indian MNEs and their internationalization. In the 2015 Fortune Global 500 list, India had seven entries, ranging from rankings of 119 (Indian Oil) to 449.

Some researchers have gone so far as to question the existence of a truly global firm. Doremus *et al.*[103] found empirical support for their contention that institutional infrastructures (the cultural heritage codified into legislation and values related to banking and financial markets, R&D capabilities and patterns of technological change, as well as governmental and managerial preferences and strategic propensities) combine to limit the ability of firms to move too far beyond their regional homes. Three regional blocks are presented for multinational firms: North America, Europe (largely British, French, German, and Dutch multinationals), and Asia (largely Japanese and Korean). The authors report economic data to support their contention that, while each of these regional powers have some impact outside of their own regions, practically no firms operate significantly in a balanced manner across all three regions of the world. Deep-seated differences in financial institutions, how technology is acquired and developed, and how products and services are consumed are all too divergent from each firm's region of origin for complete global cross-seeding to occur. According to Rugman, centers of regional competitive advantage may be created with some limited interventions outside of the regional core.[104]

Fashion or fit?

The above discussion has traced the evolution of the firm from a domestic-oriented to a global-oriented firm. A note of caution should be added. Growth in the firm's international business activity does require structural responses, but the evolutionary process will differ across multinationals. Apart from the important country-of-origin aspect (especially with countries that had colonies for a relatively long period of time), other variables – size of organization, pattern of internationalization, management policies, and so on – also play a part. As our discussion indicates, firms undergo stages of restructuring as they attempt to grapple with environment changes that require strategic responses.

CONTROL MECHANISMS

As indicated in Figure 3.1 at the beginning of this chapter, international operations place additional stresses on control mechanisms. There is also additional stress on the firm's ability to co-ordinate resources and activities. As the chairman and chief executive officer of the French hotel and travel company Accor explained in a newspaper interview:[105]

> *Accor has to be a global company, in view of the revolution in the service sector which is taking place [. . .]. National [hotel chains] cannot optimize their operations. They cannot invest enough money [. . .]. Globalization brings considerable challenges which are often underestimated. The principal difficulty is getting our local management to adhere to the values of the group [. . .]. Every morning when I wake I think about the challenges of co-ordinating our operations in many different countries.*

Figure 3.11 (overleaf) presents two strategies for global control. It is important to note these two strategies are not independent or divorced from each other. Rather they present a difference in emphasis.

Traditionally, MNEs have emphasized more formal, structural forms of control. As presented earlier in the chapter, strategy is implemented via the factoring of workflows, the articulation of control by some combination of specialization characterized by functional, global product division, national, regional (area) divisions, or matrix structures. Structure results in hierarchies, functional authority and increasingly prescribed job descriptions, selection criteria, training standards, and compensable factors. HR activities act to implement existing structural systems of control. Communication and relationships are formalized and prescribed and budgetary targets and 'rational', explicit, quantitative criteria dominate performance management systems.[106] Complementary yet definitely secondary control is developed and maintained via more informal personal and social networks – the informal organization.[107]

FIGURE 3.11 Control strategies for multinational firms

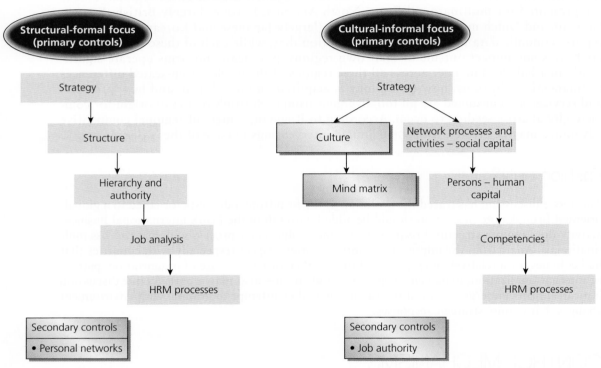

Source: Adapted from A. Engle and Y. Stedham, 'Von Nebenrolle zu Hauptrolle, von Statist ins Rampenlicht: Multinational and Transnational Strategies – Implications for Human Resource Practices', Conference Proceedings of the Sixth Conference on International Human Resource Management, Paderborn, Germany: University of Paderborn, 1998; and A. Engle, M. Mendenhall, R. Powers and Y. Stedham, 'Conceptualizing the Global Competency Cube: A Transnational Model of Human Resource', Journal of European Industrial Training, Vol. 25, No. 7, pp. 15–23.

The inadequacy of bureaucratic, structural controls when dealing with significant variations in distance and people experienced in the far-flung activities and operations of MNEs has been noted by researchers for decades. The unique cultural interactions and the contextual and physical distances that characterized multinational operations may have outstripped the capabilities of solely structural and formal forms of control.[108] As long ago as 1981, William Ouchi termed the phrase 'clan control' to describe social control as a legitimate control system to supplement or replace traditional structural, bureaucratic control.[109] A more cultural focus emphasizes the group-level potential of corporate culture, informal social processes, personal work networks, and the investment in social capital to act as sources of more complete and nimble control in a complex multiproduct, multicultural environment.

On the individual level, an emphasis on persons (as opposed to jobs), their competencies and skills, and the investment in human capital become the focus of more customized HR practices and processes.[110] Formal, structural controls still exist, but they are not the primary source of control.

Results from a survey of 390 Mexican subsidiaries of US MNEs by Gomez and Sanchez[111] led them to conclude that predicting the preferred combination of formal and informal controls a MNE might choose is problematic. The complexities related to subsidiary mandate, reliance on local or corporate technologies and skills, as well as the cultural distance between the corporate and host cultures need to be considered in determining the mix of formal and informal control. Clearly more research is called for in this topic area.[112] Returning to several of the elements in Figure 3.11, we will review informal control processes.

Control though personal relationships

A consistent theme in the descriptions of transnational and networked organization forms is the need to foster vital knowledge generation and diffusion through lateral communication via a network of working relationships. Networks are considered as part of an individual's or organization's *social capital*: contacts and ties, combined with norms and trust, that facilitate knowledge sharing and information exchanges between individuals, groups, and business units.[113] As network relationships are built and maintained through personal contact, organizations need processes and forums where staff from various units can develop types of personal relationships that can be used for organizational purposes. For example, working in cross-functional and/or cross-border teams can assist in developing personal contacts. Training and development programs, held in regional centers or at headquarters, become an important forum for the development of personal networks that foster informal communication channels.

Control through corporate culture

Some advocates of more complex structural forms regard the use of cultural control as an effective informal control mechanism. Corporate culture is variously defined, but essentially it refers to a process of socializing people so that they come to share a common set of values and beliefs that then shape their behavior and perspectives. It is often expressed as '*our way of doing things*'. Cultural control may be a contentious issue for some – there is evidence of multinational imperialism where corporate culture is superimposed upon national cultures in subsidiary operations. However, its proponents offer persuasive arguments as to its value as a management tool.[114] The emphasis is on developing voluntary adherence to corporate behavioral norms and expectations through a process of internalization of corporate values and beliefs.

The literature on corporate culture recognizes the role played by HR activities in fostering corporate culture. For example, Alvesson and Berg[115] regard HRM activities as important means of establishing corporate culture identity. The HR activities that build corporate culture include recruitment and selection practices because firms tend to hire or 'buy' people who appear to hold similar values. Training and development programs, reward systems and promotion are also activities that reinforce company value systems.[116] Such reinforcement is considered to lead to more committed and productive employees who evince appropriate behavior and therefore reduce the need for formal control mechanisms. Placement of staff is another method. Some global firms have become even more systematic in their efforts to achieve control by way of shared corporate culture. As the developmental process outlined in IHRM in Action Case 3.1 indicates, these efforts can become a central element in IHRM strategy.

IHRM in Action Case 3.1

Reflections from the shuttle tram at the
Cincinnati/Northern Kentucky
International Airport

February 14

The cold rain had changed over to wet snow as Mary Knox turned into the airport exit at Cincinnati/Northern Kentucky International Airport. Having checked in her four pieces of luggage, complete with horrible extra luggage charges, and said goodbye to her husband and three children, Mary guiltily took her place on the transfer shuttle tram going to Terminal 2.

Mary had been brought up in rural Clay County, Kentucky, near the Tennessee border. Her father was a long-haul trucker and her mother a traditional stay-at-home mom. She grew up in a rural part of the county, close to her paternal grandparent's farm. Doing well in high school, she received an Associate Degree in Nursing and had been a nurse for ten years. When her first marriage ended she took her two girls and made a new start in Midway, Kentucky.

Royoda Motor Manufacturing, USA (RMM), the North American arm of a global Japanese auto company, had built a final fabrication plant in Midway in 1985. When the six-cylinder engines were first manufactured in the USA at the Midway plant (a four billion dollar investment, employing around 4500 employees) in 2003, RMM hired a large number of people to respond to the expansion. Mary was one of those new hires. She did very well, showing a real understanding of the technical details of the production process, rising quickly to the position of line manager.

Mary's supervisor had recommended her for a new seven-week training program for managers at Royoda City in Japan. Mary was the most junior plant employee to be part of a class of 35 managers from the USA, Japan, China, and Australia. The RMM Institute was created two years earlier to provide training and deal with concerns that Royoda's corporate culture, long deemed to be a critical element in the car company's worldwide success (at last count 170,000 workers in ten Japanese plants and 21 plants outside of Japan), would be weakened by the fast pace of growth and geographic dispersion away from Japan. Some all-too-public part quality failures reinforced this concern a few years earlier. The Royoda Institute was part of a concerted effort to re-establish a strong, unifying 'Royoda Path' for the globally dispersed firm.

As the shuttle quietly but dramatically started up for Terminal 2, Mary gripped the support bar next to her and worried about how her family would cope during her seven-week absence, worried about the differences in food (she had packed plenty of Pepto-Bismol, antacids, and anti-diarrheal pills), worried about language differences (she had two years of Spanish in high school), worried about the culture shock she had seen in the preparatory orientation films the training department had shown her in Midway, and, most of all, worried about letting her production team down. As the shuttle arrived and the doors opened, she took a deep breath and stepped out into the underground concourse and awaiting gates.

April 22

Mary was very tired. Even the formidable Farbocks' 'Double Red Eye' coffee she had consumed in Los Angeles had worn off. The delays at the Los Angeles International Airport due to a security scare had made the long trip home even longer. Even though she was 12 pounds lighter than when she had left (due to long walks around the grounds of the Royoda Institute and the charming small city of Mokkibi – not in Royoda City as she had originally thought – and regular long swims in the heated Institute pool) she felt strangely at peace with the world.

The group problem-solving sessions, lectures from very senior RMM executives – including a memorable dinner meeting with Fujio Konishi, President of Royoda – exercises in devolving complex problems into their various root causes, consensus-building activities and an emphasis on how to lead and train others on *kaizen*, the five

(Continued)

(Continued)

stage philosophy of continuous improvement, had made the ten-hour days race by. Many nights she had fallen into bed in the small dormitory-like rooms too exhausted to say goodnight to her Australian and Japanese room-mates. An entire week was spent on interpreting Royoda's complex set of interactive production data displays, progress charts, and color-coded status information iconography. Mary thought to herself, "That is when I just about wanted to go home" – all that information made hospital intensive care wards look simple and placid by comparison.

Mary got to know several class members very well, hiking in the mountains with some of them on one weekend (the resurgent spring weather and flowering plants in the mountains reminded her of her home in Eastern Kentucky) and taking bullet trains to Kyoto and Tokyo on other weekends. She was very aware that her Australian, Chinese, and Japanese classmates had far more diversity in language skills than she had. She had powered through and overcome the "information overkill crisis", as she had later come to call it.

Mary recalled the first time she had hiked up the Pine Mountain as a child near her hometown in southeastern Kentucky, looking down on the town in miniature and the railway lines and roads connecting the valley, all laid out before her like a miniature train set. "Maybe that is what I got from my time in Japan – a sense of the connected-ness of Royoda", she mused. Connectedness across cultures, people, product lines, functional specializations, and geographic areas were all clearer to her now.

The shuttle was crowded with passengers and Mary could not help but note how loud and physically demon-strative the 'Americans' were. Beside her stood a Japanese family – a man, his wife, and their two daughters. Perhaps he was a salaryman coming to RMM in Midway. Mary strained to hear and only picked up three Japanese words from the conversation between the younger daughter and the mother – 'home', 'school', and 'friends'. Good words.

As the shuttle stopped at the terminal, Mary stepped lightly out of the tram to her waiting luggage (hopefully) and family. Walking down the concourse to the glass-enclosed section denoting the end of the security zone and filled with people patiently waiting, she was reminded of part of one of her grandfather's favorite poems, by that famous traveller Robert Louis Stevenson: "Home is the sailor, home from the sea, and the hunter, home from the hill".

Source: Allen D. Engle, Sr. – fictional composite case from interviews, web sources and articles related to global corporate culture and management development practices.

SUMMARY

The purpose of this chapter has been to identify the HR implications of the various options and responses that international growth places on the firm. This chapter focused on:

- The general topic of balancing standardization and localization of MNE operations and how this balancing act runs throughout all HR planning, processes, activities, and systems.

- The organizational context in which IHRM activities take place. Different structural arrangements have been identified as the firm moves along the path to multinational status – from export department through to more complex varieties such as the matrix, heterarchy, transnational, and networked structures.

- Control and co-ordination aspects. Formal and informal mechanisms were outlined, with emphasis on control through personal networks and relationships, and control through corporate culture, drawing out HRM implications.

- How international growth affects the firm's approach to HRM. Firms vary from one another as they go through the stages of international development and react in different ways to the circumstances they encounter in the various foreign markets. There is a wide variety of matches between IHRM approaches, organizational structure, and stage of internationalization. Over 28 years ago almost half the US firms surveyed by Dowling[117] reported that the operations of the HR function were unrelated to the nature of the firm's international operations. A study by Monks[118] of nine subsidiaries of multinationals operating in Ireland found that the majority adopted a local approach to the HR function, with headquarters involvement often limited to monitoring the financial implications of HR decisions.

- Stages of development and organizational forms should not to be taken as normative.[119] Research does suggest a pattern and a process of internationalization, but firms do vary in how they adapt to international operations – we use nationality of the parent firm to demonstrate this.

Through the approach taken in this chapter, we have been able to demonstrate that there is an interconnection between IHRM approaches and activities and the organizational context, and that HR managers have a crucial role to play. In order to better perform this role, it would seem important that HR managers understand the various international structural options, along with the control and co-ordination demands imposed by international growth.

DISCUSSION QUESTIONS

1   What are the issues of standardization and localization in general for MNEs and how do they particularly manifest themselves in IHRM activities?

2   What are the stages a firm typically goes through as it grows internationally and how does each stage affect the HR function?

3   What are the specific HRM challenges in a networked firm?

4   Country of origin can strongly influence a firm's approach to organization structure. As MNEs from China and India internationalize, to what extent are they likely to differ from that observed for Japanese, European, and US MNEs?

FURTHER READING

C. Bartlett and P. Beamish *Transnational Management: Text, Cases and Readings in Cross-border Management*, 7th Ed. (Boston, MA: McGraw-Hill/Irwin, 2014).

P. Caligiuri, D. Lepak and D. Bonache *Managing the Global Workforce* (Chichester, UK; John Wiley and Sons, Ltd, 2010).

W. Egelhoff and J. Wolf 'New Ideas About Organizational Design for Modern MNEs', in A. Verbeke and H. Merchant (eds.) *Handbook of Research on International Strategic Management* (Cheltenham: Edward Elgar, 2012), pp. 137–154.

M. Festing and J. Eidems 'A Process Perspective on Transnational HRM Systems – A Dynamic Capability-based Analysis', *Human Resource Management Review* Vol. 21 (2011), pp. 162–173.

E. Stiles, E. 'The International HR Department,' in G. Stahl, I. Bjorkman and S. Morris (eds.) *Handbook of Research in International Human Resource Management*, 2nd ed. (Cheltenham: Edward Elgar, 2012), pp. 36–51.

NOTES AND REFERENCES

1.   For more on the potential of strategic and structural activities to impact on international human resource processes and systems see P. Evans, V. Pucik and I. Björkman *The Global Challenge: International Human Resource Management*, 2nd ed. (Boston: McGraw-Hill, 2011), particularly Chapter 2. Also see D. Minbaeva and H. De Cieri 'Strategy and IHRM' in D. Collins, G. Wood and P. Caligiuri (eds.) The Routledge Companion to International Human Resource Management (New York: Routledge Publishing, 2015), pp. 13–28.

2.   A discussion of the 'administrative heritage' that may link MNE country of origin to a predisposition for certain strategies and structural options is presented by C. Bartlett and P. Beamish in *Transnational Management: Text, Cases and Readings in Cross-Border Management*, 7th ed. (Boston: McGraw-Hill/Irwin, 2014), pp. 292–303; T. Jackson *International HRM: A Cross-Cultural Approach* (London: Sage Publications, 2002); and P. Buckley and P. Ghauri, 'Globalization, Economic Geography and the Strategy of Multinational Enterprises', *Journal of International Business Studies*, Vol. 35, No. 2 (2004), pp. 81–98.

3.   See A. Levinson 'Organizational Design and Talent Strategies for Emerging Markets', *Organizational Dynamics*, Vol. 43 (2014), pp. 205–213. For a well-presented review of novel forms of organizing globally – described by the authors as bundles of elements in evidence – see P. Puranam, O. Alexy and M. Reitzig 'What's "New" About New Forms of Organizing?', *Academy of Management Review*, Vol. 39, no. 3 (2014), pp. 162–180.

4.   M. Svard and R. Luostarinen *Personnel Needs in the Internationalising Firm,* FIBO Publication No. 19 (Helsinki: Helsinki School of Economics, 1982).

5.   P. M. Rosenzweig and N. Nohria 'Influences on Human Resource Management Practices in Multinational Corporations', *Journal of International Business Studies,* Vol. 25, No. 2 (1994), pp. 229–51. For an empirical review of the complexities of the standardization–localization issue see R. Raffaelli and M. Glynn 'Turnkey or Tailored? Relational Pluralism, Institutional Complexity, and the Organizational Adoption of More or Less Customized Practices', Academy of Management Journal, Vol. 57, no. 2 (2014), pp. 541–562.

6. Evans, Pucik and Björkman *The Global Challenge*; R. White 'A Strategic Approach to Building a Consistent Global Rewards Program', *Compensation and Benefits Review,* Vol. 37, No. 4 (2005), pp. 23–40.

7. M. Bloom, G. T. Milkovich and A. Mitra 'International Compensation: Learning from How Managers Respond to Variations in Local Host Contexts', *International Journal of Human Resource Management,* Vol. 14, No. 8 (2002), pp. 1350–1367.

8. P. Lawrence and J. Lorsch 'Differentiation and Integration in Complex Organizations', *Administrative Science Quarterly,* Vol. 12 (1967), pp. 1–30; N. Forster and R. Whipp 'Future of European Human Resource Management: A Contingent Approach', *European Management Journal,* Vol. 13, No. 4 (1995), pp. 434–42; P. Gunnigle, K. R. Murphy, J. N. Cleveland, N. Heraty and M. Morley 'Localization in Human Resource Management: Comparing American and European Multinational Corporations', *Advances in International Management,* Vol. 14 (2002), pp. 259–284.

9. K. Kamoche 'Strategic Human Resource Management within a Resource-capability View of the Firm', *Journal of Management Studies,* Vol. 33 (1996), pp. 213–233.

10. The firm-specific complexities of this standardization–localization issue are presented in a review of dynamic structures, roles and responsibilities at Nestlé SA by M. Hird and M. Stripe 'Nestlé: Reflections on the HR Structure Debate', in P. Sparrow, M. Hird, A. Hesketh and C. Cooper (eds.) *Leading HR* (Basingstoke, UK: Palgrave Macmillan, 2010), pp. 46–67. For an empirical review of four Taiwanese multinationals that concludes that a more or less constant flux between global integration and local adaptation can be expected see Y.Y. Chang, A. Smale and S.S. Tsang 'A Diachronic Analysis of HRM transfer: Taiwanese Multinational in the UK', Cross Cultural Management, Vol. 20, no. 3 (2013), pp. 464–482.

11. A.W. Harzing *Managing the Multinationals: An International Study of Control Mechanisms* (Cheltenham: Edward Elgar, 1999).

12. E. Farndale, J. Paauwe, S. Morris, G. Stahl, P. Stiles, J. Trevor and P. Wright 'Context-Bound Configurations of Corporate HR Functions in Multinational Firms', *Human Resource Management*, Vol. 49, No. 1, (2010), pp. 45–66.

13. N. J. Adler and F. Ghadar 'Strategic Human Resource Management: A Global Perspective', in R. Pieper (ed.) *Human Resource Management: An International Comparison* (Berlin and New York: De Gruyter, 1991), pp. 235–260.

14. Bartlett and Beamish, *Transnational Management* (New York: McGraw-Hill, 2013).

15. S. Blazejewski and W. Dorow *Corporate Cultures in Global Interaction: A Management Guide* (Gütersloh, Germany: Bertlesmann Foundation, 2007).

16. J. D. Thompson *Organizations in Actions* (New York: McGraw-Hill, 1967); A. H. Aldrich *Organizations & Environments* (Englewood Cliffs, NJ: Prentice Hall, 1979); Royer and F. Kullak *When in Rome Pay as the Romans Pay? Considerations About Transnational Compensation Strategies and the Case of a German MNE,* ESCP-EAP Working Paper No. 22 (Berlin: ESCP-EAP European School of Management, 2006). Schering AG was acquired by Bayer AG in 2006 and is now Bayer Schering Pharma AG.

17. Further details can be found in M. Festing, J. Eidems, S. Royer and F. Kullak, *When in Rome Pay as the Romans Pay? Considerations About Transnational Compensation Strategies and the Case of a German MNE*, ESCP-EAP Working Paper No. 22 (Berlin: ESCP-EAP European School of Management, 2006). Schering AG was acquired by Bayer AG in 2006 and is now Bayer Schering Pharma AG.

18. P. Sparrow 'International Rewards Systems: To Converge or Not to Converge?', in C. Brewster and H. Harris (eds.) *International HRM: Contemporary Issues in Europe* (London: Routledge, 2004), pp. 102–119. See also G. T. Milkovich and M. Bloom 'Rethinking International Compensation', *Compensation and Benefits Review,* Vol. 30, No. 1 (1998), pp. 15–23.

19. H. Triandis 'Generic Individualism and Collectivism', in M. Gannon and K. Newman (eds.) *The Blackwell Handbook of Cross-cultural Management* (Oxford: Blackwell Business Pub., 2002), pp. 16–45.

20. A well-known definition for institutions is the following: institutions consist of cognitive, normative and regulative structures and activities that provide stability and meaning to social behavior. See W. R. Scott *Institutions and Organizations* (Thousand Oaks, CA: Sage, 1995), p. 33.

21. P. J. DiMaggio and W. Powell 'The Iron Cage Revisited: Institutional Isomorphism and Collective Rationality in Organizational Fields', *American Sociological Review,* Vol. 48 (1983), pp. 47–160; R. D. Whitley *European Business Systems: Firms and Markets in Their National Contexts* (London: Sage, 1992); R. D. Whitley *Business Systems in East Asia: Firms, Markets and Societies* (London: Sage, 1992). For a more concrete application of the institutional approach to a specific human resource practice see M. Festing, and I. Sahakiants 'Compensation Practices in Central and Eastern European EU Member States – An Analytical Framework Based on Institutional Perspectives, Path Dependencies and Efficiency Considerations', *Thunderbird International Business Review*, Vol. 52, No. 3 (2010), pp. 203–216.

22. A. Ferner 'Country of Origin Effects and HRM in Multinational Companies', *Human Resource Management Journal,* Vol. 7, No. 1 (1997), pp. 19–37.

23. Whitley *Business Systems in East Asia;* Whitley *European Business Systems.*

24. Federal Ministry of Education and Research (ed.) *Education in Germany* (Bonn/Berlin: Federal Ministry of Education and Research, 2004).

25. P. Sparrow 'International Rewards Systems: To Converge or Not to Converge?', in C. Brewster and H. Harris (eds.) *International HRM: Contemporary Issues in Europe* (London: Routledge, 2004), p. 103.

26. S. N. As-Saber, P. J. Dowling and P. W. Liesch 'The Role of Human Resource Management in International Joint Ventures: A Study of Australian-Indian Joint Ventures', *International Journal of Human Resource Management,* Vol. 9, No. 5 (1998), pp. 751–766.

27. S. E. Khilji 'Modes of Convergence and Divergence: An Integrative View of Multinational Practices in Pakistan', *International Journal of Human Resource Management,* Vol. 13, No. 2 (2002), pp. 232–253.

28. L. Liberman and I. Torbiörn 'Variances in Staff-related Management Practices at Eight European Country Subsidiaries of a Global Firm', *International Journal of Human Resource Management,* Vol. 11, No. 1 (2000), pp. 37–59.

29. B. Taylor, 'Patterns of Control within Japanese Manufacturing Plants in China: Doubts about Japanization in Asia', *Journal of Management Studies,* Vol. 36, No. 6 (1999), pp. 853–873.

30. Ferner 'Country of Origin Effects and HRM in Multinational Companies'.

31. Human Resource Management of US American Enterprises in the United Kingdom, published in German language as: A. Ferner, P. Almond, P. Butler, I. Cark, T. Colling, T. Edwards and L. Holden 'Das Human Resource Management amerikanischer Unternehmen in Grobbritannien', in H. Wächter and R. Peters (eds.) *Personalpolitik amerikanischer Unternehmen in Europa* (München and Mering: Hampp, 2004); A. Ferner, P. Almond and T. Colling 'Institutional Theory and the Cross-national Transfer of Employment Policy: The Case of "Workforce Diversity" in US Multinationals', *Journal of International Business Studies,* Vol. 36 (2005), pp. 304–321.

32. M. Pudelko and A.W Harzing 'Country-of-Origin, Localization or Dominance Effect? An Empirical Investigation of HRM Practices in Foreign Subsidiaries', *Human Resource Management,* Vol. 46, No. 4 (2007), pp. 535–559. Also see M. Pudelko and A.W. Harzing 'The Golden Triangle for MNCs: Standardization towards Headquarters Practices, Standardization towards Global Best Practices and Localization', *Organizational Dynamics,* Vol. 37, No. 4 (2008), pp. 394–404.

33. T. Edwards, P. Almond, I. Clark, T. Colling and A. Ferner 'Reverse Diffusion in US Multinationals: Barriers from the American Business System', *Journal of Management Studies,* Vol. 42 (2005), pp. 1261–1286.

34. A. Ferner, J. Quintanilla and M. Varul 'Country-of-origin Effects, Host-country Effects, and the Management of HR in Multinationals', *Journal of World Business,* Vol. 36, No. 2 (2001), pp. 107–127.

35. Edwards, Almond, Clark, Colling and Ferner 'Reverse Diffusion in US Multinationals: Barriers from the American Business System'.

36. For a recent tri-regional approach ('bundles' of HR practices apropos to 'North Western Europe', 'Anglo-Irish Europe' and 'Central-Southern Europe') to European HR practices and firm performance see E. Stavrou, C. Brewster and C. Charalambous 'Human Resource Management and Firm Performance in Europe Through the Lens of Business Systems: Best Fit, Best Practice or Both?', *International Journal of Human Resource Management*, Vol. 21, No. 7 (2010), pp. 933–962.

37. P. Buckley, J. Clegg and H. Tan 'The Art of Knowledge Transfer: Secondary and Reverse Transfer in China's Telecommunications Manufacturing Industry', *Management International Review,* Vol. 43, Special Issue 2 (2003), pp. 67–93.

38. Motorola company website information, December 2002.

39. Y. Yan 'A Comparative Study of Human Resource Management Practices in International Joint Ventures: The Impact of National Origin', *International Journal of Human Resource Management,* Vol. 14, No. 4 (2003), pp. 487–510.

40. For example see J. Birkinshaw and N. Hood 'Multinational Subsidiary Evolution: Capability and Charter Change in Foreign Owned Subsidiary Companies', *Academy of Management Review,* Vol. 23, No. 4 (1998), pp. 773–795; J. Birkinshaw and N. Hood (eds.) *Multinational Corporate Evolution and Subsidiary Development* (New York: St. Martin's Press, 1998); T. Ambos and J. Birkinshaw 'Headquarters' Attention and its Effect on Subsidiary Performance', *Management International Review,* Vol. 50, No. 4 (2010), p. 449–469; K. Fatehi *Managing Internationally* (London: Sage Publications, 2008), pp. 416–419.

41. See, for example, Birkinshaw and Hood, 'Multinational Subsidiary Evolution'.

42. T. Ying 'Electronics Giant to Open R&D Company', *China Daily,* 26–27 March (2005), p. 4.

43. Gupta and Govindarajan 'Knowledge Flows and the Structure of Control within Multinational Corporations'.

44. Ibid.

45. Human resource management implications are mainly based on S. Taylor, S. Beechler and N. Napier 'Toward an Integrative Model of Strategic International Human Resource Management', *Academy of Management Review,* Vol. 21, No. 4 (1996), pp. 959–985. For a more specific exposition of subsidiary mandates and HR issues (in the Hungarian context) see J. Poór, A. Engle, and A. Gross 'Human Resource Management Practices of Large Multinational Firms in Hungary, 1988–2005', *Acta Oeconomica,* Vol. 60, No.4 (2010), pp. 427–460.

46. A. Harzing and N. Noorderhaven 'Knowledge Flows in MNCs: An Empirical Test and Extension of Gupta and Govindarajan's Typology of Subsidiary Roles', *International Business Review*, Vol. 15 (2006), pp. 195–214.

47. Ibid., p. 195.

48. For an interesting study and review of centers of excellence, see M. Adenfelt and K. Lagerstrom 'The Development and Sharing of Knowledge by Centers of Excellence and Transnational Teams: A Conceptual Framework', *Management International Review,* Vol. 48, No. 3 (2008), pp. 319–338.

49. S. Morris, S. Snell and P. Wright 'A Resource-based View of International Human Resources: Toward a Framework of Integrative and Creative Capabilities', in G. Stahl and I. Bjorkman (eds.) *Handbook of Research in International Human Resource Management* (Cheltenham: Edward Elgar, 2006), pp. 433–448.

50. J. Birkinshaw and J. Ridderstråle 'Fighting the Corporate Immune System: A Process Study of Subsidiary Initiatives in Multinational Corporations', *International Business Review,* Vol. 8, No. 2 (1999), p. 154.

51. S. Michailova and K. Husted 'Knowledge-sharing Hostility in Russian Firms', *California Management Review,* Vol. 45, No. 3 (2003), pp. 59–77.

52. O. Tregaskis 'Learning Networks, Power and Legitimacy in Multinational Subsidiaries', *International Journal of Human Resource Management,* Vol. 14, No. 3 (2003), pp. 431–447.

53. Taylor, Beechler and Napier 'Toward an Integrative Model of Strategic International Human Resource Management'. For a detailed discussion of the potential complexities of the transfer of knowledge to subsidiaries in the automobile industry in India see F. Becker-Ritterspach *Hybridization of MNE Subsidiaries: The Automotive Sector in India,* (Basingstoke, UK: Palgrave Macmillan, 2009).

54. Festing, Eidems and Royer 'Strategic Issues and Local Constraints in Transnational Compensation Strategies'.

55. J. Birkinshaw and J. Ridderstråle 'Fighting the Corporate Immune System', pp. 149–80.

56. Festing, Eidems and Royer 'Strategic Issues and Local Constraints in Transnational Compensation Strategies'. For other resource-dependent-oriented analyses see Y. Kim 'Different Subsidiary Roles and International Human

Resource Management: An Exploratory Study of Austra-lian Subsidiaries in Asia', *Journal of Asia-Pacific Business,* Vol. 4 (2002), pp. 39–60; Myloni, Harzing and Mirza 'The Effect of Corporate-level Organizational Factors on the Transfer of Human Resource Management Practices'.

57. Gupta and Govindarajan 'Knowledge Flows and the Struc-ture of Control within Multinational Corporations'; Harzing *Managing the Multinationals.* For a study emphasizing the discretionary power of the headquarters in the headquarters–subsidiary relationship see T. Ambos, U. Andersson and J. Birkinshaw 'What are the Consequences of Initiative-taking in Multinational Subsidiaries?' *Journal of International Business Studies*, Vol. 41, No. 7 (2010), pp. 1099–1118.

58. J. Martinez and J. Jarillo 'The Evolution of Research on Coordination Mechanisms in Multinational Corporations', *Journal of International Business Studies,* Vol. 19 (1989), pp. 489–514. For a more wide-ranging and recent discus-sion of the many facets of coordination and control in multi-national and subsidiary relationships, see U. Andersson and U. Holm (eds.) *Managing the Contemporary Multinational: The Role of Headquarters* (Cheltenham: Edward Elgar, 2010).

59. J. I. Martinez and J. C. Jarillo 'Coordination Demands of International Strategies', *Journal of International Business Studies,* Vol. 21 (1991), p. 431.

60. For a further discussion in the context of IHRM strategies see M. Festing 'International HRM in German MNCs', *Management International Review,* Vol. 37, Special Issue No. 1 (1997), pp. 43–64. For a discussion of the possible roles corporate HR executives may take on, specific to the context of talent management aspects of global HRM, see E. Farndale, H. Scullion and P. Sparrow 'The Role of the Corporate HR Function in Global Talent Management', *Jour-nal of World Business,* Vol. 45, No. 2, (2010), pp. 161–168.

61. A PriceWaterhouseCoopers report points out that global workforce management includes the management of a respective database. For example, 70,000 employees of IBM have their profile online. PriceWaterhouseCoopers (eds.) *Technology Executive Connections: Successful Strategies for Talent Management* (USA: PriceWater-houseCoopers, 2006), p. 40. For a discussion and empirical investigation of the human capital implications of global databases see C. Ruta 'HR Portal Alignment for the Creation and Development of Intellectual Capital', *International Journal of Human Resource Management*, Vol. 20, No. 3 (2009), pp. 562–577.

62. These insights are based on an interview by one of the authors with the Head of HR of a transnational organization. For a more general view from the top of the capabilities of HRM in global coordination – from a UK perspective – see G. Maxwell and L. Farquharson 'Senior Manager's Perceptions of the Practice of Human Resource Management', *Employee Relations,* Vol. 30, No. 3 (2008), pp. 304–322.

63. The organization's structure defines the tasks of individu-als and business units within the firm and the processes that result from the intertwined tasks: identifying how the organization is divided up (differentiated) and how it is united (integrated). For a recent conceptual review of the ongoing quest for an optimal structure in an increasingly turbulent world, see J. Davis, K. Eisenhardt and C. Bingham 'Optimal Structure, Market Dynamism, and the Strategy of Simple Rules', *Administrative Science Quarterly*, Vol. 54, No. 3 (2009), pp. 413–452.

64. P. Sparrow 'Integrating People, Processes, and Context Issues in the Field of IHRM', in P. Sparrow (ed.) *Handbook of International Human Resource Management* (New York: John Wiley and Sons, 2009), pp. 3–28.

65. See M. Forsgren *Theories of the Multinational Firm* (Cheltenham, UK: Edward Elgar, 2008), particularly Chapter 5, 'The Designing Multinational: A Tale of Strate-gic Fit', pp. 71–100; J. Johanson and J. E. Vahlne 'The Mechanism of Internationalisation', *International Marketing Review,* Vol. 7, No. 4 (1990), pp. 11–24; N. Malhotra and C. Hinings 'An Organizational Model For Understanding Internationalization Processes', *Journal of International Business Studies*, Vol. 41, No. 2 (2010), pp. 330–349.

66. The willingness to entertain and success of export strategies are presented in the Chinese context by G. Gao, J. Murray, M. Kotabe and J. Li 'A "Strategy Tripod" Perspective on Export Behaviors: Evidence from Domes-tic and Foreign Firms Based in an Emerging Economy', *Journal of International Business Studies*, Vol. 14, No. 3 (2010), pp. 377–396. A study of US service firms involved in international operations showed that a wholly owned subsidiary/branch office was the most common method, though engineering and architecture firms used direct exports and consumer services used licensing/franchising (K. Erramilli 'The Experience Factor in Foreign Market Entry Behavior of Service Firms', *Journal of International Business Studies,* Vol. 22, No. 3 (1991), pp. 479–501).

67. J. Ricart, M. Enright, E Ghemawat, S. Hart and T. Khanna 'New Frontiers in International Strategy', *Journal of Inter-national Business Studies,* Vol. 35 (2004), pp. 175–200; D. Welch and L. Welch 'Pre-expatriation: The Role of HR Factors in the Early Stages of Internationalization', *International Journal of Human Resource Management,* Vol. 8, No. 4 (1997), pp. 402–413.

68. U. Zander, L. Zander and H.E. Yildiz 'Building Competitive Advantage in International Acquisitions: Grey Box Condi-tions, Culture, Status and Meritocracy', in A. Verbeke and H. Merchant (eds.) *Handbook of Research on Interna-tional Strategic Management* (Cheltenham: Edward Elgar, 2012), pp. 211–237.

69. See V. Pucik 'Strategic Human Resource Management in a Multinational Firm', in H. Wortzel and L. Wortzel (eds.) *Strategic Management of Multinational Corporations: The Essentials* (New York: John Wiley, 1985), p. 425.

70. N. Adler and A. Gundersen *International Dimensions of Organizational Behavior*, 5th ed. (Mason, OH: Thomson South-Western, 2008), Chapter 10; M. Bloom, G. Milkovich and A. Mitra 'International Compensation: Learning How Managers Respond to Variations in Local Host Contexts', *International Journal of Human Resource Management,* Vol. 14, No. 8 (2003), pp. 1350–1367.

71. For an example of the ongoing research on subsidiary roles, autonomy and overall relations with corporate headquarters see J. Birkinshwa and S. Prashantham 'Initiative in Multinational Subsidiaries', in A. Verbeke and H. Merchant (eds.) *Handbook of Research on International Strategic Management* (Cheltenham: Edward Elgar, 2012), pp. 155–168; J. Hamprecht and J. Schwarzkof 'Subsid-iary Initiatives in the Institutional Environment', *Manage-ment International Review*, Vol. 45 (2014), pp. 757–778; S. Schmid, L. Dzedek and M. Lehrer 'From Rocking the Boat to Wagging the Dog: A Literature Review of Subsidiary Initiative Research and Integrative Framework',

Journal of International Management, Vol. 20 (2014), pp. 201–218. For a more specific presentation of subsidiary HR autonomy see M. Belizon, P. Gunnigle and M. Morley ' Determinants of Central Control and Subsidiary Autonomy in HRM: the Case of Foreign-Owned Multinational Companies in Spain', *Human Resource Management Journal,* Vol. 23, No. 3 (2013), pp. 262–278.

72. Pucik 'Strategic Human Resource Management in a Multinational Firm'.

73. C. Bartlett and S. Ghoshal 'Organizing for Worldwide Effectiveness: The Transnational Solution', in R. Buzzell, J. Quelch and C. Barrett (eds.) *Global Marketing Management: Cases and Readings*, 3rd ed. (Reading, MA: Addison Wesley, 1992). For a presentation reflecting multiple possible paths and motivations for finding this balance, see P. Buckley and R. Strange 'The Governance of the Global Factory: Location and Control of World Economic Activity', Academy of Management Perspectives, Vol. 29, No. 2 (2015), pp. 237–249.

74. J. Galbraith and R. Kazanjian 'Organizing to Implement Strategies of Diversity and Globalization: The Role of Matrix Designs', *Human Resource Management,* Vol. 25, No. 1 (1986), p. 50. See also R. Daft *Organization Theory and Design*, 10th ed. (Mason, OH: South-Western Pub., 2008), Chapter 6; and R. Fitts and J. Daniels 'Aftermath of the Matrix Mania', *Columbia Journal of World Business,* Vol. 19, No. 2 (1984), for an early discussion on the matrix structure.

75. W. Taylor 'The Logic of Global Business: An Interview with ABB's Percy Barnevik', *Harvard Business Review*, March-April 1991, pp. 91–105. For a more complete presentation of ABB's strategic intent and structural and process qualities see K. Barham and C. Heimer *ABB: The Dancing Giant* (London: Financial Times/Pitman Publishing, 1998).

76. C. Bartlett and S. Ghoshal 'Matrix Management: Not a Structure, a Frame of Mind', *Harvard Business Review*, July-August 1990, pp. 138–145. Hofstede's concerns with the workability of balanced matrix structures are presented in his prescription that 'structure should follow culture' and be flexible and fluid, Hofstede, Hofstede and Minkov, *Cultures and Organizations*, pp. 402–409.

77. S. Ronen *Comparative and Multinational Management* (New York: John Wiley, 1986), p. 330.

78. P. Dowling 'International HRM', in L. Dyer (ed.) *Human Resource Management: Evolving Roles and Responsibilities,* Vol. 1, ASFA/BNA Handbook of Human Resource Management Series (Washington, DC: BNA, 1988), pp. 228–257.

79. Galbraith and Kazanjian 'Organizing to Implement Strategies', p. 50.

80. For a recent review in support of the usefulness of the matrix form see J. Qui and L. Donaldson 'Stopford and Wells were right! MNC Matrix Structures Do Fit "High-High" Strategy', *Management International Review*, Vol. 52 (2012), pp. 671–689.

81. See M. Baaij, T. Mom, F. Van den Bosch and H. Volberda 'Why Do Multinational Corporations Relocate Core Parts of their Corporate Headquarters Abroad?', *Long Range Planning*, Vol. 48 (2015), pp. 46–58.

82. G. Hedlund 'The Hypermodern MNC – A Heterarchy?', *Human Resource Management*, Vol. 25, No. 1 (1986), pp. 9–35.

83. G. Hedlund 'A Model of Knowledge Management and the N-form Corporation', *Strategic Management Journal,* Vol. 15 (1994), pp. 73–90.

84. Bartlett and Ghoshal 'Organizing for Worldwide Effectiveness', p. 66.

85. A. Engle and M. Mendenhall 'Transnational Roles, Transnational Rewards: Global Integration in Compensation', *Employee Relations*, Vol. 26, No. 6 (2004), pp. 613–625.

86. Birkinshaw and Hood *Multinational Corporate Evolution and Subsidiary Development*.

87. M. Forsgren 'Managing the International Multi-center Firm: Case Studies from Sweden', *European Management Journal,* Vol. 8, No. 2 (1990), pp. 261–267. Also see Forsgren *Theories of the Multinational Firm*, Chapter 6, 'The Networking Multinational: A Tale of Business Relationships', pp. 101–124. Much of this work has been based on the concepts of social exchange theory and interaction between actors in a network.

88. J. I. Martinez and J. C. Jarillo 'The Evolution of Research on Coordination Mechanisms in Multinational Corporations', *Journal of International Business Studies* (Fall 1989), pp. 489–514.

89. S. Ghoshal and C. Bartlett 'The Multinational Corporation as an Interorganizational Network', *Academy of Management Review,* Vol. 8, No. 2 (1990), pp. 603–625.

90. S. Ghoshal and C. Bartlett 'Building the Entrepreneurial Corporation: New Organizational Processes, New Managerial Tasks', *European Management Journal,* Vol. 13, No. 2 (1995), p. 145.

91. R. Marschan 'Dimensions of Less-hierarchical Structures in Multinationals', in I. Björkman and M. Forsgren (eds) *The Nature of the International Firm* (Copenhagen: Copenhagen Business School Press, 1997).

92. N. Nohria and S. Ghoshal *The Differentiated Network: Organizing Multinational Corporations for Value Creation* (San Francisco, CA: Jossey-Bass, 1997), pp. 28–32.

93. Y. Doz, J. Santos and P. Williamson *From Global to Metanational: How Companies Win in the Knowledge Economy* (Boston: Harvard Business Press, 2001).

94. Y. Doz, J. Santos and P. Williamson *From Global to Metanational*, p. 247.

95. H. Scullion and K. Starkey 'In Search of the Changing Role of the Corporate Human Resource Function in the International Firm', *International Journal of Human Resource Management,* Vol. 11, No. 6 (2000), pp. 1061–1081.

96. L. Leksell 'Headquarter-Subsidiary Relationships in Multinational Corporations', unpublished doctoral thesis, Institute for International Economic Studies, University of Stockholm, Stockholm (1981).

97. G. Hedlund 'Organization In-between: The Evolution of the Mother-Daughter Structure of Managing Foreign Subsidiaries in Swedish MNCs', *Journal of International Business Studies*, Fall (1984), pp. 109–123.

98. Assessment of Ford Motor Company from the *New York Times*, accessed January 27, 2011 at http://topics.nytimes.com/top/news/business/companies/ford_motor_company/index.html.

99. S. Ronen *Comparative and Multinational Management* (New York: John Wiley, 1986).

100. R. B. Peterson, J. Sargent, N. K. Napier and W. S. Shim 'Corporate Expatriate HRM Policies, Internationalisation and Performance', *Management International Review*, Vol. 36, No. 3 (1996), pp. 215–230.

101. S.K. Chai and M. Rhee 'Confucian Capitalism and the Paradox of Closure and Structural Holes in East Asian

Firms', *Management and Organizational Review*, Vol. 6, No. 1 (2010), pp. 5–29.

102. J. Shen 'Factors Affecting International Staffing in Chinese Multinationals (MNEs)', *International Journal of Human Resource Management,* Vol. 17, No. 2 (2006), pp. 295–315.

103. P. Doremus, W. Keller, L. Pauley and S. Reich *The Myth of the Global Corporation* (Princeton, NJ: Princeton University Press, 1998).

104. For additional empirical support for the idea of the regional multinational and the difficulties inherent in being a balanced, fully global firm, see A. Rugman and R. Hodgetts 'The End of Global Strategy', *European Management Journal,* Vol. 19, No. 4 (2001), pp. 333–343. For a more recent debate on the presence of absence of global as opposed to regional firms, see the special issue in the *Journal of International Business Studies*, particularly an empirical review of Japanese MNEs, 'The Regional Nature of Japanese Multinational Business', by S. Collinson and A. Rugman in *Journal of International Business Studies*, Vol. 39, No. 2 (2008), and a rejoinder to criticisms of the regional approach by A. Rugman and A. Verbeke 'The Theory and Practice of Regional Strategy: A Response to Osegowitsch and Sammartino', *Journal of International Business Studies*, Vol. 39, No. 2 (2008), pp. 326–332.

105. Interview by Andrew Jack, *Financial Times,* October 13 (1997), p. 14.

106. A. D. Engle, P. J. Dowling and M. Festing 'State of Origin: Research in Global Performance Management, a Proposed Research Domain and Emerging Implications', *European Journal of International Management*, Vol. 2, No. 2 (2008), pp. 153–169; G. Jones, *Organization Theory, Design and Change*, 6th ed. (Upper Saddle River, NJ: Pearson/Prentice-Hall, 2010, Chapters 4 and 5); Hofstede, Hofstede and Minkov *Cultures and Organizations*, Chapter 9.

107. For an empirical review of the need for a wider range of control techniques in Jordan see F. Baddar AL-Husan, F. Baddar AL-Hussan and S. Perkins 'Multilevel HRM Systems and Intermediating Variables in MNCs: Longitudinal Case Study Research in Middle Eastern Settings', *International Journal of Human Resource Management*, Vol. 25, No. 2 (2014), pp. 234–251.

108. See C. Bartlett and P. Beamish in *Transnational Management* for their discussion of a more complete form of control, more appropriate to advanced multinational firms, via a more balanced combination of structural 'anatomy', process 'physiology' and cultural 'psychology', pp. 324–330.

109. W. Ouchi *Theory Z* (New York: Avon Books, 1981).

110. A. Engle, M. Mendenhall, R. Powers and Y. Stedham 'Conceptualizing the Global Competence Cube: A Transnational Model of Human Resource Management', *European Journal of Industrial Training*, Vol. 25, No. 7 (2001), pp. 346–353.

111. R. Gomez and J. Sanchez 'Human Resource Control in MNCs: A Study of the Factors Influencing the Use of Formal and Informal Control Mechanisms', *International Journal of Human Resource Management,* Vol. 6, No. 10 (2005), pp. 1847–1861.

112. A prescriptive approach to developing a hybrid, more balanced formal and informal strategy of control is provided by F. Nilsson and N. G. Olve 'Control Systems in Multibusiness Companies: From Performance Management

to Strategic Management', *European Management Journal*, Vol. 19, No. 4 (2001), pp. 344–358. An empirical assessment of 24 international manufacturing firms in the UK provided evidence of wide variance in the degree to which multinational firms provide forums for informal control processes, some respondents appeared to rely on more formal control systems. R. Kidger 'Management Structures in Multinational Enterprises: Responding to Globalization', *Employee Relations,* Vol. 24, No. 1 (2002), pp. 69–85; for a theoretical discussion of the potential relationships between social capital, HRM and corporate strategy see S.C. Kang, S. Morris and S. Snell 'Relational Archetypes, Organizational Learning, and Value Creation: Extending Human Resource Architecture', *Academy of Management Review,* Vol. 32, No. 1 (2007), pp. 236–256.

113. J. Nahapiet and S. Ghoshal 'Social Capital, Intellectual Capital, and the Organizational Advantage', *Academy of Management Review,* Vol. 23, No. 2 (1998), pp. 242–266; M. Hitt, L. Bierman, K. Uhlenbruck and K. Shimizu 'The Importance of Resources in the Internationalization of Professional Service Firms: the Good, the Bad and the Ugly', *Academy of Management Journal,* Vol. 49, No. 6 (2006), pp. 1137–1157.

114. D. Ravasi and M. Schultz 'Responding to Organizational Identity Threats: Exploring the Role of Organizational Culture', *Academy of Management Journal,* Vol. 49, No. 3 (2006), pp. 433–458.

115. M. Alvesson and R. Berg *Corporate Culture and Organizational Symbolism* (Berlin: Walter de Gruyter, 1992). For a more recent discussion of the critical role of organizational culture and effectiveness see E. Schein *The Corporate Culture Survival Guide*, 2nd ed. (San Francisco: Jossey-Bass, 2009).

116. A. Engle and M. Mendenhall 'Transnational Roles, Transnational Rewards: Global Integration in Compensation', *Employee Relations,* Vol. 26, No. 6 (2004), pp. 613–625; D. Welch and L. Welch, 'Commitment for Hire? The Viability of Corporate Culture as a MNC Control Mechanism', *International Business Review,* Vol. 15, No. 1 (2006), pp. 14–28.

117. P. Dowling 'Hot Issues Overseas', *Personnel Administrator,* Vol. 34, No. 1 (1989), pp. 66–72. The ability or effectiveness of actually balancing standardization and localization – tilting neither one way nor the other – remains a question open to empirical assessment. See Festing and Eidems 'A Process Perspective on Transnational HRM Systems – A Dynamic Capability-based Analysis'.

118. K. Monks 'Global or Local? HRM in the Multinational Company: The Irish Experience', *International Journal of Human Resource Management,* Vol. 7, No. 3 (1996), pp. 721–735.

119. For a discussion of the search for patterns and the evolution of research in the area of international human resource management studies see R. Schuler, P. Sparrow and P. Budhwar 'Preface: Major Works in International Human Resource Management', in P. Budhwar, R. Schuler and P. Sparrow (eds.) *International Human Resource Management: Volume I – International HRM: The MNE Perspective* (Los Angeles: Sage, 2010), pp. xxiii–xxxv; also see P. Sparrow, 'Integrating People, Process, and Context Issues in the Field of IHRM', in P. Sparrow (ed.) *Handbook of International Human Resource Management* (Chichester, UK: John Wiley and Sons, 2009), pp. 3–28.

CHAPTER 4
IHRM IN CROSS-BORDER MERGERS AND ACQUISITIONS, INTERNATIONAL ALLIANCES, AND SMEs

Chapter Objectives

In the last chapter, we outlined how the international growth of multinational enterprises (MNEs) places demands on the senior management team. In this chapter, the international human resource management (IHRM) implications of other modes of international operations become our center of interest. Consequently, we move from an internal perspective on structure, control mechanisms, and managerial responses to a global perspective which includes external partners.

In this chapter we will first concentrate on cross-border alliances with a special emphasis on equity-based alliances. These alliances are given priority here due to their association with complex IHRM processes and practices,[1] which is a key area of interest in IHRM and International Management. Equity cross-border alliances include:

● mergers and acquisitions (M&As) and

● international joint ventures (IJVs).

At the end of the chapter we will address the special case of globalizing small and medium-sized enterprises (SMEs) while looking for attendant IHRM responses. SMEs represent important elements in the world economy. However, in IHRM research they are often neglected. There is evidence that their approaches to IHRM differ to a large extent from those of large MNEs and this is why we cover this topic in the present chapter. Chapters 2, 3 and 4 complement each other and are designed to deliver insights into the most important organizational contexts for IHRM.

CROSS-BORDER ALLIANCES

The strategic importance of alliances has increased in the course of globalization.[2] Cross-border alliances are co-operative agreements between two or more firms from different national backgrounds, which are intended to benefit all partners. As depicted in Figure 4.1, these comprise equity as well non-equity arrangements.[3]

● A **non-equity cross-border alliance** "is an investment vehicle in which profits and other responsibilities are assigned to each party according to a contract. Each party co-operates as a separate legal entity and bears its own liabilities".[4] Examples include international technology alliances or strategic research and development alliances,[5] as well as co-operative agreements in different functional areas such as marketing or production.[6]

● **Equity modes** involve a "foreign direct investor's purchase of shares of an enterprise in a country other than its own".[7] These include the establishment of subsidiaries as mentioned in Chapter 3, either through greenfield investments or **acquisitions**, as well as through joint ventures or **mergers**. The latter typically involve long-term collaborative strategies, which require the support of appropriate human resource (HR) practices.[8] They represent typical cross-border equity-based alliances.

FIGURE 4.1 **Equity and non-equity modes of foreign operation**

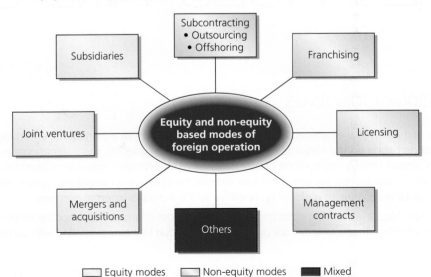

Source: Further developed from M. Kutschker and S. Schmid, *Internationales Management*, 6th ed. (Munich and Vienna: De Gruyter Oldenbourg, 2008), p. 847. Reproduced with permission.

Equity as well as non-equity cross-border alliances pose specific challenges to IHRM. Often these are crucial to the success of the international operation. As Schuler and Tarique note, "Some of the HR issues that are critical to the success of equity-based international or cross-border alliances may also rise in non-equity cross-border alliances, but they are often less central to the success of the alliance".[9] Hence, the difference in human resource management (HRM) in equity and non-equity cross-border alliances is supposed to lie in the differing extent to which specific HR measures are used.[10] However, it has to be stated that there is a research deficit with respect to HRM in non-equity cross-border alliances[11] and it is beyond the scope of this chapter to discuss the implications of all foreign entry modes in detail.[12]

CROSS-BORDER MERGERS AND ACQUISITIONS

A **merger** is the result of an agreement between two companies to join their operations together. Partners are often equals. For example, the DaimlerChrysler merger was supposed to be a merger between equals in its first stage.[13] More information about this merger and its eventual lack of success can be found in IHRM in Action Case 4.1.

An **acquisition,** on the other hand, occurs when one company buys another company with the interest of controlling the activities of the combined operations.[14] This was the case when the Dutch steel company Mittal, ranked second by volume in crude steel production in 2006, initiated a hostile takeover of the Luxembourg-based Arcelor group, ranked first in the same statistic.[15]

Figure 4.2 shows that a merger usually results in the formation of a new company while an acquisition involves the acquiring firm keeping its legal identity and integrating a new company into its own activities. The HR challenge in both cases consists of creating new HR practices and strategies that meet the requirements of the M&A.

FIGURE 4.2   The formation processes of M&As and HR challenges

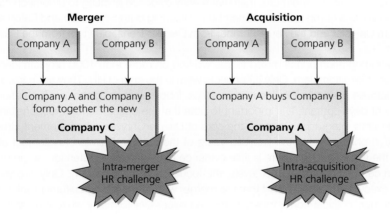

Within the context of this international volume, our focus will be on cross-border mergers and acquisitions. This means that firms with headquarters located in two different countries are the focus of our attention. Many of the HRM challenges faced in M&As are similar, and for this reason we will not further differentiate between these two entities, but summarize them and use the abbreviation M&A. The United Nations Conference on Trade and Development (UNCTAD) defines cross-border M&As as follows:[16]

Cross-border M&As involve partial or full takeover or the merging of capital, assets, and liabilities of existing enterprises in a country by TNCs [transnational corporations] from other countries. M&As generally involve the purchase of existing assets and companies.

IHRM in Action Case 4.1
HR in the DaimlerChrysler merger

The merger

The merger between Chrysler and Daimler Benz was one of the largest in history. Both companies had started to screen the automobile industry for partners in 1997. In early 1998 Jürgen E. Schrempp, Chief Executive Officer (CEO) of the German-based Daimler Benz company, took the initiative and suggested a merger to Robert J. Eaton, CEO of the American-based Chrysler corporation. The merger contract was signed in May 1998.

HR in the different phases of the M&A

At the *beginning of the merger* 'soft' people skills were not an important issue to consider. Even in the second phase when the merger was negotiated, HR issues continued to play a minor role. Negotiations were dominated by legal and financial aspects. Due to the strict secrecy at this stage, the corporate HR directors from both companies were not informed nor involved.

In the *integration planning phase* in August 1998, management teams from both firms developed strategies for the merged company. These teams identified a number of issues that had to be dealt with during the post-merger integration. With respect to HR, one important challenge was to solve the remuneration problem: the German top managers earned much less than their American counterparts. The contrary was the case for the lower management levels. It was decided that the salaries for the German top managers who had international responsibility would be raised to the US level. For a broader group of German managers a component of their salary would be linked to the company's profit and its share price. At this stage all employees were informed using various media such as letters, the intranet, or films. Furthermore, there were early evidence pointing to unforseen cultural issues in the merger. The new board was composed of 18 members, including both Schrempp and Eaton as chairmen, eight board members from Chrysler and the same number from Daimler-Benz, plus two from the Daimler subsidiaries Dasa and Debis.

During the *post-merger integration phase* mixed teams worked on more than 1000 projects identified by the post-merger integration co-ordination team. Only 43 projects were in the area of HR. They addressed topics such as corporate culture, employee profit-sharing, leadership styles, labor relations, global job evaluation, exchange programs and management development. It is important to note that the board member responsible for HR was not included in the 'Chairman's Integration Council', the core of DaimlerChrysler's management structure during the post-merger integration phase. Within the first two years of the merger, DaimlerChrysler lost about 20 top executives, mostly from the Chrysler side. There is little evidence of a systematic retention program for this level. During the information campaign for the other levels, the focus was on job security. Only two years after the merger, DaimlerChrysler executives had admitted that the merger was experiencing cultural problems. Examples included inappropriate humor, political correctness, perceived excessive formality, sexual harassment, private relationships and documentation of meetings. The company offered intercultural training for executives and management exchange programs.

Long-term effects

In 2000, profitability at Chrysler had sharply dropped and there was a 20 per cent decline in the DaimlerChrysler share price. At that time, the market capitalization of DaimlerChrysler was little more than that of Daimler-Benz before the merger. Some years later, at the beginning of 2007 and after important financial losses, mainly on the

Chrysler side, the media was discussing the possibility of a separation of Daimler and Chrysler. Although Chrysler had to close several production plants and cut around 40,000 jobs following the merger, it continuted to experi- ence problems after the merger, which was a significant problem for the combined company.[17] These problems seriously affected the success of the merger between Daimler and Chrysler and eventually led to a separation of the two partners in due course.

Source: Adapted from T. Kühlmann and P. J. Dowling, 'DaimlerChrysler: A Case Study of a Cross Border Merger', (pp. 351–363) in *Mergers & Acquistions: Managing Cultural & Human Resources* by G. K. Stahl and M. E. Mendenhall. Copyright © the Board of Trustees of the Leland Stanford Jr. University, 2005. All rights reserved. Used with the permission of Stanford University Press, www.sup.org.

Cross-border M&As have seen tremendous growth over the last two decades, in part because of the phenomenon of globalization. Although cross-border M&As are down from the historic high of 2007, "the value of cross-border M&A purchases [. . .] rose to US$441 billion, a 136% increase over the same period of 2014".[18] This is depicted in Figure 4.3.

FIGURE 4.3 **Mergers and acquisitions, 2005–2015 (billions of US$)**

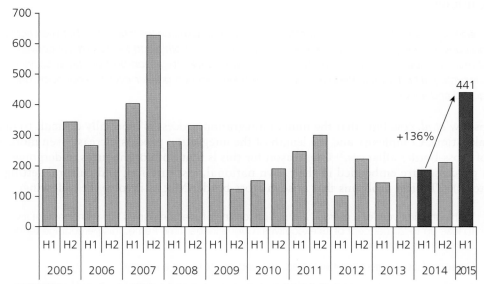

One major reason to engage in mergers or acquisitions is often to facilitate rapid entry into new markets.[19] Thus, "mergers and acquisitions are a predominant feature of the international business system as companies attempt to strengthen their market positions and exploit new market opportunities".[20] Some of the factors that a firm takes into consideration when decid- ing on a target country include: the growth aspiration of the acquiring company, risk diversi- fication, technological advantages, a response to government policies in a particular country, exchange rate advantages, favorable political and economic conditions, or an effort to follow clients.[21]

Despite the high yearly growth rates in the area of M&As, there seems to be a gap between the expected added value and the benefits realized from an M&A.[22] However, there is growing appreciation that the way in which the M&A is managed during the different phases (especially in the post-merger integration phase) has an impact on its performance, and in turn on the added value created.[23] M&A management has been investigated from many different perspectives. The work of Larsson and Finkelstein[24] provides an excellent overview of M&As from different research fields, including strategic management, economics, finance, organizational theory, and HRM.[25] Of course, all sources of research are important when explaining the phenomenon of M&A success.

For the purposes of this chapter, we are going to focus solely on HR and its role in employee relations. The quality of employee relations, ranging from employee support to employee resistance, is influenced by variables such as the similarity between the management styles of the two organizations,[26] the type of cross-border combinations, the combination potential in terms of efficiency gains or the extent of organizational integration. There is evidence that employee resistance endangers M&A performance as it may hinder synergy realization.[27] For this reason, it is important that all M&As try and effectively manage issues where employee resistance is encountered, in order that employee support can evolve. This is a process in which the HRM function can play a crucial role.

A study by Birkinshaw *et al.*[28] found that the integration of tasks[29] between two companies is interdependent with human integration. The dimensions of human integration in this study included visibility and continuity of leadership, communication processes during integration, integrating mechanisms used, acquired personnel retained, and voluntary personnel lost. Task and human integration interact in different phases to foster value creation in acquisitions:

> In phase one, task integration led to a satisfying solution that limited the interaction between acquired and acquiring units, while human integration proceeded smoothly and led to cultural convergence and mutual respect. In phase two, there was renewed task integration built on the success of the human integration that has been achieved, which led to much greater interdependencies between acquired and acquiring units.[30]

Birkinshaw *et al.* conclude that the human integration process is especially difficult to manage and takes time. Complexity and the length of the integration process increase even more in the case of cross-border alliances.[31] One reason for this is that both of the firms undergoing acquisition processes are embedded in their own national, institutional, and cultural settings (see Chapter 2).[32] Typical problems that arise in cross-border M&As involve the following:

- Within the first year of a merger, it is not uncommon for a company's top management level to lose up to 20 per cent of its executives. Over a longer time frame, this percentage tends to increase even further.[33]

- Personnel issues are often neglected, delayed or not made a priority.[34]

- Finally, a high number of M&As fail or do not produce the intended long-term results.[35]

When a firm is acquired by another firm, it constitutes an existing workforce. Considering this fact, we will describe the typical phases characterizing cross-border M&A processes and outline which HR practices are significant at each of the different stages. It is important to note that the extent to which these HR practices are carried out very much depends on the extent to which integration of the two companies is a mutual objective . In the case of low integration (e.g. if the M&A is carried out mainly for portfolio reasons) both companies remain separate cultures. However, in the case of high integration, it is crucial for the M&A to meet the HR requirements of the different phases, which will be outlined in the next section.[36]

M&A phases and HR implications

Typically, mergers and acquisitions are characterized by a series of phases. Depending on the publication, these phases will have different names. However, the M&A process usually consists of the following four steps:

1   A pre-M&A phase, including a screening of alternative partners based on an analysis of their strengths and weaknesses.

2   A due diligence phase,[37] which focuses more in-depth on analyzing the potential benefits of the merger. Here, product-market combinations, tax regulations and compatibility with respect to HR and cultural issues are of interest.[38]

3   The integration planning phase, based on the results of the due diligence phase, where planning for the new company is carried out.

4   The implementation phase, where the plans are put into action.

Various studies have shown that the HR department becomes increasingly involved in the phases of M&A integration as the process evolves. For example, a study conducted in Germany of 68 M&As revealed that HR issues are only seriously considered once the integration strategy has actually been defined.[39] Schmidt refers to a study of 447 senior HR executives who represent mainly large companies with more than 1000 employees. Most participants were from North America, supplemented by companies from Europe, Latin America and Asia. He found that those companies which involved the HR department early in the process were more successful than others with late HR involvement.[40] Both studies showed that the strongest involvement of the HR department took place in the last two phases of the M&A process. From this study Schmidt has derived best practices, which should be considered in the different M&A process phases. They are complemented by culture-specific aspects, which are of special importance in cross-border M&As (see Figure 4.4).

An analysis of the data gathered in the context of the Cranfield Network on International Human Resource Management (CRANET) shows that the following HRM measures have an

FIGURE 4.4 HR activities in the phases of a cross-border M&A

Pre-M&A phase	Due diligence phase	Integration planning phase	Implementation and assessment phase
• Identification of people-related issues • Planning for due diligence • Assessing people • Working out the organizational/cultural fit • Forming the M&A steering team • Educating the team on the HR implications	Estimating people-related • Transactional costs • Ongoing costs • Savings • Identifying and assessing cultural issues	• Developing employee culture-sensitive communication strategies • Designing key talent retention programs • Planning and leading integration efforts • Developing a new strategy for the new entity • Helping the organization cope with change • Defining an organizational blueprint and staffing plan	• Managing ongoing change, especially cultural change • Managing employee communications • Advising management on dealing with people issues • Aligning HR policies, especially total rewards • Monitoring the process of organizational and people-related integration activities • Ensuring the capture of synergies via incentives • Initiating learning processes for future M&As

Based on information in the article 'The correct spelling of M&A begins with HR by Jeffery A. Schmidt, *HR Magazine*, June 2001. (c) 2001, Society for Human Resource Management, Alexandria, VA. Used with permission. All rights reserved.'

important effect on the success of mergers and acquisitions: increasing involvement of HRM in the strategic decision-making processes of the firm, formalization of HR practices, support of the creation of organizational capabilities through training and development activities, and development of line managers and internal labor markets. These aspects seem to be independent from the consideration of specific M&A phases.[41]

IHRM in Action Case 4.1 analyzes the case of the DaimlerChrysler merger with respect to the M&A phases and briefly outlines which HR measures were taken. If you compare the information given about the DaimlerChrysler merger with the list of HR activities outlined in Figure 4.4, you can analyze the strengths and the weaknesses from an HR perspective. What lessons could be learned from this process?

Strategic HRM and the role of the HR function in M&As

Aguilera and Dencker[42] suggest a strategic approach to HR management in M&A processes. Based on strategic HRM literature suggesting a fit between business strategy and HR strategy, they argue that firms should match their M&A strategy with their HR strategy while relying on three conceptual tools:

> **Resources** are defined as tangible assets such as money and people, and intangible assets, such as brands and relationships. In the context of HRM in M&A decisions about resources involve staffing and retention issues, with termination decisions being particularly important. **Processes** refer to activities that firms use to convert the resources into valuable goods and services. For example, in our case, these would be training and development programs as well as appraisal and reward systems. Finally, values are the way in which employees think about what they do and why they do it. Values shape employees' priorities and decision-making.[43]

These ideas deliver starting points for developing HR strategies for the newly created entity and provide a basis for consideration of how to meet the intra-merger or intra-acquisition HR challenges outlined in Figure 4.1. Taking a strategic approach and aligning the HRM activities with the M&A strategy with respect to resources, processes, and values is a challenging task for the HR manager to perform: the HR manager must develop a set of integrated HR activities which are not only in line with the business strategy but with the M&A strategy as well.[44] Based on the work of Ulrich (1997),[45] the HR function can take the role of *strategic partner* (i.e. management of strategic HR), *administrative expert* (i.e. management of the firm's infrastructure), *employee champion* (i.e. management of the employee contribution), or *change agent* (i.e. management of transformation and change). In each phase of the M&A process each role involves different activities.

Rees and Edwards[46] see an emerging integrated HR strategy within M&As, mainly as the result of the interplay of the various intraorganizational micropolitical forces and the influence factors from the institutional and industrial environment. M&As may provide an excellent basis to reconsider the HR strategy of a company and to place the HR function in an important position as a key actor responsible for intercultural integration and consideration of the legal environment of the various labor markets. However, there is a danger that, due to unfavorable micropolitical conditions within the merger, a company may not utilize the full strengths of its HRM function.

The role of expatriates in M&As

The role of expatriates has been discussed with respect to **knowledge** transfer between the acquiring and the acquired company. However, the transfer of embedded knowledge is not guaranteed by each international assignment. While some studies have revealed the importance of prior working experience with a specific host country or with a particular entry mode as a success factor for expatriates involved in the integration of mergers,[47] this has not been confirmed for acquisitions. In a study by Hébert *et al.*, prior experience did not have an impact on the performance of the acquired firm.[48]

In contrast to these findings, the above-mentioned study on M&As in Germany revealed that successful integration is dependent upon managers' industry experience, experience with similar projects and, particularly in the case of cross-border alliances, level of intercultural competence.[49] An emphasis on industry experience is in line with the suggestion by Hébert *et al.*, who state that industry experience is an important asset when staffing an acquired subsidiary with an expatriate, because it can lead to a transfer of best practices.[50]

These arguments have implications for the staffing of the post-merger integration team. Hébert *et al.*[51] suggest that acquiring companies should not completely rely on the placement of expatriates within the top management team of an acquired subsidiary. They suggest creating a strong team including a mix of both groups – expatriates and local members of top management – and recommend that acquisition integration be viewed as a collective learning process.

A study by Villinger of 35 acquisitions by Western MNEs in Hungary, the Czech Republic, Slovakia and Poland found that post-acquisition managerial learning[52] highlights the importance of appropriate cross-border management skills. The author emphasizes that local language skills as well as sensitivity towards cultural differences are crucial for M&A success. It is especially important to note this when companies from developing countries represent the acquired firm in the M&A process. As Villinger[53] notes:

> *Interestingly, although language and communication problems are clearly pointed out as the key barrier to successful learning from both sides, there seems to be a consensus that the command of the partner's language is mainly a requirement for Eastern managers, and significantly less so for Western partners. This may be surprising, as it can lead to a situation in which a hundred Eastern European managers have to learn German, instead of a small number of German expatriates learning the local language. However, it may be argued that the language chosen for (future) communications will depend on the expected direction of 'the flow of learning' between the two partners.*

A comparative approach to HRM in M&A processes

While it seems possible to identify the typical phases of M&A processes across nationalities and industries, the content of the HR measures appears to depend very much on the nationality and culture of the companies involved in the M&A – a specific application of our previous discussion of 'country of origin effect' in Chapter 2. Child *et al.*[54] highlight the following HRM policy characteristics for the different countries of their investigation (USA, Japan, Germany, France, and the UK):

- **Performance-related pay** is more popular in the USA than in Japan or Germany.[55]

- Recruitment in the USA tends to be rather short-term compared to Germany, France, and the UK. In Japan the lifetime orientation is now less prevalent, but there is still a longer-term focus than in the other countries.[56]

- Training and career planning is most extensive in the USA.

Despite the fact that there are signs of convergence in HR practices across countries due to the increasing globalization of markets, the cultural and institutional differences between MNEs and the resulting impact on HR still seems to be important.[57] This seems to also hold true when M&A processes are concerned and especially in the post-integration phase. Child *et al.*[58] summarize the results of their case study research as follows:

- Convergence across nationalities in HRM policies was evident in post-acquisition moves towards performance-related pay, training, and team-based product development.

- Most acquirers also made adjustments to suit the local culture.

- American HRM reflected a short-term individualistic national business culture.

- Japanese HRM, although adopting some American methods, generally reflected long-term, consensual, team-based, collectivist national philosophies.

- French companies have been influenced by IHRM best practice but still tend to display an ethnocentric approach that gives precedence to managers of French origin.

- German companies were the most anxious to adopt international practices in their acquisitions, even when these conflict with their traditional practices. For example, they force themselves to be more informal.

INTERNATIONAL EQUITY JOINT VENTURES

International joint ventures (IJVs), the second type of equity-based cross-border alliance discussed in this chapter, have experienced tremendous growth during the last two decades and will continue to represent a major means of global expansion for MNEs.[59] In emerging economies such as China they represent the dominant operation mode for MNE market entry.[60] According to a well-known definition by Shenkar and Zeira,[61] an IJV is:

> A separate legal organizational entity representing the partial holdings of two or more parent firms, in which the headquarters of at least one is located outside the country of operation of the joint venture. This entity is subject to the joint control of its parent firms, each of which is economically and legally independent of the other.

An IJV can have two or more parent companies. Many IJVs, however, involve two parent companies. An increasing number of IJV partners leads to increasing complexity overall, including the international HR function and practices.[62] For reasons of simplification we concentrate on a constellation of two partners in the following. As will be outlined later, problems will get even more complex with more than two partners. The equity division between the parent companies of the joint venture may differ. In some cases the ratio is 50:50, in others the dominance of one partner becomes more obvious with a ratio of 51:49 or through various other combinations. This, of course, has implications for the control of the IJV – an issue which will be discussed later in this chapter. Figure 4.5 depicts the formation of an IJV. In contrast to M&As, the parent companies of an IJV keep their legal identity and an additional new legal entity representing the IJV is established. Figure 4.5 also indicates the level of complexity that an IJV represents for the HRM function. For this reason, IJVs clearly represent an important field of research for IHRM scholars.[63] The topics of research on IHRM in IJVs are very similar to those in M&As. In both cases, partners with different institutional, cultural, and national backgrounds come together and must balance their interests. However, in IJVs this challenge includes the following factors:

- HR must manage relations at the interfaces between IJV and the parent companies. The different partners that make up the IJV may possibly follow different sets of rules and this can lead to critical dualities[64] within the HR function.

- The HR department must develop appropriate HRM practices and strategies for the IJV entity itself. HR has to recruit, develop, motivate, and retain HR at the IJV level.[65]

FIGURE 4.5 Formation of an international equity joint venture

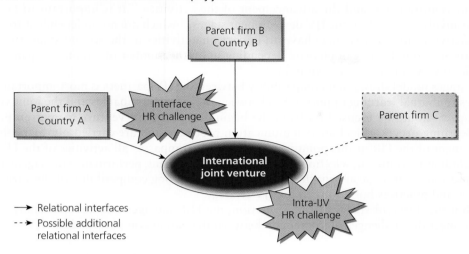

These two challenges have to be taken into consideration during the different phases of establishing and managing the joint venture[66] and will be described later in this chapter.

According to a literature analysis by Schuler, the main reasons for engaging in an IJV are as follows:[67]

- to gain knowledge and to transfer that knowledge
- host government insistence
- increased economies of scale
- to gain local knowledge
- to obtain vital raw materials
- to spread the risks (i.e. share financial risks)
- to improve competitive advantage in the face of increasing global competition
- to provide a cost-effective and efficient response required by the globalization of markets.

Special emphasis should be given to the knowledge transfer or learning objective.[68] IJVs provide an excellent opportunity to learn from another company in two ways. First, each company has the chance to 'learn the other partner's skills'. This can include gaining know-how and process knowledge in specific functional areas such as R&D, or acquiring local knowledge about a specific market or culture. Second, companies acquire working experience in co-operating with other firms. Thus, the IJV can be used as a medium for organizational learning processes as well.[69]

Unfortunately, there is evidence that many IJVs fail[70] or do not produce the expected results.[71] Some reasons for these failures can be traced back to the lack of interest in the HRM and cross-cultural management aspects of IJVs.[72] These two issues will be addressed in the following sections.

IJV development stages and HRM implications

Similar to the M&A processes discussed earlier, the development of IJVs can also be described in development stages. Schuler distinguishes four stages: the formation, in which the partnership between the parent companies is the center of interest, the development and implementation of the joint venture itself, and the advancement of the activities.[73] It is important to note that HRM is involved in each of the IJV development stages,[74] which are not independent from each other. Activities in the first stage have an impact on activities in the second stage and so on. Furthermore, complexity can increase depending upon the number of parent companies[75] and countries involved in the joint venture.[76]

The stages model shows that compatibility between the IJV partners is most important when it comes to mutual learning opportunities between the parent companies and the joint venture. This aspect should be focused on from the beginning of a joint venture formation process. As all learning processes include communication processes and are carried out by people, the management of the HR at this point is critical. This encompasses all activities of the HR function including **recruitment**, selection, **training** and **development**, performance management, and compensation. A strategic approach requires not only a strong compatibility of the various HR activities and practices but also with the IJV strategy.[77]

Within the different stages of IJV formation, the HR manager may take on many roles in order to meet the challenges of interaction between the parent company and the IJV:

- In the *partnership role*, HR managers should take the needs of all stakeholders into account and demonstrate a thorough understanding of the business and the market.

- As a *change facilitator* and *strategy implementer*, HR managers should be able to conceptualize and implement new strategies involving trust-based communication and co-operation with relevant partners. This also requires the creation of a stable learning environment.[78]

- As an *innovator*, the HR manager should be able to identify talent for executing IJV strategies and adapting to changes in the IJV stages.

- As a *collaborator*, the HR manager's strengths should lie in creating win-win situations characterized by sharing rather than competing between the different entities engaged in the joint venture.[79]

The importance of cross-cultural management in IJVs

As outlined in the previous section on 'the comparative approach of HR in M&As', the national, institutional and cultural environments of a firm do indeed matter. Here we will focus on cultural issues which play an important role in IJVs.[80] This information on comparative HRM as well as on cross-cultural HRM is relevant to both M&As and IJVs. In many studies, the implications of different cultural employee backgrounds coming together in an IJV have been the center of interest. Such a case is described in the following IHRM in Action Case 4.2, which addresses the HR-related challenges of two different institutional and cultural environments working together in a common venture. This example illustrates how cultural differences matter in collaboration, decision-making, and loyalty in the German–Chinese Joint Venture of Beijing Lufthansa Center Co. Ltd.

The top management team and the role of expatriates in IJVs

As shown in IHRM in Action Case 4.2, the IJV's top management team has a high impact on the performance of the joint venture. The team's main task is to control the daily business operations of the IJV. The case described here is typical when the two parent firms of an IJV share equal equity division. Usually, both have the right to be equally represented in the management team, and control of the key management positions is a critical issue when negotiating an IJV contract. Each firm tries to protect its own interests and to keep as much control as possible by staffing key positions with its own people.[81] Kabst[82] calls these IJV positions 'functional gatekeepers' – they try to protect their firm's assets in specific functional areas such as R&D, production, or marketing.

IHRM in Action Case 4.2

Collaboration, decision-making, and loyalty
in a German–Chinese joint venture: Beijing
Lufthansa Center Co. Ltd.

The joint venture

In 1978 the People's Republic of China opened its frontiers for foreign investors; the need for modern hotels, apartments and office space that could meet Western requirements became obvious. Deutsche Lufthansa AG, together with the government of the city of Beijing, decided to establish a multifunctional service center to provide a logistics base for international business travellers for whom China was an unknown territory at that time. The joint venture contract was signed in 1986 and in May 1992 the Beijing Lufthansa Center Co. Ltd. was opened as one of the largest Chinese–German ventures.

Requirements for the selection of the management team

According to the legal requirements for joint ventures in China, the management team of a joint venture was required to have *equal representation* of both parties. For the selection of the German members their *technical abilities, industry experience, and management know-how* were of major importance to ensure acceptance by their Chinese counterparts. Furthermore, an *understanding of Chinese culture,* combined with the ability to accept and cope with Chinese decision-making structures and lifestyle were important in creating an environment of co-operation and learning. Learning opportunities were a major motivation for the Chinese decision to work in a joint venture.

Another important aspect was *language.* As many older Chinese were not able to speak English at that time, there was often a need for a translator. All documents had to be translated into either English or Chinese. For all important meetings there were translators. German managers took into account that this was time-consuming and not all information might have been transferred. Consequently, it would be useful for the co-operation and the atmosphere within the joint venture if the Germans also had some Chinese language capabilities.

The German management team members were told that if they were able to influence the selection of their Chinese counterparts they needed to understand that *status and important contacts, as well as informal relationships within the administration and government* played an important role in ensuring an important contribution to the joint venture's success.

Collaboration

Although all parties should have a common interest in the success of a joint venture, *different perspectives* on specific topics can lead to conflict. This can have an impact on factors such as the choice of suppliers (foreign vs. Chinese instead of quality considerations) or the use of company cars as important status symbols. The use of foreign consultants was favored by the Germans for quality reasons, while the Chinese voted for local consultants for cost reasons. The same was true for discussions concerning the need of expatriates. Chinese managers tried to avoid expensive expatriates while their German counterparts were convinced that they needed people with specific qualifications, which, according to them, could only be provided by expatriates. Again, the negotiations about these issues were very time-consuming.

With respect to decision-making, the joint venture contract stated that the general manager was responsible for daily business and would be supported by a Chinese deputy. These requirementss ensured that the Chinese legal and cultural environment was sufficiently respected in the decision-making processes. However, in practice this meant that the general manager could not decide anything without the support of the Chinese deputy, and decision processes became slow and complicated. This led to a change in the decision-making relationship

(Continued)

(Continued)

between the general manager and the deputy, which gave more power to the deputy and ensured that the general manager could only take a limited number of decisions without the deputy.

Loyalty

In many situations, strong loyalty to the parent company presented a problem because the managers did not put the common project at the center of interest. For example, it was reported that the Chinese managers didn't want to take decisions without consulting their parent firm, which again led to very slow decision processes. Here, the high degree of power distance and uncertainty avoidance of the Chinese partners may have influenced this behavior. However, this approach endangers loyalty to the joint venture and discourages local employees and managers from both sides. Another issue which led to difficulties involved the way in which expatriate managers viewed their jobs in the joint venture. For them, their positions were often just another step in their careers which could possibly lead to a higher position after the assignment. In this case, loyalty to the parent company was higher than loyalty to the joint venture.

Source: Based on H. J. Probst 'Human Resources in a German-Chinese Joint Venture – Experiences from the Beijing Lufthansa Center Co. Ltd', published in German language as H. J. Probst 'Human Resources in einem deutsch-chinesischen Joint Venture: Praxiserfahrungen am Beispiel der Beijing Lufthansa Center Co. Ltd.', *Duisburger Papiere zur Ostasienwirtschaft*, Vol. 22 (1995), pp. 1–44. Reproduced with permission.

Due to the fact that the parent companies compete for these key management positions, the top management team is usually composed of individuals from different cultural contexts. As in all **multicultural** teams, diversity may provide opportunities, but the individuals may also have problems working effectively together. The critical challenge for a multicultural team heading an IJV is not only that it has to deal with different cultural expectations, but that it also has to balance the various management styles and strategic objectives of the different parent firms. Li *et al.*[83] point out that identification with both the IJV and the parent firm can lead to significant role conflicts and divided loyalty for IJV managers. In the Beijing Lufthansa case study, an exaggerated identification with the parent firm could have influenced communication and decision-making processes in the multicultural team, leading to lower commitment and, consequently, to problems in decision-making and unsatisfactory results. To avoid intercultural conflicts, companies often recruit country experts from outside the company rather than repositioning internal technical experts.

To address these problems and to increase IJV performance, Li *et al.* suggest taking explicit measures for improving organizational identity and identification at the IJV level.[84] In his study on the retention of experienced managers in IJVs in China, Li[85] notes the involvement of these managers in strategic decision-making processes and intensive social integration measures as the most important measures for reducing turnover of high potentials in IJVs. However, the effectiveness of these measures decreased with an increase in shares of the foreign partner.

INTERNATIONAL SMEs[86]

SMEs: Strategic importance and barriers to internationalization

The role of SMEs is often not discussed in the international management literature. SMEs can be defined using headcount, annual turnover, or the annual balance sheet total. Table 4.1 outlines the definition of a SME developed by the European Commission. It is important to note that there is no commonly accepted definition of a SME, and criteria and limits differ. The European Commission definition is very specific, while other definitions include companies with up to 1000 employees.[87]

TABLE 4.1 SME definition

Enterprise category	Headcount	Annual turnover	Annual balance sheet total
Medium-sized	< 250	< € 50 million	< € 43 million
Small	< 50	< € 10 million	< € 10 million

Source: European Commission (ed.) *The New SME Definition*. User Guide and Model Declaration (Brussels: European Commission, 2005), p. 14. Reproduced with permission.

It is often forgotten that SMEs play an important role in the world economy, as shown by the following figures:

- In the European Economic Area (EEA) and Switzerland there are more than 16 million enterprises. Less than 1 per cent are large enterprises; the rest are SMEs. Two-thirds of all jobs in this region are in SMEs, while one-third of all jobs are provided by large enterprises.[88] In many countries the percentage of employees working for enterprises with fewer than 20 employees amounts to more than 80 per cent.[89]

- SMEs constitute the backbone of the Asia-Pacific region, accounting for 90 per cent of enterprises, between 32 and 48 per cent of employment and between 80 and 60 per cent of gross domestic product in individual Asia-Pacific economies.[90]

- In the USA more than 80 per cent of total employment is with organizations with fewer than 20 employees.[91]

The strong position of SMEs in their national economies is not reflected to the same extent in the international business environment.[92] When internationalizing their operations, SMEs experience different challenges than large organizations. They have less experience with environmental contexts in different countries, less power to withstand the demand of host governments, less reputation, and fewer financial resources, as well as fewer resources for managing international operations.[93] The top ten barriers to access to international markets as identified by an Organisation for Economic Co-operation and Development (OECD) survey on 978 SMEs worldwide include the following:

1 shortage of working capital to finance exports

2 identifying foreign business opportunities

3 limited information to locate/analyze markets

4 inability to contact potential overseas customers

5 obtaining reliable foreign representation

6 lack of managerial time to deal with internationalization

7 inadequate quantity of and/or untrained personnel for internationalization

8 difficulty in managing competitor's prices

9 lack of home government assistance/incentives

10 excessive transportation/insurance costs.[94]

In many countries such as Singapore, Korea, and South Africa, and in the European Union (EU), SME internationalization is promoted by policies of their home countries. As the World Investment Report[95] suggests:

Policymakers need to support entrepreneurship and foster the creation of start-up MNEs, especially in knowledge-based industries. In terms of enterprise development countries make up for the lack

of entrepreneurial talents and start-up candidates through the promotion of new industries and the creation of 'seed companies'. Spin-offs from public research institutes or from leading universities may also be encouraged, backed by relevant financial institutions.

IHRM features in SMEs

Much of our knowledge generated in the area of IHRM applies to large organizations.[96] While there is evidence that some recruitment or compensation practices are applicable to small organizations as well, the management of people in small organizations often differs from practices and strategies of established large organizations.[97] Although our understanding of IHRM in SMEs is still limited, there are some key points which we outline in this section of the chapter.

The importance of the founder/owner.   Internationalization process theory, which is derived from the behavioral model of uncertainty avoidance,[98] suggests that specific features of the owner or founder of an SME have an impact on the internationalization process of this particular enterprise.[99] The **'experiential market knowledge'** of the managers is assumed to have a direct impact on the choice of foreign markets and thus, the internationalization process of the SME. This theoretical approach predicts that managers start the internationalization process in geographically and culturally close markets and that with increasing experience they move towards more distant markets. Consequently, in a globalizing SME, the top managers responsible for internationalization decisions should have sufficient international background and experience to be able to take informed decisions.

Research on global start-ups or 'born globals',[100] which are characterized by an emphasis on international orientation and growth from inception, has confirmed that:[101] "the founders of international new ventures are more 'alert' to the possibilities of combining resources from different national markets because of the competencies they developed from their earlier activities".[102] Manolova *et al.* report that person-related factors such as international experiences/skills, international orientation, environmental perceptions and demographic factors such as age, education and tenure had systematic effects on the internationalization of small firms. Summarizing the results of their own study they state:[103]

We expected that owners/founders who had international work experience, or established personal networks and relationships abroad would possess the skills necessary to conduct international business arrangements. Consistent with this, owners/founders or managers who have more positive perceptions of the international environment will also be more likely to internationalize their own small businesses.

Recruitment, selection and retention.   The above-mentioned barriers to SME internationalization included a scarcity of qualified international managers. Small firms may have more difficulties than large firms in recruiting adequate international managers.[104] It has been argued that many less-qualified employees are employed by SMEs because they do not meet the recruitment requirements of large organizations and are forced to work for SMEs as their second choice. As one interviewee in the study by MacMahon and Murphy[105] stated: "You get these big multinationals who cream off the top graduates and production operatives which leaves a small business very vulnerable in terms of the quality and availability of labor". Indeed, recruitment, selection, and staffing have been shown to be problematic for SMEs because these firms are perceived to lack legitimacy as employers with a strong international orientation.[106]

Kühlmann[107] has analyzed the image of SMEs as employers in the external labor market in Germany. He found that image advantages of SMEs as compared to large organizations included a good working atmosphere, less anonymity, a high degree of information, and low requirements for mobility. Participants of the study perceived the following factors as disadvantages: career opportunities, employee benefits, progressiveness of the company, training programs, pay, and international working opportunities. The results indicate a self-fulfilling prophecy: potential job candidates think that SMEs do not have strong international operations and do not apply. Because the SMEs cannot recruit qualified international managers, they are not as successful in international markets as they could be. In order to attract more applicants interested in international operations, Kühlmann suggests HR marketing activities for SMEs which clearly communicate that the firm has a strong position in international markets and offers international career opportunities. If the small size of the firm makes it difficult to attract sufficient interest, he recommends co-operation with other SMEs in a similar situation.

A study by Park and Ghauri[108] notes that it is not sufficient for small and medium-sized companies to employ highly qualified, internationally experienced managers in order to gain new technological knowledge from acquisitions. In addition to this, the managers must be highly motivated to acquire this knowledge. According to the authors this should be supported by a number of measures that facilitate the transfer of technological knowledge. This is in line with the results of a study on cross-border knowledge transfer by Pérez-Nordtwedt, Kedia, Datta and Rasheed.[109] For these researchers the intention to learn is decisive for understanding the relevant context, for a faster knowledge transfer and thus for a more successful learning process. Furthermore, their results indicate that, in addition to the quality of the relationships, trust as well as the attractiveness of knowledge to be acquired may have a positive effect on knowledge acquisition.

Research[110] has shown that the selection criteria of SMEs often include a general fit with the small organization or technical capabilities rather than requirements that refer to a future position with international responsibility. Small firms look for generalist knowledge rather than specialists. However, it has to be stressed that the requirements for international managers in SMEs are similar to those identified in large organizations.[111] Consequently, internationalizing SMEs should rethink their selection criteria and define a set of international competencies.[112]

With respect to retaining key employees, the perceived advantages and disadvantages of working for a SME outlined in the image study cited above provide useful information. The advantages need to be emphasized and SMEs should also consider improving, for example, the training opportunities or career paths of their key employees. Furthermore, the importance of financial benefits should be noted. In an empirical study of 449 German SMEs with up to 1000 employees, Weber and Kabst[113] found that financial participation programs were offered in more than 20 per cent of the companies – presumably to increase the manager's identification with the firm with the aim to enhance the long-term retention of key personnel.

Human resource development: the challenge of learning.   Learning processes are of critical importance in the volatile global environment of modern business. This is especially true in cross-border alliances, which are ranked third as preferred foreign market entry strategies of SMEs, after export activities and subsidiaries.[114] Although organizational learning is a neglected area in SME research[115] early evidence indicates that it may differ between small and large organizations. Training and development activities tend to be rather short-term oriented in SMEs and are not always designed to meet long-term strategic needs.[116] The distinctive cultural features of a small organization indicate an informal learning approach using local networks and socialization[117] rather than formalized training.[118] Often the focus is on acquiring tacit knowledge related to the specific context of the firm rather than on gaining explicit knowledge.

With respect to the specificities of the international environment, Brussig et al.[119] suggest that HRM should encourage staff in boundary-spanning positions,[120] (i.e. at the external interface of the SME) to pay attention to aspects relevant to internationalization decisions.

This involves improving the capacity for perceiving relevant environmental developments – e.g. training programs could include strategy and communication seminars. However, employees must be motivated to report and share their observations regularly and systematically, which requires good communication within the company. Anderson and Boocock[121] note that:

> Those involved in HRD [human resource development] in smaller organizations [. . .] should resist the temptation to impose 'large firm thinking' into a small organizational context. In small firms there is a complex interaction between scarce resources, reliance on the motivations and abilities of a few key individuals and a necessary focus on short-term priorities. The study suggests that 'smallness' does not preclude generative learning, but the achievement of this is not universally relevant.

However, there is still a lack of knowledge about the 'optimal' balance between formal and informal training in SMEs[122] and the relationship between training and firm performance is still unresolved.[123] Another problem is that training is often perceived as an 'unaffordable luxury' in SMEs, particularly with regard to the training of expatriates.[124]

Expatriate management.   As the previous sections have shown, an informal approach to HRM still dominates in SMEs,[125] especially for expatriate employees.[126] Research on this topic is relatively scarce, but an empirical study by Weber and Kabst of 449 German SMEs with up to 1000 employees shows that expatriate assignments predominantly occur in joint ventures and wholly owned foreign subsidiaries, but licensing agreements may also involve expatriates. After the challenge of recruiting people in foreign markets, the internal recruitment of employees for international jobs was perceived as the most important problem for the firms in this study. This finding is in line with the above discussion concerning problems with SME recruiting. However, a positive sign of a systematic approach to expatriate management in SMEs is that more than 16 per cent of firms indicated that they send employees abroad for management development reasons. In terms of training, the most important activities were language courses, while cross-cultural training only played a minor role.[127] When SMEs needed cross-cultural training for potential expatriates, these employees were sent to external training institutions. Given the small number of expatriates, in-house training is not a viable option for most SMEs. Clearly, the cultural integration of foreign acquisitions remains a challenge for most SMEs.[128]

Limited resources of the HR department and outsourcing.   The list of barriers to the internationalization of SMEs at the beginning of this section indicated that resources such as financial capital, qualified human capital to initiate and control internationalization processes, and time are often all too scarce. This in part explains why sophisticated management strategies are lacking and the appointment of HR specialists does not occur on the grounds that the costs cannot be justified with respect to the size of SMEs.[129] The focus of the usually small HR group in an SME is usually on transacting administrative tasks and most important HR decisions are taken by the founder/owner of the enterprise.[130] The fact that most of the important HR activities are left to line managers is problematic for two reasons:[131]

> First, the complexity of many HR activities is likely to result in them becoming a significant drain on managerial time and resources. As such, HR tasks may interfere with managerial responsibilities that are directly related to revenue production [. . .]. Second, many HR tasks involve substantial complexity and, thus, the quality of HR decisions may well be affected as the general managers often lack significant training and expertise in HR.

On the national level, professional employer organizations have been discussed as possible providers of HR-related services – based on a contractual agreement with the SME, the professional employer organization can become the outsourced HR department for the respective firm. This option can lead to improved managerial satisfaction in SMEs and higher-quality HR decisions.[132] Thus, outsourcing of HR practices represents a potentially valuable strategy to cope with the size-related deficiencies of HRM in SMEs. However, the risks of outsourcing strategically important activities should always be closely monitored. Despite these tendencies, a study of French SMEs has shown that the importance of strategic HRM has increased within this group: in the period between 1998 and 2005 more and more firms developed a strategic approach to HRM and spent less time on administrative issues.[133]

An alternative approach for SMEs can be found in the co-operation between SMEs and large MNEs in the German automobile industry. Suppliers followed the car producers into foreign locations and benefited from the HR experience of the MNE. The latter supports small suppliers with its know-how about expatriate management, the environment of the relevant markets, and its relationships with relevant governmental institutions for gaining visa and work permits. Furthermore, information about HRM issues in the local country is shared. Thus, a symbiosis can emerge between the interests of the MNE in facilitating the effective functioning of its suppliers abroad and the interests of SMEs, which need relevant, specialized information in order to prevent mistakes and reduce costs.

SUMMARY

In this chapter we have extended the discussion about the organizational context of MNEs conducted in Chapter 3 to other organizational forms, which pose specific problems to IHRM, i.e. cross-border alliances and globalizing SMEs. Cross-border M&As have seen a tremendous growth in the course of globalization. We have described their formation process as well as four important development phases: pre-M&A phase, due diligence phase, integration planning phase, and implementation phase. In each of the phases specific strategic HR requirements need to be taken into account in order to effectively manage the M&A process. The role of expatriates is mainly discussed with respect to learning effects. A comparative approach to HR in M&As indicates the complexity that emerges from the institutional and cultural environments in which the firms are embedded.

The number of IJVs has increased significantly over the last few decades. In the chapter we have outlined the IJV formation process, which poses considerable challenges for the HR function. Four stages are identified for the development of IJVs (formation; development; implementation; advancement and beyond) that require specific HR measures and roles. We also addressed the importance of cross-cultural management in IJVs, which is an important factor for effective co-operation across all levels of the IJV, including the top management team. Both types of equity-based cross-border alliances are very similar, involving both strategic, comparative and cross-cultural HRM issues, as well as specified expatriate roles.

The third organization form we addressed was the case of the internationalized SME. In this case, different challenges have been identified. First we outlined the strategic importance of SMEs in international business and examined barriers to SME internationalization. We also addressed important IHRM features distinguishing SMEs from MNEs: the founder/owner of the SME; recruitment, selection, and retention; HR development with special emphasis on learning; expatriate management; and the limited resources of the HR department in SMEs and outsourcing opportunities.

DISCUSSION QUESTIONS

1   Describe the formation process of cross-border mergers, acquisitions, and IJVs. What are the major differences?

2   Describe the development phases of an M&A and the respective HR implications.

3   Outline the development phases of an IJV and the respective HR implications.

4   How do cultural and institutional differences impact the HR integration in M&As and in IJVs?

5   What are the barriers to internationalization for SMEs?

6   What are some of the typical challenges for HRM in internationalized SMEs?

FURTHER READING

J. Li 'How to Retain Local Senior Managers in International Joint Ventures: The Effects of Alliance Relationship Characteristics', *Journal of Business Research*, 61(9) (2008), pp. 986–994.

H. Merchant 'Joint venture configurations in big emerging markets', in A. Verbeke and H. Merchant (eds.) *Handbook of research on international strategic management* (Cheltenham: Edward Elgar Publishing, 2012), pp. 188–210.

B. Park and P. Ghauri 'Key factors affecting acquisitions of technological capabilities from foreign acquiring firms by small and medium sized local firms' *Journal of World Business*, Vol. 46(1) (2011), pp. 116–125.

C. Rees and T. Edwards 'Management Strategy and HR in International Mergers: Choice, Constraint and Pragmatism',

Human Resource Management Journal, 19(1) (2009), pp. 24–39.

J. Sears, Aguilera and J. Dencker 'The role of human resource management in cross-border acquisitions' in G. Stahl, I. Björkman and S. Morris (eds.) *Handbook of research in international human resource management*, 2nd ed. (Cheltenham: Edward Elgar Publishing, 2012), pp. 415–435.

S. Teerikangas, G. Stahl, I. Björkman and M. Mendenhall 'IHRM issues in mergers and acquisitions' in D. Collins, G. Wood and P. Caligiuri (eds.) *The Routledge companion to international human resource management* (London: Routledge Publishing, 2015), pp. 423–456.

NOTES AND REFERENCES

1. R. Schuler and I. Tarique 'Alliance Forms and Human Resource Issues, Implications, and Significance', in O. Shenkar and J. J. Reuer (eds.) *Handbook of Strategic Alliances* (Thousand Oaks: Sage, 2006), pp. 219–239. Also see M. Correia, R. Campos e Cunha and M. Scholten 'Impact of M&As on organizational performance: The moderating role of HRM centrality', European Management Journal, Vol. 31 (2013), pp. 323–332.

2. Ibid.

3. W. Cascio and M. Serapio Jr. 'Human Resources Systems in an International Alliance: The Undoing of a

Done Deal?', *Organizational Dynamics*, Vol. 19, No. 3 (1991), pp. 63–74.

4. R. Schuler, S. Jackson and Y. Luo *Managing Human Resource in Cross-Border Alliances* (London, New York: Routledge, 2004), p. 2.

5. UNCTAD (ed.) *World Investment Report 2005* (New York and Geneva: United Nations, 2005), p. 126.

6. R. Schuler and I. Tarique 'Alliance Forms and Human Resource Issues, Implications, and Significance', in O. Shenkar and J. J. Reuer (eds.) *Handbook of Strategic Alliances* (Thousand Oaks: Sage, 2006), pp. 219–239.

7. UNCTAD (ed.) *World Investment Report 2005* (New York and Geneva: United Nations, 2005), p. 297.

8. J. Child and D. Faulkner *Strategies of Cooperation: Managing Alliances, Networks, and Joint Ventures* (Oxford, London: Oxford University Press, 1998).

9. R. Schuler and I. Tarique 'Alliance Forms and Human Resource Issues, Implications, and Significance', in O. Shenkar and J. Reuer (eds.) *Handbook of Strategic Alliances* (Thousand Oaks: Sage, 2006), p. 220.

10. R. Schuler and I. Tarique 'Alliance Forms and Human Resource Issues, Implications, and Significance', in O. Shenkar and J. Reuer (eds.) *Handbook of Strategic Alliances* (Thousand Oaks: Sage, 2006), pp. 219–239.

11. For recent notable exceptions see, for example, the work by P. Budhwar, H. Luthar and J. Bhatnagar, 'The Dynamics of HRM Systems in Indian BPO Firms', *Journal of Labor Research*, Vol. 27, No. 3 (2006), pp. 339–360; B. M. Lajara, F. G. Lillo and V. S. Sempere 'The Role of Human Resource Management in the Cooperative Strategy Process', *Human Resource Planning*, Vol. 25, No. 2 (2002), pp. 34–44; B. M. Lajara, F. G. Lillo and V. S. Sempere 'Human Resources Management: A Success and Failure Factor in Strategic Alliances', *Employee Relations*, Vol. 25, No. 1 (2003), pp. 61–80. See also for international HRM practices in project organizations C. L. Welch, D. E. Welch and M. Tahvanainen 'Managing the HR Dimension of International Project Operations', *The International Journal of Human Resource Management*, Vol. 19, No. 2 (2008), pp. 205–222.

12. For an overview see D. Welch and L. Welch 'Linking Operation Mode Diversity and IHRM', *International Journal of Human Resource Management*, Vol. 5, No. 4 (1994), pp. 911–926. A more recent overview is provided in 'IHRM issues in mergers and acquisitions' by S. Teerikangas, G. Stahl, I. Bjorkman and M. Mendenhall in D. Collins, G. Wood and P. Caligiuri (eds.) The Routlege Companion to International Human Resource Management (Abingdon, UK: Routledge, 2015), pp. 423–456.

13. T. Kühlmann and P. J. Dowling 'DaimlerChrysler: A Case Study of a Cross-Border Merger', in G. K. Stahl and M. E. Mendenhall (eds.) *Mergers and Acquisitions: Managing Culture and Human Resources* (Stanford, CA: Stanford Business Books, Stanford University Press, 2005), pp. 351–363.

14. For other definitions see also R. S. Schuler, S. E. Jackson and Y. Luo *Managing Human Resource in Cross-Border Alliances* (London, New York: Routledge, 2004), p. 5; and (Geneva: United Nations, 2006), p. 123–225.

15. UNCTAD (ed.) *World Investment Report 2006*. (New York and Geneva: United Nations, 2006).

16. UNCTAD (ed.), *World Investment Report 2006* (New York and Geneva: United Nations, 2006), p. 15.

17. See, for example, www.welt.de/data/2007/02/12/1209254.html; 12 February 2007.

18. UNCTAD (ed.) Global Investment Trends Monitor, No. 21, November 2015 (New York and Geneva: United Nations, 2015), p. 1.

19. 'Greenfield FDI refers to investment projects that entail the establishment of new production facilities such as offices, buildings, plants and factories, as well as the movement of intangible capital (mainly services)'. See UNCTAD (ed.) *World Investment Report 2006* (New York and Geneva: United Nations, 2006), p. 15.

20. J. Child, D. Faulkner and R. Pitkethly *The Management of International Acquisitions* (Oxford: Oxford University Press, 2001), p. 1.

21. R. S. Schuler, S. E. Jackson and Y. Luo *Managing Human Resource in Cross-Border Alliances* (London, New York: Routledge, 2004). Child, Faulkner and Pitkethly distinguish between market drivers, cost drivers, competitive drivers and government drivers for M&As. See J. Child, D. Faulkner and R. Pitkethly *The Management of International Acquisitions* (Oxford: Oxford University Press, 2001).

22. The same is true for international joint ventures. See K. W. Glaister, R. Husan and P. J. Buckley 'Learning to Manage International Joint Ventures', *International Business Review*, Vol. 12, No. 1 (2003), pp. 83–108.

23. J. Child, D. Faulkner and R. Pitkethly *The Management of International Acquisitions* (Oxford: Oxford University Press, 2001).

24. R. Larsson and S. Finkelstein 'Integrating Strategic, Organizational, and Human Resource Perspectives on Mergers and Acquisitions: A Case Survey of Synergy Realization', *Organization Science*, Vol. 10, No. 1 (1999), pp. 1–26. For the special case of acquisitions see a similar analysis by J. Birkinshaw, H. Bresman and L. Hakanson 'Managing the Post-Acquisition Integration Process: How the Human Integration and Task Integration Processes Interact to Foster Value Creation', *Journal of Management Studies*, Vol. 37, No. 3 (2000), pp. 395–425.

25. R. Larsson and S. Finkelstein 'Integrating Strategic, Organizational, and Human Resource Perspectives on Mergers and Acquisitions: A Case Survey of Synergy Realization', *Organization Science*, Vol. 10, No. 1 (1999), pp. 1–26 state that the emphasis primarily was on the post-combination integration process investigating cultural and other conflicts. In the related HRM research, psychological aspects, communication and careers were important topics.

26. This is confirmed by the work of D. K. Datta 'Organizational Fit and Acquisition Performance: Effects of Post-Acquisition Integration', *Strategic Management Journal*, Vol. 12, No. 4 (1991), pp. 281–297. In contrast, he didn't find an impact of differences in the evaluation and rewards systems on post-merger integration performance, although 'reward systems are often employed to reinforce values, beliefs, and practices in an organization' (p. 292).

27. R. Larsson and S. Finkelstein 'Integrating Strategic, Organizational, and Human Resource Perspectives on Mergers and Acquisitions: A Case Survey of Synergy Realization', *Organization Science*, Vol. 10, No. 1 (1999), pp. 1–26.

28. J. Birkinshaw, H. Bresman and L. Hakanson 'Managing the Post-Acquisition Integration Process: How the Human Integration and Task Integration Processes Interact to Foster Value Creation', *Journal of Management Studies*, Vol. 37, No. 3 (2000), pp. 395–425.

29. Task integration was measured by the initial plans for integration, integration mechanisms used, problems encountered during integration and task specialization during integration. See J. Birkinshaw, H. Bresman and L. Hakanson 'Managing the Post-Acquisition Integration Process: How the Human Integration and Task Integration Processes Interact to Foster Value Creation', *Journal of Management Studies*, Vol. 37, No. 3 (2000), pp. 395–425.

30. Ibid, p. 395.

31. J. A. Krug and D. Nigh 'Executive Perceptions in Foreign and Domestic Acquisitions: An Analysis of Foreign Ownership and its Effect on Executive Fate', *Journal of World Business*, Vol. 36, No. 1 (2001), pp. 85–105.

32. R. V. Aguilera and J. C. Dencker 'The Role of Human Resource Management in Cross-Border Mergers and Acquisitions', *International Journal of Human Resource Management*, Vol. 15, No. 8 (2004), pp. 1355–1370.

33. See, for example, the IHRM in Action Case 4.1 and the study by J. A. Krug and D. Nigh 'Executive Perceptions in Foreign and Domestic Acquisitions: An Analysis of Foreign Ownership and its Effect on Executive Fate', *Journal of World Business*, Vol. 36, No. 1 (2001), pp. 85–105.

34. R. V. Aguilera and J. C. Dencker 'The Role of Human Resource Management in Cross-Border Mergers and Acquisitions', *International Journal of Human Resource Management*, Vol. 15, No. 8 (2004), pp. 1355–1370.

35. A. Delios and P. W. Beamish 'Survival and Profitability: The Roles of Experience and Intangible Assets in Foreign Subsidiary Performance', *Academy of Management Journal*, Vol. 44, No. 5 (2001), pp. 1028–1038.

36. Schuler *et al.* differentiate between four types of integration: 1. the portfolio type, which has been mentioned in the text; 2. blending, i.e. the best elements from each culture are chosen; 3. a new company creation with a new culture that fits the new organization; 4. assimilation, where legitimacy is only assigned to one culture. See R. S. Schuler, S. E. Jackson and Y. Luo *Managing Human Resource in Cross-Border Alliances* (London, New York: Routledge, 2004), p. 90.

37. Some experts argue that the due diligence phase is part of the first phase, which they call pre-combination. This is followed by a combination and integration stage and a solidification and assessment stage. See R. S. Schuler, S. E. Jackson and Y. Luo *Managing Human Resource in Cross-Border Alliances* (London, New York: Routledge, 2004).

38. With respect to auditing human resource management see G. W. Florkowski and R. S. Schuler, 'Auditing Human Resource Management in the Global Environment', *International Journal of Human Resource Management*, Vol. 5, No. 4 (1994), pp. 827–851.

39. 'Successful M&As – The Impact of Human Resource Management', published in German language as: C. Geighardt, S. Armutat, H. Döring, M. Festing, C. Frühe, E. Nell and W. Werner *Erfolgreiche M&As? Was das Personalmanagement dazu beiträgt* (Düsseldorf: DGFP, 2007).

40. J. A. Schmidt 'The Correct Spelling of M&A Begins with HR', *HR Magazine*, Vol. 46, No. 6 (2001), pp. 102–108.

41. I. Nikandrou and N. Papalexandris 'The Impact of M&A Experience on Strategic HRM Practices and Organisational Effectiveness: Evidence from Greek Firms', *Human Resource Management Journal*, Vol. 17, No. 2 (2007), pp. 155–177.

42. R. V. Aguilera and J. C. Dencker 'The Role of Human Resource Management in Cross-Border Mergers and Acquisitions', *International Journal of Human Resource Management*, Vol. 15, No. 8 (2004), pp. 1355–1370.

43. Ibid, p. 1357.

44. E. M. Antila 'The Role of HR Managers in International Mergers and Acquisitions: A Multiple Case Study', *International Journal of Human Resource Management*, Vol. 17, No. 6 (2006), pp. 999–1020.

45. D. Ulrich *Human Resource Champions: The Next Agenda for Adding Value and Delivering Results* (Boston, MA: Harvard Business School Press, 1997).

46. C. Rees and T. Edwards 'Management Strategy and HR in International Mergers: Choice, Constraint and Pragmatism', *Human Resource Management Journal*, Vol. 19, No. 1 (2009), pp. 24–39.

47. A. Delios and P. W. Beamish 'Survival and Profitability: The Roles of Experience and Intangible Assets in Foreign Subsidiary Performance', *Academy of Management Journal*, Vol. 44, No. 5 (2001), pp. 1028–1038.

48. L. Hébert, P. Very and P. W. Beamish 'Expatriation as a Bridge over Troubled Water: A Knowledge-Based Perspective Applied to Cross-Border Acquisitions', *Organization Studies*, Vol. 26, No. 10 (2005), p. 1468.

49. 'Successful M&As – The Impact of Human Resource Management', published in German language as: C. Geighardt, S. Armutat, H. Döring, M. Festing, C. Frühe, E. Nell and W. Werner *Erfolgreiche M&As? Was das Personalmanagement dazu beiträgt* (Düsseldorf: DGFP, 2007).

50. L. Hébert, P. Very and P. W. Beamish 'Expatriation as a Bridge over Troubled Water: A Knowledge-Based Perspective Applied to Cross-Border Acquisitions', *Organization Studies*, Vol. 26, No. 10 (2005), p. 1469.

51. L. Hébert, P. Very and P. W. Beamish 'Expatriation as a Bridge over Troubled Water: A Knowledge-Based Perspective Applied to Cross-Border Acquisitions', *Organization Studies*, Vol. 26, No. 10 (2005), pp. 1455–1476.

52. R. Villinger 'Post-Acquisition Managerial Learning in Central East Europe', *Organization Studies*, Vol. 17, No. 2 (1996), pp. 181–206.

53. Ibid, p. 203.

54. J. Child, D. Faulkner and R. Pitkethly *The Management of International Acquisitions* (Oxford: Oxford University Press, 2001).

55. See R. Greene 'Effective rewards strategies for mergers, acquisitions and joint ventures/alliances.' *Compensation and Benefits Review*, Vol. 45, Nos. 5–6 (2014), pp. 287–291.

56. G. Olcott 'The Politics of Institutionalization: The Impact of Foreign Ownership and Control on Japanese Organizations', *International Journal of Human Resource Management*, Vol. 19, No. 9 (2008), pp. 1569–1587.

57. Katz and Darbishire (2001), Streeck (2001) and Pudelko (2006) discuss converging divergences in employment systems. With respect to employment systems they see an increasing divergence. However, in terms of work-place patterns at least Katz and Darbishire (2001) have identified a growing convergence. This is confirmed by research from the Cranet network mainly focusing on Europe (Brewster, 2006). Brewster, Mayrhofer and Morley (2004) give a more differentiated perspective. They distinguish between directional convergence and final convergence. The first is concerned with the question of whether the same trends can be observed in different countries; the latter addresses the results. Their conclusion based on the Cranet data is as follows: 'From a directional point of view, there seems to be a positive indication of convergence. However, when one looks at the question from a final convergence point of view, the answer is no longer a clear positive. None of the HR practices converged at the end of the decade. Rather, the maximum point of convergence is reached in the middle of the decade with signs of divergence after that' (Brewster, Mayrhofer and Morley, 2004). Thus the results concerning the convergence or divergence of HRM systems including performance management systems are mixed. There is no clear tendency, although in an empirical study concerning the convergence-divergence debate in HRM Pudelko (2005) concludes that the majority of the HR managers investigated (originated from Germany, the US and Japan) expect a convergence of HRM systems. See C. Brewster 'International Human Resource Management: If There Is no "Best Way", How Do We Manage?', in Inaugural Lecture (Henley Management College, UK, 2006); C. Brewster, W. Mayrhofer and M. Morley *Human Resource Management in Europe. Evidence of Convergence?* (London, Oxford: Elsevier Butterworth-Heinemann, 2004); H. C. Katz and O. Darbishire 'Converging Divergences: Worldwide Changes in Employment Systems', *Industrial and Labor Relations Review*, Vol. 54, No. 3 (2001), pp. 681–716; M. Pudelko 'A Comparison of HRM Systems in the USA, Japan and Germany in their Socio-Economic Context', *Human Resource Management Journal*, Vol. 16, No. 2 (2006), pp. 123–153; W. Streeck 'High Equality, Low Activity: The Contribution of the Social Welfare System to the Stability of the German Collective Bargaining Regime: Comment', *Industrial and Labor Relations Review*, Vol. 54, No. 3 (2001), pp. 698–706.

58. J. Child, D. Faulkner and R. Pitkethly *The Management of International Acquisitions* (Oxford: Oxford University Press, 2001), p. 180.

59. Y. Gong, O. Shenkar, Y. Luo and M.K. Nyaw 'Human Resources and International Joint Venture Performance: A System Perspective', *Journal of International Business Studies*, Vol. 36, No. 5 (2005), pp. 505–518.

60. K.B. Chan, V. Luk and G. Xun Wang 'Conflict and Innovation in International Joint Ventures: Toward a New Sinified Corporate Culture or "Alternative Globalization" in China', *Asia Pacific Business Review*, Vol. 11, No. 4 (2005), pp. 461–482.

61. O. Shenkar and Y. Zeira 'Human Resources Management in International Joint Ventures: Directions for Research', *Academy of Management Review*, Vol. 12, No. 3 (1987), p. 547.

62. R. S. Schuler and I. Tarique 'International Human Resource Management: A North American Perspective, A Thematic Update and Suggestions for Future Research', *International Journal of Human Resource Management*, Vol. 18, No. 5 (2007), pp. 717–744.

63. The following sources represent milestones in HRM-related IJV research: D. J. Cyr *The Human Resource Challenge of International Joint Ventures* (Westport, CT, London: Quorium Books, 1995); Y. Gong, O. Shenkar, Y. Luo and M.K. Nyaw 'Human Resources and International Joint Venture Performance: A System Perspective', *Journal of International Business Studies*, Vol. 36, No. 5 (2005), pp. 505–518; P. Lorange 'Human Resource Management in Multinational Cooperative Ventures', *Human Resource Management*, Vol. 25, No. 1 (1986), pp. 133–148; R. S. Schuler 'Human Resource Issues and Activities in International Joint Ventures', *International Journal of Human Resource Management*, Vol. 12, No. 1 (2001), pp. 1–52; R. S. Schuler, S. E. Jackson and Y. Luo *Managing Human Resource in Cross-Border Alliances* (London, New York: Routledge, 2004); O. Shenkar and Y. Zeira 'Human Resources Management in International Joint Ventures: Directions for Research', *Academy of Management Review*, Vol. 12, No. 3 (1987), pp. 546–557.

64. P. Evans, V. Pucik and J.L. Barsoux *The Global Challenge: Frameworks for International Human Resource Management* (Boston, USA: McGraw-Hill, 2002).

65. E.Vaara, P. Junni, R. Sarala, M. Ehrnrooth and A. Koveshikov 'Attributional tendencies in cultural explanations of M&A performance,' *Strategic Management Journal*, Vol. 38, (2014) pp. 1302–1317. Also see Y. Weber, D. Ranchman-Moore 'HR practices during post-merger conflict and merger performance.' *International Journal of Cross-Cultural Management*, Vol. 12, No. 1 (2011), pp. 73–99.

66. For these challenges see Y. Gong, O. Shenkar, Y. Luo and M.K. Nyaw 'Human Resources and International Joint Venture Performance: A System Perspective', *Journal of International Business Studies*, Vol. 36, No. 5 (2005), pp. 505–518. Similar ideas can be found in K. W. Glaister, R. Husan and P. J. Buckley 'Learning to Manage International Joint Ventures', *International Business Review*, Vol. 12, No. 1 (2003), pp. 83–108.

67. R. Schuler 'Human Resource Issues and Activities in International Joint Ventures', *International Journal of Human Resource Management*, Vol. 12, No. 1 (2001), p. 4.

68. See, for example, H. Barkema, O. Shenkar, F. Vermeulen and J. Bell 'Working Abroad, Working with Others: How Firms Learn to Operate International Joint Ventures', *Academy of Management Journal*, Vol. 40, No. 2 (1997), pp. 426–442; D. Cyr *The Human Resource Challenge of International Joint Ventures*. (Westport, CT, London: Quorium Books, 1995); P. Iles and M. Yolles 'International Joint Ventures, HRM and Viable Knowledge Migration',

International Journal of Human Resource Management, Vol. 13, No. 4 (2002), pp. 624–641.

69.   K. W. Glaister, R. Husan and P. J. Buckley 'Learning to Manage International Joint Ventures', *International Business Review*, Vol. 12, No. 1 (2003), pp. 83–108.

70.   However, changes in the ownership structure do not necessarily reflect a failure but can also meet the necessities of a volatile global environment.

71.   See, for example, S. H. Park and M. V. Russo 'When Competition Eclipses Cooperation: An Event History Analysis of Joint Venture Failure', *Management Science*, Vol. 42, No. 6 (1996), pp. 875–890; A. B. Sim and M. Y. Ali 'Determinants of Stability in International Joint Ventures: Evidence from a Developing Country', *Asia Pacific Journal of Management*, Vol. 17, No. 3 (2000), pp. 373–97.

72.   For an encompassing list of reasons for failures of international joint ventures see R. S. Schuler, S. E. Jackson and Y. Luo *Managing Human Resource in Cross-Border Alliances* (London, New York: Routledge, 2004). See also B. B. Barger 'Culture an Overused Term and International Joint Ventures: A Review of the Literature and a Case Study', *Journal of Organizational Culture, Communications & Conflict*, Vol. 11, No. 2 (2007), pp. 1–14, who identifies a research deficit in this area.

73.   R. S. Schuler 'Human Resource Issues and Activities in International Joint Ventures', *International Journal of Human Resource Management*, Vol. 12, No. 1 (2001), pp. 1–52.

74.   P. S. Budhwar, A. Varma, A. A. Katou and D. Narayan 'The Role of HR in Cross-Border Mergers and Acquisitions: The Case of Indian Pharmaceutical Firms', *Multinational Business Review*, Vol. 17, No. 2 (2009), pp. 89–110.

75.   See, for example P. W. Beamish and A. Kachra 'Number of Partners and JV Performance', *Journal of World Business*, Vol. 39, No. 2 (2004), pp. 107–120; D. R. Briscoe and R. S. Schuler *International Human Resource Management: Policy and Practice for the Global Enterprise*, 2nd ed. (New York: Routledge 2004); D. J. Cyr *The Human Resource Challenge of International Joint Ventures* (Westport, CT, London: Quorium Books, 1995); R. S. Schuler and I. Tarique 'Alliance Forms and Human Resource Issues, Implications, and Significance', in O. Shenkar and J. J. Reuer (eds.) *Handbook of Strategic Alliances* (Thousand Oaks: Sage, 2006), pp. 219–239.

76.   R. S. Schuler and I. Tarique 'Alliance Forms and Human Resource Issues, Implications, and Significance', in O. Shenkar and J. J. Reuer (eds/) *Handbook of Strategic Alliances* (Thousand Oaks: Sage, 2006), pp. 219–239.

77.   For fit-concepts in IHRM see, for example, J. Milliman, M. A. Von Glinow and M. Nathan 'Organizational Life Cycles and Strategic International Human Resource Management in Multinational Companies: Implications for Congruence Theory', *Academy of Management Review*, Vol. 16, No. 2 (1991), pp. 318–339. Also see F. Bauer and K. Matzler 'Antecedents of M&A success: The role of strategic complementarity, cultural fit, and degree and speed of integration', Strategic Management Journal, Vol. 35 (2014), pp. 269–291.

78.   See J. Zhang, M. Ahammad, S. Tarba, C. Cooper, K. Glaister and J. Wang 'The effect of leadership style on talent retention during merger and acquisition integration: Evidence from China.' *International Journal of Human Resource Management*, Vol. 26, No. 7 (2015), pp. 1021–1050.

79.   R. S. Schuler 'Human Resource Issues and Activities in International Joint Ventures', *International Journal of Human Resource Management*, Vol. 12, No. 1 (2001), p. 44.

80.   For conceptual work see, for example, L. McFarlane Shore, B. W. Eagle and M. J. Jedel 'China-United States Joint Ventures: A Typological Model of a Goal Congruence and Cultural Understanding and their Importance for Effective Human Resource Management', *International Journal of Human Resource Management*, Vol. 4, No. 1 (1993), pp. 67–83. For a specific example of the complexities inherent in successful cross-cultural coordination see P. Stokes, Y. Liu, S. Smith, S. Leidner, N. Moore and C. Rowland 'Managing talent across advanced and emerging economies: HR issues and challenges in a Sino-German strategic collaboration', International Journal of Human Resource Management, DOI: 10.1080/09585192.2015.1074090.

81.   Y. Gong, O. Shenkar, Y. Luo and M.-K. Nyaw 'Human Resources and International Joint Venture Performance: A System Perspective', *Journal of International Business Studies*, Vol. 36, No. 5 (2005), pp. 505–518; J. Li, K. Xin and M. Pillutla 'Multi-Cultural Leadership Teams and Organizational Identification in International Joint Ventures', *International Journal of Human Resource Management*, Vol. 13, No. 2 (2002), pp. 320–337.

82.   R. Kabst 'Human Resource Management for International Joint Ventures: Expatriation and Selective Control', *International Journal of Human Resource Management*, Vol. 15, No. 1 (2004b), pp. 1–16.

83.   J. Li, K. Xin and M. Pillutla 'Multi-Cultural Leadership Teams and Organizational Identification in International Joint Ventures', *International Journal of Human Resource Management*, Vol. 13, No. 2 (2002), pp. 320–337. See also C. A. Frayne and J. M. Geringer 'A Social Cognitive Approach to Examining Joint Venture General Manager Performance', *Group & Organization Management*, Vol. 19, No. 2 (1994), pp. 240–262. For the role of HRM policies as providers of control mechanisms see also J. Child, D. Faulkner and R. Pitkethly *The Management of International Acquisitions* (Oxford: Oxford University Press, 2001).

84.   Ibid, pp. 320–337.

85.   J. J. Li 'How to Retain Local Senior Managers in International Joint Ventures: The Effects of Alliance Relationship Characteristics', *Journal of Business Research*, Vol. 61, No. 9 (2008), pp. 986–994.

86.   This section is partly based on M. Festing 'Globalization of SMEs and Implications for International Human Resource Management', *International Journal of Globalisation and Small Business*, Vol. 2, No. 1 (2007), pp. 1–18.

87.   Internationalization of medium-sized enterprises, published in German language as: R. Kabst,

Internationalisierung mittelständischer Unternehmen (München, Mehring: Hampp, 2004a).

88. UNECE, UNECE Operational Activities: SME – Their Role in Foreign Trade, http://www.unece.org/indust/sme/foreignt.html, 17 February 2007.

89. http://stats.oecd.org/WBOS/default.aspx?Dataset-Code=CSP6, 20 February 2007.

90. UNECE, UNECE Operational Activities: SME – Their Role in Foreign Trade, http://www.unece.org/indust/sme/foreignt.html, 17 February 2007.

91. http://stats.oecd.org/WBOS/default.aspx?Dataset-Code=CSP6, 20 February 2007.

92. OECD (ed.) *OECD Keynote Paper on Removing Barriers to SME Access to International Markets* (Geneva: OECD, 2006), http://www.oecd.org/dataoecd/4/16/37818320.pdf, 17 February 2007. For empirical evidence on the UK see H. Matlay and D. Fletcher 'Globalization and Strategic Change: Some Lessons from the UK Small Business Sector', *Strategic Change*, Vol. 9, No. 7 (2000), pp. 437–449.

93. For a discussion of SME barriers to internationalization in various contexts see Z. Acs, R. Morck, J. M. Shaver and B. Yeung 'The Internationalization of Small and Medium-Sized Enterprises: A Policy Perspective', *Small Business Economics*, Vol. 9 (1997), pp. 7–20; P. J. Buckley 'International Technology Transfer by Small and Medium-Sized Enterprises', *Small Business Economics*, Vol. 9 (1997), pp. 67–78; M. Fujita 'Small and Medium-Sized Transnational Corporations: Salient Features', *Small Business Economics*, Vol. 7 (1995), pp. 251–271; D. A. Kirby and S. Kaiser 'Joint Ventures as an Internationalization Strategy for SMEs', *Small Business Economics*, Vol. 21 (2003), pp. 229–242; UNECE, UNECE Operational Activities: SME – Their Role in Foreign Trade, http://www.unece.org/indust/sme/foreignt.html, 17 February 2007; S. Vachani 'Problems of Foreign Subsidiaries of SMEs Compared with Large Companies', *International Business Review*, Vol. 14, No. 4 (2005), pp. 415–439.

94. OECD (ed.) *OECD Keynote Paper on Removing Barriers to SME Access to International Markets* (Geneva: OECD, 2006), http://www.oecd.org/dataoecd/4/16/37818320.pdf, 17 February 2007.

95. UNCTAD (ed.) *World Investment Report 2006* (New York and Geneva: United Nations, 2006), p. 80.

96. V. Anderson and G. Boocock 'Small Firms and Internationalisation: Learning to Manage and Managing to Learn', *Human Resource Management Journal*, Vol. 12, No. 3 (2002), pp. 5–24; A. Wilkinson 'Employment Relations in SMEs', *Employee Relations*, Vol. 21, No. 3 (1999), pp. 206–217.

97. V. Anderson and G. Boocock 'Small Firms and Internationalisation: Learning to Manage and Managing to Learn', *Human Resource Management Journal*, Vol. 12, No. 3 (2002), pp. 5–24; A. Wilkinson 'Employment Relations in SMEs', *Employee Relations*, Vol. 21, No. 3 (1999), pp. 206–217.

98. J. Johanson and J. E. Vahlne 'The Internationalization Process of the Firm – A Model of Knowledge Development and Increasing Foreign Market Commitments', *Journal of International Business Studies*, Vol. 8, No. 1 (1977), pp. 23–32; J. Johanson and J. E. Vahlne 'The Mechanism of Internationalisation', *International Marketing Review*, Vol. 7, No. 4 (1990), pp. 11–24; L. Melin, 'Internationalization as a Strategy Process', *Strategic Management Journal*, Vol. 13 (1992), pp. 99–118.

99. This finding is comparable to board internationalization of large companies. Knowledge and experiences gained in foreign markets are supposed to positively influence the extent and quality of firm internationalization. See, for example, N. Athanassiou and D. Nigh 'The Impact of the Top Management Team's International Business Experience on the Firm's Internationalization: Social Networks at Work', *Management International Review (MIR)*, Vol. 42, No. 2 (2002), pp. 157–181. For measurement issues of board internationalization see S. Schmid 'Measuring Board Internationalization – Toward a More Holistic Approach', in ESCP-EAP Working Paper No. 21 (ESCP-EAP European School of Management, Berlin, 2006). For empirical evidence from the UK small business sector see H. Matlay and D. Fletcher 'Globalization and Strategic Change: Some Lessons from the UK Small Business Sector', *Strategic Change*, Vol. 9, No. 7 (2000), pp. 437–449.

100. G. A. Knight and S. T. Cavusgil 'The Born Global Firm: A Challenge to Traditional Internationalization Theory', in T. K. Madsen (eds.) *Advances in International Marketing* (Greenwich, London: JAI Press, 1996), Vol. 8, pp. 11–26; M. Rennie 'Global Competitiveness: Born Global', *McKinsey Quarterly*, Vol. 4 (1993), pp. 45–52.

101. T. K. Madsen and P. Servais 'The Internationalization of Born Globals: An Evolutionary Process?', *International Business Review*, Vol. 6, No. 6 (1997), pp. 561–583.

102. P. P. McDougall, S. Shane and B. M. Oviatt 'Explaining the Formation of International New Ventures: The Limits of Theories from International Business Research', *Journal of Business Venturing*, Vol. 9 (1994), p. 475.

103. T. S. Manolova, C. G. Brush, L. F. Edelman and P. G. Greene 'Internationalization of Small Firms', *International Small Business Journal*, Vol. 20, No. 1 (2002), p. 22.

104. I. O. Williamson 'Employer Legitimacy and Recruitment Success in Small Businesses', *Entrepreneurship Theory and Practice*, Vol. 25, No. 1 (2000), pp. 27–42.

105. J. MacMahon and E. Murphy 'Managerial Effectiveness in Small Enterprises: Implications for HRD', *Journal of European Industrial Training*, Vol. 23, No. 1 (1999), p. 32.

106. M. S. Cardon and C. E. Stevens 'Managing Human Resources in Small Organizations: What do we know?', *Human Resource Management Review*, Vol. 14, No. 3 (2004), pp. 295–323.

107. 'Internationalization of Medium-Sized Enterprises as a Challenge for Recruitment and Development', published in German language as: T. M. Kühlmann 'Internationalisierung des Mittelstands als Herausforderung für die Personalauswahl und -entwicklung', in Gerhard und Lore Kienbaum Stiftung, J. Gutmann and R. Kabst (eds.) *Internationalisierung im*

Mittelstand. Chancen-Risiken-Erfolgsfaktoren (Wiesbaden: Gabler, 2000), pp. 357–371.

108. B. I. Park and P. N. Ghauri 'Key Factors Affecting Acquisition of Technological Capabilities from Foreign Acquiring Firms by Small and Medium Sized Local Firms', *Journal of World Business*, Vol. 46, No. 1 (2011), pp. 116–125.

109. L. Pérez-Nordtvedt, B. L. Kedia, D. K. Datta and A. A. Rasheed 'Effectiveness and Efficiency of Cross-Border Knowledge Transfer: An Empirical Examination', *Journal of Management Studies*, Vol. 45, No. 4 (2008), pp. 714–744.

110. This has been confirmed in literature analysis by M. S. Cardon and C. E. Stevens, 'Managing Human Resources in Small Organizations: What do we know?', *Human Resource Management Review*, Vol. 14, No. 3 (2004), pp. 295–323. However, this study does not focus explicitly on *international* SMEs.

111. 'Globalization of SMEs – Experiences and Recommendations for Human Resource Management', published in German language as: DGFP (ed.) *Globalisierung in kleinen und mittleren Unternehmen. Erfahrungen und Ansatzpunkte für das Personalmanagement* (Düsseldorf: DGFP, 2007).

112. Ibid.

113. 'Internationalization of Medium-sized Enterprises – Organization form and Human Resource Management', published in German language as: W. Weber and R. Kabst, 'Internationalisierung mittelständischer Unternehmen: Organisationsform und Personalmanagement', in Gerhard und Lore Kienbaum Stiftung, J. Gutmann and R. Kabst (eds.) *Internationalisierung im Mittelstand. Chancen-Risiken-Erfolgsfaktoren* (Wiesbaden: Gabler, 2000), pp. 3–92.

114. Ibid.

115. V. Anderson and G. Boocock 'Small Firms and Internationalisation: Learning to Manage and Managing to Learn', *Human Resource Management Journal*, Vol. 12, No. 3 (2002), pp. 5–24.

116. R. Hill and J. Stewart 'Human Resource Development in Small Organizations', *Journal of European Industrial Training*, Vol. 24, No. 2–4 (2000), pp. 105–117.

117. M. S. Cardon and C. E. Stevens 'Managing Human Resources in Small Organizations: What do we know?', *Human Resource Management Review*, Vol. 14, No. 3 (2004), pp. 295–323.

118. 'Globalization of SMEs – Experiences and Recommendations for Human Resource Management', published in German language as: DGFP (ed.) *Globalisierung in kleinen und mittleren Unternehmen. Erfahrungen und Ansatzpunkte für das Personalmanagement* (Düsseldorf: DGFP, 2007).

119. M. Brussig, L. Gerlach and U. Wilkens *The Development of Globalisation Strategies in SME and the Role of Human Resource Management*, paper presented at the Global Human Resource Management Conference, Barcelona, 2001.

120. A. H. Aldrich *Organizations & Environments* (Englewodd Cliffs: Prentice Hall, 1979); J. D. Thompson, *Organizations in Action: Social Science Bases of Administrative Theory* (New York, NY: McGraw-Hill, 1967).

121. V. Anderson and G. Boocock 'Small Firms and Internationalisation: Learning to Manage and Managing to Learn', *Human Resource Management Journal*, Vol. 12, No. 3 (2002), p. 20.

122. M. S. Cardon and C. E. Stevens 'Managing Human Resources in Small Organizations: What do we know?', *Human Resource Management Review*, Vol. 14, No. 3 (2004), pp. 295–323.

123. D. J. Storey 'Exploring the Link, among Small Firms, between Management Training and Firm Performance: A Comparison between the UK and other OECD Countries', *International Journal of Human Resource Management*, Vol. 15, No. 1 (2004), pp. 112–130.

124. J. MacMahon and E. Murphy 'Managerial Effectiveness in Small Enterprises: Implications for HRD', *Journal of European Industrial Training*, Vol. 23, No. 1 (1999), p. 29.

125. J. S. Hornsby and D. F. Kuratko 'Human Resource Management in U.S. Small Businesses: A Replication and Extension', *Journal of Developmental Entrepreneurship*, Vol. 8, No. 1 (2003), pp. 73–92; B. Kotey and P. Slade 'Formal Human Resource Management Practices in Small Growing Firms', *Journal of Small Business Management*, Vol. 43, No. 1 (2005), pp. 16–40; D. J. Storey, 'Exploring the Link, among Small Firms, between Management Training and Firm Performance: A Comparison between the UK and other OECD Countries', *International Journal of Human Resource Management*, Vol. 15, No. 1 (2004), pp. 112–130.

126. For an exception see H. Harris and L. Holden 'Between Autonomy and Control: Expatriate Managers and Strategic IHRM in SMEs', *Thunderbird International Business Review*, Vol. 43, No. 1 (2001), pp. 77–100.

127. 'Internationalization of Medium-sized Enterprises – Organization Form and Human Resource Management', published in German language as: W. Weber and R. Kabst, 'Internationalisierung mittelständischer Unternehmen: Organisationsform und Personalmanagement', in Gerhard und Lore Kienbaum Stiftung, J. Gutmann and R. Kabst (eds.) *Internationalisierung im Mittelstand. Chancen-Risiken-Erfolgsfaktoren*, (Wiesbaden: Gabler, 2000), pp. 3–92.

128. 'Globalization of SMEs – Experiences and Recommendations for Human Resource Management', published in German language as: DGFP (ed.) *Globalisierung in kleinen und mittleren Unternehmen. Erfahrungen und Ansatzpunkte für das Personalmanagement* (Düsseldorf: DGFP, 2007).

129. N. Kinnie, J. Purcell, S. Hutchinson, M. Terry, M. Collinson and H. Scarbrough 'Employment Relations in SMEs – Market-Driven or Customer-Shaped?', *Employee Relations*, Vol. 21, No. 3 (1999), pp. 218–235; B. S. Klaas, J. Mc Clendon and T. W. Gainey 'Managing HR in the Small and Medium Enterprise: The Impact of Professional Employer Organizations', *Entrepreneurship Theory and Practice*, Vol. 25, No. 1 (2000), pp. 107–124.

130. 'Internationalization of Mediums-Sized Enterprises as a Challenge for Recruitment and Development', published in German language as T. M. Kühlmann, 'Internationalisierung des Mittelstands als Herausforderung für die

Personalauswahl und -entwicklung', in Gerhard und
Lore Kienbaum Stiftung, J. Gutmann and R. Kabst (eds.)
*Internationalisierung im Mittelstand. Chancen-Risiken-
Erfolgsfaktoren* (Wiesbaden: Gabler, 2000),
pp. 357–371.

131. B. S. Klaas, J. Mc Clendon and T. W. Gainey
'Managing HR in the Small and Medium Enterprise:
The Impact of Professional Employer Organizations',
Entrepreneurship Theory and Practice, Vol. 25, No. 1
(2000), p. 107.

132. Ibid, pp. 107–124.

133. A. A. Razouk and M. Bayad 'Investigating the Use of
Strategic Human Resource Management in French Small
and Medium-Sized Enterprises: Longitudinal Study',
Human Systems Management, Vol. 28, No. 1/2 (2009),
pp. 47–56.

CHAPTER 5
SOURCING HUMAN RESOURCES FOR GLOBAL MARKETS – STAFFING, RECRUITMENT, AND SELECTION

Chapter Objectives

The previous three chapters have concentrated on the global environment and organization contexts. We now focus on the 'managing people' aspect. The aim is to establish the role of human resource management (HRM) in sustaining international business operations and growth. We first lay the foundations by covering the following:

- issues relating to the various approaches to staffing foreign operations
- the reasons for using international assignments: position filling, management development, and organizational development

- the various types of international assignments: short-term, extended and longer-term; non-standard arrangements: commuter, rotator, contractual, virtual, and self-initiated assignments

- the role of expatriates and non-expatriates in supporting international business activities.

We then concentrate more closely on recruitment and selection issues, focusing especially on:

- the debate surrounding expatriate failure as a starting point

- selection criteria and procedures for international assignments

- gender in international HRM: dual careers and the female expatriate.

INTRODUCTION

The purpose of this chapter is to expand on the role of international human resource management (IHRM) in sustaining global growth. In this context sourcing decisions are most important. We examine the various approaches taken to staffing international operations and the allocation of human resources (HR) to the various international operations of the firm to ensure effective strategic outcomes. The pivotal role of international assignments is outlined. We then concentrate on recruitment and selection as major influence factors on the success of global assignments.

APPROACHES TO STAFFING

There are staffing issues that internationalizing firms confront that are either not present in a domestic environment, or are complicated by the international context in which these activities take place. Take, for example, this scenario. A US multinational enterprise (MNE) wishes to appoint a new finance director for its Irish subsidiary. It may decide to fill the position by selecting from the finance staff available in its parent operations [that is, a parent-country national (PCN)], or by recruiting locally [a host-country national (HCN)], or by seeking a suitable candidate from one of its other foreign subsidiaries [a third-country national (TCN)].

The IHRM literature uses four terms to describe MNE approaches to managing and staffing subsidiaries. These terms are taken from the pioneering early work of Perlmutter,[1] who stated that it was possible to identify among international executives three primary attitudes – **ethnocentric, polycentric,** and **geocentric** – which influenced the development of a multinational enterprise. These primary attitudes had a significant effect on top management assumptions and decisions about key products, functional areas within the MNE, and geographical location decisions. To demonstrate these three attitudes, Perlmutter used aspects of organizational design such as decision-making, evaluation and control, information flows, and complexity within organizations. He also used the term *perpetuation*, which he defined as "recruiting, staffing, and development". A fourth attitude – **regiocentric** – was added later.[2] We shall consider the connection between these categories and staffing practices and examine the advantages and disadvantages of each approach.

Ethnocentric

In ethnocentric firms, few foreign subsidiaries have any autonomy, and strategic decisions are made at headquarters. Key positions in domestic and foreign operations are held by managers from headquarters. Subsidiaries are managed by staff from the home country (PCNs). There are often sound business reasons for pursuing an ethnocentric staffing policy:

- A perceived lack of qualified HCNs.

- The need to maintain good communication, co-ordination and control links with corporate headquarters. For firms at the early stages of internationalization, an ethnocentric approach can reduce the perceived high risks inherent in new environments. When a multinational acquires a firm in another country, it may wish to initially replace local managers with PCNs to ensure that the new subsidiary complies with overall corporate objectives and policies; or because local staff may not have the required level of competence. Thus, an ethnocentric approach to a particular foreign market situation can be perfectly valid for a very experienced multinational. Having your own person, in whom you can place a degree of trust to do the right thing, can moderate the perceived high risk involved in foreign activities. This has been well described by Bonache, Brewster and Suutari as 'assignments as control'.[3]

An ethnocentric policy, however, has a number of disadvantages:[4]

- It limits the promotion opportunities of HCNs, which may lead to reduced productivity and increased turnover within that group.

- The adaptation of expatriate managers to host countries often takes a long time, during which PCNs often make mistakes and poor decisions.

- When PCN and HCN compensation packages are compared, the often considerable income gap in favor of PCNs may be viewed by HCNs as unjustified.

- For many expatriates a key overseas position means new status, authority, and an increase in standard of living. These changes may affect expatriates' sensitivity to the needs and expectations of their host country subordinates, which may be quite different to the perceptions of the PCN manager.

Polycentric

Using a polycentric approach involves the MNE treating each subsidiary as a distinct national entity with some decision-making autonomy. Subsidiaries are usually managed by HCNs, who are seldom promoted to positions at headquarters, and PCNs are rarely transferred to foreign subsidiary operations. The main advantages of a polycentric policy, some of which reduce the shortcomings of the ethnocentric policy identified above, are:

- Employing HCNs eliminates language barriers, avoids the adjustment problems of expatriate managers and their families, and removes the need for expensive cultural awareness training programs.

- Employment of HCNs allows a multinational company to take a lower profile in sensitive political situations.

- Employment of HCNs is often less expensive, even if a premium is paid to attract high-quality local applicants.

- This approach gives continuity to the management of foreign subsidiaries and avoids the turnover of key managers that, by its very nature, results from an ethnocentric approach.

A polycentric policy, however, has its own disadvantages:

- Bridging the gap between HCN subsidiary managers and PCN managers at corporate headquarters is difficult. Language barriers, conflicting national loyalties and a range of cultural differences (for example, personal value differences and differences in attitudes to business) may isolate the corporate headquarters staff from the various foreign subsidiaries. The result may be that an MNE could become a 'federation' of independent national units with nominal links to corporate headquarters.

- Host-country managers have limited opportunities to gain experience outside their own country and cannot progress beyond the senior positions in their own subsidiary. Parent-country managers also have limited opportunities to gain overseas experience. As headquarters positions are held only by PCNs, the senior corporate management group will have limited exposure to international operations and, over time, this may constrain strategic decision-making and resource allocation.

Of course, in some cases the host government may effectively dictate that key managerial positions are filled by its nationals. Alternatively, the MNE may wish to be perceived as a local company as part of a strategy of local responsiveness. Having HCNs in key, visible positions assists a localization strategy.

Geocentric

With a geocentric approach, the MNE is taking a global approach to its operations, recognizing that each part (subsidiaries and headquarters) makes a unique contribution with its unique competence. It is accompanied by a worldwide integrated business, and nationality is less important than ability. This was a major goal that the European telecommunications company Vodafone set out to achieve. As a company speaker stated:

We want to create an international class of managers. In our view, the right way to do it is to have people close to one another, sharing their different approaches and understanding how each different part of the company now faces specific business challenges in the same overall scenario. We want to develop a group of people who understand the challenges of being global on the one hand and are still deeply rooted in the local countries on the other. Our target is to develop an international management capability that can leverage our global scale and scope to maintain our leadership in the industry.[5]

There are three main advantages to this approach:

1   It enables an MNE to develop an international executive team which assists in developing a global perspective and an internal pool of labor for deployment throughout the global organization.

2   It overcomes the 'federation' drawback of the polycentric approach.

3   This approach supports co-operation and resource sharing across units.

As with the other staffing approaches, there are challenges and disadvantages associated with a geocentric policy:

●   Host governments want a high number of their citizens employed and may utilize immigration controls in order to increase HCN employment if enough people and adequate skills are available, or require training of HCNs over a specified time period to replace foreign nationals.

●   Most countries (both advanced economies and developing economies) require MNEs to provide extensive documentation if they wish to hire a foreign national instead of a local national. Providing this documentation can be time-consuming, expensive, and at times futile. Of course, the same drawback applies to an ethnocentric policy. A related issue is the difficulty of obtaining a work permit for an accompanying spouse or partner.

●   A geocentric policy can be expensive to implement because of increased training and relocation costs. A related factor is the need to have a compensation structure with standardized international base pay, which may be higher than national levels in many countries.

●   Large numbers of PCNs, TCNs, and HCNs need to be sent abroad in order to build and maintain the international cadre required to support a geocentric staffing policy. To successfully implement a geocentric staffing policy requires relatively long lead times and more centralized control of the staffing process. This necessarily reduces the independence of subsidiary management in these issues, and this loss of autonomy may be resisted by subsidiaries.

Regiocentric

This approach reflects the geographic strategy and structure of the MNE. Like the geocentric approach, it utilizes a wider pool of managers but in a limited way. Staff may move outside their home countries but only within the particular geographic region. Regional managers may not be promoted to headquarters positions but enjoy a degree of regional autonomy in decision-making.[6] For example, a US-based MNE could create three regions: Europe, the Americas, and Asia-Pacific. European staff would be transferred throughout the European region, but staff transfers to the Asia-Pacific region from Europe would be rare, as would transfers from the regions to headquarters in the USA.

The advantages of using a regiocentric approach are:

- It facilitates interaction between managers transferred to regional headquarters from subsidiaries in that region and PCNs posted to the regional headquarters.

- It reflects some sensitivity to local conditions, since local subsidiaries are usually staffed almost totally by HCNs.[7]

There are some disadvantages in a regiocentric policy:

- It can produce federalism on a regional rather than a country basis and constrain the MNE from developing a more global perspective.

- While this approach does improve career prospects at the national level, it only moves the barrier to the regional level. Talented managers may advance to jobs in regional headquarters but less frequently to positions at the MNE headquarters.

A philosophy towards staffing

In summary, based in part on top management attitudes, a multinational can pursue one of several approaches to international staffing. It may even proceed on an ad-hoc basis,[8] rather than systematically selecting one of the four approaches discussed above. However, an ad-hoc approach is really policy by default because there is no conscious decision or evaluation of appropriate policy. The 'policy' is a result of corporate inertia, inexperience, or both. The major disadvantage here (apart from the obvious one of inefficient use of resources) is that the MNE's responses are reactive rather than proactive and a consistent HR strategy that fits the overall MNE strategy is more difficult to achieve.

Table 5.1 summarizes the advantages and disadvantages of using the three categories of staff – PCNs, HCNs, and TCNs. These approaches to staffing in part reflect top management attitudes, but it is important to keep in mind that the nature of international business often forces adaptation upon implementation. For example, an MNE may adopt an ethnocentric approach to all its foreign operations, but a particular host government may require the appointment of its own citizens to the key subsidiary positions so, for that market, a polycentric approach needs to be implemented. The strategic importance of the foreign market, the maturity of the operation and the degree of cultural distance between the parent and host country can influence the way in which the MNE makes key staffing decisions. In some cases an MNE may use a combination of approaches. For example, it may operate its European interests in a regiocentric manner and its Asia-Pacific interests in an ethnocentric way until there is greater confidence in operating in that region of the world.

TABLE 5.1 The advantages and disadvantages of using PCNs, TCNs, and HCNs

Parent-country nationals

Advantages
- Organizational control and co-ordination is maintained and facilitated.
- Promising managers are given international experience.
- PCNs may be the best people for the job because of special skills and experiences.
- There is assurance that the subsidiary will comply with MNE objectives, policies, etc.

Disadvantages
- The promotional opportunities of HCNs are limited.
- Adaptation to the host country may take a long time.
- PCNs may impose an inappropriate headquarters style.
- Compensation for PCNs and HCNs may differ.

Third-country nationals

Advantages
- Salary and benefit requirements may be lower than for PCNs.
- TCNs may be better informed than PCNs about the host-country environment.

Disadvantages
- Transfers must consider possible national animosities (e.g. India and Pakistan).
- The host government may resent hiring of TCNs.
- TCNs may not want to return to their home country after the assignment.

Host-country nationals

Advantages
- Language and other barriers are eliminated.
- Hiring costs are reduced and no work permit is required.
- Continuity of management improves, since HCNs stay longer in their positions.
- Government policy may dictate hiring of HCNs.
- Morale among HCNs may improve as they see future career potential.

Disadvantages
- Control and co-ordination of headquarters may be impeded.
- HCNs have limited career opportunities outside the subsidiary.
- Hiring HCNs limits opportunities for PCNs to gain foreign experience.
- Hiring HCNs could encourage a federation of national rather than global units.

Determinants of staffing choices

Because of these operating realities, it is sometimes difficult to precisely equate managerial attitudes towards international operations with the structural forms we presented in Chapter 3. The external and internal contingencies facing an internationalizing firm influence its staffing choices. These include the following:

- **Context specificities** – the local context of the headquarters as well as of the subsidiary can be described by cultural and institutional variables (as outlined in Chapter 2).[9] Cultural values may differ considerably between the headquarters and the host-country context. For example, Tarique, Schuler and Gong see the cultural similarity between parent country and subsidiary country as a moderator in the relationship between MNE strategy and subsidiary staffing.[10] Gong found that MNEs tend to staff culturally distant subsidiaries with PCNs, which has a positive effect on labor productivity.[11] The institutional environment includes, for example, the legal environment and the education system.[12] The education system may be directly linked to staff availability on the local labor market. Furthermore, the country-specific contextual factors in the parent country may lead to a country-of-origin effect, i.e. MNEs may try to transfer management practices from their home country to foreign locations. Another effect is the host-country effect, which implies that subsidiaries are influenced by their local environment.[13] As discussed in Chapter 1, the type of industry the firm is active in may have a significant impact as well.

- **Firm specific variables** – these variables were outlined in the framework on strategic HRM in MNEs introduced in Chapter 1. The most relevant variables are MNE structure and strategy, international experience, corporate governance, and organizational culture which describe the MNE as a whole.[14]

- **Local unit specificities** – as the staffing approach may vary with the cultural and institutional environment, it may also be dependent on the specificities of the local unit. An important factor here is the establishment method of the subsidiary, i.e. whether it is a greenfield investment, a merger, an acquisition, or a shared partnership.[15] Furthermore, the strategic role of a subsidiary, its strategic importance for the MNE as a whole and the related questions of the need for control and the locus of decision-making can influence staffing decisions.[16]

- **IHRM practices** – selection, training and development, compensation, and career management (including expatriation and repatriation) play an important role in the development of effective policies required to sustain a preferred staffing approach.

These four groups of factors systematically influence staffing practices. Due to situational factors, individual staffing decisions may be taken in an unexpected way. Further, it has to be acknowledged that there are interdependencies between these variables. Figure 5.1 illustrates the various determinants of staffing choices. This model may be helpful in drawing together the various contextual, organizational, and HR-related issues in determining staffing choices. For example, a firm that is maturing into a networked organization (firm specificity) will require IHRM approaches and activities that will assist its ability to develop a flexible global organization that is centrally integrated and co-ordinated yet locally responsive – a geocentric approach. However, a key assumption underlying the geocentric staffing philosophy is that the MNE has sufficient numbers of high-caliber staff (PCNs, TCNs, and HCNs) constantly available for transfer anywhere, whenever global management needs dictate.[17]

FIGURE 5.1   Determinants of staffing choices[18]

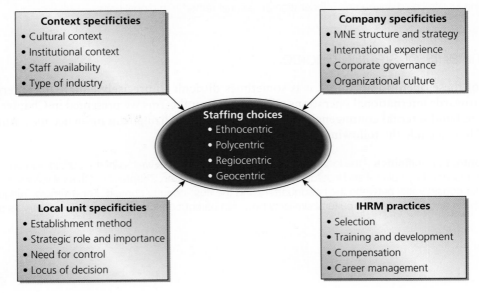

While most of the research on staffing has concentrated on movements from the head-quarters to other units of the MNE, a study by Collings, McDonnell, Gunnigle, and Lavelle has analyzed outward staffing flows in MNEs, i.e. flows of HCNs and TCNs working in Irish subsidiaries to headquarters or other units of their employer. Although the numbers of out-flow movements were quite small, they indicate a movement from ethnocentric approaches to more global staffing perspectives in many MNEs.[19] Many studies investigating the deter-minants of staffing policies have been conducted in MNEs stemming from developed coun-tries. A study of Chinese MNEs by Shen has confirmed that Western models are generally applicable to Chinese MNEs as well.[20] However, the author points out that the same catego-ries sometimes have different meanings. It is interesting to note that in this study culturally determined factors such as trust and personal ethics proved to be of special importance for staffing decisions. Overall, it seems that the different determinants of staffing choices out-lined above all have an important impact and will remain an important focus for IHRM researchers.

TRANSFERRING STAFF FOR INTERNATIONAL BUSINESS ACTIVITIES

The above discussion demonstrates the options for staffing key positions in foreign operations. We will now look at the HR consequences of these approaches and the broader implications in terms of the reasons for using international assignments, types of international assignments, the role of expatriates and non-expatriates, and the role of inpatriates.

Importance of international assignments

Given the difficulties surrounding international assignments, it is reasonable to question why multinationals persist in using expatriates. Certainly there are ebbs and flows associated with the number of staff moved internationally. Frequently, predictions are made that expatriates will become like dinosaurs as firms implement localization strategies, replacing expatriates with HCNs as a way of containing employment costs. In addition, the term 'international assignment' covers a wide variety of assignment forms, purposes, process, concerns, and HR accommodations.[21] It seems reasonable to conclude that research and practitioner inter-est with regard to the forms, strengths, weaknesses, costs, and benefits of what began some 40 years ago as 'expatriate' issues remains a major strand of IHRM.[22]

The *Brookfield Report* 2015 indicates that the use of expatriates will continue to grow in response to pressure for internationally mobile staff for a variety of purposes.[23] Some 34 per cent of the companies expected an increase, while 12 per cent were convinced of a decrease in the number of international assignments. Currently, 74 per cent of the investigated com-panies have reduced assignment expenses. Important measures to reduce costs were 'closer scrutiny of policy exceptions' (25 per cent) and 'policy provisions offered to assignees' (23 per cent).

Reasons for international assignments

The international management and IHRM literature has consistently identified three key organizational reasons for the use of various forms of international assignments:

1 **Position filling:** The organization has a need and, depending on the type of position and the level involved, will either employ someone locally or transfer a suitable candidate. Some studies[24] state that the problem of availability of qualified employees has decreased and that personnel

costs are more important when deciding about international assignments. However, the *Brookfield Global Mobility Trends Survey Report* provides evidence in 2015 that a lack of available skills is the major reason for international assignments. In many cases the most important assignment objectives were 'filling a managerial skills gap' (28 per cent) and 'filling a technical skills gap' (21 per cent).[25]

2   **Management development:** Staff are often moved into other parts of the organization for training and development purposes and to assist in the development of common corporate values. Headquarters staff may be transferred to subsidiary operations, or subsidiary staff transferred into the parent operations or to other subsidiary operations. Assignments may be for varying lengths of time and may involve project work as well as a trainee position. The perceived link between international experience and career development can be a motivator for staff to agree to such transfers.[26] The *Brookfield Global Mobility Trends Survey 2015* identified 'building international management experience' as the second most important reason for international assignments mentioned by the investigated companies.[27]

3   **Organization development:** Here the more strategic objectives of the operation come into play: the need for control; the transfer of knowledge, competence, procedures, and practices into various locations; and to exploit global market opportunities. As a result, organizational capabilities enabling a firm to compete in global markets might be developed.[28] This category can be illustrated by the three other reasons for international assignments mentioned by the *Brookfield Global Mobility Trends Survey 2015:* 'technology transfer' (7 per cent), 'launching new endeavors' (9 per cent), and 'transfer of corporate culture' (6 percent).[29]

Harzing[30] states in her study that most of the reasons for international assignment eventually lead to organization development.[31] In fact, international assignments are often undertaken to reach several goals simultaneously.[32] Furthermore, a study by Tungli und Peiperl[33] investigating the assignments policies and measures in 136 MNEs revealed that the importance of the assignment objectives also differed by country of origin. For example, the development of management skills was one of the most important reasons for international assignments in German MNEs, whereas MNEs from the USA mainly sent managers abroad to fill local skill gaps. Japanese as well as British MNEs indicated that the development of new operations abroad was their major reason to send expatriates abroad.[34]

Types of international assignments

Employees are transferred internationally for varying lengths of time depending on the purpose of the transfer and the nature of the task to be performed. MNEs tend to classify types according to the length or duration of the assignment:

● **Short-term:** Up to three months. These are usually for troubleshooting, project supervision, or a stopgap measure until a more permanent arrangement can be found.

● **Extended:** Up to one year. These may involve similar activities as those for short-term assignments.

● **Long-term:** Varies from one to five years, involving a clearly defined role in the receiving operation (e.g. a senior management role in a subsidiary). The long-term assignment has also been referred to as a 'traditional expatriate assignment'.

TABLE 5.2   Differences between traditional and short-term assignments

	Traditional assignments	Short-term assignments
Purpose	• Filling positions or skills gaps • Management development • Organizational development	• Skills transfer/problem solving • Management development • Managerial control
Duration	Typically 12–36 months	Typically up to 6 or 12 months
Family's position	Family joins the assignee abroad	Assignee is unaccompanied by the family
Selection	Formal procedures	Mostly informal, little bureaucracy
Advantages	• Good relationships with colleagues • Constant monitoring	• Flexibility • Simplicity • Cost-effectiveness
Disadvantages	• Dual-career considerations • Expensive • Less flexibility	• Taxation • Side-effects (alcoholism, high divorce rate) • Poor relationships with local colleagues • Work permit issues

Source: Adapted from M. Tahvanainen, D. Welch and V. Worm 'Implications of **Short-term International Assignments**', *European Management Journal*, Vol. 23, No. 6 (2005), p. 669, with permission from Elsevier.

Table 5.2 illustrates some of the differences between short-term and traditional expatriate assignments. It should be noted that definitions of short-term and long-term assignments vary and depend on organizational choices. The results of the 2015 *Brookfield Report* indicate that 45 per cent of the international assignments were long-term and 55 per cent were short-term.[35] Most of the research on international assignments focuses on traditional long-term assignments because these represent the highest number of international assignments. Our knowledge concerning alternative assignment types such as commuter, rotational, contractual, and virtual assignments (also termed 'non-standard assignments') is still limited,[36] but the growth of these non-standard assignments is described in further detail in the following paragraphs.[37]

- **Commuter assignments** – special arrangements where the employee commutes from the home country on a weekly or biweekly basis to the place of work in another country. Cross-border workers or daily commuters are not included. Usually, the family of the assignee stays in the home country. For example, the employee may live in London but work in Moscow. Reasons for these assignments can include that a particular problem must be solved and the assigned employee, due to their experience and qualifications, is needed in two places at the same time; or that the target country is unstable.[38] The *Brookfield Report* from 2015 indicates that 31 per cent of the investigated companies have a policy for commuter assignments in place and that this type of assignment will even gain importance in the future.[39] However, it is important to note that a non-standard assignment is not always an effective substitute for the traditional expatriate assignment: "There are real concerns about the viability of commuter arrangements over an extended period of time due to the build-up of stress resulting from intensive travel commitments and the impact on personal relationships".[40]

- **Rotational assignments** – employees commute from the home country to a place of work in another country for a short, set period followed by a break in the home country. The employee's family usually remains in the home country. This arrangement is commonly used on oil rigs and with hardship locations in the global mining industry. Eighteen per cent of the investigated companies in the *Brookfield Report* (2015) had a policy for this type of assignment.

- **Contractual assignments** – used in situations where employees with specific skills vital to an international project are assigned for a limited duration of 6 to 12 months. Research and Development (R&D) is one area that is using multinational project teams and lends itself to short-term contractual assignments in conjunction with longer-term assignments and virtual teams.[41]

- **Virtual assignments** – where the employee does not relocate to a host location but manages, from home base, various international responsibilities for a part of the organization in another country. In this case, the manager relies heavily on communication technologies such as telephone, email, or video conferences. Visits to the host country are also necessary. The main reasons for using virtual assignments are similar to that of other non-standard forms of international assignments: the shortage of experienced staff prepared to accept longer-term postings, the immobile family, and cost containment. Welch, Worm and Fenwick's[42] study into the use of virtual assignments in Australian and Danish firms suggests that, while there are certain advantages to operating virtually (such as not having to relocate a family unit), there are disadvantages that may affect successful work outcomes. For example, role conflict, dual allegiance, and identification issues occur between the person in the home location and the virtual work group in the foreign location. It is not clear to whom the virtual assignee 'belongs' – the home location where the person physically resides for most of the time, or the foreign unit. Another issue is how much time should be devoted to 'virtual' work responsibilities vs. the 'real' work. In addition, given that much of the work is done through electronic media, the potential for cultural misunderstandings increases and the geographical distance rules out normal group interaction. Communication is mainly through conference calls, videoconferencing and emails, and requires good skills in using these media.

   Visits between the two locations are necessary to support the working of this arrangement as not everything can be settled virtually. Face-to-face meetings are still needed. In summary, virtual assignments tend to be used for regional positions (e.g. European Marketing Manager) where the person is mainly co-ordinating a number of national marketing activities but is based at a regional center. Based on the results of a German/Asian case study, Holtbrügge and Schillo[43] suggest that specific intercultural training needs to be provided for the virtual assignee as well as for the team members abroad in order to avoid intercultural misunderstandings.

- **Self-initiated assignments** – while standard expatriations are usually initiated by the organization, self-initiated assignments are initiated by the individual. Many organizations do not systematically track and manage these kinds of assignments. However, often these employees are highly interested in an international challenge, have adequate language skills, an international mindset, and are quite entrepreneurial. They comprise an important resource for their employers and can increase international mobility potential in the organization.[44] It is therefore important to manage them carefully and to understand their motivation to stay in the MNE, particularly upon completion of the self-initiated international assignment.[45] According to a study by Cerdin and Pragneux,[46] organization-assigned and self-initiated expatriates are relatively similar with respect to the career anchors of internationalism, challenge, and lifestyle, with a preference for achieving a balance between work and personal life. They differ from each other with respect to other dimensions such as security. A recent example of university academics as self-initiated expatriates is reported by Selmer and Lauring.[47]

THE ROLES OF AN EXPATRIATE

As mentioned above, the reasons for using expatriates are not mutually exclusive. They do, however, underpin expectations about the roles that staff play as a consequence of being transferred from one location to another country. These roles are delineated in Figure 5.2.

FIGURE 5.2 **The roles of an expatriate**

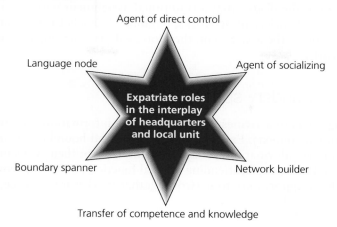

The expatriate as an agent of direct control

The use of staff transfers can be regarded as a bureaucratic control mechanism, where the primary role is that of ensuring compliance through direct supervision. Harzing[48] found that German companies tend towards this form of control. She labels expatriates who are such agents as 'bears', arguing that the analogy reflects the level of dominance of this type of expatriate control. To a certain extent, using expatriates for control reflects an ethnocentric predisposition, but this can be important in ensuring subsidiary compliance, enabling strategic objectives for local operations to be achieved.

The expatriate as an agent of socialization

There is an implicit expectation that expatriates assist in the transfer of shared values and beliefs. Harzing names expatriates who transfer corporate values as 'bumble-bees'. However, as Fenwick et al.[49] point out, there has been little empirical investigation of the effectiveness of expatriates as agents of socialization. In fact, attempts to instill corporate values and norms ritualized in the form of certain expected behaviors often have negative results at the subsidiary level.

Expatriates as network builders

As we discussed in Chapter 3, international assignments are viewed as a way of developing social capital[50] by fostering interpersonal linkages that can be used for informal control and communication purposes. Naturally, as employees move between various organizational units, their network of personal relationships changes, leading to Harzing's analogy of expatriates as 'spiders' to describe this role. How these employees are utilized is person-dependent. People tend to nurture and protect their networks, to be very selective about the way they use their connections, and to evaluate the potential damage to key individuals in their networks if the connection was to be used inappropriately. In their study of project teams and networks, Schweiger et al.[51] provide the following example of how international assignments assisted network development:

I depended heavily on the contacts I had developed over the years. The time spent in international assignments was invaluable. I knew important people in several key operations. I knew how they operated and what was important to them. They also knew that I was credible and would help them when the opportunity arose.

While short-term assignments may not allow the expatriate to develop as wide a range of contacts in one location to the degree that a traditional assignment permits, over time they can increase the number and variety of networks, building channels for the transfer of ideas and competence.[52] Duration of the assignment, therefore, will have an impact on the person's ability to develop networks.

Expatriates as boundary spanners

Boundary spanning refers to activities, such as gathering information, that bridge internal and external organizational contexts. Expatriates are considered boundary spanners because they can collect host-country information, act as representatives of their firms in the host country, and influence agents. For example, attending a social function at a foreign embassy can provide the expatriate with an opportunity to network, gather market intelligence, and promote the firm's profile at a high level.

Expatriates as language nodes

Marschan-Piekkari *et al.*[53] found that Finnish expatriates working for the elevator company Kone sometimes became what they termed 'language nodes' upon repatriation.

Transfer of competence and knowledge

International assignments do assist in knowledge sharing and competence transfer, and encourage adoption of common work practices which may strengthen elements of corporate culture. Thus, they may contribute to further developing the social capital within the MNE.[54] Staff in various organizational units also encounter different viewpoints and perspectives that will shape their behavior and may reinforce their feeling of belonging. Goodall and Roberts[55] relate the experience of a Chinese employee in the Chinese operation of a European oil company. Her time in the parent's operation in Europe enabled her to appreciate how the company valued its name and reputation, and she was able to better understand the company's code of conduct and attitude towards occupational health and safety.

Overall, international assignments are seen as an effective way of accomplishing multiple objectives. In fact, one could argue that there are elements of knowledge transfer in all the roles we have identified. However, clear empirical evidence as to the effectiveness of expatriates in conducting their numerous roles is limited. Certain factors may influence effectiveness:

- The creation of an environment of openness and support can encourage cross-fertilization of ideas and implementation of '**best practice**'.

- There is a need for knowledge and information to travel dyadically – that is, between the expatriate and the host location, and back to the expatriate's home location – if the multinational is to benefit from international assignments as a mechanism for knowledge transfer.

- Despite the recognition of the importance of personal networks in knowledge and information transfer, staffing decisions are often made without regard to their effect on network relationships. In many cases there is no strategic approach applied to control for potentially negative effects.

- There is a link between the duration of the assignment and the effective transfer of knowledge. Some knowledge may be transferred quickly while other skills and knowledge (particularly where a high level of tacitness is present) may take longer.

- Much of what is transferred depends on the expatriate concerned in terms of ability to teach others and motivation to act as an agent of knowledge transfer.

- The success of the knowledge-transfer process depends not only on the motivation and abilities of the assignee but also on the local employees and their relationships.[56]

A final point: Bolino and Feldman[57] make an interesting observation that, when expatriates are assigned for position filling due to a lack of appropriate local staff, these expatriates are often forced to take over some of the responsibilities of their colleagues due to differences in knowledge levels. Consequently, they argue, expatriates often spend a lot of time on less challenging tasks to help out local co-workers and train them. In such cases, while the expatriates may assist in skills transfer, over time their own level of competence may erode as they are not developing their own expertise. Thus, when expatriates return to their home operation, they may find that their knowledge is somewhat out of date.

THE ROLE OF NON-EXPATRIATES

The above discussion has centered on the international assignment. What has tended to be overlooked is that a considerable amount of international business involves what can be called 'non-expatriates': people who travel internationally but are not considered expatriates, as they do not relocate to another country. These non-expatriates have been called international business travelers[58] – employees who spend a large proportion of their time visiting foreign markets, subsidiary units, and international projects. Popular terms for these employees include 'road warriors', 'globetrotters', 'frequent fliers', and 'flexpatriates'.[59] International travel is an essential component of their work, such as international sales staff whose job almost totally comprises international travel; and managers whose job entails numerous visits to international operations. International sales representatives attend trade fairs, visit foreign agents and distributors, demonstrate new products to potential clients, and negotiate sales contracts. Various staff will visit foreign locations to deal with host-country government officials, alliance partners, subcontracting firms, and foreign suppliers.

Apart from the resource implications, there are issues relating to the management of international business travelers. DeFrank et al.[60] identify the following factors as stressors:

- **Home and family issues** – such as missing important anniversaries and school events. The more frequent the travel, the greater the potential for family and marital relationships to be strained.

- **Work arrangements** – the 'domestic' side of the job still has to be attended to even though the person is traveling internationally. Modern communications allow work to accompany the business traveler, who is often expected to remain up to date with home-office issues while away from the office.

- **Travel logistics** – airline connections, hotel accommodation, and meeting schedules.

- **Health concerns** – poor diet, lack of physical exercise, lack of sleep, coping with jetlag, and exposure to viruses and other health problems (e.g. Deep Vein Thrombosis from excessive air travel).

- **Host-culture issues** – as international business is conducted in other cultural settings, the person is still expected to be able to operate in unfamiliar environments and handle cultural differences effectively. However, the limited empirical and anecdotal evidence suggests that non-expatriates do not receive the same level of cross-cultural training as expatriates – if any.

Non-expatriate business travelers also perform many of the roles of expatriates, in terms of being agents for socialization, network builders, boundary spanners, and language nodes. From the limited evidence available, however, it would seem that the management of staff using these forms of arrangements falls to the functional or line managers involved rather than the HR department as such. Possible HR strategies that could better meet the demands of flexpatriates have been suggested by Demel and Mayrhofer.[61] They suggest that the specific situation of flexpatriates should be included in job descriptions and working contracts and could be part of specific HRM policies for this target group. For example, selection criteria should go beyond technical knowledge and cross-cultural skills and include, for example, health issues such as physical fitness. The issue of working and traveling time must also be addressed with respect to recognizing the need for the employee to recover from international travel (adjustment to jetlag, changes in diet, etc.). If these concerns are taken into consideration, flexpatriates can be an even more valuable alternative solution to international mobility.

THE ROLE OF INPATRIATES

As we have outlined in Chapter 1, inpatriates are mainly distinguished from expatriates by definition. They include international assignments of HCNs or TCNs from a foreign location to the parent country (usually the corporate headquarters) of the MNE. **Inpatriates** are:

> expected to share their local contextual knowledge with headquarters staff in order to facilitate effective corporate activities in these local markets. At the same time they are socialized in the headquarters corporate culture and learn firm-specific routines and behaviors that enable them to master future management tasks within the organization. As a result, inpatriates seem to act both as knowledge senders and receivers.[62]

Collings and Scullion[63] have identified the following key drivers for recruiting and transferring inpatriate managers:

- desire to create a global core competency and a cultural diversity of strategic perspectives in the top management team,[64] thus increasing the capability of organizations to 'think global and act local'

- desire to provide career opportunities for high-potential employees in host countries, i.e. HCNs and TCNs

- the emergence of developing markets which often represent difficult locations for expatriates in terms of quality of life and cultural adjustment.

However, the strategy of inpatriation also underlines that the strategic importance of the headquarters is still predominant, indicating that the knowledge of the culture, the structure, and the processes specific to the headquarters are still important requirements for vertical career advancement. Usually, the assignment to the headquarters aims at training the manager for a top management position back home in the foreign subsidiary. In many MNEs, an inpatriate assignment may be a first and limited career step, reflecting a rather ethnocentric approach. Harvey and Buckley[65] conclude that, in this case, "inpatriation may be a dangerous process". While it might be more difficult for inpatriates than for PCNs to realize a vertical career in the headquarters, they experience the same integration and repatriation problems as expatriates during and after their international assignment. Consequently, they may not receive the same return on investment for their international assignment as expatriates. This can only be guaranteed if career opportunities for inpatriate HCNs or TCNs exist within the headquarters and across the wider organization. In this case inpatriation can be an important step in realizing a geocentric orientation within the MNE and thus an 'open sky' (i.e. where career success is not dependent on an employee's nationality) for HCN and TCN managers. Based on a sample of 143 inpatriates in ten German multinationals, Reiche, Kraimer and Harzing[66] have analyzed the retention of inpatriates. They found that trust and fit with the headquarters staff, as well as firm-specific learning and career prospects, played an important role in ensuring retention of inpatriate employees.

In an international comparative study Tungli and Peiperl found significant differences in the target group of international assignments between German, British, Japanese, and US MNEs. The authors differentiate between PCNs, TCNs, and inpatriates. The study found that Japanese

MNEs rely almost solely on PCNs for international assignments, while British MNEs seem to systematically use different groups of employees (56 per cent PCNs, 37 per cent TCNs, and 7 per cent expatriates in the headquarters). The group of international assignees from German MNEs consisted of 79 per cent PCNs, 12 per cent TCNs, and 9 per cent inpatriates.[67] More research on the long-term consequences of these different practices is needed.

RECRUITMENT AND SELECTION OF INTERNATIONAL MANAGERS

Hiring and deploying people to positions where they can perform effectively is a goal of most organizations, whether domestic or international. '**Recruitment**' is defined as searching for and obtaining potential job candidates in sufficient numbers and of sufficient quality so that the organization can select the most appropriate people to fill its job needs. Here, employer branding may play a crucial role, especially in emerging countries such as China or India where it may be difficult to find enough qualified personnel for foreign companies due to the strong growth rates of these economies and the fierce competition for talent in the local labor markets. **Selection** is the process of gathering information for the purposes of evaluating and deciding who should be employed in particular jobs. It is important to note that recruitment and selection are discrete processes and both processes need to operate effectively if the firm is to effectively manage its staffing process. For example, a firm may have an excellent selection system for evaluating candidates, but if there are insufficient candidates to evaluate then this selection system is less than effective. Both processes must operate effectively for optimal staffing decisions to be made.

Some of the major differences between domestic and international staffing are first that many firms have predispositions with regard to who should hold key positions in headquarters and subsidiaries (i.e. ethnocentric, polycentric, regiocentric, and geocentric staffing orientations) and second, the constraints imposed by host governments (e.g. immigration rules with regard to work visas and the common requirement in most countries to provide evidence as to why local nationals should not be employed rather than hiring foreigners) can severely limit the MNE's ability to hire the right candidate. In addition, as Scullion and Collings[68] note, most expatriates are recruited *internally* rather than externally, so the task of persuading managers (particularly if they are primarily working in a domestic environment) to recommend and/or agree to release their best employees for international assignments remains a key issue for international HR managers. The small number of **external recruits** is confirmed by data from the *Global Relocation Trends Survey* 2010. Here, the proportion of external hires for international positions was only 8 per cent across all firms that participated in the 2010 survey. This represented the lowest figure in the history of the report (the benchmark historical average is 12 per cent of expatriates).[69]

Recruitment of internal hires for expatriate assignments is preferred because this reduces the risk of a poor selection decision. In an internal selection process performance appraisals, personal reports, interviews with colleagues, and firm-internal career plans can be used as information sources in order to reduce uncertainty. In their study of 653 Spanish companies, Bayo-Moriones and Ortín-Ángel show that the preference for **internal recruitment** is not only motivated by the minimization of selection risks but also by the wish to secure present and past investments in human capital.[70] In the case of expatriate recruitment on the external labor market, the selection risk is often managed by using specialized (and relatively expensive) consultants. The more traditional devices of recruitment and selection such as traditional job advertisements and executive search (also known as *headhunting*) can also be used (see IHRM in Action Case 5.1).

Maekelae, Björkman and Ehrnrooth[71] have identified a variety of staffing archetypes (local-internal, local-external, global-internal, and global-external) that relate to human capital

IHRM in Action Case 5.1

International headhunting

Peculiarities occur in the selection process when external service providers are assigned to undertake the search for international managers and are involved in the subsequent selection. Whereas in the scientific literature there are hardly any discussions or ideas presented addressing this topic, in practice headhunting is a commonly used method to fill international positions. According to Hewitt's HR Outsourcing Survey, which includes more than 100 US companies, these companies pursue four central aims with the transfer of most (national and international) HR activities to external service providers. Accordingly, most of the companies surveyed (65 per cent) indicated they want to reduce costs by outsourcing activities. Furthermore, access to external expertise is attractive to many companies, as well as improved service quality and the possibility to more intensively direct internal resources to strategic HRM. With reference to outsourcing IHRM, the survey reveals that 43 per cent of the companies revert to the expertise of external service providers for expatriate management matters and 56 per cent in repatriation issues; 3 to 4 per cent of the companies even plan to outsource these areas in the near future. Concerning recruiting, 10 per cent of the companies surveyed indicated that they already assigned their recruiting to external service providers; an additional 6 per cent definitely plan to outsource their recruiting. As there are no explicit figures available, one can only speculate how many firms make use of outsourcing for their international employee selection as well. However, the specialization of numerous headhunting agencies and management consultancies in the area of IHRM and executive search for international managers indicates a high demand in these areas.

An example is the management consultancy ABC Asian Business Consultants from South Korea. Not only does it support companies from different branches in the search and selection of qualified managers, it also assists firms in organizing international management training or international career planning. Currently, seven employees and 15 trainers work on international projects at the company's offices in Korea, China, India, and Germany. Every year, about 15 employee-selection projects are completed by ABC Asian Business Consultants. Headhunting selection criteria and job profiles are adjusted to the needs of the recruiting company and the requirements of the vacant position. Due to the high degree of candidates' qualifications and confidentiality of information, the selection process is very complex. First of all, potential candidates must be identified and personally contacted. Alternative forms of HR Marketing (for example, activities involving Internet-based platforms or social networks) are not used because of the need for confidentiality. Often, a *cover story* is used to identify qualified candidates, seek further information and evaluate interest. Before the first contact between the candidate and the recruiting company takes place, the candidate's *curriculum vitae* is evaluated, followed by two interviews with representatives of ABC Asian Business Consultants. Interviews via software programs such as ICQ, Skype or Windows Live Messenger may be used occasionally to bridge long distances and to conduct the interviews without national or international relocation. Based on the protocols of the interviews and the application forms, a short report on every candidate is compiled and a shortlist of the most qualified candidates is presented to the recruiting company. Ultimately, final interviews with the candidates are conducted by employees of the recruiting company, before a final decision on the filling of the international position is reached. The whole selection process may cover a period of several months. Occasionally, international assessment centers are organized using different methods such as individual presentations, role play, or presentations to the board of directors.

Based on his past experience, Dr Ulrich Hann, owner and Chief Executive Officer of ABC Asian Business Consultants, can identify cultural differences and differences in the qualifications of candidates from diverse international backgrounds. Differences depending on the respective nationality appear, for example, in the personal contact during the selection interviews. There are also differences regarding the professional qualifications and skills of candidates. Many Indian candidates have a very high level of qualifications in natural sciences, while there is a strong demand for German candidates with a degree in mechanical engineering.

There are particular challenges for HR consultants in a dynamic international environment. Dr Hann notes: "Similar to the requirements for the candidates, the requirements and criteria for a qualified HR consultant in the international business environment are also high". Notably, multilingualism is important to understand the needs of the customers and those of the candidates. In addition to a professional qualification, entrepreneurial thinking as well as international work experience are essential requirements to find a position in a recruiting company as an external service provider for IHRM.

Source: © Lena Knappert and Marion Festing. Based on personal communication with Ulrich Hann, 8 June 2010.

advantages. These are mainly concerned with knowledge and social capital advantages including a positive effect on interaction and trust within the organization.

EXPATRIATE FAILURE AND SUCCESS

Expatriate failure and success are obviously critical and related issues for global firms. Both topics have been intensively examined by IHRM researchers for decades. We will start with the more traditional focus on expatriate failure. Considering the major determinants for expatriate failure clarifies the links to expatriate success. First, there are three questions related to failure: its definition, the magnitude of the phenomenon, and the costs associated with failure.

What do we mean by expatriate failure?

The term 'expatriate failure' has been defined as the premature return of an expatriate (that is, a return home before the period of assignment is completed). In such a case, an expatriate failure represents a selection error, often compounded by ineffective expatriate management policies. There has been some discussion in the literature about the usefulness of defining expatriate failure so narrowly. For example, an expatriate may be ineffective and poorly adjusted, but if not recalled the person will not be considered a failure. Clearly, an inability to either effectively handle new responsibilities or to adjust to the country of assignment is very likely to contribute to diminished performance levels. These results may not be immediately apparent but can have long-term negative consequences in terms of subsidiary performance. However, if the expatriate remains for the duration of the assignment, to all intents and purposes the assignment will have been considered a success.

Another significant issue is that of expatriates leaving the MNE within the first or second year after repatriation (for more details on repatriation see Chapter 7) because they feel that their newly acquired knowledge is not valued.[72] Again, in this case the international assignment would be regarded as a success although it leads to the loss of a valuable employee. On the other hand, a project abroad can be completed early, which could lead to a premature return of an expatriate. According to the above-mentioned definition this would be erroneously classified as a failure. Thus, the traditional definition of premature return of an expatriate that has dominated the literature does not necessarily indicate expatriate failure. Harzing suggests that a definition of expatriate failure should include poor performance as well as repatriation problems.[73] An example of research that adopts this broader definition of expatriate failure (that is, including under performance and retention upon completion of the assignment) is a study conducted by Forster[74] on 36 British firms, which concluded:

> If we accept that a broader definition of EFRs [expatriate failure rates] is warranted, then it can be argued that the actual figure of those who are 'failing' on IAs [international assignments] could be somewhere between 8 per cent and 28 per cent of UK expatriates and their partners.

In the next section we look at the magnitude of expatriate failure in further detail.

What is the magnitude of the phenomenon we call expatriate failure?

The *Brookfield Report* 2015 provides several indicators for expatriate failure. Firms indicated that 5 per cent of expatriate assignments were regarded as failures. The survey also reported that expatriate turnover was about 12 per cent; 20 per cent left while on assignment, 25 per cent within the first year upon repatriation, 26 per cent between the first and the second year, and 29 per cent after two years. Comparing these figures to an average annual turnover rate of 12 per cent, these percentages can be considered as relatively high, especially since important investments by the assigning firm are at stake. Locations with the highest expatriate failure rates were China (12 per cent), the UK (10 per cent), and India (9 per cent).[75]

In the following section we will report some selected results from academic studies on expatriate failure. First, the analyses show that differences in expatriate failure rates by country of origin of the MNE are relatively low. Second, they indicate the historical development of expatriate failure rates. We draw on data from the important work by Tung[76] on expatriate failure in US, European, and Japanese MNEs, which initiated this discussion in the early 1980s, and recent work by Tungli and Peiperl, which reported figures from Germany, Japan, Britain, and the USA in 2009.[77] The results of both studies are presented in Table 5.3.

TABLE 5.3 Expatriate failure rates

Premature return rate	Western Europe 1982	Germany 2009	UK 2009	Japan 1982	Japan 2009	USA 1982	USA 2009
Less than 10%	97%	91%	93%	86%	94%	24%	86%
More than 10% but less than 20%	3%	0%	3%	14%	0%	69%	2%
Equal to or more than 20%	0%	9%	3%	0%	6%	7%	11%

Source: R. L. Tung 'Selection and Training Procedures of U.S., European, and Japanese Multinationals', *California Management Review*, Vol. 25, No. 1 (1982), pp. 57–71 and p. 164; Z. Tungli and M. Peiperl 'Expatriate Practices in German, Japanese, U.K., and U.S. Multinational Companies: A Comparative Survey of Changes', *Human Resource Management*, Vol. 48, No. 1 (2009), pp. 153–171. Reproduced with permission.

As Table 5.3 shows, Tung identified higher expatriate failure rates and a higher percentage of MNEs reporting more than 10 per cent failure rates in US MNEs than in European or Japanese organizations. The more recent data show that the reported figures have become more similar across the investigated countries and that premature return of expatriates still represents an ongoing challenge.[78] Harzing[79] has questioned the reported failure rates in the US literature, claiming there is "almost no empirical foundation for the existence of high failure rates when measured as premature re-entry". More recently, Christensen and Harzing have again questioned the value of the whole concept of expatriate failure, arguing that "it might well be time to abandon the concept of expatriate failure altogether and instead draw on the general HR literature to analyze problems related to turnover and performance management in an expatriate context".[80]

From the above discussion we can draw the following conclusions:

1   Broadening the definition of expatriate failure beyond that of premature return is warranted. Following up broad surveys with interviews with responding firms may assist in this exploration.

2   Regardless of the definition or precise amount of 'failure', its very presentation as a problem has broadened the issue to demonstrate the complexity of international assignments. In fact, one could argue that the so-called persistent myth of high US EFR has been a positive element in terms of the attention that has subsequently been directed towards expatriation practices. It has certainly provoked considerable research attention into the causes of expatriate failure.

What are the costs of failure?

The costs of expatriate failure can be both **direct** and **indirect**. **Direct costs** include airfares and associated relocation expenses, and salary and training. The precise amount varies according to the level of the position concerned, country of destination, exchange rates, and whether the 'failed' manager is replaced by another expatriate. The 'invisible' or **indirect costs** are harder to quantify in monetary terms but can prove to be more expensive for firms. Many expatriate positions involve contact with host-government officials and key clients. Failure at this level may result in loss of market share, difficulties with host-government officials, and demands that expatriates be replaced with HCNs (thus affecting the multinational's general staffing approach). The possible effect on local staff is also an indirect cost factor, since morale and productivity could suffer.[81]

Failure also has an effect on the expatriate concerned, who may lose self-esteem, self-confidence and prestige among peers.[82] Future performance may be marked by decreased motivation, lack of promotional opportunities, and perhaps increased productivity to compensate for the failure. Finally, the expatriate's family relationships may be threatened. These are additional costs to organizations that are often overlooked.

Reasons for expatriate failure – and what about expatriate success?

Tung[83] is recognized as the first researcher to investigate the reasons for expatriate failure. Although she found differences according to the country of origin of the MNE, important personal factors were the inability to adapt either on the part of the spouse or the manager. Other family problems, the maturity of the manager and problems coping with higher responsibilities inherent in the position abroad were also noted. The more recent comparative study by Tungli and Peiperl does not indicate any country specificities in the results. It confirms the importance of the first three reasons mentioned in the study by Tung: the inability to adapt by the family or the manager as well as other family issues. However, in addition they also find that firm-specific issues and deficient performance by the expatriate are major reasons for a premature return.[84] In his study based on 21 interviews, Lee[85] found similar reasons for expatriate failure.

However, he also found that the activities of the MNE itself and support for the expatriates and the families were major success factors for international assignments.[86]

Efforts to understand the personal factors related to expatriate success,[87] as well as how to provide the correct mix of contextual support (mentoring, work design and task sequencing, as well as an understanding of career issues)[88] are ongoing.

Finally, the *Brookfield Study* (2015) reports that spouse/partner dissatisfaction (10 per cent), the inability to adapt (9 per cent), other family concerns (14 per cent), and poor candidate selection (11 per cent) accounted for expatriate failure. In a verbatim comment they confirm the results by Lee that IHRM has an important role in creating successful international assignments: "career and talent management (before, during, and after) is the single most important factor in retaining employees after the assignment".[89]

SELECTION CRITERIA

We now have a fuller understanding of the phenomenon called 'expatriate failure', as well as the multi-faceted nature of international assignments, and why developing appropriate **selection criteria** has become a critical IHRM issue. It should be noted that selection is a two-way process between the individual and the organization. A prospective candidate may reject the expatriate assignment, either for individual reasons such as family considerations, or for situational factors such as the perceived toughness of a particular culture. It is a challenge for those responsible for selecting staff for international assignments to determine appropriate selection criteria. Figure 5.3 illustrates the factors involved in expatriate selection, both in terms of the individual and the specifics of the situation concerned. It should be noted that these factors are inter related. We base the following discussion around Figure 5.3.

FIGURE 5.3 Factors in expatriate selection

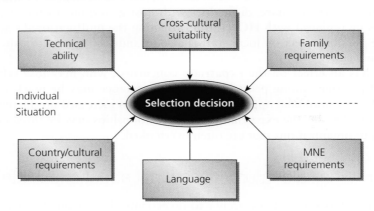

Technical ability

Naturally, an employee's ability to perform the required tasks of a particular job is an important selection factor. Technical and managerial skills are therefore an essential criterion. Indeed, research findings consistently indicate that multinationals place heavy reliance on relevant technical skills during the expatriate selection process.[90] Since expatriates are predominantly internal recruits, personnel evaluation records can be examined and checked with the candidate's past and present superiors. The dilemma is that past performance may have little or no bearing on one's ability to achieve a task in a foreign cultural environment.

Cross-cultural suitability: competence, adjustment and other indicators

As we have already discussed, the cultural environment in which expatriates operate is an important factor for determining successful performance. Here, **intercultural competence** and related concepts, as well as the ability to adjust to a foreign culture, play important roles. However, a precondition for cross-cultural suitability is soft skills that are also important in other national positions.

Soft skills.   Soft skills are a criterion which is underestimated by many MNEs.[91] They are a precondition for *intercultural competence*. As Caligiuri, Tarique and Jacobs state, they are important success factors of international managers and need to be considered in addition to technical knowledge and skills. They include psychological as well as personal features, international experience and language knowledge. Furthermore, a capacity to internalize and provide training to local personnel is an often neglected issue. However, this capacity may play a vital role for the success of an international assignment due to the crucial importance of knowledge and technology transfer.[92]

Intercultural competence.   Apart from the obvious technical ability and managerial skills, expatriates require cross-cultural abilities that enable the person to operate in a new environment and to guarantee the functioning of culturally diverse teams.[93] This is often expressed by using the term 'intercultural competence', which is defined as "the ability to function effectively in another culture".[94] There appears to be a consensus that desirable attributes should include dimensions such as cultural empathy, adaptability, diplomacy, language ability, positive attitude, emotional stability, maturity, and so on.[95] These various issues can be related to three basic structural dimensions of intercultural competence.[96] The *affective dimension* of intercultural competence reflects the emotional attitude towards a foreign culture. The *cognitive layer* relates to culture-specific knowledge.[97] Most important is the *ability* dimension because this includes the actual intercultural behavior.[98]

Intercultural competence and related concepts.   Closely related to intercultural competence is the concept of *cultural intelligence*. Ang *et al.*[99] define cultural intelligence as "a specific form of intelligence focused on capabilities to grasp, reason, and behave effectively in situations characterized by cultural diversity". While it is very similar to the concept of intercultural competence in also considering perceptual, cognitive, motivational, and ability elements, it focuses mainly on the cognitive dimension of this construct.[100] Bücker and Poutsma[101] have related the concepts of intercultural competence, intercultural sensitivity, cultural intelligence, and global mindset (ability to appreciate elements of various cultures)[102] to '*global management competencies*' and use this as a more comprehensive approach to describe what kind of management skills a global manager needs to have.

Bird *et al.*[103] see intercultural competence as one part of the terrain of *global leadership*. In their concept, cross-cultural relationship skills, traits and values, the cognitive orientation, and the global business expertise are the core pillars of intercultural competence. To map the terrain of global leadership they add global business competencies at the macro level, including global organizing expertise and visioning. To define the term 'global leadership' they adopt the definition by Osland and Bird. According to them, global leadership is "the process of influencing the thinking, attitudes, and behaviors of a global community to work together synergistically toward a common vision and common goal".[104]

The ability to adjust to a foreign culture.   This factor has been a consistent reason given for expatriate failure – and has been the subject of considerable interest to researchers.[105] The dilemma is that adjustment to a foreign culture is multifaceted, and individuals vary in terms of their reactions and coping behaviors. The concept of an adjustment cycle or curve is helpful in demonstrating the typical phases that may be encountered during cultural adjustment. The curve (sometimes referred to as the U-Curve) is based on psychological reactions to the assignment and comprises four phases.[106]

Phase 1 commences with reactions prior to the assignment – the expatriate may experience a range of positive and negative emotions such as excitement, anxiety, fear of the unknown, or a sense of adventure. There can be an upswing of mood upon arrival in the assignment country that produces what has been referred to as the '**honeymoon**' or '**tourist**' **phase**. Then, as the novelty wears off, realities of everyday life in the foreign location begin to intrude, homesickness sets in, and a downswing may commence – a feeling that 'the party is over'[107] – which can create negative appraisals of the situation and the location, leading to a period of crisis – **Phase 2**. This can be a critical time, and how the individual copes with the psychological adjustment at this phase has an important impact in terms of success or failure. There is a suggestion that 'failure as an early recall' may be triggered at this point. Once past this crisis point, as the expatriate comes to terms with the demands of the new environment, there is a pulling up – **Phase 3** – as the person begins to adjust to the new environment. This levels off over time to what has been described as healthy recovery – **Phase 4**.

However, when considering the above U-Curve, one should remember some critical points. The U-Curve is normative. Some people do not experience this U-Curve. Individuals will differ in their reactions to the foreign location and with respect to their international experience prior to this assignment.[108] The time period involved varies, and there is no conclusive statistical support for the various phases.[109] Black and Mendenhall[110] point out that the U-Curve describes these phases but does not explain how and why people move through the various phases. There may be other critical points during the assignment – beyond Phase 4 – that may produce downturns, negative reactions, and upswings (that is, a cyclical wave rather than a U-Curve). In summary, it can be stated that, despite its plausibility, the U-curve lacks theoretical foundation and empirical support and does not indicate what the results of cross-cultural adjustment may necessarily be.[111]

This critique on the U-Curve adjustment and other adjustment concepts[112] has led to important research activities and to a lot more clarity on the determinants of the adjustment process, the process itself, and its outcomes.[113] Figure 5.4 provides an overview.

FIGURE 5.4   Overview of important adjustment variables

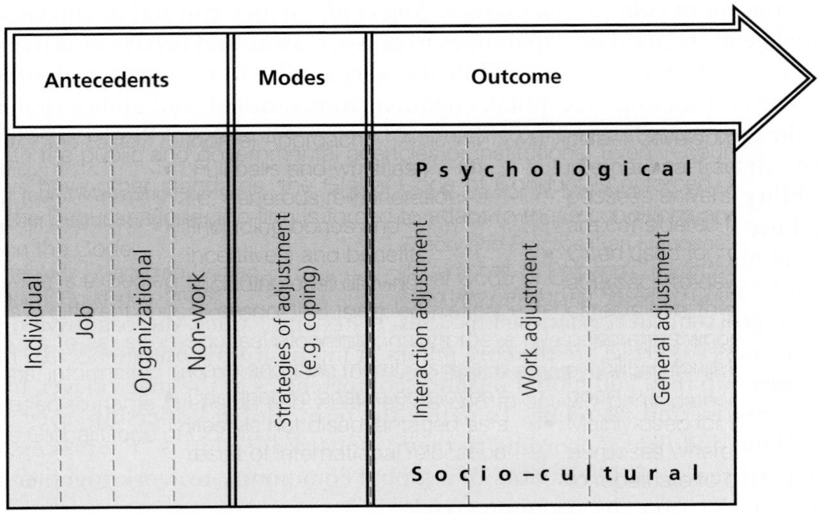

Source: M. Festing and M. Maletzky, 'Cross-Cultural Leadership Adjustment – A Framework Based on the Theory of Structuration', *Human Resource Management Review*, Vol. 21, No. 3 (2011), p. 188. With permission from Elsevier.

Today, we differentiate between two kinds of adjustment: psychological adjustment, which is measured with respect to the psychological well-being of the expatriate; and socio-cultural adjustment, which describes the ability to interact successfully in the foreign country.[114]

Antecedents of cross-cultural adjustment include:

- individual aspects (e.g. gender or goal orientation)

- work-related factors (e.g. role clarity, decision autonomy)[115]

- organizational aspects (e.g. company support)

- non-work-related factors (e.g. family issues).

Adjustment modes are strategies to achieve adjustment. Depending on the focus of the study this can, for example, be strategies for coping with stress.[116]

For *adjustment outcomes* it is often referred to the three variables identified in the popular concept by Black and Mendenhall:[117]

1 work adjustment

2 interaction adjustment, and

3 general adjustment.

Often the outcomes also include an explicit performance[118] or effectiveness dimension[119] or address the issue of commitment.[120]

Family requirements

The family is a very important influence factor on the success of an international assignment, particularly the spouse.[121] Despite the importance of the accompanying spouse/partner, as Shaffer and Harrison[122] point out, the focus has been on the expatriate. From the multinational's perspective, expatriate performance in the host location is the important factor. However, the interaction between expatriate, spouse/partner and family members' various adjustment experiences is now well documented.

It should be pointed out that the spouse (or accompanying partner) often carries a heavy burden. Upon arrival in the country of assignment, the responsibility for settling the family into its new home falls on the spouse, who may have left behind a career, along with friends and social support networks (particularly relatives). In developing countries the employment of house servants is quite common, but this is an aspect of international living that many Westerners from developed countries have some difficulty adjusting to. It is often not possible for the spouse/partner to work in the country of assignment due to immigration regulations, and the well-being and education of the children may be an ongoing concern for the spouse.

As discussed above, apart from the accompanying partner's career, there are other family considerations that can cause a potential expatriate to decline the international assignment. Disruption to children's education is an important consideration, and the selected candidate may reject the offered assignment on the grounds that a move at this particular stage in his or her child's life is inappropriate. The care of aging or invalid parents is another consideration. While these two reasons have been noted in various studies, what has been somewhat overlooked is the issue of single parents. Given increasing divorce rates, this may become a critical factor in assignment selection and acceptance where the custody of children is involved. The associated legal constraints, such as obtaining the consent of the other parent to take the child (or children) out of the home country, and visiting/access rights, may prove to be a major barrier to the international mobility of both single mothers and single fathers.

Country/cultural requirements

As discussed in Chapter 1, international firms are usually required to demonstrate that a HCN is not available before the host government will issue the necessary work permit and entry visa for the desired PCN or TCN. In some cases, the multinational may wish to use an expatriate and have selected a candidate for the international assignment, only to find the transfer blocked by the host government. Many developed countries are changing their legislation to facilitate employment-related immigration, which will make international transfers somewhat easier – for example, the European Union Social Charter allows for free movement of citizens of member countries within the European Union (EU). It is important that HR staff keep up to date with relevant legislative changes in the countries in which the MNE is involved.

An important related point is that generally a work permit is granted to the expatriate only. The accompanying spouse or partner may not be permitted to work in the host country. Increasingly, multinationals are finding that the inability of the spouse to work in the host country may cause the selected candidate to reject the offer of an international assignment. If the international assignment is accepted, the lack of a work permit for the accompanying spouse or partner may cause difficulties in adjustment and even contribute to long-term failure. For these reasons, some multinationals provide assistance in this regard.

Further, the host country may be an important determinant. Some regions and countries are considered 'hardship postings': remote areas away from major cities or modern facilities, or war-torn regions with high physical risk. Accompanying family members may be an additional responsibility that the multinational does not want to bear. There may be a reluctance to select females for certain Middle East or South East Asian regions and in some countries a work permit for a female expatriate will not be issued. These aspects may result in the selection of HCNs rather than expatriates.

To overcome this problem, a group of more than 20 large multinationals (including Shell, British Airways, Unilever, PricewaterhouseCoopers, and Siemens) has established an organization called 'Permits Foundation',[123] in an attempt to promote the improvement of work permit regulations for spouses of expatriates. It also aims to raise government awareness of the connection between work permits and employee mobility.

MNE requirements

Selection decisions are influenced by the specific situation of the MNE. For example, the MNE may consider the proportion of expatriates to local staff when making selection decisions, mainly as an outcome of its staffing philosophy. However, operations in particular countries may require the use of more PCNs and TCNs than would normally be the case, as multinationals operating in parts of Eastern Europe and China are discovering. Furthermore, the mode of operation involved needs to be considered. Selecting staff to work in an international joint venture may involve major input from the local partner, and could be heavily constrained by the negotiated agreement on selection processes.[124]

Language

Language skills may be regarded as of critical importance for some expatriate positions, but lesser in others, though some would argue that knowledge of the host country's language is an important aspect of expatriate performance, regardless of the level of position. The ability to speak the local language is an aspect often linked with cross-cultural ability. Nevertheless, mastering the local language is most often not the most important qualification with respect to languages.[125] Another component to language in the selection decision is the role of the *common corporate language*. As previously discussed, many multinationals adopt a common corporate language as a way of standardizing reporting systems and procedures.[126] This is not, perhaps, an issue for PCN selection within multinationals from the Anglo-Saxon world (Britain, the USA, Canada,

Australia, and New Zealand) where the chosen corporate language remains the same as that of the home country. However, it becomes an expatriate selection issue for multinationals from non-English speaking countries that adopt English as the corporate language, unless the posting is to a country with a shared language. For instance, a Spanish multinational using Spanish as the corporate language, selecting a PCN to head its new subsidiary in Mexico, does not face the same language issue as a Spanish multinational with English as its corporate language selecting a PCN for its US facility. For the latter, fluency in English would be required. Lack of fluency in the corporate language, therefore, can be a selection barrier. Prospective candidates may be eliminated from the potential pool due to a lack of at least competency in the common language.[127] Language ability therefore may limit the MNE's ability to select the most appropriate candidate.

EXPATRIATE SELECTION PROCESSES IN PRACTICE

Once the selection criteria for international positions have been defined, processes need to be put in place to measure these criteria. However, it is relatively common in many MNEs that international selection processes can be rather informal. As we indicated at the beginning of the section on selection criteria, most multinationals admit that technical and/or managerial skills are the dominant, sometimes only, criteria used. We have suggested that reliance on technical skills is mainly due to the fact that the reason for most international assignments is 'position filling'. Of the factors outlined in Figure 5.3, technical skills are perhaps the easiest to measure. It could be argued that Figure 5.3 represents a best practice or ideal selection model that many MNEs do not in fact use.

Harris and Brewster[128] have argued that expatriate selection, in reality, often tends to be an ad-hoc process that they describe as the '*coffee-machine system*'. They suggest that managers chatting around the coffee machine (or water cooler) can start the selection process through a casual conversation about a vacant expatriate position that needs to be filled. A colleague may volunteer the name of a potential expatriate – thus starting an informal shortlist of candidates. What happens next, according to Harris and Brewster, is that the MNE's formal selection processes are then activated to legitimize the decision that has, in effect, already been taken around the coffee machine. Harris and Brewster relate that this process is the most common form of selection process they encountered in their study of UK firms. They then derived a typology of selection systems to explain variations found in the way expatriate selection is conducted.

It is, of course, possible to find examples of formal, open selection processes in firms, as well as informal or closed systems. Harris and Brewster note that the process can be influenced by the maturity of the MNE, its stage in the internationalization process and its size or industry. The type of position involved, the role of the HR function in the process, and whether the multinational is reactive rather than proactive where international assignment selection is involved remain key factors in how selection processes work in MNEs.

Formal selection procedures

In their comparative study, Tungli and Peiperl[129] found that in Germany, the UK, and the USA structured interviews dominate the selection of expatriates in MNEs. Furthermore, recommendations and self-selection played important roles. On the contrary, in Japanese MNEs recommendations and self-selection were the most important techniques, followed by tests of intercultural skills. In comparison, psychological and cognitive tests were used much less, especially in Germany and the USA. The effectiveness of such tests as predictors of cultural adjustment is open to question. For example, Torbiörn[130] comments that, though desirable personality traits are specified and recommended, the tests or criteria to assess these traits are seldom convincingly validated. Likewise, Willis[131] states that if tests are used they should be selected with care and regard for reliability and validity because, while some tests may be useful in suggesting potential problems, there appears to be little correlation between test scores and actual performance. He further adds that most of the relevant tests have been developed in the USA and, therefore, may be culture-bound. The use of such tests outside the USA without careful modification adds another question mark to their reliability and validity as predictors of expatriate success.

For a long time assessment centers and interviews have been recommended to select personnel for international positions. In these cases a selection board (i.e. a group of internationally experienced managers and IHRM specialists) could be used to interview the candidates and assess their suitability for international assignments. Thus, questions should address the specifics of the work environment of international managers. Prior international experience, the ability to adjust to a foreign environment, soft skills in an intercultural context such as intercultural communication abilities and the personality of the candidate could be the focus of these interviews.[132]

Besides selection practices focusing on the candidate, interviews can also be conducted with the spouse of the possible future expatriate. The comparative study by Tungli and Peiperl[133] revealed no significant differences concerning this practice in Germany, the UK, the USA, and Japan. For example, 13.6 per cent of investigated MNEs conducted interviews with the spouse. The reason for introducing this practice can be found in our discussion of premature return of expatriates – the inability of the spouse to adjust plays an important role in premature return and a number of firms are trying to minimize this risk, which may lead to an expatriate failure. Approaches that are designed for international selection processes often focus on intercultural competence. For example, the *Intercultural Development Inventory* suggested by Hammer, Bennett und Wiseman[134] tests sensitivity for intercultural differences based on a 50-item questionnaire. The aim is to differentiate candidates on a dimension between *ethnocentrism* and *ethnorelativism*. While ethnocentrism is associated with denial of foreign cultures, ethnorelativism is characterized by adjustment to foreign cultures and integration. Another option to measure intercultural competence would be an intercultural assessment center. This requires a clear definition of intercultural competence and every single exercise of the assessment center would have to be designed in order to measure its dimensions. Table 5.4 provides an example of such a design used by German MNEs. Normally, a group of IHRM managers and managers with international experience observes the candidates and evaluates the results. For the validity of the selection tools it is important that there is a clear and shared understanding of the indicators to evaluate whether the results of an exercise are positive or negative. This must be provided by the MNE or the consultants responsible for conducting the intercultural assessment center.[135] The role play exercise outlined in IHRM in Action Case 5.2 illustrates one of these exercises and Table 5.5 shows evaluation criteria for a role play exercise.

TABLE 5.4   Tasks and exercises used in an assessment center

Exercise features	Presentation	Role play	Questionnaire	Group discussion	Case study
Tolerance for ambiguity					
Goal orientation					
Interpersonal skills					
Empathy					
Non-judgmentalism					
Flexibility					
Meta-communication					

Source: Based on T. M. Kühlmann and G. Stahl 'Diagnose interkultureller Kompetenz: Entwicklung und Evaluierung eines Assessment Centers', in C. I. Barmeyer and J. Bolten (eds.), *Interkulturelle Personalorganisation* (Berlin: Verlag Wissenschaft und Praxis, 1998), p. 220. Reproduced with permission.

TABLE 5.5 Evaluation scheme for a role play in an intercultural assessment center

Dimensions	Examples for high intercultural competence	Examples for low intercultural competence
Tolerance for ambiguity	• Is patient • Shows a sense of humor	• Is impatient • Is very serious
Interpersonal skills	• Takes advantage of the time for a short conversation • Speaks about himself/private issues	• Immediately says 'goodbye' • Speaks immediately about business
Empathy	• Puts himself in the place of the business partner • Avoids offensive behavior	• Is only aware of his situation • Is offensive
Non-judgmentalism	• Assumes unintended lateness • Does not compare to home-country behavior	• Assumes intended lateness • Points to the virtue of punctuality in his home country
Flexibility	• Changes the subject • Suggests a new meeting	• Repeats continuously • Speaks about wasted opportunities
Learning orientation	• Tries to clarfiy unclear issues • Takes the arguments of the Mexican	• Does not ask to clarify unclear issues • Does not take the point of the Mexican

Source: T. Kühlmann and G. Stahl 'Fachkompetenz allein genügt nicht – Interkulturelle Assessment Center unterstützen die gezielte Personalauswahl', *Personalführung Plus* (1996), p. 24. Reproduced with permission.

IHRM in Action Case 5.2

Role playing: Intercultural competence

You have been assigned to Mexico for a two-year international assignment. Your task is to support the development of a new subsidiary. During the first weeks of your stay in Mexico you experience again and again that your Mexican employees as well as your suppliers and customers are never on time.

Now you are sitting in a restaurant and waiting for the Sales Director of one of your Mexican suppliers. Your meeting was at 12.30, but it is already 13.00 and the person you were waiting for has not shown up. As you have another appointment at 13.30 you ask for the bill, still hungry! Exactly at this moment the Sales Director shows up – half an hour late.

How do you react? What reaction do you expect from your Mexican partner? Which reactions would be interculturally competent and which would not be?

Source: Based on T. M. Kühlmann and G. K. Stahl 'Fachkompetenz allein genügt nicht – Interkulturelle Assessment Center unterstützen die gezielte Personalauswahl', *Personalführung Plus* (1996), p. 24. Reproduced with permission.

DUAL CAREER COUPLES

So far, we have focused on defining profiles and selecting suitable candidates for international assignments. We will now consider an emerging constraint – the dual career couple – on the available pool of candidates, thus hindering the recruitment and selection process. The rise in dual career couples, along with the aging population and other family-related situations, combine to make more people immobile. Employees are prepared to state the grounds for refusal as 'family concerns'. That this justification has become more acceptable reflects a significant shift in thinking about the role of non-work aspects impinging on work-related matters. The importance of the dual career couple challenge becomes clear when we look at some numbers. The *Brookfield Global Mobility Trend Survey 2015* states that 48 per cent of spouses were employed before an assignment (but not during). However, only 11 per cent were employed both before and during the assignment (historical average: 13 per cent).[136]

Considering these numbers it is not surprising that while the most important reason for turning down assignments reported in the *Brookfield* study was family concerns (38 per cent), the partner's career (21 per cent) was the second most common response. MNEs are aware of the dual career challenge and have reacted by providing a series of resources. Important support measures include language training, educational assistance, employer-sponsored work permits, and assistance with career planning.[137]

Other solutions to the challenge of dual career couples include the following:

- **Inter-firm networking** – here the multinational attempts to place the accompanying spouse or partner in a suitable job with another multinational, sometimes in a reciprocal arrangement. To illustrate: a US MNE may enter into an agreement with a German MNE also operating in a city or a region, e.g. China, in order to find a position within their respective Chinese facilities for each other's accompanying partner (that is, "you find my expatriate's spouse a job and work visa, and I will do likewise for you"). Alternatively, a local supplier, distributor or joint venture partner may agree to employ the accompanying spouse/partner.

- **Job-hunting assistance** – here the MNE provides spouse/partner assistance with the employment search in the host country. This may be done through employment agency fees, career counseling, or simply work permit assistance. Some may provide a fact-finding trip to the host location before the actual assignment.

- **Intra-firm employment** – this is perhaps a logical but often somewhat difficult solution. It means sending the couple to the same foreign facility, perhaps the same department. Not all multinationals (nor all couples) are comfortable with the idea of having a husband and wife team in the same work location and there can often be significant difficulties obtaining work visas for such arrangements.

- **On-assignment career support** – some time ago Motorola[138] provided an example of how a multinational may assist spouses to maintain and even improve career skills through what Motorola called its Dual-Career Policy. This consisted of a lump-sum payment for education expenses, professional association fees, seminar attendance, language training to upgrade work-related skills, and employment agency fees. There were conditions attached, such as the spouse must have been employed before the assignment. Thus, if the spouse was unable to find suitable employment, the assignment time could be spent on career development activities.

Other examples of on-assignment assistance are providing help in establishing contacts and paying for lost spouse income. The idea is to maintain skills so that the spouse may find work upon re-entry into the home country. These attempts demonstrate that creative thinking can assist MNEs to overcome this potential barrier. It is not possible to comment with authority on how effective the above assistance schemes are in terms of overcoming the dual career barrier. However, it is clear that multinationals are attempting to address the issue and create solutions for this barrier to mobility. According to the *Brookfield Global Mobility Trend Survey 2010*:

> *Spouses and partners feel strongly that their professional lives are valid concerns – both during and after international assignments. After all, 50 per cent of spouses were employed before such assignments. Consequently, they are demanding that companies assist them in maintaining their careers – especially when economic conditions make this difficult.*[139]

Besides supporting the expatriate's spouse before, during, and after the international assignment, MNEs can also choose to offer non-standard assignments as described earlier in this chapter – commuter and virtual assignments seem to provide relevant options here.

Are female expatriates different?   Our final issue in terms of selection for international assignments is related to gender. The typical expatriate still tends to be male. The *Brookfield Global Mobility Trend Survey* found in 2015 that 19 per cent of all expatriates were female (historical average in the *Brookfield Reports*: 17 per cent). However, there is a trend towards increasing numbers of female expatriates. For example, in 1984 Adler[140] reported a survey of international HR practices in over 600 US and Canadian companies that found only 3 per cent of the 13,338 expatriates identified were female. She found that female expatriates tended to be employed by companies with over 1000 employees in the banking, electronics, petroleum, and publishing industries. Researchers have continued to examine why so few expatriates are female. Is it because they were unwilling to relocate? Is it attitudinal? Does it reflect a common preconception that men in some cultures, such as certain Asian countries, do not like reporting to female managers, particularly foreign women, and therefore women should not be posted overseas? This unspoken assumption may contribute to what has been referred to as 'the glass border that supports the glass ceiling'. However, this is a view that has no strong empirical support.[141]

A number of studies challenge some of the attitudes regarding the suitability of females for international assignments. For example, Stroh, Varma and Valy-Durbin[142] found that US and Canadian women are interested in and likely to accept international assignments, though there are response variations between those with children and those without. However, the women in this study tended to believe that their firms were hesitant to ask them to accept an international assignment, though supervisors (whether male or female) did not necessarily share that belief. Further, performance of female expatriates was found initially to be affected by host-country prejudice regarding the role of women in certain countries – considered as culturally tough assignment locations. However, the longer the women were on such assignments, the less they perceived that prejudice was a barrier to effectiveness. Caligiuri and Tung[143] in their study of female and male expatriates in a US-based multinational found that females can perform equally as well as their male counterparts regardless of a country's attitude toward women in managerial positions.

Taking a different approach in her study of Austrian female expatriates, Fischlmayr[144] used the concepts of external and self-established barriers to explore why women are underrepresented in international assignments.

Through 21 interviews with HR managers and female expatriates in Austrian multinationals from various industries and positions, Fischlmayr found that attitudes of HR directors were a major barrier to the selection of female expatriates, though self-established barriers were also very strong. Females in Austrian companies often had to specifically request an international assignment whereas their male colleagues were required to take international assignments. Further, some women regarded their age as a factor in terms of others' perceptions and expectations about their behavior. The older the woman, the easier it was to obtain a position overseas. Fischlmayr concludes that women are partly to blame for their underrepresentation.

Mayrhofer and Scullion[145] report on the experiences of male and female expatriates in the German clothing industry. They found that women were sent to a diverse range of countries, including Islamic countries. Overall, there were few differences in the experiences of both gender groups, though female expatriates placed more value on integration of spouse/family issues prior to and during the assignment than did the males in the sample. Assignment lengths in this industry tended to be shorter and involved various forms of non-standard assignments and there were generally more female managers than perhaps found in other industries. More women than men were assigned for longer assignment terms, and the authors conclude that the higher proportion of women in the industry appeared to make gender a less important issue. However, this did not apply to the top senior management positions where women were less represented. Mayrhofer and Scullion conclude that there are still barriers to female expatriates in terms of senior expatriate positions.

A further contribution comes from a study by Napier and Taylor[146] of female expatriates from various countries working in Japan, China, and Turkey. The women fell into three categories: traditional expatriates, 'trailers' who were spouses/partners of male expatriates, and 'independents' – professional women who could be called self-selected expatriates. Napier and Taylor found that gaining credibility with local clients was a major issue. Accommodating to cultural differences, maintaining a social life and a need for appropriate interpersonal skills were important factors in coping with work demands. Networks became important for both business and social contexts. Being a minority (a foreign female) meant higher visibility than they were used to and could be positive in terms of getting access to key clients and customers.

What emerges as common across the various studies on female expatriates is that assignment location, level of organization support, spouse/partner satisfaction, and intercultural experiences are important in terms of performance. The list of moderators is similar to those we discussed in general terms earlier in this chapter. What does appear to differentiate female and male expatriates is the degree to which these moderators affect individual performance and the value placed on cultural awareness training prior to the international assignment. The dual career issue may prove to be a greater barrier for female mobility as males are more reluctant to accompany their spouse/partner.

Insch, McIntyre and Napier[147] have developed strategies for breaking the glass ceiling before, during, and after an international assignment. They consider the perspectives of both the female expatriate and the MNE. Table 5.6 depicts these strategies. Overall, the performance

TABLE 5.6   Strategies for breaking the expatriate glass ceiling

Strategies	For female expatriates	For MNEs
Pre-assignment strategies	• Self-awareness • Understand her own strengths, and recognizing the values and emotions that she identifies with based on her upbringing and culture • Use those strengths and skills to the fullest advantage • Plan her life as well as her career • Develop the relationships and social networks • Find and use mentors as well as correspond with female expatriates for advice and guidance	• Begin with a thorough review of the selection criteria for overseas assignments • Eliminate, through policy and training, any overt or subtle gender biases in the selection process • Train selection decision-makers to avoid the subtle gender biases in the selection process • Trailing spouse and 'dual-career' issues should be discussed and provided for regardless of the manager's gender • Make a more concerted effort to insert women into the relevant informal and formal organizational networks
On-assignment strategies	• Find and use mentors as a key to success • Develop the willingness and skill to absorb knowledge from the local settings	• Consider assigning female expatriates to countries where they are likely to have a greater opportunity to adjust quickly, develop, and grow, particularly earlier in their careers • Consider and develop possibilities for short-term assignments • Continue training and mentoring
Post-assignment strategies	• Simply acknowledge that the likelihood of extensive use of knowledge is unlikely • Female expatriates may think and act more entrepreneurially, taking even greater responsibility for managing their careers	• A psychological contract must be fulfilled when an expatriate returns, e.g. pay particular attention to the continued mentoring and training, and opportunities for the expatriates to use their new expertise

Source: G. Insch, N. McIntyre and N. Napier, 'The Expatriate Glass Ceiling: The Second Layer of Glass', *Journal of Business Ethics*, Vol. 83, No. 1 (2008), pp. 19–28. Reproduced with permission via Rightslink.

of female expatriates is influenced by the prejudices against female managers in the respective countries. However, this influence is perceived as less strong the longer the female managers stay abroad.[148] Caligiuri and Cascio[149] argue that foreign women are often evaluated according to other criteria than local women. In countries in which females tend to be rather discriminated against in working life, foreign women are seen as neutral. Caligiuri and Cascio state that it could be a success factor if female expatriates do not emphasize too much their female role and take on typical female role behavior in the foreign country. Instead they should deliberately differentiate themselves from the behavior described as typical for local women. This should lead to the perception of being seen as an expert rather than being seen as a woman and should enable a successful and equal business relationship.

SUMMARY

This chapter has expanded on the role of staffing, recruitment, and selection in international operations for sustaining international business operations. The following issues were discussed:

- We have outlined the various approaches to staffing international operations – ethnocentric, polycentric, geocentric, and regiocentric and discussed their advantages and disadvantages. In addition, we presented a model delineating factors that may determine the choice of these options: context specificities, MNE characteristics, features of the local unit as well as IHRM practices.

- Primary reasons for using international assignments include position filling, management development, and organization development. There are indicators that the importance of management development is increasing.

- Various types of international assignments can be distinguished: short, extended, and long-term (traditional); and non-standard forms such as commuter, rotational, contractual, virtual, and self-initiated assignments. All were presented including implications for the MNE as well as for the individual.

- Roles of expatriates are complex. They can act as an agent for direct control, as an agent for socialization, as a network builder, as a boundary spanner, and as a language node. These various roles of the expatriate help to explain why expatriates are utilized and illustrate why international assignments continue to be an important aspect of international business from the organization's perspective.

- We placed emphasis on the fact that non-expatriates are also critical to international business operations. International business travelers present their own challenges, such as the effect of frequent absences on family and home life, the possible negative health effects, and other stress factors. The management of such individuals, though, does not appear to fall within the domain of the HR department.

- Another important development in IHRM is the role of inpatriates. This is a group of employees that only differs by definition from expatriates because it includes only those employees who are sent to the headquarters by foreign locations and not those who are assigned by the headquarters.

This chapter has addressed key issues affecting recruitment and selection for international assignments. We have covered:

- the debate surrounding expatriate failure and success

- important factors in the selection of expatriates, including technical ability, cross-cultural suitability (soft skills in an international context, intercultural competence, and cross-cultural adjustment), family requirements, country/cultural requirements, language, and MNE requirements

- informal selection processes that can often influence expatriate selection and, more formally, interview, assessment centers, recommendations, and self-selection

- dual career couples as a barrier to staff mobility, and a number of techniques that MNEs are utilizing to overcome this constraint

- the specific case of female expatriates and whether they face different issues than their male counterparts.

It is also clear that, while our appreciation of the issues surrounding expatriate recruitment and selection has deepened in the past 30 years, much remains to be explored. The field is dominated by US research on predominantly US samples of expatriates, though there has been an upsurge in interest from European academics and practitioners. Will the factors affecting the selection decision be similar for multinationals emerging from countries such as China and India? If more MNEs are to encourage subsidiary staff to consider international assignments as part of an intra-organizational network approach to management, we will need further understanding of how valid the issues and findings discussed in this chapter are for all categories of staff from different country locations. It is apparent, though, that staff selection remains critical. Finding the right people to fill positions, particularly key managers – whether PCN, TCN, or HCN – can significantly influence international expansion. However, effective recruitment and selection is only the first step.

DISCUSSION QUESTIONS

1 Outline the main characteristics of the four approaches to international staffing.

2 Which factors determine the choice of a staffing approach? Would a MNE choose the same staffing approach worldwide? Place your arguments in the context of the model outlining determinants of staffing choices.

3 What are the reasons for using international assignments?

4 What is the role of inpatriates? Do inpatriates guarantee a geocentric staffing policy?

5 As a newly-appointed project manager of a research team, you believe that you will be able to manage the project virtually from your office in London, even though the other six members are located in Munich. This will solve your personal dilemma as your family does not want to be relocated. The project has a six-month deadline. What factors should you consider in order to make this virtual assignment effective?

6 Should multinationals be concerned about expatriate failure? If so, why?

7 What are the most important factors involved in the selection decision?

FURTHER READING

M. Andresen and T. Biemann 'A taxonomy of internationally mobile managers', *International Journal of Human Resource Management*, Vol. 24, No. 3 (2013), pp. 533–557.

P. Caligiuri and J. Bucker 'Selection for international assignments', in D. Collings, G. Wood and P. Caligiuri (eds.) *The Routledge Companion to International Human Resource Management* (London: Routledge Publishing, 2015), pp. 275–288.

D. Collings and H. Scullion 'Global staffing', in G. Stahl, I. Bjorkman and S. Morris (eds.) *Handbook of Research in International Human Resource Management*, 2nd ed. (Cheltenham: Edward Elgar Publishing, 2012), pp. 142–161.

P. Caliguri and J. Bonache 'Evolving and enduring challenges in global mobility', *Journal of World Business*, Vol. 51, No. 1 (2016), pp. 127–141.

L. Howe-Walsh and B. Schyns 'Self-Initiated Expatriation: Implications for HRM', *International Journal of Human Resource Management*, Vol. 21, No. 2 (2010), pp. 260–273.

I. Nikandrou and L. Panayoutopoulou 'Recruitment and selection in context', in C. Brewster and W. Mayrhofer (eds.) *Handbook of Research on Comparative Human Resource Management* (Cheltenham: Edward Elgar Publishing, 2012), pp. 121–138.

H. Scullion and D. Collings *Global Talent Management* (London: Routledge, 2010).

NOTES AND REFERENCES

1. H. V. Perlmutter 'The Tortuous Evolution of the Multinational Corporation', *Columbia Journal of World Business*, Vol. 4, No. 1 (1969), pp. 9–18.

2. D. A. Heenan and H. V. Perlmutter *Multinational Organizational Development. A Social Architectual Perspective* (Reading, MA: Addison–Wesley, 1979).

3. J. Bonache, C. Brewster and V. Suutari 'Expatriation: A Developing Research Agenda', *Thunderbird International Business Review*, Vol. 43, No. 1 (2001), pp. 3–20.

4. Y. Zeira 'Management Development in Ethnocentric Multinational Corporations', *California Management Review*, Vol. 18, No. 4 (1976), pp. 34–42.

5. PricewaterhouseCoopers (eds.) *Managing Mobility Matters 2006* (London: PricewaterhouseCoopers, 2006).

6. D. A. Heenan and H. V. Perlmutter *Multinational Organizational Development. A Social Architectual Perspective* (Reading, MA: Addison–Wesley, 1979).

7. A. J. Morrison, D. A. Ricks and K. Roth 'Globalization Versus Regionalization: Which Way For the Multinational?', *Organizational Dynamics*, Vol. 19, No. 3 (1991), pp. 17–29.

8. I. Torbiörn 'Staffing Policies and Practices in European MNCs: Strategic Sophistication, Culture-Bound Policies or Ad-hoc Reactivity', in H. Scullion and M. Linehan (eds.) *International Human Resource Management. A Critical Text* (Basingtoke, UK: Palgrave Macmillan, 2005), pp. 47–68.

9. For a recent discussion based on comparative HRM data see M. Brookes, R. Croucher, M. Fenton-O'Creevy and P. Gooderham 'Measuring Competing Explanations of Human Resource Management Practices through the Cranet Survey: Cultural versus Institutional Explanations', *Human Resource Management Review*, Vol. 21, No. 1 (2011), pp. 68–79. Also see N. Ando and Y. Paik 'Institutional distance, host country and international business experience, and the use of parent country nationals', Human Resource Management Journal, Vol. 23, No. 1 (2013), pp. 52–71.

10. I. Tarique, R. Schuler and Y. Gong 'A Model of Multinational Enterprise Subsidiary Staffing Composition', *International Journal of Human Resource Management*, Vol. 17, No. 2 (2006), pp. 207–224.

11. See the results of a study among Japanese subsidiaries by Y. Gong 'Subsidiary Staffing in Multinational Enterprises: Agency, Resources, and Performance', *Academy of Management Journal*, Vol. 46, No. 6 (2003), pp. 728–739. A similar analysis has been carried out by K. Thompson and M. Keating 'An Empirical Study of Executive Nationality Staffing Practices in Foreign-Owned MNC Subsidiaries in Ireland', *Thunderbird International Business Review*, Vol. 46, No. 6 (2004), pp. 771–797.

12. For an institutional perspective see the national business systems approach by R. Whitley *European Business Systems: Firms and Markets in their National Contexts* (London: Sage, 1992).

13. For a discussion of European staffing approaches see I. Torbiörn 'Staffing Policies and Practices in European MNCs: Strategic Sophistication, Culture-Bound Policies or Ad-hoc Reactivity', in H. Scullion and M. Linehan (eds.) *International Human Resource Management. A Critical Text* (Basingtoke, UK: Palgrave Macmillan, 2005), pp. 47–68.

14. For a similar discussion see C. M. Vance and Y. Paik *Managing a Global Workforce. Challenges and Opportunities in International Human Resource Management* (Armonk, N. Y., London: M. E. Sharpe, 2006).

15. For a discussion of these factors on subsidiary HRM see Y. Kim and S. J. Gray 'Strategic Factors Influencing International Human Resource Management Practices: An Empirical Study of Australian Multinational Corporations', *International Journal of Human Resource Management*, Vol. 16, No. 5 (2005), pp. 809–830.

16. For the issue of subsidiary consideration see M. M. Novicevic and M. Harvey 'Staffing Architecture for Expatriate Assignments to Support Subsidiary Cooperation', *Thunderbird International Business Review*, Vol. 46, No. 6 (2004), pp. 709–724. For a discussion of the impact of different subsidiary strategies see J. Bonache and Z. Fernandez 'Strategic Staffing in Multinational Companies: A Resource-Based Approach', in C. Brewster and J. E. Harris (eds.) *International Human Resource Management: Contemporary Issues in Europe* (London, New York: Routledge, 2004), pp. 163–182. For a resource-dependence perspective on the emergence of international HRM strategies see M. Festing, J. Eidems and S. Royer 'Strategic Issues and Local Constraints in Transnational Compensation Strategies: An Analysis of Cultural, Institutional and Political Influences', *European Management Journal*, Vol. 25, No. 2 (2007), pp. 118–131.

17. D. E. Welch 'HRM Implications of Globalization', *Journal of General Management*, Vol. 19, No. 4 (1994), pp. 52–68.

18. This figure is informed by the work of D. E. Welch 'Determinants of International Human Resource Management Approaches and Activities: A Suggested Framework', *Journal of Management Studies*, Vol. 31, No. 2 (1994), pp. 139–164; H. De Cieri and P. J. Dowling 'Strategic International Human Resource Management in Multinational Enterprises', in G. K. Stahl and I. Björkman (eds.) *Handbook of International Human Resource Management Research* (Cheltenham, Northhampton, MA: Edward Elgar, 2006), pp. 15–35; M. Festing, J. Eidems and S. Royer 'Strategic Issues and Local Constraints in Transnational Compensation Strategies: An Analysis of Cultural, Institutional and Political Influences', *European Management Journal*, Vol. 25, No. 2 (2007), pp. 118–131; K. Thompson and M. Keating 'An Empirical Study of Executive Nationality Staffing Practices in Foreign-Owned MNC Subsidiaries in Ireland', *Thunderbird International Business Review*, Vol. 46, No. 6 (2004), pp. 771–797.

19. In their model they predict that headquarters, subsidiary, structural and HR systems factors predict these flows. The empirical findings partly support these assumptions. For details see D. G. Collings, A. McDonnell, P. Gunnigle and J. Lavelle 'Swimming against the Tide: Outward Staffing Flows from Multinational Subsidiaries', *Human Resource Management*, Vol. 49, No. 4 (2010), pp. 575–598.

20. J. Shen 'Factors Affecting International Staffing in Chinese Multinationals (MNEs)', *International Journal of Human Resource Management*, Vol. 17, No. 2 (2006), pp. 295–315.

21. See M. Andresen and T. Biemann's interesting assessment of research on differing forms of international assignments, 'A taxonomy of internationally mobile managers', *International Journal of Human Resource Management,* Vol. 24, No. 3 (2013), pp. 533–557, as well as methodological concerns raised by P. Tharenou on how research has been designed and carried out in this area, 'Researching expatriate types: The quest for rigorous methodological approaches', *Human Resource Management Journal*, Vol. 25, No. 2 (2015), pp. 149–165.

22. See M. Dabic, M. Gonzalez-Loureiro and M. Harvey 'Evolving research on expatriates: What is 'known' after four decades (1970–2012)' *International Journal of Human Resource Management*, Vol. 26, No. 3 (2015),

pp. 316–337; P. Caliguri and J. Bonache, J. 'Evolving and enduring challenges in global mobility', *Journal of World Business*, Vol., 51, No. 1 (2016) pp. 127–141.

23. Brookfield Global Relocation Services (ed.) *Global Mobility Trends Survey Report* 2015 (Woodridge, IL, 2015).

24. See PricewaterhouseCoopers (eds.) *Managing Mobility Matters 2006* (London: PricewaterhouseCoopers, 2006), *Relocation Trends Survey 2010* (2010).

25. Brookfield Global Relocation Services (ed.) *Global Mobility Trends Survey Report* 2015 (Woodridge, IL, 2015).

26. For example, Benson and Patties (2008) found that, in the case of US-American managers, international experience was associated with greater firm internal and external career opportunities. Jokinen (2010) argues that expatriates build international career capital, i.e. knowing-how, knowing-why and knowing-whom as a basis for international career development. See G. S. Benson and M. Pattie 'Is Expatriation Good for my Career? The Impact of Expatriate Assignments on Perceived and Actual Career Outcomes', *International Journal of Human Resource Management*, Vol. 19, No. 9 (2008), pp. 1636–1653; T. Jokinen 'Development of Career Capital through International Assignments and its Transferability to New Contexts', *Thunderbird International Business Review*, Vol. 52, No. 4 (2010), pp. 325–336.

27. Brookfield Global Relocation Services (ed.) Global Mobility Trends Survey Report 2015 (Woodridge, IL, 2015).

28. Based on a literature review on German IHRM studies, Harzing concludes that all key reasons for international assignments can lead to organization development 'defined as the increase of the company's potential to succeed and to compete in the international market' (Harzing 2001: 368). See A.W. Harzing 'Of Bears, Bumble-Bees, and Spiders: The Role of Expatriates in Controlling Foreign Subsidiaries', *Journal of World Business*, Vol. 36, No. 4 (2001), pp. 366–379. With respect to IHRM, Morris *et al.* distinguish between integrative and creative capabilities to meet the challenges of the global market. See S. S. Morris, S. A. Snell, P. M. Wright, G. K. Stahl and I. Björkman (eds.) 'A Resource-Based View of International Human Resources: Toward a Framework of Integrative and Creative Capabilities', *Handbook of Research in International Human Resource Management* (Northampton, MA: Edward Elgar, 2006), pp. 433–448.

29. Brookfield Global Relocation Services (ed.) *Global Mobility Trends Survey Report* 2015 (Woodridge, IL, 2015).

30. See also A.W. Harzing 'Of Bears, Bumble-Bees, and Spiders: The Role of Expatriates in Controlling Foreign Subsidiaries', *Journal of World Business*, Vol. 36, No. 4 (2001), p. 368.

31. For recent empirical evidence on organizational assignments (and individual) goals see M. Dickmann and N. Doherty 'Exploring Organizational and Individual Career Goals, Interactions, and Outcomes of Developmental International Assignments', *Thunderbird International Business Review*, Vol. 52, No. 4 (2010), pp. 313–324. They summarize their arguments by introducing the dimensions of knowing-how, knowing-whom and knowing-why on the organizational as well as on the individual side.

32. For further details see P. Sparrow, C. Brewster and J. E. Harris *Globalizing Human Resource Management* (London, New York: Routledge, 2004).

33. For further details see Z. Tungli and M. Peiperl 'Expatriate Practices in German, Japanese, U.K., and U.S. Multinational Companies: A Comparative Survey of Changes', *Human Resource Management*, Vol. 48, No. 1 (2009), pp. 153–171.

34. For further details see Z. Tungli and M. Peiperl 'Expatriate Practices in German, Japanese, U.K., and U.S. Multinational Companies: A Comparative Survey of Changes', *Human Resource Management*, Vol. 48, No. 1 (2009), pp. 153–171.

35. For further details see Brookfield Global Relocation Services (ed.) Global Mobility Trends Survey Report 2015 (Woodridge, IL, 2015).

36. For further details see D. E. Welch, V. Worm and M. Fenwick 'Are Virtual Assignments Feasible?', *Management International Review*, Vol. 43 Special Issue No. 1 (2003), pp. 95–114.

37. For further discussions about non-standard assignments see also J. Bonache, C. Brewster, V. Suutari and P. De Saá 'Expatriation: Traditional Criticisms and International Careers: Introducing the Special Issue', *Thunderbird International Business Review*, Vol. 52, No. 4 (2010), pp. 263–274; D. G. Collings, H. Scullion and M. J. Morley 'Changing Patterns of Global Staffing in the Multinational Enterprise: Challenges to the Conventional Expatriate Assignment and Emerging Alternatives', *Journal of World Business*, Vol. 42, No. 2 (2007), pp. 198–213; H. Harris, C. Brewster and C. Erten 'Auslandseinsatz, aber wie? Klassisch oder alternative Formen: Neueste empirische Erkenntnisse aus Europa und den USA', in G. K. Stahl, W. Mayrhofer and T. M. Kühlmann (eds.) *Internationales Personalmanagement: Neue Aufgaben, Neue Lösungen* (München, Mering: Hampp, 2005), pp. 271–292.

38. For more details see J. Bonache, C. Brewster, V. Suutari and P. De Saá 'Expatriation: Traditional Criticisms and International Careers: Introducing the Special Issue', *Thunderbird International Business Review*, Vol. 52, No. 4 (2010), pp. 263–274.

39. Brookfield Global Relocation Services (ed.) *Global Mobility Trends Survey Report* 2015 (Woodridge, IL, 2015).

40. Ibid, p. 11.

41. A. Mendez 'The Coordination of Globalized R&D Activities through Project Teams Organization: An Exploratory Empirical Study', *Journal of World Business*, Vol. 38, No. 2 (2003), pp. 96–109.

42. D. E. Welch, V. Worm and M. Fenwick 'Are Virtual Assignments Feasible?', *Management International Review*, Vol. 43 Special Issue No. 1 (2003), pp. 95–114, p. 98.

43. For further details see D. Holtbruegge and K. Schillo 'Intercultural Training Requirements for Virtual Assignments: Results of an Explorative Empirical Study', *Human Resource Development International*, Vol. 11, No. 3 (2008), pp. 271–286.

44. For a summary of the historical development of this type of assignment J. Bonache, C. Brewster, V. Suutari and P. De Saá 'Expatriation: Traditional Criticisms and International Careers: Introducing the Special Issue', *Thunderbird International Business Review*, Vol. 52, No. 4 (2010),

pp. 263–274. The ongoing debate on the construct and how to understand it is presented by J.L. Cerdin and J. Selmer 'Who is a self-initiated expatriate? Towards conceptual clarity of a common notion,' *International Journal of Human Resource Management*, Vol. 25, No. 9 (2015), pp. 1281–1301. The relationship between an interest in initiating an assignment and early childhood influences – a multicultural home life – is related by J. Selmer and J. Lauring, 'Self-initiated expatriates. An exploratory study of adjustment of adult third-culture kids vs. adult monoculture kids,' *Cross-Cultural Management*, Vol. 21, No. 4 (2014), pp. 422–436.

45. For a study on the impact factors on self-assigned expatriate repatriation see P. Tharenou and N. Caulfield 'Will I Stay or Will I Go? Explaining Repatriation by Self-initiated Expatriates', *Academy of Management Journal*, Vol. 53, No. 5, pp. 1009–1028.

46. For details of the study see J.L. Cerdin and M. L. Pargneux 'Career Anchors: A Comparison between Organization–assigned and Self–initiated Expatriates', *Thunderbird International Business Review*, Vol. 52, No. 4 (2010), pp. 287–299.

47. For an empirical study see J. Selmer and J. Lauring 'Self-Initiated Academic Expatriates: Inherent Demographics and Reasons to Expatriate', *European Management Review*, Vol. 7, No. 3 (2010), pp. 169–179.

48. A.W. Harzing 'Of Bears, Bumble-Bees, and Spiders: The Role of Expatriates in Controlling Foreign Subsidiaries', *Journal of World Business*, Vol. 36, No. 4 (2001), pp. 366–379.

49. M. S. Fenwick, H. L. De Cieri and D. E. Welch 'Cultural and Bureaucratic Control in MNEs: The Role of Expatriate Performance Management', *Management International Review*, Vol. 39 (1999), pp. 107–124.

50. S. S. Morris, S. A. Snell, P. M. Wright, G. K. Stahl and I. Bjoerkman (eds.) 'A Resource-Based View of International Human Resources: Toward a Framework of Integrative and Creative Capabilities', *Handbook of Research in International Human Resource Management* (Northampton, MA: Edward Elgar, 2006), pp. 433–448.

51. D. M. Schweiger, T. Atamer and R. Calori 'Transnational Project Teams and Networks: Making the Multinational Organization More Effective', *Journal of World Business*, Vol. 38, No. 2 (2003), pp. 127–140.

52. J. Birkinshaw and N. Hood 'Unleash Innovation in Foreign Subsidiaries', *Harvard Business Review*, Vol. 79, No. 3 (2001), pp. 131–137.

53. R. Marschan-Piekkari, D. Welch and L. Welch 'Adopting a Common Corporate Language: IHRM Implications', *International Journal of Human Resource Management*, Vol. 10, No. 3 (1999), pp. 377–390.

54. K. Maekelae 'Knowledge Sharing Through Expatriate Relationships', *International Studies of Management & Organization*, Vol. 37, No. 3 (2007), pp. 108–125.

55. K. Goodall and J. Roberts 'Only Connect: Teamwork in the Multinational', *Journal of World Business*, Vol. 38, No. 2 (2003), pp. 150–164.

56. For an analysis of these relationships see J. Bonache and C. Zárraga-Oberty 'Determinants of the Success of International Assignees as Knowledge Transferors: A Theoretical Framework', *International Journal of Human Resource Management*, Vol. 19, No. 1 (2008), pp. 1–18.

57. M. C. Bolino and D. C. Feldman 'Increasing the Skill Utilization of Expatriates', *Human Resource Management*, Vol. 39, No. 4 (2000), pp. 367–379.

58. D. E. Welch, L. S. Welch and V. Worm 'The International Business Traveller: A Neglected but Strategic Human Resource', *International Journal of Human Resource Management*, Vol. 18, No. 2 (2007), pp. 173–183.

59. H. Mayerhofer, L. C. Hartmann, G. Michelitsch-Riedl and I. Kollinger 'Flexpatriate Assignments: A Neglected Issue in Global Staffing', *International Journal of Human Resource Management*, Vol. 15, No. 8 (2004), pp. 1371–1389.

60. R. S. DeFrank, R. Konopaske and J. M. Ivancevich 'Executive Travel Stress: Perils of the Road Warrior', *Academy of Management Executive*, Vol. 14, No. 2 (2000), pp. 58–71.

61. For more details and empirical evidence see B. Demel and W. Mayrhofer 'Frequent Business Travelers across Europe: Career Aspirations and Implications', *Thunderbird International Business Review*, Vol. 52, No. 4 (2010), pp. 301—311; and B. Demel *Karrieren von Expatriates und Flexpatriates* (München, Mering: Hampp, 2010).

62. S. B. Reiche 'The Inpatriate Experience in Multinational Corporations: An Exploratory Case Study in Germany', *International Journal of Human Resource Management*, Vol. 17, No. 9 (2006), pp. 1572–1590, p. 1580.

63. D. Collings and H. Scullion 'Global Staffing', in G. K. Stahl and I. Björkman (eds.) *Handbook of Research in International Human Resource Management* (Cheltenham, Northampton, MA: Edward Elgar, 2006), pp. 141–157.

64. Similar ideas can be found in M. Harvey, C. Speier and M. M. Novicevic 'The Role of Inpatriation in Global Staffing', *International Journal of Human Resource Management*, Vol. 10, No. 3 (1999), pp. 459–476.

65. M. G. Harvey and M. R. Buckley 'Managing Inpatriates: Building a Global Core Competency', *Journal of World Business*, Vol. 32, No. 1 (1997), pp. 35–52.

66. For more details see S. B. Reiche, Kraimer M. L. and A.W. Harzing 'Why do International Assignees Stay? An Organizational Embeddedness Perspective', *Journal of International Business Studies*, Vol. 42, No. 4 (2011), pp. 521–544.

67. For further details see Z. Tungli and M. Peiperl, 'Expatriate Practices in German, Japanese, U.K., and U.S. Multinational Companies: A Comparative Survey of Changes', *Human Resource Management*, Vol. 48, No. 1 (2009), pp. 153—171.

68. H. Scullion and D. Collings 'International Recruitment and Selection', in H. Scullion and D. Collings (eds.) *Global Staffing* (London, New York: Routledge, 2006), pp. 59–86. Services (eds.) *Global Relocation Trends: 2010 Survey Report* (2010).

69. For further details see Brookfield Global Relocation Services (eds.) *Global Relocation Trends: 2010 Survey Report (2010).*

70. For further details see A. Bayo-Moriones and P. Ortín-Ángel 'Internal Promotion versus External Recruitment in Industrial Plants in Spain', *Industrial & Labor Relations Review*, Vol. 59, No. 3 (2006), pp. 451–470.

71. For further details see K. Maekelae, I. Björkman and M. Ehrnrooth 'MNC Subsidiary Staffing Architecture: Building Human and Social Capital within the Organisation', *International Journal of Human Resource Management*, Vol. 20, No. 6 (2009), pp. 1273–1290.

72. For further details see Brookfield Global Relocation Services (ed.) *Global Mobility Trends Survey Report 2015* (Woodridge, IL, 2015).

73. For further details see A.W. Harzing (eds.) *Composing International Staff* (London, UK: Sage, 2004).

74. N. Forster 'The Persistent Myth of High Expatriate Failure Rates: A Reappraisal', *International Journal of Human Resource Management*, Vol. 8, No. 4 (1997), p. 430.

75. For further details see Brookfield Global Relocation Services (ed.) *Global Mobility Trends Survey Report 2015* (Woodridge, IL, 2015).

76. R. L. Tung 'Selection and Training of Personnel for Overseas Assignments', *Columbia Journal of World Business*, Vol. 16, No. 1 (1981), pp. 68–78; R. L. Tung 'Selection and Training Procedures of U.S., European, and Japanese Multinationals', *California Management Review*, Vol. 25, No. 1 (1982), pp. 57–71; and R. L. Tung 'Human Resource Planning in Japanese Multinationals: A Model for U.S. Firms?', *Journal of International Business Studies*, Vol. 15, No. 2 (1984), pp. 139–149.

77. For further details see Z. Tungli and M. Peiperl 'Expatriate Practices in German, Japanese, U.K., and U.S. Multinational Companies: A Comparative Survey of Changes', *Human Resource Management*, Vol. 48, No. 1 (2009), pp. 153–171.

78. For further details see Z. Tungli and M. Peiperl 'Expatriate Practices in German, Japanese, U.K., and U.S. Multinational Companies: A Comparative Survey of Changes', *Human Resource Management*, Vol. 48, No. 1 (2009), pp. 153–171.

79. A.W. K. Harzing 'The Persistent Myth of High Expatriate Failure Rates', *International Journal of Human Resource Management*, Vol. 6, No. 2 (1995), p. 458.

80. A.W. Harzing and C. Christensen, 'Expatriate Failure: Time to Abandon the Concept?', *Career Development International*, Vol. 9, No. 7 (2004), pp. 616–626.

81. M. E. Mendenhall and G. Oddou 'The Overseas Assignment: A Practical Look', *Business Horizons*, Vol. 31, No. 5 (1988), pp. 78–84.

82. M. Mendenhall and G. Oddou 'The Dimensions of Expatriate Acculturation: A Review', *Academy of Management Review*, Vol. 10, No. 1 (1985), pp. 39–47.

83. For further details see R. L. Tung 'Selection and Training Procedures of US, European, and Japanese Multinationals', *California Management Review*, Vol. 25, No. 1 (1982), pp. 57–71.

84. For further details see Z. Tungli and M. Peiperl 'Expatriate Practices in German, Japanese, U.K., and U.S. Multinational Companies: A Comparative Survey of Changes', *Human Resource Management*, Vol. 48, No. 1 (2009), pp. 153–171.

85. H.W. Lee 'Factors that Influence Expatriate Failure: An Interview Study', *International Journal of Management*, Vol. 24, No. 3 (2007), pp. 403–413.

86. For similar results see M. L. Kraimer, S. J. Wayne and R. A. Jaworski 'Sources of Support and Expatriate Performance: The Mediating Role of Expatriate Adjustment', *Personnel Psychology*, Vol. 54, No. 1 (2001), pp. 71–99.

87. The complexities of personal factors are represented by a study by S. Remhof, M. Gunkel and C. Schlaegel 'Goodbye Germany! The influence of personality and cognitive factors on the intention to work abroad', *International Journal of Human Resource Management*, Vol. 25, No. 16 (2014), pp. 2319–2343; also P. Nguyen, J. Felfe and I. Fooken 'Interaction effects of dual organizational commitment on retention in international assignments: The case of Western expatriates in Vietnam', *International Journal of Human Resource Management*, Vol. 26, No. 11 (2015), pp. 1407–1427.

88. See W.L. Zhuang, M. Wu and S.L. Wen 'Relationship of mentoring functions to expatriate adjustments: Comparing home country mentorship and host country mentorship,' *International Journal of Human Resource Management*, Vol. 24, No. 1 (2013), pp. 35–49. Also see N. Kawai and R. Strange 'Perceived organizational support and expatriate experience: Understanding a mediated model', *International Journal of Human Resource Management*, Vol. 25, No. 12 (2014), pp. 2438–2462; M. Malek, P. Budhwar and S. Reiche 'Sources of support and expatriation: A multiple stakeholder perspective of expatriate adjustment and performance in Malaysia', *International Journal of Human Resource Management*, Vol. 26, No. 2 (2015), pp. 258–276.

89. Brookfield Global Relocation Services (ed.) *Global Mobility Trends Survey Report 2015* (Woodridge, IL, 2015).

90. I. Björkman and M. Gertsen 'Selecting and Training Scandinavian Expatriates: Determinants of Corporate Practice', *Scandinavian Journal of Management*, Vol. 9, No. 2 (1993), pp. 145–164; A. L. Hixon 'Why Corporations Make Haphazard Overseas Staffing Decisions', *Personnel Administrator*, Vol. 31, No. 3 (1986), pp. 91–94; E. Marx *International Human Resource Practices in Britain and Germany* (London: Anglo–German Foundation for the Study of Industrial Society, 1996); J. McEnery and G. DesHarnais 'Culture Shock', *Training & Development Journal*, Vol. 44, No. 4 (1990), pp. 43–47; M. E. Mendenhall, E. Dunbar and G. R. Oddou 'Expatriate Selection, Training and Career–Pathing: A Review and Critique', *Human Resource Management*, Vol. 26, No. 3 (1987), pp. 331–345; PricewaterhouseCoopers (eds.) *International Assignments. European Policy and Practice* (PricewaterhouseCoopers, 1996).

91. For further details see D. G. Collings, H. Scullion and M. J. Morley 'Changing Patterns of Global Staffing in the Multinational Enterprise: Challenges to the Conventional Expatriate Assignment and Emerging Alternatives', *Journal of World Business*, Vol. 42, No. 2 (2007), pp. 198–213.

92. For further details see P. Caligiuri, I. Tarique and R. Jacobs 'Selection for International Assignments', *Human Resource Management Review*, Vol. 19, No. 3 (2009), pp. 251–262.

93. For empirical evidence see, for example, the recent paper by S. Lloyd and C. Haertel 'Intercultural Competencies for Culturally Diverse Work Team', *Journal of Managerial Psychology*, Vol. 25, No. 8 (2010), pp. 845–875.

94. M. C. Gertsen 'Intercultural Competence and Expatriates', *International Journal of Human Resource Management*, Vol. 1, No. 3 (1990), p. 341.

95. P. M. Caligiuri 'The Big Five Personality Characteristics as Predictors of Expatriate's Desire to Terminate the Assignment and Supervisor-rated Performance', *Personnel Psychology*, Vol. 53, No. 1 (2000), pp. 67–88.

96. For further details see W. B. Gudykunst, R. L. Wiseman and M. R. Hammer 'Determinants of the Sojourner's Attitudinal Satisfaction: A Path Model', *Communication Yearbook*, Vol. 1 (1977), pp. 415–425.

97. For further details see R. L. Wiseman, M. R. Hammer and H. Nishida 'Predictors of Intercultural Communication Competence', *International Journal of Intercultural Relations*, Vol. 13, No. 3 (1989), pp. 349–370.

98. These three facets are very common elements in a discussion on intercultural competence. See, for example, M. C. Gertsen 'Intercultural Competence and Expatriates', *International Journal of Human Resource Management*, Vol. 1, No. 3 (1990), pp. 341–362; S. Lloyd and C. Haertel 'Intercultural Competencies for Culturally Diverse Work Team', *Journal of Managerial Psychology*, Vol. 25, No. 8 (2010), pp. 845–875.

99. S. Ang, L. Van Dyne, C. Koh, K. Y. Ng, K. J. Templer, C. Tay and N. A. Chandrasekar 'Cultural Intelligence: Its Measurement and Effects on Cultural Judgment and Decision-Making, Cultural Adaptation and Task Performance', *Management & Organization Review*, Vol. 3, No. 3 (2007), pp. 335–371, p. 337.

100. For further details see K.Y. Ng, L. Van Dyne and S. Ang 'Beyond International Experience: The Strategic Role of Cultural Intelligence for Executive Selection in IHRM', in P. Sparrow (eds.) *Handbook of International Human Resource Management: Integrating People, Process, and Context* (Chippenham, UK: Wiley, 2009), pp. 97–114.

101. For more details see J. Bücker and E. Poutsma 'Global Management Competencies: A Theoretical Foundation', *Journal of Managerial Psychology*, Vol. 25, No. 8 (2010), pp. 829–844.

102. T. Jokinen 'Global Leadership Competencies: A Review and Discussion', *Journal of European Industrial Training*, Vol. 29, No. 3 (2005), pp. 199–216.

103. For more details see A. Bird, M. Mendenhall, M. J. Stevens and G. Oddou 'Defining the Content Domain of Intercultural Competence for Global Leaders', *Journal of Managerial Psychology*, Vol. 25, No. 8 (2010), pp. 810–828.

104. J. S. Osland and A. Bird 'Global Leaders as Experts', in W. H. Mobley and E. Weldon (eds.) *Advances in Global Leadership* (London: Elsevier, 2006), Vol. 4, pp. 123–142, p. 123.

105. M. L. Kraimer, S. J. Wayne and R. A. Jaworski 'Sources of Support and Expatriate Performance: The Mediating Role of Expatriate Adjustment', *Personnel Psychology*, Vol. 54, No. 1 (2001), pp. 71–99.

106. For a review and assessment of the U-Curve, see J. S. Black and M. Mendenhall 'The U–Curve Adjustment Hypothesis Revisited: A Review and Theoretical Framework', *Journal of International Business Studies*, Vol. 22, No. 2 (1991), pp. 225–247.

107. H. De Cieri, P. J. Dowling and K. F. Taylor 'The Psychological Impact of Expatriate Relocation on Partners', *International Journal of Human Resource Management*, Vol. 2, No. 3 (1991), pp. 377–414; M. Kauppinen 'Antecedents of Expatriate Adjustment. A Study of Finnish Managers in the United States' (Helsinki School of Economics, 1994).

108. For a critical discussion of the adjustment concept see A. Furnham and S. Bochner *Culture Shock – Psychological Reactions to Unfamiliar Environments* (London: Routledge 1986); C. Ward, Y. Okura, A. Kennedy and T. Kojima 'The U-Curve on Trial: A Longitudinal Study of Psychological and Sociocultural Adjustment during Cross-Cultural Transition', *International Journal of Intercultural Relations*, Vol. 22, No. 3 (1998), pp. 277–291.

109. T. Hippler, C. Brewster and A. Haslberger 'The elephant in the room: The role of time in expatriate adjustment', *International Journal of Human Resource Management*, Vol. 26, No. 16 (2015), pp. 1920–1935.

110. J. S. Black and M. Mendenhall 'The U-Curve Adjustment Hypothesis Revisited: A Review and Theoretical Framework', *Journal of International Business Studies*, Vol. 22, No. 2 (1991), pp. 225–247.

111. For further details see J. S. Black and M. Mendenhall 'The U-Curve Adjustment Hypothesis Revisited: A Review and Theoretical Framework', *Journal of International Business Studies*, Vol. 22, No. 2 (1991), pp. 225–247.

112. For further details see D. C. Thomas and M. B. Lazarova 'Expatriate Adjustment and Performance: A Critical Review', in G. K. Stahl and I. Björkman (eds.) *Handbook of Research in International Human Resource Management* (Cheltenham, UK: Edward Elgar, 2006), pp. 247–264. For further details see M. Festing and M. Maletzky 'Leadership Adjustment of Western Expatriates in Russia – A Structurationalist Perspective', in 10th International Human Resource Management Conference (Santa Fe, NM, 2009); A. Haslberger 'The Complexities of Expatriates Adaption', *Human Resource Management Review*, Vol. 15 (2005), pp. 160–180; T. Hippler and P. Caligiuri 'Revisiting the Construct of Expatriate Adjustment: Implications for Theory and Measurement', in 10th International Human Resource Management Conference (Santa Fe, NM, USA, 2009).

113. For further details see P. Bhaskar-Shrinivas, D. A. Harrison, M. A. Schaffer and D. Luk 'What Have We Learned About Expatriate Adjustment? Answers Accumulated from 23 Years of Research', in Academy of Management Annual Meeting (2004); A. Haslberger 'The Complexities of Expatriates Adaption', *Human Resource Management Review*, Vol. 15 (2005), pp. 160–180; A. Haslberger 'Expatriate Adjustment. A More Nuanced View', in M. Dickmann, C. Brewster and P. Sparrow (eds.) *International HRM: A European Perspective* (New York: Routledge, 2008), pp. 130–149; G. K. Stahl *Internationaler Einsatz von Führungskräften* (München: Oldenbourg, 1998).

114. For further details see W. Searle and C. Ward 'The Prediction of Psychological and Sociocultural Adjustment during Cross-Cultural Transitions', *International Journal of Intercultural Relations*, Vol. 14, No. 4 (1990), pp. 449–464; and J. Li 'When Does Decision Autonomy Increase Expatriate Managers' Adjustment? An Empirical Test', *Academy of Management Journal*, Vol. 51, No. 1 (2008), pp. 45–60.

115. See, for example, the study by R. Takeuchi, J. Shay and J. Li 'When does decision autonomy increase expatriate managers' adjuctment? An empirical test.' *Academy Management Journal*, Vol. 51, No. 1, (2008), pp. 45–60.

116. For further details see G. K. Stahl *Internationaler Einsatz von Führungskräften* (München: Oldenbourg, 1998).

117. For further details see J. S. Black and M. Mendenhall 'The U-Curve Adjustment Hypothesis Revisited: A Review and Theoretical Framework', *Journal of International Business Studies*, Vol. 22, No. 2 (1991), pp. 225–247; Farh and S. Tangirala 'When Does Cross-cultural Motivation Enhance Expatriate Effectiveness? A Multilevel Investigation of the Moderating Roles of Subsidiary Support and Cultural Distance', *Academy of Management Journal*, Vol. 53, No. 5 (2010), pp. 1110–1130; A. M. Osman-Gani and T. Rockstuhl, 'Antecedents and Consequences of Social Network Characteristics for Expatriate Adjustment and Performance in Overseas Assignments: Implications for HRD', *Human Resource Development Review*, Vol. 7, No. 1 (2008), pp. 32–57; and J. W. Slocum 'Individual Differences and Expatriate Assignment Effectiveness: The Case of US-based Korean Expatriates', *Journal of World Business*, Vol. 43, No. 1 (2008), pp. 109–126.

118. See, for example, G. Chen, B. L. Kirkman, K. Kim and C. Farh, 'When does cross-cultural motivation enhance expatriate effectiveness? A multilevel investigation of the moderating roles of cultural distance and support." *Academy of Management Journal*, Vol. 53, No. 5 (2010), pp. 1110–1130.

119. This has, for example, been the subject of a study by K. Kim and J. Slocum, 'Individual differences and expatriate assignment effectiveness: The case of US-based Korean expatriates.' *Journal of World Business*, Vol. 43, No. 1 (2008), pp. 109–126.

120. See, for example, S.Y. Lii and S.Y. Wong 'The Antecedents of Overseas Adjustment and Commitment of Expatriates', *International Journal of Human Resource Management*, Vol. 19, No. 2 (2008), pp. 296–313.

121. See also The Economist Intelligence Unit (eds.) *Up or Out: Next Moves for the Modern Expatriate* (London, New York, Hong Kong, Geneva: *The Economist*, 2010).

122. M. A. Shaffer and D. A. Harrison 'Forgotten Partners of International Assignments: Development and Test of a Model of Spouse Adjustment', *Journal of Applied Psychology*, Vol. 86, No. 2 (2001), pp. 238–254.

123. See www.permitsfoundation.com/home.htm for the home page of the Permits Foundation.

124. S. N. As-Saber, P. J. Dowling and P. W. Liesch 'The Role of Human Resource Management in International Joint Ventures: A Study of Australian-Indian Joint Ventures', *International Journal of Human Resource Management*, Vol. 9, No. 5 (1998), pp. 751–766.

125. S. N. As-Saber, P. J. Dowling and P. W. Liesch 'The Role of Human Resource Management in International Joint Ventures: A Study of Australian-Indian Joint Ventures', *International Journal of Human Resource Management*, Vol. 9, No. 5 (1998), pp. 751–766.

126. For further information on company-specific language issues see Y. Luo and O. Shenkar 'The Multinational Corporation as a Multilingual Community: Language and Organization in a Global Context', *Journal of International Business Studies*, Vol. 37, No. 3 (2006), pp. 321–339; R. Piekkari 'Language Effects in Multinational Corporations: A Review from an International Human Resource Management Perspective', in G. K. Stahl and I. Björkman (eds.) *Handbook of Research in International Human Resource Management* (Cheltenham: Edward Elgar, 2006), pp. 536–550; D. Welch, L. Welch and R. Piekkari 'Speaking in Tongues', *International Studies of Management & Organization*, Vol. 35, No. 1 (2005), pp. 10–27.

127. R. Marschan-Piekkari, D. Welch and L. Welch 'Adopting a Common Corporate Language: IHRM Implications', *International Journal of Human Resource Management*, Vol. 10, No. 3 (1999), pp. 377–390.

128. H. Harris and C. Brewster 'The Coffee-Machine System: How International Selection Really Works', *International Journal of Human Resource Management*, Vol. 10, No. 3 (1999), pp. 488–500.

129. For further details see Z. Tungli and M. Peiperl 'Expatriate Practices in German, Japanese, U.K., and U.S. Multinational Companies: A Comparative Survey of Changes', *Human Resource Management*, Vol. 48, No. 1 (2009), pp. 153–171.

130. I. Torbiörn *Living Abroad: Personal Adjustment and Personnel Policy in the Oversea Setting* (New York: Wiley, 1982).

131. H. L. Willis 'Selection for Employment in Developing Countries', *Personnel Administrator*, Vol. 29, No. 7 (1984), p. 55; K. Y. Au and J. Fukuda 'Boundary Spanning Behaviors of Expatriates', *Journal of World Business*, Vol. 37, No. 4 (2002), pp. 285–296.

132. For further details see M. Mendenhall and G. Oddou 'The Dimensions of Expatriate Acculturation: A Review', *Academy of Management Review*, Vol. 10, No. 1 (1985), pp. 39–47.

133. For further details see Z. Tungli and M. Peiperl 'Expatriate Practices in German, Japanese, UK, and US Multinational Companies: A Comparative Survey of Changes', *Human Resource Management*, Vol. 48, No. 1 (2009), pp. 153–171.

134. For further details see M. R. Hammer, M. J. Bennett and R. Wiseman 'Measuring Intercultural Sensitivity: The Intercultural Development Inventory', *International Journal of Intercultural Relations*, Vol. 27, No. 4 (2003), pp. 421–443.

135. For further details see J. Beneke 'Vorschläge für ein interkulturelles Assessment Center', in J. Beneke (ed.) *Kultur, Mentalität, nationale Identität, Sprachen und Sprachlernen. Arbeitspapiere zur internationalen Unternehmenskommunikation*, Vol. 1, Schriftenreihe der Forschungsstelle für interkulturelle Kommunikation (Hildesheim: Universität Hildesheim, 1992).

136. Brookfield Global Relocation Services (ed.) *Global Mobility Trends Survey Report 2015* (Woodridge, IL, 2015).

137. Brookfield Global Relocation Services (ed.) *Global Mobility Trends Survey Report 2015* (Woodridge, IL, 2015).

138. The Conference Board *Managing Expatriates' Return*, Report Number 1148–98–RR (New York, 1996).

139. Brookfield Global Relocation Services (ed.) *Global Relocation Trends: 2010 Survey Report* (2010), p. 12.

140. N. J. Adler 'Women in International Management: Where are They?', *California Management Review*, Vol. 26, No. 4 (1984), pp. 78–89.

141. For further details see P. M. Caligiuri and W. F. Cascio 'Can We Send Her There? Maximizing the Success of Western Women on Global Assignments', *Journal of World Business*, Vol. 33, No. 4 (1998), pp. 394–416.

142. L. K. Stroh, A. Varma and S. J. Valy-Durbin 'Why Are Women Left at Home: Are They Unwilling to Go on International Assignments?', *Journal of World Business*, Vol. 35, No. 3 (2000), pp. 241–255.

143. P. M. Caligiuri and R. L. Tung 'Comparing the Success of Male and Female Expatriates from a US-based Multi-national Company', *International Journal of Human Resource Management*, Vol. 10, No. 5 (1999), pp. 763–782.

144. I. C. Fischlmayr 'Female Self-Perception as Barrier to International Careers?', *International Journal of Human Resource Management*, Vol. 13, No. 5 (2002), pp. 773–783.

145. W. Mayrhofer and H. Scullion 'Female Expatriates in International Business: Empirical Evidence from the German Clothing Industry', *International Journal of Human Resource Management*, Vol. 13, No. 5 (2002), pp. 815–836.

146. N. K. Napier and S. Taylor 'Experiences of Women Professionals Abroad: Comparisons across Japan, China and Turkey', *International Journal of Human Resource Management*, Vol. 13, No. 5 (2002), pp. 837–851.

147. For further details see G. Insch, N. McIntyre and N. Napier 'The Expatriate Glass Ceiling: The Second Layer of Glass', *Journal of Business Ethics*, Vol. 83, No. 1 (2008), pp. 19–28.

148. For further details see L. K. Stroh, A. Varma and S. J. Valy-Durbin 'Why Are Women Left at Home: Are They Unwilling to Go on International Assignments?', *Journal of World Business*, Vol. 35, No. 3 (2000), pp. 241–255.

149. For further details see P. M. Caligiuri and W. F. Cascio 'Can We Send Her There? Maximizing the Success of Western Women on Global Assignments', *Journal of World Business*, Vol. 33, No. 4 (1998), pp. 394–416.

CHAPTER 6
INTERNATIONAL
PERFORMANCE
MANAGEMENT

Chapter Objectives

The aim of this chapter is to draw together the relevant literature on **performance management** in the international context as it relates to international human resource management (IHRM). The concentration is on the subsidiary context, reflecting the historical bias towards subsidiary management in the international business and performance management literature, although the focus is broadening. The approach is to identify those aspects that require a substantial modification of traditional performance management (especially appraisal criteria, the roles of various actors in the processes, and the processes themselves) that are imposed by international operations. We specifically address the following aspects:

● multinational performance management at the global and local level: considering aspects such as non-comparable data, the volatility of the global environment, the effect of distance, and the level of subsidiary maturity

● performance management as part of a MNE's control system

● factors associated with expatriate performance, including compensation package, task and role, headquarters' support, host environment factors, and cultural adjustment

● performance management of expatriates and non-expatriates, and for those on non-standard tasks and assignments such as commuter and virtual work

● issues related to the performance appraisal of international employees.

INTRODUCTION

The complexities of managing performance in a multinational enterprise's (MNE's) various globally distributed facilities have received a great deal of professional and academic attention in the last decade. As presented in Chapters 2 and 3, diversity in cultures, production and operations, geographical dispersal, and varieties of modes of operations all combine to make performance measurement and the creation of performance management processes that are simultaneously locally relevant and globally comparable a major challenge for human resource management (HRM) practitioners.[1] Monitoring performance and ensuring conformity to agreed-upon standards are significant elements in the managerial control system of a multinational firm; and yet, as Cascio has stated, "the terrain of global performance management systems is largely uncharted".[2]

In this chapter, we differentiate between 'performance management' and 'performance appraisal'. *Performance management* is a process that enables the MNE to evaluate and continuously improve individual, subsidiary unit, and corporate performance against clearly defined, pre-set goals and targets. Figure 6.1 illustrates the major issues, actors, and decision processes related to performance management in the international context. This model will allow us to investigate the complex interaction between local and global contexts for performance and the tasks of the actors, performance criteria, purposes for and timing of performance management as these elements relate to individual and firm outcomes. It provides a convenient starting point for our exploration of the link between the MNE's internationalization strategies, its goals for individual units in terms of contribution to global profitability, and the performance management

FIGURE 6.1 Perspectives, issues, actions, and consequences in MNE performance management

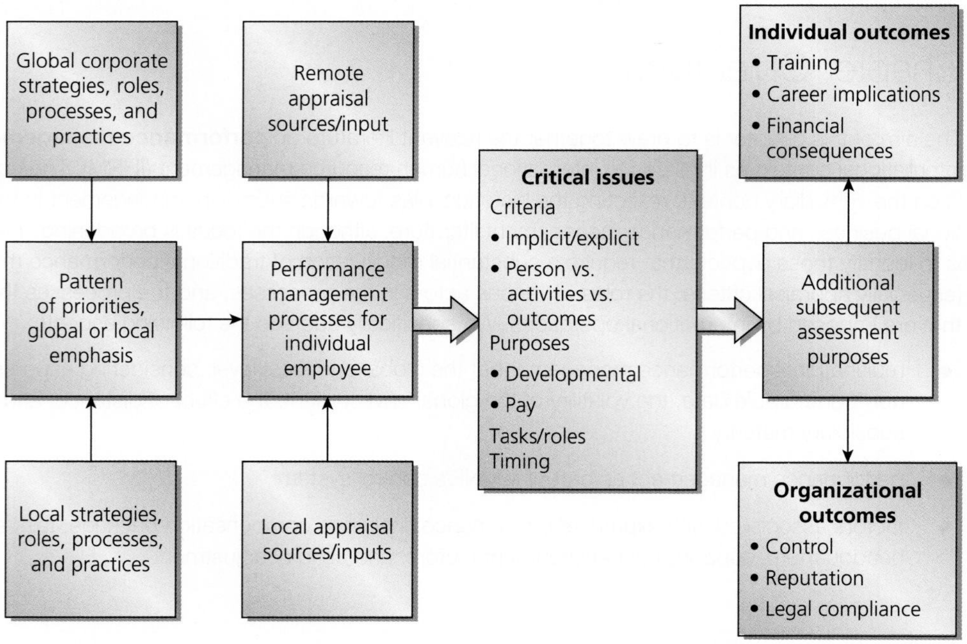

Source: Adapted from A. Engle and P. Dowling, 'State of Origin: Research in Global Performance Management: Progress or a Lost Horizon?', *Conference Proceeding of the VIIIth World Congress of the International Federation of Scholarly Associations of Management*, Berlin, September, 2006.

of individual employees, whether PCN, TCN, or HCN. The aspects of these relationships are critical as an individual's performance is *appraised* (or evaluated) according to expectations of appropriate outcomes and behavior that contribute to organizational goal attainment.

MULTINATIONAL PERFORMANCE MANAGEMENT

While a given firm's general strategic position may vary[3] (depending on, for instance, its size, industry, and geographic dispersal), a multinational makes strategic choices based on economic and political imperatives. Within this context, as indicated in Figure 6.1, the MNE has specific expectations for each of its foreign subsidiaries, co-operative ventures, and other forms of operation modes, in terms of market performance and contribution to total profits and competitiveness. When evaluating subsidiary performance against these expectations, however, it is important to recognize various constraints that may affect goal attainment. These include the following five constraints outlined below.

Whole vs. part

First, it is important to appreciate that, by its very nature, the MNE is a single entity that faces a global environment, which means that it simultaneously confronts differing national environments. Integration and control imperatives often place the multinational in the position where it decides that *the good of the whole* (i.e. the entire MNE) is more important than one subsidiary's short-term profitability. An example is provided by Pucik,[4] where a multinational establishes an operation in a particular market where its main global competitor has a dominant position. The main objective of entering the market may be to challenge the competitor's cash flow with aggressive pricing policies. Pucik explains that:

> The balance sheet of this particular subsidiary might be continually in the red, but this strategy, by tying up the competitor's resources, may allow substantially higher returns in another market. The difficulties in quantifying such a global strategy in terms of the usual return-on-investment objectives are obvious.

Another situation is where the MNE establishes a joint venture in a particular market in order to have a presence there, even though it has low expectations in the short term and may provide a relatively low level of resources to the venture. Therefore, the consequences of such global decisions for subsidiary management must be taken into consideration when considering the issue of performance appraisal of the senior managers of this joint venture.

Non-comparable data

A second key constraint is that frequently the data obtained from subsidiaries may be neither easily interpretable nor reliable. The following examples illustrate this point:[5]

> Sales in Brazil may be skyrocketing, but there are reports that the Brazilian government may impose tough new exchange controls within a year, thus making it difficult for the multinational to repatriate profits. Does this mean that the MNE is performing effectively? Is the subsidiary performing effectively? Are the senior managers of the subsidiary performing effectively?
>
> Sales in Peru may be booming, but headquarters management was unaware that under Peruvian accounting rules, sales on consignment are counted as firm sales. How should the headquarters accounting system handle these sales relative to sales from other subsidiaries, which do not consider sales on consignment as firm sales?

As Garland *et al.*[6] explain, physical measures of performance may be easier to interpret than in the above examples, but difficulties may still arise. For instance, notions of what constitutes adequate quality control checks can vary widely from one country to another, import tariffs can distort pricing schedules, or a dock strike in one country can unexpectedly delay supply of necessary components to a manufacturing plant in another country. Further, local labor laws may require close to full employment at plants that are producing below capacity. These factors can make an objective appraisal of subsidiary performance problematic, which in turn complicates the task of appraising the performance of individual subsidiary managers.

Volatility in the global business environment

A third factor that can impact on the performance of a subsidiary is the occurrence of volatility and turbulence in the global business environment. This volatility may require that long-term goals be flexible in order to respond to potential market contingencies. According to Pucik,[7] an inflexible approach may mean that subsidiaries could be pursuing strategies that no longer fit the new environment. Consider, for example, the impact on international business of major events in the past three decades or so, such as: the collapse of communist rule in the late 1980s in Eastern Europe and the former Soviet Union; the adoption of the Euro (€) as the single currency by most of the European Union (EU) countries; Chinese market reforms; the Severe Acute Respiratory Syndrome (SARS) and bird flu epidemics; the spread of international terrorism; the Gulf Wars; rising oil prices; high-profile corporate collapses; the adoption of international accounting standards (IAS); the Indian Ocean tsunami disaster in 2004; government cutbacks and austerity measures associated with the global financial crisis that began in 2008; and the Arab Spring political disturbances in 2011.

Each of these events has had profound implications for the global and local strategies of multinationals. Because subsidiaries operate under such volatility and fluctuation, they must tailor long-term goals to the specific situation in a given market. Problems arise when subsidiary managers perceive that goals and deadlines set by a distant headquarters strategy team are unrealistic and inflexible due to a failure to take into account local conditions that change as a result of a volatile environment. Obviously, involving regional and subsidiary managers in strategic planning assists in managing this perception.

Separation by time and distance

A fourth factor that can impact on the performance of a subsidiary is the effect of separation by time and distance. Judgements concerning the congruence between the MNE and local subsidiary activities are further complicated by the physical distances involved, time-zone differences, the frequency of contact between the corporate head-office staff and subsidiary management, and the cost of the reporting system.[8] Developments in sophisticated worldwide communications systems such as increasingly advanced video-conference facilities do not fully substitute for 'face-to-face' contacts between subsidiary managers and corporate staff. In some areas, the telecommunications system may be underdeveloped or impacted by an unreliable power grid and it may be necessary to meet personally with a manager and their team to fully understand the problems that these local managers must deal with. For this reason, many MNE corporate managers spend a considerable amount of time traveling in order to meet expatriate and local managers in foreign locations. It is then possible for HR corporate staff, when designing performance management systems, to more accurately account for the influence of country-specific factors.

The growing use of web-based Human Resource Information System (HRIS) platforms is in part a response to the separations of time, distance, and culture experienced by multinational firms[9]. These strategies may be driven by the complexity and inherent uncertainty of global performance and a sense that successfully competing in the global marketplace will require increased efficiency of operations. However, the potential of these technical systems to control and co-ordinate activities and processes within the MNE may be limited by unspoken or ill-articulated roles, processes, practices, criteria, and purposes.[10]

Variable levels of maturity across markets: the need for relevant comparative data

A final factor influencing the performance of a subsidiary is the variable level of maturity across markets. According to Pucik,[11] without the supporting infrastructure of the parent, market development in foreign subsidiaries is generally slower and more difficult to achieve than at home, where established brands can support new products and new business areas can be cross-subsidized by other divisions. As a result, more time may be needed to achieve results than is customary in a domestic market, and this fact ought to be recognized in the performance management process. Further, variations in customs and work practices between the parent country and the **foreign subsidiary** need to be considered. For example:

> One does not fire a Mexican manager because worker productivity is half the American average. In Mexico, that would mean that this manager is working at a level three or four times as high as the average Mexican industrial plant. Here we need relevant comparative data, not absolute numbers; our harassed Mexican manager has to live with Mexican constraints, not European or American ones, and these can be very different. The way we measure worker productivity is exactly the same, but the numbers come out differently because of that environmental difference.[12]

In summary, there are a number of significant constraints that must be taken into account when considering foreign subsidiary performance.[13] Because performance measurement is primarily based on strategic factors, it affects the appraisal and success of the subsidiary's chief executive and senior management team most directly.[14]

CONTROL AND PERFORMANCE MANAGEMENT

Although it is not often described as such, performance management is a part of a multinational's control system because performance targets are a part of formal control. Through formal control mechanisms and communication through the feedback and appraisal aspects, performance management also contributes to shaping corporate culture, both formally and informally,[15] thereby acting as an informal control mechanism as well as part of the **bureaucratic control system**. Employees are rewarded for adopting appropriate work behaviors and this in turn reinforces normative control. Figure 6.2 illustrates the performance-behavior-outcomes linkage. It is through formal and informal control mechanisms that the MNE achieves the

FIGURE 6.2 **MNE control and performance**

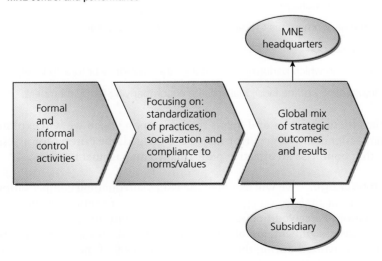

consistency, co-ordination, and compliance of desired behavior and outcomes to implement its global strategy. These behaviors and outcomes are expected at all levels and areas – at headquarters as well as in subsidiary operations.

In a sense, by adopting a performance management approach, MNEs are drawing on a number of HRM activities to realize performance goals set during the performance appraisal process. Its proponents argue, somewhat convincingly, that effective performance management is beneficial to both the individual and the firm. Strong goal setting and appraisal are key elements of an individual performance management system that also may include training and development, and performance-related pay.[16]

PERFORMANCE MANAGEMENT OF INTERNATIONAL EMPLOYEES

Having considered the broader context, we now turn our attention to individual performance management. Consistent with our general approach, we use the term 'expatriate' to cover parent-country nationals (PCNs), third-country nationals (TCNs), and those host-country nationals (HCNs) on assignment to headquarters. We also address performance management issues relating to those on non-standard and short-term assignments (such as commuter and virtual) and non-expatriates (e.g. international business travelers). Given the broad scope, and the fact that often issues are common to both expatriates and non-expatriates, we use the term 'international employees' when all these various groups are involved.

As discussed in Chapter 5, international assignments vary in terms of the duration and scope of physical relocation required. That is, from traditional expatriate assignments when expatriates and, usually, their family members relocate, to virtual assignments where no physical relocation by employees or their families is required. When attempting to manage the performance of staff working across the multinational, it is essential to consider all these variables in relation to the nature of the international assignment. The following sections also identify some performance management issues associated with both expatriate and non-expatriate international assignments.

Expatriate performance management

As noted in Chapter 5, expatriation remains a key dimension of MNE and performance. When attempting to determine expatriate performance, it is important to consider the impact of the following variables and their interrelationship:

- the compensation package
- the task – the assignment task variables and role of the expatriate
- headquarters' support
- the environment in which performance occurs – the subsidiary or foreign facility
- cultural adjustment – of the individual and the accompanying family members.

Figure 6.3 depicts these variables and forms the basis upon which we will explore the nature of the international assignment, how performance is managed, the criteria for assessment, and the other elements that comprise an effective performance management system.

Compensation package.   We will examine the issues surrounding compensation in Chapter 8. However, it is essential that we recognize the importance of **remuneration** and reward in the performance equation. Perceived financial benefits, along with the progression potential associated with an overseas assignment, are often important motives for accepting the posting. If these expectations are not realized during the assignment, the level of motivation and commitment is likely to decrease, thus affecting performance.

FIGURE 6.3 Variables affecting expatriate performance

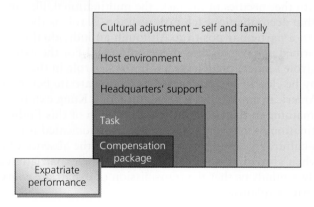

Task. As outlined earlier, expatriates are assigned to foreign operations to fulfil specific tasks. Hays[17] identified four such tasks:

- The *chief executive officer*, or subsidiary manager, who oversees and directs the entire foreign operation.

- The *structure reproducer*, who carries the assignment of building or reproducing in a foreign subsidiary a structure similar to that which he or she knows from another part of the company. He or she could be building a marketing framework, implementing an accounting and financial reporting system, or establishing a production plant, for example.

- The *troubleshooter*, who is sent to a foreign subsidiary to analyze and solve a particular operational problem.

- The *operative*, whose assignment is to perform functional job tasks in an existing operational structure, in generally lower-level, supervisory positions.

Interesting presentations on executive performance management have recently been provided as part of a wider discussion of 'corporate governance'. Issues of performance criteria (an overreliance on 'shareholder value' models of executive performance) and the evolving roles, responsibilities, and institutional safeguards to assure a complete, accurate, and unbiased assessment of top-level managers are widely cited for this critical task group.[18]

In a recent review of cross-cultural performance management systems, Caligiuri identifies four basic types of international assignments: **'technical assignments'** – short-term knowledge transference activities, said to make up 5 to 10 per cent of expatriate assignments; **'developmental assignments'** – focusing on in-country performance and the acquisition of local or regional understanding by the assignee, said to make up 5 to 10 per cent of assignments; **'strategic assignments'** – high-profile activities that focus on developing a balanced global perspective, said to make up 10 to 15 per cent of assignments; and **'functional assignments'** – described as more enduring assignments with local employees that involve the two-way transfer of existing processes and practices, said to make up between 55 and 80 per cent of assignments.[19] Accurately assessing performance in the tasks inherent in technical and functional assignments may well involve a limited number of sources and focus on more concrete output criteria (projects completed, contracts signed, etc.). Assessing progress in developmental and strategic assignments, given their more complex, subjective tasks, is likely to involve a wider variety of local and global participants and perspectives.[20]

Task variables are generally considered to be more under a multinational's control than environmental factors. Because of this relative control, task variables can be better assessed and more easily changed, depending, of course, on the level of position and the nature of the task assignment. Along with the specifics of the task, the multinational, like any other organization, determines the role that accompanies each task position. A role is the organized set of behaviors that is assigned to a particular position. Although an individual may affect how a role is interpreted and performed, the role itself is predetermined.[21] For the expatriate (role recipient), the parent company (role sender) predetermines his or her role in the foreign assignment, and role expectations may be clearly communicated to the expatriate before departure. Black and Porter[22] found that American expatriates working in Hong Kong exhibited similar managerial behavior to those remaining in the USA. In their discussion of this finding, these authors suggest that the US multinationals involved in this study communicated role expectations by omitting to provide cross-cultural training before departure. In the absence of incentives to modify their role behavior when abroad, it is not surprising that the expatriates concerned performed as they did. This study reminds us that the transmission of expatriate role conception is culturally bound. As Torbiörn[23] explains:

> The content of the managerial role, as perceived by both the individual manager and the parent company, is affected by organizational norms, in terms of parent-company expectations of the manager, and by the set of cultural norms that the manager holds in relation to other cultural and organizational norms that may be represented by other role senders. Organizational and cultural norms thus interactively determine the role content of the manager.

The difficulty this presents for the expatriate manager is that *the role is defined in one country but performed in another*. That is, the cultural norms regarding the set of behaviors that define 'a manager in the USA' may not be the same as those considered appropriate for a manager's role in an important emerging economy such as Indonesia.

Communication of role conception from the multinational to the expatriate is indicated by the straight arrows in Figures 6.4 and 6.5. Role conception is also communicated to the role recipient by host-country stakeholders (e.g. subsidiary employees, host-government officials, customers, suppliers, etc.) as shown by the dashed arrows. This, however, crosses a cultural boundary. Role behavior provides the feedback loop, again at two levels: the parent and the host-country stakeholders. Trying to perform to differing expectations may cause role conflict. If PCN managers adapt their role behavior according to the role conception communicated in the host environment, it may conflict with that predetermined at headquarters. Janssens'[24] study of expatriate performance indicated that role conflict is likely to result in situations where the international manager has an understanding of the host-country culture and realizes that the use of headquarters' procedures or actions may lead to ineffective management. She postulates that the higher the degree of intercultural interaction, the more problems the expatriate has with role conflict.

FIGURE 6.4 **PCN role conception**

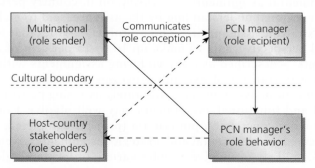

Source: Adapted from I. Torbiörn, 'The Structure of Managerial Roles in Cross-cultural Settings', *International Studies of Management & Organization*, Vol. 15, No. 1 (1985), p. 60. Reproduced with permission.

FIGURE 6.5 TCN role conception

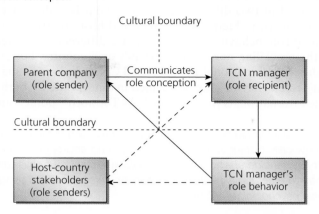

Source: Adapted from I. Torbiörn, 'The Structure of Managerial Roles in Cross-cultural Settings', *International Studies of Management & Organization*, Vol. 15, No. 1 (1985), p. 60. Reproduced with permission.

From the perspective of headquarters, commitment to the parent is perceived as important, given the part that the PCN plays in transferring know-how and 'the preferred way of doing things' into the subsidiary. This helps to explain the preference for using headquarters' standards in expatriate performance appraisal as a control mechanism.[25] If the PCN is perceived to identify too closely with host-subsidiary concerns (the term 'going native' has, in the past, often been used to describe this perception), he or she may be recalled. Some MNEs will restrict the length of stay to no more than three years to contain the possibility of PCN identification with local concerns. Because of the importance given to the parent as role sender in performance appraisal, a PCN may elect to ignore role communication sent from the host-country stakeholders if they consider that performance appraisal is determined by how role behavior conforms to headquarters' expectations. After all, the expatriate's career is with the parent firm, not the host subsidiary.

Some empirical support for such a view comes from work by Gregersen and Black[26] in their study of US expatriate retention and dual commitments (to the parent and the local organizations). They found, at the correlational level, commitment to the parent and to the local operation were both positively related to intent to stay. However, "regression analysis indicated that when controlling for certain demographic and attitudinal variables, commitment to the parent company appears to be slightly more relevant to expatriates' intention to stay". Role conflict was found to affect commitment to the parent company, but was unrelated to commitment to the host company. Another intervening variable may be that of role autonomy. For example, job discretion emerged as an important aspect from a survey of 115 US expatriates working in various countries by Birdseye and Hill.[27] They found that: "Foreign work methods may be more structured than their American counterparts (perhaps more procedures and protocols) and that individuals have less discretion in how they approach tasks and problems". These authors conclude that individuals are likely to blame this lack of discretion on the organization, the job, and the location – in that order. A similar finding emerged from an earlier study of US domestic and international relocation by Feldman and Tompson.[28] The degree of change in job duties was positively related to adjustment, while the degree of change in the organization was negatively related to adjustment. Thus, role conflict and role autonomy appear to be important elements in job satisfaction and task performance.

Role clarity emerged as an important variable in a meta-analysis of expatriate adjustment and performance. Integrating studies on expatriate adjustment, the authors[29] found that:

role clarity and work adjustment was the second largest effect [. . .] suggesting that the uncertainty regarding objectives, goals, and role requirements is the strongest stressor in expatriates' overseas work environments. In addition, role clarity also has a moderate potential to spill over and minimize non-work difficulties.

Role expectations are likely to be more complex for the TCN than the PCN, as the role is defined by and performed in two different countries. That is, role conception crosses two cultural boundaries, as shown in Figure 6.5. Parent and host-country role senders may have differing expectations of role behavior that, in turn, are different to the accepted managerial behavior defined by the prevailing norms in the TCN's own country. For example, a US manager working for a Dutch multinational posted as a TCN in Indonesia may face added difficulties. The American's role behavior may be deemed inappropriate by both the parent (Dutch multinational) and the host nationals (Indonesians). As Torbiörn[30] points out:

> *The task of the PCN manager could be described as one of realizing the expectations of a psychologically close, but physically distant stakeholder [parent] in an environment containing other role senders [host-country stakeholders] who are psychologically distant, but physically close [. . .]. The TCN manager must try to meet the expectations of role senders who are all psychologically distant in a context that is also psychologically distant.*

However, as you may recall from our discussion of the rationale for using TCNs, often the country of assignment is perceived by headquarters as culturally close and this may be an important factor which influences the decision to use a TCN (e.g. a German multinational decides to transfer a Canadian into the USA, rather than a German). As there are very few studies that specifically examine TCN performance management issues,[31] we can only assume that many of the aspects relating to PCNs discussed above will apply to the TCN situation. An American manager working in Indonesia, for instance, whether as a PCN or TCN, may encounter lack of job discretion – with perhaps the same effect in terms of performance – depending on the strength of other intervening variables. For example, differing role senders may exacerbate the situation through conflicting role expectations.

The preceding discussion demonstrates the importance of considering the role that accompanies each task position. Given that task performance is a core component of expatriate appraisal, it is also necessary to recognize that it does not occur in isolation. Many individuals and firms rank job ability as the primary ingredient relating to their expected probability of success in the international assignment, as discussed in Chapter 5. Certain types of tasks, however, require significantly more interaction with host-country stakeholders. Thus, the task variables should not be evaluated in isolation from the subsidiary environment context.

Another factor relating to task variables that warrants consideration is the similarity of the job the individual is assigned abroad to the job that they held domestically. Some types of tasks require an individual to operate within a given structure, while other tasks demand the creation of the structure. Individuals vary greatly in their ability to conceive and implement a system, and their tolerance for lack of structure and ambiguity. Some MNEs have experienced failure abroad because they assumed that an individual could be effective in setting up a structure, such as a marketing system, based on evidence of good performance within the existing marketing structure in the domestic corporation.[32]

Headquarters' support.   The expatriate assignment differs from a domestic relocation as it involves the transfer of the individual (and possibly accompanying family members) into a foreign environment, outside their normal cultural comfort zones. The individual's primary motivation for accepting the assignment may be career- or finance-orientated, but this is often mixed with a genuine feeling of loyalty and commitment to the sending organization. As mentioned previously, the process of adjustment to the foreign location typically produces, to varying degrees, a range of emotional and psychological reactions to unfamiliar situations encountered over the period of the stay in the host country. The level of headquarters' support provided to the individual and the family is an important performance variable.

Host environment.   The environment has an impact on any job, but it becomes of primary importance with regard to expatriate management. According to Gregersen *et al.*,[33] the international context – with its differing societal, legal, economic, technical, and physical demands – can be a major determinant of expatriate performance. Consequently, expatriate performance should be placed within its international as well as its organizational context. Therefore, the five major constraints identified above in terms of multinational strategy and goal setting for the subsidiary are important considerations for expatriate performance management.

The type of operation to which the expatriate is assigned is important. For instance, it may be relatively easier to perform in a wholly owned subsidiary than in a joint venture with a state-owned enterprise in China. Conflicting goals between the parent companies are a common problem within international joint ventures (IJVs) and can make the expatriate's job more difficult. An expatriate IJV manager may have difficulty trying to serve two masters and experience a high level of uncertainty regarding the effect of differing goal expectations for the IJV upon their performance appraisal. Similarly, the stage of the international business will influence the success of the expatriate. An expatriate overseeing the establishment of a new facility in a foreign country, especially in a developing or emerging market, will face different challenges and constraints to an expatriate manager who is posted into an established operation.

Cultural adjustment.   The process of cultural adjustment may be a critical determinant of expatriate job performance. Indeed, much of the literature reviewed in our discussion of the cause of expatriate 'failure' covers the process of adjustment. It is likely that expatriates and their families will have some difficulty adjusting to a new environment, and this will impact on the manager's work performance. The dilemma is that adjustment to a foreign culture is multi-faceted, and individuals vary in terms of their reactions and coping behaviors. Determining the relevance of adjustment to the new environment when assessing expatriate work performance may be problematical.

The five variables – compensation package, task, headquarters' support, host environment, and cultural adjustment – reviewed above, and shown in Figure 6.3, are not mutually exclusive but interact in a way that has significant implications for the appraisal of international employees' performance. Designers and users of performance management systems need to be conscious of, and responsive to, the impact of these variables.[34]

A cross-cultural context for performance management

As noted in Figure 6.1, corporate and local strategies and role expectations create much of the potential for complexity and conflict in the definitions underlying criteria, processes, and standards that make up performance management. Regional and national institutional, regulatory, and historical contexts can impact the character of the criteria selected, task definitions, the timing, and even the purposes of performance management. We present three examples of the relationship between national context and firm-level practices. Chinese performance management systems have been described as personalized, network-driven, focused on pay decision consequences, often implicit or under-spoken, and largely historical and critical in nature.[35]

In France, legal and cultural factors combine to create a performance management system characterized by administrators with a high level of legal expertise – even though France's labor laws allow some flexibility in assessing performance within a merit-based and non-discriminatory framework. It is seen as a system linked to motivation and developing intellectual capital via coaching and competency-based assessments, with tasks often facilitated by the acceptance of advanced forms of technology. Centralization in processes, implicit or non-transparent procedures, a propensity to have more or less favorable impressions of individuals based on the prestige of their previous university-corporate-governmental experiences, and a strong link between assessment and hierarchical remuneration may be seen to result from widely held cultural norms and values within certain segments of French society.[36] As with any national assessment, care must be taken not to overgeneralize. Practices in France vary by size of the firm – with larger firms being more open to a wider variety of performance management practices and criteria than smaller firms – as well as by industry, level of internationalization, and occupational level of employee.[37]

By contrast, and with the same caveats against overgeneralization, performance management in Germany must adjust to a much more precisely delineated set of legal and institutional factors. A strong tradition of **collective bargaining** – be it on the plant, firm, or industry level – plant level co-determination and a centuries-old tradition of vocational training all contribute to performance management systems characterized by a high level of worker input via works councils, consensus-building processes and activities, long-term career focus, value placed on flexibility in task capability to enhance long-term job security, and high value placed on specialized technical knowledge.[38] Processes tend to be more consensual, explicit, ongoing, and informal in a day-to-day setting, yet roles, standards, criteria, purposes, schedules, and consequences are explicitly formalized and regulated via co-determination. Performance-based pay as a consequence or outcome of the performance management system has been much slower to gain widespread acceptance among German firms. This may be due to the use of short-term performance criteria often applied to trigger British and US models of performance-based pay. German firms tend to focus on linking performance management results to drive long-term training and development activities.[39]

Performance management of non-expatriates

In Chapter 5, non-expatriates (i.e. the international business traveler, or 'frequent flyer') were described as employees whose work involved international travel but who were not considered international assignees because they did not relocate to another country. Performance management issues may also impact upon the performance of another group: commuters. This is a form of non-standard assignment outlined in Chapter 5 where the person does not completely relocate but commutes between their home country and their office in another country. An example would be an executive who considers 'home' to be a suburb of London, but who, from Monday morning to Friday night, lives and works in Germany while the family remains in London.[40] In Chapter 5 we also discussed the trend towards the use of virtual assignments to overcome staff immobility. Instead of moving into the host environment, the person manages the international position from the home country using a combination of regular communication link-ups and frequent trips to the foreign location.

As yet, little is really known about the implications of such international business travel – whether as part of a non-standard assignment or as a component of a specific job – for individual performance. However, it is possible to suggest some performance management challenges:

- How to determine performance criteria and goals related to the effective conduct of non-standard assignments, especially **virtual assignees**. As indicated in Figure 6.1, agreement on performance criteria is an important component of the performance management process. This requires the link between each employee's performance and the achievement of the MNE's strategic goals and objectives to be clearly established and understood. However, as the role conceptions in Figures 6.4 and 6.5 show, shared conceptions of roles and expectations are complicated by the number of cultures and organizational contexts involved. With virtual assignees, monitoring and evaluating a physically and geographically distant group of employees is problematical. It is 'management by remote control'. In addition, the virtual assignee may be faced with dual goals – that of the domestically located job and the virtual work group. Therefore, the perennial challenge of effectively communicating the strategic links between the assignee's performance and organizational strategy is likely to be magnified.[41]

- An understanding of the criteria for performance is generally advocated as a highly participative process between supervisor and employee.[42] As with the traditional expatriate assignment, work conducted through non-standard assignments and international travel is still conducted across cultural and national boundaries, and thereby subject to cultural differences in norms about acceptable or preferred levels of participation.

- Isolating the international dimensions of job performance might not be as straightforward as in traditional expatriate assignments. It may depend on the level of difficulty inherent in the performance criteria set and how individual performance levels are determined.

- Outstanding performance, under performance or failure in non-expatriate and non-standard assignments will challenge the performance appraisal process.

- As we shall explore in a later section of this chapter, regular feedback on progress towards those performance goals is most usually provided through the performance appraisal activity. Performance feedback for assignees will only be relevant if it reflects the international contexts in which it is performed.[43] Those enduring concerns of who conducts performance appraisals, how and based on what performance data, may be intensified when it involves increasing numbers of others outside head office with whom the assignee is working.

- One key function of performance appraisal feedback is that it provides opportunities to improve performance by identifying performance gaps that might be eliminated with training and development. Cross-cultural awareness and competence training will still be relevant for non-expatriates. However, detailed analysis and study of other pre-departure and ongoing training that might be required for non-expatriate assignments is yet to be conducted.

- Employee expectations about rewards for performance and as elements of their working conditions, together with motivation are important aspects of individual performance. In MNEs, the management of links between performance and rewards is already complex, due to the specialized local knowledge required across multiple employment and legal environments. The challenges for IHRM are to determine what to reward when dealing with non-expatriate assignments, and the way compensation for each type of international assignment fits with the multinational's global compensation strategy.

- The impact of non-standard assignments on host-country national co-workers should also be considered – particularly in terms of the impact on these staff of international business travelers and commuters who 'drop in, drop out'.

PERFORMANCE APPRAISAL OF INTERNATIONAL EMPLOYEES

Now that we have an understanding of the variables likely to influence performance, including the nature of the international assignment being performed, we can discuss the criteria by which performance is to be appraised (or evaluated – the terms are used interchangeably in the relevant literature). We note that the focus on expatriate management is also reflected in the literature about the performance appraisal of international staff, and much of the following discussion reflects that emphasis. However, aspects of expatriate performance appraisal are also relevant to the appraisal of non-expatriates and these, along with the aspects that distinguish between the two categories of international staff, will be highlighted.

As shown in Figure 6.1, individual performance management involves a set of decisions on the dimensions and level of performance criteria, task and role definitions, and the timing of the formal and informal aspects of the appraisal. Traditionally, it comprises a formal process of goal setting, performance appraisal, and feedback. Data from this process is often used to determine pay and promotion, and training and development requirements. MNE goals influence the individual's salient task set, against which job goals and standards are established and measured. There are differences in the way this process is handled within MNEs. For example, in Germany and Sweden it is common for employees to have input into job goal setting, whereas in other countries such as the USA job goals tend to be assigned.[44] In addition, the type and length of assignment appears to influence how performance management is handled. For example, a study of Finnish firms revealed that those on short-term assignments were treated the same as any other employee in the company, and there was more flexibility in the timing of the performance review for those assigned to projects.[45]

Performance criteria

The global firm's ability to measure an employee's individual contribution to performance and to assess the aggregate contribution of human capital to strategic progress is a complex and timely topic in organizational studies.[46] Goals tend to be translated into performance appraisal criteria so specificity and measurability issues are important aspects, and we need to recognize that hard, soft, and contextual goals are often used as the basis for performance criteria. *Hard goals* are objective, quantifiable, and can be directly measured – such as return-on-investment (ROI), market share, and so on. *Soft goals* tend to be relationship- or trait-based, such as leadership style or interpersonal skills. *Contextual goals* attempt to take into consideration factors that result from the situation in which performance occurs. For example, MNEs commonly use arbitrary transfer pricing and other financial tools for transactions between subsidiaries to minimize foreign-exchange risk exposure and tax expenditures. Another consideration is that all financial figures are generally subject to the problem of currency conversion, including sales and cash positions. Further complications could arise because some host governments (usually emerging economies) may decide to place restrictions on repatriation of profits and currency conversion. The nature of the international monetary system and local accounting differences may also preclude an accurate measurement of results. The dilemma this poses is that the use of transfer pricing and other financial tools is necessary because of the complexity of the international environment. Multinationals cannot allow subsidiaries to become autonomous in financial management terms and place controls on subsidiary managers. Thus, the financial results recorded for any particular subsidiary do not always accurately reflect its contribution to the achievements of the MNE as a whole. Therefore, such results should not be used as a primary input in performance appraisal.[47] For this reason, a performance management approach is now advocated, rather than traditional performance appraisal, as it allows for clarification of goals and expectations of performance against those goals.

Janssens[48] suggests that performance appraisal of subsidiary managers against hard criteria is often supplemented by frequent visits by headquarters staff and meetings with senior managers from the parent company. Soft criteria can be used to complement hard goals, and take into account areas that are difficult to quantify such as leadership skills, but their appraisal is somewhat subjective and, in the context of both expatriate and non-expatriate assignments, more complicated due to cultural exchanges and clashes. However, relying on hard criteria such as financial data to evaluate how well a manager operates a foreign subsidiary does not consider the way results are obtained and the behaviors used to obtain these results.[49] Concern with questionable ethical practices led to the enactment of the US Foreign Corrupt Practices Act (FCPA), which may prompt an increased use of behavioral as well as results data to appraise the performance of managers in foreign subsidiaries.[50] However, an appraisal system that uses hard, soft, and contextual criteria builds upon the strengths of each while minimizing their disadvantages.[51] Using multiple criteria wherever possible is therefore recommended in the relevant literature. In addition, job analysis must, as Harvey[52] suggests, generate criteria that adequately capture the nature of international work as opposed to the domestic context, in order to provide valid appraisal information.

Who conducts the performance appraisal?

Another issue is who conducts the performance appraisal. Typically, employees are appraised by their immediate superiors, and this can pose problems for subsidiary chief executive officers (or senior managers). They work in countries geographically distant, yet are evaluated by superiors back at headquarters who are not in a position to see on a day-to-day basis how the expatriate performs in the particular situation. Consequently, subsidiary managers tend to be assessed according to subsidiary performance, with a reliance on hard criteria similar to that applied to heads of domestic units or divisions. Of course, there is a danger that a subsidiary manager will take decisions and implement local strategies that favor short-term performance to the detriment of longer-term organizational goals.

Appraisal of other employees is likely to be conducted by the subsidiary's Chief Executive Officer, or the immediate host-country supervisor, depending upon the nature and level of the position concerned. [53] With regard to expatriate performance appraisal, host-country managers may have a clearer picture of expatriate performance and can take into consideration contextual criteria. However, they may have culturally bound biases (e.g. about role behavior) and lack an appreciation of the impact of the expatriate's performance in the broader organizational context. As the IHRM in Action Case 6.1 illustrates, some expatriates may prefer to have parent-company evaluators, given that their future career progression may depend on how the appraisal data are utilized back at headquarters. This may be especially so in cases where foreign operations are relatively less important than, say, domestic US operations.[54] Others may prefer a host-country appraisal if they perceive it as a more accurate reflection of their performance.

Multiple raters are sometimes used in the domestic context – e.g. the 360-degree feedback process. It has been argued that, given the cross-cultural complexity of the foreign assignment, a team of evaluators should be used for performance appraisal. For example, Gregersen *et al.*[55] found that most firms (81 per cent) in their survey of HR directors in 58 US multinationals used more than one rater when assessing expatriate performance. The immediate superior (in either the home or host country), the expatriate as self-rater, and the HR manager (either home or host-country based) were commonly used as multiple evaluators of US expatriate performance. The *2010 Brookfield Global Relocation Trends Survey Report* found that 35 per cent of respondents reported using performance reviews in the host country, 27 per cent used reviews in both host and home countries, and 10 per cent used performance reviews in the home country.[56] For the virtual assignment situation, the use of multiple appraisers would most likely be the most accurate way to determine performance. However, the availability of knowledgeable, trained raters may constrain the approach taken in the international context.

Standardized or customized performance appraisal forms

Domestic firms commonly design performance appraisal forms for each job category, particularly those using a traditional performance appraisal approach rather than performance management. Such standardization assists in the collection of accurate performance data on which HR decisions can be made and allows for cross-employee comparisons. The question often posed is: should these standardized forms be adapted when used for appraising international managers? As Gregersen *et al.*[57] argue:

In principle, performance appraisal systems are designed carefully and often presumed to be static. Valid reasons exist for maintaining standard, traditionally used appraisals (e.g., when the system has been tested, has identified baselines, and reduces future development costs). These reasons are valid as long as the context of the performance does not change. In the expatriate setting, however, the performance context does change, and sometimes it changes dramatically. Given a global context, previous testing and established baselines grounded in domestic situations can become meaningless.

Despite this, they found that, in their sample of US firms, 76 per cent used the same standardized appraisal forms for expatriate appraisal.[58] Employees who relocate within the multinational, and non-expatriate assignees who also cross cultural boundaries in their performance context, do not always feel headquarters-based appraisal forms allow for consideration of the critical success factors of their performance like cross-cultural competence.[59]

IHRM in Action Case 6.1
A rainy expatriate performance appraisal

Richard Hoffman, a Québécois chemical engineer working for a Canadian-based energy firm, was given a three-year expatriate assignment in Venezuela as a technical liaison and environmental protection project manager. His local project supervisor was Jean, a French engineer who had lived in French Guiana and then Venezuela for over 20 years. Richard thought that, as a Francophone from Quebec, he and Jean would be able to build a quick working relationship. Rich sent Jean an early email (in French, and not the usual corporate English) containing what he thought of as the five most significant goals associated with his assignment – similar to the management-by-objectives section of the more or less standard performance appraisal forms he had filled out for years during earlier assignments in Edmonton, Toronto and at corporate headquarters in Montreal. After several months with no response from Jean, Richard caught Jean in the hallway between meetings and asked him about the email and his progress to date. "Don't worry about that", Jean responded blandly. "Just keep working to the deadlines and I will check with your co-workers and the other project managers on your work. Where did you go to engineering school, by the way?".

Richard waited another six months and was becoming increasingly anxious as the firm's annual review week approached. He finally caught up with Jean on a rainy Friday in the lobby of the office building as they both waited for their drivers to arrive. When asked about the upcoming performance review, Jean snorted and said, *"C'est tout fini*, it's all been taken care of. Make an appointment with my assistant, Louisa, next week and we can go over the report we have sent to Montreal". As Jean stepped gingerly into the rainy Caracas parking lot, Richard thought back to the last few weeks with his team, the sometimes loud disagreements with his fellow project managers, and wondered if it was too late in the day to call his old supervisor in Toronto.

Source: Based on the synthesis of a series of expatriate experiences.

Frequency of appraisal

In practice, formal appraisal is commonly carried out on a yearly basis, and this appears to extend to international performance systems, even though the domestic-oriented literature on this topic recommends an ongoing combination of formal and informal performance appraisal and feedback. For example, the majority of the US companies in the Gregersen *et al.* study referred to above reported annual appraisal practices. It is interesting to note that the US companies using annual appraisal systems were more likely to use standard appraisal forms and hard criteria. In their discussion of this finding, Gregersen *et al.* comment that replicating domestic practices requires less effort in collecting and interpreting the data, and that the preference for following the domestic system might reflect a lack of international experience within the companies in the sample. It is important to note that only 28 per cent of the HR respondents in their study reported having actually been on an international assignment themselves, so it is reasonable to assume that they might not be fully aware of the need to take contextual criteria into consideration, or see a need for the customization of their expatriate performance systems. Limited research suggests that gender differences may also impact preferences in the form and nature of reviews, in some studies even more significantly as do cultural differences.[60]

Performance feedback

An important aspect of an effective performance management system is the provision of timely feedback of the appraisal process. One of the problems with annual appraisal is that employees do not receive the consistent frequent feedback considered critical in order to maintain or improve their performance. The performance literature also suggests that regular feedback is an important aspect in terms of meeting targets and revising goals, as well as assisting in motivation of work effort. The difficulty for the expatriate who is being evaluated by a geographically distant manager is that timely, appropriate feedback is only viable against hard criteria.

For virtual assignees, this is further complicated when geographic dispersion dictates reliance on email communication. Interpersonal relations and an effective choice of **communication medium** are two factors influencing virtual workgroup relations.[61] Milliman *et al.*[62] reported two critical incidents involving miscommunication between managers working on a virtual assignment in the USA and Malaysia. Email feedback about his Malaysian counterpart's good performance provided to the Malaysian by the American head of the project generated a cycle of cross-cultural conflict. This threatened the virtual team's performance when the Malaysian sought to transfer out of the team. Adopting an organizational learning approach, the researchers analyzed the miscommunication and its consequences. They concluded that the two managers concerned had different views about what constituted "the primary source of job performance, how performance feedback is provided, what role the subordinate will have in communicating with a superior, how conflict is handled, and what communication styles are expected". The approach used to analyze these incidents provides a useful IHRM starting point for developing effective cross-cultural performance feedback communication skills.

Appraisal of HCN employees

The discussion so far has omitted the issue of appraising the performance of HCN employees. To a certain extent, this reflects the limited research on the topic in the context of IHRM, though there is a growing body of literature on comparative HRM practices. What is important to mention here is that the practice of performance appraisal itself confronts the issue of *cultural applicability*.[63] Performance appraisal in different nations can be interpreted as a signal of distrust or even an insult. In Japan, for instance, it is important to avoid direct confrontation to 'save face', and this custom affects the way in which performance appraisal is conducted. A Japanese manager cannot directly point out a work-related problem or error committed by a subordinate:

> *Instead, he is likely to start discussing with the subordinate the strong points of that person's work, continuing with a discussion about the work on a relatively general level. Then he might continue to explain the consequences of the type of mistake committed by the subordinate, still without directly pointing out the actual mistake or the individual employee. From all this, the subordinate is supposed to understand his mistake and propose how to improve his work.*[64]

One way to overcome the dilemma of cultural adaptation is to use HCNs to assist in devising a suitable system for appraising subsidiary employees and to advise on the conduct of the appraisal. At times, the need for local responsiveness may affect the multinational's ability to effectively implement a standardized approach to performance management at all levels within the global operation.[65]

As we discussed in relation to PCNs and TCNs, the level of position involved is an important consideration. Should a multinational appoint a HCN as its subsidiary manager, much of what we covered in terms of goals (particularly hard goals) and performance measures could be expected to apply to the HCN. In terms of task performance and potential role conflict, as can be seen from Figure 6.6, Torbiörn[66] recognizes that HCN managers face particular role concerns that are different from those of PCN and TCN managers. The HCN manager is expected to perform a role that is conceptualized by a psychologically and physically distant parent company but enacted in an environment with other role senders who are both psychologically and physically close.

FIGURE 6.6 **HCN role perception**

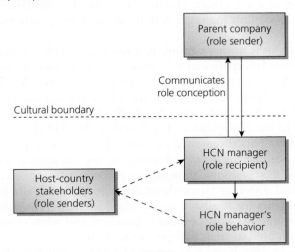

Source: Adapted from I. Torbiörn, 'The Structure of Managerial Roles in Cross-cultural Settings', *International Studies of Management & Organization*, Vol. 15, No. 1 (1985), p. 60. Reproduced with permission.

Parent-company role conception is communicated to the HCN, but it crosses the cultural boundary, as does feedback expressed as the HCN's role behavior (the straight arrows in Figure 6.6). Input from 'host-country' role senders, though, does not cross a cultural boundary. The HCN receives role expectations and enacts role behaviors in his or her own cultural environment. For subsidiary staff below the top management level, one would expect that the performance management system be localized to take into consideration local behavioral norms of work behavior. Torbiörn's model depicts only HCN managerial role conception and communication.

Conflict may arise in cases where HCNs report to a PCN expatriate manager who also conducts their performance appraisal. In a way, this is the reverse of the discussion surrounding local managers appraising the performance of expatriates in terms of cultural bias. The difference, of course, is the impact that parent-company standards have on the performance management system and the degree to which localization is permitted in a standardized approach.[67] It may not be culturally sensitive to use appraisal techniques such as 360-degree feedback, for instance. In practice, US multinationals have often used the same appraisal form for HCNs as for their domestic employees. Sometimes the forms are translated from English; sometimes they are not. Both approaches have drawbacks. As discussed above, while some MNEs are developing information systems to assist in performance appraisal, the widespread use of computer-generated data is hampered by the legal constraints imposed by some host governments or by concerns about personal privacy.

One aspect that is overlooked in the limited literature on this topic is the potential for role conflict for those HCNs transferred into the parent's operations.[68] For that period, the HCN may be evaluated according to role behavior expectations communicated by role senders that are physically close but psychologically distant, in an environment that is also psychologically distant. The HCN is then transferred, usually back into his or her home country, and may experience difficulties in readjusting role behavior.

In relation to performance appraisal generally, it seems that the process remains problematic, irrespective of cultural impacts. For example, a study by Gerringer *et al.* reported a common finding across ten countries/regions, which was the failure of performance appraisal to fulfil its development purpose. The study formed part of the Best Practices in International HRM project – a multiple-year, multiple-researcher, multinational project.[69] The ten countries/regions were Australia, Canada, China, Indonesia, Japan, Korea, Latin America, Mexico, Taiwan, and the USA. The researchers noted: "It appears that the potential of appraisal is not fully realized in current practice, not only (as widely believed) in the USA, but also in most other countries".[70]

Reviews on global performance management describe a more widespread use of performance management systems by multinational firms. Formal reviews tend to be annual or biannual, online systems are still in the minority (20 per cent of responding firms), but one-third of the firms stated they had plans to move to online systems. Objective and subjective criteria are used, and training based on the results of the performance management process is growing. Systems capabilities related to consistency within the far-flung system in the firm, integrating performance management into other HR activities (such as succession planning and compensation) and linking performance management to strategic planning while incorporating the leadership of senior management, are seen as critical if performance management is to contribute to the control of MNEs.[71]

The criticality of balancing global (parent) processes, practices, roles and norms with local or regional equivalents is of ongoing interest to students of global performance management. Investigating the impact of high-context cultures on selecting and valuing implicit, explicit-subjective, or explicit-objective forms of performance criteria is the theme of some research in this area. Preliminary research has begun on operationalizing these kinds of dimensions and gathering cross-cultural empirical data – most certainly a non-trivial task.[72]

Research is also ongoing into contrasting the standardized system of global performance management as envisioned at MNE headquarters and the locally or regionally customized 'systems in use' as holistically practiced on site.[73] The effects of legal and regulatory contexts on the aforementioned processes, practices and norms, and the widening range of tasks and assignments required of employees in MNEs, all combine to make performance management a complex yet critical area of HRM.[74]

A systemic review of published research may lead one to conclude that, whereas many cross-cultural issues have been presented in the research, a more strategic view of MNE performance management, particularly how the systems are rolled out across continents, business divisions and elements of dispersed global value chains, remains to be taken. Of particular interest is the question of how performance results are used at the macro level to guide or otherwise impact MNE strategic action.[75]

SUMMARY

Technical competence is a necessary but not sufficient condition for successful international performance. Cross-cultural interpersonal skills, sensitivity to foreign norms and values, and ease of adaptation to unfamiliar environments are just a few of the managerial characteristics most multinationals seek when selecting international managers. The added challenge is the effective management and appraisal of performance across all of the MNE's operations. In this chapter we have explored:

- the basic components of a performance management system that is conscious of and responds to the organizational, national, and international elements

- multinational performance aspects – whole (global) vs. part (subsidiary); non-comparable data; the volatility of the global environment; the effect of distance; and the level of maturity – and, briefly, performance management as a control mechanism

● factors associated with expatriate performance: the compensation package; task and role; level of headquarters support; host-environment factors; and cultural adjustment

● the performance management of non-expatriates and those on non-standard assignments, using the virtual assignment as an illustration of some of the aspects that need to be considered in these non-traditional assignment types

● the issues relating to the performance appraisal of international employees

● appraisal of HCN managers and employees in subsidiary operations.

Broadening out the discussion to the multinational level and addressing performance management and appraisal concerns related to non-expatriates and those on non-standard assignments has been useful to remind us that there are many dimensions to international business operations that need to be considered when designing an effective performance management system in the multinational context.

DISCUSSION QUESTIONS

1 In the section on the volatility of the global environment, several world events were listed that have had profound implications for the global and local strategies of MNEs. Select a recent world event, identify the specific HR implications that may arise from this and devise policies as to how these may be handled.

2 Discuss the major factors associated with appraisal of expatriate managerial performance.

3 One of the dangers of performance appraisal is that, because the focus is so much on a particular individual, the teamwork aspect gets lost. In an international location, it is perhaps desirable to focus more on how the PCN has settled in and is operating as part of a team rather than as an individual. What are the difficulties and special circumstances experienced in team performance management?

4 Why is it important to include hard, soft, and contextual goals when assessing managerial performance?

5 In what ways would the role of a manager working in a non-standard international assignment arrangement differ from that of a typical expatriate manager?

FURTHER READING

P. Boselie, E. Farndale and J. Paauwe 'Performance management', in C. Brewster and W. Mayrhofer (eds.) *Handbook of Research on Comparative Human Resource Management*, (Cheltenham: Edward Elgar, 2012), pp. 369–392.

W. Cascio 'Global Performance Management Systems', in G. Stahl, I. Björkman and S. Morris (eds.) *Handbook of Research in International Human Resource Management*, 2nd ed. (Cheltenham: Edward Elgar, 2012), pp. 183–204.

A. Engle, P. Dowling and M. Festing 'State of Origin: Research in Global Performance Management, a Proposed Research Domain and Emerging Implications', *European Journal of International Management*, 2 (2) (2008), pp. 153–169.

A. Engle, M. Festing and P. Dowling 'Gaining altitude on global performance management processes: A multilevel analysis', *International Journal of Human Resource Management*, 26 (15) (2015), pp. 1955–1964.

C. Fey, Y. Morgulis, S. Park, J. Hyeon and I. Björkman 'Opening the black box of the relationship between HRM practices and firm performance: A comparison of MNE subsidiaries in the USA, Finland and Russia', *Journal of International Business Studies* 40 (2009), pp. 690–712.

M. Iqbal, S. Akbar and P. Budhwar 'Effectiveness of performance appraisal: An integrated framework', *International Journal of Management Reviews*, 17 (2015), pp. 510–533.

H. Shih, Y. Chiang and I. Kim 'Expatriate Performance Management from MNEs of Different National Origins', *International Journal of Manpower*, 26(2) (2005), pp. 157–176.

NOTES AND REFERENCES

1. Excellent overviews of research in this area are provided by P. Caligiuri 'Performance Measurement in a Cross-cultural Context', in W. Bennett, C. Launce and J. Woehr (eds.) *Performance Management: Current Perspectives and Future Challenges* (Mahwah, NJ: Lawrence Erlbaum Associates, 2006), pp. 227–244; and W. Cascio 'Global Performance Management Systems', in G. Stahl, I. Björkman and S. Morris (eds.) *Handbook of Research in International Human Resource Management*, 2nd ed. (Cheltenham: Edward Elgar, 2012), pp. 183–204.

2. Cascio 'Global Performance Management Systems', p. 201.

3. C. A. Bartlett and S. Ghoshal 'Managing Across Borders: New Strategic Requirements', *Sloan Management Review* (Summer, 1987), pp. 7–17.

4. V. Pucik 'Strategic Human Resource Management in a Multinational Firm', in H. Y. Wortzel and L. H. Wortzel (eds.) *Strategic Management of Multinational Corporations: The Essentials* (New York: John Wiley, 1985), pp. 429-430. For a specific example of the issue of complex interpretations of what constitutes performance in interdependent, dispersed MNEs, in this case particular to Taiwan, see L.H. Lin 'Subsidiary performance: The contingency of multinational corporation's international strategy', European Management Journal, 32 (2014), pp. 928-937.

5. J. Garland, R. N. Farmer and M. Taylor *International Dimensions of Business Policy and Strategy*, 2nd ed. (Boston, MA: PWS–KENT, 1990), p. 193.

6. Ibid.

7. Pucik 'Strategic Human Resource Management in a Multinational Firm', p. 430.

8. Ibid.

9. For a sense of issues related to the potential of and pitfalls inherent in sophisticated HRIS systems to provide nuanced performance information, see N. Boyd and B. Gessner 'Human resource performance metrics: methods and processes that demonstrate you care', *Cross Cultural Management*, Vol. 20, No. 2 (2013), pp. 251–273; J. Dulebohn and R. Johnson 'Human resource metrics and decision support: A classification framework', *Human Resource Management Review*, Vol. 23 (2013), pp. 71–83.

10. A. Engle, P. Dowling and M. Festing 'State of Origin: A Proposed Research Domain and Emerging Implications', *European Journal of International Management*, Vol. 2, No. 2 (2008), pp. 153-169; and B. Campbell, A. Peterson and J. Correa 'Performance Management: Rewired for the Recovery', *Workspan,* Vol. 53, No. 7 (2010), pp. 43–48.

11. Pucik 'Strategic Human Resource Management in a Multinational Firm'.

12. Garland, Farmer and Taylor *International Dimensions of Business Policy and Strategy*, p. 193.

13. K. Mellahi, J. Frynas and D. Collins found evidence supporting the unifying effect of universal "best practices" in an assessment of Brazilian MNEs, 'Performance management practices within emerging market multinational enterprises: the case of Brazilian multinationals', *International Journal of Human Resource Management,* DOI: 10.1080/09585192.2015.1042900.

14. For a cross-cultural discussion of the interactive relationship between executive understanding of performance management and the effectiveness of performance management processes for the firm, see C. Lakshman 'Leveraging human capital through performance management process: The role of leadership in the USA, France and India', *International Journal of Human Resource Management*, Vol. 25, No. 10 (2014), pp. 1351–1372.

15. Engle, Dowling and Festing 'State of Origin: A Proposed Research Domain and Emerging Implications'; M. Fenwick, H. De Cieri and D. Welch 'Cultural and Bureaucratic Control in MNEs: The Role of Expatriate Performance Management', *Management International Review*, Vol. 39, Special Issue No. 3 (1999), pp. 107–124.

16. A. Varma, P. Budhwar and A. DeNisi (eds.) *Performance Management Systems: A Global Perspective* (New York: Routledge, 2008).

17. R. Hays 'Expatriate Selection: Insuring Success and Avoiding Failure', *Journal of International Business Studies*, Vol. 5, No. 1 (1974), pp. 25-37. Tung appears to have based her initial studies on these categories (see R. Tung 'Selection and Training of Personnel for Overseas Assignments', *Columbia Journal of Word Business,* Vol. 16, No. 1 (1981), pp. 68–78).

18. See L. Gomez-Mejia, P. Berrone and M. Franco-Santos *Compensation and Organizational Performance: Theory, Research and Practice* (London: M. E. Sharpe, 2010), particularly Chapters 4 through 7; E. Lawler *Talent: Making People Your Competitive Advantage* (San Francisco: Jossey-Bass, 2008), particularly Chapters 5 and 8; M. Hilb *New Corporate Governance: Successful Board Management Tools*, 2nd ed. (Berlin: Springer Publishing, 2006); and F. Malik *Effective Top Management* (Frankfurt: Wiley-VCH, 2006).

19. Caligiuri 'Performance Measurement in a Cross-cultural Context'.

20. For more on how the purposes and roles inherent in assignments may impact upon the characteristics of performance management systems see Engle, Dowling and Festing 'State of Origin'.

21. H. Mintzberg *The Nature of Managerial Work* (Englewood Cliffs, NJ: Prentice-Hall, 1973), p. 54. Also see W. Cascio and H. Aguinis *Applied Psychology in Human Resource Management*, 7th ed. (Upper Saddle River, NJ: Prentice Hall-Pearson, 2011), particularly Chapter 1 and pp. 405–407.

22. J. S. Black and L. Porter 'Managerial Behaviors and Job Performance: A Successful Manager in Los Angeles May Not Succeed in Hong Kong', *Journal of International Business Studies*, Vol. 22, No. 1 (1991), pp. 99–113.

23. I. Torbiörn 'The Structure of Managerial Roles in Cross-Cultural Settings', *International Studies of Management & Organization*, Vol. 15, No. 1 (1985), pp. 52–74, quote from p. 59.

24. M. Janssens 'Evaluating International Managers' Performance: Parent Company Standards as Control Mechanism', *International Journal of Human Resource Management,* Vol. 5, No. 4 (1994), pp. 853-873. Also see D. Briscoe and L. Claus 'Employee Performance Management: Policies and Practices in Multinational Enterprises', in A. Varma, P. Budhwar and A. DeNisi (eds.) *Performance Management: A Global Perspective* (London: Routledge, 2008), pp. 15–39.

25. Janssens 'Evaluating International Managers' Performance'.

26. H. B. Gregersen and J. S. Black 'A Multifaceted Approach to Expatriate Retention in International Assignments', *Group & Organization Studies*, Vol. 15, No. 4 (1990), p. 478. Also see I. Björkman, W. Barner-Rasmussen, M. Ehrnrooth and K. Makela 'Performance Management Across Borders', in P. Sparrow (ed.) *Handbook of International Human Resource Management* (New York: John Wiley and Sons, 2009) pp. 229–249 for a very lucid discussion of researching the tension of interests and loyalties inherent in locally adopting or adjusting standardized global performance management systems, processes and activities.

27. M. G. Birdseye and J. S. Hill 'Individual, Organization/Work and Environmental Influences on Expatriate Turnover Tendencies: An Empirical Study', *Journal of International Business Studies*, Vol. 26, No. 4 (1995), p. 800.

28. D. C. Feldman and H. B. Tompson 'Expatriation, Repatriation, and Domestic Geographical Relocation: An Empirical Investigation of Adjustment to New Job Assignments', *Journal of International Business Studies*, Vol. 24, No. 3 (1993), pp. 507-529.

29. P. Bhaskar-Shrinivas, M. Shaffer and D. Luk 'Input-Based and Time-Based Models of International Adjustment: Meta-Analytic Evidence and Theoretical Extensions', *Academy of Management Journal*, Vol. 48, No. 2 (2005), p. 272.

30. Torbiörn 'The Structure of Managerial Roles in Cross-cultural Settings', p. 59.

31. For example, in one of the few articles on this topic, Chadwick looks at the TCN assignment in general and does not specifically address performance. Rather, the focus is on fair treatment and equity regarding compensation. See W. Chadwick 'TCN Expatriate Manager Policies', in J. Selmer (ed.) *Expatriate Management: New Ideas for International Business* (Westport, CT: Quorum Books, 1995).

32. Cascio 'Global Performance Management Systems'; A. Engle, P. Dowling and M. Festing 'State of Origin: A Proposed Research Domain and Emerging Implications'.

33. H. B. Gregersen, J. M. Hite and J. S. Black 'Expatriate Performance Appraisal in US Multinational Firms', *Journal of International Business Studies*, Vol. 27, No. 4 (1996), pp. 711-738.

34. For the significance of incremental negotiation in resolving this complex process see E. Moren 'The negotiated character of performance appraisal: How interrelations between managers matter,' *International Journal of Human Resource Management*, Vol. 24, No. 4 (2013), pp. 853-870; bridges across differences due to varying perceptions of systems fairness and the need to see the performance management system in terms of wider issues of MNE culture are presented by K. Dewettinck and H. van Dijk 'Linking Belgian employee performance management system characteristics with performance management system effectiveness: Exploring the mediating role of fairness,' *International Journal of Human Resource Management*, Vol. 24, No. 4 (2013), pp. 806–825; and H. Hofstetter and I. Haraz 'Declared versus actual organizational culture as indicated by an organization's performance appraisal', *International Journal of Human Resource Management*, Vol. 26, No. 4 (2015), pp. 445-466.

35. See C. Bailey and C. Fletcher 'International Performance Management and Appraisal: Research Perspectives', M. Harris (ed.) *Handbook of Research in International Human Resource Management* (London: Lawrence Erlbaum, 2008), pp. 125–143; and M. Festing, L. Knappert, P. Dowling and A. Engle 'Country-Specific Profiles in Global Performance Management – A Contribution to Balancing Global Standardization and Local Adaptation', Conference Proceedings of the 11th Conference on International Human Resource Management, June 2010.

36. C. Barzantny and M. Festing 'Performance Management in Germany and France', in A. Varma, P. Budhwar and A. DeNisi (eds.) *Performance Management Systems: A Global Perspective* (London: Routledge, 2008), pp. 147-167; and P. Gooderham, O. Nordhaug and K. Ringdal 'Institutional and Rational Determinants of Organizational Practices: Human Resource Management in European Firms', *Administrative Science Quarterly,* Vol. 44 (1999), pp. 507–531.

37. Barzantny and Festing 'Performance Management in Germany and France'; and M. Tahrvanainen and V. Suutari 'Expatriate Performance Management in MNCs', in H. Scullion and M. Lineham (eds.) *International HRM: A Critical Text* (Basingstoke: Macmillan, 2005), pp. 91-113.

38. M. Dickmann 'Implementing German HRM Abroad: Desired, Feasible, Successful?' *International Journal of Human Resource Management*, Vol. 34, No. 2 (2003), pp. 265-283.

39. For more on Anglo-Saxon approaches to performance-based pay see H. Aguinis *Performance Management* (Upper Saddle River, NJ: Pearson Education, 2007), particularly Chapter 10. For more information related to German performance management see Barzantny and Festing 'Performance Management in Germany and France'; and M. Pudelko 'A Comparison of HRM Systems in the USA, Japan and Germany in their Socioeconomic Context', *Human Resource Management Journal*, Vol. 16, No. 2 (2006), pp. 123-153.

40. M. Fenwick 'On International Assignment: Is Expatriation the Only Way to Go?', *Asia Pacific Journal of Human Resources*, Vol. 42, No. 3 (2003), pp. 365-377; V. Suutari and C. Brewster 'Beyond Expatriation: Different Forms of International Employment', in P. Sparrow (ed.) *Handbook of International Human Resource Management* (New York: John Wiley and Sons, 2009), pp. 131-149.

41. M. Maznevski, S. Davison and K. Jonsen 'Global Virtual Team Dynamics and Effectiveness', in G. Stahl and I. Bjorkman (eds.) *Handbook of Research in International Human Resource Management* (Cheltenham, UK: Edward Elgar, 2006), pp. 364-384; P. Caligiuri 'Performance Measurement in a Cross-cultural Context'.

42. See, for example, G. Dessler *Human Resource Management*, 12th ed. (Upper Saddle River, N.J.: Prentice Hall, 2011), particularly Chapter 9; C. Vance and Y. Paik *Managing a Global Workforce* (London: M. E. Sharpe, 2011).

43. P. Dowling, A. Engle, M. Festing and C. Barzantny 'Proposing Processes of Global Performance Management: An Analysis of the Literature', Conference Proceedings of the IFSAM 2010 World Congress, Paris, France, July 2010; Cascio 'Global Performance Management Systems'.

44. Tahvanainen *Expatriate Performance Management*; Engle, Dowling and Festing 'State of Origin'.

45. Suutari and Brewster 'Beyond Expatriation: Different Forms of International Employment'; M. Tahvanainen, D. Welch and V. Worm 'Implications of Short-term International Assignments', *European Management Journal*, Vol. 23, No. 6 (2005), pp. 663-673.

46. For a well-presented and far-reaching discussion of the relationship between strategic purpose and talent management, see J. Boudreau and P. Ramstad *Beyond HR: The New Science of Human Capital* (Boston, MA: Harvard Business School Press, 2007); S. Brutus' 'Word Versus Numbers: A Theoretical Exploration of Giving and Receiving Narrative Comments in Performance Appraisal', *Human Resource Management Review*, Vol. 20, No. 2 (2010), provides a series of hypotheses in support of the contention that narrative comments in otherwise 'hard' and standardized performance management systems may provide a rich source of information for practitioners and researchers alike. Ironically, this potentially useful narrative may be more problematic to accurately decipher across cultural boundaries.

47. Pucik 'Strategic Human Resource Management'.

48. Janssens 'Evaluating International Managers' Performance'.

49. R. W. Beatty 'Competitive Human Resource Advantages through the Strategic Management of Performance', *Human Resource Planning*, Vol. 12, No. 3 (1989), pp. 179–194. Also see Cascio 'Global Performance Management Systems'.

50. K. F. Brickley *Corporate Criminal Liability: A Treatise on the Criminal Liability of Corporations, Their Officers and Agents*, Cumulative supplement (Deerfield, IL: Clark Boardman Callaghan, 1992). Enacted in 1977, the FCPA addresses the problem of questionable foreign payments by US multinationals and their managers. The act was amended by Congress in 1988 to include substantial increases in the authorized criminal fines for organizations and new civil sanctions for individuals violating the FCPA. See www.justice.gov/criminal/fraud/cfpa/ (as accessed on 28 October 2010) for details, amendments, interpretations and worksheets.

51. Tahvanainen *Expatriate Performance Management*; and Gregersen, Hite and Black 'Expatriate Performance Appraisal in U.S. Multinational Firms'.

52. Harvey 'Focusing the International Personnel Performance Appraisal Process'.

53. Tahvanainen *Expatriate Performance Management*.

54. E. Naumann 'Organizational Predictors of Expatriate Job Satisfaction', *Journal of International Business Studies*, Vol. 24, No. 1 (1993), pp. 61–80.

55. Gregersen, Hite and Black 'Expatriate Performance Appraisal in US Multinational Firms'.

56. Brookfield Global Relocation Services, Global Relocation Trends: 2010 Survey report, p. 46.

57. Gregersen, Hite and Black 'Expatriate Performance Appraisal in US Multinational Firms', p. 716.

58. It should be noted that these authors take a traditional performance appraisal approach, rather than utilize the newer performance management literature that we discuss in this chapter. It may be that the goal setting stressed in the performance management literature will assist standardization.

59. Cascio 'Global Performance Management Systems'; and Engle and Dowling 'State of Origin'.

60. See M. Festing, L. Knappert and A. Kornau 'Gender-specific preferences in global performance management: An empirical study of male and female managers in a multinational context,' *Human Resource Management*, Vol. 54, No. 1 (2015), pp. 55–79.

61. See W. Cascio and S. Shurygailg 'E-leadership in Virtual Firms', *Organizational Dynamics,* Vol. 31 (2003), pp. 362-375; also see M. Kavanaugh and M. Thite *Human Resource Information Systems* (Thousand Oaks, CA: Sage, 2009), particularly pp. 381–382.

62. J. Milliman, S. Taylor and A. Czaplewski 'Cross-Cultural Performance Feedback in Multinational Enterprises: Opportunity for Organizational Learning', *Human Resource Planning*, Vol. 25, No. 3 (2002), pp. 29–43.

63. See, for example, N. Adler and A. Gundersen *International Dimensions of Organizational behavior*, 5th ed. (Cincinnati, OH: South Western/Thomson, 2008); S. Schneider 'National vs. Corporate Culture: Implications for Human Resource Management', *Human Resource Management*, Vol. 27 (1988), pp. 231-246; and G. R. Latham and N. K. Napier 'Chinese Human Resource Management Practices in Hong Kong and Singapore: An Exploratory Study', in G. Ferris, K. Rowland and A. Nedd (eds.) *Research in Personnel and Human Resource Management*, Vol. 6 (Greenwich, CT: JAI, 1989).

64. J. V. Koivisto 'Duality and Japanese Management: A Cosmological View of Japanese Business Management', paper presented at the European Institute of Advanced Studies in Management Workshop, *Managing in Different Cultures*, Cergy Group Essec, France, 23–24 November 1992. Also see M. Morishima 'Performance Management in Japan', in A. Varma, P. Budhwar and A. DeNisi (eds.) *Performance Management Systems: A Global Perspective* (Abingdon, UK: Routledge, 2008), pp. 223–238 for an institutional and historical review of this subject.

65. Caligiuri 'Performance Measurement in a Cross-cultural Context'; Dowling, Engle, Festing and Barzantny 'Proposed Processes'; and Engle, Dowling and Festing 'State of Origin'.

66. Torbiörn 'The Structure of Managerial Roles in Cross-Cultural Settings'.

67. Engle, Dowling and Festing 'State of Origin'; also Dowling, Engle, Festing and Barzantny 'Proposing Processes of Global Performance Management: An Analysis of the Literature'.

68. The performance appraisal of 'inpatriates' is briefly covered in M. Harvey and M. Buckley 'Managing Inpatriates: Building a Global Core Competency', *Journal of World Business*, Vol. 32, No. 1 (1997), pp. 35–52. For a more general overview of the role of 'inpatriates' in control processes for multinational firms, see M. Harvey and M. Novicevic 'The Evolution from Repatriation of Managers in MNEs to "Inpatriation" in Global Organizations', in G. Stahl and I. Björkman (eds.) *Handbook of Research in International Human Resource Management* (Cheltenham: Edward Elgar, 2006), pp. 323–346.

69. J. Gerringer, C. Frayne and J. Milliman 'In Search of "Best Practices" in International Human Resource Management: Research Design and Methodology', *Asia Pacific Journal of Human Resources,* Vol. 40, No. 1 (2002), pp. 9–37.

70. J. Milliman, S. Nason, C. Zhu and H. De Cieri 'An Exploratory Assessment of the Purposes of Performance Appraisals in North and Central America and the Pacific Rim', *Asia Pacific Journal of Human Resources*, Vol. 40, No. 1 (2002), p. 117. For an alternative perspective, questioning the applicability of 'Western logics' to performance management processes in the Middle East, see A. Giangreco, A. Carugati, M. Pilati and A. Sebastiano 'Performance Appraisal Systems in the Middle East: Moving Beyond Western Logics', *European Management Review*, Vol. 7, No. 3 (2010), pp. 155–168.

71. See Cascio's 'Global Performance Management Systems' discussion as well as a survey of 278 firms from 15 countries reported in P. Bernthal, R. Rogers and A. Smith's *Managing Performance: Building Accountability for Organizational Success* (Pittsburgh, PA: Development Dimensions International, 2003).

72. Dowling, Engle, Festing and Barzantny 'Proposing Processes of Global Performance Management: An Analysis of the Literature'; Engle, Dowling and Festing 'State of Origin: A Proposed Research Domain and Emerging Implications'.

73. Björkman, Barner-Rasmussen, Ehrnrooth and Makela 'Performance Management Across Borders'; Dowling, Engle, Festing and Barzantny 'Proposing Processes'.

74. Institutional context, cultural values and history – as these variables impact on performance management – are an ongoing subject of cross-cultural research related to performance assessment. For examples see A. Dhiman and S. Maheshware 'Performance appraisal politics from appraise perspective: A study of antecedents in the Indian contest', *International Journal of Human Resource Management*, Vol. 24, No. 6 (2013), pp. 1202–1235; C.-J. Tsai and W.L. Wang 'Exploring the Factors Associated with Employees' Perceived Appraisal Accuracy: A Study of Chinese State-owned Enterprise', *International Journal of Human Resource Management*, Vol. 24, No. 11 (2013), pp. 2197–2220.

75. See A. Engle, M. Festing and P. Dowling 'Proposing Processes of Global Performance Management: An Analysis of the Literature', *Journal of Global Mobility*, Vol. 2, No. 1 (2014) pp. 5-25; and A. Engle, M. Festing and P. Dowling 'Gaining Altitude on Global Performance Management Processes: A Multilevel Analysis', *International Journal of Human Resource Management*, Vol. 26, No. 15 (2015), pp. 1955–1964.

CHAPTER 7
INTERNATIONAL TRAINING, DEVELOPMENT, CAREERS, AND TALENT

Chapter Objectives

Training aims to improve employees' current work skills and behavior, whereas **development** aims to increase abilities in relation to some future position or job. In this chapter, we examine how the international assignment is a vehicle for both training and development, as reflected in the reasons why international assignments continue to play a strategic role in international business operations. The role of training in preparing and supporting personnel on international assignments is also considered. We examine the following issues:

- the role of training in supporting expatriate adjustment and on-assignment performance

- components of effective pre-departure training programs such as cultural awareness, preliminary visits and language skills; as well as relocation assistance and training for trainers

- the effectiveness of pre-departure training

- the developmental aspect of international assignments

- training and developing international management teams

- trends in international training and development.

Reflecting the general literature on this topic, the focus of the chapter is on the traditional expatriate assignment. However, where possible we will draw out training and development aspects relating to short-term assignments, non-standard assignments, and international business travelers.

The chapter concludes with what could be called the post-assignment stage and its wider impact on the careers of employees who have been on an international assignment. Re-entry raises issues for both the expatriate and the multinational enterprise (MNE), some of which may be connected to events that occurred during the international assignment. We examine:

- the process of re-entry or repatriation

- job-related issues

- social factors, including family factors that affect re-entry and work adjustment

- MNE responses to repatriate concerns

- staff availability and career issues

- return-on-investment (ROI) and knowledge transfer

- designing a repatriation program

- broader international career issues.

At the end of the Chapter we make the link between global careers and Global Talent Management (GTM), a major challenge for multinational organizations.

INTRODUCTION

In order to compete successfully in a global market, more firms are focusing on the role of human resources (HR) as a critical part of their core competence and source of competitive advantage. As Kamoche[1] comments: "the human resource refers to the accumulated stock of knowledge, skills, and abilities that the individuals possess, which the firm has built up over time into an identifiable expertise". Training and development activities are part of the way in which the MNE builds its stock of HR – its human capital. An indication of the importance of this is the increasing number of MNEs that have established their own 'universities' or 'schools'. Motorola, McDonald's, Oracle, and Disney universities are good examples of these in-house training centers. Several European, Japanese, and Korean firms have similar arrangements (e.g. the Lufthansa School of Business).[2]

The international assignment in itself is an important training and development tool:

- Expatriates are trainers, as part of the transfer of knowledge and competence between the various units – a major rationale for the use of international assignments. Whether implicitly or explicitly stated, they are expected to assist the MNE to train and develop HCNs – that is, train their replacements.

- Expatriates are also expected to ensure that systems and processes are adopted, and inevitably they will be engaged in showing how these systems and processes work, as well as monitoring the effective performance of HCNs.

- One of the reasons for international assignments is management development. A move into another area internationally (job rotation) is a useful way for employees to gain a broader perspective. It assists in developing capable people who form the required pool of global operators, as discussed in earlier chapters.[3]

Therefore, the way in which an MNE anticipates and provides suitable training for international assignments is an important first step. This is reflected in the growth of interest in, and provision of, pre-departure training to prepare expatriates and accompanying family members for their international assignment.

Figure 7.1 is a schematic representation of the international training and development process. It shows the link between international recruitment and selection, and training and development activities. Most expatriates are *internal hires*, selected from within the MNE's existing operations. However, as indicated by the dotted arrow in Figure 7.1, some expatriates may be hired externally for an international assignment. We will now consider the various elements related to expatriate training and development in the context of managing and supporting international assignments.

FIGURE 7.1   International training and development

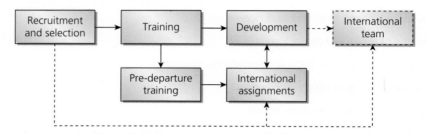

The role of expatriate training

Given that the primary selection criterion for most MNEs is technical ability of existing employees,[4] it is not surprising to find that most of the literature on expatriate training is devoted to expatriate pre-departure training activities that are mainly concerned with developing cultural awareness. Therefore, once an employee has been selected for an expatriate position, pre-departure training is considered to be the next critical step in attempting to ensure the expatriate's effectiveness and success abroad, particularly where the destination country is considered culturally tough. In Figure 7.1 pre-departure training is indicated as a subset of general training. Effective cultural training, it is advocated, assists individuals to adjust more rapidly to the new culture. As Earley[5] points out, a major objective of intercultural training is to help people cope with unexpected events in a new culture. They should learn from their intercultural experiences in order to improve cross-cultural collaboration.[6]

The limited, predominately US-based research into this area reveals that a large number of US multinationals have been reluctant to provide even a basic level of pre-departure training, though this is now changing. Particular interest in the area began with Tung's[7] seminal study on expatriation practices, including the use of pre-departure training programs. MNEs appear to be more positive about the provision of training over the last few years than at the time when Tung's study was conducted, possibly in part due to the growth in numbers of providers of pre-departure training that multinationals can access. Today we see different patterns emerging. For example, in 2015 Brookfield reports[8] from a sample of 143 MNEs stemming mainly from the Americas and EMEA that 83 per cent provided cross-cultural training (CCT), with 45 per cent offering preparation on *some* assignments and 38 per cent on *all* assignments (see source at Table 7.1). Furthermore, where cross-cultural preparation is offered only on some assignments, 17 per cent make it available based on host location and the familiarity of the assignee with the host country (29 per cent), and 17 per cent based on the type of assignment. Here we see that type of assignment and intended location have considerable influence on when CCT is offered.

TABLE 7.1 Availability of CCT in MNEs

	Brookfield 2009	Brookfield 2015
CCT available	81 %	83 %
CCT attendance optional provided to:	78 %	75 %
• Employee only	7 %	7 %
• Employee and spouse	32 %	35 %
• Whole family	56 %	55 %

Source: Brookfield Global Relocation Services. Global Relocation Trends Survey Reports, 2009; and Global Mobility Trends Survey Report, 2015. Woodridge, IL. All rights reserved.

Previously, multinational firms placed less priority on providing pre-departure training for the spouse and family.[9] However, perhaps due to increasing recognition of the interaction between expatriate performance and family adjustment, more multinationals have now extended their pre-departure training programs to include the spouse/partner and children. This result reflected in Table 7.1 seems to have become stable over the last few years. However, as Table 7.1 shows, the percentage of firms that make CCT *optional* remains very high (75 per cent in 2015) so it is possible that many expatriates still receive very little training. In a review of CCT, Littrell and Salas suggest that a lack of synthesis in the area of CCT research has made it difficult for managers to implement CCT. Their review provides a number of research-based guidelines as to how MNEs can enhance the success of their CCT programs.[10]

It is also important to note that the provision of pre-departure training appears to vary across industries: Mercer[11] reports that chemical, pharmaceutical, healthcare, and consumer firms are overall the most generous in terms of pre-assignment support, while information technology (IT) firms are the least generous. For example, 56 per cent of chemical, pharmaceutical, healthcare, and consumer firms provide language training to assignees' children, but only 14 per cent of IT companies do.

COMPONENTS OF EFFECTIVE PRE-DEPARTURE TRAINING PROGRAMS

Studies indicate that the essential components of pre-departure training programs that contribute to a smooth transition to a foreign location include: cultural awareness training, preliminary visits, language instruction, assistance with practical day-to-day matters, and security briefings.[12] We will look at each of these in turn.

Cultural awareness programs

It is generally accepted that, to be effective, the expatriate employee must adapt to and not feel isolated from the host country. A well-designed cultural awareness training program can be extremely beneficial, as it seeks to foster an appreciation of the host country's culture so that expatriates can behave accordingly, or at least develop appropriate coping patterns. Without an understanding (or at least an acceptance) of the host-country culture in such a situation, the expatriate is likely to face some difficulty during the international assignment. Therefore, cultural awareness training remains the most common form of pre-departure training.

The components of cultural awareness programs vary according to country of assignment, duration, purpose of the transfer, and the provider of such programs. As part of her study of expatriate management, Tung[13] identified five categories of pre-departure training, based on different learning processes, type of job, country of assignment, and the time available. These were: area studies programs that included environmental briefing and cultural orientation; culture assimilators (a training device whereby various cultural encounters can be discussed and analyzed); language training; sensitivity training; and field experiences. To understand possible variations in expatriate training, Tung proposed a contingency framework for deciding the nature and level of rigor of training. The two determining factors were the degree of interaction required in the host culture and the similarity between the individual's native culture and the new culture. The related training elements in her framework involved the content of the training and the rigor of the training. Essentially, Tung argued that:

- if the expected interaction between the individual and members of the host culture was low, and the degree of dissimilarity between the individual's native culture and the host culture was low, then training should focus on task- and job-related issues rather than culture-related issues. The level of rigor necessary for effective training should be relatively low.

- if there was a high level of expected interaction with host nationals and a large dissimilarity between the cultures, then training should focus on cross-cultural skill development as well as on the new task. The level of rigor for such training should be moderate to high.

Tung's model specifies criteria for making training-method decisions – such as *degree of expected interaction* and *cultural similarity*. One limitation of the model is that it does not assist the user to determine which specific training methods to use or what might constitute more or less rigorous training.

More than a decade later, Tung[14] revisited her earlier work and reported that her original recommendations held, though with some changes:

- Training should be more orientated to lifelong learning than 'one-shot' programs with an area-specific focus.

- There should be more emphasis on provision of foreign language training.

- There should be emphasis on the levels of communication competence, not just verbal communication, so the person becomes bicultural and bilingual, which enables an easier transition between one culture and another.

- CCT assists in managing diversity.

- The preview of the expatriate position should be realistic, as this facilitates effective performance.

Mendenhall and Oddou extended Tung's model and this was refined subsequently by Mendenhall, Dunbar, and Oddou,[15] who proposed three key dimensions in their CCT model:

1   training methods

2   levels of training rigor

3   duration of the training relative to degree of interaction and culture novelty.

This model provides excellent guidelines for managers to determine an appropriate program. For example, if the expected level of interaction is low and the degree of similarity between the individual's home culture and the host culture is high, the length of the training could probably be less than a week to provide the appropriate level of training rigor.[16] Training methods would emphasize an information-giving approach. Examples of such an approach would be:

- area or cultural briefings

- lectures, movies, or books

- use of interpreters
- 'survival-level' language training.

If the individual is to work in a foreign location for a period of 2 to 12 months and is expected to have some interaction with members of the host culture, the level of training rigor should be higher and the length of training longer (at least 1–4 weeks). Training methods would emphasize an affective approach. Examples of such an approach would be:

- role playing
- critical incidents
- culture assimilator training[17]
- case studies
- stress reduction training
- moderate language training.

If the individual is going to a fairly novel and different host culture and the expected degree of interaction is high, the level of CCT rigor should be high and training should be for two months or longer. Depending on the level of fluency required for language training, some training programs may extend up to a year. Training methods would emphasize an immersion approach. Examples of such an approach would be:

- assessment centers
- field experiences
- simulations
- sensitivity training
- intercultural web-based workshops
- extensive language training.

One obvious practical limitation of Black and Mendenhall's model is that there may be insufficient time for an expatriate to undertake CCT, which is often given as a reason why MNEs do not provide pre-departure training or why the uptake for such training is low. It would therefore be difficult to develop appropriate pre-departure training programs in such cases. Other contextual and situational factors – such as cultural toughness, length of assignment, and the nature/type of the job – may have a bearing on the content, method and processes involved in the cultural awareness training program. More importantly, monitoring and feedback should be recognized as important components of individual skill development, particularly as adjustment and performance are the desired outcomes of cultural awareness training.

Preliminary visits

One technique that can be very useful in orienting international employees is to send them on a **preliminary visit** to the host country. A well-planned visit for the candidate and spouse provides a preview that allows them to assess their suitability for and interest in the assignment. Such a visit also serves to introduce expatriate candidates to the business context in the host location and helps encourage more informed pre-departure preparation. It is essential to note that such a visit must be *relevant to the intended position that the international employee will be taking up* and not simply a 'tourist' experience. When used as part of a pre-departure training program, visits to the host location can assist in the initial adjustment process (for details on expatriate adjustment see Chapter 5).

Opinion Research Corporation (ORC),[18] in its survey of 916 MNEs, reported that three-quarters provide a pre-assignment trip to expatriates to allow them to become familiar with the new location, secure housing, child education, and other such items that are necessary for a successful transition to the host country: 49 per cent offer a preliminary visit to the expatriate and spouse, 20 per cent for all family members, and 6 per cent for the expatriate only. Furthermore, the majority of firms typically provide four to six days for such a trip, with all actual expenses for hotel, transportation, meals, and miscellaneous expenses reimbursed.

Obviously, the prospective assignee may reject the assignment on the basis of the preliminary visit. Most firms that utilize preliminary visits, though, weigh the cost of a preliminary visit against premature recall and underperformance risks. A potential problem arises if the aim of the preliminary visit is twofold – part of the selection decision and part of pre-departure training. For example, the MNE could be sending mixed signals to the prospective assignee if it offers the preliminary visit as part of the selection process, but upon arrival in the proposed country of assignment the prospective assignee is expected to make decisions regarding suitable housing and schools. Such treatment could be interpreted as accepting the preliminary visit equals accepting the assignment, thus negating its role in the decision-making process.

Where MNEs use the preliminary visit to allow the assignee (and spouse) to make a more informed decision about accepting the overseas assignment, it should be used solely for that purpose. Combined with cultural awareness training, the preliminary visit is a useful component of a pre-departure program. Exposure to the expatriate community (if one exists in the proposed host location) can also be a positive outcome. Brewster and Pickard[19] found that an expatriate community has an influence on expatriate adjustment.

Language training

Language training is a seemingly obvious, desirable component of a pre-departure program. However, it is consistently ranked below that of the desirability for cultural awareness training. In trying to understand why language skills are given a lower priority we should consider the following aspects related to language ability that need to be recognized.

The role of English as the language of world business.   It is generally accepted that English is the language of world business, though the form of English is more 'international English' than that spoken by native speakers of English.[20] India is an attractive location for foreign call centers due, in part, to the availability of a large local English-speaking population from which to recruit employees. The willingness of Chinese nationals to acquire English fluency is confirming the dominance of English. Multinationals from the Anglo-Saxon or English-speaking countries such as Britain, the USA, Canada, Australia, and New Zealand often use the dominant role of English as a reason for not considering language ability in the selection process, and for not stressing language training as part of pre-departure programs. However, more firms are including language training, as evidenced by recent surveys. The 2015 Brookfield Report shows that now 75 per cent of the investigated MNEs now provide language training to spouses as well. In fact, it was the most common form of spousal assistance.[21]

Host-country language skills and adjustment.   Clearly, the ability to speak a foreign language can improve the expatriate's effectiveness and negotiating ability, as well as improve the adjustment of family members. As has been pointed out for a long time, it can improve managers' access to information regarding the host country's economy, government, and market.[22] Of course, the degree of fluency required may depend on the level and nature of the position that the expatriate holds in the foreign operation, the amount of interaction with external stakeholders such as government officials, clients, trade officials, as well as with host-country nationals.

In a survey of 400 expatriates by Tung,[23] the importance of language skills was identified as a critical component in assignment performance. Respondents indicated that the ability to speak the local language, regardless of how different the culture was to their home country, was as important as cultural awareness in their ability to adapt and perform on assignment. Knowledge of the host-country language can assist expatriates and family members to gain access to new social support structures outside of work and the expatriate community. For example, McNulty[24] found that learning the host-country language was rated by 71 per cent of spouses as an important adjustment activity during international assignments, with one spouse suggesting that "language proficiency is power".

Language skills are therefore important in terms of task performance and cultural adjustment. Their continued omission from pre-departure training can be partly explained by the length of time it takes to acquire even a rudimentary level of language competence. Hiring language-competent staff to enlarge the language pool from which potential expatriates may be drawn is one answer, but its success depends on up-to-date information being kept on all employees, and frequent language auditing to see whether language skills are maintained.[25]

Knowledge of the corporate language.   As previously mentioned, multinationals tend to adopt (either deliberately or by default) a common company language to facilitate reporting and other control mechanisms. Given its place in international business, quite often English becomes the common language within these multinationals. Expatriates can become language nodes, performing as communication conduits between subsidiary and headquarters, due to their ability to speak the corporate language.[26] It also can give added power to their position in the subsidiary, as expatriates – particularly parent-country nationals (PCNs) – often have access to information that those not fluent in the corporate language are denied. An expatriate fluent in the parent-company language and the language of the host subsidiary can perform a gate-keeping role, whatever formal position the expatriate may hold.

Most MNEs use staff transfers as part of a corporate training program, with host-country national (HCN) recruits spending time at corporate headquarters as inpatriates (see Chapter 5). These training programs will normally be conducted in the corporate language.[27] Fluency in the corporate language is, therefore, usually a prerequisite for international training assignments and may constrain the ability of subsidiary employees to attend and benefit from such training.

Practical assistance

Another component of a pre-departure training program is that of providing information that assists in relocation. Practical assistance makes an important contribution toward the adaptation of the expatriate and his or her family to their new environment. McNulty, Hutchings and De Cieri,[28] in a study of 31 expatriates based in Asia, found that being left to fend for oneself resulted in a short-term negative impact on overall return on investment, as well as a perceived breach of the psychological contract. One important problem identified in their study was poor HR support such as a lack of mobility expertise and a poor attitude towards international assignees among locally trained (host-country) HR staff. HR support was found to matter most in the first weeks or months because most stressors were related to settling in rather than the new job. Also problematic for expatriates was not having a central area or person to go to for advice and information; seeking help from a dozen or more different departments was considered time-consuming and inefficient, and a distraction from doing their job adequately.

Practical assistance includes all manner of support both before and during an assignment.[29] For example, pre-departure practical support can include preparing official papers/visas, shipping assignee's goods to the host country, shipping additional baggage by air, interim accommodation in the home and host country, additional moving allowances to help cover incidental and out-of-pocket expenses otherwise not reimbursed or covered in the policy (e.g. connection and installation of appliances and utilities, purchase of small electrical appliances, replacement of non-fitting furniture or clothes), furniture storage in the home country, and consultations with a tax adviser and a relocation agent. On-assignment practical support can include ongoing language training, administrative support in filling in tax and official administration forms, assistance in opening a bank account, and finding and negotiating a housing lease. On-assignment practical support to help expatriates socially integrate is also needed but less common according to the Mercer 2010 survey, with only 12 per cent of companies introducing assignees to other expatriates living in the host location, 10 per cent providing membership to a sport/fitness club, and 5 per cent to a private/social club.

Many multinationals now take advantage of relocation specialists to provide this practical assistance, for example in finding suitable accommodation and schools.[30] Usually during the assignment, host-country HR staff will organize any further orientation programs and language training. However, as McNulty *et al.* show, it is important that corporate human resource management (HRM) staff act as a liaison to the sending line manager as well as the HR department in the foreign location to ensure that adequate practical assistance is provided.

Security briefings

A relatively new type of pre-departure training is the security briefing. This has become necessary as expatriates increasingly relocate to locations where personal safety may be a concern, and therefore present increased and unfamiliar threats to their health, safety, and security. We will return to this evolving topic area in Chapter 10. Risks and threats to expatriates range from hostile political environments (terrorism, kidnapping, hijacking, coup, war), natural disasters, exposure to disease (pandemics), travel accidents, and other common travel problems (scheduling delays, passport problems). ORC[31] reported in 2008 that 21 per cent of companies provided security briefings to expatriates dependent on the location of their assignment, with 43 per cent having established formal programs or broad guidelines for security and 63 per cent having either a formal or informal program in the case of emergencies. Security plans include evacuation procedures, assignment tracking systems, ongoing security briefings, and continuous improvements in overall security in all at-risk locations. In 19 per cent of participating companies, ORC reported that expatriates had been repatriated from locations deemed unsafe. In these instances, particularly for medical evacuations, 64 per cent of companies used an emergency evacuation service (e.g. SOS International), while 15 per cent covered the costs on an ad-hoc basis. In the event of death or serious illness in the expatriate's family, 41 per cent of companies paid the full cost of travel to the home country for the entire family. Interestingly, ORC found that, in companies where expatriates were assigned to dangerous locations, the overwhelming majority (71 per cent) did not pay a danger pay allowance. Just 15 per cent offered this allowance, and a further 14 per cent handled it on a case-by-case basis. However, the 2015 Brookfield Report showed that only 3 per cent of the investigated companies indicated that the security situation at the foreign location was a reason to refuse the international assignments or to return prematurely.[32]

Training for the training role

Expatriates are often used for training because of a lack of suitably trained staff in the host location. Consequently, expatriates often find themselves training HCNs as their replacements. The obvious question is: how are expatriates prepared for this training role? There is little research on this question. We do know from the cross-cultural management literature that there are differences in the ways people approach tasks and problems, and that these can have an impact on the learning process.[33] The ability to transfer knowledge and skills in a culturally sensitive manner perhaps should be an integral part of pre-departure training programs, particularly if training is part of the expatriate's role in the host country.

One way that MNEs could improve the quality and content of the training offered to expatriates in their role of training HCNs as their replacements would be to better utilize the knowledge-transfer process when expatriates are repatriated. A paper by Lazarova and Tarique[34] has examined this issue and argues that effective knowledge transfer occurs when there is a fit between individual readiness to transfer knowledge and organizational receptivity to knowledge. Specifically they propose that:

> *Organizations should try to match the level of intensity of their knowledge transfer mechanisms to the type of knowledge gained abroad. Thus, highly intense extraction tools (e.g. assigning repatriates to strategic teams) should be used to acquire international knowledge with high tacitness and high specificity [. . .]. Such knowledge would be transferred most effectively through rich mechanisms involving frequent communication between the repatriate and other organizational members. Organizations can use low intensity extraction tools (e.g. presentations, intranet) to acquire explicit international knowledge (e.g. information on banking laws and regulations in a particular foreign market).*

TCN and HCN expatriate training

Anecdotal evidence suggests that in some firms pre-departure training may not be provided to third-country nationals (TCNs) being transferred to another subsidiary, or for HCNs (inpatriates) transferred into the parent-country operations. Where it is provided, it may not be to the extent of that available to PCNs. This omission could create perceptions of inequitable treatment in situations where PCNs and TCNs work in the same foreign location, and affect adjustment to the international assignment. Not considering the needs of HCNs transferred to the parent organization reflects an ethnocentric attitude.[35]

There may be a link between the amount of training, particularly cross-cultural, and assignment length. HCNs transferred to either headquarters or to another subsidiary are often for short-term, project-based assignments or for management development purposes. As such, they may not be regarded as 'genuine' expatriate postings, thus falling outside the ambit of the HR function. In order to design and implement TCN and HCN pre-departure training, local management, particularly those in the HR department, need to be conscious of the demands of an international assignment – just as we have discussed in terms of corporate/headquarters HR staff. There perhaps needs also to be recognition and encouragement of this from headquarters, and monitoring to ensure that sufficient subsidiary resources are allocated for such training.

Provision of training for non-traditional expatriate assignments

In theory, all staff should be provided with the necessary level of pre-departure training given the demands of the international assignment. Cultural adjustment is inherent in international staff transfers. Pre-departure training should also be provided for employees on short-term assignments, on non-standard assignments such as commuting, and to international business travelers. However, there is a paucity of information regarding pre-departure training for non-standard assignments.

Short-term and non-standard assignments

Given the generally low level of provision of pre-departure training to traditional expatriates, it is not surprising to find that those on short-term and non-standard assignments receive little or no preparation before departure. The oversight may be due to lack of time, which is a standard reason for non-provision of pre-departure training.

This may be why multinationals are increasingly using modern technology to overcome time and resource constraints. For example, Brookfield[36] reports that 44 per cent of companies now use media-based or web-based alternatives to face-to-face CCT, of which:

- 34 per cent use it for portability (anytime, anywhere)

- 23 per cent use media or web-based programs as additional forms of support for in-person programs

- 23 per cent use it for cost reasons

- 11 per cent use it as stand-alone alternatives, and

- 5 per cent use it for time efficiency.

International business travelers

Non-expatriates tend to be a forgotten group, yet for many firms they may comprise the largest contingent of employees involved in international business. International business travelers are flying into and out of foreign operations, performing a myriad of tasks including training. For example, explaining a new product's development, service, or process to HCN employees that will involve demonstrations, seminar presentations and other methods of information dissemination. Such internal MNE interaction will usually involve the use of the corporate language. Therefore, non-expatriates need to be aware that HCNs will differ in their level of competence. It is easy to equate intelligence with language fluency, perceiving lack of fluency as a sign of stupidity. Internal MNE briefings and training sessions will need to take into account local variances in how people conduct themselves in formal situations and approach the 'classroom' situation.

International business travelers may be providing new product information to foreign agents or distributors. These activities naturally involve cross-cultural interaction. Competence in the local language, or at least an ability to work with and through interpreters, may be required. The same applies to those conducting negotiations with host-government officials, prospective clients, suppliers, and subcontractors. All these activities are strategically important, yet there is little in the literature regarding the provision of training for these roles. From the limited, mainly anecdotal information available, it would seem that non-expatriates learn on the job and gradually acquire the knowledge and skills to function effectively in various countries and situations.[37] For a review of the international business traveler literature see Welch and Worm.[38]

THE EFFECTIVENESS OF PRE-DEPARTURE TRAINING

The objective of pre-departure training is to assist the expatriate to adjust to the demands of living and working in a foreign location. The question is: how effective is such training and what components have been considered to be essential by those who have been provided pre-departure training?

The Brookfield surveys ask firms to indicate the value of intercultural training for international assignee success, as shown in Table 7.2. For the 2015 survey,[39] 83 per cent of companies report CCT as being of 'good' or 'great value' for expatriate success, with no one indicating it has little or no value, and 17 per cent reporting a neutral value. However, it should be noted that information on how the responding firms evaluated their training was not provided – a common problem with many surveys of training utilization.

TABLE 7.2 Perceived value of cross-cultural preparation of expatriates

Value rating	Brookfield 2015	Brookfield 2011	Brookfield 2009
Of great value	32%	25%	19%
Of good/high value	51%	64%	60%
Of neutral value	17%	11%	19%
Of poor value	0%	0%	2%

Source: Brookfield Global Relocation Trends, 2009 and 2011. LLC. Global Mobility Trends Survey Report, 2015. Woodridge, IL. All rights reserved.

Several academic studies have attempted to assess the effectiveness of pre-departure training. Eschbach, Parker and Stoeberl[40] report the results of a study of 79 US repatriates. They measured cognitive, affective, and experiential CCT and language training provided by the company or self-initiated. The amount and type of training, based on the models of Tung and Black *et al.* described earlier in this chapter, were included. Expatriates with integrated CCT exhibited cultural proficiency earlier, and appeared to have greater job satisfaction, than those with less training. Repatriates commented that there was a need for accurate, up-to-date cultural and language training for expatriates and spouses, and many considered that preliminary visits should be used.

Another study represents a meta-analysis of the CCT literature.[41] The conclusion reached was that the effectiveness of CCT was somewhat weaker than expected due to:

- limited data, as few organizations systematically evaluate or validate the effectiveness of their training programs or make them available to the public
- the use of a mixture of different training methods, making evaluation of which method is most effective difficult to isolate
- the large diversity in cultures that expatriates face
- the interaction between individual differences between expatriates and the work environment they face; what works for one person may not work for another, thus the effects of CCT can be as diverse as the countries to which expatriates are assigned.

The authors add that traditional training methods may underestimate the complexity of international business life, where expatriate managers are required to perform complex jobs across multiple cultural contexts, sometimes on the same day or even within the hour. Training programs that capture this reality are difficult to find and many existing CCT programs have yet to prove their utility.[42]

DEVELOPING STAFF THROUGH INTERNATIONAL ASSIGNMENTS

International assignments have long been recognized as an important mechanism for developing international expertise (see also Chapter 5). The expected outcomes are:

- *Management development.* Individuals gain international experience, which assists in career progression, while the multinational gains through having a pool of experienced international operators on which to draw for future international assignments.

- *Organizational development.* International assignments also provide a MNE with a way of accumulating a stock of knowledge, skills, and abilities upon which it can base its future growth. A global mindset is an important side benefit, as key personnel take a broader view. Further, as discussed previously, expatriates are agents of direct control and socialization and assist in the transfer of knowledge and competence.

We shall now consider these outcomes, first from the perspective of the individual, and then from the multinational's viewpoint.

Individual development

An international assignment can be compared to job rotation, a management development tool that seeks to provide certain employees with opportunities to enhance their abilities by exposing them to a range of jobs, tasks, and challenges. It is therefore not surprising to find an implicit assumption that an international assignment almost always has management development potential. Along with expected financial gain, perceived career advancement is often a primary motive for accepting international assignments. This is particularly the case in small-population, advanced economies (e.g. Austria, the Netherlands, Australia, Finland, Sweden, and New Zealand) where the relatively small local economy is not big enough to generate growth, and international activities provide the opportunity for ongoing revenue growth.[43] In such a situation, employees (particularly younger employees who are motivated to build their careers) understand that international experience is often an essential requirement for further career advancement. A recent review by Kerr, McNulty and Thorn,[44] outlining how Australians and New Zealanders pursue global careers, reports that expatriates from these countries not only pursue company-assigned opportunities but increasingly pursue *self-initiated opportunities* as well.

Overall, there is a paucity of research that demonstrates a link between an international assignment and career advancement. There remains a need for research that establishes career paths as a direct consequence of international assignments.[45] There are two possible explanations for this lack of interest in the career outcomes of international assignments:

- MNEs and researchers have been somewhat preoccupied with the process of expatriation from the organization's perspective. It is important to understand the roles played by the various international human resource management (IHRM) activities so that proper management and support for expatriates can be provided to reduce underperformance and improve cost-effectiveness.

- Surveys consistently report that expatriates consider career progression as a primary motive for accepting international assignments. Such a consistency of response – that is, career advancement as a reason for accepting an overseas assignment – has masked the issue of whether these career expectations are, indeed, met. In other words, we know why people accept international assignments, but we do not have a clear picture of when and how these expectations are met, and the consequences to both the individual and the multinational if the expected career outcomes are not met. McNulty, Hutchings and De Cieri[46] provide some recent evidence that Asia-based expatriates are somewhat dissatisfied with their career progression as a result of undertaking international assignments, showing that changing patterns of mobility in the Asia-Pacific region has contributed to a decrease in loyalty and commitment, with implications for MNEs in terms of expatriate retention and overall corporate ROI.

Developing international teams

Expatriates may gain individual management development from the international assignment, as we have previously discussed. The international assignment is often the 'training ground' for the **international cadre** in Figure 7.2. For MNEs, this term usually refers to a group of high-potential employees who have been selected for specialized management training to enable the MNE to continue to expand its international operations. International teams can be formed from those who have had international experience, though the international assignment itself may be an assignment to an international team or to form an international team. It is frequently argued that multinationals, especially in networked organizations, would benefit from using international teams as:

- a mechanism for fostering innovation, organizational learning, and the transfer of knowledge

- a means of breaking down functional and national boundaries, enhancing horizontal communication and information flows

- a method for encouraging diverse inputs into decisions, problem solving, and strategic assessments

- an opportunity for developing a global perspective

- a technique for developing shared values, thus assisting in the use of informal, normative control through socialization.

FIGURE 7.2 Developing international teams through international assignments

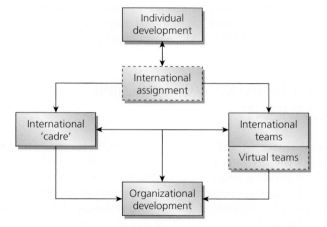

Research and development and international projects are common situations in which teamwork is utilized and forms the basis of much of the literature on multinational teams, a subset of which is the *virtual team*, where members are geographically dispersed (see Figure 7.2). To a certain extent, international assignments achieve team building by exposing employees to various parts of the global organization. Consequently, expatriates develop local networks that often persist after completion of the assignment. These predominantly informal networks can later be activated for work situations, such as providing membership of project teams.[47] Not everyone will wish to become part of an international cadre, but to create an effective global pool of international operators, many MNEs are conscious that they need to provide international experience to many levels of managers, regardless of nationality. A small cadre comprised only of PCNs may defeat the purpose of having a team of experienced employees who are capable of operating in multiple environments on various types of tasks and jobs. For example, Peterson[48] found that Western-based multinationals operating in Central and Eastern Europe were increasing the use of TCN and HCN expatriate transfers as a way of widening the 'corporate talent pool'.

While the international assignment plays an important role in both management and organizational development, its effectiveness depends on the individuals concerned, the type of multinational and contextual factors. For example, Caligiuri and Di Santo[49] argue that certain personality characteristics that have been identified as expatriate predictors of success cannot be developed through international assignments. In other words, individual characteristics such as dogmatic or authoritarian tendencies are not likely to be altered through an expatriate experience. However, Caligiuri and Di Santo do suggest that individuals can learn to be more sensitive to the challenges of working in another country – that is, to become more culturally aware. This knowledge and experience would prove valuable when working in an international team comprising colleagues from other countries.

Whereas a complete review of the growing topic of global leadership development is outside of the purview of this book, the authors note that the strands of professional development, cadre building, strong global corporate culture, and a well-thought-out pattern of international assignments for groups of executives that show potential have combined to build practitioner and academic interest in the subfield of global leadership.[50] Alternative research lenses, measures, definitions, and causal linkages to effective leadership on the global stage are widely discussed.[51] The role of the executive development unit within HR is far less understood.

The MNE needs to be able to provide the resources and support for those working in international teams such as research and development (R&D) projects. Managers supervising international teams, for example, will need to understand processes such as group dynamics, especially how national cultures affect group functioning. Those who have previous experience of international assignments and teams will be better placed than those who have not. Perhaps this is why some MNEs are placing greater stress on the need for international experience and are prepared to use expatriates despite the costs and difficulties often associated with international assignments. For reviews of the literature on developing international teams see Gibbs,[52] Maznevski *et al.*[53], and Caligiuri and Tarique.[54]

TRENDS IN INTERNATIONAL TRAINING AND DEVELOPMENT

There are a number of emerging and continuing trends in international training and development. First, although the pressure from globalization continues to push MNEs towards a convergent approach to training and development, there is a continuing pressure from many countries (particularly developing countries) for localization of training and development initiatives, of which MNEs must be mindful. Al-Dosary and Rahman[55] have reviewed the benefits and problems associated with localization of training and development. Second, there is a growing realization that, although globalization is having a major impact on business processes and associated training and development efforts in MNEs, there is evidence that for competence development and learning it is still necessary to consider the impact and importance of the national context and institutions on such efforts (see Geppert).[56] Third, there is increasing awareness of the important role of non-governmental organizations (NGOs) in international training and development (see Chang, and Brewster and Lee for reviews).[57] Fourth, with the rise of China as an economic superpower, there is increasing interest in all aspects of training and development with a focus on China (see Wang *et al.*, Zhao, Zhang *et al.*, Zhu, and Wang and Wang for reviews).[58] Finally, there is a realization in the training and development literature that the field must address global, comparative and national level contexts for training and development, just as the international HRM field is beginning to do (see Metcalfe and Rees[59] for a review).

RE-ENTRY AND CAREER ISSUES

It is evident from the material covered in this book that there have been considerable advances in our understanding and knowledge of the issues surrounding the management and support of expatriates in terms of recruitment and selection, pre-departure training, and compensation.

As Figure 7.3 indicates, the expatriation process also includes **repatriation:** the activity of bringing the expatriate back to the home country. While it is now more widely recognized by managers and academics that repatriation needs careful managing, attention to this aspect of international assignments has been somewhat belated. In the past, the unpredictable and incremental nature of globalization led to reactive assignments, and re-entry to the firm was left unspoken or dealt with informally on an ad-hoc basis. As more expatriates completed their assignments, firms were faced with organizing these returns in a more planned pattern that allowed for a more strategic and complete use of the repatriate's newfound experiences and insights, while at the same time easing the return to their home country and firm.[60]

FIGURE 7.3 Expatriation includes repatriation

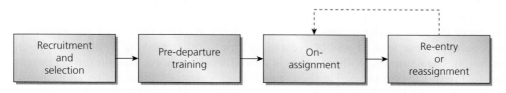

Re-entry into the home country presents new challenges. The repatriate is coping with what has been termed 're-entry shock', or 'reverse **culture shock'**. While people frequently expect life in a new country to be different, they may be less prepared for the experience of returning home to present problems of adjustment. As a consequence, it can be a surprising and traumatic experience for some[61] – perhaps more difficult than what was encountered in the foreign location. From the MNE's perspective, repatriation is frequently considered as the final stage in the expatriation process (as indicated in Figure 7.4), but it is important to note that the MNE's ability to attract future expatriates is affected by the manner in which it handles repatriation.[62]

FIGURE 7.4 Repatriation activities and practices

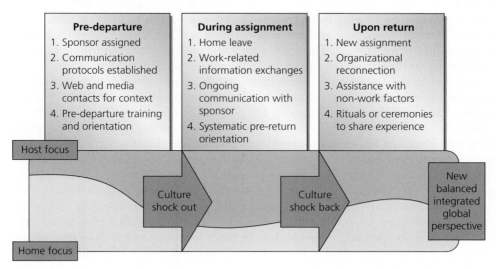

In this section, we focus on the key factors associated with re-entry, including how the repatriation process is handled by the individual and the receiving work unit, as well as family adjustment. We will also explore how repatriation affects the successful 'closure' of the foreign assignment, its impact on future career paths within the MNE, and the effect on staff mobility. The reasons for the international assignment and its outcomes are assessed – that is, how the MNE recoups its investment in human capital, and the process of knowledge and competence transfer upon re-entry. It should be noted that what is written about the re-entry process centers on the traditional expatriate assignment, based predominantly on experiences of repatriated PCNs.

THE REPATRIATION PROCESS

Typically, on completion of the international assignment the MNE brings the expatriate back to the home country, though not all international assignments end with a transfer home. Some expatriates may agree to become part of the multinational's international team of managers (as indicated by the dotted arrow in Figure 7.3) and thus have consecutive overseas assignments. In the event that one of these consecutive assignments involves the expatriate returning to the home-country operations, it will be treated as 'just another posting' rather than re-entry or repatriation. For example, William Jones is moved from his home base in the US parent operations to Japan for two years. He then spends four years in China, followed by one year in headquarters in the USA before moving on to another position in the British operations. That one-year period spent at headquarters is not treated as re-entry back into the home-country operations. In contrast, Mary Smith has spent three years working in China and is repatriated back to the USA into a defined position at headquarters.

As outlined in Figure 7.4, repatriation can be seen to encompass three phases. First, before the global assignment, MNEs may act to assign home sponsors or **mentors** and hold them responsible for keeping the expatriate in touch with changing conditions in the home country. Ideally, such sponsors might have relevant expatriate assignments as part of their own work history. Web-based indices of relevant national, regional, industrial, or firm websites may be provided. These ongoing communication protocols may be formal or informal.[63] Mercer[64] reports that 22 per cent of companies have put in place a mentoring program to assist assignees in the expatriation and repatriation process. But for over half of these, the mentor system is applied only in specific cases and not to the entire assignee population. By initially creating this network of personal and media links, the expatriate may be able to keep up with the changes in the home country, work unit, and the larger firm, as well as changes in the local or regional community while on assignment. This more systematic updating may contribute to more realistic expectations on the part of the expatriate, reducing culture shock upon return.

Second, during the assignment, 'home leave', work-related information exchanges, sponsor communications, and a systematic pre-return orientation process can all facilitate realistic expectations and ease the return. Allowing for periodic returns to the home country will help the expatriate and his or her family to reconnect with firm employees, family and friends, and catch up with changing business, economic, and political conditions. Some MNEs allow their expatriates to use their holidays to visit more exotic, once-in-a-lifetime locations closer to the host country.[65] In some cases, this is not a wise policy for the employer as, by doing this, some expatriates lose their perspective of how things may be changing in their home country and may develop a somewhat 'rose-colored' view of life back at home. The first author has, over a number of years, been given numerous examples by managers with international experience of expatriate families spending their holidays in other locations rather than returning to their home country and subsequently developing a rather unrealistic view of life in their home country, which led to difficulties when the reality of subsequent repatriation resulted in adjustment difficulties. For this reason, ORC[66] reports that 58 per cent of MNEs enforce a policy whereby expatriates are required to take home leave in their home country.

Work-related information exchanges are part of any expatriate assignment. Through these regular and ongoing task-related communications, a considerable amount of information about changes in home personnel, power politics, strategic developments, and less work-related updates can be passed on to the expatriate. These activities may become more intense in the months or weeks immediately prior to the return. Upon return, a series of immediately practical and more long-term activities combine during what is normally a very restricted time frame. MNEs can be less effective in their use of expatriates by either being too vague and unfocused about repatriates, or they can try to be too efficient by expecting the returning expatriate to jump back into the home assignment before the issues and processes related to return are resolved – literally before their 'bags are unpacked'.[67] Immediate practical issues upon return include housing and schools for children. Returning expatriates need to be assigned office space and given an orientation to the new job assignment and local work group. On a broader scale, the repatriate must reconnect with the local social network of the MNE and personal and career dynamics may have to be adjusted in new and potentially unpredictable ways.[68] Changes and adjustments for societal, firm, and job dynamics on the personal, family, job, organizational, and career levels are involved in this final stage.

Note the two stages of culture shock represented at the bottom in Figure 7.4. An over-emphasis on the home focus, at the expense of a focus on the host assignment, can lead to problems with performance while on assignment and premature return. At the same time, an overemphasis on host activities, at the expense of some awareness of changes at home, can lead to a second culture shock upon return. The goal of any set of expatriation/repatriation practices should result in the successful integration of home and host experiences. Achieving this more balanced set of transitions is not always easy. For example, Harzing[69] has conducted a comprehensive survey of 287 subsidiaries of nearly 100 different multinationals and reported that 52 per cent of sampled firms experienced repatriate re-entry problems. IHRM in Action Case 7.1 provides an example of some of these problems.

Re-entry and repatriation problems

The problems outlined above and in the IHRM in Action Case 7.1 may lead to staff turnover, with repatriates opting to leave the organization. As we have reported in Chapter 5, according to the latest Brookfield report,[70] expatriate turnover increases after the assignment. While 20 per cent leave while on assignment, the percentage grows to 25 per cent within the first year upon repatriation, 26 per cent between the first and the second year, and 29 per cent after two years. Comparing these figures to an average annual turnover rate of 12 per cent, these percentages can be considered as relatively high, especially since important investments by the assigning firm are at stake. As has been reported before the employee exits mainly because of job opportunities in other firms, due to inadequate job performance or because of various family issues.

When asked about practices to minimize international assignee's attrition the respondents of the 2015 Brookfield report[71] listed the following:

- position guarantee after the assignment (14 per cent)
- repatriation support for the family (11 per cent)
- opportunities to use international experience (11 per cent)
- repatriation career support (10 per cent)
- recognition (8 per cent).

Given the reasons why international assignments are used, the direct and indirect costs involved and the various roles that are assigned to expatriates, it seems important to understand why re-entry is problematic yet of seemingly lesser importance to researchers and managers than other stages of the international assignment. To this end, we now examine factors that may contribute to re-entry problems, considering the process first from the individual's perspective and then the MNE's viewpoint.

IHRM in Action Case 7.1

Repatriation and loss prevention at ISCAM

On his last day of work at ISCAM, Wayne Bullova wrote up his letter of resignation, took the five weeks of vacation he was due, and walked through the February snow across the downtown Denver street to open his own safety and security consulting firm. Only three years earlier, Wayne had jumped at the chance to take the assignment as Loss Prevention and Safety Director at ISCAM's new regional center in Peru. As a global mining engineering firm with decades of international activities, ISCAM had done a very good job of preparing Wayne and his family for the differences between Lima and Denver. The children had quickly adjusted to the American school, surprisingly his Mexican-born wife had enjoyed being involved in both the expatriate community and the local Peruvian church group associated with the cathedral, and Wayne had immediately enjoyed the increased responsibilities and centrality of his new role. As an ex-US Army Ranger Captain, his security role did provide occasional adrenaline rushes as he responded to Sendero Luminoso activities in mine sites around Huaneayo, but the evident success of the counterterrorism and security protocols he developed were gratifying.

His return to Denver some six months ago was a different matter. He knew that things would be different at home after the corporate restructuring that occurred a year into his expatriate assignment. His long-time mentor and friend, Herman Balkin, had taken a reportedly very generous early retirement package after a long-simmering executive power struggle unpredictably came to a head. Several restructuring 'aftershocks' relocated many of his colleagues outside of Colorado. During his assignment in Peru, Wayne was more and more frustrated as his informal corporate intelligence network dissolved and the role of his liaison was passed around among a series of increasingly junior and, to his mind, clueless executives.

The assignment he was promised by the company president was 'rethought' and when he returned six months ago he spent the better part of a month trying to get an office and understand his new job. Everyone he talked to had a different perspective on what he was being asked to do. He felt claustrophobic and, to make matters worse, the new counterterrorism and security protocols he had developed and used with great success in Peru were either systematically ignored or so modified by his supervisors that they were unrecognizable.

At a Bronco's football game he shared his growing frustrations with Balkin. On the home front, the new house they had purchased upon return – having sold their home at the advice of the HR director at the time of the international assignment – was expensive, hard to heat and placed them in a city school district that the children were having problems with. He had looked at private schools, but the tuitions were astronomical and his salary was not much more than it had been three years ago. His wife had started to complain about Denver winters again. At work, Wayne felt as if he had returned to a totally different world. Balkin asked if ISCAM had asked Wayne to renew his executive non-competition agreement. Wayne replied that ISCAM had not. "Well, there you go", said Balkin. "Let's do what we have talked about for years. With your technical expertise and my industry contacts, we can work for ourselves – at least we will know who our bosses are and what the job is".

Source: Fictionalized synthesis from several interviews.

INDIVIDUAL REACTIONS TO RE-ENTRY

As with cross-cultural adjustment, the re-entry process is a complex interaction of several factors. It is possible to group the major factors that have been identified as moderators of re-entry readjustment into two categories – job-related factors and social factors – as depicted in Figure 7.5, which we now discuss.

FIGURE 7.5 Factors influencing repatriate adjustment

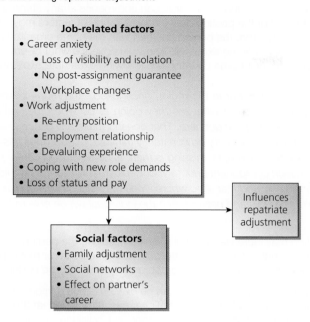

Job-related factors

These factors center around future employment prospects as a consequence of the international assignment, the value being placed on the person's international experience, coping with new role demands and the loss of status and financial benefits upon re-entry. We shall examine these factors in turn.

Career anxiety.   When surveyed, expatriates consistently list two motivators for accepting an international assignment: career advancement and financial gain.[72] The Brookfield 2015 Survey asked about the value of international experience to an employee's career and respondents gave the following responses, which seem to reflect a bit more optimism than in former surveys:[73]

- 43 per cent of respondents said that expats were promoted faster.

- 29 per cent believed that expats obtained positions in the firm more easily.

- 19 per cent of respondents noted that expats changed employers more often.

It is not surprising then that a prime factor in re-entry is career anxiety. This can emerge prior to the physical relocation, even before Phase 1 in Figure 7.4, and can affect productivity during the last few months of the international assignment as the person contemplates the re-entry process. So, what prompts career anxiety? The causes range across the following and are often interrelated:

- *No post-assignment guarantee of employment*. This is becoming the reality for perhaps the majority of employees on international assignments. The Brookfield 2015 Survey[74] asked respondents how the company most commonly helps to identify new jobs within the company after the international assignment, if their firm required a clear statement about what the expatriate would do following an assignment. The answers included informal networking (33 per cent), mandatory identification of a job by the department that authorized the assignment (27 per cent), and formal job postings (18 per cent).

● *A fear that the period overseas has caused a loss of visibility and isolation* – as captured in the phrase 'out of sight, out of mind'.[75] This fear can commence at any stage during an assignment and not just as the end of the posting draws near. A range of factors may influence this process: (1) the amount of contact that the person has had with the home organization, (2) the seniority of the position, and (3) whether the expatriate knows in advance what re-entry position they will take up when they return to their home country. The following expatriate explains this challenge well:

> *One very senior partner out in the region once joked, "the moment you get off the plane everybody starts thinking about what are they going to do when they go back". I remember laughing that off, thinking, "I just got here. That doesn't make any sense at all". And then after a while I went, "Oh, I get it". You really do constantly think about how does this all fit into the bigger picture [so] I think what is explicitly missing is there is no advanced career planning that would include the repatriation component prior to your deployment. There is no mid-term and certainly no long-term thinking around that. And where it needs to start is pre-trip [. . .] to start thinking to take advantage of the skills and network that the individual will be able to bring back.[76]*

● *Lack of information* may increase the level of anxiety, leaving the person with a decided impression that the firm has not planned adequately, or that a mediocre or makeshift job awaits.[77] If there is no post-assignment job guarantee, the anxiety level may be understandably high.

● *Changes in the home workplace.* Anxiety can be exacerbated by informal communication from home-based colleagues about organizational changes. It may be that the MNE is in the process of a major restructuring, the aftermath of a merger or acquisition, or sale of divisions or business units. These changes are often accompanied by job shedding. Knowledge of such changes and potential or real job loss may add to the level of anxiety – particularly if the expatriate does not have a guaranteed job upon repatriation.

Another issue here is that restructuring can affect the host-country operations – such as closure of a plant, dissolving of a joint venture, or merging of operations post-acquisition. This may leave the expatriate stranded, or force an early, unplanned repatriation.[78] If similar changes are also occurring in the home country, then availability of suitable positions may be reduced. One repatriate who was placed in such a position explains:

> *The division I worked for was reorganized, and the subsidiary I worked for was placed under stringent cost-cutting guidelines, which forced me to return earlier than anticipated. My re-entry was very cold, with little support in finding a job since previous management had been fired.[79]*

All of these factors combine to suggest that expatriates can be deeply affected by career anxiety. In a recent study examining expatriates' views relating to the perceived benefits gained at the individual level from international assignments, McNulty *et al.* found that 87 per cent of expatriates in an Asia-Pacific study perceived career enhancement as increasing their marketability to *other* employers and not just their own. These views were largely based on inadequate career planning provided by MNEs. Specific benefits from international assignments included:

> *"being more visible; it should open up doors to the future", "exhibiting a broader mindset which should make me better suited for advancement" and "giving me loads of experience to bring back to [my home country]".[80]*

Work adjustment.   Black, Gregersen and Mendenhall[81] argue that work adjustment has an important impact on a person's intent to stay with the organization (see also Chapter 5). Career anxiety is one moderating factor, but other factors may also lead to readjustment problems:

● *The employment relationship.* An individual's career expectations may be based on clear messages sent by top management to the effect that an international assignment is a condition for career progression. That is, verbal or written statements such as: "We are an international company and we need internationally oriented people who have worked in our overseas facilities". These pronouncements can be made in the context of the need for a global orientation or mindset where a definite link is made between international experience and global managers.

Perceptions regarding expected career outcomes also are influenced by comments made by HR or line managers during the recruitment and selection stage. For example, the line manager may suggest to a younger employee: "You should volunteer for that international assignment. It would be a smart career move at this stage in your life". If others have been promoted upon repatriation, it may be perceived to be the 'norm', thus reinforcing the perception that international assignments lead to promotion upon re-entry.

For these reasons, the person believes promotion should follow based on successful performance while abroad, and if the re-entry position does not eventuate within a reasonable time frame then career anxiety is justified. A study by Lazarova and Caligiuri[82] of 58 repatriates from four North American-based companies found that repatriation support practices are positively related to perceptions of organizational support, and these affect repatriates' intention to stay or leave the organization. The psychological contract is a moderator of re-entry readjustment as well as on-assignment adjustment and performance. The repatriate may believe that their performance overseas warrants promotion: that signals were given by the organization that effective performance in the international assignment would result in career advancement. When the expected promotion does not eventuate, the repatriate may feel there is no option but to exit the organization. It is important to note that the psychological contract concerns perceptions and expectations, complicated by the fact that the MNE representative making statements about career outcomes prior to the international assignment is not necessarily the person who is responsible for re-entry decisions about job placement and promotion.

- *Re-entry position.* It would seem for some that promotion is a primary issue, as the following comment from a repatriate reveals:[83]

  Get a promotion before the return! You are forgotten while overseas, and you start all over on the return. The promotions go to people who have been in a position for extended periods; nothing done overseas counts in this company.

Fears surrounding future employment and career development can materialize. Peers are promoted ahead of the repatriated manager, and the repatriate sometimes is placed in a position that is, in effect, a demotion. The situation may be exacerbated if the repatriate had held a senior position in the foreign location and now finds himself (or herself) at a less senior level. As a consequence, the re-entry position is frequently judged by whether it matches the repatriate's career expectation, particularly when the international assignment has caused considerable family disruption such as a forced break in the career of the accompanying partner, or difficulties experienced with the education of the children involved. Put simply, the repatriate wants the 'end to justify the means', so that the family unit is fully compensated for the sacrifices it has made in expectation of career advancement.

Suutari and Brewster, in their study of Finnish expatriates, report that most repatriates left only after they felt that they had given the firm sufficient time to find more suitable positions. These authors identified an 'external pull factor': external recruiters were actively headhunting repatriates either during the assignment or upon return.[84] A question put to responding firms in the Brookfield surveys concerned the career impact of international experience. Firms were asked to compare the careers of expatriates with those of employees without international experience. It seems clear from the discussion about career anxiety above that the value to employees of remaining with their firm after an international assignment may not be particularly compelling, but it may well be that employees believe that their international experience may increase their marketability to other employers. Stroh[85] found that the best predictors of repatriate turnover were whether the company had a career development plan and whether the company was undergoing turbulence such as downsizing. She argues that lower rates of repatriate turnover are more likely in organizations that planned for the repatriation of their employees and provided career development planning for them.

- *Devaluing the overseas experience.* Career progression is important, but to be promoted upon re-entry signifies that international experience is important and valued by the organization. However, the re-entry position may be a less challenging job with reduced responsibility and status than that held either during the international assignment, or prior to the period overseas, in 'holding' positions such as a task force or project team, or in temporary positions engaged in duties that do not appear to exploit their newly gained international expertise.[86] For some, the return position is frequently a lateral move rather than a promotion.[87] The positions do not seem to be related to, nor draw upon, experiences and skills the person may have acquired during the international assignment – that is, giving the impression that such experience is devalued.

Coping with new role demands.   Along with career issues, a mismatch of expectations can affect the repatriate's perception of the role associated with a new position. A role is the organized set of behaviors that are assigned to a particular position. Although an individual may affect how a role is interpreted and performed, the role itself is predetermined, usually defined in the job description.[88] Effective role behavior is an interaction between the concept of the role, the interpretation of expectations, the person's ambitions and the norms inherent in the role. Readjustment problems may occur because, although the repatriate is attempting to function back in the home country, his or her role conception remains influenced by the experience of the foreign assignment. Torbiörn[89] contends that, as long as the repatriate's "identity and basic values are still bound up in the culture of the home country, the strain of adjusting to conditions at home will be slight". However, while the repatriate may retain the role conception, and the cultural norms regarding behavior appropriate to that role, the foreign subsidiary's influence may linger, and what is communicated to the home company, in the form of role behavior, may not fully conform to the home firm's expectations.

Social factors

The familiar surroundings of the home environment may ease the transition, or at least the cultural adjustment will not be as demanding as that confronted in the foreign country. However, the international experience can distance the repatriate, and his or her family, socially and psychologically. If the expatriate position gave the person a higher profile, involving interaction with the local, national, social, and economic elite, the return home may bring with it some measure of social disappointment. The financial loss of the compensation premium, housing subsidy, and related benefits may also exacerbate these feelings.

Family adjustment.   It must be stressed here that, where spouses, partners, and children are involved, each family member is experiencing his or her own readjustment problems.[90] For some returnees, re-entry is a shock. It is as if they had pressed the 'pause' button as they flew out of the country, and expected life at home to remain in the 'freeze frame'. Re-entry reminds them that life is not static. Others may have, as a coping behavior in the foreign location, glamorized life back home, and now have to come to terms with reality, to accept the negative as well as the positive aspects of home. For example, the foreign country may have appeared more expensive in relative terms, but upon repatriation the family is confronted with a higher level of inflation in the home country than was previously the case. Conversely, life at home may now seem dull and unexciting in contrast, and the family unit may begin to glamorize the life they left behind in the foreign location. These reactions can be compounded if the family income has been reduced upon repatriation. Of course, the income level depends on whether spouses/partners worked while in the foreign location, and how quickly they find suitable jobs upon repatriation.

Social networks. In the past, impressions generated about changes in the home country may have depended on how effectively the family was able to keep up to date with events back home. In the twenty-first century this is much less of a problem as the coverage by satellite television news channels such as CNN and BBC World, widespread access to the internet, email, social media, mobile phone technology, the low cost of communication via Skype and global-oriented newspapers such as the *International Herald Tribune*, make it significantly easier for expatriates to follow events in their home country and stay in touch with their extended family. This in turn assists with re-establishing social networks, which can be difficult, especially if the family has been repatriated to a different state or town in the home country.

Children may also find re-entry difficult. Coming back to school, attempting to regain acceptance into peer groups and being out of touch with current sport and fashion can cause some difficulties. One can speculate that the more difficult the re-entry process for the children, the greater the 'spillover' effect for the repatriate.

Effect on partner's career. Partners encounter difficulties in re-entering the workforce, particularly if the partner has not been able to work outside the home prior to, or during, the foreign assignment but now desires to find outside employment, either as part of a re-entry coping strategy or due to altered family circumstances. Negative experiences during the job search may affect the partner's self-worth, compounding the readjustment process and even causing tension in the relationship. For those who held positions prior to the overseas assignment, difficulties in re-entering the workforce may depend on occupation,[91] length of time abroad, unemployment levels in the home country, and personal characteristics such as age and gender.[92]

There is limited research into the effects of the foreign assignment and repatriation upon the partner's career, and many questions surrounding this issue remain unexplored:

- Do new employers consider the value of the time overseas to 'compensate' for the forced career disruption?

- Have those partners who were able to work during the foreign assignment found employment in career-related jobs and been able to progress upon repatriation?

- What effect does not working during an assignment have on partners' self-esteem and confidence to re-enter the workforce upon repatriation? McNulty[93] found that expatriate partners were quite distressed during assignments when they were unable to work, often leading to serious consequences:

  I know for a fact a number of the female partners of my husband's male colleagues who have all relocated here have had serious problems adjusting due to their inability to work and make friends in this location. Many wish to return home, others are really stressed, and two are potential suicide cases [. . .] should I not be able to obtain work after a reasonable amount of time, I will seriously consider breaking the contract because I can think of a half dozen expat wives who are on anti-depressants because of it and I won't be joining them.

- Do male 'trailing' partners face different challenges upon repatriation than do females? In one of the few reported studies into dual-career expatriates, Harvey[94] found a difference between female expatriate managers' expectations prior to and after expatriation, exposing the need for support for the male trailing partner. The overseas assignment was the focus of Harvey's study, but one could assume that the same results would hold true upon repatriation. More recently, Linehan and Scullion[95] looked at the repatriation process of female expatriates working in various European companies but did not consider the career aspect of the accompanying spouse/partner.

Readjustment of the expatriate, whether male-led or female-led, may be linked with concerns about the effect that the foreign assignment might have on the partner's career. Given that dual-career couples are on the increase, and that more females expect overseas assignments, the issue of the partner's career is likely to become a major factor determining staff availability for future overseas assignments. Yet ORC[96] reported that, while pre-assignment and on-assignment assistance to spouses was relatively good, the likelihood of multiple types of support was smaller upon repatriation. Our analysis has revealed how various factors influence re-entry and readjustment at the individual level. These moderating factors can combine in hard-to-predict ways, creating a volatile situation that may lead to the repatriate's unforeseen and debilitating exit from the multinational.

RESPONSES BY THE MNE

The above sections have considered the re-entry and career issues from the perspective of the individual repatriate. We shall now examine the issues from the viewpoint of the multinational enterprise. Early studies into the issue of repatriation indicated that it was somewhat neglected by MNEs. For example, Mendenhall, Dunbar and Oddou[97] concluded that US HR professionals may be unaware of the challenges facing repatriated managers. Commenting on the results of his 1989 study, Harvey[98] noted that: "Even though many executives have experienced difficulties upon repatriation, [US] multinationals have seemingly not addressed the issues related to repatriation with the same level of interest as preparing executives for expatriation".

However, it appears that there has been some slight recent progress on this issue. For example, the Brookfield data shows that, in 2015, 93 per cent of responding firms held re-entry discussions, compared with a historical average of 92 per cent. The timing and formality of these re-entry discussions varies. For example, 7 per cent of respondents discussed repatriation before leaving on the assignment, 34 per cent did so at least six months before return, and 52 per cent discussed repatriation less than six months before assignment completion. The Brookfield surveys do not report on spousal or family involvement in re-entry discussions, but these aspects were raised in the ORC Worldwide 2005 report on dual-careers, which reported job search assistance, résumé preparation and career counseling as the most common forms of assistance. However, the report does not indicate if this was negotiated before or during the international assignment or upon re-entry, and if it was part of a re-entry discussion.

Managing the process of repatriation should be of concern to MNEs that desire to maximize the benefits of international assignments and create a large internal labor market.[99] A well-designed repatriation process is important in achieving these objectives for three main reasons: staff availability, ROI, and knowledge transfer. These are now discussed.

Staff availability and career expectations

The way a multinational enterprise handles repatriation has an impact on staff availability for current and future needs, as indicated in Figure 7.6. Re-entry positions signal the importance given to international experience. If the repatriate is promoted or given a position that obviously capitalizes on international experience, other managers interpret this as evidence that international assignments are a positive career move. On the other hand, if a MNE does not reward expatriate performance, tolerates a high turnover among repatriates, or is seen to terminate a repatriate's employment upon re-entry, then it is likely that younger managers will conclude that acceptance of an international assignment is a relatively high-risk decision in terms of future career progression within the organization. The MNE's ability to attract high-caliber staff for international assignments is thereby lessened, and this can have a negative effect on the firm's international activities in the long term.

FIGURE 7.6 Linking repatriation process to outcomes

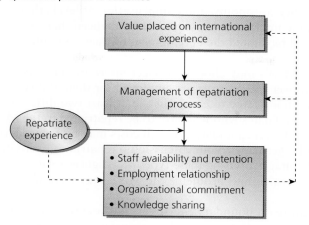

Recently, there has been some discussion in the management literature about international assignments and *boundaryless careers*. The term 'boundaryless career' appears to have been coined in recognition of shifts occurring in the employment relationship, particularly in Western countries. The traditional hierarchical career path, with definable stages (such as junior, middle, and senior manager), assumed long-term employment within one organization – the so-called 'job for life', where one climbed the corporate ladder. Employees now tend to switch jobs more frequently, either voluntarily or involuntarily due to economic changes or organizational restructuring. "*The* **boundaryless careerist** *[. . .] is the highly qualified mobile professional who builds his or her career competencies and labor market value through transfers across boundaries*".[100]

Careers are becoming discontinuous in the sense that individuals move between organizations and may have periods of contract work, self-employment, or unemployment interspersed with more traditional employment arrangements. International assignments, particularly for career expatriates or global managers, are sometimes regarded as boundaryless in that the assignment places the person in another organization, most commonly a subsidiary or an international joint venture. Accompanying this view is the notion that the individual rather than the organization is responsible for career management: the term 'protean' (after the Greek god Proteus, who could change into any form)[101] is sometimes used to reflect the idea of a self-directed career with continuous learning.

Multinationals are reinforcing the notion of protean and boundaryless careers when they do not guarantee repatriates positions upon re-entry. As Stahl *et al.*[102] found in their large study of 494 German managers posted to 59 countries: "the vast majority of expatriates viewed their international assignment as an opportunity for skill development and future career advancement, even though it may not be with their current company, [which] supports the notion of boundaryless careers". The McNulty *et al.* study cited earlier displays similar findings in their study of 31 Asia-based expatriates, where 87 per cent perceived that undertaking an international assignment would benefit their long-term career prospects but not necessarily their continued employment with their firm. In such cases, commitment and loyalty to the organization is instead replaced by commitment and loyalty to one's career, i.e. a 'free agent' mentality. Such a change may restrict the ability of the organization to retain high-caliber individuals to successfully complete international assignments, thus affecting the quality as well as the quantity of suitable candidates and the development of a cadre of global operators.

Similar results were found in a study of German and Singaporean expatriates. Both of these groups reported concerns with their firms' ability to facilitate their careers upon return from international assignments, provide further opportunities to use the new knowledge and skills they had gained during their international assignments, or provide them with new positions having the responsibility, autonomy, and compensation at levels that met their expectations. They did feel as if these international assignments enhanced their opportunities among other possible employers and facilitated the development of their own intercultural and professional or managerial skills.[103]

In some instances MNEs may choose to select *international itinerants* – that is, "professional managers who over their careers are employed for their ability, by at least two business organizations that are not related to each other, in at least two different countries",[104] instead of selecting in-house candidates who will have to be repatriated to the MNE. By selecting these individuals in lieu of internal candidates, overall costs may be reduced, ongoing support costs can be managed, and – germane to our discussion – repatriation activities can be eliminated. The two main disadvantages of using these types of assignees relate to a lack of in-depth firm knowledge by the itinerants and problems the MNE may have in selecting and controlling itinerants.[105]

Much of the literature on boundaryless careers has focused on domestic business, particularly in the USA. Some researchers suggest that expatriate careers still correspond very much to the traditional model of the organizational career, especially in the case of a global corporate philosophy that places some emphasis on the development of global leaders.[106] Festing and Müller[107] found in a study of 168 alumni of a European business school that, in cases where international assignments had an important strategic value for the MNE and were accompanied by a high level of IHRM activity, expatriates had rather traditional career expectations aiming at a long-term employment relationship with their employer. In these cases the retention rates of international managers after the international assignment were high. This indicates that the organizational context at least partly influences the emergence of expatriate career patterns and confirms the relationships outlined in Figure 7.5, i.e. that IHRM measures such as repatriation programs influence the outcomes in terms of the employment relationship in general and specifically employee retention rates and commitment.

How actively an MNE manages an international assignee's career may vary substantially, with decisions made on the basis of strategy or simply reaction to circumstances. Career management is conceptualized in an analysis of 194 UK-based firms by Baruch and Peiper as being more or less sophisticated and with more or less involvement by the firm in an employee's career. 'Basic' and 'formal' practices, comprised less sophisticated career practices and low levels of involvement, are characterized by practices such as common career paths, written personal career planning, job posting, and lateral moves. More sophisticated practices with higher levels of firm involvement in an employee's career are described as 'multidirectional' and 'active planning' forms of career management. These models are characterized by practices such as in-depth career counseling, succession planning, a strong link between performance management systems and career planning, peer appraisals, and upward appraisal processes.[108] Surprisingly little is known about the factors that determine how much time, energy, and effort returning expatriates and executives in MNEs will put into career practices designed to maintain existing work relationships, as opposed to simply accepting repatriation turnover as an inevitable cost of doing business globally.

Return-on-investment

Expatriates are expensive, especially expatriates from first-world advanced economies. Where possible, multinationals try to localize positions through the employment of HCNs, but not all positions can or should be localized. Similarly, MNEs are increasingly using local-plus compensation for PCNs or TCNs as a way to reduce costs.[109] One alternative, which more MNEs are utilizing or experimenting with, is a short-term or non-standard assignment to replace the traditional expatriate assignment. Cost containment is the driver here along with staff immobility, as the discussion in Chapter 5 has shown.

Getting a return on the investment related to an international assignment would appear to be an important objective but not easy to achieve. First, there is a matter of definition. In one of the few articles that considered ROI on international assignments, McNulty and Tharenou[110] recognize that a meaningful definition should include a cost-benefit analysis of financial and non-financial data, measured against the purpose of the assignment. Identifying direct costs is relatively easy as relocation expenses, an itemized compensation package, and other international assignee entitlements are accessible. The indirect, intangible, non-financial costs are more problematical. These include the non-direct costs of expatriate failure or underperformance and the opportunity cost of not using a HCN.

Placing monetary value on the benefits of the international assignment is also a challenge as the intangibles (e.g. knowledge and skills transfer, management development, and relationship/network building) are somewhat invisible, often tacit and person-bound. It is difficult to measure intellectual, social, and human capital gains[111] – improvements in the stock of knowledge and competence that result from a successful repatriation process. ROI analysis also focuses on the international assignment period, and can be an exercise to justify cost-reduction measures (such as replacing expatriates with HCNs) rather than considering gains that accrue to the organization through repatriated staff.

Although firms participating in the Brookfield surveys tracked assignment costs, only 5 per cent of respondents in the 2015 survey[112] formally measured ROI of assignments, the lowest in the history (9 per cent) of the 20-year report. Difficulties encountered in attempts to measure ROI were:

- not being sure how to measure ROI (53 per cent)

- lack of importance of ROI to organizational goals (not required) (11 per cent)

- no time to measure (8 per cent).

More importantly, when asked to rate their firm's international assignments in terms of ROI, 14 per cent rated ROI as excellent, 43 per cent as very good, and 43 per cent as good. The historical average for excellent/very good (combined) is 23 per cent, for good alone 44 per cent, and for fair/poor (combined) 33 per cent. So, we see some current changes here.[113] The measures included in the ROI were the expatriate compensation package (71 per cent), the relocation support costs (71 per cent), the completion of the assignment objectives (43 per cent), the business revenue generated (43 per cent), the administration costs (29 per cent), the costs of possible attrition (29 per cent), employee development (29 per cent), and others.

Further, employees will perform their own ROI calculations (what McNulty *et al.* call *individual ROI*) based on perceived and actual costs and benefits, and these calculations will influence their willingness to accept an international assignment (or repeat the experience) either with their current firm or another employer.[114] Aligning corporate objectives with individual expectations is not an easy task, and compounds attempts to balance costs and benefits for both parties.[115]

Knowledge transfer

A common theme in current international business that is stressed by managers is the need for cross-fertilization of ideas and practices that assist in developing and maintaining competitive advantage. International assignments are a primary method of achieving this objective. As the Economist Intelligence Unit 2010[116] report concludes:

> If globalization is seen as inexorable then companies, to a greater or lesser extent, will need a globally mobile workforce tasked with administering their far-flung but rapidly growing operations [. . .] but getting the right people in the right place for the right length of time to execute that international

strategy is no simple matter. The expatriate experience provides a valuable insight into globalization's big trends, while touching many of the business operational dilemmas that companies encounter when investing abroad.

Given the roles played by expatriates, along with their cost, it is reasonable to expect that MNEs would endeavor to retain key staff and to extract and build upon their international experience. However, as we have seen in our examination of re-entry and career issues, a relatively high turnover of repatriate staff seems acceptable. More telling is the continuing trend not to guarantee post-assignment positions so that the organization has greater flexibility over employment levels. We can draw several conclusions regarding repatriate attrition rates. First, despite the rhetoric, knowledge transfer is treated as a one-way activity. Expatriates are sent on international assignments and effectiveness is determined on the performance of their ascribed roles and work responsibilities. Any transfer of knowledge and competence occurs in the host location and remains there. Expatriates return to their home base and are reassigned or resign.

Although some MNEs have attempted to capture knowledge acquired in international assignments, research on this area is limited by modelling issues and a paucity of robust, dynamic investigations.[117] The point here is that, while performing their tasks in the host location, expatriates develop skills and gain experience, knowledge, and network relationships that can then be used upon repatriation in some way or another. For example, a project manager working in Russia can report, on re-entry to his UK home base, technical problems encountered and solutions that were developed to overcome these problems, thus sharing the experience. However, not all of the knowledge about that project is explicit. Much will remain tacit and person-bound. What is codified and made explicit often is retained within the project team, even though some of the information and knowledge could be applicable to other projects or types of business concerning Russia, such as important contacts, management styles, and some technical solutions. In addition, international assignments vary in terms of purpose, duration, location, and nature and these differences affect the acquisition and transfer of knowledge and skills.

HCNs transferred to headquarters for developmental reasons, for example, may benefit through such exposure, but the experience will remain person-bound if the home unit does not allow the repatriated HCN opportunities to share knowledge and information. Contacts at headquarters can be used for personal advantage. A similar case can be made for TCNs transferred from another subsidiary. The aims of cross-fertilization of ideas and best practices given to justify cross-border movement of staff require the right environment to facilitate sharing of information and knowledge. The 'not-invented-here' mindset (or xenophobia) can operate to devalue repatriate contributions.

What knowledge and skills are acquired through a typical international assignment? A study of 19 Austrian repatriates provides some answers. Based on in-depth interviews, Fink *et al.*[118] classified repatriate knowledge into five categories:

- *Market-specific knowledge.* Local system (political, social, economic), local language, and local customs.

- *Personal skills.* Intercultural knowledge, self-confidence (that is, ability to make quick decisions), flexibility, tolerance.

- *Job-related management skills.* Communication, project management, problem solving.

- *Network knowledge.* Meeting diverse people – clients, suppliers, subsidiary personnel, other expatriates.

- *General management capacity.* An enlarged job description, broader job responsibilities, exposure to other parts of the organization.

The range of knowledge and skills listed comprise both tacit and explicit knowledge. The authors consider that the first four categories are useful for the sending organization, while the last (general management capacity) is most beneficial to the individual. Fink *et al.* conclude that repatriate knowledge may be useful in enhancing a firm's competitiveness but acknowledge the difficulties in capitalizing on this, particularly if repatriates exit before such knowledge has been transferred. They also point out that the size of the firm, and its stage in the internationalization process, is a critical factor. The Austrian firms in their sample were small and medium-sized enterprises (SMEs) that did not have need for a large number of 'general managers' and thus were unable to meet repatriate expectations based on their newly acquired skills and knowledge.

The trend towards not providing a post-assignment position guarantee suggests that multinationals accept loss of experience, knowledge, and competence; that repatriates effectively forced to leave the organization will take with them what could be vital and valuable, allowing competing firms to reap the benefits of a substantial investment in human capital. Those who remain in the organization may not be motivated to share.[119] Perhaps this apparent downgrading of the repatriate experience is partly due to the fact that many firms are unaware of the benefits of the international assignment to both the firm and the individual, as ROI calculations, clearly linked to the nature and purpose of the assignment, are not performed. As Downes and Thomas[120] found, MNEs that valued international experience were rewarded by loyal employees who contributed to the intellectual capital base of their firms. Unfortunately, the finding that repatriates become an underutilized resource has been a consistent result in studies and surveys examining repatriation.[121]

Blakeney, Oddou and Osland recommend that HR practitioners in multinational firms take a wider, more systemic view of the expatriate-repatriate cycle, and focus on: (1) identifying the critical, implicitly held knowledge assets inherent in expatriation/repatriation; and (2) reducing the sources of resistance to knowledge transfer inherent in the motivation and capabilities of the repatriate as well as the structural and cultural impediments inherent in the receiving unit at home. This can be done by building trust and enhancing the shared sense of social identity between the repatriate and the receiving unit.[122] Practically speaking, HR practices that combine a unified expatriation/repatriation cycle that explicitly emphasizes knowledge transference in each stage of the process (i.e. in selection, pre-departure and in-country training, mentoring or coaching, designing the international assignment, re-entry training, returnee job assignment and selection, as well as the training of the returnee's own manager) would clearly assist in the successful transfer of knowledge. More formal activities, including seminars by repatriates as post-assignment 'action learning' exercises and the development of knowledge-disseminating teams and databases made up to index the expertise of repatriates, can facilitate progress.[123]

Empirical research by Tung points out the potential for patterns of international careers – in this case, careers in MNEs moving back and forth between China and North America – to contribute to outward foreign direct investment strategies for MNEs.[124] These human capital flows are only now being documented and a rudimentary understanding of the complex relationships between government policies, cultural solidarity in the face of diasporas, and personal career ambition is beginning to emerge.

DESIGNING A REPATRIATION PROGRAM

While there is no simple, quick solution, preparing the repatriate and family for re-entry appears to have some value. The potential for mismatch of expectations regarding the future may be addressed as part of re-entry training before the return, and discussed during re-entry counseling sessions (sometimes referred to as debriefing) between the receiving organization in the home country and the repatriate. In common parlance, such sessions would enable both parties to 'take a reality check'. What should be covered in formal repatriation programs? Table 7.3 is an amalgam of the lists suggested by respondents in the various surveys referred to above.

TABLE 7.3 Topics covered by a repatriation program

- Preparation, physical relocation, and transition information (what the MNE will help with).
- Financial and tax assistance (including benefit and tax changes; loss of overseas allowance).
- Re-entry position and career path assistance.
- Reverse culture shock (including family disorientation).
- School systems and children's education, and adaptation.
- Workplace changes (such as corporate culture, structure, decentralization).
- Stress management, communication-related training.
- Establishing networking opportunities.
- Help in forming new social contacts.

Some MNEs assign the expatriate a *mentor* (also referred to as a sponsor). The mentor is usually in a more senior position than the expatriate, from the sending work unit, and often knows the expatriate personally. The rationale behind the use of a mentor is to alleviate the 'out-of-sight, out-of-mind' feeling discussed earlier through the provision of information (such as, workplace changes) on a regular basis, so that the expatriate is more prepared for conditions faced upon re-entry. A mentor should also ensure that the expatriate is not forgotten when important decisions are made regarding positions and promotions. Linehan and Scullion[125] found that 40 of the 50 females in their study had experienced mentoring relationships and believed that their management positions were partially due to that relationship. The mentors provided contact and support from the home organization that also facilitated re-entry and reduced the 'out-of-sight, out-of-mind' syndrome. Their experiences led them to adopt mentoring roles in their new domestic positions.

It is reasonable to suggest that the practice of mentoring, to be effective, has to be managed. For example, what happens when the mentor retires or leaves the firm? Who monitors the mentor's performance? In the 2015 Brookfield Survey, 9 per cent of the investigated companies indicated that they used mentoring programs for improving ROI. Mentoring duties include the following examples[126]:

- maintaining contact with the expatriate throughout the assignment
- ensuring expatriates are kept up to date with developments in the home country
- ensuring expatriates are retained in existing management development programs
- being responsible for assisting expatriates with the repatriation process, including assisting them to obtain a repatriation position.

It may be that having a mentor assists the expatriate to adjust during the foreign assignment but, by itself, does not necessarily help re-entry. Stroh[127] concludes that her study "did not show that having a mentoring program would make an independent contribution to the repatriate retention rate", but there was a suggested link between assignment of a mentor, career development, and repatriate retention. In other words, an effective mentor is likely to alert the firm with regard to the imminent return of the repatriate and this influences the provision of a suitable re-entry position; or the mentor role is part of a managed repatriation program.

Caligiuri and Lazarova[128] recommend a number of proactive strategies to maximize the likelihood that the professional, financial, and emotional issues faced by repatriates and their families will be dealt with and repatriates will be able to return with an integrated and balanced set of experiences which will be available to the MNE (see the right-hand box of Figure 7.4). These proactive strategies include:

- managing expectations via pre-departure briefings on what can be expected during the assignment and upon return

- multiple career-planning sessions focusing on career objectives and performance indicators, carried out by HR managers or a purpose-built team of past repatriates and relevant executives

- written repatriate agreements when feasible to clarify the types of assignments available upon return

- mentoring programs that continue on into the repatriate's post-assignment career; this practice may act to notify the firm of any post-assignment dissonance and reduce turnover

- extended home visits to keep up with social, family, and organizational changes

- reorientation programs to provide the repatriate with a briefing on changes in strategy, policies, and organization

- personalized reorientation by the MNE so the repatriate and his or her family may deal with the emotionally charged issues of social readjustment, schools, family dynamics, and lifestyle changes inherent in return

- personalized financial and tax advice, as well as access to interim financial benefits such as short-term loans

- providing some kind of an adjustment period upon return that may or may not include a vacation or reduced workload

- visible and concrete expressions of the repatriate's value to the firm (in the form of promotion, public ceremonies, or a completion bonus), required to seal and reinforce this new, more globally encompassing relationship between the MNE and the repatriate.

The Brookfield 2015 Survey[129] reports that 64 per cent of companies had a formal repatriation policy in place, compared to a historical average of 71 per cent. Only 14 per cent had a repatriation strategy linked to career management in place (historical average: 18 per cent).

While recognition of the importance of repatriation programs should be increasing, and MNEs are experimenting with other measures such as mentors, other avenues could be explored such as using repatriates as an important information source. Inviting repatriates to assist in developing repatriation programs may contribute to relevant and effective policies. It may also have a desirable side-effect upon readjustment simply by giving participating repatriates a sense that they are not an underutilized resource, and that the MNE recognizes they can make a valuable contribution to the expatriation process. It is, naturally, important that wherever possible the multinational ensures equity of treatment between PCN, TCN, and HCN expatriates.

Global Careers and GTM[130]

Within the area of IHRM and due to the *war for talent*,[131] referring to demographic shifts, declining birth rates, ageing workforce labor shortage, and increased need for international managers in some countries, the field of Global Talent Management (GTM) has emerged.[132]

Talent management has been consistently cited as one of the top priorities for executives around the world in the last years.[133] It has also caught researchers' attention, so the research field has rapidly developed in the last decade.[134] There are various definitions and forms of managing talent; however, in this chapter we use Hugh Scullion and David Collings'[135] definition of GTM, meaning: "all organizational activities for the purpose of attracting, selecting, developing, and retaining the best employees in the most strategic roles on a global scale".

What becomes clear is that managing international talent is most often about key employees, also referred to as *high potentials*, in strategic positions in the company, and therefore differs from IHRM, which addresses all employees in the whole organization. Furthermore, GTM focuses on a smaller subset of practices, while IHRM encompasses a wider variety of HR policies and practices (e.g. compensation, labor relations, health and safety, etc.) and thus IHRM also includes more stakeholders (e.g. customers, investors, labor unions).[136] GTM can therefore be examined as being part of IHRM.

In their research studying global talent management processes and practices of a large sample of 37 multinational, successful and well-known corporations in North America, Europe, and Asia, Stahl et al.[137] identify several talent management best practices (practices, which the companies report work well for them) in the areas of: (1) recruitment, staffing, and succession planning; (2) training and development; and (3) retention management. However, what these authors also state is, in order to be successful, merely implementing these practices is not sufficient; they need to be properly aligned with the company's business strategy, internally consistent and integrated in other elements of the talent management system, and deeply embedded in the corporate culture.[138]

Despite the wide variety of practices and varying focuses of talent management systems, there is a general consensus amongst practitioners and academics alike that training and development play a crucial role in retaining high potentials and internally grooming future leaders.[139] So, talent development programs, job rotation, coaching, investments, corporate academies and programs delivered by leading business schools have increasingly taken on the talent management approach.[140]

Further global talent challenges pertain to the sufficient supply of talent inflows – meeting the increasing need for international managers with a specific skill set, the integration of skilled ethnic minorities,[141] global mobility, the management of multiple generations in the workplace (e.g. Generations X, Y and Z),[142] as well as workforce diversity.[143]

To conclude, managing this pivotal group of employees in a global context is similarly complex as is IHRM for a multinational enterprise, trying to balance global standardization and local adaptation between the headquarters and international subsidiaries.[144] Extracts and peculiarities on how to manage talent in different national and cultural settings such as Brazil, China, the Association of South Eastern Asian Nations (ASEAN), India, the Middle East, and Central and Eastern Europe can be found in Scullion and Collings' manual on GTM,[145] or the summary of GTM by Akram Al Ariss.[146] However, research also suggests that Talent Management is context-specific and the national environment and business system[147] highly influence the way Talent Management is conducted. Therefore, another challenge for GTM for MNEs is to consider these industries' regional or national (e.g. European Union) specific peculiarities.

SUMMARY

This chapter has concentrated on the issues relating to training and developing expatriates for international assignments and the repatriation process. With regard to training and development we have discussed:

- the role of expatriate training in supporting adjustment and on-assignment performance

- the components of effective pre-departure training programs such as cultural awareness, preliminary visits, language skills, relocation assistance, and training for trainers

- how cultural awareness training appears to assist in adjustment and performance and therefore should be made available to all categories of staff selected for overseas postings, regardless of duration and location

- the need for language training for the host country and in the relevant corporate language
- the impact that an international assignment may have on an individual's career
- the international assignment as an important way of training international operators and developing the international 'cadre'; in this sense, an international assignment is both training (gaining international experience and competence) and managerial and organizational development.

With regard to the repatriation process we have discussed:

- the overall process of repatriation. With re-entry, the broader socio-cultural context of the home country takes a backstage position – unlike in the expatriation adjustment phase, where the foreign culture can be overwhelming. For the majority of repatriates, coming home to the familiar culture may assist in readjustment
- the more profound effect that job-related factors appear to have, and how *re-entry shock* is perhaps a more accurate term to describe the readjustment process experienced upon repatriation
- the particular importance of career issues upon re-entry to repatriates. Factors that affect career anxiety are: no post-assignment guarantee of employment; fear that the period overseas has caused a loss of visibility; changes in the home workplace that affect re-entry positions; and the employment relationship
- the re-entry position as an important indicator of future career progression and the value placed on international experience. Coping with new role demands is another factor in readjustment, along with loss of status and pay
- social factors that can include loss of social standing and the accompanying loss of the expatriate lifestyle. Family readjustment is also important. A specific aspect is the effect of the international assignment upon the spouse/partner's career, such as being re-employed and having international experience recognized
- MNE responses to repatriates' concerns focusing on re-entry procedures. Issues covered include: how repatriation affects staff availability, whether companies are measuring and obtaining a return on investment through international assignments, and the contribution of repatriates to knowledge transfer. The concepts of protean and boundaryless careers were introduced in terms of the international assignment and career outcomes
- the design of effective repatriation programs, including the use of mentors and available forms of technology
- the view of repatriation as part of the expatriation process, as suggested in Figure 7.4, which should remind those responsible for expatriation management of the need to prepare repatriates for re-entry and to recognize the value of the international experience to both parties.

Further, we highlighted the meaning of GTM in MNEs.

DISCUSSION QUESTIONS

1 Summarize the key challenges faced in training expatriate managers.

2 Assume you are the HR director for a SME that has begun to use international assignments. You are considering using an external consulting firm to provide pre-departure training for employees, as you do not have the resources to provide this 'in-house'. What components will you need covered? How will you measure the effectiveness of the pre-departure training program provided by this external consultant?

3 How does an international assignment assist in developing a 'cadre' of international operators? Why is it necessary to have such a cadre?

4 Why do some MNEs appear reluctant to provide basic pre-departure training?

5 What factors contribute to re-entry shock?

6 What are the objectives of a good mentoring system for international assignees?

7 Placing value on the international assignment assists repatriate retention. Discuss this statement.

8 Why is it important to measure ROI for international assignments? Which indicators can be used?

9 How do practices related to Talent Management differ from more general HRM activities? What special issues or concerns must be faced by MNEs in terms of a unified yet responsive GTM program?

FURTHER READING

P. Caligiuri and J. Bonache 'Evolving and Enduring Challenges in Global Mobility', *Journal of World Business*, 51 (1) (2016), pp. 127–141.

P. Caligiuri and I. Tarique 'International Assignee Selection and Cross-cultural Training and Development', in G. Stahl, I. Björkman and S. Morris (eds.) *Handbook of Research in International Human Resource Management*, 2nd ed. (Cheltenham: Edward Elgar, 2012), pp. 321–342.

M. Dickmann and Y. Baruch *Global Careers* (New York: Routledge, 2011).

A. McDonnell, P. Gunnigle and J. Lavelle 'Learning Transfer in Multinational Companies: Explaining Inter-organization Variation', *Human Resource Management Journal*, 20 (1) (2010), pp. 23–43.

R. Poeli, T. Rocco and G. Roth (eds.) *The Routledge Companion to Human Resource Development* (London: Routledge Publishing, 2015).

H. Scullion and D. Collings *Global Talent Management* (London: Routledge, 2011).

P. Tharenou and N. Caulfield 'Will I Stay or Will I Go? Explaining Repatriation by Self-Initiated Expatriates', *Academy of Management Journal*, 53 (5) (2010), pp. 1009–1028.

NOTES AND REFERENCES

1. K. Kamoche 'Strategic Human Resource Management with a Resource-Capability View of the Firm', *Journal of Management Studies*, Vol. 33, No. 2 (1996), p. 216.

2. verantwortung.lufthansa.com/fileadmin/downloads/en/LH-school-of-business.pdf.

3.   For recent reviews of developments in the field of global mobility in general see Y. McNulty and H. De Cieri's introductions in 'Advances in the Field of Global Mobility: Complexity and Challenges', *International Studies of Management and Organization*, Vol. 44, No. 2 (2014), pp. 3–8 and 'Advances in the Field of Global Mobility: Reflection, Reaction and Redirection', *International Studies of Management and Organization*, Vol. 44, No. 3 (2014), pp. 3–7.

4.   See Brookfield *Global Relocation Services (ed.) Global Mobility Trends Survey Report*, 2015 (Woodridge, IL, 2015).

5.   P. C. Earley 'Intercultural Training for Managers: A Comparison', *Academy of Management Journal*, Vol. 30, No. 4 (1987), p. 686.

6.   M. C. Gertsen, A.M. Söderberg and M. Zölner (eds.) *Global Collaboration: Intercultural Experiences and Learning* (Palgrave Macmillan, 2012); especially Festing, M. 'State of the Art: International Human Resource Management and Cultural Learning' (2012) pp. 59–76 in the same volume.

7.   R. Tung 'Selection and Training Procedures of US, European, and Japanese Multinationals', *California Management Review*, Vol. 25, No. 1 (1982), pp. 57–71.

8.   Brookfield Global Relocation Services (ed.) *Global Mobility Trends Survey Report*, 2015 (Woodridge, IL, 2015).

9.   K. Barham and M. Devine *The Quest for the International Manager: A Survey of Global Human Resource Strategies*, Ashridge Management Research Group, Special Report No. 2098 (London: The Economist Intelligence Unit, 1990). See also D. Welch 'Determinants of International Human Resource Management Approaches and Activities: A Suggested Framework', *Journal of Management Studies*, Vol. 31, No. 2 (1994), pp. 139–164.

10. I. Littrell and E. Salas 'A Review of Cross-Cultural Training: Best Practices, Guidelines, and Research Needs', *Human Resource Development Review*, Vol. 4, No. 3 (2005), pp. 305–334.

11. Mercer HR, 2010 International Assignments Survey, Geneva.

12. See, for example, M. Mendenhall and G. Oddou 'Acculturation Profiles of Expatriate Managers: Implications for Cross-Cultural Training Programs', *Columbia Journal of World Business*, Winter (1986), pp. 73–79. For a more recent and updated discussion see G. Stahl, M. Mendenhall, and G. Oddou (eds.) *Readings and Cases in International Human Resource Management and Organizational Behavior*, 5th ed. (New York: Routledge Publishing, 2012).

13. R. Tung 'Selecting and Training of Personnel for Overseas Assignments', *Columbia Journal of World Business*, Vol. 16 (1981), pp. 68–78.

14. R. Tung 'A Contingency Framework of Selection and Training of Expatriates Revisited', *Human Resource Management Review*, Vol. 8, No. 1 (1998), pp. 23–37.

15. M. Mendenhall and G. Oddou 'Acculturation Profiles of Expatriate Managers'; M. Mendenhall, E. Dunbar and G. Oddou 'Expatriate Selection, Training and Career-Pathing: A Review and Critique', *Human Resource Management*, Vol. 26 (1987), pp. 331–345.

16. Earley advocates the use of both documentary and interpersonal methods to prepare managers for intercultural assignments (see P. Earley 'International Training for Managers: A Comparison of Documentary and Interpersonal Methods', *Academy of Management Journal*, Vol. 30, No. 4 (1987), pp. 685–698). Baliga and Baker suggest that the expatriates receive training that concentrates on the assigned region's culture, history, politics, economy, religion and social and business practices. They argue that only with precise knowledge of the varied components of their host culture can the expatriate and family grasp how and why people behave and react as they do (see G. Baliga and J. C. Baker 'Multinational Corporate Policies for Expatriate Managers: Selection, Training, and Evaluation', *Advanced Management Journal*, (Autumn 1985), pp. 31–38).

17. For further information on the use of cultural assimilators see R. Brislin 'A Culture General Assimilator: Preparation for Various Types of Sojourns', *International Journal of Intercultural Relations*, Vol. 10 (1986), pp. 215–234; and K. Cushner 'Assessing the Impact of a Culture General Assimilator', *International Journal of Intercultural Relations*, Vol. 13 (1989), pp. 125–146.

18. ORC '2008 Worldwide Survey of International Assignment Policies and Practices', New York.

19. C. Brewster and J. Pickard 'Evaluating Expatriate Training', *International Studies of Management and Organization*, Vol. 24, No. 3 (1994), pp. 18–35. For a more abstract discussion on the impact of community on an expatriate's global capabilities see K.Y. Ng, M. Tan and S. Ang 'Global Cultural Capital and Cosmopolitan Human Capital', in A. Burton-Jones and J.C. Spender (eds.) *The Oxford Handbook of Human Capital* (Oxford: Oxford University Press, 2011), pp. 96–119.

20. C. Wright and S. Wright 'Do Languages Really Matter? The Relationship between International Business Success and a Commitment to Foreign Language Use', *Journal of Industrial Affairs*, Vol. 3, No. 1 (1994), pp. 3–14. These authors suggest that international English is perhaps a better term than 'poor' or 'broken' English.

21. Brookfield Global Relocation Services (ed.) *Global Mobility Trends Survey Report*, 2015 (Woodridge, IL, 2015).

22. Baliga and Baker 'Multinational Corporate Policies'. For a presentation of more indirect, contextual impact at the level of the subsidiary see S. Reiche, A.W. Harzing and M. Pudelko 'Why and How Does Shared Language Affect Subsidiary Knowledge Inflows? A Social Identify Perspective', *Journal of International Business Studies*, Vol. 46 (2015), pp. 528–551.

23. R. Tung and Arthur Andersen *Exploring International Assignees' Viewpoints: A Study of the Expatriation/ Repatriation Process* (Chicago, IL: Arthur Andersen, International Executive Services, 1997).

24. Y. McNulty 'Being Dumped in to Sink or Swim: An Empirical Study of Organizational Support for the Trailing Spouse', *Human Resource Development International*, Vol. 15, No. 4 (2012), pp. 417–434.

25. R. Marschan, D. Welch and L. Welch 'Language: The Forgotten Factor in Multinational Management', *European Management Journal*, Vol. 15, No. 5 (1997), pp. 591–597; see also Fixman 'The Foreign Language Needs of US-Based Corporations'. For an interesting alternative argument against the 'Babel' of myriad language use in

the MNE, see S. Volk, T. Kohler and M. Pudelko 'Brain Drain: The Cognitive Neuroscience of Foreign Language Processing in Multinational Corporations', *Journal of International Business Studies*, Vol. 45 (2014), pp. 862–885.

26. A.W. Harzing and M. Pudelko 'Hablas Vielleicht un peu la Mia Language? A Comprehensive Overview of the Role of Language Differences in Headquarters-subsidiary Communication', *International Journal of Human Resource Management*, Vol. 25, No. 5 (2014), pp. 696–717.

27. See R. Chebium 'A Common Language: Training Across Borders', *HR Magazine*, Vol. 60, No. 1 (2015), pp. 53–58.

28. Y. McNulty, H. De Cieri and K. Hutchings 'Expatriate Return on Investment in Asia Pacific: An Empirical Study of Individual ROI versus Corporate ROI', *Journal of World Business*, 48 (2013), pp. 209–221.

29. Mercer HR, 2010 International Assignments Survey, Geneva.

30. Relocation specialist companies include Cartus, Brookfield and Pricoa-Prudential, among others.

31. ORC '2008 Worldwide Survey of International Assignment Policies and Practices', New York.

32. Brookfield Global Relocation Services (ed.) *Global Mobility Trends Survey Report*, 2015 (Woodridge, IL, 2015).

33. See, for example, H. Park, S. D. Hwang and J. K. Harrison 'Sources and Consequences of Communication Problems in Foreign Subsidiaries: The Case of United States Firms in South Korea', *International Business Review*, Vol. 5, No. 1 (1996), pp. 79–98; and A. Rao and K. Hashimoto 'Intercultural Influence: A Study of Japanese Expatriate Managers in Canada', *Journal of International Business Studies*, Vol. 27, No. 3 (1996), pp. 443–466.

34. M. Lazarova and I. Tarique 'Knowledge Transfer Upon Repatriation', *Journal of World Business*, Vol. 40 (2005), pp. 361–373, quotation from p. 370.

35. M. Harvey '"Inpatriation" Training: The Next Challenge for International Human Resource Management', *International Journal of Intercultural Relations*, Vol. 21, No. 3 (1997), pp. 393–428.

36. Brookfield Global Relocation Services (ed.) *Global Mobility Trends Survey Report*, 2015 (Woodridge, IL, 2015), p.82.

37. An exception is an article by R. DeFrank, R. Konopaske and J. M. Ivancevich 'Executive Travel Stress: Perils of the Road Warrior', *Academy of Management Executive*, Vol. 14, No. 2 (2000), pp. 58–71. However, the authors only devote one paragraph to host-culture issues.

38. D. Welch and V. Worm 'International Business Travelers: A Challenge for IHRM', in G. Stahl and I. Björkman (eds.) *Handbook of Research in International Human Resource Management* (Cheltenham: Edward Elgar, 2006), pp. 283–301.

39. Brookfield Global Relocation Services (ed.) Global Mobility Trends Survey Report, 2015 (Woodridge, IL, 2015).

40. D. Eschbach, G. Parker and P. Stoeberl 'American Repatriate Employees' Retrospective Assessments of the Effects of Cross-Cultural Training on their Adaptation to International Assignments', *International Journal of Human Resource Management*, Vol. 12, No. 2 (2001), pp. 270–287.

41. M. Morris and C. Robie 'A Meta-Analysis of the Effects of Cross-Cultural Training on Expatriate Performance and Adjustment', *International Journal of Training and Development*, Vol. 5, No. 2 (2001), pp. 112–125. The authors define meta-analysis as 'a method developed in the late 1970s to summarize and integrate research findings from multiple articles [. . .] to resolve conflicting findings of multiple studies on the same topic by combining their results in a systematic fashion', pp. 113–114.

42. J. Selmer, I. Torbiön and C. de Leon 'Sequential Cross-Cultural Training for Expatriate Business Managers: Pre-departure and Post-arrival', *International Journal of Human Resource Management*, Vol. 9, No. 5 (1998), pp. 831–840.

43. See 'Small Nations in the Global Economy: An Overview', in D. Van Den Bulke, A. Verbeke and W. Yuan (eds.) *Handbook on Small Nations in the Global Economy: The contribution of multinational enterprises to national economic success* (Cheltenham: Edward Elgar, 2009).

44. K. Inkson, Y. McNulty and K. Thorn 'The Global Careers of Australians and New Zealanders', in Y. Baruch and C. Reis (eds.) *Careers Without Borders* (UK: Routledge, 2013).

45. The delimiting effects of national culture, at least within Europe, are presented in a review of executive careers by E. Davoine and C. Ravasi 'The Relative Stability of National Career Patterns in European Top Management Careers in the Age of Globalization: A Comparative Study in France/Germany/Great Britain and Switzerland', *European Management Journal*, Vol. 31 (2013), pp. 152–163. Robust ongoing efforts continue to capture complex, 'protean' career opportunities associated with globalization and track the career impact of the growing forms of international assignments noted in earlier chapters. For examples see Y. Baruch 'The Development and Validation of a Measure for Protean Career Orientation', *International Journal of Human Resource Management*, Vol. 25, No. 19 (2014), pp. 2702–2724; Y. Baruch, M. Dickmann, Y. Altman and F. Bournois 'Exploring International Work: Types and Dimensions of Global Careers', *International Journal of Human Resource Management*, Vol. 24, No. 12 (2013), pp. 2369–2393; and A. Fee, S. Gray and S. Lu 'Developing Cognitive Complexity from the Expatriate Experience: Evidence from a Longitudinal Field Study', *International Journal of Cross Cultural Management*, Vol. 13, No. 3 (2013), pp. 299–318.

46. Y. McNulty, H. De Cieri and K. Hutchings 'Expatriate Return on Investment in Asia Pacific: An Empirical Study of Individual ROI Versus Corporate ROI', *Journal of World Business*, Vol. 48, No. 2 (2013), pp. 209–221.

47. See P. Evans 'Management Development as Glue Technology', *Human Resource Planning*, Vol. 14: 4 (1992).

48. R. Peterson 'The Use of Expatriates and Inpatriates in Central and Eastern Europe Since the Wall Came Down', *Journal of World Business*, Vol. 38 (2003), pp. 55–69.

49. P. Caligiuri and V. Di Santo 'Global Competence: What is It, and Can It be Developed Through Global Assignments?', *Human Resource Planning*, Vol. 24, No. 3 (2001), pp. 27–35.

50. See P. Caligiuri 'Developing Culturally Agile Global Business Leaders', *Organizational Dynamics*, Vol. 42 (2013), pp. 175–182; M. Mendenhall and A. Bird 'In Search of Global Leadership', *Organizational Dynamics*, Vol. 42

(2013), pp. 167–174; and R. Steers and W. Shim 'Strong Leaders, Strong Cultures: Global Management Lessons From Toyota and Hyundai', *Organizational Dynamics*, Vol. 42 (2013), pp. 217–227.

51. A discussion of how leaders may adjust their leadership style across assignments is provided by M. Festing and M. Maletzy on 'Cross Cultural Leadership Adjustment – A Multilevel Framework Based on the Theory of Structuration', *Human Resource Management Review*, Vol. 21 (2011), pp. 186–200. For the proffering of a measure of the capabilities of global leaders see M. Stevens, A. Bird, M. Mendenhall and G. Oddou 'Measuring Global Leader Intercultural Competency: Development and Validation of the Global Competencies Inventory (GCI)', *Advances in Global Leadership*, Vol. 8 (2014), pp. 115–154. For a well-written example of leadership as the independent variable and its possible links to other firm qualities, in this case how a well-developed global leadership perspective may relate to corporate social responsibility on the part of the MNE, see C. Miska, G. Stahl and M. Mendenhall 'Intercultural Competencies as Antecedents of Responsible Global Leadership', *European Journal of International Management*, Vol. 7, No. 5 (2013), pp. 550–569.

52. J. Gibbs 'Decoupling and Coupling in Global Teams: Implications for Human Resource Management', in G. Stahl and I. Björkman (eds.) *Handbook of Research in International Human Resource Management* (Cheltenham: Edward Elgar, 2006), pp. 347–363.

53. M. Maznevski, S. Davison and K. Jonsen 'Global Virtual Team Dynamics and Effectiveness', in G. Stahl and I. Björkman (eds.) *Handbook of Research in International Human Resource Management* (Cheltenham: Edward Elgar, 2006), pp. 364–384.

54. P. Caligiuri and I. Tarique 'International Assignee Selection and Cross–cultural Training and Development', in G. Stahl and I. Björkman (eds.) *Handbook of Research in International Human Resource Management* (Cheltenham: Edward Elgar, 2006), pp. 302–322.

55. A. Al-Dosary and S. Rahman 'Saudization (Localization) – A Critical Review', *Human Resource Development International*, Vol. 8, No. 4 (2005), pp. 495–502.

56. M. Geppert 'Competence Development and Learning in British and German Subsidiaries of MNCs: Why and How National Institutions Still Matter', *Personnel Review*, Vol. 34, No. 2 (2005), pp. 155–177.

57. W. Chang 'Expatriate Training in International Nongovernmental Organizations: A Model for Research', *Human Resource Development Review*, Vol. 4, No. 4 (2005), pp. 440–461; C. Brewster and S. Lee 'HRM in Not-for-profit International Organizations: Different, But Also Alike', in H. Larsen and W Mayrhofer (eds.) *European Human Resource Management* (London: Routledge, 2006). For a presentation of how universities may provide global leadership capabilities in a more traditional classroom setting see M. Mendenhall, A. Arnardottir, G. Oddou and L. Burke 'Developing Cross-cultural Competencies in Management Education Via Cognitive-behavior Therapy', *Academy of Management Learning & Education*, Vol. 12, No. 3 (2013), pp. 436–451.

58. J. Wang, G. Wang, W. Ruona and J. Rojewski 'Confucian Values and the Implications for International HRD', *Human Resource Development International*, Vol. 8, No. 3 (2005), pp. 311–326; C. Zhao 'Management of Corporate Culture through Local Managers' Training in Foreign Companies in China: A Qualitative Analysis', *International Journal of Training and Development*, Vol. 9, No. 4 (2005), pp. 232–255; D. Zhang, Z. Zhang and B. Yang 'Learning Organization in Mainland China: Empirical Research on its Application to Chinese State-owned Enterprises', *International Journal of Training and Development*, Vol. 8, No. 4 (2004), pp. 258–273; C. Zhu *Human Resource Management in China: Past, Current and Future HR Practices in the Industrial Sector* (London: Routledge, 2004); J. Wang and G. Wang 'Exploring National Human Resource Development: A Case of China Management Development in a Transitioning Context', *Human Resource Development Review*, Vol. 5, No. 2 (2006), pp. 176–201.

59. B. Metcalfe and C. Rees 'Theorizing Advances in International Human Resource Development', *Human Resource Development International*, Vol. 8, No. 4. (2005), pp. 449–465.

60. See L. Stroh, J. S. Black, M. Mendenhall and H. Gregersen *International Assignments: An Integration of Strategy, Research and Practice* (Mahiwah, NJ: Lawrence Erlbaum, 2005); M. Harvey and M. Novicevic 'The Evolution from Repatriation of Managers in MNEs to "Patriation" in Global Organizations', in G. Stahl and I. Björkman (eds.) *Handbook of Research in International Human Resource Management* (Cheltenham: Edward Elgar, 2006), pp. 323–343.

61. R. Moran 'Coping with Re-entry Shock', *International Management* (December 1989), p. 67; M. G. Harvey 'Repatriation of Corporate Executives: An Empirical Study', *Journal of International Business Studies*, Vol. 20, No. 1 (Spring 1989), pp. 131–144.

62. Stroh *et al. International Assignments* (Endnote 63); Harvey 'Repatriation of Corporate Executives'.

63. Y. Paik, B. Segand and C. Malinowski 'How to Improve Repatriation Management: Are Motivations and Expectations Congruent Between the Company and Expatriates?', *International Journal of Management*, Vol. 23 (2002), pp. 635–648; Stroh *et al. International Assignments.*

64. Mercer HR, 2010 International Assignments Survey, Geneva.

65. J. S. Black, H. Gregersen and M. Mendenhall 'Towards a Theoretical Framework for Repatriation Adjustment', *Journal of International Business Studies*, Vol. 23 (1992), pp. 737–760.

66. ORC '2008 Worldwide Survey of International Assignment Policies and Practices', New York.

67. Stroh *et al. International Assignments*, pp. 215–216.

68. W. Mayrhofer, M. Meyer, A. Lellatchitch and M. Schiffinger 'Careers and Human Resource Management: A. European Perspective', *Human Resource Management Review*, Vol. 14 (2004), pp. 473–498; Stroh *et al. International Assignments,* pp. 199–217.

69. A.W. Harzing *Environment, Strategy, Structure, Control Mechanisms, and Human Resource Management in*

Multinational Companies, Company Report (Limburg, The Netherlands: University of Limburg, 1996).

70. Brookfield Global Relocation Services (ed.) *Global Mobility Trends Survey Report*, 2015 (Woodridge, IL, 2015).

71. Brookfield Global Relocation Services (ed.) *Global Mobility Trends Survey Report*, 2015 (Woodridge, IL, 2015).

72. R. Tung and Arthur Andersen *Exploring International Assignees' Viewpoints: A Study of the Expatriation/Repatriation Process* (Chicago, IL: Arthur Andersen, International Executive Services, 1997); D. Feldman and D. Thomas 'Career Issues Facing Expatriate Managers', *Journal of International Business Studies*, Vol. 23, No. 2 (1992), pp. 271–294.

73. Brookfield Global Relocation Services (ed.) *Global Mobility Trends Survey Report*, 2015 (Woodridge, IL, 2015).

74. Brookfield Global Relocation Services (ed.) *Global Mobility Trends Survey Report*, 2015 (Woodridge, IL, 2015).

75. Harzing *Environment, Strategy, Structure, Control Mechanisms*; D. Osborn 'The International Mobility of French Managers', *European Management Journal*, Vol. 15, No. 5 (1997), pp. 584–590.

76. Y. McNulty, H. De Cieri and K. Hutchings 'Expatriate Return on Investment in Asia Pacific: An Empirical Study of Individual ROI Versus Corporate ROI', *Journal of World Business*, Vol. 48, No. 2 (2012) [dx.doi.org/10.1016/j.jwb.2012.07.005].

77. S. Black and H. Gregersen 'When Yankee Comes Home: Factors Related to Expatriate and Spouse Repatriation Adjustment', *Journal of International Business Studies*, Vol. 22, No. 4 (1991), pp. 671–694.

78. M. Bolino and D. Feldman 'Increasing the Skill Utilization of Expatriates', *Human Resource Management*, Vol. 39, No. 4 (2000), pp. 367–379.

79. L. Stroh, H. Gregersen and J. Black 'Closing the Gap: Expectations Versus Reality Among Repatriates', *Journal of World Business*, Vol. 33, No. 2 (1998), p. 119.

80. Y. McNulty, H. De Cieri and K. Hutchings, ibid.

81. J. Black, H. Gregersen and M. Mendenhall 'Toward a Theoretical Framework of Repatriation Adjustment', *Journal of International Business Studies*, Vol. 23, No. 4 (1992), pp. 737–760.

82. M. Lazarova and P. Caligiuri 'Retaining Repatriates: The Role of Organizational Support Practices', *Journal of World Business*, Vol. 36, No. 4 (2001), pp. 389–401.

83. Stroh, Gregersen and Black 'Closing the Gap', p. 119.

84. V. Suutari and C. Brewster 'Repatriation: Empirical Evidence from a Longitudinal Study of Careers and Expectations among Finnish Expatriates', *International Journal of Human Resource Management*, Vol. 14, No. 7 (2003), pp. 1132–1151.

85. L. Stroh 'Predicting Turnover among Repatriates: Can Organizations Affect Retention Rates?', *International Journal of Human Resource Management*, Vol. 6, No. 2 (1995), p. 450.

86. Stroh, Gregersen and Black 'Closing the Gap'. See also R. L. Tung 'Career Issues in International Assignments', *Academy of Management Executive*, Vol. 2, No. 3 (1988), pp. 241–244; and H. Gregersen 'Commitments to a Parent Company and a Local Work Unit during Repatriation', *Personnel Psychology*, Vol. 45, No. 1 (Spring 1992), pp. 29–54; R. Tung 'A Contingency Framework Revisited',

87. *Human Resource Management Review*, Vol. 8, No. 1 (1998), pp. 23–37.

R. Tung and E. Miller 'Managing in the Twenty-first Century: The Need for Global Orientation', *Management International Review*, Vol. 30, No. 1 (1990), pp. 5–18; D. Allen and S. Alvarez 'Empowering Expatriates and Organizations to Improve Repatriation Effectiveness', *Human Resource Planning*, Vol. 21, No. 4 (1998), pp. 29–39.

88. H. Mintzberg *The Nature of Managerial Work* (Englewood Cliffs, NJ: Prentice-Hall, 1973), p. 54.

89. I. Torbiörn 'The Structure of Managerial Roles in Cross-cultural Settings', *International Studies of Management & Organization*, Vol. 15, No. 1 (1985), p. 69.

90. For an excellent, if not somewhat irreverent illustration of spouse repatriation challenges, see Robin Pascoe's book *Homeward Bound: A Spouse's Guide to Repatriation* (Vancouver: Expatriate Press, 2000).

91. G. Stevens and S. Black 'The Impact of Spouse's Career-Orientation on Managers During International Transfers', *Journal of Management Studies*, Vol. 28, No. 4 (1991), pp. 417–428.

92. Black and Gregersen 'When Yankee Comes Home'.

93. Y. McNulty 'Being dumped in to sink or swim: An empirical study of organizational support for the trailing spouse', *Human Resource Development International*, Vol. 15, No. 4 (2012), pp. 417–434.

94. M. Harvey 'Dual-Career Expatriates: Expectations, Adjustment and Satisfaction with International Relocation', *Journal of International Business Studies*, Vol. 28, No. 3 (1997), pp. 627–658.

95. M. Linehan and H. Scullion 'Repatriation of European female corporate executives: An empirical study', *International Journal of Human Resource Management*, 13(2) (2002), pp. 254–267.

96. ORC '2005 Dual Careers and International Assignments Survey', New York.

97. M. Mendenhall, E. Dunbar and G. Oddou 'Expatriate Selection, Training and Career-pathing: A Review and a Critique', *Human Resource Planning*, Vol. 26, No. 3 (1987), pp. 331–345.

98. Harvey 'The Other Side of Foreign Assignments'.

99. As discussed by G. Oddou, B. Szkudlarek, J. Osland, J. Deller, R. Blakeney and N. Fufuya in 'Repatriates as a Source of Competitive Advantage: How to Manage Knowledge Transfer', *Organizational Dynamics*, Vol. 42 (2013), pp. 257–266. Also see J. Gonzalez and S. Chakraborty 'Expatriate Knowledge Utilization and MNE Performance: A Multilevel Framework', *Human Resource Management Review*, Vol. 24 (2014), pp. 299–312.

100. D. Thomas, M. Lazarova, and K. Inkson 'Global Careers: New Phenomenon or New Perspectives?', *Journal of World Business*, Vol. 40, No. 4 (2005), p. 341.

101. See, for example, J. Mezias and T. Scandura 'A Needs Driven Approach to Expatriate Adjustment and Career Development: A Multiple Mentoring Perspective', *Journal of International Business Studies*, Vol. 36, No. 5 (2005), pp. 519–539.

102. G. Stahl, E. Miller and R. Tung 'Toward the Boundaryless Career: A Closer Look at the Expatriate Career Concept and the Perceived Implications of an International Assignment', *Journal of World Business*, Vol. 37 (2002), p. 222.

103. See G. Stahl and C. Chua 'Global Assignments and Boundaryless Careers: What Drives and Frustrates International Assignees?', in M. Morley N. Heraty and D. Collins (eds.) *International Human Resource Management and International Assignments* (Basingstoke: Palgrave Macmillan, 2006), pp. 133–152.

104. M. Banal and W. Harry 'Boundaryless Global Careers: The International Itinerants', in M. Morley, N. Heraty and D. Collins (eds.) *International Human Resource Management and International Assignments* (Basingstoke: Palgrave Macmillan, 2006), pp. 153–180, especially p. 157.

105. Ibid.

106. Y. Baruch and Y. Altman 'Expatriation and Repatriation in MNCs: A Taxonomy', *Human Resource Management*, Vol. 41, No. 2 (2002), pp. 239–259.

107. M. Festing and B. Müller 'Expatriate Careers and the Psychological Contract – An Empirical Study on the Impact of International Human Resource Management', in M. Festing and S. Royer (eds.) *Current Issues in International Human Resource Management and Strategy Research* (München and Mering: Hampp, 2008), pp. 93–118.

108. For more on the sophistication and commitment to career management see Y. Baruch and M. Peiper 'Career Management Practices: An Empirical Survey and Implications', *Human Resource Management*, Vol. 39, No. 4 (2000), pp. 347–366; J. Richardson and M. Mallon 'Career Interrupted: The Case of the Self-Directed Expatriate', *Journal of World Business*, Vol. 40, No. 4 (2005), pp. 409–420; and D. Thomas, M. Lazarova and K. Inkson 'Global Careers: New Phenomenon or New Perspectives?', *Journal of World Business*, Vol. 40 (2005), pp. 340–347.

109. P. Stanley 'Local-plus Packages for Expatriates in Asia: A Viable Alternative', *International Human Resource Journal*, Vol. 3 (2009), pp. 8–11.

110. Y. McNulty and P. Tharenou 'Expatriate Return on Investment', *International Studies of Management & Organization*, Vol. 34, No. 3 (2004), pp. 68–95.

111. See D. Welch, A. Steen and M. Tahvanainen 'All Pain, Little Gain? Reframing the Value of International Assignments', *International Journal of Human Resource Management*, Vol. 20, No.6 (2009), pp. 1327–1343. An effort to operationalize social capital is provided by O. Levy, M. Peiperl and C. Bouquet 'Transnational social capital: A conceptualization and research instrument', *International Journal of Cross Cultural Management*, Vol. 13, No. 3 (2013), pp. 319–338.

112. Brookfield Global Relocation Services (ed.) *Global Mobility Trends Survey Report*, 2015 (Woodridge, IL, 2015).

113. Ibid.

114. Y. McNulty 'Expatriate Return on Investment: Past, Present and Future', in D. Collings, G. Wood and P. Caligiuri (eds.) *The Routledge Companion to International Human Resource Management*, New York: Routledge Publishing, pp. 399–420.

115. McNulty, Hutchings and De Cieri 'How Expatriates in Asia View Expatriate Return on Investment: An Empirical Study of Individual ROI Versus Corporate ROI'. For a lucid review of potential differences in the timing and calculated nature of ROI on the part of the employee and the MNE,

see Y. McNulty and H. De Cieri 'Linking Global Mobility and Global Talent Management: The Role of ROI', *Employee Relations*, Vol. 38, No. 8 (2016), pp. 3–30.

116. D. Bolchover '2010 Up or Out: Next Moves for the Modern Expatriate' (London, UK: Economist Intelligence Unit).

117. See D. Minbaeva 'IHRM's Role in Knowledge Management in Multinational Corporations', in D. Collings, G. Wood and P. Caligiuri (eds.) *The Routledge Companion to International Human Resource Management* (London: Routledge Publishing, 2015), pp. 457–468.

118. G. Fink, S. Meierewert and U. Rohr 'The Use of Repatriate Knowledge in Organizations', *Human Resource Planning*, Vol. 28, No. 4 (2005), pp. 30–36.

119. M. Lazarova and I. Tarique 'Knowledge Transfer upon Repatriation', *Journal of World Business*, Vol. 40, No. 4 (2005), pp. 361–373.

120. M. Downes and A. Thomas 'Managing Overseas Assignments to Build Organizational Knowledge', *Human Resource Planning*, Vol. 22, No. 4 (1999), pp. 31–48. Systemic effort to incorporate 'learning-organization' capabilities into the MNE are presented by H. Shipton, Q. Zhou and E. Mooi 'Is There a Global Model of Learning Organizations? An Empirical, Cross Nation Study', *International Journal of Human Resource Management*, Vol. 24, No. 12 (2013), pp. 2278–2298.

121. See, for example, R. Tung and Arthur Andersen *Exploring International Assignees' Viewpoints*; Price Waterhouse Europe 'International Assignments: European Policy and Practice'; Lazarova and Caligiuri 'Retaining Repatriates'.

122. R. Blakeney, G. Oddou and J. Osland 'Repatriate Assets: Factors Impacting Knowledge Transfer', in M. Morley, N. Heraty and D. Collings (eds.) *International Human Resource Management and International Assignments* (Basingstoke: Palgrave Macmillan, 2006), pp. 181–199.

123. As reported by Blakeney *et al.* 'Repatriate Assets'. Colgate-Palmolive developed a database of repatriate skills, as 'the company saw the value of having information on each manager's knowledge/experience with particular cultures and disseminating knowledge about local markets throughout its global operations', p. 194. For a more in-depth discussion of potential relationships between knowledge-mapping processes, career development and strategic activities in transnational firms see A. Engle, P Dowling and M. Mendenhall 'Transnational Trajectories: Emergent Strategies of Globalization and a New Context for Strategic HRM in MNEs' (working paper, 2007).

124. R. Tung 'The Human Resource Challenge to Outward Foreign Direct Investment Aspirations from Emerging Economies: The Case of China', *International Journal of Human Resource Management*, May, Vol. 18, Issue 5 (2007), pp. 868–889.

125. Linehan and Scullion 'Repatriation of European Female Corporate Executives'.

126. PriceWaterhouse Europe 'International Assignments', p. 32.

127. Stroh 'Predicting Turnover among Repatriates', p. 454.

128. P. Caligiuri and M. Lazarova 'Strategic Repatriation Policies to Enhance Global Leadership Development', in M. Mendenhall, T Kuhlmann and G. Stahl (eds.) *Developing Global leaders: Policies, Processes and Innovations* (Westport, CT: Quorum Books, 2001), pp. 243–256.

129. Brookfield Global Relocation Services (ed.) *Global Mobility Trends Survey Report*, 2015 (Woodridge, IL, 2015).

130. The authors would like to thank Lynn Schäfer, Head of the Talent Management Institute at the ESCP-Europe campus in Berlin, Germany for her significant assistance in this presentation. The topic of talent management is complex and dynamic; its relationship to employee development activities in MNEs is doubly so. For a further sense of these issues see escpeurope-talentmanagementinstitut.de/

131. E.G. Chambers, M. Foulton, H. Handfield-Jones, S.M. Hankin and E.G. Michaels III 'The War for Talent', *McKinsey Quarterly*, Issue 3 (1998), pp. 44–57; E. Michaels, H. Handfield-Jones and B. Axelrod *The War for Talent* (Boston, Mass: Harvard Business School Press, 2001).

132. G.K. Stahl, I. Björkman, E. Farndale, S.S. Morris, J. Paauwe, P. Stiles, J. Trevor and P.M. Wright 'Global talent management: How leading multinational build and sustain their talent pipeline', *INSEAD Faculty and Research Working Paper 34/OB* (2007); I. Tarique and R.S. Schuler 'Global Talent Management: Literature Review, Integrative Framework, and Suggestions for Further Research', *Journal of World Business*, 45 (2010), pp. 122–133; H. Scullion and D. Collings (eds.) *Global Talent Management* (London, New York: Routledge, 2011); D. Collings 'Integrating Global Mobility and Global Talent Management: Exploring the Challenges and Strategic Opportunities', *Journal of World Business*, Vol. 49 (2014), pp. 253–261.

133. BCG and WFPMA *Creating People Advantage in 2012. Mastering HR Challenges in a Two-Speed World*, www.bcgperspectives.com/content/articles/people_management_human_resources_leadership_creating_people_advantage_2012/, 10 February 2016; BCG and EAPM, *Creating People Advantage 2013. Lifting HR Practices to the next level*, www.bcg.de/documents/file147615.pdf, 10 February 2016.

134. C. Tansley, P.A. Turner, C. Foster, L.M. Harris, J. Stewart, A. Sempik *et al. Talent: Strategy, Management, Measurement* (Plymouth, UK: Chartered Institute of Personnel and Development, 2007); E. Gallardo-Gallardo, P. Gallo and N. Dries 'A Bibliometric Analysis of TM Research from 1990–2013: Productivity, Impact and Collaboration', in 2nd EIASM Workshop on Talent Management (Brussels, Belgium, 2013).

135. H. Scullion and D. Collings (eds.) *Global Talent Management* (London, New York: Routledge, 2011), p. 6.

136. I. Tarique and R.S. Schuler 'Global Talent Management: Literature Review, Integrative Framework, and Suggestions for Further Research', *Journal of World Business*, Vol. 45 (2010), pp. 122–133.

137. G. Stahl, I. Björkman, E. Farndale, S.S. Morris, J. Paauwe, P. Stiles, J. Trevor and P.M. Wright 'Global Talent Management: How Leading Multinational Build and Sustain Their Talent Pipeline', INSEAD Faculty and Research Working Paper 34/OB (2007), p. 10.

138. G. Stahl, I. Björkman, E. Farndale, S.S. Morris, J. Paauwe, P. Stiles, J. Trevor and P.M. Wright, ibid; G. Stahl, I. Björkman, E. Farndale, S.S. Morris, J. Paauwe, P. Stiles, J. Trevor and P.M. Wright 'Six Principles of Effective Global Talent Management', *MIT Sloan Management Review*, Vol. 53 (2012), pp. 25–32.

139. V. Vaiman and D. Collings 'Global Talent Management' in D. Collings, G. Wood and P. Caligiuri (eds.) *The Routledge Companion to International Human Resource Management*. (London: Routledge Publishers, 2015), pp. 210–225.

140. G. Stahl, I. Björkman, E. Farndale, S.S. Morris, J. Paauwe, P. Stiles, J. Trevor and P. Wright, ibid. For a well-written review of the relationship between leadership development activities and the area of talent management, see P. Iles 'Talent Management and Leadership Development', in R. Poell, T. Rocco and G. Roth (eds.) *The Routledge Companion to Human Resource Development* (London: Routledge Publishing, 2015), pp. 212–222.

141. A. Al Ariss, J. Vassilopoulou, M.F. Özbilgin and A. Game 'Understanding Career Experiences of Skilled Minority Ethnic Workers in France and Germany', *International Journal of Human Resource Management*, Vol. 24 (2013), pp. 1236–1256.

142. See also M. Festing and L. Schäfer 'Generational Challenges to Talent Management: A Framework for Talent Retention Based on the Psychological Contract Perspective', *Journal of World Business*, Vol. 49 (2014), pp. 262–271.

143. I. Tarique and R. Schuler 'Global Talent Management: Literature Review, Integrative Framework, and Suggestions for Further Research', *Journal of World Business*, Vol. 45 (2010), pp. 122–133; H. Scullion and D. Collings (eds.) *Global Talent Management* (London, New York: Routledge, 2011); D. Collings 'Integrating Global Mobility and Global Talent Management: Exploring the Challenges and Strategic Opportunities', *Journal of World Business*, Vol. 49 (2014), pp. 253–261.

144. J. Boudreau, P. Ramstad and P. Dowling 'Global Talentship: Toward a Decision Science Connecting Talent to Global Strategic Success', *Advances in Global Leadership*, Vol. 3 (2003), pp. 63–99.

145. H. Scullion and D. Collings (eds.) *Global Talent Management* (London: Routledge, 2011). p. 6.

146. A. Al Ariss (ed.) *Global Talent Management: Challenges, Strategies and Opportunities* (Cham, Heidelberg, New York, Dordrecht, London: Springer Science + Business Media, 2014).

147. M. Festing, L. Schäfer and H. Scullion 'Talent Management in Medium-sized German Companies: An Explorative Study and Agenda for Future Research', *International Journal of Human Resource Management*, Vol. 24, No. 9 (2013), pp. 1872–1893.

CHAPTER 8
INTERNATIONAL
COMPENSATION

Chapter Objectives

In the introductory chapter we described international HR managers as grappling with complex issues. International managers must: (1) manage more activities from a broader perspective; (2) be more involved in the lives of their far-flung employees; (3) balance the needs of parent-country nationals (PCNs), host-country nationals (HCNs), and third-country nationals (TCNs); (4) control exposure to financial and political risks; and (5) be increasingly aware of and responsive to host-country and regional influences. All of these issues and concerns are highlighted in stark contrast in a discussion of compensation issues. In this chapter we:

- examine the complexities that arise when firms move from compensation at the domestic level to compensation in an international context

- detail the key components of an international compensation program

- outline the two main approaches to international compensation (Going Rate and Balance Sheet) and the advantages and disadvantages of each approach

- introduce a third emerging approach to international compensation: Local Plus

- examine the special problem areas of taxation, valid international living cost data, and the problem of managing TCN compensation

- examine recent developments and global compensation issues.

INTRODUCTION

Global compensation practices have recently moved far beyond the original domain of expatriate pay. Compensation is increasingly seen as: a mechanism to develop and reinforce a global corporate culture,[1] a primary source of corporate control, explicitly linking performance outcomes with associated costs,[2] and the nexus of increasingly strident, sophisticated, and public discourses on central issues of corporate governance in an international context.[3] All of these goals are simultaneously pursued across a range of legal and regulatory environments.[4]

Increased *complexities* in global pay include the growing use of outsourced activities and subsequent labor-pricing needs,[5] balancing centralization and decentralization of incentives, benefits and pensions, given the technical capabilities of web-based human resource information systems (HRIS),[6] and balancing the need for more accurate and detailed performance metrics on international assignees with the realities of a cost-sensitive environment resulting from maturing global competitiveness.[7]

Increasingly, domestic pay practices of long-standing have been questioned as firms move into the global arena. These overt *challenges* to deeply held national and corporate values and pay systems include challenges to the universal applicability of incentive pay programs[8] and what some critics view as out-of-control executive compensation programs, often driven by US-based multinational pay systems.[9] Critiques of US-based MNE pay for executives have recently expanded to include challenges to the effectiveness of legal and institutional forms of corporate governance and the roles, responsibilities, and pay practices of corporate boards, compensation committees, and the use of executive pay consultants.[10]

Greater *choice,* the growing ability to systematically identify and implement heretofore novel or unrecognized pay practices, may be seen to result from increases in the transparency of pay practices around the world due to increased global media attention and reach, changes in corporate reporting regulations, the sheer number of assignments across borders, as well as the impact of the World Wide Web.[11] It remains to be seen if this increased choice will translate into a predictable set of global pay practices.

These complexities, challenges, and choices facing managers involved in global compensation decisions do not change two primary areas of focus. These individuals must manage highly complex and turbulent local details, while concurrently building and maintaining a unified, strategic pattern of compensation policies, practices, and values.[12]

For MNEs to successfully manage compensation and benefits requires knowledge of employment and taxation law, customs, environment, and employment practices of many foreign countries; familiarity with currency fluctuations and the effect of inflation on compensation; and an understanding of why and when special allowances must be supplied and which allowances are necessary in what countries – all within the context of shifting political, economic, and social conditions. The level of local knowledge needed in many of these areas requires specialist advice and many multinationals retain the services of consulting firms that may offer a broad range of services or provide highly specialized services relevant to human resource management (HRM) in a multinational context.[13]

Because of its complexity and expense, much of the discussion in this chapter addresses PCN compensation. However, issues relevant to TCNs and HCNs are also described because they are becoming more important to the success of many multinational enterprises (MNEs).[14] Indeed, expatriate compensation – long the preoccupation of global HR executives – is increasingly seen more as a component of a more balanced, albeit complex system of worldwide pay.[15] National and regional differences in the meaning, practice, and tradition of pay remain significant sources of variation in the international firm. Yet these contextual sources of complexity must be balanced with strategic intent and administrative economy.[16] Rather than seeing pay as an ethnocentric extension of an essentially domestic strategy, pay systems are increasingly becoming truly global – with truly global objectives.[17]

Objectives of international compensation

When developing international compensation policies, an MNE seeks to satisfy several objectives. First, the policy should be consistent with the overall strategy, structure, and business needs of the multinational. Second, the policy must work to attract and retain staff in the areas where the MNE has the greatest needs and opportunities. Thus, the policy must be competitive and recognize factors such as incentive for foreign service, **tax equalization,** and reimbursement for reasonable costs. Third, the policy should facilitate the transfer of international employees in the most cost-effective manner for the firm. Fourth, the policy must give due consideration to equity and ease of administration.

The international employee will also have a number of objectives that need to be achieved from the firm's compensation policy. First, the employee will expect the policy to offer financial protection in terms of benefits, social security and living costs in the foreign location. Second, the employee will expect a foreign assignment to offer opportunities for financial advancement through income and/or savings. Third, the employee will expect issues such as the cost of housing, education of children, and home leave to be addressed in the policy.

If we contrast the objectives of the MNE and the employee, we of course see the potential for many complexities and possible problems, as some of these objectives cannot be maximized on both sides. The 'war stories' about problems in international compensation that we see in HR practitioner magazines are testimony to these complexities and problems. McNulty et al. also allude to these problems in their studies of expatriation, particularly in the Asia-Pacific region.[18]

However, if we take away the specialist jargon and allow for the international context, are the competing objectives of the firm and the employee *fundamentally* different from that which exists in a domestic environment? We think not. We agree with the broad thrust of an influential article by Milkovich and Bloom[19] which argues that firms must rethink the traditional view that local conditions dominate international compensation strategy. This is again another application of the ongoing balancing act between global standardization and local customization. We will return to these issues at the end of the chapter after we have covered some of the technical aspects and complexities of compensation in an international context.

KEY COMPONENTS OF AN INTERNATIONAL COMPENSATION PROGRAM FOR EXPATRIATES

The area of international compensation is complex primarily because multinationals must cater to three categories of employees: PCNs, TCNs, and HCNs. In this section, we discuss key components of international compensation as follows.

Base salary

The term **base salary** acquires a somewhat different meaning when employees go abroad. In a domestic context, base salary denotes the amount of cash compensation serving as a benchmark for other compensation elements (such as bonuses and benefits). For expatriates, it is the primary component of a package of allowances, many of which are directly related to base salary (e.g. foreign service premium, cost-of-living allowance, housing allowance) as well as the basis for in-service benefits and pension contributions. It may be paid in home or local-country currency or a combination of both. The base salary is the foundation block for international compensation whether the employee is a PCN or TCN. Major differences can occur in the employee's package depending on whether the base salary is linked to the home country of the PCN or TCN, or whether an international rate is paid. (We will return to this issue later in the chapter.)

Foreign service inducement and hardship premium

PCNs often receive a salary premium as an inducement to accept a foreign assignment, as well as a **hardship premium** to compensate for challenging locations. Under such circumstances, the definition of hardship, eligibility for the premium, and amount and timing of payment must be addressed. For example, where a host country's work week may be longer than that of the home country, a differential payment may be made in lieu of overtime, which is not normally paid to PCNs or TCNs. In cases in which hardship is determined, US firms often refer to the US Department of State's *Hardship Post Differentials Guidelines* to determine an appropriate level of payment. As a number of researchers in this field have noted over many decades,[20] making international comparisons of the cost of living is problematic. It is important to note, though, that these payments are more commonly paid to PCNs than TCNs. Foreign service inducements, if used, are usually made in the form of a percentage of salary, usually 5 to 40 per cent of base pay, but are also sometimes offered as a lump-sum incentive (i.e. as a one-off payment made at some point during an assignment). Such payments vary, depending upon the assignment location, tax consequences, and length of assignment.

Allowances

Issues concerning allowances can be very challenging to a firm establishing an overall compensation policy, partly because of the various forms of allowances that exist. In this section we will discuss the six most common allowances.

Cost-of-living allowance.   The cost-of-living allowance (COLA), which typically receives the most attention, involves a payment to compensate for differences in expenditures between the home country and the foreign country. COLA payments are intended to compensate for cost differentials between an expatriate's home and host country – for example, the costs of transportation, furniture and appliances, medical expenditures, alcohol and tobacco, automobile maintenance, and domestic help. Family size is the predominant method for determining COLA payments, with increments provided for each child. Often this allowance is difficult to determine, so companies may use the services of organizations such as Mercer (a US-based firm)[21] or ECA International (based in Britain).[22] These firms specialize in providing COLA information on a global basis, regularly updated, to their clients. The COLA may also include payments for housing and utilities, and discretionary items.[23] Various COLA indices exist, which, for example, allow an American to live like an American in Paris or which presume that the American will adapt to the assignment location by adjusting to the local lifestyle and international living costs.

Housing allowance.   The provision of a **housing allowance** implies that employees should be entitled to maintain their home-country living standards (or, in some cases, receive accommodation that is equivalent to that provided for similar foreign employees and peers). The amount of housing allowance is determined predominantly by family size and, to some extent, job level. Other alternatives include: company-provided housing (either mandatory or optional); a fixed housing allowance across a particular job level, with the expatriate 'topping up' according to personal preferences; or assessment of a portion of income, out of which actual housing costs are paid. Housing issues are often addressed on a case-by-case basis, but as a firm internationalizes, formal policies become more necessary and efficient. Financial assistance and/or protection in connection with the leasing of an expatriate's former residence is offered by many MNEs, but less so for selling a house, as many MNEs encourage their employees to retain a presence in their home-country real estate market. Those in the banking and finance industry tend to be the most generous, offering assistance in sale and leasing, payment of closing costs, payment of leasing management fees, rent protection, and equity protection. Generally, TCNs tend to receive these benefits less frequently than PCNs.

Home leave allowances.   Many MNEs also have a provision for home leave allowances, where employers cover the expense of one or more trips back to the home country each year. The primary purpose of paying for such trips is to give expatriates the opportunity to renew family and business ties, thereby helping them to minimize adjustment problems when they are repatriated. Although firms traditionally have restricted the use of leave allowances to travel home, some firms give expatriates the option of applying home leave to foreign travel rather than returning home. Firms allowing use of home leave allowances for foreign travel need to be aware that expatriate employees with limited international experience who opt for foreign travel rather than returning home may become more homesick than other expatriates who return home for a 'reality check' with fellow employees and friends. Without the benefit of returning home to mix with employees and friends, it is possible to idealize what they remember of their experience at work and home and fail to come to a measured judgement of what is good and bad in both their host and home environments. Overall, it would seem prudent for MNEs to take the view that home leave allowances should normally be used for the purpose for which they are provided – to give employees and their families the opportunity to renew family and business ties, thereby increasing the probability of reduced adjustment problems when they are repatriated.

Education allowances.   The provision of education allowances for the children of expatriates is frequently an integral part of an international compensation policy. Allowances for education can cover items such as tuition (including language classes), application and enrolment fees, books and supplies, meals, transportation, excursions and extracurricular activities, parent association fees, school uniforms and, if applicable, room and board. Although school uniforms are not common in the USA, it is common practice (and in many countries compulsory) for schoolchildren to wear uniforms, particularly in international schools. PCNs and TCNs usually receive similar treatment concerning educational expenses, but the level of education provided for and the adequacy of local public schools vs. international schools may present problems for multinationals. International schools (e.g. United World College of South East Asia; British International School, Shanghai) are far more expensive than local public schools but are preferred by many expatriates because these schools follow the home-country curriculum and cater to a globally diverse student body more capable of supporting 'third-culture kids'. The costs of local and international schools for dependent children from kindergarten through to high school are typically covered by the employer. Opinion Research Corporation (ORC) reports that 95 per cent of MNEs contribute to the educational expenses of expatriate children.[24] However, there may be restrictions depending on the age of the children (pre-school, day care and university are typically not covered), availability of school places, and their fees. In a number of countries, attendance at schools in the host location may be seen as unsuitable and the MNE may cover (or contribute towards) the costs of children attending a private boarding school elsewhere (e.g. the costs of room and board as well as other transportation costs to cover parental visits and school holiday travel).[25] The costs of attendance at a university may also be provided for by multinationals when deemed necessary, but this is rare.

Relocation allowances.   Items typically covered by relocation allowances include moving, shipping, and storage charges; temporary living expenses; subsidies regarding appliance or car purchases (or sales); and down payments or lease-related charges. Allowances regarding perquisites (cars, drivers, club memberships, servants[26], and so on) may also need to be considered (usually for more senior positions, but this varies according to location). These allowances are often contingent upon tax-equalization policies and practices in both the home and the host countries. For example, in most Western countries a driver is considered a luxury, only available to very senior managers. In developing economies a driver is economical in terms of cost, effectiveness, and safety. Apart from the expectation that managers use drivers, parking is frequently chaotic in developing countries (especially in large cities) and the driver also performs the function of a parking attendant. In some developing countries it is quite common for the police to arrest drivers involved in traffic accidents and leave them in detention while responsibility and damages are assessed. Such a risk is unacceptable to many MNEs which do not allow their expatriate employees to drive at all in specific developing countries and provide local drivers for both the expatriate and spouse.

Spouse assistance.   Increasingly, many MNEs are also offering **spouse assistance** to help guard against or offset income lost by an expatriate's spouse as a result of relocating abroad. Payments, on average, are capped at US$7000 per family but vary according to region. Although some MNEs may pay a one-time allowance to make up for a spouse's lost income (averaging US$11,000 per family according to ORC[27]), US multinationals are beginning to focus on providing spouses with employment opportunities abroad, either by offering job-search assistance, career counseling, cultural orientation, resume/CV preparation, work-permit assistance, and language tuition, or in more unusual cases employment in the MNE's foreign business (subject of course to a work visa being approved by the host-country government for this purpose).

To summarize, MNEs generally pay allowances in order to encourage employees to take international assignments and to keep employees 'whole' (i.e. relatively comparable) to home standards. We will present more about this concept later in the chapter.

Benefits

The complexity inherent in international benefits often brings more difficulties than when dealing with compensation. Expatriate 'benefits' include healthcare, pension plans/social security, life insurance, child allowances, and profit sharing/stock option plans.

Pension plans are very difficult to deal with country-to-country as national practices vary considerably. Transportability of pension plans/social security and medical coverage benefits are very difficult to normalize. Therefore, MNEs need to address many issues when considering benefits, including:

● whether or not to maintain expatriates in home-country programs, particularly if the multinational does not receive a tax deduction for it

● whether MNEs have the option of enrolling expatriates in host-country benefit programs and/or making up any difference in coverage

● whether expatriates should receive home-country or are eligible to receive host-country social security benefits.

Most US PCNs typically remain under their home-country benefit plan, with the exception of medical benefits: more than half of the MNEs surveyed by ORC assign their expatriates to an international healthcare plan. In some countries, expatriates cannot opt out of local social security programs. In such circumstances, the firm normally pays for these additional costs. European PCNs and TCNs enjoy portable social security benefits within the European Union. Laws governing private benefit practices differ from country to country, and firm practices also vary. Not surprisingly, multinationals have generally done a good job of planning for the retirement needs of their PCN employees, but this is generally less the case for TCNs.[28] There are many reasons for this: TCNs may have little or no home-country social security coverage; they may have spent many years in countries that do not permit currency transfers of accrued benefit payments; or they may spend their final year or two of employment in a country where final average salary is in a currency that relates unfavorably to their home-country currency. How their benefits are calculated and what type of retirement plan applies to them may make the difference between a comfortable retirement in a country of their choice or a forced and financially less comfortable retirement elsewhere.

In addition to the already discussed benefits, multinationals also provide vacations and special leave. Included as part of the employee's regular vacation, annual home leave usually provides airfares for families to return to their home countries. Rest and rehabilitation leave is also frequently available if the conditions of the host country are clearly below the standards of the home country. Typically, rest and rehabilitation leave provides the employee's family with paid airfares to a more comfortable location near the host country. In addition to rest and rehabilitation leave, emergency provisions are available in case of a death or illness in the family. Employees in hardship locations generally receive additional leave expense payments and rest and rehabilitation periods.

APPROACHES TO INTERNATIONAL COMPENSATION OF EXPATRIATES

There are two main options in the area of international compensation – the **Going Rate Approach** (also referred to as the Market Rate Approach) and the **Balance Sheet Approach** (sometimes known as the Build-up Approach). In this section we describe each approach and discuss the advantages and disadvantages inherent in each approach.[29]

The Going Rate Approach

The key characteristics of this approach are summarized in Table 8.1. With this approach, the base salary for the international transfer is linked to *the salary structure in the host country*. The multinational usually obtains information from local compensation surveys and must decide whether local nationals (HCNs), expatriates of the same nationality, or expatriates of all nationalities will be the reference point in terms of benchmarking. For example, a Japanese bank operating in New York would need to decide whether its reference point would be local US salaries, other Japanese competitors in New York, or all foreign banks operating in New York. With the Going Rate Approach, if the location is in a low-pay county, the multinational usually supplements base pay with additional benefits and payments.

TABLE 8.1 Going Rate Approach

- Based on local market rates
- Relies on survey comparisons among:
  - Local nationals (HCNs)
  - Expatriates of the same nationality
  - Expatriates of all nationalities.
- Compensation based on the selected survey comparison
- Base pay and benefits may be supplemented by additional payments for low-pay countries

There are advantages and disadvantages of the Going Rate Approach, summarized in Table 8.2 (overleaf). The advantages are: there is equality with local nationals (very effective in attracting PCNs or TCNs to a location that pays higher salaries than those received in the home country); the approach is simple and easy for expatriates to understand; expatriates are able to identify with the host country; and there is often equity among expatriates of different nationalities.

TABLE 8.2 **Advantages and disadvantages of the Going Rate Approach**

Advantages	Disadvantages
• Equality with local nationals	• Variation between assignments for the same employee
• Simplicity	• Variation between expatriates of the same nationality in different countries
• Identification with host country	• Potential re-entry problems
• Equity among different nationalities	

The disadvantages of the Going Rate Approach are as follows. First, there can be variation between assignments for the same employee. This is most obvious when we compare an assignment in an advanced economy with one in a developing country, but also when we compare assignments in various advanced economies where differences in managerial salaries and the effect of local taxation can significantly influence an employee's compensation level using the Going Rate Approach. Not surprisingly, individual employees are very sensitive to this issue. Second, there can be variation between expatriates of the same nationality in different locations. A strict interpretation of the Going Rate Approach can lead to rivalry for assignments to locations that are financially attractive, and little interest in locations considered financially unattractive. Finally, the Going Rate Approach can pose problems upon repatriation when the employee's salary reverts to a home-country level that is below that of the host-country. This is not only a problem for firms in developing countries but also for MNEs from many countries where local managerial salaries are well below that of the USA, which has long been the world market leader in managerial salaries, although the gap between US and some European salaries has been narrowing.[30]

The Balance Sheet Approach

The key characteristics of this approach (which is the most widely used approach for international compensation) are summarized in Table 8.3. The basic objective is to 'keep the expatriate whole' (that is, maintaining relativity to PCN colleagues and compensating for the costs of an international assignment)[31] through maintenance of the home-country living standard plus a financial inducement to make the package attractive. This approach links the base salary for expatriates to the salary structure of the relevant home country. For example, a US executive taking up an international position would have his or her compensation package built upon the US base-salary level rather than that applicable to the host country. The key assumption of this approach is that foreign assignees should not suffer a material loss due to their transfer, and

TABLE 8.3 **The Balance Sheet Approach**

• Basic objective is maintenance of home-country living standard plus financial inducement

• Home-country pay and benefits are the foundations of this approach

• Adjustments to home package to balance additional expenditure in host country

• Financial incentives (expatriate/hardship premium) added to make the package attractive

• Most common system in usage by multinational firms

this is accomplished through the utilization of what is generally referred to as the Balance Sheet Approach. According to Reynolds:

The balance sheet approach to international compensation is a system designed to equalize the purchasing power of employees at comparable position levels living overseas and in the home-country and to provide incentives to offset qualitative differences between assignment locations.[32]

There are four major categories of outlays incurred by expatriates that are incorporated in the Balance Sheet Approach:

1   *Goods and services* – home-country outlays for items such as food, personal care, clothing, household furnishings, recreation, transportation, and medical care.

2   *Housing* – the major costs associated with housing in the host country.

3   *Income taxes* – parent-country and host-country income taxes.

4   *Reserve* – contributions to savings, payments for benefits, pension contributions, investments, education expenses, social security taxes, etc.

Where costs associated with the host-country assignment exceed equivalent costs in the parent country, these costs are met by both the MNE and the expatriate to ensure that parent-country equivalent purchasing power is achieved.

Table 8.4 shows a typical spreadsheet for an expatriate assignment using the Balance Sheet Approach. In this example, an Australian expatriate is assigned to a hypothetical country called New Euphoria, which has a cost-of-living index of 150 relative to Australia and an exchange rate of 1.5 relative to the Australian dollar. In addition to a foreign service premium, a hardship allowance is also payable for this location. Housing is provided by the MNE, and a notional

TABLE 8.4   Expatriate compensation worksheet

Employee:	Brian Smith		
Position:	Marketing Manager		
Country:	New Euphoria		
Reason for change:	New Assignment		
Effective date of change	1 February 2018		
Item	**Amount (A$ PA)**	**Paid in Australian dollars (A$ PA)**	**Paid in local currency (NE$ PA)**
Base salary	200,000	100,000	150,000
Cost of living allowance	50,000		75,000
Overseas service premium (20%)	40,000	40,000	
Hardship allowance (20%)	40,000	40,000	
Housing deduction (7%)	−14,000	−14,000	
Tax deduction	−97,000	−97,000	
TOTAL	219,000	69,000	225,000

COLA Index = 150

cost for this is recognized by a 7 per cent deduction from the package, along with a notional tax deduction (we discuss taxation later in the chapter). The expatriate can see from this spreadsheet what components are offered in the package and how the package will be split between Australian currency and New Euphoria currency.

There are advantages and disadvantages of the Balance Sheet Approach, summarized in Table 8.5. There are three main advantages. First, the Balance Sheet Approach provides equity between all foreign assignments and between expatriates of the same nationality. Second, repatriation of expatriates is facilitated by this emphasis on equity with the parent country as expatriate compensation remains anchored to the compensation system in the parent country. Third, this approach is easy to communicate, as Table 8.4 illustrates.

TABLE 8.5 Advantages and disadvantages of the Balance Sheet Approach

Advantages	Disadvantages
• Equity	• Can result in great disparities
• Between assignments	• Between expatriates of different nationalities
• Between expatriates of the same nationality	• Between expatriates and local nationals
• Facilitates expatriate re-entry	• Can be quite complex to administer
• Easy to communicate to employees	

There are two main disadvantages of the Balance Sheet Approach. First, this approach can result in considerable disparities – both between expatriates of different nationalities and between PCNs and HCNs. Problems arise when international staff are paid different amounts for performing the same (or very similar) job in the same host location, according to their different home base salary. For example, in the Singapore regional headquarters of a US bank, a US PCN and a New Zealand TCN may perform the same (or similar) banking duties, but the American will receive a higher salary than the New Zealander because of the differences in US and New Zealand base-salary levels. As noted above, differences in base-salary levels can also cause difficulties between expatriates and HCNs. Traditionally, this has referred to the problem of highly paid PCNs being resented by local HCN employees because these 'foreigners' are perceived as being excessively compensated (and because they are blocking career opportunities for locals).[33]

However, feelings of resentment and inequity can also run in the other direction. For instance, as indicated above, the USA has the highest level of managerial compensation in the world. Thus, a multinational that establishes a subsidiary in the USA (or acquires a US business) may find that, if it uses a Balance Sheet Approach, its expatriates may be substantially underpaid compared to local American employees. While the logic of the balance sheet states that being tied to the home country assists in repatriation because the expatriate identifies with the home country, research in equity theory[34] suggests that employees do not always assess compensation issues in a detached way.

The issue of base-salary differences is also a concern for US employees working for foreign firms operating in the USA. Many non-US multinationals are reluctant to pay high US salaries to US employees who are offered international assignments (as HCNs into the firm's home-country operations, or as TCNs in a regional subsidiary). US employees are equally reluctant to accept the lower salaries paid in the firm's home country. Thus, the Balance Sheet Approach can produce disparities and may also act as a barrier to staff acceptance of international assignments. A second problem with the Balance Sheet Approach is that, while this approach is both elegant and simple as a concept, it can become quite complex to administer. Complexities particularly arise in the areas of tightly integrated private and government fund transfers (e.g. taxes and pensions).

A third emerging approach to international compensation: Local Plus

Over the past decade, a third approach to international compensation, summarized in Table 8.6 (overleaf) and called 'Local Plus', has begun to emerge, particularly in the Asia-Pacific region. A **Local Plus Approach** is one in which expatriate employees are paid according to the prevailing salary levels, structure, and administration guidelines of the host location, plus provide 'expatriate-type' benefits such as assistance with transportation, housing, and dependents' education in recognition of the employee's 'foreign' status. Benefits may be paid in kind (directly by the MNE) or as add-ons to local salary levels at a grossed-up rate to account for host taxes. Local Plus compensation does *not* typically include tax equalization, COLA, mobility premiums, hardship allowances, familiarization visits, home leave, cross-cultural training and other pre-departure programs, or spouse assistance. Pension benefits are optional depending on the nature of the assignment and whether the transfer is temporary or permanent.

The driving force behind a Local Plus Approach for many MNEs is to reduce their international assignment costs. Developing low-cost alternative salary packages, such as Local Plus, is one way to achieve this. With many companies also seeing an increase in the number of developmental assignees,[35] many expatriates (especially junior and middle management staff) are often willing to accept a reduced package such as Local Plus in return for the international experience that will enhance their future careers. Typically, Local Plus is used for long-term assignments, permanent transfers, intraregional transfers (e.g. as in Asia-Pacific), and for assignments from low- to high-wage locations.

In many respects, Local Plus compensation is a hybrid version of both the Balance Sheet (home-based) and Going Rate (host-based) approaches, often containing the optimum benefits of both. As such, it is a compensation approach that can frequently solve some of the problems encountered in more traditional compensation approaches and therefore has some unique benefits. For example, because the expatriate benefits of a Local Plus package are not 'fixed' as in the Balance Sheet Approach, there is considerable flexibility to tailor each 'plus' component (i.e. add or a remove a benefit) according to a variety of individual and corporate objectives. This is advantageous for a number of reasons. First, if we take the Balance Sheet Approach, this is based on the notion that expatriate employees can identify a 'home' country, but with more expatriates undertaking multiple assignments, often back to back and frequently over a decade or more (some with no intention to return or retire there), identifying 'home' is becoming increasingly difficult. Using a Balance Sheet Approach under these circumstances does not make sense, but a Local Plus Approach does. Second, companies that recruit employees from locations where they have no presence (e.g. TCNs) and therefore no payroll facilities will find it very difficult to administer either a home- or host-based approach. Again, a Local Plus Approach will solve this problem by offering 'plus' benefits based on what is appropriate given the employee's experience and skills, rather than where they come from or where they are going to.

The benefits of the Local Plus Approach can be seen in the increasing use of this type of compensation in Asia-Pacific.[36] AIRINC reports that companies headquartered in Asia are more likely to have a formal Local Plus policy in place and have more assignees on a Local Plus policy than in any other region in the world.[37] This may be due in large part to Asia's economic growth over the past decade, which is fuelling the demand for a more globalized workforce;[38] as such, MNEs must entice hundreds of thousands of expatriates to the region while also facilitating the transfer of international employees in the most cost-effective manner.

Although the benefits of Local Plus compensation are numerous, there are also some disadvantages for firms that use the approach. In a recent study of expatriates' views about international assignments across five regions, McNulty and colleagues found that Local Plus compensation tends to shift the power balance in the employment relationship in expatriates' favor.[39] This is because, by its nature, Local Plus compensation has a more normalizing effect on how expatriates live in a host-country in comparison to expatriates' on more generous salary packages. It means that the lifestyle of expatriates on Local Plus compensation is generally more closely aligned with the lifestyle and socioeconomic habits of locals in the host country, i.e. the disparity in purchasing power between themselves and HCNs is marginal given that the choices they make about their standard of living (where to live, which schools to attend) are determined *less* by the MNE. As a result of their greater sacrifice and being forced to rely less on the organization to support some of their fundamental employment needs, which are often not compensated for in other non-financial ways (e.g. through improved career management support), Local Plus compensation can impact on expatriates' job embeddedness in terms of commitment and loyalty. In sum, Local Plus compensation tends to decrease the ties that bind expatriates to their firm.

The shift in power in the employment relationship in favor of expatriates can have significant implications for MNEs. The most significant problem is expatriate retention. For instance, if Local Plus compensation is ideally suited to expatriates' willingness to accept a reduced salary package in exchange for the opportunity to acquire valuable international skills, it is necessary to also consider that, once these skills have been acquired, employees' marketability on the international labor market will likely increase. As Local Plus expatriates are less reliant on firms to fund their expatriate lifestyle, and because they are living a largely 'local' lifestyle to begin with, their willingness to consider other job offers that may afford them even an incremental increase in their current salary is higher. This may be because they feel 'pushed' to find better employment opportunities, or because they have (or are developing) a self-initiated career orientation (i.e. pursuing a protean, global, or boundaryless career – as discussed in Chapter 7) that is prompting them to initially accept a Local Plus package. Either way, there is an increased risk of losing expatriates to competitors, particularly during an international assignment, which can have a devastating effect on MNEs' broader global staffing objectives. See Table 8.6 for a comparison of some long-term assignment options we have discussed.

TABLE 8.6   Compensation approaches and strategies for long-term international assignments

Policy name	Strategy	Description of policy	Purpose used for
Full International	Development	• Based on Balance Sheet (home) Approach • 'Full bells and whistles', i.e. generous remuneration (including bonus and incentives) and benefits (including cost of living allowance, housing, education, spousal allowance, car, home leave and club memberships) • Designed to ensure employee's lifestyle not disadvantaged as a result of international relocation	• Targeted at executives for career development or on international track who possess universal skills and are considered high potential • Often used for 'cadre' approach to developing careers of elite group of high performers whose permanent mobility is long-term strategic goal • Mainly used for retention purposes where goal is to repatriate to corporate headquarters or business group headquarters • Used sparingly and as a reward for key individuals

(Continued)

(Continued)

Policy name	Strategy	Description of policy	Purpose used for
Expat Lite	Skills/ Secondment	• Based on reduced Balance Sheet (home) Approach • Reduced version of 'full bells and whistles', i.e. generous remuneration with/without bonus and incentives, and inclusion of some benefits (e.g. housing, education, car, home leave) but not others (e.g. club memberships, spousal allowance, cost of living)	• Expatriates with deep technical skills or competencies needed in another location • Specific goal is to transfer skills and knowledge for duration of assignment only (no more than two years) • Expatriate relocates for fixed period and repatriates with no intention to relocate again unless a specific skill need arises • Often used to service clients in locations where local skills are not available
Local Plus	Cost savings	• Based on Going Rate (host) Approach • Provides some benefits of developmental policy but on greatly reduced basis • Expatriates often localized with some additional benefits provided to sustain retention • No ongoing allowances (e.g. cost of living) • Initial allowances typically phased out over period of assignment (100% benefit year one, 50% benefit year two, 20% benefit year three)	• Combination of developmental and skills/ secondment expatriates, but generally targeted at middle management executives who are specialized, functional people, or broad business managers and/or generalists who move between a variety of different positions (and locations) throughout their career • Typically offered to managers initiating relocation or indicating willingness to relocate
Localization	Cost savings, functional turnover and retention	• Based on Going Rate (host) Approach • Initial allowances from any of the above strategies phased out over period of assignment (100% benefit year one, 50% benefit year two, 20% benefit year three) to achieve full 'local' remuneration	• Typically offered to managers initiating a relocation or indicating willingness to relocate, and long-term assignees who have exceeded term of contract (i.e. beyond initial three- or five-year assignment) but who wish to remain in location or whose firm does not wish to repatriate
One-way International	Self-initiated transfers	• Based on Going Rate (host) Approach • One-way relocation package to host destination • Salary, incentives, and benefits paid from local payroll	• Self-initiated/employee-initiated relocation

Source: Table 8.6 was created by the author team specifically for this textbook.

Taxation

Taxation is probably the one aspect of international compensation that causes the most concern to HR practitioners and expatriates because taxation generally evokes emotional responses.[40] No one enjoys paying taxes, and this issue can be very time-consuming for both the MNE and the expatriate. To illustrate the potential problems, an assignment abroad for a US expatriate may result in being taxed in the country of assignment and in the USA. This dual tax cost, combined with all of the other expatriate costs, makes some US multinationals think twice about making use of expatriates. It is important to note that Section 911 of the US Internal Revenue Service Code contains provisions permitting a substantial deduction on foreign-earned income, but US expatriates must file with the Internal Revenue Service and usually also with the host-country tax office during their period of foreign service. This requirement is more onerous than for citizens of some other Organization for Economic Cooperation and Development countries who are not required to declare their total global income to their home-country taxation authority.

Multinationals generally select one of the following approaches to handling international taxation:

- *Tax equalization.* Firms withhold an amount equal to the home-country tax obligation of the expatriate, and pay all taxes in the host country.

- *Tax protection.* The employee pays up to the amount of taxes he or she would pay on compensation in the home country. In such a situation, the employee is entitled to any windfall received if total taxes are less in the foreign country than in the home country. In her classic review of global compensation, Stuart[41] adds two other approaches: (1) *ad hoc* (each expatriate is handled differently, depending upon the individual package agreed to with the MNE); and (2) *laissez-faire* (employees are 'on their own' in conforming to host-country and home-country taxation laws and practices). However, neither of these approaches are recommended and we shall focus on tax equalization and tax protection, as these are the most common approaches.

Tax equalization is by far the more common taxation policy used by multinationals.[42] Thus, for an expatriate, tax payments equal to the liability of a home-country taxpayer with the same income and family status are imposed on the employee's salary and bonus. Any additional premiums or allowances are paid by the firm, tax-free to the employee. As multinationals operate in more and more countries, they are subject to widely discrepant income tax rates. For example, if we look at selected maximum federal marginal tax rates (see Table 8.7), the 'top five' highest taxation countries are the Netherlands, Sweden, France, Denmark, and Japan. The USA is below the rates for these five countries.[43]

Many MNEs have responded to this complexity and diversity across countries by retaining the services of international accounting firms to provide advice and prepare host-country and home-country tax returns for their expatriates. Increasingly, multinationals are also outsourcing the provisions of further aspects of the total expatriate compensation packages including a variety of destination services in lieu of providing payment in a package.[44] When multinationals plan compensation packages, they need to consider to what extent specific practices can be modified in each country to provide the most tax-effective, appropriate rewards for PCNs, HCNs, and TCNs within the framework of the overall compensation policy of the MNE.

As one international HRM manager noted some years ago, the difficulties in international compensation "are not compensation so much as benefits". Pension plans are very difficult to compare or equalize across nations, as cultural practices vary considerably. Transportability of pension plans, medical coverage, and social security benefits are very difficult to normalize.[45] This observation remains relevant today and MNEs need to actively monitor a range of issues when considering benefits, including:

TABLE 8.7 Maximum marginal federal tax rates

Country	Maximum marginal rate (%)
Australia	46.5
Belgium	45.3
Canada	49.5
Chile	39.5
Denmark	55.6
France	54.0
Germany	47.5
Italy	47.8
Japan	50.5
Korea	39.4
Mexico	35.0
Netherlands	50.1
New Zealand	33.0
Poland	20.9
Spain	52.0
Sweden	56.9
Switzerland	36.1
Turkey	35.8
UK	45.0
USA	46.3

Source: Adapted from the Organization for Economic Cooperation and Development (OECD), Table 1.7 'Top statutory personal income tax rate and top marginal tax rates for employees, 2014'. Reproduced with permission.[46]

- whether or not to maintain expatriates in home-country programs, particularly if the MNE does not receive a tax deduction for it
- whether MNEs have the option of enrolling expatriates in host-country benefit programs and/or making up any difference in coverage
- whether host-country legislation regarding termination affects benefit entitlement
- whether expatriates should receive home-country or host-country social security benefits
- whether benefits should be maintained on a home-country or host-country basis, who is responsible for the cost, whether other benefits should be used to offset any shortfall in coverage, and whether home-country benefit programs should be exported to local nationals in foreign countries.

Differences in national sovereignty are also at work in the area of mandated public and private pension schemes – what many nations refer to as 'social security' programs. Table 8.8 highlights the differences in mandated degree of contribution (ranging from a low of 0 per cent to a high of nearly 60 per cent), as well as the mix of employer-employee contribution.

For many international firms, expatriate assignments are likely to increase in distance, number, and duration over an employee's career, and more and more firms may create cadres of permanent international assignees – called 'globals' by some firms. The inherent complexity and dynamism of culturally embedded and politically volatile national tax and pension processes promise to tax the resources, time, and attention of international human resource (HR) managers for the foreseeable future. Seamless networks of global firms, their specialist consultants and local and regional public and private interests are a goal rather than a reality.

TABLE 8.8 Social security contributions by employers and employees

Country	Employer contribution rate (%)	Employee contribution rate (%)	Total contribution rate (%)
Australia*	0.00	0.00	0.00
Belgium	34.79	13.07	47.86
Canada	7.58	6.83	14.41
Chile	0.00	7.00	7.00
France	41.86*	14.05**	55.91
Germany	19.28	20.18	39.46
Italy	32.08**	10.49**	42.57**
Japan	14.60	14.45	29.05
Korea	10.29	3.84	14.13
Mexico	7.59**	1.65**	9.24**
Netherlands	11.31	31.15	42.46
Poland	16.78	10.06	26.84
Singapore	13.00	8.00	21.00
Spain	29.90	6.35	36.25
Sweden	31.42	6.25	37.67
Switzerland	6.25	6.25	12.5
Turkey	17.50	15.00	32.50
UK	13.80	12.00	25.80
USA	7.65	7.65	15.30

* When the contributions are at zero, they are funded out of the General Tax Revenue and range from zero to very high values.
** Varies idiosyncratically.

Source: Adapted from the Organization for Economic Cooperation and Development (OECD), Tables 3.1 and 3.2 'Social Security Contribution Rates and Related Provisions, 2014'. Reproduced with permission.[47]

International living costs data

Obtaining up-to-date information on international living costs is a constant issue for multinationals. As we noted at the beginning of this chapter, the level of local knowledge required in many areas of international human resource management (IHRM) requires specialist advice. Consequently, many MNEs retain the services of consulting firms that may offer a broad range of services or provide highly specialized services relevant to HRM in a multinational context. With regard to international living costs, a number of consulting firms offer regular surveys calculating a cost-of-living index that can be updated in terms of currency exchange rates. A recent survey of living costs[48] in selected cities ranked the ten most expensive cities (including rent) as New York, Oslo, Geneva, Zurich, Tokyo, Dubai, Copenhagen, Singapore, Toronto, and London. The first US city in the index was New York, ranked as the most expensive city including rent costs, but only the sixth most expensive city if you exclude rent costs. The least expensive city was Mumbai in India (formerly known as Bombay). Price differentials between Eastern and Western Europe closed in 2009 to an average of 26 per cent higher prices in Western Europe.

MNEs using the Balance Sheet Approach must constantly update compensation packages with new data on living costs, which is an ongoing administrative requirement. This is a very important issue for expatriate employees and forms the basis of many complaints if updating substantially lags behind any rise in living costs. Multinationals must also be able to respond to unexpected events such as the currency and stock market crash that suddenly unfolded in a number of Asian countries in late 1997. Some countries such as Indonesia faced a devaluation of their currency (the ruphiah) by over 50 per cent against the US dollar in a matter of weeks. This event had a dramatic impact on prices, the cost of living, and the cost of servicing debt for Indonesian firms with loans denominated in a foreign currency such as the US dollar.

There is also much debate about what should be in the 'basket of goods' which consulting firms use as the basis for calculating living costs around the world. For example, the Swiss Bank UBS uses the 'Big Mac Index' to measure living costs around the world.[49] According to Table 8.9, it takes almost three hours for the average worker in Nairobi to earn enough for a Big Mac. In Chicago, Berlin, and Taipei the global burger can be bought for less than 15 minutes' effort.[50]

It is also possible to take a wider view and focus on *business costs* rather than living costs for expatriates, because the multinational firm is interested in the overall cost of doing business in a particular country, as well as the more micro issue of expatriate living costs. *The Economist* Intelligence Unit[51] calculates such indices, which measure the relative costs of doing business in different economies by compiling statistics relating to wages, costs for expatriate staff, air travel and subsistence, corporation taxes, perceived corruption levels, office and industrial rents, and road transport. Generally, the developed countries tend to rank as more expensive than developing countries because their wage costs are higher.

Differentiating between PCNs and TCNs

As we have indicated, one of the outcomes of the Balance Sheet Approach is to produce differentiation between expatriate employees of different nationalities because of the use of nationality to determine the relevant home-country base salary. In effect, this is a differentiation between PCNs and TCNs. Many TCNs have a great deal of international experience because they often move from country to country in the employ of one multinational (or several) headquartered in a country other than their own (for example, an Indian banker may work in the Singapore branch of a US bank). As Reynolds[52] long ago observed, there is no doubt that paying TCNs according to their home-country base salary can be less expensive than paying all expatriates on a PCN scale – particularly if the multinational is headquartered in a country which has both

TABLE 8.9 Range of working times required to buy one Big Mac

City	1 Big Mac in min
Zurich, Sydney, Chicago	11
Taipei, Berlin, Montreal	13
Ljubljana, Dublin, Toronto	15
Amsterdam, Lyon, Helsinki	16
Stockholm, Johannesburg, Dubai	17
Seoul, Rome, Doha	18
Oslo, Madrid	19
Copenhagen, Manama, Moscow	20
Barcelona, Tel Aviv	21
Kuala Lumpur	23
Bratislava	24
San Paulo, Warsaw	25
Athens	26
Bueno Aires, Tallinn, Vilnius	29
Prague	30
Rio de Janeiro, Santiago de Chile	32
Riga	34
Bogotá, Shanghai	35
Bangkok	37
Lima	38
Mumbai	40
Beijing	42
Budapest, Bucharest	44
Delhi	50
Kiev	55
Cairo	62
Jakarta	67
Mexico City	78
Manila	87
Nairobi	173

Notes: Price of one Big Mac divided by weighted average hourly pay across 14 professions

Source: UBS, Prices and Earnings, 2015.[53]

high managerial salaries and a strong currency. However, justifying these differences to TCNs can be difficult. Clearly, many MNEs take the view that a significant reduction in expenses outweighs the difficulty of justifying any negative pay differentials. However, as MNEs expand and international revenue becomes more significant, TCN employees often become more valuable. A focus on retaining talented TCNs often requires rethinking the existing approach to compensating TCNs.

As a starting point, multinationals need to match their compensation policies with their staffing policies and general HR philosophy. If, for example, an MNE has an ethnocentric staffing policy, its compensation policy should be one of keeping the expatriate *whole* (that is, maintaining relativity to PCN colleagues plus compensating for the costs of international service). If, however, the staffing policy follows a geocentric approach (that is, staffing a position with the 'best person', regardless of nationality), there may be no clear 'home' for the TCN, and the multinational will need to consider establishing a system of **international base pay** for key managers, regardless of nationality, that is paid in a major reserve currency such as the US dollar or the euro. This system allows MNEs to deal with considerable variations in base salaries for managers. Conceptualizing, creating, co-ordinating, and communicating such a system across diverse divisions, cultures, and employee groups is a daunting task.[54]

TENTATIVE CONCLUSIONS: PATTERNS IN COMPLEXITY, CHALLENGES, AND CHOICES

While, so far, some of this chapter has concentrated on expatriate compensation, we will now draw conclusions for the larger group of (international) managers in MNEs. As outlined at the opening of the chapter, international compensation administration may be more complex than its domestic counterpart, but is only slowly and fitfully evolving from a dominant domestic state of origin.[55] Domestic pay patterns – that is, norms and assumptions, **pay strategies** and practices, as well as pay forms and administration – are increasingly challenged as executives in MNEs are exposed to alternative pay forms, varying legal and institutional contexts, and the rapidly changing realities of global competitiveness.

Recent developments in the study of global pay issues may be seen to operate at three distinct vertical levels: the basic level of cultural values and assumptions; the intermediate level of pay strategy, practices, and systems design; and the surface (artefact) level of pay administration and form[56] – see Figure 8.1 (overleaf). On a second, horizontal level, firms must individually determine how to strike a balance between traditional, internally based models and explanations of pay, and those more externally focused models and explanations of pay that comprise a global challenge to the status quo.[57] Globalizing firms must individually choose between internally and externally focused assumptions, strategies, and practices. This combined choice is the complex 'context' of pay for any given multinational. Pay context is the pivotal center column in Figure 8.1.

On the level of basic explanations, firms can choose to emphasize firm-specific theories of job worth (such as resource-based views of the firm,[58] behavioral theory[59], or new institutional economics models)[60] or they may emphasize firm-external theories of job worth (such as cultural and institutional perspectives).[61] These theories may be implicit and not articulated by pay practitioners, and yet these assumptions may indirectly drive all other pay processes. On the more explicit and more widely investigated level of norms and values, pay strategy may be seen as some combination of internal, corporate norms (derived from and consistent with pay strategy, IHRM strategy, and traditional employment relationships – practiced 'psychological contracts') and external, environmental norms (derived from labor unions, educational systems, and local or regional institutional sources) that may vary significantly by geographic region.

FIGURE 8.1 Complexity, challenges, and choices in global pay

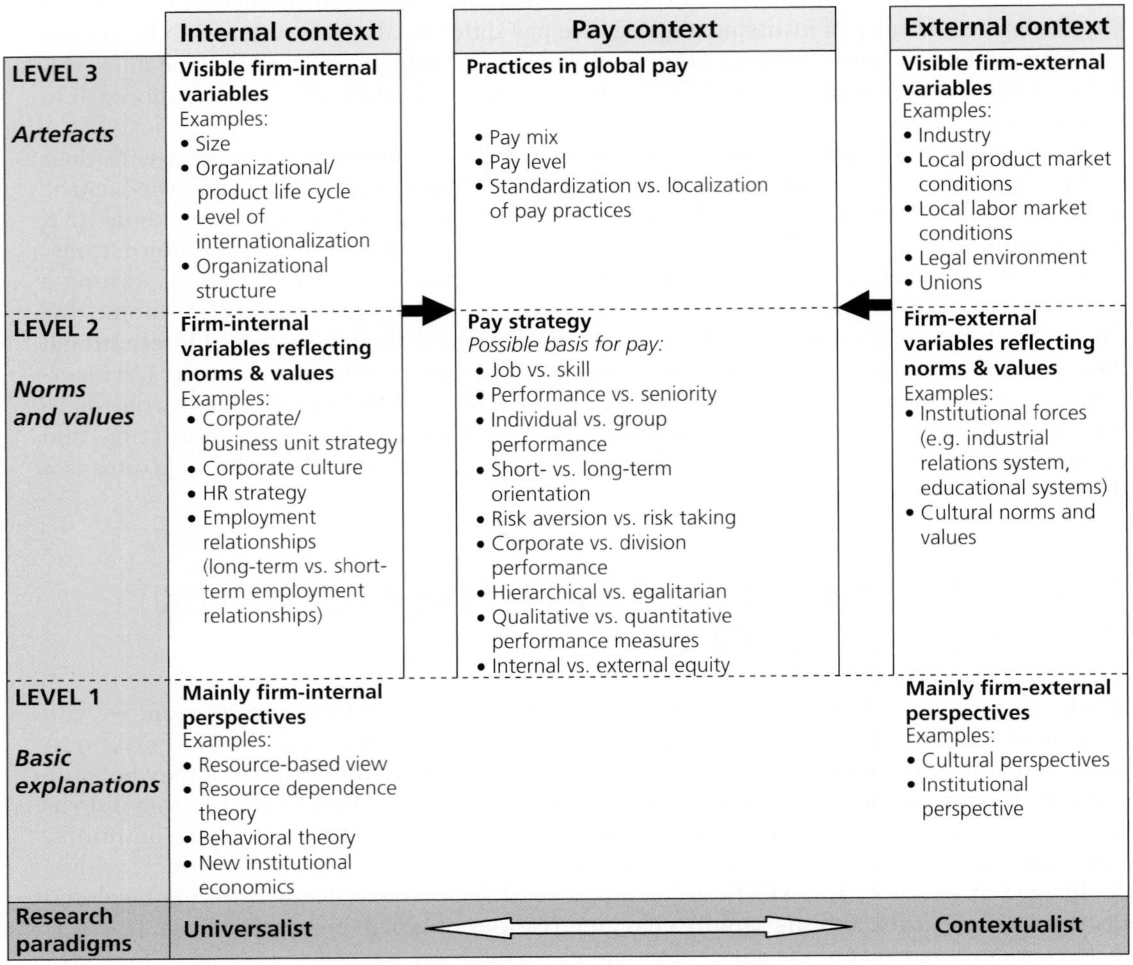

	Internal context	Pay context	External context
LEVEL 3 *Artefacts*	**Visible firm-internal variables** Examples: • Size • Organizational/ product life cycle • Level of internationalization • Organizational structure	**Practices in global pay** • Pay mix • Pay level • Standardization vs. localization of pay practices	**Visible firm-external variables** Examples: • Industry • Local product market conditions • Local labor market conditions • Legal environment • Unions
LEVEL 2 *Norms and values*	**Firm-internal variables reflecting norms & values** Examples: • Corporate/ business unit strategy • Corporate culture • HR strategy • Employment relationships (long-term vs. short-term employment relationships)	**Pay strategy** *Possible basis for pay:* • Job vs. skill • Performance vs. seniority • Individual vs. group performance • Short- vs. long-term orientation • Risk aversion vs. risk taking • Corporate vs. division performance • Hierarchical vs. egalitarian • Qualitative vs. quantitative performance measures • Internal vs. external equity	**Firm-external variables reflecting norms & values** Examples: • Institutional forces (e.g. industrial relations system, educational systems) • Cultural norms and values
LEVEL 1 *Basic explanations*	**Mainly firm-internal perspectives** Examples: • Resource-based view • Resource dependence theory • Behavioral theory • New institutional economics		**Mainly firm-external perspectives** Examples: • Cultural perspectives • Institutional perspective
Research paradigms	**Universalist**	⟵⟶	**Contextualist**

Pay strategy may be defined in terms of a series of interlocking strategic choices on: basis of pay (job vs. skill, performance vs. seniority),[62] unit of aggregation (paying individuals, groups, organizations, short- vs. long-term orientation to pay),[63] patterns of variation in pay (variability or risk in pay, hierarchical vs. egalitarian pay orientation)[64], and an overall focus on internal equity – as captured by job-evaluation systems – as opposed to external equity, as captured by market surveys.[65] 'Universal' pay systems may be preferred by corporate pay planners rather than having to deal with myriad 'local' systems. Ease of administration and the standardization of practices are attractive and can contribute to simplicity in global assignments, resolving disputes related to perceived inequities or policy inconsistencies, and so on. However, local or regional 'host contexts' and/or MNE strategy may influence senior managers to compromise these global preferences and strategically align pay practices more or less in conformance with local or regional requirements.[66] Strategic necessity and contextual requirements may incrementally grudgingly 'move' pay practices away from a universalized and toward a more localized character.[67]

It should be noted that in the center column of Figure 8.1, under 'possible basis for pay', a number of levels of analysis have emerged to supplement or augment traditional job-based pay. Firms may provide *an individual employee* with personal 'choice' in pay and pay for his or her skills or competencies.[68] Alternately, a firm may pay at the traditional *job level*, realizing that even standard jobs may vary tremendously across geographic regions. Firms may also pay at the *task group or plant level* of aggregation.[69] Finally, firms may provide 'customized' pay at the *national level* or provide standardized 'core' pay for all employees in the global firm.[70] Increasingly, we may combine pay packages across these vertical levels of analysis and pay for a combination of personal, job, group, national, or corporate purposes.[71] These composite pay systems are more complex, but they are also more flexible and responsive to diverse employee demands and changing global business conditions.[72]

MNEs face global challenges to executive compensation practices and forms of corporate governance.[73] These challenges may be seen as an ongoing debate between advocates of pay systems that value competitive individualism and result in 'hierarchical' pay systems with large pay differentials for executives, market-sensitive professions and other 'critical' employee groups[74], and the advocates of pay systems that value co-operative collectivism and result in more 'egalitarian' pay systems with smaller pay differentials and more shared group or firm-wide reward practices.[75] Increasingly, multinationals that violate corporate or local norms in one location in order to respond to local norms in a second location do so at their own risk.[76]

At the final level of pay form and administration (artefacts), MNEs may determine that pay practices such as pay mix (between base pay, the nature and extent of benefits, use of long-term and short-term incentives, etc.), overall level of pay and the degree to which pay is standardized across all units or customized to local conditions should be the result of internal or external influences.[77] Firm-specific realities (such as operating in a monopolistic industry, a low degree of internationalization, and simple organizational design) may mitigate for standardized pay practices. Conversely, strongly held local values, institutions and regulations, an advanced level of internationalization, and decentralized organizational designs may mitigate for more flexible, localized pay practices.[78]

SUMMARY

In this chapter, we have examined the complexities that arise when firms move from compensation at the domestic level to compensation in an international context. It is evident from our review that compensation policy becomes a much less precise process than is the case in the domestic HR context. To demonstrate this complexity, we have:

- detailed the key components of an international compensation program

- outlined the two main approaches to international compensation (the Going Rate and the Balance Sheet) and introduced a third new approach – Local Plus – and explained its components as well as its advantages and disadvantages

- outlined special problem areas such as taxation, obtaining valid international living-costs data, and the problems of managing TCN compensation

- presented a model of global pay that highlights the complexity and yet familiarity of pay practices in the global context; it is this combination of pay decisions based on strategic global standardization and sensitivity to changing local and regional conditions that characterizes the state of international pay practices

- posited that a strategic yet sensitive balance can only be achieved by creating and maintaining professional networks comprising home-office and local-affiliate HR practitioners, outsourcing selected activities through specialist consultants, and close co-operation with local and regional governments and other key local institutions.

DISCUSSION QUESTIONS

1 What should be the main objectives for a multinational with regard to its compensation policies?

2 Describe the main differences in the Going Rate and Balance Sheet approaches to international compensation.

3 What are the key differences in salary compensation for PCNs and TCNs? Do these differences matter?

4 Describe Local Plus compensation and explain the major challenges MNEs face when using the approach.

5 What are the main points that MNEs must consider when deciding how to provide benefits?

6 Why is it important for MNEs to understand the compensation practices of other countries?

7 Explain how balancing the interests of global and local, occupational and functional perspectives might play out in a compensation decision scenario.

FURTHER READING

J. Bonache and L. Stirpe 'Compensating Global Employees', in G. Stahl, I. Björkman and S. Morris (eds.) *Handbook of Research in International Human Resource Management*, 2nd ed. (Cheltenham: Edward Elgar, 2012), pp. 162–182.

M. Festing 'International Human Resource Management and Economic Theories of the Firm', in G. Stahl, I. Björkman and S. Morris (eds.) *Handbook of Research in International Human Resource Management*, 2nd ed. (Cheltenham: Edward Elgar, 2012), pp. 453–471.

M. Festing, A. Engle, P. Dowling and I. Sahakiants 'HRM Activities: Pay and Rewards', Chapter 7 in C. Brewster and W. Mayrhofer (eds.) *Handbook of Research in Comparative Human Resource Management* (Cheltenham, UK: Edward Elgar, 2012), pp. 93–118.

B. Gerhart 'Compensation and National Culture', in L. Gomez-Mejia and S. Werner (eds.) *Global Compensation: Foundations and Perspectives*, (New York: Routledge, 2008), pp. 142–157.

C. Tornikoski, V. Suutari and M. Festing 'Compensation packages of international assignees', in D. Collings, G. Wood and P. Caligiuri (eds.) *The Routledge Companion to International Human Resource Management* (London: Routledge, 2015), pp. 289–307.

NOTES AND REFERENCES

1. See J. Kerr and J. Slocum 'Managing Corporate Culture Through Reward Systems', *Academy of Management Executive*, Vol. 19, No. 4 (2005), pp. 130–138; and P. Evans, V. Pucik and I. Björkman *The Global Challenge: International Human Resource Management*, 2nd ed. (New York: McGraw–Hill, 2011), particularly pp. 365–381.

2. E. Locke 'Linking Goals to Monetary Incentives', *Academy of Management Executive*, Vol. 18, No. 4 (2004), pp. 130–133; W. Mannering and D. Fischetti 'Engaging Employees Through Performance Markets', *WorldatWork Journal*, Vol. 18, No.4 (2009), pp. 83–92; and A. Pomeroy 'Executive Briefing: Global Pay for Performance', *HR Magazine*, Vol. 51, No. 4 (April 2006), p. 18.

3. Martin Hilb presents a well-written and thorough introduction to this interesting topic area in *New Corporate Governance: Successful Board Management Tools,* 2nd ed. (Berlin: Springer Publishing, 2006); a fascinating critique of contemporary executive pay and governance is provided by L. Bebchuck and J. Fried in *Pay Without Performance: The Unfulfilled Promise of Executive Compensation* (Cambridge, MA: Harvard University Press, 2004).

4. See M. Finkin and J. Crutcher-Gershenfeld (eds.) *Multinational Human Resource Management and the Law: Common Workplace Problems in Different Legal Environments*, (Cheltenham, UK: Edward Elgar, 2013), particularly part VI Compensation and Benefits Administration; I. Fulmer and Y. Chen 'How Communication Affects Employee Knowledge of and Reactions to Compensation Systems', in V. Miller and M. Gordon (eds.) *Meeting the Challenge of Human Resource Management: A Communication Perspective* (New York: Routledge Publishing, 2014), pp.167–178.

5. F. Cooke and P. Budhwar 'HR Offshoring and Outsourcing: Research Issues for IHRM', in P. Sparrow (ed.) *Handbook of International Human Resource Management* (Chichester, UK: John Wiley and Sons, 2009), pp. 341–361.

6. M. Kavanagh and J. Michel 'International Human Resource Management', in M. Kavanagh and M. Thite (eds.) *Human Resource Information Systems* (Thousand Oaks, California: Sage Publications, 2009), pp. 361–391; D. Robb 'Unifying Your Enterprise With a Global HR Portal', *HR Magazine*, Vol. 51, No. 3 (March 2006), pp. 109–115.

7. K. Chou and H. Risher 'Point/Counterpoint: Pay for Performance', *Workspan*, Vol. 48, No. 9 (September 2005), pp. 28–37; S. Troutman and S. Ross 'Rationalizing Global Incentive Pay Plans: Look At the Big Picture, Part One', *Workspan*, Vol. 48, No. 8 (August 2005), pp. 18–22; 'Part Two', *Workspan*, Vol. 48, No. 9 (September 2005), pp. 52–56; 'Part Three', *Workspan*, Vol. 48, No. 10 (October 2005), pp. 30–33. Also see E. Krell 'Evaluating Returns on Expatriates', *HRMagazine*, Vol. 50, No. 3 (March 2005), pp. 60–65; and S. Nurney 'The Long and The Short of It: When Transitioning From Short-term to Long-term Expatriate Assignments, Consider the Financial Implications', *HRMagazine*, Vol. 50, No. 3 (March 2005), pp. 91–94.

8. Chou and Risher 'Point/Counterpoint'; D. Green 'In the Global Reward Environment One Size Doesn't Fit All', *Workspan*, Vol. 48, No. 10 (October 2005), pp. 34–38; and P Gooderham, M. Morley, C. Brewster and W. Mayrhofer 'Human Resource Management: A Universal Concept?', in C. Brewster, W. Mayrhofer and M. Morley (eds.) *Human Resource Management in Europe: Evidence of Convergence?* (Oxford: Elsevier Butterworth-Heinemann, 2004), pp. 1–26. For a well-presented review of European reward practices and patterns see 'European Reward Governance Survey 2015' by T. Alewed, M. Festing, and M. Tekieli, Aon Hewitt-ESCP Europe.

9. See Hilb *New Corporate Governance*; Bebchuck and Fried *Pay Without Performance*; as well as A. Pomeroy 'Executive Briefing: With Executive Comp Go Your Own Way', *HRMagazine*, Vol. 50, No. 1 (November 2005), p. 14; E. Poutsma, P. Ligthart and R. Schouteten 'Employee Share Schemes in Europe – The Influence of US Multinational', *Management Revue*, Vol. 16, No. 1 (2005), pp. 99–122; E. E. Lawler *Talent: Making People Your Competitive Advantage* (San Francisco: Jossey-Bass, 2008), particularly Chapter 4 'Managing Talent' and Chapter 8 'Governing Corporations'. M. Hope's 'An Interview with Geert Hofstede', *Academy of Management Executive*,

Vol. 18, No. 1 (2004), pp. 75–79 includes the provocative quote from Hofstede: 'A present fad is the myth of the magical powers of top executives. The importance of management in general, and top management in particular, is overrated and top managers are overpaid. In many cases top managers have been brought in who turn out to be parasites on their corporation rather than assets to its real success. The importance of the people who do the work is underrated, although this trend differs between countries and parts of the world' (p. 78). Challenges indeed. The criticality of executive boards in ensuring value for executive investments is found in B. Ellig's 'Role of the Board Compensation Committee', *Compensation and Benefits Review*, Vol. 46, Nos. 5 and 6 (2014), pp. 262–275.

10. See Hilb *New Corporate Governance*; as well as S. Tyson and F. Bournois (eds.) *Top Pay and Performance: International and Strategic Approach* (Oxford: Elsevier Butterworth-Heinemann, 2005); 'New Ideas-Compensation: US CEO and Director Pay On the Rise', www.conferenceboard.org, in *Workspan*, Vol. 49, No. 1 (January 2006), p. 14; M. Thompson 'Investors Call For Better Disclosure of Executive Compensation in Canada', *Workspan Focus: Canada*, supplement to *Workspan* (February 2006), pp. 4–6; B. Florin, K. Hallock and D. Webber 'Executive Pay and Firm Performance: Methodological Considerations and Future Directions' (posted at digital commons@ILR, digitalcommons.ilr.cornell.edu/cri/15 Compensation Research Initiative 2010). For a more theoretically based assessment of agency dilemmas see T. Clark 'Dangerous Frontiers in Corporate Governance', *Journal of Management and Organization*, Vol. 20, No. 3 (2014), pp. 268–286. Evidence for a more positive correlation between firm performance and executive rewards – if appropriate measures, comparisons and time frames are assessed – is presented by M. Farmer and G. Alexandrou 'CEO Compensation and Relative Company Performance Evaluation: UK Evidence', *Compensation and Benefits Review*, Vol. 45, No. 2 (2013), pp. 88–96.

11. For an ongoing discussion of transparency in pay see L. Gomez-Mejia, P. Berrone and M. Franco-Santos *Compensation and Organizational Performance: Theory, Research and Practice* (London: M.E. Sharpe, 2010), particularly Chapter 5 on the 'Determinants and Consequences of Executive Pay'; and A. Engle and P. Dowling 'Global Rewards: Strategic Patterns in Complexity', Conference Proceedings of the International Conference of Human Resource Management in a Knowledge Based Economy, Ljubljana, Slovenia, June 2004.

12. For a well-articulated review of transformations in reward practices, albeit predominantly from a US perspective, see G. Ledford 'The Changing Landscape of Employee Rewards: Observations and Prescriptions', *Organizational Dynamics*, Vol. 43 (2014), pp. 168–179. An argument is made by N. Gupta and J. Shaw that reward topics are largely under-researched by academics in 'Employee Compensation: The Neglected Area of HRM Research', *Human Resource Management Review*, Vol. 24 (2014), pp. 1–4.

13. For example, specialized firms such as P-E International in Britain provide a survey of Worldwide Living Costs

while Price Waterhouse offers a worldwide consulting service called 'Global Human Resource Solutions', which covers a broad range of international HR issues. Also see Mercer's widely used 'Expatriate Calculator' at www.imercer.com/default.aspx?page=home&contentId=1082.

14. J. Dunning and S. Lundan *Multinational Enterprises and the Global Economy*, 2nd ed. (Northampton, Mass.: Edward Elgar, 2008).

15. U. Krudewagen and S. Eandi 'Designing Employee Policies for an International Workforce', *Workspan*, Vol. 53, No. 6 (2010), pp. 74–78; Y.-S. Hsu 'Expatriate Compensation: Alternative Approaches and Challenges', *WorldatWork Journal*, Vol. 16, No. 1 (2007), pp. 15–19.

16. See K. Lowe, J. Milliman, H. DeCeiri and P. Dowling 'International Compensation Practices: A Ten-Country Comparative Analysis', *Human Resource Management*, Vol. 41, No. 1 (Spring 2002), pp. 45–66; S. Overman 'In Sync: Harmonizing Your Global Compensation Plans May Be Done More "In Spirit" Than to the Letter', *HR Magazine*, Vol. 45, No. 3 (March 2000), pp. 86–92; and E. Scott and R. Burke 'Taming the Beast: Aligning Global Sales Incentives', *Workspan*, Vol. 50, No. 3 (March 2007), pp. 44–49.

17. M. Bloom and G. T. Milkovich 'A SHRM Perspective on International Compensation and Reward Systems' *Research in Personnel and Human Resource Management*, Supplement 4, (Greenwich, CT: JAI Press, 1999), pp. 283–303; M. Festing, A. Engle, P. Dowling and I. Sahakiants 'HRM Activities: Pay and Rewards', in C. Brewster and W. Mayrhofer (eds.) *Handbook of Research in Comparative Human Resource Management* (Cheltenham, UK: Edward Elgar, 2012), pp. 139–163.

18. Y. McNulty, H. De Cieri *et al.* 'Do Global Firms Measure Expatriate Return on Investment? An Empirical Examination of Measures, Barriers and Variables Influencing Global Staffing Practices', *International Journal of Human Resource Management*, 20(6) (2009) 1309–1326. Also see Y. McNulty, K. Hutchings *et al.* 'How Expatriate Employees View Expatriate Return on Investment', *Proceedings of the Academy of International Business* Annual Meeting, Nagoya, Japan, 2011.

19. G. T. Milkovich and M. Bloom 'Rethinking International Compensation', *Compensation and Benefits Review*, Vol. 30, No. 1 (1998), pp. 15–23.

20. H. J. Ruff and G. I. Jackson 'Methodological Problems in International Comparisons of the Cost of Living', *Journal of International Business Studies*, Vol. 5, No. 2 (1974), pp. 57–67. For a more recent discussion of the complexities of this issue see G. T. Milkovich, J. Newman and B. Gerhart, *Compensation* 10th ed. (New York: McGraw-Hill, 2011), particularly pp. 536–540.

21. Acquired by Mercer in July 2010, see the webpage www.orcworldwide.com/. For specifics on the level of detail of available cost-of-living services provided by global consulting firms (for a fee) see www.imercer.com/products/2010/cost-of-living.aspx#col.

22. To view the webpage of ECA International see www.eca-international.com/.

23. Ibid.

24. Boarding schools are relatively common in Britain, former British colonies and a number of European countries. See, for example, the Association of Boarding Schools, www.boardingschools.com/about-tabs.

25. ORC Worldwide 'Worldwide Survey of International Assignment Policies and Practices' (New York: ORC Worldwide, 2008).

26. It is common in Asia and many developing countries in other regions for expatriates and local business people to employ maids and cooks in their houses. As stated in an earlier note when discussing employment of drivers, it may be expected that an expatriate would employ servants and to not do so would be judged negatively as this would be depriving local people of employment. Not surprisingly, this is one benefit which expatriate spouses miss when they return to their home country.

27. ORC Worldwide 'Dual Career Couples and International Assignments Survey' (New York: ORC Worldwide, 2005). Local legal requirements and traditional practices can be made by nation and region. For example see 'Global Benefits and Employment Terms and Conditions Reports'.

28. Extensive comparisons of international benefits components, series, fee accessible, as described in the '2010/2011 Global Catalog of Compensation, Benefits, and Policies and Practices Survey Reports', Towers Watson Data Service, Rochelle Park, New Jersey. For a more general discussion of the complexities of benefits and pension issues in international mergers and acquisitions see A. Rosenberg and N. Lasker 'Beyond Borders: Mastering Pension and Benefit Issues in Global M&A Transactions', *WorldatWork Journal*, Vol. 17, No. 4 (2008), pp. 28–36. The need to provide this coverage and still be cost-sensitive given the new economic realities of the 21st century is discussed in a web article by *WorldatWork* 'Companies Juggle Cost Cutting with Maintaining Competitive Benefits for International Assignees', accessed September 29, 2010 from www.worldatwork.org/waw/adimComment?id=42613&id=wsw092810.

29. The material in the tables describing the two main approaches to international compensation is based on various sources – the research and consulting experience of the first author and various discussions on this topic with a range of HR managers and consultants in Australia and the USA.

30. See C. Mestre, A. Rossier-Renaud and M. Berger 'Better Benchmarks for Global Mobility', *Workspan*, Vol. 52, No. 4 (2009), pp. 72–77; as well as D. Balkin 'Explaining CEO Pay in a Global Context: An Institutional Perspective', in L. Gomez-Mejia and S. Werner (eds.) *Global Compensation: Foundations and Perspectives* (New York: Routledge, 2008), pp. 192–205. In interviews conducted a number of years ago by the first author with senior management of Australian firms operating internationally, repatriation difficulties were one of the major reasons cited for not following a Going Rate Approach with Australian expatriates.

31. See B. W. Teague *Compensating Key Personnel Overseas* (New York: The Conference Board, 1972); and J. J. Martoccho *Strategic Compensation*, 6th ed. (Upper Saddle River, NJ: Pearson/Prentice-Hall, 2011), particularly

Chapter 14, for a more detailed discussion of the concept of keeping the expatriate 'whole'.

32. This discussion of the Balance Sheet Approach follows the presentation in Chapter 5 of the *2000 Guide to Global Compensation and Benefits*, ed. C. Reynolds (San Diego, CA: Harcourt Professional Publishing, 2000).

33. For a discussion of the complexities of this topic specific to China see K. Leung, X. Lin and L. Lu 'Compensation Disparity Between Locals and Expatriates in China: A Multilevel Analysis of the Influence of Norms', *Management International Review*, Vol. 54 (2014), pp. 107–128.

34. See Chapter 8 of J. Martocchio *Strategic Compensation*, 6th ed. (Upper Saddle River, NJ: Pearson/Prentice Hall, 2011) for a review of equity theory applied to compensation.

35. M. Neijzen and S. De Bruyker *Diverse Expatriate Populations: Alternative Remuneration Packages* (New York: AIRINC, 2010).

36. See ORC Worldwide 'Survey on local-plus packages in Hong Kong and Singapore' (New York, 2008); ORC Worldwide 'Survey on local-plus packages for expatriates in China' (New York, 2009).

37. AIRINC 'Mobility Outlook Survey' (New York, 2011), AIRINC.

38. D. Bolchover 'Up or Out: Next Moves for the Modern Expatriate' (London, UK: Economist Intelligence Unit, 2010).

39. Y. McNulty, K. Hutchings *et al.* 'How Expatriate Employees View Expatriate Return on Investment', *Proceedings of the Academy of International Business* (Nagoya, Japan, June 2011).

40. R. Cui 'International Compensation: The Importance of Acting Globally', *WorldatWork Journal*, Vol. 15, No. 4 (2006), pp. 18–23; R. Herod *Global Compensation and Benefits: Developing Policies for Local Nationals* (Alexandria, Va.: Society for Human Resource Management, 2008).

41. P. Stuart 'Global Payroll – A Taxing Problem', *Personnel Journal* (October, 1991), pp. 80–90. For a discussion of the comparative international tax status of incentive elements of pay see J. George 'Do Performance Awards Work Outside the US?' *Workspan*, Vol. 53, No. 1 (2010), pp. 12–14.

42. Ibid.; tax equalization can become a potential area of familial contention and more complex when dual-career families seek tandem international assignments, as presented by G. Aldred in 'Dual Career Support: Strategies for Designing and Providing Career Support for International Assignee Partners', *GMAC Strategic Advisor*, 2, 6 (February 2006), pp. 1–4 (www.gmacglobalrelocation.com). No fewer than 78 per cent of surveyed MNEs applied a tax equalization policy according to the Brookfield Survey 2010.

43. *Organization for Economic Co-operation and Development*; see www.oecd.org under 'OECD Tax Database' for a complete listing of tax rates and other fiscal policy comparisons for member nations.

44. 'Brookfield Global Relocation Trends 2010 Survey', Brookfield GMAC Global Relocation Services (2010), www.brookfieldgrs.com/insights_ideas.grts/.

45. R. Schuler and P. Dowling *Survey of SHRM Members* (New York: Stern School of Business, New York University, 1988).

46. Ibid.

47. *Organization for Economic Co-operation and Development*.

48. 'UBS Prices and Earnings, Wealth Management Research, August 2010, A Global Purchasing Power Comparison', accessed 3 October 2010 from www.ubs.com. The arcane complexities of attempting to forecast exchange rates can be found in an interesting article by K. Clements and Y. Lan 'A New Approach to Forecasting Exchange Rates', *Journal of International Finance*, Vol. 29 (2010), pp. 1424–1437. For an updated European perspective see ec.europa.eu/eurostat/statistics-explained/index.php/Comparative_price_levels_of_consumer_goods_and_services; and from UBS www.ubs.com/microsites/prices-earnings/edition–2015.html.

49. 'Price and Earnings: A Comparison of Purchasing Power Around the Globe' (Zurich: UBS AG, Wealth Management Research, 2015).

50. See UBS.com.

51. See www.eiu.com/index.asp for *The Economist* Intelligence Unit website.

52. C. Reynolds 'Cost-Effective Compensation', *Topics in Total Compensation*, Vol. 2, No. 1 (1988), p. 320.

53. Accessed from www.UBS.com 'UBS, Prices and Earnings 2015', PDF document, p. 12, accessed on 13 February 2016.

54. The difficulties of communicating a globally standardized equity share plan at Siemens are reported by R. Knells, M. Muntermann, K. Wolff and U. Zschoche 'The Importance of Communication When Implementing Global Share Plans: The Siemens Experience', *Compensation and Benefits Review*, Vol. 45, No. 5 (2013), pp. 272–277.

55. J. Newman, B. Gerhart and G. Milkovich *Compensation*, 12th ed. (Boston, MA: McGraw-Hill Pub., 2017), Chapter 16.

56. See E. Schein *Organizational Culture and Leadership* (San Francisco, CA: Jossey-Bass Pub., 1985). For a specific regional discussion of this issue see M. Festing and I. Sahakiants 'Compensation Practices in Central and Eastern European EU Member States – An Analytic Framework Based on Institutional Perspectives, Path Dependencies and Efficiency Considerations', *Thunderbird International Business Review*, Vol. 52, No. 3 (2010), pp. 203–216.

57. See M. Festing, A. Engle, P. Dowling and I. Sahakiants 'HRM Activities: Pay and Rewards'; P. Dowling, A. Engle, M. Festing and B. Mueller 'Complexity in Global Pay: A Meta-Framework', *Conference Proceedings of the 8th Conference on International Human Resource Management*, (Cairns, Australia, June 2005), CD-ROM indexed by title and first author's name; C. Brewster 'Comparing HRM Policies and Practices Across Geographical Borders', in G. Stahl and I. Björkman (eds.) *Handbook of Research in International Human Resource Management* (Cheltenham, UK: Edward Elgar, 2006), pp. 68–91.

58. J. Barney 'Firm Performance and Sustained Competitive Advantage', *Journal of Management*, Vol. 17, No. 1 (1991), pp. 99–120.

59. See J. G. March and H. A. Simon *Organizations* (New York: Wiley and Sons, Inc., 1958).

60. O. Williamson 'Efficient Labor Organization', in F. Stephens (ed.) *Firms, Organization and Labor* (London: MacMillan, 1984), pp. 87–118; G. Marin 'The Influence of Institutional and Cultural Factors on Compensation Practices Around the World', in L. Gomez–Mejia and S. Werner (eds.) *Global Compensation: Foundations and Perspectives* (New York: Routledge, 2008), pp. 3–17. Also see M. Festing and I. Sahakiants 'Compensation Practices in Central and Eastern EU Member States – An Analytical Framework Based on Institutional Perspectives, Path Dependencies and Efficiency Considerations', *Thunderbird International Business Review*, Vol. 53, No. 3 (2010), pp. 203–216.

61. As in M. Armstrong and H. Murlis *Reward Management: A Handbook of Remuneration Strategy and Practice* (London: Kogan Page Limited, 1991). Also see G. T. Milkovich and M. Bloom 'Rethinking International Compensation', *Compensation and Benefits Review*, Vol. 30, No. 1 (1998), pp. 15–23; M. Festing, J. Eidems and S. Royer 'Strategic Issues and Local Constraints in Transnational Compensation Strategies: An Analysis of Cultural, Institutional and Political Influences', *European Management Journal*, Vol. 25, No. 2 (2007), pp. 118–131; M. Brookes, G. Wood and C. Brewster 'Variations in Financial Participation in Comparative Context', in G. Wood, C. Brewster and M. Brookes (eds.) *Human Resource Management and the Institutional Perspective* (London: Routledge Publishing, 2014), pp. 39–58.

62. A. Engle and M. Mendenhall 'Transnational Roles, Transnational Rewards: Global Integration in Compensation', *Employee Relations*, Vol. 26, No. 6 (2004), pp. 613–625. For a more basic discussion of competency-based rewards see P. Zingheim and J. Schuster 'Competencies replacing Jobs as the Compensation/HR Foundation', *WorldatWork Journal*, Vol. 18, No. 3 (2009), pp. 6–20. For a North American-based empirical review of skills based pay systems and their impact on workforce flexibility, employee membership behaviors and productivity see A. Mitra, N. Gupta and J. Shaw 'A Comparative Examination of Traditional and Skills-based Pay Plans', *Journal of Managerial Psychology*, Vol. 26, No. 4 (2011), pp. 278–296. For a Spanish empirical sample of the relationship between competencies and rewards see M. Diaz-Fernandez, A. Lopez-Cabrales and R. Valle-Cabera 'In Search of Demanded Competencies: Designing Superior Compensation Systems', *International Journal of Human Resource Management*, Vol. 24, No. 3 (2013), pp. 643–666.

63. L. Gomez-Mejia and T. Welbourne 'Compensation Strategies In a Global Context', *Human Resource Planning*, Vol. 14, No. 1 (1991), pp. 29–41; R. Heneman, C. von Hippel, D. Eskew and D. Greenberger 'Alternative Rewards in Unionized Environments', in R. Heneman (ed.) *Strategic Reward Management* (Greenwich, CT: Information Age Pub., 2002), pp. 131–152. The use of variable group pay and benefits is presented as positively impacting innovations in an empirical review of a wide range of Canadian firms by B. Curran and S. Walsworth 'Can You Pay Employees to Innovate? Evidence From the Canadian Private Sector,' *Human Resource Management Journal*, Vol. 24, No. 3 (2014), pp. 290–306.

64. Gomez-Mejia and Welbourne 'Compensation Strategies in a Global Context'; M. Bloom and G. T. Milkovich 'A SHRM Perspective on International Compensation and Reward Systems', *Research in Personnel and Human Resource Management*, Supplement 4 (Greenwich, CT: JAI Press, 1991), pp. 283–303. For a review of efforts by the Chartered Institute of Personnel and Development (CIPD) in the United Kingdom to more systematically assess the potential cost and financial liability inherent in employee incentive schemes – in the light of a widespread perception that risky executive incentives led to dysfunctional decisions in the period 1995– 2008 – see C. Cotton and J. Chapman 'Rewards in the U.K.: Top 10 Risks', *Workspan*, Vol. 53, No. 1, (2010), pp. 52–57.

65. Milkovich and Newman 'A SHRM Perspective on International Compensation and Reward Systems'.

66. M. Festing, J. Eidems and S. Royer 'Strategic Issues and Local Constraints in Transnational Compensation Strategies: An Analysis of Cultural, Institutional and Political Influences'. An earlier version of this was presented by Marion Festing, Allen D. Engle, Peter Dowling and Bernadette Muller in the Conference Proceedings of the 8th Conference on International Human Resource Management, Cairns, Australia, 2005. For more on the tension between standardization and globalization see M. Festing, A. Engle, P. Dowling and I. Sahakiants 'HRM Activities: Pay and Rewards'.

67. M. Festing and A. Engle 'Contextualism in Rewards: Constructs, Measures and the Discretion of Multinational Enterprises', in C. Brewster and W. Mayrhofer 'Comparative Human Resource Management – Current Status and Future Development', Professional Development Workshop, HR Division, Academy of Management (Montreal, August 2010); M. Bloom, G. T. Milkovich and A. Mitra 'International Compensation: Learning From How Managers Respond to Variations in Local Host Contexts', *International Journal of Human Resource Management*, Vol. 14 (2003), pp. 1350–1367. Also see A. Mitra, M. Bloom and G. T Milkovich 'Crossing a Raging River: Seeking Far-Reaching Solutions to Global Pay Challenges', *WorldatWork Journal*, Vol. 11, No. 2 (2002), pp. 6–17. For a lucid argument that international scholars may have overestimated the forces associated with localization of rewards see B. Gerhart 'Compensation and National Culture', in L. Gomez-Mejia and S. Werner (eds.) *Global Compensation: Foundations and Perspectives* (New York: Routledge, 2008), pp. 142–157.

68. J. Boudreau, P. Ramstad and P. Dowling 'Global Talentship: Toward a Decision Science Connecting Talent to Global Strategic Success', in W. H. Mobley and P. W. Dorfman (eds.) *Advances in Global Leadership*, Vol. 3 (Oxford: Elsevier Science, 2003), pp. 63–99. Also see A. Engle, M. Mendenhall, R. Powers and Y. Stedham 'Conceptualizing the Global Competency Cube: A Transnational Model of Human Resource', *Journal of European Industrial Training*, Vol. 25, No. 7 (2001), pp. 346–353.

69. E. E. Lawler III *Rewarding Excellence* (San Francisco, CA: Jossey-Bass Pub., 2000); C. Garvey 'Steer Teams With the Right Pay', *HR Magazine*, Vol. 47, No. 5 (May 2002), pp. 71–78.

70. G. T. Milkovich and M. Bloom 'Rethinking International Compensation', *Compensation and Benefits Review*, Vol. 30, No. 1 (1998), pp. 15–23.

71. G. T. Milkovich and M. Bloom 'Rethinking International Compensation'. Also see A. Engle and M. Mendenhall 'Transnational Roles and Transnational Rewards: Global Integration in Compensation', *Employee Relations*, Vol. 26, No. 6 (2004), pp. 613–625.

72. An additional advantage of these composite systems is the potential for the pay system to act as a more nuanced and meaningful 'signal' to attract and hold employees with certain capabilities. Recall the 'talent management' discussion from Chapter 7 and the need to gain and maintain critical skills in a highly competitive global environment. The potential signaling advantage of a performance-focused pay system is presented by B. Gerhart and M. Fang 'Pay for (Individual) Performance: Issues, Claims, Evidence and the Role of Sorting Effects', *Human Resource Management Review*, Vol. 24 (2014), pp. 41–52.

73. For an interesting and rather complete cross-cultural review of corporate governance roles, processes and activities, organized by geographic regions, see the *Handbook on International Corporate Governance: Country Analyses*, 2nd ed., edited by C. Mallin (Cheltenham, UK: Edward Elgar Publishers, 2011).

74. See Newman, Gerhart and Milkovich *Compensation*, pp. 74–79, 82–88. Also see R. Greene *Rewarding Performance: Guiding Principles; Custom Strategies*

(New York: Routledge, 2010), particularly the discussion on Chapter 10 on global rewards and national and regional cultural clusters and norms, a discussion based on Fons Trompennars' *Managing People Across Cultures* (Chichester, UK: John Wiley and Sons, 2004) research on the patterns to values and preferences of various regions of the world.

75. Newman, Gerhart and Milkovich, 2017, particularly pages 74 through 79 and 82 through 88.

76. Post-hoc home country executive financial liabilities for questionable activities that may or may not have been locally *de rigueur* are an interesting application of this greater question of values across very different cultures. See M. Bartiromo 'Siemen's CEO Loscheer looks to the Future', *Business Week* (19 October 2009), pp. 17–18. For a well-written introduction to the issue of convergence or divergence in pay practices that may be associated with increasing transparency in pay practices around the world see C. Fay 'The Global Convergence of Compensation Practices', in L. Gomez-Mejia and S. Werner (eds.) *Global Compensation: Foundations and Perspectives* (New York: Routledge, 2008), pp. 131–141.

77. A. Katsoudas, S. Olsen and P. Weems 'New Trends in Global Equity Rewards', *Workspan*, Vol. 50, No. 3 (2007), pp. 28–33.

78. See Dowling, Engle, Festing and Mueller 'Complexity in Global Pay'; Bloom, Milkovich and Mitra 'International Compensation'.

CHAPTER 9
INTERNATIONAL INDUSTRIAL RELATIONS AND THE GLOBAL INSTITUTIONAL CONTEXT*

Chapter Objectives

In this chapter we:

- discuss the key issues in international industrial relations and the policies and practices of MNEs

- examine the potential constraints that trade unions may have on MNEs

- outline key concerns that trade unions have with regard to the activities of MNEs

*The contribution of Associate Professor Peter Holland (Monash University, Melbourne, Australia) to this chapter is gratefully acknowledged.

- outline strategies adopted by trade unions when dealing with MNEs
- discuss recent trends and issues in the global workforce context
- discuss the formation of regional economic zones such as the European Union (EU) and the impact of opponents to globalization
- present issues of codes of conduct and non-governmental organizations as multinational enterprises (MNEs)
- discuss human resource (HR) implications of offshoring strategies.

INTRODUCTION

In this chapter we will use the more traditional term 'industrial relations' to describe the broad field of study that looks at wider issues of work and employment. We recognize that newer terms such as 'employee relations' and 'employment relations' are also used in the literature but prefer to use the traditional term in the global context because this is consistent with international organizations such as the International Organization of Employers and the International Labor Organization.[1]

Before we examine the key issues in industrial relations as they relate to MNEs, we need to consider some general points about the field of international industrial relations.[2] First, it is important to realize that it is difficult to compare industrial relations systems and behavior across national boundaries; an industrial relations concept may change considerably when translated from one industrial relations context to another.[3] The concept of collective bargaining, for example, in the USA is understood to mean negotiations between a local trade union and management; in Sweden and Germany the term refers to negotiations between an employers' organization which represents the major firms in a particular industry and the trade union covering employees in that industry. Cross-national differences also emerge as to the objectives of the collective bargaining process and the enforceability of collective agreements. Many European unions continue to view the collective bargaining process as an ongoing class struggle between labor and capital, whereas in the USA union leaders take a very pragmatic economic view of collective bargaining rather than an ideological view. Second, it is very important to recognize in the international industrial relations field that no industrial relations system can be understood without an appreciation of its historical origin.[4] As Schregle[5] has observed,

> A comparative study of industrial relations shows that industrial relations phenomena are a very faithful expression of the society in which they operate, of its characteristic features, and of the power relationships between different interest groups. Industrial relations cannot be understood without an understanding of the way in which rules are established and implemented and decisions are made in the society concerned.

An interesting example of the effect of historical differences may be seen in the structure of trade unions in various countries. Poole[6] has identified several factors that may underlie these historical differences:

- the mode of technology and industrial organization at critical stages of union development
- methods of union regulation by government
- ideological divisions within the trade union movement
- the influence of religious organizations on trade union development
- managerial strategies for labor relations in large corporations.

As Table 9.1 shows, union structures differ considerably among Western countries. These include industrial unions, which represent all grades of employees in an industry; craft unions, which are based on skilled occupational groupings across industries; conglomerate unions, which represent members in more than one industry; and general unions, which are open to almost all employees in a given country. These differences in union structures have had a major influence on the collective bargaining process in Western countries. Some changes in union structure are evident over time; for example, enterprise unions are increasingly evident in industrialized nations. Enterprise unions are common in Asia-Pacific nations, although there are national variations in their functions, and in the proportion of enterprise unions to total unions.

TABLE 9.1   Trade union structure in leading Western industrial societies

Australia	general, craft, industrial, white-collar
Belgium	industrial, professional, religious, public sector
Canada	industrial, craft, conglomerate
Denmark	general, craft, white-collar
Finland	industrial, white-collar, professional, technical
Germany	industrial, white-collar
Great Britain	general, craft, industrial, white-collar, public sector
Japan	enterprise
The Netherlands	religious, conglomerate, white-collar
Norway	industrial, craft
Sweden	industrial, craft, white-collar, professional
Switzerland	industrial, craft, religious, white-collar
USA	industrial, craft, conglomerate, white-collar

Source: M. Poole *Industrial Relations: Origins and Patterns of National Diversity* (London: Routledge & Kegan Paul, 1986), p. 79.

The less we know about how a structure came to develop in a distinctive way, the less likely we are to understand it. As Prahalad and Doz[7] note, the lack of familiarity of multinational managers with local industrial and political conditions has sometimes needlessly worsened a conflict that a local firm would have been likely to resolve. Increasingly, MNEs are recognizing this shortcoming and admitting that industrial relations policies must be flexible enough to adapt to local requirements.

In line with research findings,[8] the transfer of industrial relations and other policies and practices from host countries to foreign subsidiaries is strongly influenced by a variety of factors and actors.[9] Black[10] states that national culture is found to be significantly associated with the characteristics of industrial relations, which is not always well articulated in the research. This is also supported by Hunter and Katz,[11] who looked at the globalization of the US banking and automotive industry and noted the important need to pay attention to the national industry systems of industry relations, as this will provide more insight into how best to manage these relationships. In addition, further research on country of origin (see Tuslemann *et al.*)[12] found that organizations are likely to adopt a variety of industrial relations strategies. This is best summed up by the example of Hyundai developing a production plant in China – see IHRM in Action Case 9.1.

IHRM in Action Case 9.1

MNC and industrial relations in China – The case of Hyundai Motor Company (HMC)

Despite initial attempts to maintain control over policies and practices, the transfer of industrial relations policies and practices from HMC in Korea to its China subsidiary has been influenced by the host country and various actors both inside and outside HMC. An overview of these policies and patterns are outlined below. Because of the high unemployment in the sector when HMC was setting up, the local government strongly supported the development of a low-skilled labor-intensive plant. Because of the weak union this system was adopted. However, despite HMC's attempts to curb the role of unions in other countries such as Canada and India, in China the plant union membership was 100 per cent as the union was a sub-branch of the plant's Communist Party Committee. These differences have resulted in the hybrid development of work patterns and practices including industrial relations highlighted in the table below.

CASE 9.1 TABLE A comparison of employment policies and practices between plants in China and Korea

	China	Korea
Production	Semi-automated and labor-intensive	Fully-automated
Work organization	Flat hierarchical structure Team working the focus	Highly centralized with many organizational levels
Skill training	Low to unskilled production training	Strong focus on training and higher-order skill development
Remuneration	Collective agreement but unions weak and under state control	Strong unions able to achieve higher wages. Collective bargaining
Job security	Production workers on one-year contracts usually renewed and low turnover	Greater job and security for longevity of service
Labor–management relations	All workers belong to union (ACFTU) which is under state control and acts more as an agent of management; however, signs of change towards more independent and stronger role for unions and Workers Representative Congresses	Strong unions and industrial reforms have given unions greater bargaining power

Source: Adapted from Zou and Lansbury, 2009.[13]

KEY ISSUES IN INTERNATIONAL INDUSTRIAL RELATIONS

The case of HMC in China leads us into the focus of this section of this chapter, on the industrial relations strategies adopted by multinationals rather than the more general topic of comparative industrial relations.[14] Later in this chapter we will cover the emerging topic of 'offshoring of labor', but first we examine the central question for industrial relations in an international context, which concerns the orientation of MNEs to organized labor.

Industrial relations policies and practices of multinational firms

Because national differences in economic, political, and legal systems produce markedly different industrial relations systems across countries, MNEs generally delegate the management of industrial relations to their foreign subsidiaries. However, a policy of decentralization does not keep corporate headquarters from exercising some co-ordination over industrial relations strategy. Generally, corporate headquarters will become involved in or oversee labor agreements made by foreign subsidiaries because these agreements may affect the international plans of the firm and/or create precedents for negotiations in other countries. Further, Marginson et al.[15] found that the majority of the firms in their study monitored labor performance across units in different countries. Comparison of performance data across national units of the firm creates the potential for decisions on issues such as unit location, capital investment, and rationalization of production capacity. The use of comparisons would be expected to be greatest where units in different countries undertake similar operations. For reviews of the literature in this area, see the work of Gunnigle and his colleagues.[16]

Much of the literature on the industrial relations practices of MNEs tends to be at a more cross-national or comparative level. As with the HMC case, there is, however, some research on industrial relations practices at the firm level. Empirical research has identified a number of differences in multinational approaches to industrial relations. Indeed, a number of studies have examined differences in the propensity of multinational headquarters to intervene in, or to centralize control over, matters such as industrial relations in host locations. Multinational headquarters involvement in industrial relations is influenced by several factors, as detailed below.

The degree of intersubsidiary production integration.   According to Hamill,[17] a high degree of integration was found to be the most important factor leading to the centralization of the industrial relations function within the firms studied. Industrial relations throughout a system become of direct importance to corporate headquarters when transnational sourcing patterns have been developed – that is, when a subsidiary in one country relies on another foreign subsidiary as a source of components or as a user of its output.[18] In this context, a co-ordinated industrial relations policy is one of the key factors in a successful global production strategy.[19] One early example of the development of an international policy for industrial relations can be seen in the introduction of employee involvement across Ford's operations.[20]

Nationality of ownership of the subsidiary.   There is evidence of differences between European and US firms in terms of headquarters' involvement in industrial relations.[21] A number of studies have revealed that US firms tend to exercise greater centralized control over labor relations than do British or other European firms.[22] US firms tend to place greater emphasis on formal management controls and a close reporting system (particularly within the area of financial control) to ensure that planning targets are met. In his review of empirical research of this area, Bean[23] showed that foreign-owned multinationals in Britain prefer single-employer bargaining (rather than involving an employer association), and are more likely than British firms to assert managerial prerogative on matters of labor utilization. Further, Hamill[24] found US-owned subsidiaries to be much more centralized in labor relations decision-making than British-owned. Hamill attributed this difference in management procedures to the more integrated nature of US firms, the greater divergence between British and US labor relations systems than between British and other European systems, and the more ethnocentric managerial style of US firms.

IHRM approach.   In earlier chapters, we discussed the various international human resource management (IHRM) approaches utilized by multinationals; these have implications for international industrial relations. Interestingly, an ethnocentric predisposition is more likely to be associated with various forms of industrial relations conflict.[25] Conversely, it has been shown that more geocentric firms will bear more influence on host-country industrial relations systems, due to their greater propensity to participate in local events.[26]

MNE prior experience in industrial relations.   European firms have tended to deal with industrial unions at industry level (frequently via employer associations) rather than at firm level. The opposite is more typical for US firms. In the USA, employer associations have not played a key role in the industrial relations system, and firm-based industrial relations policies tend to be the norm.[27]

Subsidiary characteristics.   Research has identified a number of subsidiary characteristics to be relevant to centralization of industrial relations. First, subsidiaries that are formed through acquisition of well-established indigenous firms tend to be given much more autonomy over industrial relations than are greenfield sites set up by a multinational firm.[28] Second, according to Enderwick, greater intervention would be expected when the subsidiary is of key strategic importance to the firm and the subsidiary is young.[29] Third, where the parent firm is a significant source of operating or investment funds for the subsidiary – that is, where the subsidiary is more dependent on headquarters for resources – there will tend to be increased corporate involvement in industrial relations and human resource management (HRM).[30] Finally, poor subsidiary performance tends to be accompanied by increased corporate involvement in industrial relations. Where poor performance is due to industrial relations problems, multinationals tend to attempt to introduce parent-country industrial relations practices aimed at reducing industrial unrest or increasing productivity.[31]

Characteristics of the home product market.   An important factor is the extent of the home product market[32] – an issue that was discussed in Chapter 1. If domestic sales are large relative to overseas operations (as is the case with many US firms), it is more likely that overseas operations will be regarded by the parent firm as an extension of domestic operations. This is not the case for many European firms, whose international operations represent the major part of their business. Lack of a large home market is a strong incentive to adapt to host-country institutions and norms. There is evidence of change in the European context: since the implementation of the single European market in 1993, there has been growth in large European-scale companies (formed via acquisition or joint ventures) that centralize management organization and strategic decision-making. However, processes of operational decentralization with regard to industrial relations are also evident.[33]

Management attitudes towards unions.   An additional important factor is that of management attitudes or ideology concerning unions.[34] Knowledge of management attitudes concerning unions may provide a more complete explanation of multinational industrial relations behavior than could be obtained by relying solely on a rational economic model. Thus, management attitudes should also be considered in any explanation of managerial behavior along with such factors as market forces and strategic choices. This is of particular relevance to US firms, since union avoidance appears to be deeply rooted in the value systems of American managers.[35] Commenting on labor relations in the USA, the noted Harvard labor law scholar, Derek Bok, has observed that:

> A look at the forces that shape our labor laws does tell us something about our own society – or at least it brings some old truths into sharper focus. Consider the individualism, the pragmatism and the decentralization that pervades our system of labor relations. These qualities have been much praised and doubtless contribute much to labor relations in America. They permit great flexibility in a diverse country and provide abundant opportunities for initiative [. . .]. At the same time, these national traits

have also produced a system of labor law that is uniquely hard on the weak, the uneducated, the unorganized, and the unlucky.[36]

Table 9.2 shows Organization for Economic Cooperation and Development (OECD) data on trade union density of 18 developed economies from 2005 to 2013. Sweden, Denmark and Norway have the highest levels of union membership, while France, the USA, and Korea have low levels of union density. Hence, managers from these countries may be less likely to have extensive experience with unions than managers in many other countries. Overall, Table 9.2 shows that union density has slightly declined in the period 2005 to 2010, with the OECD average declining from 18.8 in 2005 to 16.9 in 2013. This decline in union density in many countries may be explained by economic factors such as reduced public-sector employment, reduced employment in manufacturing industries as a share in total employment, and increased competition; it is also suggested to be associated with decentralization of industrial relations to business-unit level, changes in governance, and legislative changes. Union membership decline is also linked to the introduction of new forms of work organization, globalization of production, and changes in workforce structure.[37]

TABLE 9.2 Trade union density

Country	2005	2013
Australia	22.3	17.0
Austria	33.3	27.4
Canada	27.7	27.2
Chile	13.5	15.3 in 2012*
Denmark	70.7	66.8
France	7.7	7.7 in 2012*
Germany	21.7	17.7
Hungary	17.5	10.6 in 2012*
Ireland	34.0	29.6
Italy	33.6	36.9
Japan	18.8	17.8
Mexico	16.9	13.6
Norway	54.9	53.5
Poland	21.5	12.5 in 2012*
Spain	14.8	17.5 in 2012*
Sweden	76.5	67.7
UK	28.4	25.4
USA	12.0	10.8
OECD countries	18.8	16.9

* Data not available for 2013.

Source: OECD Database www.OECD.Stat extracted 9 September 2015. Trade union density is the ratio of wage and salary earners that are trade union members divided by the total number of wage and salary earners.

Although there are several problems inherent in data collection for a cross-national comparison of union density rates, several theories have been suggested to explain the variations among countries. Such theories consider economic factors such as wages, prices, and unemployment levels; social factors such as public support for unions; and political factors. In addition, studies indicate that the strategies utilized by labor, management, and governments are particularly important.[38]

Another key issue in international industrial relations is industrial disputes. Hamill[39] examined the strike-proneness of multinational subsidiaries and indigenous firms in Britain across three industries. Strike-proneness was measured via three variables: strike frequency, strike size, and strike duration. There was no difference across the two groups of firms with regard to strike frequency, but multinational subsidiaries did experience larger and longer strikes than local firms. This may be as noted due to the lack of familiarity with the industrial relations environment or, as Hamill suggests, this difference indicates that foreign-owned firms may be under less financial pressure to settle a strike quickly than local firms – possibly because they can switch production out of the country.

Overall, it is evident that international industrial relations are influenced by a broad range of factors. Commenting on the overall results of his research, Hamill[40] concluded that:

> general statements cannot be applied to the organization of the labor relations function within MNEs. Rather, different MNEs adopt different labor relations strategies in relation to the environmental factors peculiar to each firm. In other words, it is the type of multinational under consideration which is important rather than multinationality itself.

TRADE UNIONS AND INTERNATIONAL INDUSTRIAL RELATIONS

Trade unions may limit the strategic choices of multinationals in four ways, by: (1) influencing wage levels to the extent that cost structures may become uncompetitive; (2) constraining the ability of multinationals to vary employment levels at will; (3) hindering or preventing global integration of the operations of multinationals;[41] and (4) campaigning and mobilizing against multinationals.[42] We shall briefly examine each of these potential constraints.

Influencing wage levels

Although the importance of labor costs relative to other costs is decreasing, labor costs still play an important part in determining cost competitiveness in most industries. The influence of unions on wage levels is therefore, important. Multinationals that fail to successfully manage their wage levels will suffer labor-cost disadvantages that may narrow their strategic options.

Constraining the ability of multinationals to vary employment levels at will

For many multinationals operating in Western Europe, Japan, and Australia, the inability to vary employment levels 'at will' may be a more serious problem than wage levels. Many countries now have legislation that limits considerably the ability of firms to carry out plant closure, redundancy, or layoff programs unless it can be shown that structural conditions make these employment losses unavoidable. Frequently, the process of showing the need for these programs is long and drawn-out. Plant closure or redundancy legislation in many countries also frequently specifies that firms must compensate redundant employees through specified formulae such as two week's pay for each year of service. In many countries, payments for involuntary terminations are quite substantial, especially in comparison to those in the USA.

Trade unions may influence this process in two ways: by lobbying their own national governments to introduce redundancy legislation; and by encouraging regulation of multinationals by international organizations such as the OECD. Multinational managers who do not take these restrictions into account in their strategic planning may well find their options to be considerably limited.

Hindering or preventing global integration of the operations of MNEs

In recognition of these constraints (which can vary by industry), some multinationals make a conscious decision not to integrate and rationalize their operations to the most efficient degree, because to do so could cause industrial and political problems. Prahalad and Doz[43] cite General Motors (GM) as an example of this 'sub-optimization of integration'. GM was alleged in the early 1980s to have undertaken substantial investments in Germany (matching its new investments in Austria and Spain) at the demand of the German metalworkers' union (one of the largest industrial unions in the Western world) in order to foster good industrial relations in Germany. One observer of the world auto industry suggested that car manufacturers were sub-optimizing their manufacturing networks partly to placate trade unions and partly to provide a 'redundancy in sources' to prevent localized industrial relations problems from paralyzing their network. This suboptimization led to unit manufacturing costs in Europe that were 15 per cent higher, on average, than an economically optimal network would have achieved. Prahalad and Doz[44] drew the following conclusion from this example:

> Union influence thus not only delays the rationalization and integration of MNEs' manufacturing networks and increases the cost of such adjustments (not so much in the visible severance payments and 'golden handshake' provisions as through the economic losses incurred in the meantime), but also, at least in such industries as automobiles, permanently reduces the efficiency of the integrated multinational corporation network. Therefore, treating labor relations as incidental and relegating them to the specialists in the various countries is inappropriate. In the same way as government policies need to be integrated into strategic choices, so do labor relations.

THE RESPONSE OF TRADE UNIONS TO MNEs

Trade union leaders have long seen the growth of multinationals as a threat to the bargaining power of labor because of the considerable power and influence of large multinational firms. While it is recognized that multinationals are 'neither uniformly anti-union nor omnipotent and monolithic bureaucracies',[45] their potential for lobbying power and flexibility across national borders creates difficulties for employees and trade unions endeavoring to develop countervailing power. There are several ways in which multinationals have an impact upon trade union and employee interests. Kennedy[46] has identified the following seven characteristics of MNEs as the source of trade union concern about multinationals:

1   *Formidable financial resources.* This includes the ability to absorb losses in a particular foreign subsidiary that is in dispute with a national union and still show an overall profit on worldwide operations. Union bargaining power may be threatened or weakened by the broader financial resources of a multinational. This is particularly evident where a multinational has adopted a practice of *transnational sourcing and cross-subsidization of products or components* across different countries. "The economic pressure which a nationally based union can exert upon a multinational is certainly less than would be the case if the company's operations were confined to one country".[47]

2   *Alternative sources of supply.* This may take the form of an explicit 'dual-sourcing' policy to reduce the vulnerability of the multinational to a strike by any national union. Also, temporary

switching of production in order to defeat industrial action has been utilized to some extent, for example, in the automotive industry.[48]

3   *The ability to move production facilities to other countries.* A reported concern of employees and trade unions is that job security may be threatened if a multinational seeks to produce abroad what could have, or previously has, been manufactured domestically. National relative advantages provide MNEs with choice as to location of units. Within the European Union (EU), for example, evidence suggests that MNEs locate skill-intensive activities in countries with national policies promoting training and with relatively high labor costs. Conversely, semi-skilled, routinized activities are being located in countries with lower labor costs.[49] Threats by multinationals, whether real or perceived, to reorganize production factors internationally with the accompanying risk of plant closure or rationalization, will have an impact on management-labor negotiations at a national level. However, technical and economic investments may reduce a multinational's propensity to relocate facilities.

4   *A remote locus of authority* (i.e. the corporate head office management of a multinational firm). While many MNEs report decentralization and local responsiveness of HRM and industrial relations, trade unions and works councils have reported that the multinational decision-making structure is opaque and the division of authority obscured. Further, employee representatives may not be adequately aware of the overall MNE organizational strategy and activities.[50]

5   *Production facilities in many industries.* As Vernon[51] has noted, many multinationals operate multiple product lines across a range of industries.

6   *Superior knowledge and expertise in industrial relations.*

7   *The capacity to stage an 'investment strike',* whereby the multinational refuses to invest any additional funds in a plant, thus ensuring that the plant will become obsolete and economically non-competitive.

Many of the points made by Kennedy would now be recognized as characteristics of the process described as *offshoring,* as presented later in this chapter. This topic will remain a key issue within the broader debate concerning globalization and the employment consequences of globalization. For reviews of offshoring, see Auer *et al.,*[52] Cooke,[53] and Pyndt and Pedersen.[54]

Another issue reported by trade unions is their claim that they have difficulty accessing decision-makers located outside the host country and obtaining financial information. For example, according to Martinez Lucio and Weston:

> *Misinformation has been central to the management strategy of using potential investment or disinvestment in seeking changes in certain organizations [. . .]. For example, in companies such as Heinz, Ford, Gillette, and General Motors, workers have established that they had on occasions been misinformed by management as to the nature of working practices in other plants.*[55]

The response of labor unions to multinationals has been fourfold: to form international trade secretariats (ITSs); to lobby for restrictive national legislation; to try and achieve regulation of multinationals by international organizations; and finally, to undertake a mobilization or corporate campaign against the MNE.

CAMPAIGNING AND MOBILIZING

Where trade unions believe a MNE has acted in a way that is not to the benefit of its members or society as a whole, it may institute a campaign around this issue and recruit like-minded organizations (for example religious groups, government, and non-government organizations (NGOs)) in a public campaign on the issue to pressure the MNE to reconsider its decisions. The interesting aspect about this approach is that the issue(s) can be wide and varied, from union recognition and terms and conditions through to issues of social injustice. The issues or injustices become a focal point for the collective groups.[56]

International trade secretariats

ITSs function as loose confederations to provide worldwide links for the national unions in a particular trade or industry (e.g. metals, transport, and chemicals). The secretariats have mainly operated to facilitate the exchange of information.[57] The long-term goal of each ITS is to achieve transnational bargaining with each of the multinationals in its industry. Each ITS has followed a similar program to achieve the goal of transnational bargaining.[58] The elements of this program are: (1) research and information; (2) calling company conferences; (3) establishing company councils; (4) companywide union-management discussions; and (5) co-ordinated bargaining. Overall, the ITSs have met with limited success, the reasons for which Northrup[59] attributes to: (1) the generally good wages and working conditions offered by multinationals; (2) strong resistance from multinational firm management; (3) conflicts within the labor movement; and (4) differing laws and customs in the industrial relations field.

Lobbying for restrictive national legislation

On a political level, trade unions have for many years lobbied for restrictive national legislation in the USA and Europe. The motivation for trade unions to pursue restrictive national legislation is based on a desire to prevent the export of jobs via multinational investment policies. For example, in the USA, the American Federation of Labor-Congress of Industrial Organizations (AFL-CIO) has in the past lobbied strongly in this area.[60] A major difficulty for unions when pursuing this strategy is the reality of conflicting national economic interests. In times of economic downturn, this factor may become an insurmountable barrier for trade union officials. To date, these attempts have been largely unsuccessful, and, with the increasing internationalization of business, it is difficult to see how governments will be persuaded to legislate in this area.

Regulation of multinationals by international organizations

Attempts by trade unions to exert influence over multinationals via international organizations have met with some success. Through trade union federations such as the European Trade Union Confederation (ETUC) the labor movement has been able to lobby the International Labor Organization (ILO), the United Nations Conference on Trade and Development (UNCTAD),[61] the OECD and the EU. The ILO has identified a number of workplace-related principles that should be respected by all nations: freedom of association, the right to organize and collectively bargain, abolition of forced labor, and non-discrimination in employment. In 1977 the ILO adopted a code of conduct for multinationals (Tripartite Declaration of Principles Concerning MNEs and Social Policy).[62] The ILO code of conduct, which was originally proposed in 1975, was influential in the drafting of the OECD guidelines for multinationals, which were approved in 1976. These voluntary guidelines cover disclosure of information, competition, financing, taxation, employment and industrial relations, and science and technology.[63]

A key section of these guidelines is the *umbrella* or *chapeau clause* (the latter is the more common term in the literature) that precedes the guidelines themselves. The purpose of a chapeau clause is to serve as a summary or 'lead-in statement' for guidelines or agreements. For the OECD guidelines this clause states that multinationals should adhere to the guidelines "within the framework of law, regulations and prevailing labor relations and employment practices, in each of the countries in which they operate". Campbell and Rowan[64] state that "employers have understood the chapeau clause to mean compliance with local law supersedes the guidelines while labor unions have interpreted this clause to mean that the guidelines are a 'supplement' to national law". The implication of this latter interpretation is significant: a firm could still be in violation of the OECD guidelines even though its activities have complied with national law and practice. Given the ambiguity of the chapeau clause and the fact that the OECD guidelines are voluntary, it is likely that this issue will continue to be controversial.

There is also some controversy in the literature as to the effectiveness of the OECD guidelines in regulating multinational behavior.[65] This lack of agreement centers on assessments of the various challenges to the guidelines. The best known of these challenges is the *Badger* case. The Badger Company was a subsidiary of Raytheon, a US-based multinational. In 1976 the Badger Company decided to close its Belgian subsidiary, and a dispute arose concerning termination payments.[66] Since Badger (Belgium) NV had filed for bankruptcy, the Belgian labor unions argued that Raytheon should assume the subsidiary's financial obligations. Raytheon refused and the case was brought before the OECD by the Belgian government and the International Federation of Commercial, Clerical, Professional and Technical Employees (FIET), an international trade secretariat. The Committee on International Investments and MNEs (CIIME) of the OECD indicated that paragraph six of the guidelines (concerned with plant closures) implied a 'shared responsibility' by the subsidiary and the parent in the event of a plant closing. Following this clarification by the CIIME and a scaling down of initial demands, Badger executives and Belgian government officials negotiated a settlement of this case.

Blanpain[67] concludes that the *Badger* case made clear the responsibility of the parent company for the financial liability of its subsidiary but that this responsibility is not unqualified. As to whether the *Badger* case proved the 'effectiveness' of the OECD guidelines, Jain,[68] and Campbell and Rowan[69] point out that the Belgian unions devoted considerable resources to make this a test case and had assistance from both American unions (which, through the AFL-CIO, lobbied the US Department of State) and the Belgian government in their negotiations with the OECD and Badger executives. Liebhaberg[70] is more specific in his assessment:

> Despite an outcome which those in favor of supervision consider to be positive, the Badger Case is a clear demonstration of one of the weaknesses in the OECD's instrument, namely that it does not represent any sort of formal undertaking on the part of the 24 member states which are signatories to it. The social forces of each separate country must apply pressure on their respective governments if they want the guidelines applied.

A recent development with the OECD guidelines has been the follow-up procedures. The system of National Contact Points promotes observance of the guidelines by MNEs operating in or from the governments' territories. It appears that this system is now having some influence on MNE behavior in the industrial relations area. In May 2011 ministers from the OECD and developing economies agreed on new guidelines to promote more responsible business conduct by multinational enterprises, and a second set of guidance designed to combat the illicit trade in minerals that finances armed conflict. The OECD statement noted that:

> Forty-two countries will commit to new, tougher standards of corporate behavior in the updated Guidelines for Multinational Enterprises: the 34 OECD countries plus Argentina, Brazil, Egypt, Latvia, Lithuania, Morocco, Peru, and Romania. The updated Guidelines include new recommendations on human rights abuse and company responsibility for their supply chains, making them the first inter-governmental agreement in this area.
>
> The Guidelines establish that firms should respect human rights in every country in which they operate. Companies should also respect environmental and labor standards, for example, and have appropriate due diligence processes in place to ensure this happens. These include issues such as paying decent wages, combating bribe solicitation and extortion, and the promotion of sustainable consumption.[71]

Recognizing the limitations of voluntary codes of conduct, European trade unions continue to lobby the Commission of the EU to regulate the activities of multinationals.[72] Unlike the OECD, the Commission of the EU can translate guidelines into law, and has developed a number of proposals concerning disclosure of information to make multinationals more 'transparent'. These are discussed in more detail in the next section.

Corporate campaigning and mobilization

A relatively new approach by the trade union movement in response to globalization is to develop a campaign with like-minded groups and highlight the issues to the organization and its various stakeholders of particular (social) issues. A key catalyst for the development of this approach by unions has been the mobility of capital. This focus on MNE corporate (global) citizenship behavior has provided a new strategic approach to union-based campaigns. In a globalized economy this is seen as one strategy in dealing with the power imbalances between MNE and employees (highlighted above) to achieve corporate accountability. As Holland and Pyman note, this form of resistance and opposition to global corporations on social grounds has been one of the most significant geopolitical forces emerging in the twenty-first century.[73]

As Willis[74] points out, questions of economic inequality and corporate power have influenced political and economic change, including the development of the UN Global Compact, which includes principles that support human rights trade unionism, anti-discriminatory practices, and environmental protection. As a result, MNEs have become signatories to corporate codes of conduct (which are discussed later), committing themselves to responsible management practices regarding employment and labor standards and the environment in globalized communities.

The underlying reason for the success of this approach is the use of stakeholders such as consumers, suppliers, and political players which can affect the decision-making and reputation of the MNE in the marketplace. As such, trade unions are playing an increasing role in the emerging network of global campaigns on working conditions. One of the most recent examples of such a campaign led by unions was against the James Hardie Industries Limited, which is highlighted in IHRM in Action Case 9.2.

REGIONAL INTEGRATION: THE EU

Regional integration such as the development of the EU has brought significant implications for industrial relations.[75] In the Treaty of Rome (1957), some consideration was given to social policy issues related to the creation of the European Community. In the EU, the terms 'social policy' or 'social dimension' are used to cover a number of issues including in particular labor law and working conditions, aspects of employment and vocational training, social security and pensions. There have been a number of significant developments in EU social policy over the past four decades. The Social Charter of the Council of Europe came into effect in 1965. In 1987, the major objective of the implementation of the Single European Act was to establish the Single European Market (SEM) on 31 December 1992, in order to enhance the free movement of goods, money, and people within the SEM. The social dimension aims to achieve a large labor market by eliminating the barriers that restrict the freedom of movement and the right of domicile within the SEM. The European Community Charter of the Fundamental Social Rights of Workers (often referred to simply as the Social Charter) was introduced in 1989 and guided the development of social policy in the 1990s.[76] Naturally, the social dimension has been the subject of much debate: proponents defend the social dimension as a

IHRM in Action Case 9.2

James Hardie Industries Limited (JHIL) corporate campaign

JHIL is a MNE in the fiber-cement industry, originally established in Australia and the largest manufacturer of products containing asbestos until the mid-1980s. Evidence emerged of the company's knowledge of the dangers of asbestos for many years, from which it did little to protect employees or customers. As evidence mounted on the links between asbestos and cancer, it was estimated the JHIL was liable for 76 per cent of the claims in Australia. JHIL set up a compensation fund for asbestos victims and then undertook a restructure which resulted in the headquarters moving from Australia to the Netherlands. It was subsequently revealed that the compensation funds were not adequately funded and the restructure had meant the ability to seek redress was limited as Australia and the Netherlands did not have a legal treaty, meaning victims could not enforce claims.

The campaign

The subsequent corporate campaign was led by the Australian Council of Trade Unions (ACTU), and focused on adequate compensation against JHIL. This ACTU campaign also gained the support of the Labor state government of New South Wales, and an inquiry into the shortfall in the compensation scheme was established. As well as the public and political pressure, economic pressure came from the New South Wales Government as a major customer of JHIL. A key feature in the public campaign was victims turning up to the inquiry with their oxygen bottles and masks, highlighting the impact of the asbestos-related diseases. The report from the inquiry found that JHIL were responsible for the shortfall.

The campaign escalates

The company, through a variety of communications, sought to downplay the findings of the government report. The ACTU called for a boycott of JHIL products and built an alliance with US-based trade unions, which was JHIL's largest market, to highlight the issues in the USA. This was followed by national rallies in major Australian cities and shareholder pressures at annual general meetings of JHIL. At the height of the union campaign JHIL management publicly made a commitment to negotiate with the ACTU. However, after a year, when negotiations were still ongoing, a threat by the ACTU of a second wave of action brought a resolution to the campaign.

 The use of public pressure on JHIL on moral and ethical grounds was the core of the campaign underpinned by political and economic pressure on both a local and global scale, which encouraged and engaged a cross-section of society to become involved. This proved to be crucial in the campaign on community and social values.

 Whilst issues still reoccur regarding the compensation fund due to the fact that victims are still emerging, the fund has been re-established in Australia to support current and future victims.

Source: Holland and Pyman, 2012.

means of achieving social justice and equal treatment for EU citizens, while critics see it as a kind of 'social engineering'.[77]

 The current treaty for the EU is the Treaty of Lisbon, which came into force in December 2009.[78] The Treaty of Lisbon guarantees the enforcement of a Charter of Fundamental Rights that covers civil, political, economic, and social rights, which are legally binding not only on the

EU and its institutions but also on the member states as regards the implementation of EU law. It also reaffirms important steps to outlaw discrimination on the grounds of gender, race, and color, and mentions social rights applied within companies, e.g. workers' rights to be informed, to negotiate and take collective action – in other words, the right to strike. The European Commission department responsible for social policy is the Directorate-General for Employment, Social Affairs and Inclusion.[79] For many firms, whether non-European MNEs with businesses operating within the EU or smaller European firms, the legal complexity of operating within the EU increases the utility of belonging to an employer association such as the Federation of European Employers[80] to facilitate the challenge of managing across European national boundaries and accessing relevant information.

The issue of social 'dumping'

The growing importance of the MNE on a global scale has created increasing concerns about competitiveness. The focus of competitive advantage for the MNE is increasingly moving away from the firm level and toward employee cost and government support. This has been described by some as a 'race to the bottom'.[81] One of the early concerns related to the formation of the EU was its impact on jobs. There was alarm that those member states that have relatively low social security costs would have a competitive edge and that firms would locate in those member states that have lower labor costs. The counter alarm was that states with low-cost labor would have to increase their labor costs, to the detriment of their competitiveness. There are two industrial relations issues here: the movement of work from one region to another and its effect on employment levels; and the need for trade union solidarity to prevent workers in one region from accepting pay cuts to attract investment, at the expense of workers in another region.

With the expansion of the EU in 2004 to include ten new members (most relatively low-income states, some of whom are still working to overcome the heritage of state socialist economic systems and limited recent experience with parliamentary democracy) there has been an increased sensitivity to the problem of social dumping.[82] This is particularly so since the global financial crisis in 2009. An Internet search using the term 'social dumping' will turn up web pages reflecting concerns from multiple perspectives – trade union, societal, and business. We examine these multiple perspectives in the next section of this chapter, where we look at the issue of monitoring global HR practices.

CODES OF CONDUCT – MONITORING HRM PRACTICES AROUND THE WORLD

An issue that has been somewhat overlooked in the IHRM literature is the need to monitor the HRM practices used in a variety of social, legal, and regulatory contexts. An increasingly common way to address these issues is with a code of conduct. This is a policy document that provides rules and boundaries and stipulates acceptable standards of behavior. A well-structured and thought-through code of conduct can provide a fair, consistent, and valuable set of signals to those inside and outside the organization – in other words, the core values of that organization. It is clear therefore that a code of conduct needs to be ethical and underpinned by integrity. Whilst these values can be argued as being subjective, such codes provide guidelines on how the organization is expected to operate.

This is of particular relevance to MNEs involved in cross-border alliances in industries such as textile, clothing, and footwear (TCF) and other consumer goods industries such as electrical goods where MNEs do not establish their own manufacturing operations. A critical issue in the management of the international supply chain is ensuring that quality standards are met. This has been problematic for some MNEs with global brands such as Nike, Levi Strauss, Benetton, Reebok, and Adidas. A major management challenge for these firms has been the reaction of Western consumers to allegations of unfair employment practices used by their subcontractors in countries such as India, Bangladesh, China, Turkey, Indonesia, El Salvador, Honduras, the Dominican Republic, and the Philippines.

Various MNEs have been accused of condoning work practices such as the use of child labor, long working hours for minimal pay, and unsafe working environments – conditions that would not be permitted in the home countries of leading Western MNEs. Public uproar in the 1990s resulted in various actions by governments, the United Nations (UN) and NGOs to try to enforce codes of conduct also for subcontractors through their multinational partners.[83] Some multinationals, with corporate reputations and valuable brands at stake, quickly introduced their own codes of conduct.[84] These codes of conduct included, for example, acceptable working conditions, no child labor, and minimum wages. There is now a universal standard, similar to the ISO 9000 quality standard, called the *Social Accountability 8000*, whose principles are drawn from the UN human rights conventions.[85]

However, as the recent Rana Plaza disaster in Bangladesh in April 2013 illustrated, whilst health and safety issues were central to the deaths of over 1100 employees and the serious injury of 1000 workers, industrial relations issues also came to the fore in subsequent investigations. Evidence emerged of employees working over 100 hours a week with two days off a month and standard wages in the range of US$10 to US$13 a week for producing many household brands for a wide variety of advanced market economies. The Institute for Global Labour and Human Rights also reported evidence of intimidation against workers attempting to undertake collective bargaining and unionization.

While the code of conduct approach initially appeared to handle the public relations issue, as the Rana Plaza example illustrates, ongoing enforcement has proven difficult. The role of HRM related to a global code of conduct may include the following:

- drawing up and reviewing codes of conduct
- conducting a cost-benefit analysis to oversee compliance of employees and relevant alliance partners
- championing the need to train employees and alliance partners in elements of the code of conduct
- checking that performance and rewards systems take into consideration compliance to codes of conduct.

IHRM in Action Case 9.3 illustrates one example of a firm that has established a global code of conduct. On the basis of this case, you can discuss what internal and external effects such a code of conduct may have for the MNE.

Non-government organizations

The globalization of trade and business has provoked a vigorous debate within national states and is often expressed in anti-globalization rallies and protests. The activities of environmental groups such as Greenpeace highlight how these organizations have also become internationalized. They tend to have national 'managers' in various countries, and variations of structural forms for co-ordination and accountability. Aid agencies such as the Red Cross, the Red Crescent, World Vision, and Médecins Sans Frontieres (Doctors without Borders) are prominent examples of NGOs. They may utilize different organizational structures and have members who may internalize to a greater degree the shared values and beliefs, due to the nature of the organization's mission and activities, than may be found in a for-profit

IHRM in Action Case 9.3

Degussa's global code of conduct

The firm

Degussa group is a multinational corporation with a market leadership position in the sector of specialty chemistry. The group is represented worldwide on all five continents and based in more than 300 locations. The cornerstone for Degussa was placed in 1843 in Frankfurt, Germany; after several acquisitions, today 44 000 employees work for this company worldwide. Since June 2004, the Degussa group has been a 100 per cent subsidiary of Rag AG. Due to its important size and long history, as well as its broad international experience, Degussa operates relatively independently from the parent company. Key production facilities, sales and marketing offices of Degussa can be found in around 60 countries, whereas the business activity focuses on Europe, North America, and Asia. Degussa generates almost three-quarters of its sales volume outside of Germany.

The organization

Degussa has a decentralized organization within a global business framework. This is achieved through business units, which have full accountability for local operations. However, to maintain strategic control of its international business, strategic management decisions are mainly made in the headquarters – this philosophy is also reflected in the structure of the management board, which consists solely of German managers.

To foster a corporate strategy and a new corporate culture known as 'Blue Spirit', a set of supporting principles including Degussa's Global Social Policy, guiding missions which are incorporated in management practices (e.g. a bonus system for executives linked to corporate goals), as well as a Global Code of Conduct were developed. The aim was to bring together several different corporate cultures and to create one company in which every employee at every site feels as though he or she is part of a common whole.

The Global Code of Conduct

The Global Code of Conduct aims at supporting the employees in their daily work and providing them with reference points. In the course of growing globalization, the variety of relevant markets and cultures has increased. The expectations of employees as well as customers are becoming more complex, and different national and cultural backgrounds gain importance in the day-to-day work in this multinational company. The Code of Conduct is binding for every Degussa staff member and is applied in all subsidiaries as well as in the parent company. In addition, the code includes guidelines which control interactions with the corporate environment as well as with the public and governmental agencies or institutions. Even in countries (e.g. India) where local rules and laws have other standards, the Global Code of Conduct is enforced. In case regional requirements go beyond the Degussa Code, the firm is forced to adapt to these conditions and has to include respective deviations within the Code.

Every employee worldwide is expected to comply with the Global Code of Conduct. Degussa has appointed various compliance officers in different units to ensure that the rules are respected. In addition, these officers might answer any related questions to assist employees in complying with these rules. Beyond this, local HR departments offer training sessions, information and publications to ensure that all employees are familiar with the Code. All employees are encouraged to name strengths and weaknesses and to actively participate in the continuing further development of this Global Code of Conduct.

Content of the Global Code of Conduct: compliance rules for the Degussa group

1. Scope and objectives

2. Business conduct

   2.1 Managing business transactions

   2.2 Business relations

   2.3 Conflicts of interest

   2.4 Insider trading

   2.5 Maintaining the confidentiality of internal information

   2.6 Political involvement and contributions

   2.7 Ethics

3. Technical issues

   3.1 Competition and anti-trust law

   3.2 Foreign trade, export, and terrorism controls

   3.3 Tax law

   3.4 Environmental protection, safety, occupational health, and quality

   3.5 Data protection

   3.6 IT security

4. Practical implementation of compliance rules

Source: Based on information obtained from Degussa's website, and 'Consult' – Kienbaum Kundenmagazin, Kienbaum Human Resources Management Consulting, 1/2007, pp. 1–7.

multinational. Nonetheless, in terms of global control and operations, there may be similar managerial concerns to those of, for instance, oil companies. Physical risk – such as the danger of staff being taken hostage and of having property damaged – is common to firms operating in hostile contexts. As Fenwick[86] identifies, non-profit organizations have been largely ignored in IHRM research, possibly because IHRM "reflects the traditional management ethos of effectiveness and efficiency rather than the non-profit ethos of values-driven, charitable, and philanthropic ideals".[87] It would seem that the need to broaden the focus of the IHRM field to include NGOs will be necessary, as the impact and influence of NGOs is more than likely to continue well into the twenty-first century. For an excellent review of the role of NGOs in international business, see the paper by Lambell *et al.* (2008) in the Further Reading list at the end of this chapter.

MANAGING HR IN 'OFFSHORING COUNTRIES'

The concept of offshoring and its strategic importance

'Offshoring' is an increasingly common term used to describe the outsourcing of business activities. Contemporary offshoring, also known as service offshoring, reflects the emergence of a global economy based on service and knowledge and epitomized by the concept of the call center. What has been of interest in advanced economies has been the increasing amount of high-skilled work being offshored, which has created political, economic, employment and industrial relations tension in the home country. From an employment perspective, offshoring has been used to outsource work to contractors in countries where unionization is less developed and as such reduces the potential for disputes disrupting the production process. As such, industrial relations are transferred to a third party overseas, thereby side-stepping industrial agreement in higher wages/costs in the home countries and legal protection (as the Rana Plaza case above highlights). These countries often have very low wage rates as a further incentive to offshore.[88]

Whereas the uptake of service offshoring has been rapid, the uptake occurred starting from a relatively low-base. Even given global economic irregularities, offshoring continues to be an important trend for reaching competitive advantage in the globalized economy.[89] In this section we will give special emphasis to the context of host countries, which are typical recipients for offshoring activities of MNEs. For these offshoring countries we will discuss HRM implications[90] because this trend leads to a revolution in the global division of labor. New interfaces emerge that need to be managed.[91] However, we will first look at some of the HRM barriers and implications of offshoring.

In terms of operational issues, the lack of management expertise in dealing with the complexities that offshoring can throw up are important.[92] For example, how do you assess the knowledge skills and ability of the offshored workforce on a continuous basis? In China and India, university graduates are widely dispersed and the quality is varied – particularly the quality of language skills. Also in countries like India customer quality has never been seen as a high priority. As Shiu[93] pointed out, at best this requires issues of culture, language, service integration, and maintenance to be managed closely, which cost time and money.

Other issues include security, privacy, and legal issues as increasing volumes of sensitive data and information cross international borders. In this context, the EU has developed extensive protection mechanisms where personal data can only be offshored to countries deemed to have equivalent standards of protection and enforcement in privacy laws. Many of these issues are related to professional standards of training and development and the management of Human Resource Information Systems (HRIS). However, despite this, as Table 9.3 points out, India and China remain the top destinations for offshoring.

In India the development of offshoring was a result of strong support by the government to help the country meet those requirements that have an impact on the choice of the location for offshored activities. This choice depends on costs (labor and trade costs), the quality of institutions (particularly legislation) and infrastructure (particularly telecommunications), the tax and investment regime, and the skills of the employees (particularly language and computer skills).[94] A prominent example for offshoring activities are international call centers. However, offshoring of services also includes more sophisticated, high value-added activities, such as accounting, billing, financial analysis, software development, architectural design, testing, and research and development.[95]

As mentioned previously, in this chapter we will concentrate on the two most important countries for future foreign operations, India and China. Although it is beyond the scope of this chapter to deliver an encompassing description and analysis of the employment relations systems and approaches to HRM, we will analyze the situation with respect to offshoring and draw implications for HRM in each country. Finally, emerging issues for HRM in offshoring countries will be discussed.

TABLE 9.3 Offshoring nations, 2014

+ Move up   − Moved down

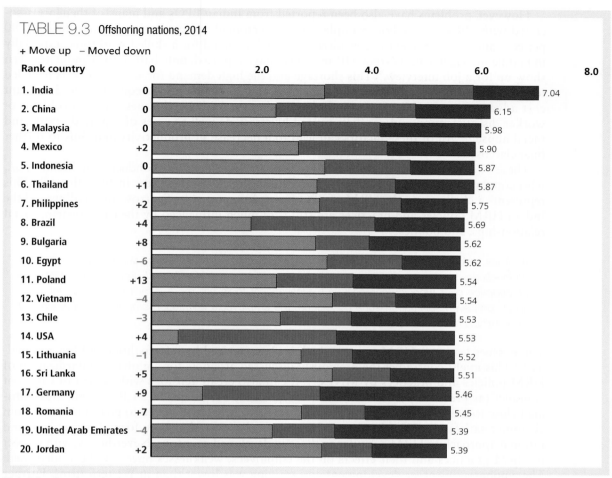

Rank country		0	2.0	4.0	6.0	8.0
1. India	0					7.04
2. China	0				6.15	
3. Malaysia	0				5.98	
4. Mexico	+2				5.90	
5. Indonesia	0				5.87	
6. Thailand	+1				5.87	
7. Philippines	+2				5.75	
8. Brazil	+4				5.69	
9. Bulgaria	+8				5.62	
10. Egypt	−6				5.62	
11. Poland	+13				5.54	
12. Vietnam	−4				5.54	
13. Chile	−3				5.53	
14. USA	+4				5.53	
15. Lithuania	−1				5.52	
16. Sri Lanka	+5				5.51	
17. Germany	+9				5.46	
18. Romania	+7				5.45	
19. United Arab Emirates	−4				5.39	
20. Jordan	+2				5.39	

Global Services Location Index

The 'Global Services Location Index' (GSLI) 2014 by A.T. Kearney is the sixth edition of the report in which the consulting firm examines the offshoring landscape in 51 countries around the globe, and ranks the top destinations for global offshoring. To come to this ranking, three main categories were researched; financial attractiveness, people skills and availability, and business environment. The weight given to these metrics is based on their importance to the location decision. 'Financial factors' constitute for 40% of the published index. 'People skills and availability' and 'business environment' both account for 30% of the total weight.

Source: A.T. Kearney, 2014.

Offshoring and HRM in India

India has developed a flourishing business process outsourcing (BPO) industry[96] and respective competencies. The technological infrastructure and the qualification as well as the motivation of the employees are perceived as benefits by Western investors and partners.

Furthermore, each year 3.1 million graduates enter the workforce and 20 per cent of the population speaks English.[97] Indian graduates are prepared to work for salaries which are lower than those of their Western counterparts. To capitalize on this cost advantage, US firms such as IBM, Hewlett-Packard and Electronic Data Systems have outsourced software development to Indian suppliers.[98] Other multinationals, such as General Electric, have used the availability of a highly educated yet relatively cheap labor force to establish their call centers in various parts of India. Local staff employed in these call centers are trained to speak English complete with a particular accent and use of appropriate idioms, so that US, UK, and Australian customers are often unaware that their local call has been diverted to a call center in India.

However, problems have also been reported from Indian BPOs and many of them are associated with HRM issues. For example, annual personnel turnover rates range from 20 to 80 per cent and a shortage exists considering the high demand for a skilled workforce, especially in middle management. As some HR managers have reported, only half of the candidates even show up for a job interview.[99] This shortage and the high demand for skilled workers have led to an annual increase in salaries of between 10 and 20 per cent. Consequently, the significant cost advantages of offshoring to India are in danger. Additional issues are the problems of worker dissatisfaction and conflicts caused by stress, as well as cases of reported sexual and racial abuse.[100] All of these factors can lead to a decrease in productivity and thus to further financial losses.[101]

These findings are confirmed by the results of an empirical study conducted by Mehta *et al.*, who concluded that HRM issues are perceived as a major weakness in BPO firms.[102] This represents a challenge to the HRM of BPO firms. As reported by Sparrow and Budhwar,[103] the Indian HRM policies and practices are still very much influenced by the caste system, social relationships, and politics:

> At times, selection, promotion, and transfer are based on ascribed status and social and political connections, so there is a strong emphasis on collectivism – family and group attainments take precedence over work outcomes [. . .]. Motivational tools are more likely to be social, interpersonal, and even spiritual. In such conditions, the employee's orientation emphasizes personalized relationships rather than performance.[104]

These issues lead to a HRM system which is characterized by informalities and less rationality.[105] This might contradict the previously discussed attempts for a global standardization of HRM policies and practices by MNEs.[106] It can also create tensions with regard to Codes of Conduct (as previously discussed). However, a study conducted in 51 BPO companies situated close to New Delhi revealed that the work settings were designed to guarantee maximum customer satisfaction. Furthermore, the authors discovered a more formal, structural, and rational approach to HRM – similar to those in developed countries. Nevertheless, with respect to HRM practices and their effects on the employees, weaknesses have also been identified. The emphasis on career development and training was lower than in Western firms. Further HRM issues to be addressed in the future included: increasing attrition rates, the prevention of psychological and stress-related problems, more flexibility in the workplace (part-time jobs do not currently exist), and the creation of a more interesting work environment to help build long-term relationships with well-qualified employees.[107] Only if the employees' needs are met by HRM measures is retention possible.[108]

Offshoring and HRM in China

China is one of the fastest growing economies in the world. It is a country well known for inexpensive manufacturing, although costs in this sector are reported to be rising.[109] Currently, salaries in China are even lower than in India. However, the total number of graduates is only half that which India produces, and the percentage of English-speaking graduates is also much lower.[110] While Chinese universities produce a high number of science and technology graduates, students come from an educational system in which they were rarely encouraged to take the initiative and deliver creative solutions, although these are major requirements by MNEs.[111] Consequently, the Chinese economy suffers from a skill shortage similar to that in India, especially for those jobs which require both technical as well as management know-how.[112] Similar turnover rates and the same tendency to increase salaries for highly skilled employees can also be observed in China.[113] Reported problems or barriers to working with local entities not only include difficulties of staff recruitment and retention but also problems in cross-cultural communication, poor working practices in supplier firms, and corrupt staff behavior.[114]

For Western MNEs who are planning to offshore activities to China, it is important to understand the role played by network connections called *guanxi:* dyadic personal relationships between people. Tung and Worm[115] explain that, while these relationships bear similarities to the Western practice of networking, there are differences: *guanxi* relationships are contingent upon conditions such as asymmetry, reciprocity, and necessity. The authors stress the importance of *guanxi* for successful business operations in China but recognize the difficulties this poses for Western managers. They suggest that *hiring practices* for key positions should take into account prospective Chinese employees' *guanxi*. The difficulty is being able to assess the extent to which prospective employees have *guanxi* that would be valuable in their enterprise.

Multinationals find that they need to invest in *training* so that employees learn how to properly use equipment, operate systems, and the like. What actions can these firms take to gain the benefits of this investment in human capital? Obviously it is not easy to prevent employees from leaving the operation. The poaching of skilled employees is a significant problem for MNEs in China. Shanghai Bell was an early entrant into the Chinese market and became the 'academy for the industry', experiencing high staff turnover to both Chinese and foreign-owned competitors.[116] In post-reform China, employees tend to change jobs frequently in pursuit of higher wages and not in an effort to develop their skills.[117] To a certain extent this may be traced back to the employment system that existed prior to reforms associated with the transition to a market economy. Guaranteed continuation of employment, along with various welfare and benefits offered to employees such as accommodation, medical treatment, childcare, and pensions, has been referred to as the *iron rice bowl*.[118] In exchange for job security, employees had little freedom to move to another work unit – that is, they were unable to quit or transfer jobs and were locked into a dependency relationship with their enterprises. Respectively, managers were deprived of their right to fire or lay off unqualified or non-productive employees.[119]

While companies operating in China are endeavoring to *reduce their attrition rates* through the provision of additional benefits and staff development programs, Chinese employees are beginning to recognize compensation differentials and that is having an impact upon job attitudes. A fair environment and good management practices are emerging as the essential tools for retaining Chinese employees, rather than above-market compensation alone. Goodall and Roberts,[120] in their study of a European oil company operating in China, cite the example of one employee who found that being part of a wider organizational network was incentive enough to stay with the multinational.

The above-mentioned recruitment, qualification, and retention problems require HRM practices which meet the needs of highly skilled HR socialized in the Chinese context. However, HRM in China has only recently evolved and is challenging the former administrative system.[121] The transition is difficult because of the previous strong influence of the state and a current highly competitive situation:[122]

> Until quite recently, the personnel function in SOEs [state-owned enterprises] was confined to job allocation, personnel record filing, and the provision of welfare benefits. The primary task for personnel management was to keep the employees politically and ideologically sound. Many of the HR practices which are familiar to their Western counterparts were beyond the experience of personnel staff in China.[123]

From this analysis Cooke derives key features that describe the current state of HRM in China:[124]

- There is no systematic approach for linking HRM with the business strategy.
- Despite a surplus of labor, many companies face recruiting and retention problems.
- There is no systematic link between performance management, reward, and long-term motivation.
- There is a lack of coherence and continuity of enterprise training.

However, research also shows differences between different types of enterprises.[125] Venter[126] points out that resource-rich companies, often characterized by foreign ownership, have a more encompassing approach to HRM, which includes formal education as a selection mechanism selecting the educational elite and continuing to develop them through extensive training programs. To cope with the problem of high turnover rates it is suggested that procedural justice as well as measures for increasing commitment within the organization may be helpful.[127] To sum up, employee needs must be met by respective HRM practices and the creation of a satisfying work environment.

Summarizing emerging issues

From this brief analysis of the situation in offshore countries, important issues emerge with respect to the role of HRM as well as skill shortages and the resulting issues. A consequence of this is the emergence of nearshoring to enhance the benefits of this form of outsourcing. In the EU, for example, continental European countries have assessed the complexities of offshoring and have developed offshoring facilities in central and Eastern Europe. The advantages of this form of outsourcing include language, time zones, and skill base – what might be described as a close cultural fit. Table 9.4 identifies the most suitable sites to which German organizations can relocate.

TABLE 9.4 Offshoring attractiveness ranking: a German perspective

Ranking of potential offshore locations from the perspective of a German company
Preference weights: cost 35%, business environment 35%, risk profile 20%, quality of infrastructure 10%

Country	Score	Rank
Czech Republic	2.3	1
Hungary	2.3	2
Poland	2.5	3
India	2.5	4
Germany	2.6	5
Malaysia	2.6	6
China	2.8	7
Ireland	2.8	8
Russia	2.8	9

Source: EIU, 2006.

Two examples which illustrate the emergence of these locations for MNEs are Hewlett-Packard (HP) and Oracle, who have developed BPOs in Poland and Romania respectively, and DHL, which has set up its European support service center in the Czech Republic. The maturing of the offshoring process reflects the increasing understanding of the complex and diverse decision-making and requirements businesses must assess before undertaking offshoring. Interestingly, whilst offshoring is often seen as a cost-cutting process, countries like Canada are increasingly identified as destinations of choice for organizations who seek high-skilled employees and stable economic and political systems, as well as a strong governance and legal system. This high end of the market appeals to EU countries, who (as noted) can only offshore to countries with at least the same standard of protection as the EU.

A possible role for HRM.   As we have seen from the discussion above, offshoring activities can fail. Common reasons for this include the unsatisfactory quality of products or services, problems of management control, the rapid turnover of local staff, and language problems. A Chartered Institute of Personnel and Development (CIPD) survey on offshoring and the role of HR conducted in more than 600 British companies revealed that the involvement of the HR department in offshoring decisions and processes was limited. Based on the survey results, CIPD identified the following roles for HRM:[128]

- consultation with unions/employee representatives

- manpower planning, considering the scope for employee redeployment[129]

- contributing to the internal communication strategy

- identifying training needs

- designing new jobs which stem from offshoring operations

- highlighting potential risks, such as the implications of employment regulation both in the home country and in foreign locations.

This discussion clearly shows that there are still starting points for strengthening the local HRM systems in Indian and Chinese firms. This measure would be further supported if HRM played a more important role in offshoring decisions and processes.

Skill shortages and the resulting consequences in a broader regional context.   Skill shortages represent a major problem in the offshoring countries of India and China. According to a widely publicized PricewaterhouseCoopers survey,[130] 41 per cent of 153 respondents from all over the world have reported problems in recruiting technical talent in emerging countries. Even more companies (47 per cent) find it difficult to retain well-qualified staff. However, this is not a phenomenon that only exists in these countries. For a long time, skill shortage has also been the focus of discussion in the context of developed Western countries – examples include Ireland[131] and Canada.[132]

Coping with skill shortages: the role of returning host-country nationals.   Another important issue that might be addressed when discussing skill shortages in emerging countries points to a group of people who originate from these countries, have studied abroad, and return back to their home countries. These individuals have been described as 'ex-host-country nationals' (EHCNs) by Tung and Lazarova[133] in an empirical study of EHCNs in Central and Eastern Europe. They state that, especially in these transitional economies "where there is a significant shortage of local talent [. . .] EHCNs appear to be a good source of supply for much needed competencies and skills to enable these countries to survive and thrive in the global economy".[134] This is confirmed by Saxenian: she states that, "if those highly skilled employees decide to return home, they are accelerating the technological developments in their home countries".[135] In her research, she discusses the cases of China and India. In an empirical investigation of Chinese university students in Canada, Tung found that the majority was receptive to the idea of returning to China.[136] However, in their study of Eastern European EHCNs, Tung and Lazarova report readaptation problems when EHCNs return to their home countries. This indicates that there is a risk as to whether the EHCNs will stay in their countries of origin and whether they will be as effective and successful as they are supposed to be. If they decide not to return to their home country after their studies there is a danger of 'brain drain'.[137] This is critical in a situation of skill shortage in an emerging country.[138] The findings by Tung and Lazarova of reintegration problems for EHCNs have important implications for HRM practitioners because they indicate that EHCNs might expect to be treated in a similar way to expatriates with careful reintegration into their countries of origin. According to Tung and Lazarova, returning HCNs can be regarded as a 'brain gain' and represent a valuable measure to cope with the challenge of skill shortages in host-country locations.

SUMMARY

In this chapter we have covered a range of institutional issues that confront MNEs in the global environment in which they conduct their business. In terms of international industrial relations, the discussion surrounding the formation of regional economic zones such as the EU and the Asia-Pacific Economic Cooperation (APEC)[139] supports the conclusion that transnational collective bargaining has yet to be attained by trade unions.[140] As Enderwick[141] has noted:

> *The international operations of MNEs do create considerable impediments in effectively segmenting labor groups by national boundaries and stratifying groups within and between nations. Combining recognition of the overt segmentation effects of international business with an understanding of the dynamics of direct investment yields the conclusion that general multinational collective bargaining is likely to remain a remote possibility.*

Enderwick argues that trade unions should opt for less ambitious strategies in dealing with multinationals, such as: (1) strengthening national union involvement in plant-based and company-based bargaining; (2) supporting research on the vulnerability of selective multinationals; and (3) consolidating the activities of company-based ITSs. Despite setbacks, especially with the regional economic integration issues discussed in this chapter, it is likely that trade unions and the ILO will pursue these strategies and continue to lobby where possible for the regulation of multinationals via the European Commission and the United Nations.

It is also likely that opponents of globalization will continue to attempt to influence public opinion in the developed economies, with campaigns against selected MNEs with industrial relations policies and practices being a particular target. The campaign against Wal-Mart, utilizing the documentary film *Wal-Mart: The High Cost of Low Price*, is an example of such a campaign. One of the key points made in the film is that Wal-Mart employees have either poor medical coverage or none at all. However, as the business magazine *Fortune*[142] notes:

> *in a globalized economy, American companies can't continue paying the world's highest health-care costs. Don't blame Wal-Mart; blame America's inability to devise a national health care plan that takes the burden off employers.*

With globalization, what was once a domestic issue has now become in part an international issue and in turn raises public policy questions as to what healthcare costs US firms can be expected to fund in a globalized economy.[143] With continuing change impacting on MNEs due to globalization and the pressure to reduce costs by offshoring, the risks to corporate reputation inherent in failure to comply with internal and external codes of conduct are unlikely to diminish and these factors will be ongoing issues in the foreseeable future.

DISCUSSION QUESTIONS

1 Why is it important to understand the historical origins of national industrial relations systems?

2 In what ways can trade unions constrain the strategic choices of multinationals?

3 Identify four characteristics of MNEs that give trade unions cause for concern.

4 How have trade unions responded to MNEs? Have these responses been successful?

5 What evidence is there to show that corporate codes of conduct are effective?

FURTHER READING

G. Bamber, R. Lansbury and N. Wailes (eds.) *International and Comparative Employment Relations*, 5th ed. (London: Sage, 2011).

D. Collings 'Multinational corporations and industrial relations: A road less travelled', *International Journal of Management Reviews*, Vol. 10, No.2 (2008), pp. 173–193.

R. Lambell, G. Ramia, C. Nyland and M. Michelotti 'NGOs and international business research: Progress, prospects and problems', *International Journal of Management Reviews*, 10(1) (2008), pp. 75–92.

G. Tsogas *Labor Regulations in a Global Economy* (Abingdon, UK: Routledge Publishing, 2015).

G. Wood, C. Brewster and M. Brookes (eds.) *Human Resource Management and the Institutional Perspective* (Abingdon: Routledge Publishing, 2014).

Y. Zhu, M. Warner and T. Feng 'Employment relations with "Chinese characteristics": The role of trade unions in China', *International Labour Review*, 150 (1–2) (2011), pp. 127–143.

NOTES AND REFERENCES

1. See www.ioe-emp.org/en/policy-areas/international-industrial-relations/index.html for the International Organisation of Employers and www.ilo.org/ for the International Labour Organization.

2. These introductory comments are drawn from J. Schregle 'Comparative Industrial Relations: Pitfalls and Potential', *International Labour Review*, Vol. 120, No. 1 (1981), pp. 15–30. For a sense of the complexity and fluidity of comparative industrial relations efforts, see B. Kaufman 'The Theoretical Foundations of Industrial Relations and Its Implications for Labor Economics and Human Resource Management', *Industrial and Labor Relations*, Vol. 64, No. 6 (2010), pp. 74–108; for an interesting analysis of 'shades of unionization' see M. Mironi 'Reframing the Representation Debate: Going Beyond Union and Non-Union Options', *Industrial and Labor Relations*, Vol. 63, No. 3 (2009), pp. 367–83.

3. This point is also referred to as the 'emic-etic problem'. See Chapter 1 for a detailed discussion of this point.

4. O. Kahn-Freund *Labour Relations: Heritage and Adjustment* (Oxford: Oxford University Press, 1979). Also see R.B. Peterson and J. Sargent 'Union and Employer Confederation Views on Current Labour Relations in 21 Industrialized Nations', *Relations Industrielles*, Vol. 52, No. I (1997), pp. 39–59. Interestingly, these national patterns – specifically in the area of pay dispersion and a premium paid for union status – continue in even what many consider the 'flattened' high technology call center industry; see R. Blatt and H. Nohara 'How Institutions and Business Strategies Affect Wages: A Cross-National Study of Call Centers', *Industrial and Labor Relations Review*, Vol. 62, No. 4 (2009), pp. 533–552.

5. J. Schregle 'Comparative Industrial Relations', p. 28.

6. M. Poole *Industrial Relations: Origins and Patterns of National Diversity* (London: Routledge, 1986).

7. C. Prahalad and Y. Doz *The Multinational Mission: Balancing Local Demands and Global Vision* (New York: The Free Press, 1987).

8. T. Edwards, T. Collings and A. Ferner 'Conceptual Approaches to the Transfer of Employee Relations Practices in Multinational Companies: An Integrated Approach', *Human Resource Management Journal*, Vol. 17, No. 3 (2007), pp. 201–217.

9. M. Zou and R. Lansbury 'Multinational Corporations and Employment Relations in the People's Republic of China: The Case of the Hyundai Motor Company', *The International Journal of Human Resource Management*, Vol. 20, No. 11 (2009), pp. 2349–2369.

10. See B. Black 'Comparative Industrial Relations Theory: The Role of National Culture', *The International Journal of Human Resource Management*, Vol. 16, No.7 (2007), pp.1137–1158.

11. L. Hunter and H. Katz 'The Impact of Globalization on Human Resource Management', *International Journal of Human Resource Management*, Vol. 23, No. 10 (2012), pp. 983–1998.

12. H. Tuselmann, M. Allen, S. Barrett and F. MacDonald 'Varieties and Variables in Employee Relations Approaches in US Subsidiaries', *International Journal of Human Resource Management*, Vol. 19, No. 9 (2008), pp. 1622–1635.

13. Adapted from M. Zou and R. Lansbury, 'Multinational corporations and employment relations in the People's Republic of China: The case of Beijing Hyundai Motor Company,' *International Journal of Human Resource Management*, Vol. 20, No. 11 (2009), pp. 2349–2369.

14. For general reviews of the comparative industrial relations literature see P. Blyton, N. Bacon, J. Fiorito and E. Heery (eds.) *The SAGE Handbook of Industrial Relations* (London: SAGE, 2008); R. Bean *Comparative Industrial Relations: An Introduction to Cross-National Perspectives*, rev. ed. (London: Routledge, 1994); Poole *Industrial Relations*; G. Bamber, R. Lansbury and N. Wailes (eds.) *International and Comparative Employment Relations*, 5th ed. (London: Sage, 2011).

15. P. Marginson, P. Armstrong, P. Edwards and J. Purcell 'Extending Beyond Borders: Multinational Companies and the International Management of Labour', *International Journal of Human Resource Management*, Vol. 6, No. 3 (1995), pp. 702–719; also see M. Martinez Lucio and S. Weston 'New Management Practices in a Multinational Corporation: The Restructuring of Worker Representation and Rights', *Industrial Relations Journal*, Vol. 25 (1994), pp. 110–121.

16. See the following publications by Gunnigle and his colleagues: P. Gunnigle, D. Collings and M. Morley 'Accommodating Global Capitalism: Industrial Relations in American MNCs in Ireland', in A. Ferner, J. Quintanilla and C. Sanchez-Runde (eds.) *Multinationals and the Construction of Transnational Practices: Convergence and Diversity in the Global Economy* (London: Palgrave Macmillan, 2006); P. Gunnigle, D. Collings and

M. Morley 'Exploring the Dynamics of Industrial Relations in US Multinational: Evidence from the Republic of Ireland', *Industrial Relations Journal*, Vol. 36, No. 3 (2005), pp. 241–256; P. Almond, T. Edwards, T. Colling, A. Ferner, P. Gunnigle, M. Muller-Camen, J. Quintanilla and H. Waechter 'Unraveling Home and Host Country Effects: An Investigation of the HR Policies of an American Multinational in Four European Countries', *Industrial Relations*, Vol. 44, No. 2 (2005), pp. 276–306; I. Clark, R. Almond, P. Gunnigle and H. Waechter 'The Americanisation of the European business system?', *Industrial Relations Journal*, Vol. 36, No. 6 (2005), pp. 494–517.

17. J. Hamill 'Labour Relations Decision-making within Multinational Corporations', *Industrial Relations Journal*, Vol. 15, No. 2 (1984), pp. 30–34.

18. S. Robock and K. Simmonds *International Business and Multinational Enterprises*, 4th ed. (Homewood, IL: Irwin, 1989); Marginson, Armstrong, Edwards and Purcell 'Extending Beyond Borders'.

19. D. Hefler 'Global Sourcing: Offshore Investment Strategy for the 1980s', *Journal of Business Strategy*, Vol. 2, No. 1 (1981), pp. 7–12; D. Grimshaw, J. Rubery and P. Almond 'Multinational companies and the host country environment', in A.W. Harzing and A. Pinnington (eds.) *International Human Resource Management*, 3rd ed. (London: SAGE, 2011), pp. 227–266.

20. K. Starkey and A. McKinlay *Strategy and the Human Resource: Ford and the Search for Competitive Advantage* (Oxford: Blackwell, 1993).

21. B. Roberts and J. May 'The Response of Multinational Enterprises to International Trade Union Pressures', *British Journal of Industrial Relations*, Vol. 12 (1974), pp. 403–416.

22. See J. La Palombara and S. Blank *Multinational Corporations and National Elites: A Study of Tensions* (New York: The Conference Board, 1976); A. Sim 'Decentralized Management of Subsidiaries and Their Performance: A Comparative Study of American, British and Japanese Subsidiaries in Malaysia', *Management International Review*, Vol. 17, No. 2 (1977), pp. 45–51; and Y. Shetty 'Managing the Multinational Corporation: European and American Styles', *Management International Review*, Vol. 19, No. 3 (1979), pp. 39–48.

23. Bean, *Comparative Industrial Relations*.

24. Hamill, 'Labour Relations Decision-making'.

25. See P Marginson 'European Integration and Transnational Management-Union Relations in the Enterprise', *British Journal of Industrial Relations*, Vol. 30, No. 4 (1992), pp. 529–545.

26. Martinez Lucio and Weston 'New Management Practices in a Multinational Corporation'.

27. See Bean *Comparative Industrial Relations*; H. Katz and A. Colvin 'Employment Relations in the United States', in G. Bamber, R. Lansbury and N. Wailes (eds.) *International and Comparative Employment Relations*, 5th ed. (London: SAGE, 2011), pp. 62–87; and L. Alonso and M. Martinez Lucio (eds.) *Employment Relations in a Changing Society* (London: Palgrave, 2006).

28. Hamill 'Labour Relations Decision-making'.

29. P. Enderwick 'The Labour Utilization Practices of Multinationals and Obstacles to Multinational Collective Bargaining', *Journal of Industrial Relations*, Vol. 26, No. 3 (1984), pp. 354-364.

30. P.M. Rosenzweig and N. Nohria 'Influences on Human Resource Management Practices in Multinational Corporations', *Journal of International Business Studies*, Vol. 25, No. 2 (1994), pp. 229-251.

31. Hamill 'Labour Relations Decision-making'.

32. Also see Bean *Comparative Industrial Relations*.

33. P. Marginson and K. Sisson 'The Structure of Transnational Capital in Europe: The Emerging Euro-Company and its Implications for Industrial Relations', in R. Hyman and A. Ferner (eds.) *New Frontiers in European Industrial Relations* (Oxford: Blackwell, 1994); K. Williams and M. Geppert 'The German Model of Employee Relations on Trial: Negotiated and Unilaterally Imposed Change in Multi-national Companies', *Industrial Relations Journal*, Vol. 37, No. 1 (2006), pp. 48–63.

34. For an interesting discussion of the importance of understanding ideology see G.C. Lodge 'Ideological Implications of Changes in Human Resource Management', in D. Walton and P.R. Lawrence *HRM Trends and Challenges* (Boston, MA: Harvard Business School Press, 1985). Also see G. Bamber *et al. International and Comparative Employment Relations*, Chapter 1.

35. See Katz and Colvin 'Employment Relations in the United States'; also T. Kochan, R. McKersie and P. Cappelli 'Strategic Choice and Industrial Relations Theory', *Industrial Relations*, Vol. 23, No. 1 (1984), pp. 16-39.

36. D. Bok 'Reflections on the distinctive character of American labor laws', *Harvard Law Review*, Vol. 84 (1971) pp. 1394-1463.

37. See V. Frazee 'Trade Union Membership is Declining Globally', *Workforce*, Vol. 3, No. 2 (1998), p. 8; *World Labour Report 1997-98: Industrial Relations, Democracy and Social Stability* (Geneva: ILO, 1997); W Groot and A. van den Berg 'Why Union Density has Declined', *European Journal of Political Economy*, Vol. 10, No. 4 (1994), pp. 749–763. For an interesting micro view of factors associated with employee commitment to union membership in Poland see P. Zientara and G. Kuczynski 'Employees' Desire to Join or Leave a Union: Evidence From Poland', *Industrial Relations*, Vol. 48, No. 1 (2009), pp. 185–192.

38. See Bean *Comparative Industrial Relations*; Poole, *Industrial Relations*; and J. Visser 'Trade Unionism in Western Europe: Present Situation and Prospects', *Labour and Society*, Vol. 13, No. 2 (1988), pp. 125–182.

39. J. Hamill 'Multinational Corporations and Industrial Relations in the UK', *Employee Relations*, Vol. 6, No. 5 (1984), pp. 12–16.

40. Hamill 'Labour Relations Decision-making', p. 34.

41. This section is based in part on Chapter 5, 'The Impact of Organized Labour', in Prahalad and Doz *The Multinational Mission*.

42. J. Kelly and P. Wilman *Union Organization and Activity* (London: Routledge, 2004).

43. Prahalad and Doz, *The Multinational Mission*.

44. Ibid., p. 102.

45. M. Allen 'Worldly Wisdom', *New Statesman and Society*, Vol. 6 (1993), pp. xii.

46. Kennedy *European Labour Relations*.

47. Bean *Comparative Industrial Relations*, p. 191.

48. Ibid.

49. Marginson, Armstrong, Edwards and Purcell 'Extending Beyond Borders'.

50. B. Mahnkopf and E. Altvater 'Transmission Belts of Transnational Competition? Trade Unions and Collective Bargaining in the Context of European Integration', *European Journal of Industrial Relations*, Vol. 1, No. 1 (1995), pp. 101–117.

51. R. Vernon *Storm over the Multinationals: The Real Issues* (Cambridge, MA: Harvard University Press, 1977).

52. P. Auer, G. Besse and D. Meda (eds.) *Offshoring and the Internationalization of Employment: A Challenge for a Fair Globalization?* (Geneva: International Labour Organization, 2006).

53. W. Cooke 'Exercising Power in a Prisoner's Dilemma: Transnational Collective Bargaining in an Era of Corporate Globalization?', *Industrial Relations Journal*, Vol. 36, No. 4 (2005), pp. 283–302.

54. J. Pyndt and T. Pedersen *Managing Global Offshoring Strategies* (Copenhagen: Copenhagen Business School Press, 2006).

55. M. Martinez Lucio and S. Weston 'Trade Unions and Networking in the Context of Change: Evaluating the Outcomes of Decentralization in Industrial Relations', *Economic and Industrial Democracy*, Vol. 16 (1995), p. 244.

56. J. Kelly 'The Future of Trade Unionism: Injustice, Identity and Attribution', *Employee Relations*, Vol. 19, No. 4 (1997), pp. 400–414.

57. For a detailed analysis of ITSs see R. Neuhaus *International Trade Secretariats: Objectives, Organization, Activities*, 2nd ed. (Bonn: Friedrich-EbertStiftung, 1982). For an overview of international labour politics and organizations see T. Boswell and D. Stevis 'Globalisation and International Labour Organizing: A World-System Perspective', *Work and Occupations*, Vol. 24, No. 3 (1997), pp. 288–308.

58. N. Willatt *Multinational Unions* (London: Financial Times, 1974). Also see K. Fatehi *Managing Internationally* (Thousand Oaks, Cal.: SAGE, 2008), Chapter 12, particularly pp. 622–623.

59. H. Northrup 'Why Multinational Bargaining Neither Exists Nor Is Desirable', *Labour Law Journal*, Vol. 29, No. 6 (1978), pp. 330–342. Also see J. Gallagher 'Solidarity Forever', *New Statesman & Society* (1997), p. 10.

60. See Kennedy *European Labour Relations*; and R. Helfgott 'American Unions and Multinational Enterprises: A Case of Misplaced Emphasis', *Columbia Journal of World Business*, Vol. 18, No. 2 (1983), pp. 81–86.

61. Up until 1993 there was a specialized UN agency known as the United Nations Centre on Transnational Corporations (UNCTC), which had published a number of reports on MNEs (see, for example, *Transborder Data Flows: Transnational Corporations and Remote-sensing Data* (New York: UNCTC, 1984); and *Transnational Corporations and International Trade: Selected Issues* (New York: UNCTC, 1985). Since 1993, the responsibilities of the UNCTC have been assigned to UNCTAD. For further information see the UNCTAD website at www.unctad.org/

Templates/StartPage.asp?intItemID=2068. See Boswell and Stevis 'Globalisation and International Labour Organizing' for more information on these international organizations.

62. See www.ilo.org/global/lang--en/index.htm as well as B.Leonard 'An Interview with Anthony Freeman of the ILO', *HRMagazine*, Vol. 42, No. 8 (August 1997), pp. 104–109. Also see R.N. Block, K. Roberts, C. Ozeki and M.J. Roomkin 'Models of International Labour Standards', *Industrial Relations*, Vol. 40, No. 2 (April 2001), pp. 258–286; and A.W. Harzing and A. Pinnington (eds.) *International Human Resource Management*, 3rd ed. (London: Sage, 2011), pp. 594–596.

63. For a detailed description and analysis of the OECD Guidelines for Multinational Enterprises see D. Campbell and R. Rowan *Multinational Enterprises and the OECD Industrial Relations Guidelines*, Industrial Research Unit (Philadelphia, PA: The Wharton School, University of Pennsylvania, 1983); and R. Blanpain *The OECD Guidelines for Multinational Enterprises and Labour Relations, 1982–1984: Experiences and Review* (Deventer, The Netherlands: Kluwer, 1985). See www.oecd.org/department/0,3355, en_2649_34889_1_1_1_1_1,00.html for the latest version of the Guidelines for MNEs.

64. Campbell and Rowan *Multinational Enterprises and OECD.* For another example of an international chapeau clause related to the World Trade Organization see www. wto.org/english/tratop_e/envir_e/envt_rules_exceptions_e.htm. See also J. Murray 'A New Phase in the Regulation of Multinational Enterprises: The Role of the OECD', *Industrial Law Journal*, Vol. 30, No. 3 (2001), pp. 255–270.

65. J. Rojot 'The 1984 Revision of the OECD Guidelines for Multinational Enterprises', *British Journal of Industrial Relations*, Vol. 23, No. 3 (1985), pp. 379–397.

66. For a detailed account of this case see R. Blanpain *The Badger Case and the OECD Guidelines for Multinational Enterprises* (Deventer, The Netherlands: Kluwer, 1977).

67. R. Blanpain *The OECD Guidelines for Multinational Enterprises and Labour Relations, 1976-1979: Experience and Review* (Deventer, The Netherlands: Kluwer, 1979).

68. H.C. Jain 'Disinvestment and the Multinational Employer: A Case History from Belgium', *Personnel Journal*, Vol. 59, No. 3 (1980), pp. 201–205.

69. Campbell and Rowan *Multinational Enterprises and OECD.*

70. B. Liebhaberg *Industrial Relations and Multinational Corporations in Europe* (London: Cower, 1980), p. 85.

71. New OECD Guidelines to Multinational Enterprises (May 2011) see www.oecd.org/document/19/0,3746, en_21571361_44315115_48029523_1_1_1_1,00.html.

72. C. Jensen, J. Madsen and J. Due 'A Role for a Pan-European Trade Union Movement? Possibilities in European IR-regulation', *Industrial Relations Journal*, Vol. 26, No. 1 (1995), pp. 4-18; Mahnkopf and Altvater 'Transmission Belts of Transnational Competition?'.

73. Holland, P. and Pyman, A. 'Trade Unions and Corporate Campaigning in a Global Economy: The Case of James Hardie', *Economic and Industrial Democracy*, Vol. 33, No.4 (2012), pp. 555–579.

74. Willis, J. 'Bargaining for the Space to Organize in the Global Economy: A Review of the Accor – IUF Trade Union Rights Agreement', *Review of Political Economy*, Vol. 9, No. 4 (2002), pp. 675–700.

75. See, for example, P. Teague 'EC Social Policy and European Human Resource Management', in C. Brewster and A. Hegewisch (eds.) *Policy and Practice in European Human Resource Management* (London: Routledge, 1994); and L. Ulman, B. Eichengreen and WT Dickens (eds.) *Labour and an Integrated Europe* (Washington, DC: The Brookings Institution, 1993) for an early analysis of integration issues and labor practices. For current information on EU Employment and Social policies see europa.eu/pol/socio/index_en.htm.

76. Commission of the European Communities *Community Charter of the Fundamental Social Rights of Workers* (Luxembourg: Office for Official Publications of the European Communities, 1990).

77. For early examples of these concerns see J. Lodge 'Social Europe: Fostering a People's Europe?', in J. Lodge (ed.) *European Community and the Challenge of the Future* (London: Pinter, 1989); J. Addison and S. Siebert 'The Social Charter of the European Community: Evolution and Controversies', *Industrial and Labour Relations Review*, Vol. 44, No. 4 (1991), pp. 597–625; and M. Hall 'Industrial Relations and the Social Dimension of European Integration: Before and After Maastricht', in R. Hyman and A. Ferner (eds.) *New Frontiers in European Industrial Relations* (Oxford: Blackwell, 1994).

78. For information on the Treaty of Lisbon see europa.eu/ abc/treaties/index_en.htm. To access a copy of the Charter of Fundamental Rights see europa.eu/lisbon_treaty/glance/rights_values/index_en.htm. For matters related to the European Parliament see www.europarl. europa.eu/en/headlines/.

79. See ec.europa.eu/social/home.jsp?langId=en.

80. See www.fedee.com.

81. D. Leahy and C. Montagna 'Temporary Social Dumping, Unions Legislation and FDI: A Note on the Strategic Use of Standards', *The Journal of International Trade & Economic Development: An International Comparative Review*, Vol. 9, No. 3 (2000), pp. 243–259.

82. See M. Morley, N. Heraty and S. Michailova (eds.) *Managing Human Resources in Central and Eastern Europe* (Abingdon, UK: Routledge, 2009); M. Ingham, H. Ingham, H. Bicak and M. Altinay 'The Impact of (More) Enlargement on the European Employment Strategy', *Industrial Relations Journal*, Vol. 36, No. 6 (2005), pp. 456-477; P. Marginson and G. Meardi 'European Union Enlargement and the Foreign Direct Investment Channel of Industrial Relations Transfer', *Industrial Relations Journal*, Vol. 37, No. 2 (2006), pp. 92–110.

83. T. Hildy, J. Doh and S. Vachani 'The Importance of Nongovernmental Organization (NGOS) in Global Governance and Value Creation: An International Business Research Agenda', *Journal of International Business Studies*, Vol. 35, No. 6 (2004), pp. 463–483.

84. J. Sajhau *Business Ethics in the Textile, Clothing and Footwear (TCF) Industries: Codes of Conduct*, Working Paper (Geneva: International Labour Office, Sectoral Activities Programme, 1997). For a broader and more

conceptual treatment of codes of conduct see D. Ardagh 'The Ethical Basis for HRM Professionalism and Codes of Conduct', in A. Pinnington, R. Macklin and T. Campbell (eds.) *Human Resource Management: Ethics and Employment* (Oxford: Oxford University Press, 2007) pp. 152–170.

85. For standards for codes of conduct refer also to L. Paine, R. Deshpande, J. Margolis and K. Bettcher 'Up to Code: Does Your Company's Conduct Meet World-class Standards?', *Harvard Business Review*, Vol. 83, No. 12 (2005), pp. 122–133. See also www.bsigroup.co.in/en-in/Assessment-and-certification-services/Management-systems/Standards-and-schemes/SA-8000/.

86. M. Fenwick 'Extending Strategic International Human Resource Management Research and Pedagogy to the Non-Profit Multinational', *International Journal of Human Resource Management*, Vol. 16, No. 4 (2005), pp. 497–512. Also see M. Fenwick and M.A. McLean 'IHRM in Non-Governmental Organizations: Challenges and Issues', in P. Sparrow (ed.) *Handbook of International Human Resource Management* (Chichester, UK: John Wiley and Co., 2009), pp. 391–412.

87. M. Fenwick 'Extending Strategic International Human Resource Management Research and Pedagogy to the Non-Profit Multinational', p. 508.

88. See P. Holland, C. Sheehan, R. Donohue, A. Pyman and B. Allen *Contemporary Issues and Challenges in HRM* (Melbourne: Tilde University Press, 2015).

89. UNCTAD (ed.) *World Investment Report 2010* (New York and Geneva: United Nations, 2010).

90. For a general discussion on entry mode choice including offshoring refer to WTO (ed.) *World Trade Report 2005*, III - Thematic Essays, C - Offshoring Services: Recent Developments and Prospects (Geneva: World Trade Organization, 2005). For a more systematic, if academic, review of offshoring and wages see H. Brucker 'Offshoring and Labor Demand: Questions, Research Strategies and Data Sources', WTO/ILO Workshop on Global Trade and Employment (31 August 2009), www.wto.org/english/res_e/reser_e/wkshop_aug09_e/brucker_e.pdf.

91. UNCTAD *World Investment Report 2010*. See as well S. Schmid and M. Daub *Service Offshoring Subsidiaries – Towards a Typology*, Working Paper No. 12 (Berlin: ESCP-EAP European School of Management, 2005).

92. See D. Farrell, M. Laboissiere, R. Pascal, J. Rosenfeld, C. de Sagundo, S. Sturze and F. Umezawa *The Emerging Global Labor Market* (McKinsey Global Institute, McKinsey and Company, June 2005).

93. As in K. Shiu 'Outsourcing: Are You Sure of Offshore? Identifying Risk in Offshoring', *Society for Computers and the Law*, Issue 56 (June 2004).

94. UNCTAD *Service Offshoring Takes Off in Europe*.

95. UNCTAD (ed.) *Offshoring – At the Tipping Point?* (Geneva and New York: UNCTAD, 2004). Also see UNCTAD (ed.) 'Information Economy Report 2009: *Trends and Outlooks in Turbulent Times*' (Geneva and New York: UNCTAD, 2009) for a presentation of the growth of broad banding and IT enabled outsourcing.

96. For different types of outsourcing in India see S. Bhowmik 'Work in a Globalizing Economy: Reflections on Outsourcing

in India', *Labour, Capital and Society*, Vol. 37, No. 1 (2004), pp. 76–96.

97. I. Hunter *The Indian Offshore Advantage: How Offshoring is Changing the Face of HR* (Aldershot: Gower Publishing, 2006).

98. See P. Budhwar and A. Varma (eds.) *Doing Business in India: Building Research-Based Practice* (London: Routledge, 2011); D. Saini and P. Budhwar 'HRM in India' in P. Budhwar (ed.) *Managing Human Resources in Asia-Pacific* (London: Routledge, 2004) pp. 113–140.

99. *Financial Times* (London, England, 20 July 2006).

100. With these examples, the importance of the global codes of conduct mentioned earlier in this chapter is supported.

101. P. Budhwar, H. Luthar and J. Bhatnagar 'The Dynamics of HRM Systems in Indian BPO Firms', *Journal of Labor Research*, Vol. 27, No. 3 (2006), pp. 339–360.

102. A. Mehta, A. Armenakis, N. Mehta and F. Irani 'Challenges and Opportunities of Business Process Outsourcing in India', *Journal of Labor Research*, Vol. 27, No. 3 (2006), pp. 323–338.

103. P. Sparrow and P. Budhwar 'Competition and Change: Mapping the Indian HRM Recipe Against World Wide Patterns', *Journal of World Business*, Vol. 32 (1997), pp. 224–242. See also Saini and Budhwar 'HRM in India'.

104. Budhwar, Luthar and Bhatnagar 'The Dynamics of HRM Systems in Indian BPO Firms', p. 345.

105. For further information about the Indian HRM systems refer to Saini and Budhwar 'HRM in India'.

106. I. Björkman 'Transfer of HRM to MNC Affiliates in Asia-Pacific', in P. Budhwar (ed.) *Managing Human Resources in Asia-Pacific* (London: Routledge, 2004), pp. 253–267. For a recent review of Indian performance appraisal practices and management values see T. Sharma, P. Budhwar and A. Varma 'Performance Management in India' in A. Varma, P. Budhwar and A. DeNisi (eds.) *Performance Management Systems, A Global Perspective* (London: Routledge, 2008), pp. 180–192; As-Saber, Dowling and Liesch 'The Role of Human Resource Management in International Joint Ventures'.

107. Budhwar, Luthar and Bhatnagar 'The Dynamics of HRM Systems in Indian BPO firms'.

108. PricewaterhouseCoopers *Technology Executive Connections: Successful Strategies for Talent Management*, p. 42.

109. 'Rising China Labor Costs Could Create New Inflation Headache for the West', *The Daily Star* (25 January 2011).

110. Budhwar, Luthar and Bhatnagar 'The Dynamics of HRM Systems in Indian BPO firms'.

111. B. Einhorn 'A Dragon in R&D: China's Labs May Soon Rival its Powerhouse Factories – and Multinationals are Flocking in for Tech Innovation', *Business Week* (26 October 2006); B. Brockie 'China Leaves the World in its Wake as it is Transformed into a Science Superpower', *The Dominion Post*, retrieved 28 February 2011, www.dompost.co.nz.

112. PricewaterhouseCoopers *Technology Executive Connections: Successful Strategies for Talent Management; Financial Times* (London, England, 20 July 2006).

113. *International Herald Tribune*, (20 April 2005).

114. B. Wilkinson, M. Eberhardt, J. McLaren and A. Millington 'Human Resource Barriers to Partnership Sourcing in

China', *International Journal of Human Resource Management*, Vol. 16, No. 10 (2005), pp. 1886–1900. For well-written and insightful more global presentations on the daunting topic of Chinese HRM from arguably the expert in the field see Malcolm Warner's lucid *Understanding Management in China: Past, Present and Future* (London: Routledge, 2014). For more insights see M. Warner and C. Rowley (eds.) *Demystifying Chinese Management: Issues and Challenges* (London: Routledge, 2014).

115. R. Tung and V. Worm 'Network Capitalism: The Role of Human Resources in Penetrating the China Market', *International Journal of Human Resource Management*, Vol. 12, No. 4 (2001), pp. 517–534.

116. P. Buckley, J. Clegg and H. Tan 'The Art of Knowledge Transfer: Secondary and Reverse Transfer in China's Telecommunications Manufacturing Industry', *Management International Review*, Vol. 43, No. 1 (2003), pp. 67–93.

117. C.J. Zhu 'Human Resource Development in China During the Transition to a New Economic System', *Asia Pacific Journal of Human Resources*, Vol. 35, No. 3 (1997), pp. 19–44. See R. Tung 'Brain Circulation, Diaspora, and International Competitiveness', *European Management Journal*, Vol. 26, No. 5 (2008), pp. 298–304; and P. Dowling and A. Engle '"Transnational Thermals": A Discussion of the Interaction of the Combined Effects of Outward FDI Via Chinese SOEs and the Chinese Diaspora to the United States and Other Advanced Economies', Conference Proceedings of the Second Annual Conference of the Chinese Economic Association-Europe (Oxford University, Oxford, UK, July 2010). The same is true in other Asian countries, as reported by N. Kathri, C.T Fern and P. Budhwar 'Explaining Employee Turnover in an Asian Context', *Human Resource Management Journal*, Vol. 11, No. 1 (2001), pp. 54–74.

118. C. Zhu CJ and P Dowling 'The impact of the economic system upon human resource management practices in China', *Human Resource Planning*, Vol. 17, No. 4 (1994), pp. 1–21; M. Warner 'Human Resource Management in China Revisited: Introduction', *International Journal of Human Resource Management*, Vol. 15, No. 4 (2004), pp. 617–634.

119. C. Zhu and P. Dowling 'Staffing Practices in Transition: Some Empirical Evidence from China', *International Journal of Human Resource Management*, Vol. 13, No. 4 (2002), pp. 569–597.

120. K. Goodall and J. Roberts 'Only Connect: Teamwork in the Multinational', *Journal of World Business*, Vol. 38, No. 2 (2003), pp. 150-164.

121. F. Cooke 'HRM in China', in P. Budhwar *Managing Human Resources in Asia-Pacific* (London: Routledge, 2004), pp. 17–34.

122. Zhu and Dowling 'Staffing practices in transition'.

123. Cooke 'HRM in China', p. 26.

124. Cooke 'HRM in China'. This is confirmed by an empirical study by Glover and Siu. These authors have discussed the need for a better quality management initiative in China. In their study they found poor standards of training, dissatisfaction with the pay level and inadequate communication structures. L. Glover and N. Siu 'The Human Resource Barriers to Managing Quality in China', *International Journal of Human Resource Management*,

Vol. 11, No. 5 (2000), pp. 867-882. For a recent review of the development, challenges and complexities of Chinese HRM from a talent management perspective see F. Cooke 'Talent Management in China', in H. Scullion and D. Collins (eds.) *Talent Management* (London: Routledge, 2011), pp. 132–154.

125. See, for example, F. Cooke 'Foreign Firms in China: Modeling HRM in a Toy Manufacturing Corporation', *Human Resource Management Journal*, Vol. 14, No. 3 (2004), pp. 31–52. Also see Ding, Goodall and Warner 'The End of the "Iron Rice-bowl"'.

126. K. Venter 'Building on Formal Education: Employers' Approaches to the Training and Development of New Recruits in the People's Republic of China', *International Journal of Training and Development*, Vol. 7, No. 3 (2003), pp. 186–202.

127. N. Khatri, C. Fern and P. Budhwar 'Explaining Employee Turnover in an Asian Context', *Human Resource Management Journal*, Vol. 11, No. 1 (2001), pp. 54-74. Empirical evidence of some flexibility in unionization approaches applied by the All China Federation of Trade Unions (ACFTU) is provided by M. Liu in 'Union Organizing in China: Still a Monolithic Labor Movement?' *Industrial and Labor Relations Review*, Vol. 64, No. 1 (2010), pp. 30–52.

128. Survey report: 'Offshoring and the Role of HR' CIPD Survey: www.cipd.co.uk, retrieved 28 February 2011.

129. Both strategic decisions taken at corporate headquarters such as plant rationalization can result in the closure of host-country operations as multinationals divest and withdraw, as well as more tactical reallocations of products, functions and processes in dynamic, globally dispersed value chains.

130. PricewaterhouseCoopers *Technology Executive Connections: Successful Strategies for Talent Management.* The survey generated responses from senior executives based in five principal regions: 30 per cent Asia, 41 per cent Europe, 23 per cent North America, 5 per cent Middle East and Africa and 1 per cent Latin America. More recently see Scullion and Collins *Global Talent Management.*

131. S. McGuiness and J. Bennett 'Examining the Link between Skill Shortages, Training Composition and Productivity Levels in the Construction Industry: Evidence from Northern Ireland', *International Journal of Human Resource Management*, Vol. 17, No. 2 (2006), pp. 265–279.

132. R. Burke and E. Ng 'The Changing Nature of Work and Organizations: Implications for Human Resource Management', *Human Resource Management Review*, Vol. 16, No. 1 (2006), pp. 86–94.

133. R. Tung and M. Lazarova 'Brain Drain versus Brain Gain: An Exploratory Study of Ex-host Country Nationals in Central and Eastern Europe', *International Journal of Human Resource Management*, Vol. 17, No. 11 (2006), pp. 1853–1872.

134. Ibid., p. 1871.

135. A. Saxenian 'From Brain Drain to Brain Circulation: Transnational Communities and Regional Upgrading in India and China', *Studies in Comparative International Development*, Vol. 40, No. 2 (2005), pp. 35–61.

136. R. Tung 'The Human Resource Challenge to Outward Foreign Direct Investment Aspirations from Emerging Economies: The Case of China', *International Journal of Human Resource Management*, Vol. 18, No. 5 (2007), pp. 868–889.

137. Y. Baruch, P. Budhwar and N. Kathri 'Brain Drain: Inclination to Stay Abroad After Studies', *Journal of World Business*, Vol. 42, No. 1 (2007), p. 99–112. For a critical view on the topic of brain drain see S. Carr, K. Inkson and K. Thorn 'From Global Careers to Talent Flow: Reinterpreting "Brain Drain"', *Journal of World Business*, Vol. 40, No. 4 (2005), pp. 386–398.

138. However, as skill shortages exist in many countries, Carr *et al.* replace the term 'brain drain' by describing talent flows across borders, and Tung and Lazarova at least see a positive notion of brain gain. Carr, Inkson and Thorn 'From Global Careers to Talent Flow'; Tung and Lazarova 'Brain Drain versus Brain Gain'.

139. M. Zanko 'Change and Diversity: HRM Issues and Trends in the Asia-Pacific Region', *Asia Pacific Journal of Human Resources*, Vol. 41, No. 1 (2003), pp. 75–87.

140. See H. Ramsey 'Solidarity At Last? International Trade Unionism Approaching The Millenium', *Economic and Industrial Democracy*, Vol. 18, No. 4 (1997), pp. 503-537; and Jensen, Madsen and Due 'A Role for a Pan-European Trade Union Movement?'.

141. Enderwick 'The Labour Utilization Practices of Multinationals', p. 357.

142. G. Colvin 'Don't Blame Wal-Mart: The Giant Retailer Isn't Evil – Just Caught Up in the Global Economy', *Fortune* (28 November 2005), p. 41.

143. See www.cfr.org/health-science-and-technology/health-care-costs-us-competitiveness/p13325 for a discussion of this issue by the (US) Council on Foreign Relations; see also J. Pfeffer 'Building sustainable organizations: The human factor', *Academy of Management Perspectives*, 24 (1) (2010), pp. 34–45.

CHAPTER 10
IHRM TRENDS AND
FUTURE CHALLENGES

Chapter Objectives

In this final chapter we identify and comment on observed trends and future directions regarding:

- international business ethics and human resource management (HRM)

- mode of operation and international human resource management (IHRM)

- ownership issues relating to IHRM requirements of organizations other than the large multinational, such as non-government organizations (NGOs)

- safety, security, and terrorism issues.

INTRODUCTION

In this book, we have explored the IHRM issues relating to managing people globally. To that end, we have focused on the implications that the process of internationalization has for the activities and policies of HRM. We now turn our attention to developments that have not previously been emphasized in the general IHRM literature and the challenges they present to IHRM: international business ethics, mode of operation, NGOs and the developing role of IHRM in contributing to safety, security, and dealing with global terrorism. In a sense, a number of these topics reflect what some Japanese multinational enterprises (MNEs) refer to as the 'general affairs' aspect of IHRM – in Japan it is common to use the term 'Human Resources and General Affairs' for the human resource (HR) function[1] because there is an expectation that the HR function will be the first line of defense in dealing with unpredictable and emergent issues from the many and varied environments and constituency groups that make up the complexity of MNEs.

In the sections that follow we return to a discussion of some issues that distinguish HRM in MNEs and revisit the framework of strategic HRM in MNEs presented in Chapter 1 – see Figure 10.1. These topics include issues associated with *external factors* and *organizational factors* that impact on the HR function and HR practices in terms of strategic HRM in the MNE.

FIGURE 10.1 A model of strategic HRM in MNEs

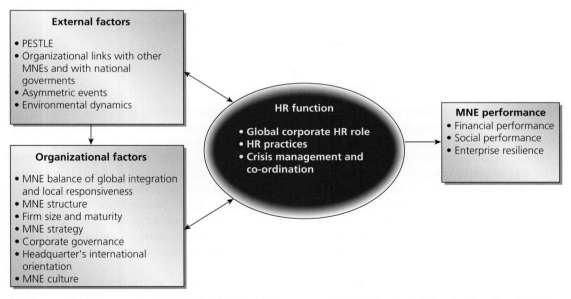

Source: H. De Cieri and P.J. Dowling 'Strategic human resource management in multinational enterprises: Developments and directions', in G. Stahl, I. Björkman and S. Morris (eds.) *Handbook of Research in International Human Resource Management*, 2nd ed. (Cheltenham, UK: Edward Elgar, 2012). Reproduced with permission from Helen De Cieri and Peter J Dowling.

External factors: International business ethics and HRM

Global business organizations face a key challenge: should they apply their own values everywhere they do business, irrespective of the cultural context and standard of local practices? To appreciate the dilemma, take the situation of a multinational that has assigned a parent-country national (PCN) to manage its operations in a host country where bribery is commonly practiced, child labor is used, and workplace safety is inadequate by Western standards. Whose standards should prevail? Should they be the standards of the MNE's parent country or the host country?

There are three main responses to this question. The first involves *ethical relativism*, the second *ethical absolutism*, and the third, *ethical universalism*. For the *ethical relativist* there are no universal or international rights and wrongs, it all depends on a particular culture's values and beliefs. For the ethical relativist, *"when in Rome, one should do as the Romans do"*. Unlike the relativist, the *ethical absolutist* believes that *"when in Rome, one should do what one would do at home, regardless of what the Romans do"*. This view of ethics gives primacy to one's own cultural values. Opponents of this view argue that ethical absolutists are intolerant individuals who confuse respect for local traditions with ethical relativism. It must be noted that, while some behaviors are wrong wherever they are practiced (e.g. bribery of government officials), other behaviors may be tolerated in their cultural context (e.g. the practice of routine gift-giving between Japanese business people). In contrast to the ethical relativist, the *ethical universalist* believes there are fundamental principles of right and wrong which transcend cultural boundaries and MNEs must adhere to these fundamental principles or global values.

The existence of universal ethical principles can also be seen in the agreements that exist among nations that are signatories to the *United Nations Declaration of Human Rights* and a number of international accords such as the *Guidelines for Multinational Enterprises* adopted by the Organization of Economic Cooperation and Development (OECD). The need for international accords and corporate codes of conduct has grown commensurately with the spread of international business and the considerable growth of offshoring (as noted in Chapter 9). However, translating ethical principles and values into practice in the international business domain is a complex and difficult task in the absence of a supranational legislative authority. Efforts to make progress in this area have centered on three factors: *regulation*, the *development of international accords*, and the *use of education and training programs*.

New global developments on the criminalization of bribery and corruption

Bribery and corruption tend to top the list of the most frequent ethical problems encountered by international managers.[2] Bribery involves the payment of agents to do things that are inconsistent with the purpose of their position or office in order to gain an unfair advantage. Bribery can be distinguished from so-called 'gifts' and 'facilitating' or 'grease' payments. The latter are payments to motivate agents to complete a task they would routinely do in the normal course of their duties. While most people do not openly condone bribery, many argue for a lenient approach based on the view that bribery is necessary to do business (the ethical relativist's argument). However, it is now generally agreed that bribery undermines equity, efficiency, and integrity in the public service; undercuts public confidence in markets and aid programs; adds to the cost of products; and may affect the safety and economic well-being of the general public.

For these reasons, there has been an international movement to criminalize the practice of bribery. In 1977 the USA enacted the Foreign Corrupt Practices Act (FCPA) to prohibit US-based firms and US nationals from making bribery payments to foreign government officials. In addition, payments to agents violate the Act if it is known that the agent will use those payments to bribe a government official. The Act was amended in 1988 to permit *facilitating* payments but mandates record-keeping provisions to help ensure that illegal payments are not disguised as entertainment or business expenses. The FCPA has in the past been criticized for placing US firms at a competitive disadvantage since European and Asian firms did not face criminal prosecution for paying bribes to foreign officials,[3] but the evidence on the competitive disadvantage of the FCPA is mixed. The FCPA has also been criticized by some for being ethnocentric, while others see this law as evidence of moral leadership on the part of the USA.[4]

In the absence of adequate international self-regulation to control bribery and corruption, the USA has lobbied other nation states over many years to enact uniform domestic government regulation to provide a level playing field. These efforts met with some success in December 1996 when the United Nations (UN) adopted the *Declaration Against Corruption and*

Bribery in International Commercial Transactions, which committed UN members to criminalize bribery and deny tax deductibility for bribes. A year later, the Declaration was endorsed by 30 OECD member nations and four non-member nations with the adoption of the *Convention on Combating Bribery of Foreign Public Officials in International Business Transactions* (*OECD Convention*). Under the OECD Convention members agreed to establish domestic legislation by the end of 1998 criminalizing the bribing of foreign public officials on an extraterritorial basis. The OECD Convention came into force in February 1999 and as of 2009 had been ratified by 38 countries. Each member state is required to undergo a peer review and to provide a report reviewing its implementation of the Convention. Country reports are available on the OECD website. The OECD Convention requires sanctions to be commensurate with domestic penalties applicable to bribery of public officials.

Given the seriousness of offences and penalties in the OECD Convention, it is imperative that enterprises involved in global business take active steps to manage their potential exposure. Also, although the OECD Convention currently addresses the supply side of corruption in the public sector, it is likely that the scope of the Convention will be expanded to include bribery in the private sector as well as the demand side of bribery. HR professionals have an important role to play in instituting a strategic plan for legal compliance and developing corporate codes for voluntary compliance. They can also provide training in understanding the difference between corrupt bribery payments, gifts and allowable facilitation payments, and the development of negotiation skills to handle problem situations that may arise in sensitive geographical regions and industries. The debate over payments to foreign officials is likely to continue for many years to come.[5]

The Berlin-based non-government lobby group Transparency International (TI) publishes an annual Corruption Perceptions Index. The index measures *perceptions*, not actual levels of corruption, for over 50 countries and is based on international surveys of business people and financial journalists. Each country is scored from 10 (highly clean) to 0 (highly corrupt). In the 2015 listing, Denmark, Finland, and Sweden (all small-population advanced economies) are the top three *least corrupt* countries. The three countries perceived to be *most corrupt* are Afghanistan, North Korea, and Somalia, which are ranked at the bottom of the list of 167 countries.[6]

The public and financial consequences of a bribery scandal can be significant for an MNE. The IHRM in Action Case 10.1 provides a sense of the actual and reputational costs of unethical conduct for a MNE. This case was first made public in late 2006 and in December 2008 US authorities fined Siemens a record US$800 million and German authorities issued a fine for 395 million euros over the failure of its former board to fulfill its supervisory duties. The total cost of this case for Siemens was 2.5 billion euros. Action was also taken against individual Siemens managers by German authorities in early 2010 when two former managers were given suspended prison sentences and large fines for their roles in this corruption scandal.[7] *The Economist* magazine entered into the debate on international bribery and corruption, noting that, "Firms are increasingly fed up with the way America's Foreign Corrupt Practices Act (FCPA) is written (confusingly) and applied (vigorously)".[8] Comparing the FCPA to the British Bribery Act passed in 2010, which covers both domestic and international bribery cases, *The Economist* stated that, although the British law makes no allowance for 'facilitation payments', it does allow a 'compliance defense' that allows a firm to avoid the harshest penalties if the wrongdoer is a junior employee and the firm otherwise has a strict anti-bribery policy that is clearly communicated to employees and effectively administered.

Ethics-related challenges for the HR function of the MNE

Managers involved in international business activities face many of the same ethical issues as those in domestic business, but the issues are made more complex because of the different social, economic, political, cultural, and legal environments in which MNEs operate. Firms which opt consciously or by default to leave ethical considerations up to individual employees not only contribute to the pressures of operating in a foreign environment (and perhaps contribute to poor performance or early recall of the expatriate), but also allow internal inconsistencies that affect total global performance.

When MNEs select international assignees, their ability to manage with integrity could be a job-relevant criterion and any pre-departure training or orientation program should include an ethics component that includes discussion of ethical dilemmas that expatriates may encounter. In designing training programs to meet the challenges of multinational business, the HR function should not only raise the issue of cultural relativities but also the extent to which moral imperatives transcend national and cultural boundaries. To avoid the temptation to cut 'ethical corners', expatriates should not be placed under unreasonable pressure to deliver good financial results and they must be given feedback and reinforcement. Performance appraisals, compensation programs, and regular trips home are important instruments in developing and maintaining ethical cultures.

The difficulties involved when massive, highly standardized firms attempt to be sensitive to local customs and values while becoming more international is personified by Wal-Mart, the giant US retailer. The highly successful low-cost strategy (with its attendant standardization plus scale and scope economies) that characterizes this would-be MNE has become a magnet for concerns, protests, and social commentary all over the world. Issues related to offshoring procurement (especially from China) are increasingly generating problems in terms of highly publicized product recalls that indicate multifaceted problems that are not limited to one functional management area such as supply chain management. For an excellent analysis of the interconnection of supply chain management issues with other functional areas of management, see Lyles *et al.*[9] The consequences of a relentless low-cost strategy on direct employee and contractor wages, healthcare benefits, working conditions and job security, and the competitive impact of Wal-Mart's 'super-stores' on traditional local retail establishments, city-center infrastructure and small-population communities have initiated a worldwide discussion of the economic, social, and political consequences of global business.[10]

Little is presently known about the evolving roles and responsibilities for HRM in balancing the economic imperatives of cost control and global standardization with the social and institutional realities of citizenship in a widening range of diverse contexts – particularly in terms of the development of labor sourcing, compensation, and employee relations strategies.[11] However, it seems clear that these are likely to remain dominant issues in international business in the twenty-first century – particularly with regard to the complex issue of evaluating the overall performance of foreign subsidiaries and their senior management teams.[12]

Organizational factors: Structure, strategy, and IHRM

We have stressed the need to broaden the scope of IHRM beyond that of subsidiary operations. While not downplaying its importance, for many MNEs, managing and staffing subsidiary units is only one aspect of international business operations, though the weighting given to subsidiary management will vary significantly according to the nature of international activities and the size of the internationalizing firm (see Chapters 1 and 3). The fact that external parties are involved in contractual modes, joint ventures, and strategic alliances imposes management and HR constraints that are not usually present in wholly owned operations. While the HR implications of international joint ventures have received considerable attention in the literature,[13] there remains a need for studies that consider the HR implications of contractual modes where the firm is operating at arm's length. Training, for instance, is often an important part of contractual modes, playing a key role in the transfer of technology and systems, inculcation of company culture, and in acting as a screening process (for example, in selecting suitable franchisees). As a result, staff may be primarily involved in short-term assignments to deliver training in foreign locations, rather than as traditional expatriates.[14] Issues related to

IHRM in Action Case 10.1

'Too little too late?' Siemens belatedly wakes up to reputation risk

Dateline: Frankfurt

It is a dense, dramatic account of police raids, arrests, and the investigation into allegations that at least 200 million euros (US $265 million) was siphoned out of secret bank accounts in Liechtenstein, Austria, and Switzerland. A page-turning airport thriller? No, the 20-F filing submitted by Siemens, a German conglomerate, to the Securities and Exchange Commission in Washington, DC on 11 December, 2006. At the same time, the firm restated its earnings to take account of uncertainties over transactions being investigated by state prosecutors in at least three countries.

The purpose of these murky dealings remains unclear: was it a case of self-enrichment by crooked employees or something more sinister – carefully laundered bribes to win Siemens business in some of the 190 countries in which it operates? Siemens insists that it was a victim of crime, not an accessory to it. It is investigating 420 million euros of suspicious payments to consultants over the past seven years. Meanwhile, six present and former employees, including one former board member arrested on 12 December, are in custody.

In the flow of adverse publicity since police raided 30 of its offices a month ago, Siemens has tried to show that it is taking appropriate action. It announced the formation of a 'task force' to clarify and standardize its employees' business practices. It also appointed an ombudsman to encourage internal whistleblowing. But for Transparency International (TI), an anti-corruption campaign group, this was not enough. It had already suspended Siemens' membership of its German chapter in 2004 because of the company's reluctance to be transparent about an unresolved bribery case in Italy. (The case was settled last month without admission of guilt.) Siemens's sluggish reaction to investigations in Liechtenstein triggered a letter last month from TI warning that the firm's membership would be liable for termination after 15 December.

At an emergency board meeting this week Siemens announced new measures to show how determined it is to change its culture. It appointed a law firm to investigate the company's compliance and control systems. And it appointed Michael Hershman, an anti-corruption expert and one of the founders of TI (a nice touch), to review anti-corruption controls and training at Siemens. Some of Siemens' problems stem from the 1990s, before Germany and other nations signed the OECD's anti-bribery convention in 1999. Yet the Italian case post-dates the convention and another case in Greece concerns preparations for the 2004 Olympics. Siemens and the Munich prosecutors point to evidence that in the latest shenanigans the suspects 'banded together' to defraud the firm. "There is only so much one can do", sighs a Siemens' spokesman, against 'criminal energy'.

But even poor supervision and control, rather than connivance with bribery, are bad enough. It cannot help appearances that Heinrich von Pierer, who was chief executive of Siemens in the 1990s before bribery was outlawed, still heads the supervisory board. He was supposed to steer the company through its transition to OECD anti-bribery rules and compliance with America's Sarbanes-Oxley Act, which requires greater disclosure and personal responsibility from executives. Worst of all for Germany's reputation as export champion of the world is the suspicion that it may owe some of its prowess to secret bank accounts and slush funds.

Source: Update based on *The Economist*, 16 December 2006, Vol. 381, Issue 8508, pp. 65–66.

the particular problems experienced with lean manufacturing operations and globally distant value chains[15] and people issues for international project management[16] are gaining interest under the heading of organizational factors.

Non-government organizations

We have already identified the importance of NGOs in Chapter 9 when discussing the importance of the institutional context in influencing the strategies and decisions of MNEs. We noted that the globalization of trade and business has provoked a vigorous debate within national states with events such as anti-globalization rallies and protests. The activities of environmental groups illustrate how these organizations have also become internationalized and interact with the key MNEs in a range of global industries. For example, a visit to the home page of Greenpeace International illustrates the range of issues and industries that this NGO is focusing on and the key MNEs in various global industries that Greenpeace is seeking to influence. Some well-known NGOs include the Wikimedia Foundation, Oxfam, and Care International. Less well-known NGOs include BRAC (formerly known as the Bangladesh Rural Advancement Committee), which is now a global organization with over 110 million beneficiaries, the Danish Refugee Council, and Mercy Corps. This diversity of activities and focus across a range of industries further illustrates the impact and influence of NGOs, which will continue to be of importance to the activities of MNEs.

External factors: Challenges in an uncertain world – safety, security and counterterrorism[17]

Traditionally, many domestic and international HR managers have been responsible for legal compliance and training issues related to safety in the workplace.[18] As national and international regulations related to workplace safety expanded, specific professional standards of practice, reporting mechanisms and roles were specified in the area of corporate risk management.[19] Risk categories associated with natural **disaster protocols**, emergency and disaster preparedness plans for MNE plant and facilities, **workplace violence** policies, **industrial theft** and sabotage protocols, and 'hardening' individual facilities to enhance **in-house security** have emerged and a growing body of professional and academic literature exists. Less clear are the particular roles, expectations, and portfolios of responsibilities that IHRM managers and directors have been called upon to incorporate into their existing responsibilities.[20] Intuitively, in smaller MNEs – operating in less sensitive industries and less turbulent markets – the IHRM generalists will be called on to incorporate these protocols by outsourcing technical security systems and personnel as required.[21] In larger organizations – particularly MNEs operating in more public and sensitive industries and/or more socially and politically turbulent regions of the world – significant investment in developing integrated, co-ordinated, and specialized **risk management** practices within the HR function is warranted. Many MNEs have developed their own idiosyncratic systems and processes in response to a history of 'critical incidents' which the firm has experienced over years or even decades – e.g. the kidnapping of an executive, a natural disaster impacting a key facility, or an airline or private aircraft disaster that decimated the executive cadre of the MNE.

Not surprisingly, executives in most MNEs are unwilling to discuss the protocols, processes, systems, and structures in place in this sensitive area. More recently emerging risk categories relate to cyber-terrorism, political terrorist groups targeting specific firms and industries and the risks inherent in pandemics such as SARS, avian flu, and airborne contaminants (as discussed in Chapter 1). Increasingly, global HR executives are held at least partially responsible for contributing to what one risk analysis consultant has called 'the business of resilience'.[22] For an overview of the area of conflict, security and political risk in international business, see the Special Issue of *Journal of International Business Studies* edited by Henisz, Mansfield and Von Glinow.[23]

As a working set of corporate risk assessment categories, a starting point for a MNE-specific audit would include the following five areas:

1 **In-facility emergency and disaster preparedness** – including being in compliance with local safety laws and standards (e.g. occupational safety and health administration rules in the USA), creating a command center and triage area, protocols for transport evacuation and the systematic location of employees, liaison with public-sector emergency workers, and media relations.

2 **In-facility security** – comprised perimeter security, search protocols into and out of facilities (truck inspections, deliveries, etc.), internal search protocols (lockers, etc.), bomb threat procedures, risk control for violence in the facility and threats to management (including training on warning signs, protection of property and equipment, and safeguarding executives), protection and lighting in parking areas, and the use of cameras in the workplace.

3 **Industrial espionage, theft, and sabotage** – activities to secure internal communications (emails, telephones, etc.), open records protection, employee privacy regulations, clearly defined physical inspections, and search processes.

4 **Cyber-terrorism** – hardware, software, and human systems to deal with hacking, information theft, internal sabotage, the sabotage of software systems and the development and maintenance of an architecture of back-up systems, and multiple independent operations for information systems.

5 **Out-of-facility fire and travel risks** – providing traveling managers with portable five-minute air packs, travel policies prohibiting employees staying in hotel rooms above the seventh floor (most aerial ladders on fire trucks only reach to the sixth floor), policies prohibiting top-level managers from traveling on the same airline flight/private aircraft, hotel evacuation training if traveling teams of employees are staying at the same hotel.[24]

According to Czinkota *et al.*, analytically, IHRM managers may be able to assess the potential risk from terrorist threats at three levels of analysis: *primary* – "at the level of the individual person and firm"; at the *micro level* – "specific regions, industries, or levels in international value chains"; and at the *macro level* – "the effect of a terrorist attack on the global environment [...] the world economy, consumer demand for goods and services, and reactions by supranational organizations such as the United Nations".[25] As an example of micro-level risk analysis, the travel/hospitality industry is particularly sensitive to terrorist events or natural disasters that may inhibit travel in general, travel to a certain region or country, or to specific travel destinations.[26] On the primary and micro levels:

> It is useful to distinguish the most vulnerable links in firm's value chains. From the individual [firm's] perspective, it is more useful to view terrorism at the micro level wherein input sourcing, manufacturing, distribution, and shipping and logistics are likely to be the most vulnerable areas.[27]

There is little doubt that global security is perceived to be a significant risk by MNEs. *The World Economic Forum Global Risks Report 2016* reports the perceived likelihood of large-scale terrorist attacks and state collapse or crisis as two likely global risks.[28] A Delphi study in 2008 by Czinkota and Ronkainen found that the five business functions within MNEs that will have the most influence on global business in the future will be: (1) logistics; (2) marketing; (3) HR; (4) finance; and (5) communications.[29] By systematically analyzing people and processes, IHRM professionals may contribute to 'stabilizing risk'[30] through recommendations that 'harden' processes in the value chain, recruit people with capabilities and skills relevant for these kinds of processes, and train employees in these processes and systems.

In a similar vein, Gillingham presents risk analysis in terms of partitioning security risk into an external environmental dimension (geographic region of operation) and an internal firm dimension (industry, firm media profile, national affiliation associated with the MNE).

Low-risk firms in low-risk environments do not need to invest as heavily in security systems and protocols. High-risk firms in low-risk environments should follow security strategies that focus on hardening individual sites. Low-risk firms in high-risk environments can follow security strategies that disperse activities across the region and build redundant infrastructure, so that value chain activities in the high-risk region can be provided by out of region units. High-risk firms in high-risk environments must invest much more in quite elaborate risk management strategies.[31] Issues related to planning, preparation, training and physical, emotional, and social support to expatriates and their families is an ongoing area of research interest.[32] Much remains to be understood in this rapidly evolving area, and the expectations, standards and practices of IHRM executives and professionals as they relate to safety and security are in flux. According to Czinkota *et al.*:

> In-depth case studies on firms directly affected by terrorism will also serve to provide grounded information as to the nature of the relationships between types of terrorism and their specific effects, and facilitate the development of models and theory.[33]

A similar conclusion can be reached in terms of the need for a better understanding of these challenges facing IHRM in MNEs.

The authors of this book have initiated a systematic review of the role of HR professionals in the complex and confidential area of global security for MNEs.[34] By developing an encompassing vocabulary of terms and outlining a standardized set of the particular dimensions that describe providing security for far-flung global value chains, people, physical assets, and information networks[35] we may better understand the issues, decisions, and roles played by international HR managers in global firms. In any event, responsibilities for people-security issues in the MNE of today and for the foreseeable future will grow in complexity and criticality.

It would appear that empirical research and modelling by IHRM and international business academics now lag behind practitioner practice and priority. This is an issue that needs to be addressed by IHRM academics in business schools.[36]

The evolving field of IHRM

The field of IHRM has been criticized as being slow to develop as a rigorous body of theory. There are a number of reasons for this. One reason is that, compared to studies in one national context, there are major methodological problems involved in the area of international management and IHRM. These problems greatly increase the complexity of doing international research and, as Adler[37] noted some years ago, it is often quite difficult to solve these problems with the rigor usually required of within-culture studies by journal editors and reviewers.

A second reason why IHRM has developed rather slowly as a field of study is that until relatively recently many management and HR researchers have regarded the IHRM field as a marginal academic area. This attitude was reflected in the relatively small number of courses on IHRM in business school curricula – a situation which is now changing, particularly in business schools in Europe and the Asia-Pacific region. A strong positive development was the establishment of a dedicated journal in the field (*International Journal of Human Resource Management*) in 1990 by the late Professor Michael Poole at Cardiff University in the UK. This journal has had a significant impact on the development of research in the field of IHRM. A more recent very positive development has been the decision of the Human Resources Division of the Academy of Management to offer an International HRM Scholarly Research Award.[38] An increasing number of books focused on HRM in particular regions such as Latin America,[39] Central and Eastern Europe,[40] the Middle East,[41] Europe,[42] Africa[43], and the Asia-Pacific region[44] have also made a valuable contribution to the IHRM literature.

The evolving role of the HRM function in MNEs

As presented in Chapter 1, the sheer complexity of the HRM function in MNEs has led to a fundamental re-examination of the purposes, actors, roles, and relationships between line managers and staff HR specialists, between subsidiary HR staff and corporate HR specialists, between MNE employees and outsourced contractors, and between the various HR actors within the MNE hierarchy (e.g. HR managers on the Board of Directors, at Vice President level or reporting directly to a board member).[45] Clearly, disentangling the complex relationships between those institutional, industrial, and historical contingencies that may contribute to the pattern of IHRM philosophies, strategies, policies, practices, and capabilities of an MNE, industry, or nation remains a rich area for future research. It does appear very likely that the challenges of international business will continue and IHRM issues will remain high on the 'problems list' of senior managers of MNEs.[46]

SUMMARY AND CONCLUDING REMARKS

Throughout this book, we have endeavored to highlight the challenges faced by firms as they confront HRM concerns related to international business operations. This chapter has been concerned with identified trends and future challenges – both managerial and academic – that are likely to have an impact on IHRM as a function and as a scientific field of study. We specifically addressed:

- international business ethics and HRM

- modes of operation other than wholly owned subsidiaries, and the IHRM activities that are required, such as training for contractual and project operations

- ownership issues relating to family-owned firms, and NGOs and the IHRM challenges specific to these organizations as they grow internationally that have remained relatively underidentified, despite their continuing importance in international business and global activities

- the complex assessment and planning activities related to safety, security, and counterterrorist efforts

- research issues in IHRM, and developments that are endeavoring to assist in understanding the intricacies and interrelationships between the IHRM function and IHRM activities, firm internationalization and strategic directions and goals.

A consistent theme throughout this book has been the way in which IHRM requires a broader perspective of what operating internationally involves, and a clear recognition of the range of issues pertaining to all categories of staff operating in different functional, task, and managerial capacities is essential. As Michael Poole[47] stated in his editorial in the first issue of the *International Journal of Human Resource Management* in 1990: "IHRM archetypically involves the worldwide management of people in the MNE".

This seventh edition marks over 25 years since the publication of the first edition of this textbook in 1990. Since such a period of time is often recognized as a milestone into adulthood in Western societies, IHRM researchers and academics should indeed celebrate the 'coming of age' of this discipline area. People issues in MNEs have never been as strategically, economically, socially, and environmentally critical as they are today.[48] Practitioners – both specialists and executives – have a vast array of technical, conceptual, and programmatic resources at their fingertips. Massive governmental and consulting systems may be tapped. Academics may pursue in their research and teaching activities any one of a number of functionalities in IHRM, across cultures, regions, institutional contexts, levels of economic development, and industries. The number of choices is indeed daunting.

Given this period of time we should both celebrate the success of the discipline area and be wary of the dangers of prematurely deciding that we have uncovered the last word on what IHRM is, or presume we have discovered the ultimate model of IHRM.[49] It may be that for now an open, systematic, comprehensive, curious, and engaged state of mind (the qualities many researchers have associated with successful international careers in industry) is more critical to the continued effective development of the discipline area of IHRM than any single model, research stream, or perspective.[50]

In Chapter 1 we stated that IHRM came out of three areas – cross-cultural management, comparative HRM and industrial relations, and HRM in multinational firms. Just as all rivers have one or more headwaters – streams or creeks that begin the river – so IHRM has a number of potential points of origin. In the nineteenth century there was a great rush to discover the source of the Nile River. What the scientists, explorers, and adventurers did at the end of their search was to come to grips with a vast, complex, and changing ecosystem. What started out as a journey to a specific, unknown destination became an increasingly sophisticated geographical odyssey that continues in Africa to this day. The ongoing process of discovery, a mapping of the *complexities* of IHRM, the *challenges* to our existing corporate and academic systems and models of people processes resulting from international activities, and the difficult *choices* practitioners must make every day in order to pursue MNE goals make up the only reasonable conclusions we can draw about this fascinating and compelling academic field after over 25 years of observation.

DISCUSSION QUESTIONS

1   What is your view of international initiatives to criminalize foreign bribery?

2   Identify a number of HRM problems that typically arise with expatriate assignments. In what ways might the core ethical values and guidelines identified in this chapter apply to them?

3   Beyond checklists and systemic analysis, what actions can MNEs take to reduce risks related to terrorism? What roles can HRM take in these processes?

4   What IHRM activities would be pertinent to the sending, by Médecins Sans Frontieres, of a medical team into a country such as Bangladesh?

FURTHER READING

R. Burke and C. Coopers (eds.) *International Terrorism and Threats to Security: Managerial and Organizational Challenges* (Cheltenham, UK: Edward Elgar Publishing, 2008).

J. Selmer and V. Suutari (guest eds.) *Cross Cultural Management: An International Journal*, Special Issue, Theme: 'Expatriation – Old Issues, New Insights', Volume 18 (2) (2011).

J. Crum *Corporate Security Intelligence and Strategic Decision Making* (Boca Raton, FLA: CRC Press, 2015).

F. Fortanier, A. Kolk and J. Pinkse 'Harmonization in CSR Reporting: MNEs and Global CSR Standards', *Management International Review*, 51 (5) (2011), pp. 665–696.

K. Lundby and J. Jolton (eds.) *Going Global: Practical Applications and Recommendations for HR and OD Professionals in*

the Global Workspace (San Francisco, USA: Jossey-Bass, 2010).

A. Moore (ed.) *Privacy, Security and Accountability: Ethics, Law and Policy* (Lanham, Maryland: Rowman and Littlefield, 2016).

S.S. Morris, P.M. Wright, J. Trevor, P. Stiles, G.K. Stahl, S. Snell, J. Paauwe and E. Farndale 'Global Challenges to Replicating HR: The Role of People, Processes, and Systems', *Human Resource Management*, 48 (6) (2009), pp. 973–995.

D. Wernick and M. Von Glinow 'Reflections on the Evolving Terrorist Threat to Luxury Hotels: A Case Study on Marriott International', *Thunderbird International Business Review*, 54 (5) (2012), pp. 729–746.

NOTES AND REFERENCES

1.   See T. Jackson *International HRM: A Cross-cultural Approach,* Chapter 5, 'The Motivating Organization: The Japanese Model' (London: Sage Publications, 2002), pp. 107–126; E. Ikegami *The Taming of the Samurai: Honorific Individualism and the Making of Modern Japan* (Cambridge, MA: Harvard University Press, 1995); and J. Abegglen and G. Stalk *Kaisha: The Japanese Corporation* (New York: Basic Books, 1985).

2.   See www.oecd.org/daf/anti-bribery/ for a comprehensive list of the most recent resources offered by the OECD on bribery in international business.

3.   L. Carson 'Bribery Extortion, and the Foreign Corrupt Practices Act', *Philosophy and Public Affairs* (1984) pp. 66–90. See also www.justice.gov/criminal-fraud/

foreign-corrupt-practices-act for up-to-date information on the FCPA as of July 2016. For a review of ethics programs as a training topic and the potential responsibilities of IHRM staff in creating and maintaining such programs see A. Vadera and R. Aguilera 'The Role of IHRM in the Formulation and Implementation of Ethics Programs in Multinational Enterprises' in P. Sparrow (ed.) *Handbook of International Human Resource Management* (Chichester, UK: John Wiley and Sons, 2009) pp. 413–438.

4.   W. Bottiglieri, M. Marder and E. Paderon 'The Foreign Corrupt Practices Act: Disclosure Requirements and Management Integrity', *SAM Advanced Journal*, (Winter 1991), pp. 21–27.

5. For an interesting empirical paper on bribery see S. H. Lee, K. Oh, and L. Eden 'Why do Firms Bribe?: Insights from Residual Control Theory into Firms' Exposure and Vulnerability to Corruption', *Management International Review*, Vol. 50, No. 6 (2010), pp. 775-796). See also 38 Suffolk Transnational Law Review 419 (2015) Beyond Good Intentions: The OECD anti-Bribery Convention's Pursuit of Prescriptive Enforcement.

6. For the most up-to-date TI Corruption Index consult the internet at www.transparency.org.

7. *The Guardian* (16 Dec 2008); *Deutsche Welle* (21 April 2010).

8. 'Bribery Abroad: A tale of two laws', *The Economist* (17 September 2011).

9. M. Lyles, B. Flynn, and M. Frohlich 'All Supply Chains Don't Flow Through: Understanding Supply Chain Issues in Product Recalls', *Management and Organization Review*, Vol. 4, No.2 (2008), pp. 167–182.

10. W. Cascio 'The High Cost of Low Wages', *Harvard Business Review*, Vol. 84, Issue 12 (2006), p. 23; W. Cascio 'Decency Means More Than "Always Low Prices": A Comparison of Costco to Wal-Mart's Sam's Club', *Academy of Management Perspectives*, Vol. 20, No. 3 (2006), pp. 26–37; R. Ghemawat 'Business, Society and the "Wal-Mart Effect"', *Academy of Management Perspectives*, Vol. 20, No. 3 (2006), pp. 41–43; A. Harrison and M. McMillan 'Dispelling Some Myths About Offshoring', *Academy of Management Perspectives*, Vol. 20, No. 4 (2006), pp. 6–22; and D. Farrell, M. Laboissiere and J. Rosenfeld 'Sizing the Emerging Global Labor Market', *Academy of Management Perspectives*, Vol. 20, No. 4 (2006), pp. 23–34. See also websites such as www.walmartmovie.com and www.wakeupwalmart.com which are highly critical of Wal-Mart, and www.walmartfacts.com where Wal-Mart responds to this criticism.

11. H. De Cieri and P.J. Dowling 'Strategic human resource management in multinational enterprises: Developments and directions', in G. Stahl, I. Björkman and S. Morris (eds.) *Handbook of Research in International HRM*, 2nd ed. (Cheltenham, UK: Edward Elgar, 2012); P. Rosenzweig 'The Dual Logics Behind International Human Resource Management: Pressures for Global Integration and Local Responsiveness', in G. Stahl and I. Björkman (eds.) *Handbook of Research in International Human Resource Management* (Cheltenham: Edward Elgar, 2006), pp. 36-48; and P. Stiles and J. Trevor 'The Human Resource Department: Roles, Coordination and Influence', in G. Stahl and I. Björkman (eds.) *Handbook of Research in International Human Resource Management* (Cheltenham: Edward Elgar, 2006), pp. 49-67.

12. S. Schmidt and K. Kretschmer 'Performance Evaluation of Foreign Subsidiaries: A Review of the Literature and a Contingency Framework', *International Journal of Management Reviews*, Vol. 12, No. 3 (2010), pp. 219-258. The issue of ethical contracting, corporate social responsibility and contingent workers at MNEs is presented by M. Zang, T. Bartram, N. McNeil and P. Dowling 'Towards a Research Agenda on the Sustainable and Socially Responsible Management of Agency Workers through a Flexicurity Model of HRM', *Journal of Business Ethics*, Vol. 127 (2015), pp. 513-523. A historical review of the developing topic of corporate social responsibility over the last 50 years is provided by Ans Kolk 'The Social Responsibility of International Business: From Ethics and the Environment to CSR and Sustainable Development', *Journal of World Business*, Vol. 51 (2016), pp. 23-34. The author concludes that three subthemes emerge in the international business literature over the last 50 years: poverty and sustainability; ethics, rights and responsibility; and the environment.

13. R. Schuler and I. Tarique 'International Joint Venture System Complexity and Human Resource Management', in G. Stahl and I. Björkman (eds.) *Handbook of Research in International Human Resource Management* (Cheltenham: Edward Elgar, 2006), pp. 385-404.

14. See R. Schuler and I. Tarique 'International Joint Venture System Complexity and Human Resource Management', in G. Stahl and I. Björkman (eds.) *Handbook of Research in International Human Resource Management* (Cheltenham, UK: Edward Elgar, 2006), pp. 385-404; and K. Lundby and J. Jolton (eds.) *Going Global: Practical Applications and Recommendations for HR and OD Professionals in the Global Workspace* (San Francisco, USA: Jossey-Bass, 2010).

15. For more on job-design effects and lean manufacturing, see S.J. Cullinane, J. Bosak, P. Flood and E. Demerouti 'Job Design Under Lean Manufacturing and the Quality of Work Life: A Job Demands and Resources Perspective', *International Journal of Human Resource Management*, Vol. 25, No. 21 (2014), pp. 2996-3015. A more HR-centered presentation by P. Sparrow and L. Otaye-Ebede 'Lean Manufacturing and HR Function Capability: The Role of HR Architecture and the Location of Intellectual Capital', *International Journal of Human Resource Management*, Vol. 25, No. 21 (2014), pp. 2892-2910 emphasizes appropriate HR skills and competencies, the specific implications for role behaviors and the essential role behaviors required for success in the lean manufacturing environment.

16. See C. Welch and D. Welch 'What Do HR Managers Really Do? HR Roles on International Projects', *Management International Review*, (2012), DOI 10.1007/s11575-011-0126-8.

17. The authors would like to acknowledge the assistance of Tom Schneid, Professor of Loss Prevention and Safety, and Larry Collins, Associate Professor of Loss Prevention and Safety and Chair of the Department of Loss Prevention and Safety in the College of Justice and Safety at Eastern Kentucky University in Richmond, Kentucky, USA in the preparation of this section of Chapter 10. Like all growing professional areas, security has its own set of jargon and acronyms, see J. Goldman's *Words of Intelligence: An Intelligence Professional's Lexicon for Domestic and Foreign Threats*, 2nd ed., (Lanham, Maryland: Scarecrow Press, 2011) for a taste of the vocabulary.

18. Although much of this material is specific to national or industry regulations, see R. Mathis and J. Jackson, *Human Resource Management*, 12th ed. (Mason, OH: South-Western/Thomson, 2008), Chapter 15 for a US perspective.

19. M. Schumann and T. Schneid *Legal Liability: A Guide for Safety and Loss Prevention Professionals* (Gaithersburg, MD: Aspen Publishers, 1997).

20. For a broad, macro perspective on global security issues, see S. Kay's thorough *Global Security in the Twenty-First Century*, 3rd ed. (Lanham, Maryland: Rowman & Littlefield, 2015). Another valuable review, focusing on intelligence gathering and the interaction between technology and security, is provided by B. Akhgar and S. Yates (eds.) *Strategic Intelligence Management: National Security Imperatives and Information and Communications Technologies* (Boston: Elsevier Books, 2013).

21. For a review of the range of services available to firms see '2007 Loss Prevention Resource Guide', *Loss Prevention: The Magazine for LP Professionals*, Vol. 6, No. 1 (2007), pp. 67–98.

22. This term was originally coined by the UK security consultants R. Briggs and C. Edwards in a 2006 think-tank paper and is quoted by J. Crump in his very interesting and thorough review of corporate security issues *Corporate Security Intelligence and Strategic Decision Making* (Boca Raton, Florida: CRC Press, 2016), pp. 15–18.

23. W. Henisz, E. Mansfield and M. A. Von Glinow 'Conflict, Security and Political Risk: International Business in Challenging Times', *Journal of International Business Studies*, Vol. 41, No. 5 (2010), pp. 759–764.

24. Personal correspondence and interview with Tom Schneid, 12 February 2007. Also see T. Schneid and L. Collins *Disaster Management and Preparedness* (Boca Raton, FA: Lewis Publishers/CRC Press, 2001). For a very similar discussion on the dimensions of risk-management practices and the degree to which multinational enterprises are viewing security and terrorism as critical strategic issues, planning for these forms of risks and allocating resources for training and protocol enhancements, see D. Wernick, 'Terror Incognito: International Business in an Era of Heightened Geopolitical Risk', in G. Suder (ed.) *Corporate Strategies Under International Terrorism and Adversity* (Cheltenham: Edward Elgar, 2006), pp. 59–82, as well as R. Burke 'International Terrorism and Threats to Security: Implications for Organizations and Management', in R. Burke and C. Cooper (eds.) *International Terrorism and Threats to Security: Managerial and Organizational Challenges* (Cheltenham, UK: Edward Elgar, 2008), pp. 3–33.

25. M. Czinkota, G. Knight and P. Liesch 'Terrorism and International Business: Conceptual Foundations', in G. Suder (ed.) *Terrorism and the International Business Environment: The Security-Business Nexus* (Cheltenham: Edward Edgar, 2004), p. 48. See also M. Czinkota, G. Knight, P. Liesch and J. Steen 'Terrorism and International Business: A Research Agenda', *Journal of International Business Studies*, Vol. 41, No. 5, (2010), pp. 826–843.

26. F. Dimanche 'The Tourism Sector', in G. Suder (ed.) *Terrorism and the International Business Environment: The Security-Business Nexus* (Cheltenham: Edward Elgar, 2004), pp. 157–170.

27. Czinkota *et al.* 'Terrorism and International Business: Conceptual Foundations', p. 55. For a very similar analysis specific to SARS see W. J. Tan and P. Enderwick 'Managing Threats in the Global Era: The Impact and Responses to SARS', *Thunderbird International Business Review*, Vol. 48, No. 4 (2006), pp. 515–536. J. McIntyre and E. Travis provide a thorough albeit general discussion of MNE practices related to hardening global supply chains in 'Global Supply Chain Under Conditions of Uncertainty: Economic Impacts, Corporate Responses and Strategic Lessons', in G. Suder (ed.) *Corporate Strategies under International Terrorism and Adversity* (Cheltenham: Edward Elgar, 2006), pp. 128–160

28. *The Global Risks Report 2016*, 11th ed. (Geneva: World Economic Forum, 2016).

29. M. Czinkota and I. Ronkainen 'Trends and Indications in International Business: Topics for Future Research', *Management International Review*, Vol. 49, No. 2 (2009), pp. 249–266.

30. Czinkota *et al.* 'Terrorism and International Business', p. 55.

31. D. Gillingham 'Managing in an Era of Terrorism', in G. Suder (ed.) *Corporate Strategies Under International Terrorism and Adversity* (Cheltenham: Edward Elgar, 2006), pp. 196–203, particularly Table 1.2, p. 199. For a highly detailed and integrated look at measuring and assessing security risks see A. Jaquith *Security Metrics: Replacing Fear, Uncertainty, and Doubt* (Upper Saddle River, NJ: Addison-Wesley, 2007).

32. For examples of the variety of these kinds of approaches being published see the firm-level systems approaches provided by L. Dai, L. Eden, and P. Beamish 'Place, Space, and Geographic Exposure: Foreign Subsidiary Survival in Conflict Zones', *Journal of International Business Studies*, Vol. 44, (2013) pp. 554–578; P. Bromiley, M. McShane, A. Nair and E. Rustambekov 'Enterprise Risk Management: Review, Critique and Research Directions', *Long Range Planning*, Vol. 48 (2015), pp. 265–276; A. Fee, S. McGrath-Camp and H. Lui 'Human Resources and Expatriate Evacuation: A Conceptual Model,' *Journal of Global Mobility*, Vol. 1, No. 3 (2013), pp. 246–263; and B. Bader and N. Berg 'The Influence of Terrorism on Expatriate Performance: A Conceptual Approach', *International Journal of Human Resource Management*, Vol. 25, No. 4 (2014), pp. 539–557. For more micro-level presentations see B. Bader, N. Berg and D. Holtbrugge 'Expatriate Performance in Terrorism-Endangered Countries: The Role of Family and Organizational Support', *International Business Review*, Vol. 24 (2015), pp. 849–860; K. Fisher, K. Hutchings and L. Pinto 'Pioneers Across War Zones: The Lived Acculturation Experiences of US Female Military Expatiates', *International Journal of Intercultural Relations* (2015) dx.doi.org/10.1016/jj.jintrel.2015.05.005; and J. Ramirez, S. Madero and C. Muniz 'The Impact of Narcoterrorism on HRM Systems', *International Journal of Human Resource Management* (2015) dx.doi.org/10.1080/09585192.2015.1091371.

33. Czinkota *et al.* 'Terrorism and International Business', pp. 55-56.

34. A. Engle, N. Spain, and P. J. Dowling 'Redesigning Edo Castle: A Sociotechnical Systems Approach to Security for Multinational Enterprises in an Age of Asymmetric Threats', *Program and Abstracts of the 2014 International Federation of Scholarly Associations of Management, World Congress in Tokyo* (Meiji University, Tokyo,

Japan, September 2014), pp. 127-128. Of particular interest is the growing interconnectivity between security for people (traditionally part of the HR portfolio) as this security subsystem interacts with security for IT systems. See H. Zafar 'Human Resource Information Systems: Information Security Concerns for Organizations', *Human Resource Management Review*, Vol. 23 (2013), pp. 105–113; as well as an interesting set of readings on privacy and people issues by A. Moore (ed.) *Privacy, Security and Accountability: Ethics, Law and Policy* (Lanham, Maryland: Rowman and Littlefield, 2016).

35. Not unexpectedly, IT security and HRM mandates increasingly blend together, as more and more HRM processes are webbed up and become part of the technical, administrative and processual 'glue' holding MNEs together. See S. Strohmeier and R. Kabst 'Configurations of e-HRM – An Empirical Exploration', *Employee Relations*, Vol. 36, No. 4 (2014), pp. 333–353; D. Stone, D. Deadrick, K. Lukaszewski and R. Johnson 'The Influence of Technology on the Future of Human Resource Management, *Human Resource Management Review*, Vol. 25 (2015), pp. 216–231; and J. Marler and S. Fisher 'An Evidence-based Review of e-HRM and Strategic Human Resource Management', *Human Resource Management Review*, Vol. 23 (2013), pp. 18–36.

36. See the following papers in a special issue of *Journal of World Business* which relate to this issue: P. Dowling and N. Donnelly 'Managing People in Global Markets – The Asia Pacific Perspective', *Journal of World Business*, Vol 48, No. 2 (2013), 171–174; and N. Haworth 'Compressed Development: Global Value Chains, Multinational Enterprises and Human Resource Development in 21st Century Asia', *Journal of World Business*, Vol 48, No. 2 (2013), 251–259.

37. N. Adler 'Cross-Cultural Management Research: The Ostrich and the Trend', *Academy of Management Review*, Vol. 8, No. 2 (1983), pp. 226–232.

38. See www.hrdiv.org/hrdivision/awards/ihrm for information on this award and recent winners.

39. M. Elvira and A. Davila (eds.) *Managing Human Resources in Latin America* (London: Routledge, 2005).

40. M. Morley, N. Heraty and S. Michailova (eds.) *Managing Human Resources in Central and Eastern Europe* (London: Routledge, 2007).

41. P. Budhwar and K. Mellahi (eds.) *Managing Human Resources in the Middle-East* (London: Routledge, 2006).

42. H. Larsen and W. Mayrhofer (eds.) *Managing Human Resources in Europe* (London: Routledge, 2006).

43. K. Kamoche, Y. Debrah, F. Horwitz and G. Nkombo Muuka (eds.) *Managing Human Resources in Africa* (London: Routledge, 2003).

44. P. Budhwar (ed.) *Managing Human Resources in Asia-Pacific* (London: Routledge, 2004); P. Budhwar and J. Bhatnagar (eds.) *The Changing Face of People Management in India* (Abingdon, UK: Routledge, 2009); and M. Thite, A. Wilkinson and P. Budhwar (eds.) *Emerging Indian Multinationals: Strategic Players in a Multipolar World* (New Delhi: Oxford University Press, 2016).

45. See P. Sparrow 'Integrating People, Process and Context Issues in the Field of IHRM', in P. Sparrow (ed.) *Handbook of International Human Resource Management* (Chichester, UK: Wiley, 2009); S. Morris, P. Wright, J. Trevor, P. Stiles, G. Stahl, S. Snell, J. Paauwe and E. Farndale 'Replicating HR: The role of People, Processes and Systems', *Human Resource Management*, Vol. 48, No. 6 (2009), pp. 973–995; E. Farndale, J. Paauwe, S. Morris, G. Stahl, P. Stiles, J. Trevor and P. Wright 'Context-Bound Configurations of Corporate HR Functions in Multinational Corporations', *Human Resource Management*, Vol. 49, No. 1 (2010), pp. 45–66. For recent research that focuses on the role of MNE headquarters see the Special Issue guest edited by B. Ambos and V. Mahnke, 'How Do MNC Headquarters Add Value?', *Management International Review*, Vol. 50, No. 4 (2010); and U. Andersson and U. Holm (eds.) *Managing the Contemporary Multinational: The Role of Headquarters* (Cheltenham, UK: Edward Elgar, 2010).

46. W. Cascio and J. Boudreau 'The Search for Global Competence: From International HR to Talent Management', *Journal of World Business*, Vol. 51, No. 1 (2015), pp. 103–114.

47. M. Poole 'Editorial: Human Resource Management in an International Perspective', *International Journal of Human Resource Management*, Vol. 1, No. 1 (1990), pp. 1–15.

48. See M. Pudelko, S. Reiche and C. Carr 'Recent Developments and Emerging Challenges in International Human Resource Management', *The International Journal of Human Resource Management*, Vol. 26, No. 2 (2015), pp. 127–135."

49. S. Jackson, R. Schuler and K. Jiang 'An Aspirational Framework for Strategic Human Resource Management,' *Academy of Management Annals*, Vol. 8, No. 1 (2014), pp. 1–56.

50. See E. Lawler, A. Mohrman, S. Mohrman, G. Ledford and T. Cummins (eds.) *Doing Research That is Useful for Theory and Practice* (San Francisco: Jossey-Bass, 1985); J. Campbell, R. Daft and C. Hulin *What to Study: Generating and Developing Research Questions* (Beverly Hills, CA: Sage Publications, 1982); and J. McGrath, J. Martin and R. Kulka *Judgment Calls in Research* (Beverly Hills, CA: Sage Publications, 1982).

CASES

CASE 1

SPANNING THE GLOBE

By Allen D. Engle, Sr.

Eric Christopher, Associate Director for Global HR Development at Tex-Mark, was sitting in his car in an early-morning traffic jam. He had thought that by leaving his home at 7.00 a.m. he would have been ahead of the heavy commuter traffic into San Antonio's city center. The explanation for the long queue was announced by the radio traffic service. A large portable crane, used to set up concrete barriers around roadworks, had overturned, and inbound and outbound traffic would be at a dead stop for at least an hour.

Eric had ended up at Tex-Mark, a computer input-output manufacturer and supplier, through an indirect career route. Brought up in the Hill Country Village district of San Antonio, Eric had graduated from Churchill High School and Baylor University in Waco, Texas with a major in History and a minor in Spanish. His maternal grandmother lived in Tennessee but was born and grew up in Edinburgh, Scotland, and Eric had spent several summers while in high school and at university backpacking around Europe.

His facility for languages was impressive and he had an excellent working use of Spanish, French, Italian, and German. He could converse in Cantonese, as the result of working in a noodle restaurant during university, and had started a tutorial course in Mandarin last fall.

Upon graduation, Eric backpacked around Europe and South America until his money ran out. Returning to Dallas he took a ticketing job with SouthWest Airlines and was quickly moved to the training unit. After four successful years at SouthWest, he was contacted by a headhunter about a position as Global Development Assistant with Tex-Mark. The promised combination of global travel, more money, and a return to San Antonio proved irresistible, and now Eric had been with Tex-Mark for five years. His career progress to date was outstanding, despite the extra workload self-imposed by undertaking MBA studies at UT, San Antonio as a part-time student.

Tex-Mark had started out as a 'spin-off' firm from IME Computers in the late 1970s. Patents, combined with an excellence in engineering, an outstanding institutional sales staff and cost-sensitive production and pricing all combined to make Tex-Mark a major force in the printer and optical scanner industry. Tex-Mark inherited a production facility in San Antonio from IME, but the company also had international production facilities operating in three countries: Monterrey, Mexico, Leith, Scotland and, more recently, Jaipur, India. A major new facility was planned to start production in Wuhu, China late next year.

Research and new product development activities were split between the home offices in San Antonio, a printer center in Durham, North Carolina and an optical research 'center of excellence' in Edinburgh, Scotland. Major sales, distribution and customer service centers had recently expanded into Asia and were now located in Rheims in France; Memphis, Tennessee; Sydney, Australia; Rio de Janeiro, Brazil; Hong Kong; and Tel Aviv, Israel.

Faced with the long delay, Eric turned the radio volume down, turned up the air conditioning and telephoned his office on his hands-free car phone to advise them of his situation. Fortunately, his personal assistant was already at work, so Eric was able to rearrange his schedule. He asked that the 10.30 meeting with Fred Banks, a plant engineer recently repatriated from Jaipur, be pushed back an hour. His major concern was a teleconference meeting at 2.00 with his director, who was currently visiting the sales center in Memphis, and the other four members of the executive career development team in San Antonio. The general topic was a review and evaluation of training and development strategies for expatriate professionals and managers resulting from Tex-Mark's growth and the new production shift to Asia. Eric had indirectly heard that Juanita Roberto, the Vice President for HR, wanted costs cut and her delegates on the team would be pushing for streamlined (Eric had mentally translated that as cheaper) training programs, shorter expatriate assignments and a faster appointment of host-country nationals (HCNs) whenever possible. While Eric had prepared for this crucial meeting, he needed to incorporate some information from his office files.

The radio announcer broke into Eric's thoughts, commenting that overextension or carrying too much weight had probably caused the crane to overturn. "I can identify with that," Eric thought to himself.

Eric's meeting with Fred Banks had not gone well. Fred was one of the last of the 'IME legacies', an IME engineer that had stayed on with Tex-Mark after the spin-off in 1978. Fred had been a bright and promising young engineer back then, and was one of the first people chosen to go to Scotland in 1983. He was so successful in bringing that facility online in an 11-month assignment that he was made lead engineer of the team that went into Mexico in 1989. The three-year Mexican project did not go as smoothly. Certainly there were many unavoidable economic uncertainties during that period.

Reviewing the files, Eric felt that a large part of the problem was that Fred's team did not relate well to their Mexican counterparts. Furthermore, the Tex-Mark team did not treat the local and national government agencies with enough respect and sensitivity. Eric noted that permits and authorizations that should have taken weeks instead took six months or more.

After the Mexican project Fred stayed in San Antonio with occasional trips to Durham, North Carolina. His assignment to India in 1999 was by sheer chance, as a last-minute replacement for another engineer whose father was diagnosed with a serious cancer some two weeks before the family was to set off on assignment. Eric had helped design the pre-departure training program for the original candidate and had even included a one-week visit for the candidate and his wife.

Today Fred had been angry and disappointed that an 18-month assignment in India had turned into a three-year assignment, and that a research position in Durham 'promised' to him by a previous Vice President (two Vice Presidents ago) had been filled by a younger Durham resident employee. Eric bluntly countered that the 18-month assignment had become a three-year assignment largely due to Fred's unwillingness to train and hand over responsibilities to local engineers and his inability to work constructively with district and federal regulators in India.

The conversation took a hostile turn and, although Eric did not lose his temper, he was troubled by Fred's final comment: "If this is how you treat the people willing to go abroad, you'll never get your best engineers to leave San Antonio".

Preparing for the 2.00 meeting, Eric reviewed the unofficial yet 'standard' expatriate training program he had been instrumental in developing over the last three years (see Exhibit A). Though Eric recommended that all pre-departure activities should be undertaken, it was not compulsory.

With the Chinese operation adding to the number of expatriate destinations, Eric realized that Tex-Mark should have a more formal policy regarding international assignments. Feedback regarding the interviews and conversations with Tex-Mark employees with country experiences was mixed. Some had developed into longer-term mentoring arrangements, but other expatriates had not found it useful. Still, it was a low-cost way of providing information. Language courses were problematical. On too many occasions there was not the time – employees left the country midway through their language courses. He recalled the idea of more 'extensive' assignments requiring more 'complete' and 'rigorous' preparation from an MBA course he had taken last year. Obviously China would be a more challenging and difficult assignment than France, but could they differentiate treatment on the grounds of cultural difficulty?

More importantly, Eric asked himself, how can I suggest we make our training more rigorous given Juanita Roberto's focus on cost? Even if I win on this point, what will I answer when asked what methods or activities make up more 'rigorous' training? Finally, what is the role of language training? Eric knew not everyone took to languages the way he did, and that Mandarin is not Spanish.

Finally, was now the time to raise the issue of repatriation? The meeting with Fred had been disturbing. Eric knew that the current debriefing and counselling sessions had a reputation for being more 'tell and sell' than a meaningful exchange of ideas and insights. Top management had recently signalled this as a growing 'problem'. Eric had planned to gather data on repatriate turnover. Perhaps this should be given a higher priority. After all, how could Tex-Mark decide to plan for international assignments, involving more third-country national (TCN) movements and the transfer of HCNs into its US operations for training and development, without considering repatriation?

EXHIBIT A   Tex-Mark Corporation's Policy for Expatriate Preparation and On-assignment Support

Pre-departure activities:

1 'Country briefings'. Outsourced to a consulting firm in San Antonio that has experience dealing with the countries in which Tex-Mark operated. Tex-Mark is prepared to pay for four sessions, each lasting one hour.

2 'Reading assignments'. Three to four books (depending on region of assignment) on national or regional culture and/or doing business in the focal region. Accompanying spouses/partners have access to a similar library.

3 Interviews and conversations with Tex-Mark employees with country experiences.

4 Language courses. Attendance at elective 'survival-level' language classes. These courses last from 8 to 12 weeks, with three course meetings a week. Tex-Mark will pay for spouses/partners as well.

In-country training and development:

Upon arrival, Tex-Mark staff in the local operation will assist the accompanying spouse/partner with job-search activities. They will assist with finding children acceptable schooling situations. Where possible, Tex-Mark staff will endeavor to provide a social support network.

Repatriation:

Upon return, all expatriates are required to go through a debriefing and career counselling session with HR staff. This should be held within two months of the person's re-entry to the home location.

In the role of Eric:

1 Summarize your thoughts on the problems at hand, alternative solutions and your strategy on how to proceed at the forthcoming meeting.

2 How will your proposal solve the problems you have defined?

3 How can you defend your solution from budgetary concerns? In what way is your approach both a solution to the problems of expatriates at Tex-Mark and a good economic investment?

Step back out of the role and answer the following:

1 Does Eric's personal background assist in his assessment of the problems he faces?

2 Would you have approached this situation differently? If so, what benefits would your different approach provide for Tex-Mark?

QUALITY COMPLIANCE AT THE HAWTHORN ARMS

By Allen D. Engle, Sr.

Sitting in his room at the Hawthorn Arms Hotel in Shannon, Ireland, waiting for a morning flight to London and then on to Marseilles, Alistair Mackay reflects on how uninspiring hotel rooms are. He has just completed a series of meetings with Irish officials in Limerick, concluding with a debriefing session over a Guinness with his Irish colleagues to plan their next move. Negotiations over a potential contract are proceeding well, but there will be labor implications that will require a formal response. Consequently, Alistair had missed the last evening flight out to London. "Another night away from the family. Thank goodness I am not missing our wedding anniversary tomorrow. I must remember to find something really special in the duty-free shop."

Six months ago, Alistair was appointed Director of Personnel Development, European Division, for Trianon, an Anglo-French avionics firm. Trianon had begun as a subcontractor for the Concorde and had gradually gained a reputation in the 1970s and 1980s as a high-quality, if sometimes undependable subcontractor for major French and British aerospace defense contractors. Attempts to expand into civilian markets by gaining contracts for the original European Airbus were unsuccessful, though today nearly 30 per cent of Trianon's sales are through civilian contracts. Now, under new executive management, Trianon is focused on major navigational display contracts for the next generation of Airbus production. Prior to joining Trianon, Alistair had worked in the legal department of a Scottish bank. European Union (EU) employment requirements had become his speciality and provided a springboard into his current position.

His cellphone rings and he receives an unexpected call from his colleague Henri Genadry, General Director of Joint Ventures, Mergers and Acquisitions, Display Division. Henri informs him that the expected outright purchase of a scanner cathode ray tube production facility in Vecses, outside of Budapest, Hungary is not going ahead. Instead, the decision has been made at

corporate headquarters in Marseilles for a ten-year joint venture with a Hungarian government-backed firm.

Henri goes on to explain that the Hungarian control and equity interests in this project are expected to make ministry officials in Budapest happy. Henri is hopeful the decision will make executives and administrators at Malév, the state-supported airline, friendly to Trianon in the long term. "We will now need a 'Quality Compliance Manager' for a three-year assignment in Hungary. It is an important position as we will need to keep tight control on this joint-venture operation. There will be some travel to France and Germany – at least in the first year – until we see how things are working out with these new partners."

Alistair asks, "When do you expect this 'Quality Compliance' manager to be available?" There is a pause on the other end of the line, after which Henri blandly responds, "Five or six weeks if we are to meet corporate timetables. We expect the person to be in on the ground, so to speak. We will need a realistic assessment of current processes, for a start. The person will need to be familiar with the joint venture's objectives and targets. We have some details through the due diligence process, but skills audits were somewhat rushed." Alistair then asks that details, including a job description, be emailed to his intranet address.

"Well," Henri admits, "this is the first joint venture our firm has been involved in outside of the UK, Germany, or France. The job description will be very precise on the technical 'quality' side but vague on the administrative 'compliance' side. You may need to fill in the missing pieces as you see fit."

After a few more minutes of general chatting, Henri finishes the phone call. Alistair plugs his laptop into the telephone port on his room's desk and, after a few false starts, logs onto the secure corporate website and accesses three personnel files from a folder he prepared some weeks ago in expectation that he would be asked for a decision. Of course, he had expected the position to be that of Project Engineer in an operation of which the firm would have

100 per cent ownership. Now he is looking for a Quality Compliance Manager in a joint venture.

Alistair doesn't like making these kinds of decisions when feeling so remote and 'disconnected' from the firm. He considers calling his friend and mentor, Gunther Heinrich, in Frankfurt, Germany and asking him about the Hungarian project, as the German-based divisions have more experience dealing with Hungarian issues. He looks at his watch. It is 10.30 p.m. "Not a civilized time to call anyone, let alone Gunther." Alistair knows that Gunther's wife, Britt, had presented them with a son three weeks ago, and they were having trouble getting the child to sleep through the night. "I will call him from the airport and set up a meeting. I will have the job description by then."

He is also feeling uncomfortable with the process he is going through. Surely we can do better than react like this after the event, he thinks. Why were we not part of the decision-making process on the Hungarian venture?

Questions:

1 Consider the three candidates in Exhibit A. If forced to make a decision tomorrow, which candidate should Alistair choose for the job? What major factors should determine his choice?

2 We are told nothing of the process that Trianon uses to recruit candidates for this level of final selection. Given what you know about the firm from the case, outline a general recruitment and selection process for Trianon. Describe how your proposed process fits with 'best' selection practices as well as the strategic needs of this company.

3 Should HR staff be involved in strategic decisions relating to international business operations, such as finalizing a joint venture agreement?

EXHIBIT A   Alistair Mackay's short list of possible candidates

First candidate: Marie Erten-Loiseau. Born in Prague, her family moved to Toulon when Marie was 12 years old. Brought up in France, she was educated as an aeronautical engineer in France and Germany. Marie worked for Trianon for 13 years, in two divisions within France and Germany, with increasing levels of project responsibility. Her leadership of two projects over the last three years in Lodz, Poland and two sites in the Czech Republic and Slovakia has been marked by remarkable success. Married, her husband is semi-retired. They have one child in university.

Second candidate: Janos Gabor. Born in Gyor, Hungary, Janos was educated at the University of Pécs, Hungary. He has a good background in the production of cathode ray tube and display system technologies, albeit from the central European perspective. He has worked at Trianon for nearly four years and has just been transferred into the cathode ray tube division as a Senior Engineer. His family is reportedly very well connected with national government officials, particularly the old, ex-party members of multiple ministerial bureaucracies. Janos is single.

Third candidate: Sinead Marrinan-McGuire, a production engineer on loan to Trianon's London office for joint-venture analyses and due diligence reviews on technical and legal grounds. She has spent three years in the Research and Development (R&D) development team in Dublin and London, working on the very technologies to be applied in this Hungarian joint venture project. Alistair met and talked with her today in Limerick and was very impressed with her understanding of corporate-level concerns and strategic issues. Most of her career has been in Ireland and around London, with only short, tactical trips to France. Married, her husband is a solicitor in Dublin. They have three children aged seven, nine, and thirteen.

CASE 3

WOLFGANG'S BALANCING ACT: REWARDING HEALTHCARE *EXECUTIVES IN A DISPERSED YET INTEGRATED FIRM*[1]

By Marion Festing and Allen D. Engle, SR.

Healthcare – a successful global player in the pharmaceutical market

Healthcare is one of the largest European pharmaceutical companies. The headquarters is situated in Hamburg, Germany and today there are about 200 subsidiaries all over the world. In 2016, throughout the globe, 30,000 people were working for *Healthcare*. Net sales amounted to €5.9 billion, with a net profit of €750 million.

The company was founded more than 100 years ago. It started in a small shop in Elmshorn, a little town north of Hamburg. In the beginning, the main business was retailing with only a small part of the product range, resulting from in-house production. The founder himself had a background in pharmaceutics. He was very dedicated to science and naturally interested in research and the development of new drugs.

Over the years in-house production was expanded and soon the founder distributed his products all over Germany and, later on, in many European countries. Overseas, the activities started in the USA with a small affiliate in New York. Over time *Healthcare* acquired several local pharmaceutical companies, which later became 100 per cent subsidiaries. Today, the US market is one of the core markets for *Healthcare*. However, the first affiliate in the USA was only the beginning of the firm's globalization. After this initial success, *Healthcare* began to enter other lucrative markets of the world such as Japan, China, Latin America, and Australia.

Over time the headquarters in Germany grew dramatically. Headquarters' activities centered on research and the production and distribution of pharmaceutical products that were largely developed within the firm. While in the past the product range was highly differentiated, today *Healthcare* concentrates on a few business areas such as oncology and dermatology. Within these business areas the firm is now recognized globally as one of the industry's leaders. The firm intends to continue to build and extend this leading position in these worldwide specialized markets.

Discontinuous changes in the environment – such as increasing costs for research and development and increasing pressure on prices due to cost containment by national authorities, and generic competition – have forced innovative pharmaceutical companies such as *Healthcare* to operate their key business processes globally. The firm has developed a multicentered company in order to ensure the effective utilization of the resources and provide nimble market penetration and product ramp-up. Critical capabilities include corporate-wide R&D processes, a concentration on a few production sites with worldwide supply responsibility and a fast penetration of the key markets. These capabilities will allow *Healthcare* to ensure the faster and more cost-effective development of innovative products, reduce production costs and thereby provide for significant sales growth and increased profitability.

In the past, *Healthcare*'s situation was characterized by worldwide activities but mainly local business processes (e.g. development and production focusing on local/regional markets). Local issues were aggregated to the four significant regions in which *Healthcare* has organized operations. These regions are Europe, the USA/Canada, Latin America, and Asia-Pacific. Consequently, the human resource management (HRM) processes were adapted to country- or region-specific conditions, and global integration was not a major issue. For example, executives and high potentials were recruited, selected, assessed, and compensated based on different regional standards.

International human resource (HR) activities concentrated on only a few international managers that acted as co-ordination agents.

Wolfgang Hansen: The new HR manager

Wolfgang Hansen has been recruited as a HR manager at *Healthcare*. Wolfgang holds a master's degree in International Management from the University of Hamburg. During his studies he has participated in a study-abroad program, spending a year in London. He has specialized in Human Resource Management and Compensation Strategies. Wolfgang's initial assignment upon graduation was in the HR department of a medium-sized German technical company. However, he missed the international dimension in this job and decided to pursue an executive MBA with a transnational orientation in order to prepare for this ideal career. His first job after having completed his transnational MBA program was at *Healthcare.*

For one year Wolfgang has been with *Healthcare,* beginning as an HR manager. Three months ago he was placed in charge of global compensation policies, with the newly created title of 'Personalreferent für globale Vergütungsstrategien'. His first project is reviewing existing policies and practices. He has been asked to make a series of recommendations on further co-ordination of global pay systems at the next meeting of the Board of Directors in Frankfurt in January. Preparing for the board meeting, Wolfgang reviews a series of documents such as recent annual reports, the Leadership Competency Set, the new Global Performance Management System and firm-internal strategic documents on the development of the corporate and HRM strategies. Each document set has been placed in its own folder. These six folders contain the following items:

Folder one: The *Healthcare* Group

In 2016, *Healthcare* again had a very successful year and reached records for key financial ratios (see Table 1). Thus, the firm was well prepared for reaching new ambitious targets for 2017. The *Healthcare* Group's very positive business development is based on the sustained

TABLE 1   Key data on the *Healthcare* Group

Values expressed in €m	2016	2015	Change
Net sales	634	583	+ 8%
Gross profit	3951	3625	+ 9%
R&D costs	981	916	+ 7%
Operating profit	891	736	+ 21%
Net profit	750	577	+ 23%
Return on sales	12.5%	11.2%	+ 1.3%
Cash flows from operating activities	982	702	+ 40%
Basic earnings per share (€)	3.33	2.52	+ 23%
Total equity	3134	2725	+ 15%
Equity ratio	52.6%	47.5%	+ 5.1%
Personnel costs	1376	1336	+ 3%
Number of employees (annual average)	30,680	29,875	+ 2.7%

growth of their top products in all-important markets (see Table 2). Both the strategic reorientation and the improvement in operational efficiency have contributed to the growth of their business. *Healthcare*'s aim is to create a solid base in order to further improve the company's profitability by optimizing the cost structure.

TABLE 2 Net sales by region of the *Healthcare* Group

	in €m		% of total	
	2016	**2015**	**2016**	**2015**
Europe	2512	2394	42%	44%
USA/Canada	2079	1856	35%	34%
Asia-Pacific	308	275	5%	5%
Latin America	667	565	11%	10%
Other Activities	365	326	6%	6%
Total	**5931**	**5416**	**100%**	**100%**

Folder two: Personnel structure of the *Healthcare* Group

The *Healthcare* Group has employed 32,185 people worldwide as of 31 December 2016, which is an increase of more than 10 per cent compared to the previous year (28,854). The number of employees working for the headquarters of *Healthcare* has increased by 232 and now accounts for roughly 33 per cent of the Group's worldwide personnel, while the number of employees worldwide has increased by 3331 employees (see Table 3). Personnel costs have risen accordingly, amounting to €1699 million in 2016 (see Table 4).

Folder three: The Leadership Competency Set of the *Healthcare* Group

The corporate Leadership Competency Set defines the critical competencies managers need to possess to master the future challenges of the *Healthcare* Group.

TABLE 3 Employees by region of the *Healthcare* Group in 2016

	2016	**2015**
Healthcare headquarters	9853	9621
Europe	8732	7956
USA/Canada	4869	4523
Asia-Pacific	2569	1956
Latin America	3706	2944
Other employees	2456	1854
Total	**32,185**	**28,854**

TABLE 4 Personnel costs of the *Healthcare* Group

Values expressed in €m	2016	2015
Wages and salaries	1365	1266
Social security and support payments	272	269
Pensions	62	61
Total	**1699**	**1596**

It has been developed based on an analysis of the business needs and by asking key players and HR people in nearly all locations of the company worldwide for their contributions. It is the basis for all HR practices and policies and is intended to ensure consistency across businesses and locations. It comprises business-related competencies, people-related competencies, and personal competencies.

Business-related competencies include:

- achievement orientation: sets and works towards achieving challenging business objectives and targets and delivers outstanding results for the *Healthcare* Group

- innovation and change: identifies the need for change and generates novel ideas to create or improve processes, systems or products, and builds commitment to change

- decision-making: makes sound, timely, and courageous decisions while balancing the risks and benefits to the *Healthcare* Group.

People-related competencies include:

- team leadership: inspires team members to maximize team output by providing clear direction, empowering them, establishing oneself as a leader, and balancing team resources with assignments

- capability development: develops people and the organization to ensure that the *Healthcare* Group has the capabilities needed for future success

- relationship building: establishes mutually trusting relationships with people both inside and outside

of the *Healthcare* Group in order to foster open communication and advance the goals and business

- impact and influence: influences others to gain their support for driving the *Healthcare* Group's strategy and goals forward and enters conflicts if necessary.

Personal competencies include:

- business understanding: demonstrates an understanding of the implications of the *Healthcare* Group's strategies, industry dynamics, market trends, the competitive environment, and one's function/profession in the accomplishment of business objectives

- analytical thinking: approaches situations by identifying the best information available and systematically assessing it for meaning and impact

- self-development: maintains a critical awareness of one's own working style and performance; takes steps to build strengths and addresses development needs in line with the strategic objectives of the *Healthcare* Group.

Folder four: Corporate HR policies

The corporate HR policies, which center around these leadership competencies, are outlined in Table 5. These policies have triggered changes in the structures and processes of HR as practiced across the firm's regions.

Folder five: The global performance system

Within the context of the new strategic orientation, *Healthcare* has also implemented a global performance system, comprising of common standards for individual performance management, as well as a bonus system common to all executives. With this new global performance system *Healthcare* intends to strengthen the performance culture within the company and facilitate a common orientation for all managers.

The individual performance management system contains two elements:

1 *Goal setting and appraisal.* The new system ensures that every manager gets a precise orientation on expectations and priorities, clear feedback on individual achievements, and contingent rewards.

2 *Leadership feedback.* In order to ensure a systematic development of each manager, the system envisages differentiated feedback on leadership behavior (based on the corporate leadership competencies), identification of development needs, and a real consensus built for targeted development activities.

TABLE 5 HR policies of the *Healthcare* Group

HR area	Policy direction
Recruitment of key talents	Good recruitment practices Strategic workforce planning
Management development	Corporate management development system based on corporate Leadership Competency Set
Transfer/mobility	Enhanced cross-functional mobility Well-balanced cross-regional mobility
Executive compensation	Attractive and competitive compensation Aligned bonus system
Pension system	Move to a defined contribution system
Organizational development	Clear structures, efficient processes Corporate announcements on managerial and structural changes
Performance management	Balanced goal setting Measuring performance Clear feedback Linkage to variable pay

The individual performance management is based on consistent goal categories, a rating scale, a template and a performance management cycle which is standardized at all sites, and co-ordinated to critical corporate processes. To ensure equal application, all managers belonging to the target group are trained on the system, its philosophy, procedures, and goals.

Closely linked to the individual performance system is the *compensation policy* of the firm and the newly developed bonus system. The compensation policy is characterized by a balance of corporate standards and local applications for cash-related compensation. Fringe benefits are organized solely on a local or regional level.

The most centralized compensation element is *long-term incentives.* Following traditional industry practice, *Healthcare* grants share options to its managers. The size of the options is largely dependent on the level of management the position holds in the hierarchy. For every level a possible range of options is defined.

With respect to base pay and *short-term incentives* the situation is different. Global standards define an orientation for the level of total cash (fixed pay plus variable pay) to local/regional market standards. This means that the total cash a manager receives depends mainly on his or her local/regional compensation levels. Corporate standards define the market standards (based on target benchmark firms and target quartile positions). Pay level is largely defined according to local standards, while taking into consideration *Healthcare*'s industry-specific positioning targets.

The bonus of managers at *Healthcare* is based on three components:

- *Individual* component. Based on results of six to ten individual objectives in the respective area of responsibility. The weight of this component is 50 per cent.

- '*My unit*' component for regions, countries, global business units, or regional business units. Reflects the performance of the organizational unit for which a manager is responsible or in which they are working. The weight of this component is 25 per cent. The goal achievement is measured by deviation between contribution margin and net sales goals and the actual numbers. Note that for headquarter functions (e.g. controlling or HR) which have no profit and loss account the 'my unit' component is replaced by an additional individual component, which accounts for 25 per cent as well.

- '*Broader context*' component. This reflects the joint responsibility for performance of a higher organizational level, i.e. the corporate level. The weight of this component is 25 per cent. The evaluation of goal achievement on corporate level is based on the degree of corporate goal achievement. Corporate goals are decided by the Board each year; the leading parameter is corporate contribution margin.

Both the 'broader context' and the 'my unit' components are leveraged. As a consequence, a goal achievement of, for example, 120 per cent will lead to a 200 per cent payout for this component. On the other hand a goal achievement of less than 100 per cent will decrease the payout for the respective component significantly. In this manner unit and broad context components have potential variance in payoffs and/or shortfall that are disproportionate to their simple weights. For every component a payout is calculated, and the sum of the three components is the total bonus a manager receives.

Folder six: An overview of the corporate and HRM strategy

As stated above, the competitive situation in the pharmaceutical industry has required *Healthcare* executives to redesign cross-border activities. While the company has always been active in a high number of foreign markets, business processes were traditionally locally oriented in the past. Wolfgang recalls a typology of international firms developed by Christopher Bartlett and the late Sumantra Ghoshal. Thinking in student terms, realigning or rebalancing *Healthcare*'s pay system means increasing global integration. In an abstract sense, *Healthcare* is attempting to develop a transnational strategy now by globally integrating certain activities while leaving room for local responsiveness. Figure 1 shows the developments in *Healthcare*'s cross-border strategy.

This tendency is reflected in the HR strategy. While recruitment, selection, performance management, and compensation policies for executives were designed according to local standards in the

FIGURE 1 **Recent developments in the internationalization strategy of *Healthcare***

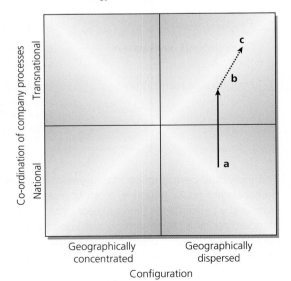

a *Healthcare*'s past situation
b *Healthcare*'s current situation
c *Healthcare*'s future situation

past, these processes have been replaced by new solutions. These solutions focus on furthering global consistency of HR systems in order to respond to strategic changes on the corporate level. The overall goal is to strengthen an aligned performance orientation and to support global co-ordination, which is essential for globally integrated business processes. Elements indicating a stronger global integration include the above-mentioned common set of leadership competencies. This concept has been developed by the headquarters' HR department in co-operation with local HR representatives and managers from different regions and business units.

Bumps on the road to international co-ordination at the *Healthcare* Group

Some of his colleagues in the HR department have told Wolfgang about problems with a standardized compensation model, which was supposed to be implemented two years ago. *Healthcare*'s aim was to have the same compensation system in each country. They wanted to have the highest possible degree of standardization in order to make transnational processes easier and more efficient. They planned to split the salary in two parts: 65 per cent fixed income and 35 per cent variable income depending on individual performance. The plan was to introduce this system not only for managers but for all employees.

Shortly after announcing the new plans, several of *Healthcare*'s regional HR managers and employees vocally opposed the new system. In France, managers even called for a strike. In Germany, the situation was difficult as well because the worker's council (*Betriebsrat*) did not agree to the new system and many negotiations followed. Many employees were frightened by the new 'risky' system as they had become dependent on a high percentage of fixed (guaranteed) income. They panicked at the thought of losing nearly half of their income and were afraid that they would never reach the 100 per cent they had gained before.

As a consequence the implementation of this system was never realized. In designing the new compensation system, *Healthcare*'s management board had only considered economic issues, while disregarding existing yet unspoken cultural frames of reference and perceptions. Wolfgang knew he had to be careful to avoid oversimplification and an overstandardization, and develop a more country-specific system which could be adjusted to local characteristics.

From his international background Wolfgang knows how important it is to include his HR counterparts from the different countries and regions in the process of further developing the HR policies and systems. This would allow him to more accurately understand the cultural and legal particularities at hand, as well as ensure him a higher level of political support in *Healthcare*'s regions and countries.

For example, as a first step, Wolfgang has been in close contact with the HR representatives in the most important strategic markets, which are currently the USA and Japan. Here, he has negotiated exceptions for the standardized currency base of performance-based pay elements. He has learned that the local currency is most important because local managers are not used to considering a foreign currency and would not accept this as a major element of the compensation system.

Another issue for discussion was the percentage dedicated to fixed and variable pay. Wolfgang had problems understanding the Japanese opposition to the new global performance management system. During *Healthcare*'s yearly HR conference he felt that Mr Okubayashi, the Japanese head of HR at *Healthcare*, was not happy with the global performance system but did not really engage in discussions about how to improve or adapt the system. Thus, one evening, Wolfgang invited him for dinner in a nice sushi bar in Düsseldorf where *Healthcare*'s yearly HR conference took place. Over innumerable cups of saki Okubayashi patiently outlined traditional compensation systems in Japan. Upon sobering up the next day Wolfgang slowly realized that, given culture and firm traditions, it would be very difficult to introduce a high level of variable pay based on individual performance in Japan. He attributed this to a higher level of risk aversion characterizing the Japanese culture as compared to many other cultures. From his studies he knew about Hofstede's dimensions describing cultural differences. As he recalled, one of them was uncertainty avoidance, which points out the extent to which people are risk averse or are prepared to take risks. He thought that risk-taking managers were probably ready to accept large incentive payments while risk-averse managers were not prepared to accept a high income variability which may be involved in performance-based pay. The latter may be the case in Japan.

When Wolfgang talked to the American head of HR at *Healthcare*, Thomas Miller, in a very late afternoon video conference, he received a different message. Miller loudly and repeatedly asserted that, from an American perspective, the global performance management system suggested by the headquarters was 'wimpy' and would not reward the outstanding achievements of 'franchise player' star managers. Compared to the big US pharmaceutical companies' percentage of variable pay for top managers, Thomas declared the monetary incentive system of *Healthcare* 'ridiculous' and demanded a higher proportion of variable pay. Wolfgang had to turn the video link sound down twice by the end of the web-enabled teleconference meeting. Was this a sign of a higher level of risk taking as a result of the underlying culture in the USA?

Step-by-step Wolfgang learned how important it is to ensure acceptance in the important strategic markets and to consider local labor market regulations. He came to realize that country-specific determinants such as cultural values or the legal environment of the firm must be considered if problems with cultural acceptance or legal conflicts are to be minimized. This newly acquired awareness made his mandate even more complicated. He had some general ideas about the contextual situation in some countries, yet he was unaware of the conditions in other countries. Implementing a new system always runs the risk of losing political support and insulting the perspectives of the local HR administrators and the business unit heads.

Thinking about the positive effects of the international HR conference, as well as his individual discussions with Okubayashi and Miller, Wolfgang took the opportunity of visiting some of *Healthcare*'s subsidiaries and taking out the HR managers for lunch. He diligently tried to identify their relative positions as to the strengths and weaknesses of the current compensation system and collected ideas for his presentation to the board.

Conclusion: A not so happy Christmas

It is Christmas Eve. Wolfgang is sitting in a newly built ski hotel in Garmisch-Partenkirchen, overlooking the snowy mountains and preparing the final draft of his presentation for the management board meeting at the beginning of January. The six file folders lie spread out across the large blonde-ash table and even across the oak floor

as thick, heavy snowflakes silently fall outside. He is thinking about reorganizing *Healthcare*'s compensation system. His task is to find the right mixture of standardization and flexibility. On the one hand, he has to implement a new compensation system in order to reduce costs. On the other, he has to take into account the traditional local HR practices. As he considers all he has learned at *Healthcare* over the last few months, he asks himself a series of questions. A visual learner, Wolfgang writes out a chart on a writing tablet that captures his sense of integration and local responsiveness at *Healthcare*. We present his sketch as Figure 2.

Question block A: Standardization vs. local responsiveness of compensation systems

Wolfgang reconsiders the degree of global standardization and local responsiveness of the current global compensation system.

1   Should he move some of the existing pay elements across the T account in Figure 2, shifting them from globally standardized to locally customized?

2   Should he add or delete some existing practices from the T account?

3   Should he change the weights or emphases (percentages) of existing elements of the pay system?

Question block B: Job-based vs. competency-based compensation

If *Healthcare*'s job-based pay dominates the existing system, while other approaches such as competency-based compensation have not been pursued, then what advantages might a competency-based system have for *Healthcare*?

1   How can the firm communicate to the geographically dispersed executives the need to acquire and maintain those management competencies that have been defined in the competency set (in folder three)?

2   Would a purely competency-based pay system be somehow more flexible?

3   But then again, what about the standardization *Healthcare* has just achieved through standardizing the job descriptions across units?

FIGURE 2 Balancing global integration and local responsiveness in *Healthcare*'s compensation strategy

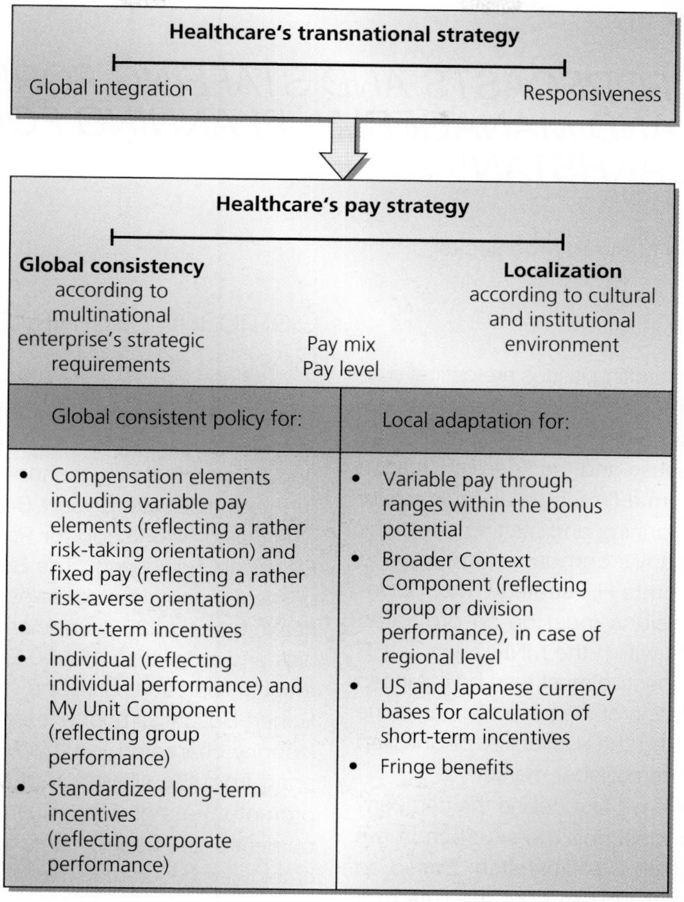
Healthcare's transnational strategy
Global integration
Responsiveness
Healthcare's pay strategy
Global consistency according to multinational enterprise's strategic requirements
Pay mix
Pay level
Localization according to cultural and institutional environment
Global consistent policy for:
Local adaptation for:
• Compensation elements including variable pay elements (reflecting a rather risk-taking orientation) and fixed pay (reflecting a rather risk-averse orientation)
• Short-term incentives
• Individual (reflecting individual performance) and My Unit Component (reflecting group performance)
• Standardized long-term incentives (reflecting corporate performance)
• Variable pay through ranges within the bonus potential
• Broader Context Component (reflecting group or division performance), in case of regional level
• US and Japanese currency bases for calculation of short-term incentives
• Fringe benefits

4 How would Wolfgang take these three competency categories and use them to develop a series of measurable, behavioral indicators to be used to assess an executive's contributions to *Healthcare*? In what sense should these new behavioral indicators be customized to local (regional) contexts? How can Wolfgang go about this process to ensure a balance of organizational standardization and local relevance?

Frustrated with the complexities he is facing, Wolfgang is planning a telephone conference with regional compensation administrators and other executives in order to expand his analysis with this group and to build political support for a new policy. Does he have the time to deal with all the inevitable differing perspectives that will emerge, and can they together create a systematic set of recommendations before his report is due to the *Healthcare* board? As a member of Wolfgang's telephone conference, please comment on the question blocks A and B.

NOTE

1. The authors would like to thank Frank Kullak, Judith Eidems, Susanne Royer, Andrea Nägel and Sinnet Lorenzen for support.

STRATEGIC FORECASTS AND STAFFING FORMULATION: EXECUTIVE AND MANAGERIAL PLANNING FOR BOSCH-KAZAKHSTAN[1]

By Marion Festing and Manfred Froehlecke[2]

Introduction

Personnel planning and staffing issues are critical success factors in foreign subsidiaries of multinational enterprises. They must be designed in the context of corporate goals and issues and the specific situation in the host country. From a firm-internal perspective, human capital/talent planning and staffing decisions are related to a company's corporate strategy and embedded in the corporate HR strategy. Thus, planning and staffing decisions must be co-ordinated with other HR activities within the MNE, such as HR development. This perspective must then be balanced with a careful consideration of the particularities in the host-country context and the availability of qualified individuals within the external labor market.

In this case study, we will first outline the company background and then describe the situation in the country of interest, which is Kazakhstan. Based on this information **it is your part to take the role of a Bosch corporate HR manager**. You are supposed to analyze both, the company- and country-specific context, and outline a proposed model for personnel planning and staffing of the Bosch subsidiary in Kazakhstan. By drawing on the ethnocentric, polycentric, regiocentric, geocentric (EPRG) Model of Perlmutter (see Chapter 5), please decide which staffing strategy would be the best choice. Discuss on this basis how many expatriates and how many local employees you would plan in the short or medium term at the different hierarchical levels. If you should perceive any further information needs please explicitly define a realistic set of supporting assumptions. Please justify your decision. Which are the advantages and disadvantages of your decision?

Company background: Robert Bosch Group[3]

The Bosch Group is a leading global manufacturer of automotive and industrial technology, consumer goods, and building technology. It was founded in the year 1886 by Robert Bosch (1861–1942) and was called 'Workshop for Precision Mechanics and Electrical Engineering'. The Bosch Group today comprises a manufacturing, sales and after-sales service network of over 350 subsidiaries and regional companies and more than 15,000 Bosch service centers in roughly 150 countries.[4] One statement by the founder Robert Bosch is important to understand the HR philosophy characterizing this MNE: "It is my intention, apart from the alleviation of all kinds of suffering, to promote the moral, physical, and intellectual development of the people". In fiscal 2016, some 283,507 employees generated sales of 47.3 billion euros.[5]

FIGURE 1   Bosch sales by region in 2016

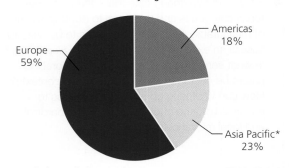

*Including other countries

Source: modified from original 2011 data, Robert Bosch GmbH (2011: 18).

TABLE 1 Bosch employees by region

Worldwide	283,507
Europe	186,602
Of these in Germany	113,557
Americas	33,689
Asia-Pacific (including other regions)	63,216

Source: Robert Bosch GmbH (2011: p. 19).

Even if 77 per cent[6] of the business volume has been generated outside Germany (see Figure 1), about 40 per cent of the total numbers of employees are working in Germany (see Table 1).

Executive and managerial planning (EMP)

The international executive and managerial planning (EMP) activity at Bosch is part of the Strategic Planning Process of the company. Once a year, the global executive staffing needs for selected countries are derived from each division's long-term strategic planning activities. Starting from the current local structure, the required number of managerial positions is determined within the parameters of a rolling eight-year forecast. Various measures are taken to meet the managerial staffing needs. They can be short-term (e.g. hiring of managerial staff from the external labor market, assignment of expatriates) or rather medium/long-term (e.g. development of high-potential employees – see the employee development discussion below), or special programs like Junior Managers Programs (JUMP).

EMP is carried out using a standardized tool from the divisional HR department in co-operation with the various regional HR departments. Aggregated results are analyzed from division, regional, and Robert Bosch World (corporate) levels. Continuous comparisons of the planned vs. actual labor staffing situations provide feedback on those assignments which have to be initiated or redefined.

The planning period of eight years consists of two parts: the input for the first four years stems from business plans and succession planning. The forecast for the last four years is based on more global-macro assumptions, e.g. changes in the leadership projected at a figure of 5 per cent. Therefore, EMP is linked to instruments of employee development in the Bosch Group.

Employee development in the Bosch Group

Bosch understands that employee development is a continuous process of maintaining and further developing those employees' qualifications needed to cope with present and future challenges. A major principle in this respect is the promotion of employees from within Bosch rather than the acquisition of new hires from outside.

HR departments support employees and managers by providing tools and programs and giving guidance. The universally standardized systems and processes for employee development are depicted in Figure 2 (overleaf).

An important procedure for the development of employees is the Management Potential Review (MED, see Figure 2),[7] which is conducted on a worldwide level. It pursues the following objectives:

- full utilization of the company's reserves of high-potential employees without compromising performance standards
- staffing requirements and development planning (middle and upper management) for the upcoming four years (succession planning – see EMP above)
- consistency in planning and a systematic tracking of employee development and career advancement measures
- use of overseas assignments, project tasks, and cross-functional moves as common development measures.

Employees who show an above-average development potential with regard to specialist and management positions will be systematically prepared for the next management level by way of the 'manager development plan' (MDP). Besides outstanding performance, Bosch expects ideal employees to meet a task- or role-relevant personality profile, show a preparedness

FIGURE 2   Instruments of employee development

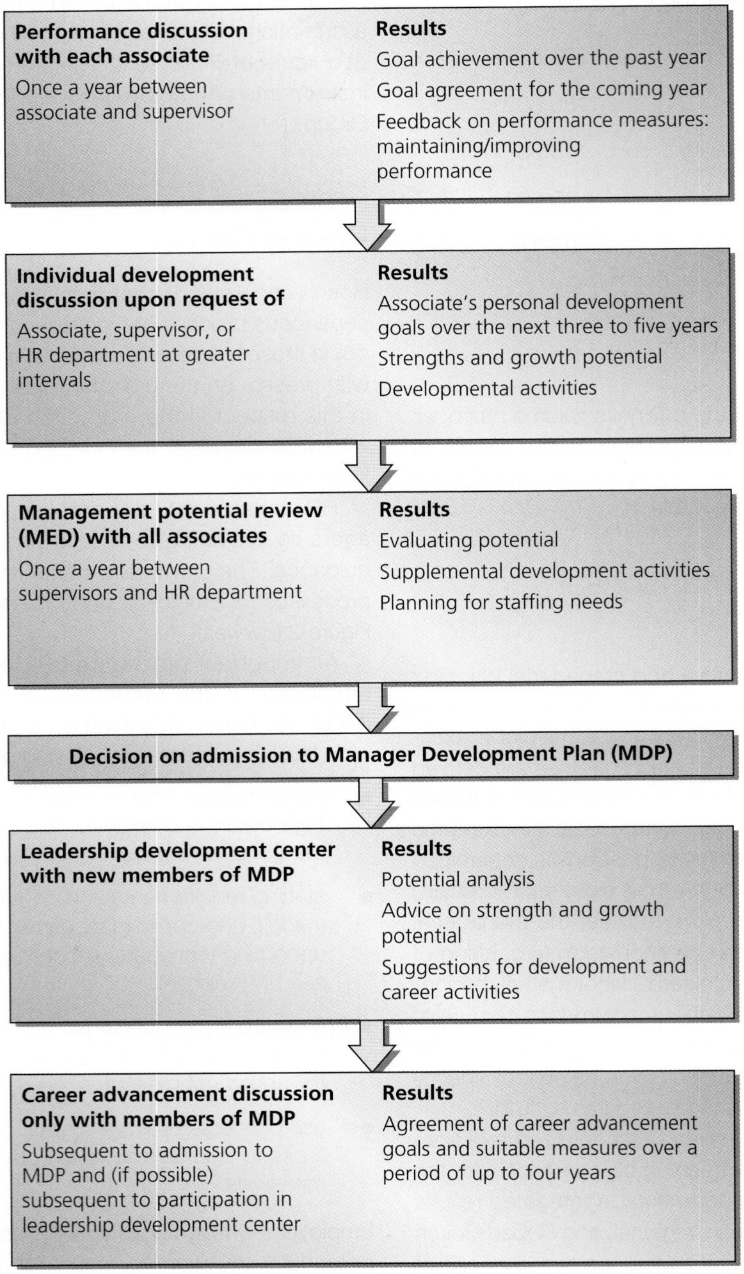

Performance discussion with each associate	Results
Once a year between associate and supervisor	Goal achievement over the past year
	Goal agreement for the coming year
	Feedback on performance measures: maintaining/improving performance

Individual development discussion upon request of	Results
Associate, supervisor, or HR department at greater intervals	Associate's personal development goals over the next three to five years
	Strengths and growth potential
	Developmental activities

Management potential review (MED) with all associates	Results
Once a year between supervisors and HR department	Evaluating potential
	Supplemental development activities
	Planning for staffing needs

Decision on admission to Manager Development Plan (MDP)

Leadership development center with new members of MDP	Results
	Potential analysis
	Advice on strength and growth potential
	Suggestions for development and career activities

Career advancement discussion only with members of MDP	Results
Subsequent to admission to MDP and (if possible) subsequent to participation in leadership development center	Agreement of career advancement goals and suitable measures over a period of up to four years

to take on new tasks and greater responsibilities, and demonstrate general mobility potential as well as a willingness to take on international assignments. MDP is a prerequisite for promotion into managerial ranks.

The preparation of the MDP candidates is a mixture of on-the-job and off-the-job measures with the goal of bringing the employees into the next management level in no more than four years. In many cases the achievement of the career advancement objective is connected with a transfer to a new assignment.

Talent management

As stated before, Bosch mainly relies on hiring and developing talent from within the firm. Consequently, it is important to focus on the acquisition of qualified university graduates and professionals to meet a wider range of potential future managerial requirements. Besides direct entries and local programs, Bosch has a standardized Bosch-wide entry program for junior managers (JUMP).[8] The goal of the program is to recruit junior managers (master's degree with up to three years of professional experience) with the potential to assume a middle management position in six to eight years.

The program lasts one and a half to two years and comprises three to four stages, including a six-month stay abroad as well as a cross-divisional assignment. This form of training emphasizes a common set of worldwide standards, experiences, and activities, and is designed to permit more rigorous and systematic preparations for a range of management tasks.

Expatriates

Currently more than 2200 expatriates[9] are working for Bosch worldwide. An expatriate, as defined by Bosch, is an employee working for more than 24 months outside his or her home country with special contractual conditions (contract in the host country for a limited period of time – normally three to five years – special allowances for hardship, cost of living, etc.). Over 1100 Germans are working in more than 40 countries, approximately 400 employees from Bosch subsidiaries are working in Germany (inpatriates) and roughly 400 TCNs are assigned to locations outside their home countries for limited periods of time. A majority of these employees were assigned due to technical and process expertise, yet some assignments were made for career development or training reasons. Two-thirds of the expatriates are assigned in managerial ranks.

Bosch requires all top managers, beside their other experiences, to have at least two years' international work experience. This international experience is an explicit prerequisite for promotion.

Country-specific features of Kazakhstan[10]

Kazakhstan is located in Central Asia with China, Russia, Kyrgyzstan, Turkmenistan, and Uzbekistan as neighbor states (as shown in Figure 3 overleaf). It covers a total of 2,727,300 sq. km.

The population is 16.4 million inhabitants (1 January 2011), including wide ethnic diversity (with 64.03 per cent Kazakhs, 24.78 per cent Russians and Ukrainians, and 11.19 per cent other ethnic minorities). 54.5 per cent live in cities.[11] Main religions are Islam (70.2 per cent) and Christianity (26.2 per cent).[12] The state language is Kazakh, but Russian is used in everyday business by most of the people and has a status of an official language. Kazakhstan became independent from the former Soviet Union in 1991 and is now a republic characterized by an authoritarian presidential rule. The capital is Astana.

Economic data: the economic situation of the country can be described by a GDP of roughly US$148.1 billion in 2010 versus US$115.3 billion in 2009. The country has an unemployment rate of 5.8 per cent (2010), an economically active population of 8.6 million persons, and comparably low labor cost. The average salary in 2010 equaled about US$527 per month. The export volume in 2010 amounted to US$59.8 billion.[13] Main exports include oil, ferrous and non-ferrous metals, machinery, chemicals, grain, wool, meat, and coal.

Education system: the education system is one of the major concerns of the country. However, this is not reflected in the public expenses for education. Today, the education system consists to a high degree of private education institutions. Funding of research is low and these institutions are dependent on foreign investments. However, a reform of the education system is one part of the strategic planning of the Kazakh Republic. To date, the universities have been restructured according to the guidelines of the Bologna Reform. Even if a relatively high number of persons hold a university degree, companies have problems finding adequately prepared personnel that have skill sets which correspond to the company's needs.

FIGURE 3 Kazakhstan's geographic location

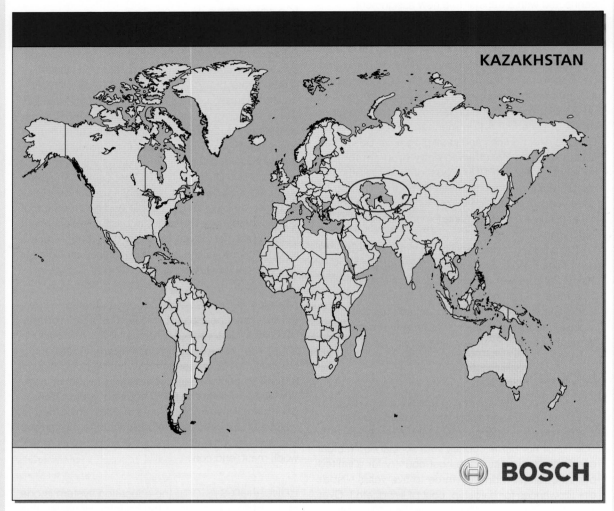

Your task: Executive and managerial planning (EMP) for a subsidiary in Kazakhstan[14]

The Board of Management of the Bosch Group has requested an EMP for Kazakhstan in line with the yearly strategic long-term planning (eight-year forecast – see the third section above). The plan should predict the demand for executive staffing at all levels and for all divisions. It should also specify how the demand will be met, including staffing sources such as the use of expatriates, local MDPs, and special programs, e.g. JUMP or external hires.

As seen from Bosch's corporate perspective, the situation in Kazakhstan is as follows:

● There are four production sites in different rural locations. Each one belongs to a different product division: Gasoline, Bosch-Rexroth, Security Systems, and Diesel Motors.

● Organizations are characterized by different market/product maturity stages: Gasoline, Bosch-Rexroth, and Security Systems are consolidated. Only small or no growth in headcount is planned over the next ten years. In contrast, Diesel is still growing fast, with present headcount plus 30 per cent estimated in the next three years.

FIGURE 4 **Form for situation analysis**

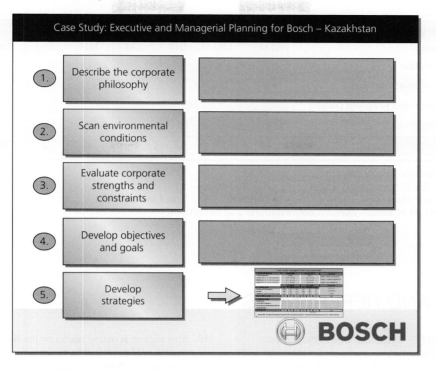

- The labor market for qualified managers and specialists is very small. External hires in Kazakhstan will take much longer to begin work than in equivalent hiring processes operating in Germany. Local candidates have very little mobility and largely lack broader national or international experiences.

- Bosch's major production sites are by and large not attractive locations to most qualified employees.

The high numbers of expatriates were the result of rapid in-country growth, especially for the Diesel site. Higher management positions are currently all filled by expatriates.

Taking the role of HR manager at Bosch, you must address the following three questions:

1 Considering the facts about Kazakhstan, please discuss which staffing strategy – according to the EPRG Model by Perlmutter – would be the most suitable for Kazakhstan. Please justify your answer.

Comment on advantages and disadvantages of your decision.

2 Analyze the company and country-specific situation by using the steps outlined in Figure 4. Plan the number and nature of short/medium-term (2017–2020) as well as long-term (2021–2023) staffing requirements for Bosch Kazakhstan in analogy to the strategic company goals. The staffing plan should consider the sources of staffing (expatriates, employees of the local MDP, or special programs such as the JUMP program or external local staff).

3 Fill in your figures in the planning chart below (see Figure 5 overleaf).

4 Finally, prepare an action plan describing how you will meet managerial staffing targets. Look especially at information provided in the 'Employee development' and 'Talent management' sections of the case for activities and timetables. Write down your action plan.[15]

FIGURE 5 Planning chart

Staffing need	Current 2013–2016			Prognosis 2017–2020			
Sources	LM	MM	UM	LM	MM	UM	Total
Expatriates							
Local MDP attendents							
Development program (JUMP)							
External hires							
Total staffing need	74	35	2	54	36	2	203

MDP: Manager Development Program
JUMP = Junior Managers Program
LM = Lower Management, MM = Middle Management, UM = Upper Management
Source: List of Bosch-specific abbreviations and definitions:

NOTES AND REFERENCES

1. The case study is imaginary. Bosch has no such activities in Kazakhstan. However, the described HR measures reflect current practices within this MNE. Management and Intercultural Leadership, ESCP Europe, Berlin/Germany; Manfred Froehlecke, Vice President, Corporate Department Human Resources Management – Executives, Robert Bosch GmbH, Stuttgart, Germany.

2. Marion Festing is Professor of Human Resource.

3. See also www.bosch.com and Robert Bosch GmbH (2011). Annual Report 2010. Retrieved 10 October 2011 from www.bosch.com/worldsite_startpage/flashbook/GB2010_EN.pdf.

4. Robert Bosch GmbH (2011: 41, 80).

5. Robert Bosch GmbH (2011: 19, 82).

6. Robert Bosch GmbH (2011: 139).

7. MED is the German abbreviation for 'Mitarbeiterentwicklungs-Durchsprache' or, in English, 'Management Potential Review'.

8. The standardized entry program JUMP is still in the implementation phase. Other, comparable programs, e.g. Management Trainee Programs, have been in place for some time.

9. Robert Bosch GmbH (2011: 59).

10. This section is mainly based on the Agency of Statistics of the Republic of Kazakhstan (2011a), Demographic Yearbook of Kazakhstan [in Russian]. Retrieved 18 November 2011 from www.stat.kz/publishing/20111/Dem2010.rar; and Agency of Statistics of the Republic of Kazakhstan (2011b). Kazakhstan in 2010. Retrieved 18 November 2011 from www.eng.stat.kz/publishing/DocLib/2011/Statyear2010.pdf.

11. Agency of Statistics of the Republic of Kazakhstan (2011a: 8, 25).

12. Agency of Statistics of the Republic of Kazakhstan (2010). 2009 Population Census Results [in Russian]. Retrieved 18 November 2011 from www.stat.kz/news/Pages/n2_12_11_10.aspx.

13. Agency of Statistics of the Republic of Kazakhstan (2011b: 9, 10, 167, 400).

14. The case study is imaginary. Bosch has no such activities in Kazakhstan.

15. The case study is simplified. A detailed planning of functional areas is not the intent of this case exercise. The student should learn to ask the right questions about how to source manpower, what challenges the company faces in a difficult environment and what measures must be taken to meet the future demands.

CASE 5

LOCAL AND INTERNATIONAL? MANAGING COMPLEX EMPLOYMENT EXPECTATIONS[1]

By Maike Andresen[2]

Akiko Nishimura is upset and exhausted. She prepares a fresh juice and wants to relax a bit. It is three o'clock in the afternoon and she has just come back to her apartment, situated in a suburb of New Delhi. Today she had an appointment with her HR manager, Mrs Puja Malik, that lasted three hours. Akiko is more than upset about the offer the HR manager made and does not understand the world anymore.

Akiko is 40 years old and was born in Tokyo. After studying management at the University of Tokyo and Wharton Business School in the USA, she started her career with a German multinational manufacturing company in Tokyo in the controlling department. Two years ago her boss offered her an expatriate assignment to New Delhi, India in order to gain international experience and develop her talent further. Her husband, Hiroshi, and two daughters, at that time 12 and 10 years old, immediately agreed to change locations and followed her. Hiroshi interrupted his career as a broker in a multinational bank.

After two years in New Delhi, Hiroshi still could not find an adequate job. Although the whole family enjoyed living in India and Akiko liked her job, Hiroshi became impatient and could not stand his inactivity any more. Through a former client he got to know about a challenging job opportunity in Singapore and successfully applied for the position. Akiko shared Hiroshi's happiness and felt that she wanted to follow him to Singapore, so she contacted her HR manager, Puja Malik, a few weeks ago and started to talk to various people within the organization in her personal network to find out what the options would be and let people know that she was looking. Yesterday, Puja Malik called her and asked for an appointment. They met today in order to talk about several opportunities and the conditions. Whereas the positions were very appealing to Akiko, the conditions were absolutely unreasonable from her perspective. After two hours

Akiko became angry, but her HR manager defended the offer, citing the restructuring of the company and new policies that came up.

"As you know, Akiko, the company started up as a technology venture about 120 years ago with its production located in Germany. In order to be profitable their production and sales needed to increase. Due to limitations in the home market, they expanded internationally in the 1920s, starting with France and quickly followed by several other countries in each of the five continents. In the 1970s the company employed 300,000 people, with more than two-thirds of these outside Germany. Due to this extensive expansion worldwide, as well as an increasingly diverse product line, the idea of controlling the entire organization from the German headquarters was seen as an impossible task. There was a need to organize into smaller, more flexible and more manageable units. Hence, the decision was made to set up a 'national organization' in every country where there were active enterprises. These national organizations were supported by the international organization at headquarters. In the course of the last 20 years these national organizations have grown to be very independent. The executive board saw the need to start focusing on a more user-oriented policy of globalization. In this reorganization process the product divisions gained a more prominent role in the structure. Today, you still see a clear role of both the product divisions but also the country organizations in the corporate structure." Puja Malik pointed a finger at the annual report and outlined the organizational chart (see Figure 1 overleaf).

Puja Malik continued: "Although the company wants to act as one company, it always has to focus on the challenge to work with three quite independent sectors. Today, the company is situated in around 60 countries worldwide with more than 116,000 employees. The HR department is currently involved

FIGURE 1

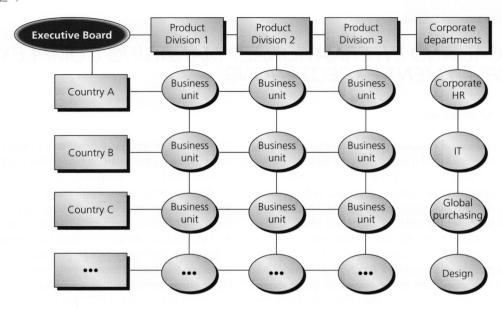

in a change process, moving toward offering more services from shared service centers. One reason for this is the request to be more effective and efficient in the process, especially with the vision to be 'one company'."

Up to the current time, when people have been moving across countries through the company, the standard has been that people mostly moved on a home-based expatriate contract. This rule also applied to Akiko when she expatriated to New Delhi. However, her HR manager recently informed her that there are new rules and that, according to this new policy, her expatriate contract would not be renewed when going to Singapore. Puja Malik argued: "I think in terms of transfer, until a few years ago we were quite generous with our expat policy. So when there was a need to, let's say, shift talent – just like you, Akiko – or people with scarce knowledge around the globe, we just gave them an expat package. But I think people in general are more open for moving around the globe, instead of going for a few years and then wanting to come back. I can see that more people are looking for a career across borders. And this may not be in the form of full expat packages in our company."

Puja Malik obviously saw the need to give a further explanation. She added that, after a long upturn period, the company also has to face the problems of the current economic crisis. This tendency is now forcing the company to rethink their strategy in regard to what they are providing for their employees who are going abroad, in order to manage the costs involved. Until recently, handling international assignments mostly with expatriates seemed the right way of doing things. But the company is facing a new population, those who stay abroad for a longer term or even permanently. "You need to know, Akiko," Puja Malik went on, "we have employees that have been in the same country for eight years on an expat package. But they are not expats anymore! And then you have the globetrotter, those who have had three or four different expat assignments. So they have left their country for more than ten years and we don't know when and if they are coming back. What do you do with them?"

Puja emphasized that this change was placing the company in a position where they were forced to go through and analyze their current policies in regard to international mobility. The intention was to create a cost-effective alternative for this new emerging population.

Akiko's first expatriate assignment to New Delhi

Akiko thinks back to her first move from Tokyo to New Delhi. Things were dealt with differently two years ago. She was part of the talent pool (and still is) and received special treatment. Today this expatriate population comprises about 750 people.

The company uses expatriation for two main reasons: first, as a career assignment for talent to gain international experience, and second, as a job assignment to transfer knowledge across borders. Whereas the company wishes to have 70 per cent of expatriates in a career assignment and 30 per cent on a job assignment, it is now evenly distributed. Moreover, to be able to give an international assignment to as many employees as possible, the company has implemented a policy saying that assignments should be a maximum of three years, and that one employee should not cumulate too many different assignments. Although Akiko originally asked for an assignment of five years in order to facilitate the change of jobs for her husband, this request was turned down. She remembers that she has been told, "If you stay longer in a country, then you block the career of someone else". Akiko agreed and signed a contract for three years.

Her expatriate package is home-based. This means that she was meant to return home to Tokyo after the assignment. Akiko was kept under her home social security, health insurance, and pension plan. The expatriate package comprises all the usual expatriate facilities and services. Akiko got to know that this expatriate package has additional costs for the company of about three times the base salary. That is also why the company wants to limit the extent of these expensive expatriate assignments only to critical positions.

"Akiko," Puja Malik argued, "the company has created different types of packages for different types of international work. When you move to Singapore, the balance between the business and the employee interest leans more in the direction of you. Hence, we offer a different contract and package to you that is called a local international contract." Akiko knows what all this is about and she gets upset. She feels that the company wants to minimize a number of costs by making some of them optional. She thinks that this is not fair as she is still growing in her career and investing a lot into the company in terms of energy and working hours, while giving up her easy life in Tokyo. It was the firm's idea to send her to New Delhi! Moreover, her husband risked his career and her two daughters had to change school and lost contact with their grandparents back in Tokyo.

What is this new local international policy about?

Puja Malik expanded on the new policy: "The local international policy came about last year as a response to an emerging need, especially in Asia. We saw that, due to globalization, there were many foreigners coming here on an expatriate assignment, and many of these foreigners also had a wish to stay. This resulted in a need for using a locally based contract but one that would still attract foreigners to travel. As a pure local contract would not be able to attract these employees, we decided to provide some extra benefits to these local international hires. The local international contract fits between an expatriate and a local package. Even though these transfers are partly employee-initiated, we provide a slow landing into the new country. This means that the host country provides some kind of support" (see Table 1 overleaf).

Akiko understands that the thought behind the local international package is to provide an alternative to the expatriate package for those cases where it is a permanent relocation of an international manager. As the local international package is really a locally based package, the salary is also based on the local salary system in the host country. Puja Malik added: "For the expat package, you know from your own experience, Akiko, that we have a balance sheet approach, where we want to ensure that the purchasing power from the home country is maintained in the host country. . . But for the local international contract, we do not want to link to the home country." Akiko saw a major problem in that and immediately asked what would happen if an international hire moves from a high-income country to a low-income country; Puja Malik confirmed that this would lead to a lowering of the salary, although the company is aware of the fact that under these conditions it might be difficult to attract foreigners on a purely local salary.

TABLE 1   The local international policy

Costs to be covered by the company:

- individual host country-based salary and incentives according to local scheme
- settling-in allowance (to cover the incidental miscellaneous expenses of a move, e.g. temporary accommodation and meals on arrival, school uniforms, and books for school-age children)
- medical check-up
- visa and permits (based on country standards)
- travel costs (outward journey; one home trip during first year)
- optional: allowance for housing and school (50 per cent after year 1, 0 per cent after year two)
- optional: retention bonus
- optional: allowances according to local needs.

FIGURE 2

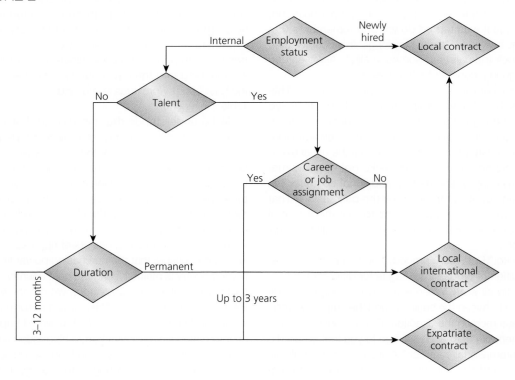

Akiko was irritated and concluded that she would not accept a decrease in her income when going to Singapore. Still, she wanted to understand why all this happens. "Puja, apart from the salary level, what do you mean by the 'slow landing' that you mentioned before?" Puja replied, "This means that, in addition to your salary, the company will give you some extra benefits such as relocation support, settling-in allowance, and one home trip during the first year." Puja pointed to her computer screen and showed Akiko what she could expect when moving to Singapore.

Akiko became aware that, in contrast to her current expatriate contract, no pre-assignment visit would be paid for, she would need to arrange the house-hunting, negotiation, school search, and so on by herself, and all 'normal' costs of living, such as housing or schooling, were to be handled by herself; any financial support would end after two years, when she would be on a normal local contract. "But, Puja, why does this new rule apply to me? I am currently on an expatriate contract – why should I opt out of it now?" Akiko interjected. "This is," replied Puja, "due to our rules. The following elements justify a local international contract: the person in question is an internal employee who is relocated. And the person is not what the company considers a talent or a top-potential employee. Your case, Akiko, is exceptional as you are a talent or top potential, but," Puja Malik emphasized, "your relocation to Singapore is not a career or job assignment. You know, Akiko, your position in Singapore could just as well be filled by a local employee. In addition, we expect these employees to localize." Akiko intervened resolutely: "But things can change fast and I might want to make another move after three to five years if a great opportunity comes up!" Puja Malik reacted: "Yes, but for the time being we treat it like a permanent relocation. And, finally, it is based more on your own initiative and decision to move. Look and see – this is our decision tree" (see Figure 2). Once again, Puja Malik pointed to her computer screen, where she uploaded the decision-making tree on assignment type.

Puja Malik stressed that these decisions are not easy to make. She illustrated that, first of all, in a constantly changing environment it is of key importance for the company to keep their employees mobile. Akiko understands that in a localization process it is therefore of great importance to think ahead about whether the person that is to be put on a local

contract is likely to get a new assignment in another country later on in his or her career. If first a person is localized, the bonds to the new country may often be stronger as some might buy a house or send the children to local schools.

"So, you see, we have our idea and rules. However," Puja Malik added, "I have to admit that I and some of my colleagues in other countries alter the content of the package, and thereby also the applicability, according to where one is coming from. We say that we have a local international contract, but it might not be applicable for Chinese or Indians to Singapore because these are lower-salary countries. I mean, the high salary in Singapore should be able to take care of your cost of living without having to compensate it . . . The business unit in Singapore may just pay for the one way ticket and the shipment to get you there, but they will not be giving you support for the housing and education."

It seemed Puja Malik was in her element as she continued without drawing a breath: "By the way, a major challenge with the local international contract appears to be its applicability in China! China has a lower income rate and a lower social security system than other countries. A current solution to this issue is to provide some extra support for those on a local international contract in China, like extension of education support and housing. Nevertheless, there are still some issues regarding social security which need to be addressed. With China having much lower social security, the risk is that we might lose possible employees as they feel they are sacrificing too much of their own security. This is also the case for pensions. In some countries, foreigners are not obliged to contribute to a state pension, and in others they are not allowed. Local international employees are therefore given a cash equivalent to the state pension and are encouraged to invest in a private fund. But this is a different story. In principle, we need a more standardized practice when it comes to pensions in the future. . ."

Do these new rules make sense?

Akiko zoned out at that point in the extensive conversation and did not follow Puja Malik's explanations as attentively as she should have done. She realized that some of the challenges of her local international package will only be apparent after the first year, when the scaling down starts and the package becomes more like a local package. At that time she will truly start to notice the difference. Before this point, the package is very similar to her current expatriate package. "I will practically be 'poorer' after the scale-down of the benefits," Akiko reflected silently. "The only way out would be to start looking for another local international assignment elsewhere to start on a full local international package again or to go on an expatriate assignment. But Hiroshi and the two girls will not like it."

She started to think about her family: "The two girls will perceive the language barrier to be very scary when going to Singapore. They will need to attend the international school – at least in a transition period. The company needs to realize that it's not just about moving an employee, it's about moving a whole family!" Akiko saw the relocation of the family as the biggest hurdle for her. "We need to feel safe, and know that we are covered if anything happens." Akiko remembered her relocation to New Delhi two years ago. Just the practical things that needed to be taken care of when they moved seemed endless: where to live, schooling, visa, and so on, and all the paperwork they needed to fill out. Meanwhile they had to deal with a new language and new customs.

Akiko summarized in her mind: "These are very practical things that will not be organized for me when going to Singapore. I will have to do everything on my own. So that will be a big challenge and it is very time-consuming, keeping me from doing my actual job!" She realized the difference between moving as an expatriate and moving on a local contract. Moving on expatriate conditions means that more or less everything is taken care of by the company, whereas going on a local contract you need to take care of most things yourself.

Akiko was startled out of her thoughts. "Akiko?" Puja Malik looked directly into her eyes. "Just let me be very honest. Of course, corporate has made it very clear that the number of people put on expat contracts has to be reduced. The background for this is to cut down the costs for these very expensive expatriates. But it is also about creating more equity with the local employees. Put yourself into the shoes of the local employees. Would you, as a local person, accept that you ceaselessly earn less than a foreigner although you do the same job?" Akiko murmured: "No, of course not". She thought that this was an interesting and important aspect.

She asked herself which contract her husband would get according to this system when going to Singapore. Akiko gazed at the decision tree on the computer screen. She realized that, as Hiroshi is changing employers and would therefore enter the company as a new employee, he would automatically get a local contract without any extras. The family's situation would be even worse! She asked herself whether this new further distinction of different types of assignments is really fair or whether it is about creating a second and third class of expatriates.

Akiko felt that she was not concentrating any more and was overloaded with information. And somehow she was also overtaxed by these implications. She did not really know what to do. She wanted to finish the conversation but Puja Malik was already continuing. "I think that in these localization processes it is important that the pros and cons are explained carefully to people because things are difficult to compare. You need to understand that you will maybe have to give up something but in return get something else. For example, you might face a decrease in salary in return for a more favorable pension model, social security system, or lower cost of living. It takes a lot of time and needs to be explained by someone who has a deep understanding of all the aspects that are part of a package." For a second Akiko wondered whether Puja Malik was fishing for compliments and was expecting her to admire her competence. Akiko decided not to react at all.

Puja Malik continued to lecture her about the policies: "For some it might be an attractive opportunity to organize themselves, but for others this will definitely be something they expect the company to take care of. And of course we need to be self-critical: even if this approach seems simpler it is unclear whether such a policy corresponds with the present culture of the company where it is an aim to take care of and support people in a moving process. We need to explain to people what the consequences might be," Puja Malik repeated herself.

Akiko took the chance to end the appointment and stressed that the most important factor with regard to the conversion in contracts has to do with communication. She felt that the loss of the benefits she would receive on a local international contract would not affect her much if she received adequate information about what a change in contract would involve before the move. Akiko stressed that, "It is more important to be clear on managing expectations from both sides since the very beginning, rather than the actual amount in the end". She stood up, said goodbye to her HR manager Puja Malik and left the office silently. She was confused and felt that she was not in the mood to continue her daily work today. Akiko decided to go back home to her apartment situated in a suburb of New Delhi and talk to her husband Hiroshi that night about the situation in order to get an additional perspective.

Questions:

1 Describe the content of a 'traditional' expatriate package, and the reasons of the company to provide such benefits. What limitations do you see in this contract when it comes to handling the company's emerging needs?

2 Make a SWOT analysis of the local international policy using information from the case study.

3 Compare the employers' and employees' needs regarding international mobility on a local international contract. What elements would have to be included in a package if they were to answer to these needs?

4 To what extent do you believe the distinction between the three groups of assignment packages (expatriate contract for expatriates, local international contract for local international hires, and local contract for external international new recruits) to be fair? To this end, (a) refer to equity theory and determine the referent person in each of the three cases; and (b) discuss the role of procedural justice. What can the company do to provoke positive behavioral intentions in reaction to the packages?

5 What does the company need to take into consideration in order to make the local international policy for this new international employee population applicable on a global basis? Formalize your arguments and propose a suggestion of a policy framework.

NOTES AND REFERENCES

1. Copyright Maike Andresen 2016.
2. The case study is inspired by a project done by an international group of four students – Camille Devautour, Tobias Falck, Christina Lindner and Jenny Karine Sundsbø – within the framework of the 'Master Programme in European Human Resource Management' (www.ehrm.de).

CASE 6

EXPATRIATE COMPENSATION AT ROBERT BOSCH GMBH: COPING WITH MODERN MOBILITY CHALLENGES[1]

By Ihar Sahakiants, Marion Festing, Manfred Froehlecke

"I would rather lose money than trust."
Robert Bosch

It was raining in Stuttgart. The new task which Klaus Meier, an employee of Robert Bosch GmbH's German headquarters' central International Assignments department, received last week from his direct supervisor Michael Stein was simultaneously interesting and extremely challenging: a new international assignment policy had to be designed for the whole Bosch Group.

The importance of a new international assignment policy is hard to overestimate. First it may be useful to take a look at some statistics for 2010 from the latest annual report of the Bosch Group.[2] The report, citing 2010 as 'a year of historic recovery' after 'recession on a historic scale', highlighted that Bosch Group sales had skyrocketed by about 24 per cent to 47.3 billion euros. About 41 per cent of the company's total sales were made outside Europe (see Figure 1).

Out of 283,597 worldwide employees, 169,950 – or about 60 per cent of the total headcount – were located outside Germany, the home country of the corporation. Moreover, 34.18 per cent of these personnel were located outside Europe (see Figure 2).

Statistics on the importance of international operations for Robert Bosch were indeed impressive, but the figures on international mobility within the Bosch Group were even more so. In 2010, there were approximately 2200 managers on international projects requiring relocation to a foreign country and lasting over two years, while the number of inpatriates from Asia, the Americas, and Europe on assignments in Germany over the same two-year period reached 400 employees.

Each new location and new market meant additional flows of expatriate and inpatriate employees within the Bosch group. Klaus opened pages 12-13 of the report, which described the highlights of 2010 with respect to new markets, particularly noting:

- *January 18. New presence in Southeast Asia: Bosch Communication Center opens branch in the Philippine capital Manila*

- *May 13. Bosch steps up its activities in Southeast Asia: new headquarters opened in Singapore*

- *July 5. Indian software subsidiary expands its operations: Robert Bosch Engineering and Business Solutions opens location in Vietnam*

- *September 13. Market entry in China. Bosch delivers 40,000 start-stop systems to the automaker ChangAn*

- *October 11. Bosch builds new plant in India: Packaging Technology invests four million euros in a facility near Goa; SB LiMotive opens a new production plant: in Ulsan, Korea, lithium-ion battery cells for hybrid and electric vehicles will be manufactured*

- *November 16. New proving ground in Japan: in the north of Hokkaido, an extended proving ground has been inaugurated – twice as big as the predecessor.*

(Robert Bosch GmbH, 2011: pp. 12–13).

Although a whole range of issues related to international mobility needed to be addressed in the new international assignment policy, Klaus wanted to start with the financial aspects of the operation. As an international mobility professional himself, he knew only too well about the high costs of expatriation. These costs included not only expensive expatriate compensation packages but also huge administration expenses and the costs of expatriate failure, e.g. the premature termination of an assignment. These total costs had the potential to make long-term assignments prohibitively expensive.

FIGURE 1 Bosch Group sales by region, 2010

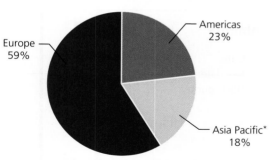

*Including other countries

FIGURE 2 Headcount at Bosch Group by region, as per 1 January 2011

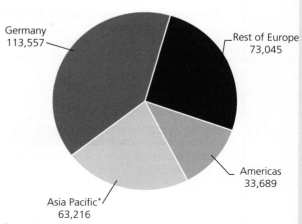

*Including other countries
Source: Robert Bosch GmbH (2011: p. 19).

To gain an overview of the situation at Bosch, Klaus planned to study the details of several actual assignments in various locations. First of all, he examined the personnel file of Hendryk van den Bosch, an old friend of his. He took the first and the last balance sheet calculations prepared for Hendryk's international assignments: an inpatriate assignment to Germany in 1999 and an expatriate assignment to Korea in 2009.

Hendryk van den Bosch started his career at Robert Bosch BV, Noofddorp (Netherlands) as a SAP project coordinator in 1994. In only two years he became manager of the data processing department for the regional subsidiary in Holland. From 1997, he was responsible for the whole Benelux region (Belgium, the Netherlands, and Luxembourg). In 1999, he accepted the position of system planning department manager at the company's headquarters in Stuttgart, Germany.

The balance sheet calculation for his new position in Germany was a standard one used for expatriate assignments within the Bosch Group (see Figure 3 overleaf). At that time, there was no single currency in Europe. Thus, according to the company rule, expatriate compensation had to be paid in the host country, although was calculated both in Holland florins (HFL) and Deutsche marks (DEM) – the national currencies before the Euro. In doing so, 35 per cent of the net income was guaranteed in the home-country currency in order to minimize any currency exchange risks for the expatriate employee. The host-country currency portion of pay was adjusted at the end of each year to eliminate possible negative effects arising from exchange rate fluctuations. Klaus knew about the importance of currency adjustment for expatriates. Although the exchange rate between HFL and DEM had been relatively stable over the years, it was a big issue in many other countries, where the exchange rate of local currencies fluctuated significantly in relation to the Deutsche mark or euro.

The host-country component of Hendryk's net salary (65 per cent of the salary paid in host-country currency) was adjusted for cost-of-living expenses, on top of which a foreign assignment bonus was provided. There were no further costs related to the foreign assignment in the host country. It was Hendryk's decision to remain in the Dutch social security system in accordance with Regulation (EEC) No. 1408/71, while housing expenses in Germany were covered by the employer. As the rent costs in the home country had been previously borne by Hendryk from his net income, and would not be incurred during his assignment in Germany, a housing expenses *'Rent in Home Country'* equivalent (i.e. an equivalent apartment rent in the home country to the amount of 18,600 HFL) was deducted from the benefits component. Hendryk's rent in the host country was therefore zero because, in line with the assignments guideline, this amount was paid directly by Bosch.

On 1 September 2003, Hendryk van den Bosch returned to Stuttgart, Germany as the Head of the Organization and Information Systems unit from his most recent assignment in Brazil. In 2009, he was expatriated again, this time to Korea as Regional Sales Director.

FIGURE 3 Balance sheet for the assignment to Germany[3]

Remuneration for International Assignments　⊕ BOSCH

Surname:	van den Bosch	Date:	18.12.1998
First name:	Hendryk	Key date:	01.01.1999
Home country:	Netherlands	Host country:	Germany
Family status:	Married		

	HFL 1=	**DEM** 0.8872

Home country annual salary

	HFL	DEM
Gross domestic salary equivalent salary (BIVE I)	155,000	
+ Annual bonus		
= BIVE II	155,000	
× work time factor　　40.0 ÷ 40.0　　1.00		
= BIVE III	155,000	
− Income Tax	46,945	
− Employee's social security contributions to pension insurance	13,801	
− Employee's social security contributions to unemployment insurance	3316	
− Employee's social security contributions to health insurance	1715	
= Net domestic equivalent	89,223	

Host country component

	HFL	DEM
65% of net domestic equivalent	57,995	51,453
× Cost of living index: Home country = 100, Host = 101.4182		52,183

Host country component

	HFL	DEM
35% of net domestic equivalent　*(guaranteed in HFL)*	31,228	27,706

Benefits component

	HFL	DEM
+ Foreign assignment bonus	31,000	
+ Child allowance	0	
+/− Company car	0	
− Rent in home country	18,600	
(Total guaranteed in HFL)	12,400	11,001
+ Rent in host country		0
+ Extra costs in host country		0
		11,001

Payment of expatriate salary

	HFL	DEM
Total net remuneration		90,889
+ Employee's social security contributions to pension insurance	13,801	12,244
+ Employee's social security contributions to unemployment insurance	3316	2942
+ Employee's social security contributions to health insurance	1715	1522
Total net remuneration including home country social security		107,597
Of which amount guaranteed in HFL	*43,628*	*38,707*

The pay calculation for his assignment to Korea was more complex (see Figure 4 overleaf). At that point, Hendryk had two children, which meant additional expenses in the host country as well as the loss of child allowance in Germany (then 1848 euros per child, per year). However, the latter was compensated by Robert Bosch GmbH in accordance with internal company policy, while housing expenses in the host country were again borne by the company.

A couple of years prior to that, several changes were introduced in the assignment policy, triggered initially by increasingly refined market data comparisons. For instance, a change of the cost-of-living data provider made it possible to make a differentiated use of indices and technically sophisticated and detailed calculations. Although this also contributed to a reduction in assignment costs for the Bosch Group, the primary goal of these changes in the compensation policy was to offer assignment conditions in line with local market conditions.

According to the new policy, the foreign assignment allowance was determined and frozen at the beginning of the assignment. As such, cost-of-living calculations were based on two indices: a more generous *Standard Home Base Index* and a so-called *Cost Effective Home Base* (CEHB) *Index*. The Standard Home Base Index was used in the first and second years of the assignment, whereas, only starting from the third year, expatriate compensation was calculated based on the CEHB Index. The decision to use the latter index was based on the assumption that cost of living decreases during the course of an assignment. This logic was based on the notion that, over time, an expatriate employee would be expected to use less expensive shopping opportunities and to refrain from expensive imports by increasingly using cheaper local products. However, calculations for the first year were also based on the CEHB Index in order to indicate to the expatriate his future income and to make clear that using the Standard Home Base Index represented more generous support at the start of an international assignment. Therefore, the difference between CEHB-based and Standard Home Base Index-based income was compensated as a *cost-of-living supplement.* Furthermore, lump-sum payments were used in order to facilitate cost control.

Klaus knew all too well how a group discussion on ways to reduce expatriation costs might proceed. One of the proposed solutions was to use increasingly alternative forms of international assignments, including short-term international assignments lasting up to one year, frequent flyer assignments, commuter and rotational assignments, global virtual teams, and so on. Many of these forms were becoming more and more popular due to the rapid development of telecommunication technologies and transport, and they were being used increasingly at Bosch. Moreover, one of the explicit goals of the Bosch Group was to increase the percentage of local senior executives in its foreign locations to at least 80 per cent. However, although it was a strong cost-reducing factor, this measure could not possibly hinder the rapid increase of standard expatriate assignments given the importance of international markets. Thus, Klaus had to consider first and foremost a number of cost reduction opportunities related to standard expatriate assignments.

Based on an analysis of multiple sources stemming from the academic literature, as well as management consulting and practitioner publications, Klaus made a list of feasible potential cost-reducing solutions. In order to form an idea of the prevalence of these measures among leading international companies, he checked the latest 'Global Assignment Policies and Practices' survey by KPMG.[4] He started his analysis with the top five positions on the list:

- **Relocation allowance.** A way to reduce costs related to the relocation allowance is to provide lump-sum payments at the beginning and at the end of an assignment. According to the KPMG survey about 54 per cent of all companies, including 47 per cent of European participants, implement this policy. Only 13 per cent of respondents worldwide do not provide any relocation allowance at all.

- **Efficient calculations of the cost-of-living allowance.** There is a clear trend among multinationals to increasingly implement an 'efficient purchaser index' in their cost-of-living calculations. According to the KPMG survey, 32 per cent of all responding companies use this index, a 10 per cent increase since 2003.

- **Cap on allowances.** Capping expatriate allowances makes it possible to reduce significantly the overall costs of foreign assignments. All allowances, including the cost-of-living, hardship, or other company-specific allowances, can be frozen for expatriates with an expatriate income exceeding a certain level. The KMPG survey shows that the majority of companies still do not cap the major allowances.

FIGURE 4   Balance sheet for the assignment to Korea

Remuneration for International Assignments   ⊚ BOSCH

Name:	Hendrik van den Bosch	Reason for calculation:	Start of assignment
Personnel number:	70186740	Valid from:	01.01.2009
Job level:	SL3		Start of assignment
Sending unit:	DS	Comment:	
Receiving unit:	RBKR	Foreign assignment allowance:	20.00% frozen at start of contract
Family status:	With spouse in Host Country	COL-factor CEHB:	1.4189
No of accompanying children:	2.0	Exchange rate:	1 EUR 1,281.000 KRW

	EUR	KRW
Basic calculation – home country annual salary		
Comparative gross domestic salary (BIVE I)	**127,000**	
BIVE II	**127,000**	
× working time factor (40.0–> 40.0 hours)	127,000	
BIVE III (total gross)	**127,000**	
– Income tax (III/2.0)	34,984	
– Reunification surcharge	1656	
– Employee's social security contributions to pension insurance	6328	
– Employee's social security contributions to unemployment insurance	1049	
– Employee's social security contributions to health insurance	3370	
– Employee's social security contributions to nursing insurance	367	
Comparative net domestic salary	79,246	
Expatriate salary		
65% host country (spendable) component	73,087	93,624,956
+ Cost of living supplement		14,448,180
35% home country (savings) component (of net = guaranteed in home currency)	27,736	
Expatriate allowances		
+ Foreign assignment allowance	15,849	
+ Child allowance	3696	
+ Compensation for Bosch Vorsorge Plan	600	
+ Additional payments I	3810	
+ Health insurance	5904	
+ Reimbursement minimal contribution to health insurance	439	
+ Reimbursement minimal contribution to nursing care insurance	51	
– Standard deduction for home country housing costs	15,240	
+ Extra costs in host country		6,900,000
Amount guaranteed in host currency		115,005,136
Amount guaranteed in home currency	42,845	54,884,573
Total net remuneration in host currency		169,889,709
+ Employee's social security contributions to pension insurance	6328	8,106,168
+ Employee's social security contributions to unemployment insurance	1049	1,343,769
Total net remuneration in host currency including home social security		179,339,646
Amount guaranteed in home currency including social security	50,222	
Payment of expatriate salary		
Payment of amount guaranteed in home currency annual	42,845	
Payment of amount guaranteed in home currency monthly	3570	
Remaining amount paid in host currency annual		115,005,136
Remaining amount paid in host currency monthly		9,583,761
One-time payments on beginning of assignment		
Relocation allowance		13,860,959
Electrical allowance	5000	

- **Housing allowance and/or costs.** There are several ways to reduce housing costs. One way is to select residence areas comparable to those used by local employees in comparable positions, thus avoiding expensive residence areas being used mainly by expatriate employees. Another way is to follow the recommendations of housing data providers and to offer additional incentives for finding housing less expensive than the standard cost recommendations. However, as reported by KPMG, the overwhelming majority of companies (82 per cent) still do not provide this type of incentive.

- **Travel expenses.** There is a trend to provide 'economy-class' travels to expatriate employees. About 56 per cent of companies surveyed by KMPG implement such a policy, 3 per cent more than in 2010.

Many of the above cost reduction measures were already being implemented at Bosch. Apart from the allowances, yearly economy-class flights to the home country had become the standard option for company travel. However, longer flights for business reasons could still be carried out using business class. The challenge, however, was to further improve existing policies by comparing several cost options, data providers, and outsourcing alternatives. This would be just the first step towards designing an all-encompassing assignment policy, as further steps would analyze tax-efficient ways of providing expatriate perquisites, as well as organize taxation and social security coverage during international assignments in co-operation with a team of international legal advisors.

Nevertheless, enthusiastic and confident of success as he was, Klaus knew that designing a new international assignment policy was going to be a long and drawn-out process involving multiple calculations as well as negotiations with colleagues and external mobility services providers. This was especially the case because the cost issue was only one aspect of the wider issue of the co-ordinated and strategically effective use of international assignments. There were many more related concerns – such as motivating potential expatriates, the impact of international assignments on professional careers, repatriation management, dual-career issues, and family income. The more Klaus thought about it, the more he saw the linkages and implications operating across multiple HR practices and multiple product and geographic units.

The rain had passed through the city and shafts of sunlight appeared through the grey clouds. Klaus recalled the themes of 'courage, curiosity, and change' at the recent corporate meeting he had attended in Berlin. The Berlin conference was one of some 850 activities staged worldwide in 2011 to mark the 125th anniversary of the Bosch company and the 150th anniversary of Robert Bosch's birth. He returned to his desk and began working to apply these themes.

Questions:

1 Why did Bosch state the cost-of-living allowance amount as a CEHB-based sum and a separate cost-of-living supplement in the first and the second years of the assignment in the balance sheet for Korea?

2 Which expatriate compensation elements at Bosch Group were already based on cost-reduction considerations listed in the case study? Please suggest ways in which these could be improved further.

3 What further cost-reduction measures could be implemented?

4 Do you believe it is possible to design a Bosch Group international assignment policy covering both expatriate and inpatriate employees at all international locations?

5 One of the measures used to reduce the costs of expatriation was to outsource elements of the administration function to external service providers. Please discuss the advantages and disadvantages of such a policy.

6 Do you believe that alternative assignments can substitute for traditional expatriate assignments in the long run? Please discuss the major opportunities and barriers.

7 What are the major barriers to the localization of expatriate managers?

8 Many international companies do not provide any additional foreign assignment allowances (e.g. relocation or hardship allowance). Do you think it would have been feasible to implement this system at Bosch? What would be the related advantages and disadvantages?

NOTES AND REFERENCES

1. While general information about the Bosch Group and sheets for calculating expatriate salaries reflect real Bosch examples, the Klaus Meier story regarding his task to further develop the organization's international assignment policy has been invented for instructive reasons.

2. Robert Bosch GmbH (2011). Annual Report 2010. Retrieved 10 October 2011 from www.bosch.com/ worldsite_startpage/flashbook/GB2010_EN.pdf.

3. BIVE is a German-language abbreviation internally used within the Bosch Group and denoting comparative gross domestic salary. As no bonus was provided and the hours worked equalled the predetermined plan, the same amounts were indicated under BIVE I, BIVE II and BIVE III.

4. KPMG (2011). Global Assignment Policies and Practices. Survey 2011. Retrieved 12 October 2011 from www .kpmginstitutes.com/taxwatch/insights/2011/pdf/ gapp-survey-2011.pdf.

CASE 7

BALANCING VALUES: AN INDIAN PERSPECTIVE ON CORPORATE VALUES FROM SCANDINAVIA

By Martine Cardel Gertsen and Mette Zølner

ACT 1

Bangalore, 17 October 2016, 8.45 a.m.

Amrita Chopra, a senior financial manager in Pharmaz India, is sitting in the back seat of one of the company cars while the driver slowly but skilfully manoeuvers the car forward through Bangalore's dense traffic jam, using the horn diligently. This morning, Amrita is on her way to a meeting with her new immediate superior, a recently arrived expatriate, Niels Nielsen. He has told her that he wants them to discuss the alignment of local work procedures with Pharmaz's corporate values.

Pharmaz India

Pharmaz India in Bangalore is a subsidiary of a multinational pharmaceutical company headquartered in Denmark. Pharmaz employs around 6 000 people; 2 500 work in Denmark, the rest in subsidiaries in more than 30 countries around the world. Pharmaz's top management, and the Chief Executive Officer (CEO) in particular, like to characterize the company as 'value-driven'. At Pharmaz the corporate culture is taken very seriously, not least at the headquarters. It has developed slowly as the company has grown over the years, for the first many years primarily within the borders of Denmark. But now, as the company finds itself in a process of rapid globalization, the headquarters is making very conscious efforts to disseminate the corporate culture across borders.

Pharmaz is strongly focused on research, and this is reflected in its corporate culture and values. The company attempts to create a learning environment for all employees, not just those working in R&D. Pharmaz's website and latest annual report state: "New ideas are our business and what we live from. Therefore our corporate culture strongly encourages all our employees, regardless of their position, to learn continuously and to work together creatively." In accordance with this ideal, three corporate core values have been formulated:

- empowerment, implying that all employees should be able to make independent decisions within their respective areas of responsibility

- equal opportunities for all employees to develop their competences and advance in their careers

- openness in communication between employees at all levels in order to further free exchange of knowledge and ideas.

Pharmaz India has been in existence since 1983, but until 2005 it was a local sales office with 10–15 employees. The local management was allowed considerable latitude since the subsidiary's strategic importance to the company was limited. In 2005 this situation changed when Pharmaz established an offshore financial services center in Bangalore. This location, known as the 'Silicon Valley of India', offers low costs and qualified, English-speaking professionals in the relevant fields. The process was initiated with two local employees, and gradually more employees were recruited to form teams responsible for registration of invoices and various accounting and controlling tasks. At first, the center only performed tasks for the headquarters in Denmark. After a couple of years, the center began expanding more rapidly, and tasks requiring collaboration with employees in other subsidiaries were gradually introduced. Today, the center employs 50 people and this number is expected to grow to more than 130 employees in the course of the next two years as more financial activities will be transferred from other parts of Pharmaz to India.

In 2007, Pharmaz acquired a part of a locally owned Indian company in order to be able to establish its own production facilities, including some R&D activities, in Bangalore. The acquisition added more than 100 employees to Pharmaz India's workforce. So today Pharmaz India comprises, in addition to various staff functions such as HR, a production unit, a R&D department, a sales department, and a financial services center. The subsidiary employs more than 200 and, according to Pharmaz's plans, a considerable number of new people will be recruited in the years to come, not just in the services center. Thus, Pharmaz India has achieved crucial strategic importance and has become a center for growth. This increased focus on Pharmaz India means that the management at headquarters is very keen that the corporate values of empowerment, equal opportunities and openness are fully implemented, or 'lived', as the top managers like to put it, in the subsidiary.

The senior financial manager and the challenges she is facing

Amrita Chopra is 45 years old and she has worked for Pharmaz for three years. One of the company drivers takes her to the office in the morning around 8 a.m. and picks her up in the evening around 6 p.m. Although she lives only 20 km away the journey takes about an hour. She prefers not driving herself on the bumpy and chaotic roads, where holes in the asphalt, motorbikes, bikes, dogs, cows, and pedestrians abound. Amrita also appreciates the opportunity to arrive home without being too stressed, especially because she has a family to take care of; she is married and has two sons who are 12 and 15 years old.

The financial services center where Amrita works is divided in two sections: one providing financial services to the headquarters and subsidiaries in Europe, and one providing services to the Pharmaz subsidiaries Asia, the USA, and Latin America. Amrita heads the first section where currently 20 people work; they are divided into four teams. As for Amrita's background, she has a master's degree in finance from a reputable Indian university and is a chartered accountant. She was born in Delhi, where she lived until she got married. Her husband is in the hi-tech business, and Bangalore seemed to be the best place for him to

be in terms of enhanced chances for career progress, so the couple decided to move there.

Until Amrita got the job as a senior financial manager with Pharmaz, she worked in the finance department of a locally owned information technology (IT) company. She achieved good results in her former job, but she often felt that she had to struggle to obtain respect in the company that was very male dominated and managed in a way she thinks of as 'traditionally Indian'. She was the first employee ever in the company to take maternity leave and some of her male colleagues seemed genuinely surprised when she came back to work after her leave. She did not receive any training, the pay was average and her working hours were long. Still, she was not unhappy in her former job. Her work was interesting and she always felt that she had the support of the CEO, who did his best to help her when problems occurred. By comparison, Pharmaz offers more advantageous working conditions. The salary is better, though admittedly not quite as good as in some other international companies in the area. Amrita has been on various types of training in Denmark and she appreciates that the company invests in her professional development in this way. At Pharmaz there is a lot of talk about work–life balance, especially from the headquarters. The idea is that employees should be able to have shorter working days and more flexibility in their schedules because of more efficient organization of work. As a manager, Amrita is rarely able to leave very early, but her working days are still shorter than they used to be, which makes it possible for her to spend more time with her family.

Although Amrita likes her job, her family is her first priority. Her husband earns enough for all of them to live comfortably, and she has at times been tempted to stay at home and be a full-time housewife. But it seems to her that it would somehow be a waste, considering her education. Also, since they live with her in-laws, there is always someone at home to look after the children and the house, and they have a live-in maid who does most of the housework. Like her own family, Amrita's in-laws are quite liberal in their attitudes to women's roles. When they moved in, they told Amrita: "You just go ahead and look for a job; we will take care of the children." Amrita is glad that they have given her this opportunity to continue her career.

Still, life in Pharmaz is not uncomplicated. Amrita finds that the corporate values are in line with her own ideas of what management ought to be, at least ideally, but she finds them difficult to implement in an Indian context. As a middle manager she often feels squeezed between the headquarters' wishes and the expectations of her employees. Visiting managers from headquarters have voiced that they find her management style a little too authoritarian and have encouraged her to "act more like a coach, delegate more, and give fewer orders". Amrita has argued that, as the senior financial manager, the results of the section are her responsibility. Therefore, she sees it as her job to tell her subordinates what is good and what is not good enough so that they can improve their performance. The managers from headquarters have answered that of course she should intervene if someone keeps making mistakes, but in general they believe the employees would learn more from being empowered to work independently. Amrita remains unconvinced, but as a manager in a subsidiary she feels compelled to follow directions from the headquarters. So she delegates more and gives fewer orders. Yet, her employees complain that she expects too much of them when she tries to adjust her behavior to the headquarters' suggestions in this way. If she leaves it up to them how to carry out their tasks and how to organize their work, some of them just keep coming back to her and asking for directions anyway. Others appear to interpret this approach as an indication that she does not find their work important and, consequently, they get very little done. There are exceptions, of course – a few of the most competent financial analysts seem to thrive without managerial interference.

Instilling and maintaining a collaborative spirit in the teams can be quite a challenge, too. At the moment three of the teams function well, but the situation has become quite tense in the fourth team. Recently, the team has made a few regrettable mistakes that appeared to be due to internal misunderstandings and lack of communication. Amrita has been told that this resulted in open quarrels between the team members, but she did not witness this herself. So far, no one has been willing to tell her exactly what the problem is and the team leader, Balvinder Singh, is evading her questions. It is clear to her, though, that communication has not flown easily between the team members since the arrival of her section's newest employee, Shankar Savarkar, a competent chartered accountant. Shankar comes from a Brahmin family and thus belongs to the highest-ranking caste according to the traditional Indian view. Amrita is concerned that he tends to act in a rather standoffish manner with Balvinder and two other members of his team, and she has noticed that he never eats lunch with them. She thinks that the team members' different backgrounds may be at the root of the team's problems, even though she feels that this ought not to be so in a professional working environment. It is a delicate issue. According to Indian legislation, the higher castes are not to enjoy any special privileges in the workplace, and caste is never openly discussed in Pharmaz. Amrita is at a loss at what to do to address the team's difficulties.

The car arrives at Bangalore's largest technology park and stops at the entrance to wait while the security guards check the vehicles in front. Next to the line of cars, employees queue up and move slowly through the gates as the guards finish checking their entrance cards. As a senior manager and a familiar face, Amrita simply nods to the security guards and her car enters the technology park, which offers quite a change of scenery compared to the buzzing, dusty road lined with the shacks of the poor in front of the larger houses. In the park, all the buildings are tall and sleek, constructed in glass and steel, and between them the green lawns are dotted with well-kept flower beds.

The company car lets Amrita off in front of the building where Pharmaz India is located, now occupying three full floors. Amrita gets out of the car, habitually taking care not to disarrange her clothes in the process. She almost always dresses in a traditional Indian sari, and today she has chosen one of her best, a bright pink one, to feel as confident as possible during the important meeting. She wears a bindi (a dot of color, usually red, applied in the center of the forehead) of a matching shade. Her hair style is the same as always: a long black plait. Generally, the employees in Pharmaz dress smartly but relatively informally. A few women wear jeans and Western-style shirts or blouses, but the majority are dressed traditionally in either a salwar kameez (loose trousers and a long tunic) or a sari. The men wear shirts with long sleeves and dark trousers, but normally jackets and ties are only worn for the occasions of important external meetings. Amrita takes the lift to go to the ninth floor where the financial services center is located.

On her way to the meeting she stops by to say hello to the regional manager, Ganesh Karanth. The regional manager has been in Pharmaz India since the subsidiary was founded and has worked his way to the top. His long career in Pharmaz has given him a lot of insight into the company and Amrita likes talking things through with him before important meetings such as the one she has today. She would like to get an idea of what the rest of the management in Pharmaz India thinks of Niels' approach and plans. Also, she would like to ask the regional manager for advice on how to solve the problems in Balvinder's team. Although Ganesh has of course never said so, she knows that he is a Brahmin because of his name, his food preferences, and his social network of other Brahmins. Amrita would not want to raise the topic of caste explicitly with Ganesh. But she thinks that he will understand without her having to spell it out. And she has seen him chatting with Shankar several times, so he may already be familiar with the situation in the team. But unfortunately, Ganesh is not in his office this morning.

Niels texts her that he is delayed. Stuck in a traffic jam. Amrita asks the new 'chai wallah' to bring her a tea. He is a thin, quiet man of middle age, and as she expects him to speak poor English she addresses him in Hindi. She is still not comfortable with the local language, Kannada, since she is not from Bangalore originally. Not that it matters very much in her daily life, otherwise she would probably have learned it by now. But most people in the fast-growing city of Bangalore seem to be from somewhere else, especially the professionals. English is Pharmaz's official corporate language and here everybody except the 'chai wallahs' and the janitors speaks it fluently and uses it for all work-related purposes. Amrita gets her hot tea, and as she sips at her cup absentmindedly she is getting increasingly impatient and nervous.

The expatriate finance director and his plans

Amrita is always apprehensive before meeting with Niels, and she knows that today's discussion will be difficult. His direct and demanding way of communicating was initially a bit of a shock to Amrita and several of her colleagues, and she still finds it a challenge. Niels urges and expects a free exchange of ideas, and Amrita finds that discussions with him can be quite inspirational. He is good at showing his appreciation when he likes the viewpoints and ideas presented. Sometimes, however, he can be difficult to convince. This, in Amrita's experience, is especially the case when your arguments refer to the particularities of the Indian context and the need to bend Pharmaz's corporate values in order to put them into practice in a realistic manner.

Niels took up his position as finance director in Pharmaz India three months ago. He is Danish, 40 years old, and he already has many years of experience in Pharmaz, not only from headquarters but also from the subsidiaries in Mexico, China, and Spain. He insists that everybody should use his first name and dislikes it when subordinates address him as 'Sir'. Amrita remembers when he first corrected her in this regard with the explanation that "what counts and deserves respect is not a person's title, but his or her skills and competences". Niels' management style is strongly embedded in the company's ideas about empowerment, equal opportunities, and openness. And, in line with Pharmaz headquarters' aspirations, he never misses a chance to practice these values conspicuously within the Indian organization. Though Niels' knowledge of the organizational context is limited after just three months in Bangalore, he has strong opinions about what to do and what not to do. He believes in implementing the corporate culture by managing explicitly through the values – for instance, with a view to speeding up decision-making processes by minimizing control and bureaucracy. As far as practically possible, he believes that decisions are to be made by the people who will carry them out and live with them in their daily work. Now he finds that the time has come to reorganize the work processes in the financial services teams so that they reflect Pharmaz's business model and values better. And he has decided to start with the four teams in Amrita's section.

Amrita is not against changes being made in her teams, but she hopes to be able to make Niels realize that you cannot go all the way with Pharmaz's management style and values right away. Moreover, she would also like to use the opportunity to suggest that a way of motivating employees to accept more responsibility in their daily work would be promotions and prices. She has already mentioned this idea briefly to Niels, but she is not sure what he thought about it. He seemed to find it a bit amusing, somehow, so maybe he just did not get the point. So this time, perhaps, she should also emphasize that promotions and prices can be important instruments for Pharmaz to use in order to retain their qualified employees in the competitive and dynamic Bangalorian labor market for financial experts.

Question:

● Identify the main issues raised and discuss how they may be explained in terms of the cultural and institutional contexts of Pharmaz in general and Pharmaz India in particular.

ACT 2

Pharmaz India's office in Bangalore, 17 October 2016, 9.30 a.m.

Amrita and Niels meet to discuss challenges and possible courses of action

Niels arrives 30 minutes late. He is dressed in jeans, a short-sleeved blue shirt and sandals. Amrita reflects that, with his laidback attire, one could almost mistake him for one of the American tourists she saw in Goa last month when she spent a long weekend there with her family. He apologizes so profusely for having kept her waiting that it almost makes Amrita feel as if he is the subordinate and she the superior. Although it makes her slightly uncomfortable, it also makes her feel that he respects her as a person, so she is a little more at ease when Niels comes straight to the point and addresses the issues he would like to see solved.

Niels begins by showing her a long email sent to him by Sebastian Skram, the corporate finance director. It is in Danish (and Amrita is tempted to remind him that the corporate language is English, but she checks herself), so Niels translates for her. The mail reads:

Dear Niels,
[Some initial small talk about the bleak weather in Copenhagen and enquiries about the well-being of Niels' family; he leaves this part out when translating to Amrita.] As you no doubt remember, we took some measures last year here in the corporate finance department at headquarters to make sure that our corporate values of empowerment and open knowledge sharing are implemented as fully as possible. Among other things we
redefined the team leaders' job descriptions so that they now spend less time on supervision and more time on development of new services and procedures in dialogue with our colleagues from the departments involved. They do, of course, still involve themselves in the teams' tasks, especially the more complex ones, but they spend less time following up and checking the team members' work. Although this means that an occasional minor error slips through from time to time, we have found that it has freed up a lot of resources for more creative purposes. In addition, we have also introduced a team bonus to promote the collaborative spirit. It is a very minor part of the employees' pay, so the psychological aspect of the incentive has probably been more important than the money in itself. The team leaders as well as the team members find that the changes have made their jobs more interesting – as clearly reflected in our latest employee satisfaction survey. I mentioned this to Emil [Emil Bistrup, the corporate CEO of Pharmaz] when we had lunch together yesterday, and he was very enthusiastic about it – you know how much weight he attaches to our corporate values. He suggested that similar efforts be made in the financial services center in Bangalore; with the plans for its growth it will soon be more important to the company than our corporate finance department here. I promised to take it up with you, but I realize that other measures may be more appropriate in Bangalore, so I leave that up to your judgement entirely. What matters is the result: the best possible implementation of our corporate values. If you believe it will be helpful I'm sure we can find the means in the budget to put the center's employees through a more elaborate course in our corporate values. Anyway, think about it and let me know what you plan to do and how I can assist you.
Best regards,
Sebastian

The mail makes it clear to Amrita that the financial services center has the attention of the top management, and although this may be an advantage in her future career, she cannot help feeling a little apprehensive about it. Also, she finds it puzzling that the corporate finance director appears to say in his mail that he does not see an occasional error as a problem. She thinks that is a risky attitude in a finance department, but she decides not to mention this to Niels as she does not wish to appear overly critical of her superiors. She asks Niels what he intends to do, and he says that the mail only underlines the need for changes that would be necessary anyway. He elaborates: the growth plans for the financial services center mean that the future and present employees need to be empowered to work out more solutions independently – or together in their teams, but without constant managerial input and follow-up. As long as the center's tasks primarily consisted in invoicing for the headquarters and other relatively routine-oriented tasks, this was less important. But now the center is expected to carry out more and more complicated tasks, not just for the headquarters but also for many different subsidiaries.

Colleagues from all over the world call the center when they need help to solve a wide variety of financial issues. And Niels has received some complaints that, although everybody is very friendly on the phone, it sometimes takes several days to get an answer to a fairly straightforward question. Niels knows that the center's employees have all been very carefully selected and, as he sees it, their technical qualifications as financial experts cannot be questioned. So the problem, he says, is not that they are unable to respond, but rather that their work procedures are too bureaucratic and that the employees do not feel empowered to do much without the explicit approval of their team leader. In many cases they will also wait for the approval of their senior financial manager, Amrita. He would like her to spend less of her time exercising micromanagement and more time on actively empowering her subordinates.

In addition, Niels goes on, it has been mentioned by several of the center's users that the team members do not seem to know very much about each other's work, so when the person they have talked to previously is off or at a meeting, no one else on the team seems to be able to help them or to know anything about the issue. He concludes that more knowledge sharing is called for – in line with Pharmaz corporate principles.

As always, Niels Nielsen asks Amrita for her opinion and feedback on his thoughts. The question is how he and Amrita can ensure that the employees get the corporate values under their skin and act accordingly, ideally without even thinking about it. Amrita feels embarrassed because her management style

has been criticized, and she finds it difficult to come up with solutions right away. She tells him that, in principle, she agrees, the values are not implemented fully and some changes may be called for. She does not, however, believe that another course in the corporate values – which the employees have been told about so often that they know the exact wordings from the annual report by heart – will change very much. Niels agrees; something else is needed to teach the employees how to "live" the values.

Amrita tells Niels that she has actually done her best to put the corporate values, especially the value of empowerment, into practice in her dealings with her subordinates. She has left a lot up to them and given fewer orders. But so far it has not been a success. Indeed, the latest anonymous employee satisfaction survey in her section showed, as Niels already knows, that she was rated poorly as a manager. Naturally, this worries and frustrates Amrita. Previously she was rated much better, and she thinks that her low score can be attributed to the attempts she has made to empower her subordinates. With some exceptions, Amrita does not believe that the employees in her section share Pharmaz's ideas of what a boss should be like. She suspects that they expect a good boss to know all the answers and not wait for the employees to come up with good ideas. He or she should take on the responsibility for everything, give explicit orders and follow them up. When Amrita thinks back on her own experiences in the Indian educational system, she tells Niels, she does not find their attitude very surprising. She believes it may be different in some educational institutions today, but the way she remembers it she was not rewarded for being critical or coming up with new approaches when doing her assignments. On the contrary, the easiest way to get good grades was to stick as closely as possible to the teachers' or professors' exact instructions, maybe even repeating their wordings where appropriate. Amrita is not convinced that all her subordinates are eager to take on more responsibility in daily work.

Niels reflects on this. Her interpretation of her low score surprises him. He finds it strange that employees should complain about a boss who gives them too much freedom, but on the other hand what she says may make sense here in India. He thinks to himself that he has probably been too optimistic – the implementation of Pharmaz's corporate culture will take time and hard work. Niels says to Amrita that he appreciates that she has taken headquarters' wish to practice empowerment seriously and that she should not be discouraged; they must expect the process to take some time. And maybe she went about it too abruptly so that her subordinates felt suddenly left to their own devices? Amrita nods – this could well have been the case. Niels specifies that empowerment does not imply that the employees are expected to be able to figure everything out entirely on their own right away, but he would like her to coach the employees so that they understand why things are done in certain ways. The idea is to explain the background and the reasoning behind Pharmaz's business model, financial guidelines, and principles for collaboration so that they will, eventually, be able to reason in the same way themselves and make more independent decisions. Amrita is still hesitant but says that maybe, after a phase of very close managerial monitoring to help employees understand how to adapt to the new demands, Niels' ideas might work, eventually.

Amrita has given less thought to the value of open communication and knowledge sharing, but she tells Niels that sometimes it is a little difficult to motivate team members to share what they know. All her subordinates have good credentials and experiences from other offshore centers. As she and Niels both know, the labor market for professionals in Bangalore is highly competitive and, generally, her employees are eager to advance their individual careers. This may lead some of them to view knowledge as a strictly personal resource that can be depleted if it is shared with colleagues. Amrita realizes that this is not the way Pharmaz would see it, but in a sense she understands her employees' concerns in this respect. After all, colleagues are competitors, too, since not everyone is likely to get promoted to head a team, for instance.

Another problem, as Amrita sees it, is that the organization is very flat compared to most Indian companies. There, it is clear who refers to whom in the hierarchy and, when you make progress in your work, you are promoted to the next level on the career ladder. At Pharmaz, her employees are all officially "financial analysts", even the team leaders, although their wages are higher. Amrita believes that it would have a motivating effect to introduce more titles. It would give people something to work towards and it would make them feel appreciated, in a manner visible to all, and also to their family and friends outside the company, when they reach a goal.

Why should the team leaders not be called "financial managers", for instance? And the best of the team members, "senior financial analysts"? She has suggested this to headquarters before but was told that her idea did not fit into Pharmaz's title structure.

Amrita also suggests that they could nominate an "employee of the quarter" in the services center and give him or her a small symbolic prize, maybe a small amount of money, as well as a certificate to frame and hang on the wall in his or her cubicle. She believes that her employees would appreciate such a gesture, and she also knows that they would probably like to be able to attach such a certificate to their CVs to document that they have done well.

Niels ventures a remark that there is no tradition for prizes at Pharmaz's headquarters and that, there, most people would find it presumptuous or even slightly ridiculous to flaunt such a certificate on their wall. Otherwise, he listens carefully without interrupting. Finally, he says that he finds her ideas interesting, also considering that a couple of the center's most qualified and ambitious financial analysts have recently handed in their resignations and accepted positions with major US-owned companies. Then Niels asks Amrita to come back the following week with a proposal for integrating Pharmaz's values, especially empowerment and knowledge sharing, in a more explicit manner in her section. Also, he asks her to elaborate on her ideas about how to motivate and retain employees.

Question:

- Imagine yourself in Amrita's position. Which proposal would you make to Niels Nielsen and how would you argue in order to convince him?

ACT 3

Pharmaz India's office in Bangalore, 17 January 2017, 2.00 p.m.

Amrita and Niels meet to evaluate the process so far

Amrita and Niels are seated at the meeting table in Niels' office. They have been told to expect a visit from Sebastian, the corporate finance director, next week. In preparation, he has asked them to evaluate the last three months' developments in the center so that they can discuss the progress made, especially as to the implementation of the corporate values, and decide what else needs to be done.

Amrita has worked very hard to change the way in which her section works. She suggested in her proposal that new job descriptions would have to be written for everyone, specifying exactly their areas of responsibility and explaining the types of decisions they would be expected to make on their own. Also, each team is to hold a short meeting every morning to inform each other of what they are doing, and everyone is expected to contribute. Other than that, Amrita suggested that, as a first step, most of the focus should be concentrated on the team leaders to make sure that they understand what empowerment and knowledge sharing means and that they practice it in their teams. They have all read about the values and attended several presentations of them, so the challenge is the daily practice, not the theory. Therefore, Amrita suggested in her proposal that she should dedicate some days each week to follow a team leader, observe his or her work, and afterwards discuss with him or her how the corporate values can be promoted more. Niels accepted Amrita's suggestions in these respects and told her to go ahead.

This afternoon Amrita tells Niels that she is satisfied with the results. The employees appear to be much happier now that it has been made clearer to them what Pharmaz expects from them. Some still ask their team leaders or Amrita for approval before they make decisions or send their reports to the center's users, but most do it less frequently now. And all the team leaders try hard to follow Amrita's new directions. Niels replies that Amrita has done a good job, but adds that when he saw the many pages with job descriptions she had produced he could not help worrying that they were creating more bureaucracy instead of reducing it. Amrita argues that they are necessary: if empowerment is to make sense to her subordinates, they must know exactly what they are empowered to do. Otherwise it is just an abstract notion. Also, when Niels comes to visit Amrita's section, he has noted that she monitors the team leaders very closely indeed and gives them detailed instructions on how to plan their days and how to delegate tasks to different team members, for instance. To Niels, this close monitoring does not seem like empowerment, and he knows that Sebastian would probably agree. But

after six months in Bangalore, Niels begins to feel that it may not be worthwhile insisting on implementing the corporate values in completely the same manner as at headquarters. Maybe different versions of empowerment, equal opportunities, and knowledge sharing are possible – and even necessary? He shares these thoughts with Amrita, who is clearly pleased that he finally understands this. Niels is not so sure that Sebastian will agree, though. It may not fit his vision of Pharmaz as a global, value-driven company – they will have to discuss it next week.

In accordance with Amrita's suggestion, Niels introduced a more differentiated title structure for the center in late October. He is not personally enthusiastic about it and he finds that, in principle, people ought to pay more attention to the content of their job than to the title it entails. This is also an opinion he has frequently heard expressed by his colleagues at headquarters. But he decided to be pragmatic in this matter. After some months in the center he was already well aware of the local employees' impatience to advance visibly in the company hierarchy, so he did not doubt that Amrita was right in assuming that new titles would have a motivational effect and probably result in more willingness to take on responsibility. But at the same time, he was wary of creating titles that would be incompatible with the company's overall global title structure and create misunderstandings in other parts of the organization. Now, the team leaders have been promoted to "financial managers", and the best of the team members have been encouraged to apply for positions as "senior financial analysts". Several local employees, including all the team leaders, have expressed their satisfaction with this decision, and although it is too early to judge the effect for sure, Amrita tells Niels that the team leaders are eager to prove that they have earned their promotions. So Niels believes it was the right thing to do, although some of his colleagues at headquarters have been joking a bit about the apparent inflation in titles in Pharmaz India.

Niels was very surprised, however, when he was approached the other day by Pavan Surin, one of the team leaders in Amrita's section, who suggested that the title structure should be expanded further. He felt that he needed an additional category between "financial analyst" and "senior financial analyst" in order to be able to reward a team member who was very good, but not quite at the "senior financial analyst" level. Frankly, Niels found this slightly ludicrous – how many hierarchical levels are necessary in a team of five people? One for each individual? But since he knows Pavan to be competent and respected by his colleagues, he would like to discuss it with Amrita before dismissing it altogether. And since he has consistently told all his subordinates to feel free to approach him any time with any ideas they might come up with as to how the center's work can be improved, he thanked Pavan for his suggestion and promised him that he would give it some thought.

Amrita is not very pleased that Pavan chose to discuss this directly with Niels instead of taking it up with her first. She knows better than to mention this to Niels, however. She knows that he sets great store by the corporate value of "openness in communication between employees at all levels", and she does not feel like being lectured about it. She hesitates to take a very firm stand regarding Pavan's suggestion but, as she says to Niels, he is probably right that the introduction of an additional step on the career would motivate some team members.

In her proposal to Niels, Amrita suggested the introduction of a reward system where employees are rated for their performance by their immediate superiors in order to give a bonus prize to the employee with the highest score each quarter. In this matter, Niels did not quite follow her suggestion. He felt that a reward system would indeed be appreciated by the local employees, and he had been told that it is customary in most companies in Bangalore. He worried, however, that Amrita's idea would not be conducive to teamwork. Therefore, he has devised a system whereby people are not only rated by their superiors for their individual performance but also by their colleagues for their ability to share knowledge and collaborate. In this way the reward system can serve not just to motivate hard work but to promote Pharmaz's values of openness and knowledge sharing, too. The system was introduced recently so no one has received a bonus prize yet. When it was presented he felt it was well received, but Niels is eager to hear Amrita's opinion on whether or not it has had any impact yet.

Amrita tells him that she believes the employees are genuinely happy with the introduction of a bonus prize, something which they had long found to be missing in Pharmaz. But she proceeds to tell him of a problematic recent episode: Balvinder's team has been given a special assignment by headquarters. It consists of a thorough, critical financial analysis of a business unit in Germany that is experiencing some severe difficulties. The financial report will form part of the basis of the strategic decision as to whether or not to close the unit down. Because of his excellent qualifications, Shankar has been asked to take on the main responsibility for this task, and he has very happily accepted. The problem is that he has become very possessive of this task and discloses next to nothing about it at the team's daily morning meetings.

Balvinder finds – and Amrita agrees – that everyone on the team could learn something about Pharmaz's business from this important, strategic assignment. Therefore, he asked Shankar last week to involve his colleagues and delegate some of the less complicated tasks involved. This, however, did not happen. When the team leader took it up with Shankar again after some days, he seemed rather annoyed. Amrita, who overheard their conversation as she passed Shankar's cubicle, was shocked to hear Shankar tell Balvinder that he intends to rate him as poorly as possible – and tell Shivesh [one of his colleagues on the team] to do the same – if he keeps nagging him. Balvinder has not brought the issue up with Amrita, but she would like to do something about it. When she raised the issue during an informal chat with Ganesh this morning, he defended Shankar. He pointed out that he has exceptional qualifications and is very hardworking, so he will be able to do the job better and faster on his own without spending time on involving the others. Amrita had to agree, this is probably true, but somehow she finds it beside the point.

Niels says that they have to find a way to deal with the problems in Balvinder's team, but he needs some time to think about it. Right now, they have to decide what to tell Sebastian about their progress, the issues that remain to be solved and their suggestions for future action.

Questions:

Step out of Amrita's role and answer the following:

1 Do you feel that the measures taken to implement the corporate values and reorganize work in the financial services center have been appropriate?

2 Would you have done anything differently?

3 How should one proceed now to achieve the best possible result for Pharmaz India's financial services center?

JUST ANOTHER MOVE TO CHINA? THE IMPACT OF INTERNATIONAL ASSIGNMENTS ON EXPATRIATE FAMILIES

By Yvonne McNulty

Lisa MacDougall looked at her desk calendar and realized it was the first-year anniversary of her employment at John Campbell College. "How ironic," she thought, "that I might resign today, exactly one year after I started here." As her colleagues dropped by her office throughout the morning to discuss a new research project that she was leading, Lisa felt both elated and sad. She was excited to be embarking on a new chapter in her career, but upset to be leaving behind her first full-time job in nearly a decade. To ease her mind, she took a morning tea break at the campus cafeteria and ordered a latte.

Then her cellphone beeped to alert an incoming message from her husband, Lachlan. As she nervously picked up the phone and read the four-word message – "it's done, go ahead" – she realized in that instant that there was no going back now: Lachlan had just signed a two-year contract with his employer to move their family to China, and it was happening in six weeks' time.

Taking a deep breath as she walked back to her office, the first task was to write a resignation letter, after which Lisa emailed her boss to request an immediate meeting to tell him she was leaving. Although he took the news in his stride, Lisa knew her boss was upset to be losing her after only a year. The college was building up its research agenda and Lisa, along with a couple of other early career researchers, had been employed as an integral part of that plan. Lisa knew that her leaving would likely disrupt those plans a little but, she reminded herself, if her boss had ever really understood what made her tick, he perhaps could have seen it coming.

Although it had been roughly six months in the planning to move to China, the decision to go had not been an easy one to make for the MacDougalls. This surprised Lachlan and Lisa, given that they were seasoned expatriates who had moved internationally, as a married couple, at least twice before – first, from Sydney to Chicago and then Philadelphia, and six years later a second international move to Singapore, their current home. After 12 straight years "on the road" and two successful international moves on two continents under their belt, the anticipation of a third move – to China, no less – seemed simple enough, and in many ways it was. Good for Lachlan's career? Check – yes. Good for their two young daughters? Check – yes. A wonderful, perhaps life-changing cultural experience for the whole family? Check – definitely, yes. Yet in many ways this move was anything *but* simple; there were so many issues to consider, and so many important decisions to be made that would likely impact their family for years to come, if not for the rest of their lives.

Foremost in Lisa's mind was whether she could work in China. The mere thought of being a stay-at-home 'trailing spouse' again was out of the question. Another concern was going back to the transience of living in rented housing again; needing permission from a landlord to put up a picture or paint the walls would be hard to get used to after having lived in their own home in Singapore for the past four years. Then there was the children's education and the change to a new school. This would be the MacDougalls' first international move with school-aged children and Lisa had no idea whether international schools in China offered the types of music and sports programs her children enjoyed. As she mulled over the China decision, Lisa also reflected on what had drawn their family into the expatriate life to begin with. Doing so, she hoped, might help her to understand how their past might now be drawing them to a new adventure in Shanghai.

All expatriate journeys start somewhere, and some even in childhood

To many of their friends, Lachlan and Lisa seemed to be made for each other. That they married quite soon after they met, and very soon after that left on their first international assignment to Chicago, came as no surprise to anyone. Lisa was born and raised in Melbourne as the daughter of European migrants and, after an eight-year commission in the Royal Australian Navy, living and working on naval establishments all over Australia, she settled in Sydney at the age of 26 to pursue a career in management consulting. She met Lachlan on a rather ordinary Saturday morning at a café in Mosman, when he politely asked if he could borrow the *International Herald Tribune* when she was done reading it. Lachlan wasn't born in Australia; he'd come to Sydney some seven years earlier as a UK backpacker on a three-month holiday that turned into a year-long sojourn, then permanent residency, and finally citizenship. Born and raised mostly in Scotland as the eldest son of a second-generation property developer, Lachlan was an architect by trade, with a bachelor's degree and an MBA from Heriot-Watt University. He'd had an interesting childhood, having moved house (and school) a dozen or more times around Scotland and Ireland as his father bought and sold various properties to expand the family business. Although his father had hoped he would take over the business one day, Lachlan had other ideas.

When exactly does a global career begin?

Their first move to Chicago was a completely out-of-the-blue opportunity but one that Lisa and Lachlan accepted immediately and without hesitation. They were newly married, had no family ties in Sydney, and shared a mutual love of travel. Lachlan had changed careers a year earlier into the IT industry and now worked for a large American technology company with offices around the globe. Although the Chicago job was on local terms – no 'expat package' – the company was willing to pay relocation expenses, and US salaries were much higher than those in Australia. With an expensive mortgage and looking to kick-start

a second career, Lachlan knew the opportunity was too good to pass up. Lisa needed no convincing – moving to the USA was the fulfillment of a life long ambition to live and work overseas and she didn't really care where that was. So, they rented out their house and waved goodbye to friends with the promise to "be back in two years".

It didn't take long once in Chicago for the MacDougalls to realize that their 'two-year plan' wasn't going to happen. Lachlan was an instant success in his new role, while Lisa relished in her newfound status as 'trailing spouse'. Despite the fact that Lisa was not permitted to work in the USA (they had not known – nor thought to ask – about the availability of work permits for accompanying partners when they accepted the job), she nonetheless found herself loving the freedom to explore a new city without the constraints of a busy, all-consuming and demanding job. They didn't need her salary anyway; Lachlan's career was flourishing, so much so that within 18 months of arriving in Chicago he was promoted into a regional US role and offered the opportunity to move to Philadelphia. They gladly accepted the move even though, again, it was on local terms with only relocation expenses paid by the company.

By the time they arrived in Philadelphia, Lisa knew that something had changed for her and Lachlan. Their expected return to Sydney in a few months' time was no longer something they talked about. Instead of renting an apartment they bought a house on the 'main line' in leafy, middle-class Montgomery County about 30 minutes drive from downtown Philly. They replaced their IKEA household goods with more expensive, longer-lasting pieces of furniture, bought two cars, and adopted a dog. Rather than seek out an expatriate community, they joined Bryn Mawr Country Club where they made many American friends and became active in golf and sailing. Because Lachlan's salary was on local terms, they lived and acted like locals and immersed themselves in the local community with a mindset that they were 'here to stay'. Of course, that would never be the case, given that their H1B visa restricted them to a maximum of six years' residency in the USA. But they had another four and a half years until the visa expired, and they intended to stay in Philadelphia until the very last month.

Their move to Asia four years later was, of course, necessary as their US visa was about to expire with no opportunity to renew. By now the MacDougalls had an 11-month old daughter, Amelia, who had been born in Philadelphia. Leaving the USA was hard for Lisa; their family had put down so many roots over the past six years and made so many American friends, and although they did have the opportunity to apply for a green card which could provide permanent residency, to the surprise of their friends the MacDougalls rejected this option in favor of another international move. They chose Asia because it would be good for both their careers and yet still close enough to Australia to maintain family and professional ties without having to repatriate. Lachlan approached his company about an internal transfer, and secured a new role in Singapore.

Singapore had been everything Lachlan and Lisa had hoped for and they had lived there – again, on a local package – much like they had lived in the USA: they bought a condo, secured permanent residency, sent their daughter to a local pre-school, hired a maid, and joined a local sailing club. Work permits for spouses were easy to get in Singapore so Lisa had been able to secure part-time employment. Because he had Permanent Resident status, Lachlan had been able to change employers three years after moving there and was now a regional expert in his field, being routinely approached by headhunters trying to poach him to accept other job offers. The expatriate community was very well established, so the MacDougalls enjoyed a thriving social life. And it was here, in Singapore, that their second daughter, Emily, was born.

Now a third move to China was looming, and as Lisa reflected on their expatriate life so far, she knew that this move, more than any before, was a game changer – for her, for Lachlan and, most importantly, for their family. They didn't *have* to leave Singapore; they were permanent residents and they owned their own home, so they could stay as long as they wished and life there was very good. It became abundantly clear that moving to China was a *choice* unlike any other they had had before. Lachlan's employer had asked him to consider a transfer to Shanghai – on a local-plus package no less, with housing and schooling – but if he did not wish to go the company maintained there would be no repercussions, as he was their most senior Asia executive and they didn't want to lose him. China was, nonetheless, a key strategic market for the company and Lachlan was, by all accounts, perfect for the job. Lisa considered that her husband's career would undoubtedly flourish if they went to China, but she was struck by the fact that, his career aside, there was no other compelling reason to leave Singapore. With this in mind, she knew that if they were to move again, it would need to benefit everyone in the family and not just one person.

Being a dual-career trailing spouse is harder than you think

In the months leading up to the China decision, Lisa spent a lot of time reflecting on her trailing spouse journey, trying to piece together what it all meant and what it could mean in a new city like Shanghai. She knew now that without a doubt she was, and probably always would be, the trailing spouse in their family, the person whose job would *not* take them to their next destination, and whose career would require more compromises than Lachlan would need to make in his. After all, he was now a Regional Vice President for an small and medium-sized enterprises (SME) technology firm in Singapore and earning more money than she could ever hope to even as a tenured professor, and that was ok with both of them; his career supported their lifestyle, and she supported their growing family. She was surprised that her trailing spouse status didn't seem to bother her anymore, whereas even a year earlier it had been all she could think about.

Since marrying Lachlan and moving to Chicago, Lisa had not worked full-time for over a decade. The first six years they had spent in the USA had been challenging. Chicago had been easy, almost like a long holiday, but that had changed once they moved to Philadelphia and committed to staying in the USA for the full duration of their visa. The career she had put 'on hold' back in Sydney, with the intention that she would return to it in a couple of years, was now a thing of the past. With no prospects to legally work in Philly, a husband frequently away on regional business trips and a waning interest in charity work (which she stereotyped as something 'old ladies' did), Lisa found herself increasingly frustrated and constrained by a trailing spouse life that she had once so willingly embraced. She was bored. Life seemed dull, meaningless and oppressive – and she hadn't yet reached the age of 35! Without a business card and a job title, she felt invisible at the many functions she attended as 'Lachlan's wife'. Instinctively she knew that their decision to move to Philadelphia had resulted in a major loss of her identity, much of which Lisa painfully realized had been tied up in a career that was now impossible for her to continue. She had two choices – commit to a life of resigned acceptance as 'Mrs Nobody' until they repatriated, or do something about it.

Like many trailing spouses often do, Lisa resolved her boredom by turning a negative situation into a life-affirming achievement: she went back to school and obtained a doctorate. On the advice of her doctoral supervisor, she chose a field of research she knew something about – expatriates. As it turned out, Lisa *loved* research and was quite good at it. Being an 'insider' to the expatriate community had many advantages – invitations to speak at international conferences, opportunities to write about her research for industry periodicals, and the chance to start a global mobility website. Slowly, year by year, as her research progressed and her expatriate journey continued, Lisa built a new career for herself and, as she would soon discover, a relatively portable one at that.

It was telling that when the move to Singapore arose she was the one pushing them to go, rather than repatriating to Sydney as Lachlan had thought they would do. As a 'global mobility academic', she perceived there would be few negatives – personally *or* professionally – if they undertook another international assignment, and she had been right: in Singapore she had easy access to a work permit and so was able to do part-time consulting for major corporations as well as adjunct teaching. When she graduated with her PhD, Lisa took a tenure-track position at John Campbell College with the intention that she would spend between three and five years there before considering a move elsewhere. It had been important that she re-enter the full-time workforce, not only professionally but also for her self-esteem and confidence. She felt a deep obligation to financially contribute to the family again, to regain some balance and equality in her marriage, and to be a strong role model as a working mother for her two young daughters. Like many trailing spouses before her, Lisa believed that the longer she remained a 'supportive non-working wife', the harder it would be for her to have a 'voice' in major family decisions where financial considerations would be an overriding concern.

Now all her thoughts turned to Shanghai. It seemed quite remarkable that in little more than a decade both she and Lachlan had somehow turned their 'expatriate adventure' into thriving global careers – and they weren't done yet. She already had two job offers to consider at local universities in China, having interviewed with institutions when the family had gone on their familiarization trip a couple of months earlier, but these were predominantly teaching jobs much like the one at John Campbell had turned out to be. Getting a spouse work permit in China would be relatively simple, so she found out, but her passion was research and, if she was to stand any chance of building an academic career, she needed to be in a job that allowed her to publish in good journals. As a foreigner in China with only 'hobby' Mandarin to get her by, how quickly could she establish a new network of contacts to find such a job? And what employment stereotypes and barriers would she face as an 'expat wife'? Although another international move would certainly deepen Lisa's mobility knowledge and experience, moving to China was a career risk – and one that she wasn't sure she needed to take.

Raising 'third-culture kids'

The children were also a major source of concern to Lisa. Their daughters, Amelia and Emily, were now six and seven years of age and had been born overseas. Although they had dual citizenship (Australian and British), the girls had never really known a home other than Singapore and had been attending 'real' school there for nearly two years. In fact, it had taken nearly two years on a wait list to get the girls *into* their school – the United World College of South East Asia (UWCSEA) – given it was the best international school in the region. As parents, Lisa and Lachlan were drawn to UWC because it was well known for striking a balance between a 'privileged childhood' and a focus on service to the global community. UWC also paid special attention to the needs and interests of 'third-culture kids' (TCKs). Although Lisa didn't consider herself a school 'snob', the reality was that there was only one UWC in Asia, and it wasn't in Shanghai. Given her deep theoretical knowledge about TCKs, along with the fact that she and Lachlan were raising two of their own, Lisa knew that Singapore meant a lot to her children and that they had incorporated its culture into their everyday life and sense of who they were. But Amelia and Emily had simultaneously developed a sense of relationship to *all* of the cultures with which they identified – where they were born, where their extended families lived and they frequently vacationed, where Mom and Dad came from – and they didn't really have full ownership in any. In reality, their sense of belonging was mostly in relation to others of an experience similar to theirs – Mom and Dad, each other, school friends, teachers – a special kind of 'in-group'. Was this a good or a bad thing?

On the one hand, Amelia and Emily were constructing and reconstructing their identities during the formative 'fragile' years of their childhood and at the same time across various foreign cultures. Lisa recognized that 'home' for her children would likely be an emotional place that couldn't be found on a map, and that the question 'where am I from?' would require a response from an atlas not an anatomy book! She also recognized that children don't move by choice and they aren't trained for it; they experience the same losses as adults but very often cannot articulate their feelings. Having been a listening ear to a number of expatriate friends over the years whose own children had experienced unresolved issues of grief resulting from the relentlessness of frequent goodbyes, Lisa was keenly aware that her girls would likely have similar experiences, and it was a distressing thought. Was it fair to impose these sorts of stressors on her children and at such a young age? What long-lasting impact would it have on their emotional and psychological well-being as they moved into adulthood?

On the other hand, Amelia and Emily seemed to possess more than a textbook understanding of global culture; they were living it every day. With frequent international travel, access to foreign languages, and exposure to transition and change, they had a rare opportunity to see the world in a way that was closed to most people their age. Lisa was proud that her children integrated well in their community, but she knew that they would never fully penetrate the local culture because it would never be their 'passport country'. She also knew that her children were likely developing a deep sense of rootlessness and possibly a migratory instinct that would be exacerbated by each and every subsequent international move. These weren't negatives per se, as Lachlan had grown up much the same in Scotland and Ireland, and it could well be that, in these formative years, Lachlan and Lisa were already setting up their children for their own global

careers, which by all accounts they perceived to be a positive outcome. Still, did they have the right to be making decisions for their children that could impact their adult lives in such unimaginable ways? Would their children's lives be better if the family lived in one neighborhood, in one city, close to their relatives and friends, and never moved?

Yes, money does actually matter

Lisa's last remaining concern about moving to China centered on their financial situation. The relocation package offered to Lachlan included a housing allowance, school fees, and tax equalization benefits as part of a 'local-plus' arrangement. For all intents and purposes the compensation package for the China move was attractive, given that for the past 12 years Lisa and Lachlan had been expatriates on local terms, with no additional benefits. Tax equalization was especially beneficial given that China's income tax rate was approximately 50 per cent, compared to 20 per cent in Singapore; for this reason Lachlan had nominated Singapore as his home country and purposely retained his and Lisa's Singapore permanent residency (PR) status. But, in doing so, the MacDougalls soon discovered that departing Singapore as PRs was a more complicated process than they had anticipated. Because they were non-citizens of Singapore, the MacDougalls would be required, by law, to settle their tax bill with the Singapore government in advance of their temporary two-year absence, including taxable income on stocks and shares offered as part of Lachlan's pay-for-performance salary scheme that would be accrued over the ensuing two years. This included existing as well as anticipated stocks and shares.

Although the technical details of Singapore's tax laws were complicated and for the most part beyond Lisa's basic understanding, the final outcome for the MacDougalls was that their tax bill prior to departure was significantly large, taking into account both their taxable earnings. Additionally, Singapore law dictated that Lachlan's existing and anticipated company shares and stocks would need to be frozen during their two-year absence (i.e. they could not sell them) in order to mitigate any financial windfall he might otherwise accrue. In theory it sounded reasonable enough, but the reality was that the MacDougalls could emerge from their China assignment in two years time with shares worth only half the value, without any opportunity to stem the loss by selling them. As a senior Vice President, Lachlan's share portfolio was substantial; about 20 per cent of the MacDougalls overall net worth consisted of company shares. Given the ongoing economic crises in Europe and the USA, and their impending retirement in 15 years' time, Lisa wasn't sure it was worth the financial risk to lock in their company share portfolio at the existing share price and to possibly suffer a loss from which it could be difficult to recover.

Coming full circle to embrace Shanghai

As Lisa drove home from John Campbell College having resigned from her job earlier that day, she turned on the car radio and listened to a BBC World Service program in which well-known author and publisher Robin Pascoe was being interviewed about her newly released book on 'Global Nomads'. As Ms Pascoe recalled her life as a foreign service spouse, raising two children in four Asian countries during the 1980s and 1990s, and spoke of the many times she had reinvented her career as a journalist, author, public speaker, and now publisher, Lisa was struck by how common global careers had become – and for women, no less. Although she herself had at times felt somewhat alone in her own journey as a trailing spouse, Lisa nonetheless knew that international mobility was inevitable for many employees as talent management became critical for multinational firms. She and Lachlan were no exception to this phenomenon: they may not have intentionally set out to pursue global careers a decade earlier, but once they had arrived on the international labor market it made sense that they remain there. They had benefited immensely by doing so, despite the many personal and professional hurdles she had overcome, and even though repatriation to Australia had been an ongoing talking point for years over the dinner table, somehow it just never seemed to factor into any of their plans.

Lisa now clearly saw for the first time that moving to China signalled an important change in their family dynamic: the MacDougalls had acquired the relatively rare skill of 'family mobility' and she instinctively knew that it was a skillset likely to be highly sought after by many global companies. Their 'united nations' global family was, in reality, a valuable commodity. Although she had always had the opportunity to return to a relatively comfortable and stable 'north shore life' in Sydney had she wanted to, Lisa had never really seriously considered it an option; instead, she knew now that she and Lachlan would probably pursue global careers in one form or another for the rest of their lives, as would their children. As Ms. Pascoe continued to tell her story on the radio, Lisa began to slowly let go of her fears and to once and for all embrace the Shanghai opportunity. And then she began to wonder . . . retaining their Singapore permanent residency status might not have been necessary after all, given that there were so many other cities they could move to when the Shanghai assignment was complete.

Questions:

1 In what ways does the MacDougall family represent a rare and valuable resource to a multinational firm?

2 Reflecting on Lisa's dual-career trailing spouse journey, how would you have approached the situation differently?

3 What problems do you foresee for Amelia and Emily if the MacDougall family undertakes another move after Shanghai?

4 Although not discussed, what impact do you think international mobility has had on the MacDougalls' marriage?

CASE 9

FINDING THE RIGHT VIEW: DEVELOPING LOCAL TALENT IN LOCAL MARKETS

By Claudia Fischer and Allen D. Engle, Sr.

A still February morning in Shanghai. The view from the 15th floor of the New Shanghai International Tower on Pudong Road South is obscured by silver-grey pollution. Thomas' practiced eye has calibrated the index at over 100 already, perhaps going to 200 plus by late afternoon. The top of the World Finance Mansion is obscured as he looks up into the fog. He cannot see to the top of the 38-floor China Merchants Tower. His sliced view of the heavy traffic on the Lujiazui Ring Road is softened by the haze.

Thomas Mueller is thinking about yesterday, today, and tomorrow. Well into ten years at Bombardier Transportation (BT), a market leader in train manufacturing, he is currently on assignment in Shanghai as General Manager of the company's Best Cost Country Sourcing subsidiary. The office in Shanghai is the key interface between procurement teams and project managers all around the world and the Chinese suppliers. He reports to the Head of Global Commodity Management, based in Headquarters in Germany.

Thomas was put on the assignment with a clear mandate to stabilize the supplier relations, standardize processes and – most critically – to implement Key Performance Indicators (KPIs) for the Shanghai office to make the unit's business performance transparent and measurable. He has completed two and a half years of his three-year assignment. According to BT's annual talent calendar, it is time to prepare the annual performance management process (PMP) reviews with his direct reports as well as the talent review input for the procurement functional 'talent day'.

Thomas feels like he is between the Devil and the deep blue sea. Firstly, one of his main assignment objectives is to develop a local successor in his role, but the employee number one on his succession list is not ready to step into Thomas' role now. Hence, he has toyed with the idea of an alternative solution in which he asks for a one-year assignment extension. On a more personal level, as BT's strategy is clearly to develop deep roots in local markets, Thomas has just started to discuss with the European management team the potential for a new role for him becoming available in a few months. This reassignment would be the perfect repatriation opportunity. His family is keen on moving back to Europe. His wife and the two kids have adapted well in China, but they still miss the extended family and some of their old friends. How would a one-year extension affect his long-term career goals? What would his family think?

Putting his dilemma aside for a while, Thomas takes his role as people manager seriously, to act as talent champion and to prepare for the outstanding performance reviews properly.

In BT, talent reviews and annual PMPs are important – more critically, they go hand in hand. The information obtained from the PMP discussions – e.g. career aspirations and interests – is used as the basis for management's preparation in the talent review process. Thomas will also listen to ideas about short- and long-term development objectives from his employees, and he and they will build or adjust the individual development plans together.

As people manager and talent champion he is expected to (1) communicate and cascade business objectives to ensure alignment between individual, team, and business objectives; (2) integrate long-term development objectives into PMP development plans; (3) actively assist employees in achieving their objectives by providing open and honest feedback regularly; (4) conduct meaningful discussions resulting in agreed-upon objectives fulfilling SMART (Specific, Measurable, Achievable, Relevant and Time-bound) criteria and, finally; (5) develop objectives for each annual cycle and review and rate employee performance and behavior at the end of each cycle. A daunting but critical set of linkages is required. Thomas helped develop the system in Berlin; it was much clearer on paper four years ago than it may be today.

Working through the system: The case of Mr Wei

As usual, Thomas perceives the office atmosphere as harmonious and calm. Co-workers are discussing topics here and there in low voices so as not to disturb the others sitting nearby in the open office space. Only far away, from the kitchen, does he hear some giggling, where a group of young employees meet up for daily lunch and share the latest news, enjoy their ordered meals and some good jokes. Hence, Thomas starts to prepare for his performance review with Mr Li Wei, his potential successor and right hand in the past years. Mr Li has worked in the office for nine years and is well respected by every employee. During the last 12 months Thomas has noted several positive performance characteristics and some areas for potential improvement in order to be ready for the year-end performance review. These informal incident reports were collected as situations developed over the year, and stored in the secure personnel folder for Mr Wei.

1 Positive feedback examples

- Business acumen: Wei is very much appreciated in the office as 'the expert', having been around from the first minute and knowing the company very well. Colleagues like to ask him for advice on business topics such as how to address an internal stakeholder.

- Holding people accountable and driving for results: Wei follows up his team plan according to the strategic initiatives he planned with Thomas during last year. His direct reports provide him with updates on a bi-weekly basis and if one is late he reminds this employee in person.

- Negotiation: Wei has led the negotiations for the newly selected supplier Xie Xie Co., Ltd. to bring this supplier on the supplier panel for global rolling stock projects on aluminum material. He has ensured this supplier offers the parts 15 per cent below competition but at the same quality and delivery standards. This means a saving of several million euros per year in future using Xie Xie as the new preferred supplier.

2 Competencies to further improve

- Skills in building partnerships: this is the core competence for this role. Unfortunately Wei has significant gaps in that area. He fails to align within the matrix with Western colleagues and misses important points during supplier negotiations. More proactivity is needed to drive his relationships to influence potential outcomes of discussions, even though he has great ideas.

- Communication: Wei needs to improve written and oral communication and to align better with Procurement Project Managers on specifications of material needed. One repeated comment from co-workers is that his presentations are too number-driven, with overly crowded slides and a lack of structure and logic such as executive summaries. Verbally his command of English is limited and has a notable accent which makes it hard for colleagues from other countries to properly understand him.

- Change leadership: Wei focuses very much on the past successes and the status quo of his office with regard to local unit strategy, targets, and climate. BT is undergoing considerable change. Wei needs to face these realities of 'tomorrow'. It is critical for the local incumbent to adapt to the changing situation and embrace the future more, leaving old habits behind and not defending the past.

After weighting the pros and cons of Li Wei's performance and behavior, Thomas decides to give him a rating of 3 – fully satisfactory. He knows Li Wei will not like it and expects a higher rating. Thomas feels a bit helpless about how to tell him of what may be seen as a disappointing assessment, but he is sure about his decision. He knows from his current experience in China how sensitive the culture is towards feedback and rating scales. Harmony is important, even in 'informal' meetings. Intangibles such as tone, gestures, and body language are carefully noted. In China, failure implies a shameful loss of face; only in rare circumstances will an official risk it.

In addition to the performance review of his direct reports, he also needs to come up with a proposal for his own succession. His supervisor is awaiting it until the end of next week. Li Wei has been seen in the last several years as being groomed as Thomas' successor. Here, at the moment of truth, Thomas has severe doubts if Li Wei is 'ready now' to fill in for him when his assignment ends in six months' time.

Furthermore, Thomas has collected feedback from some key stakeholders and everybody agrees with his judgement. Alternatives are not available – no other person in the Shanghai office can be considered to be ready for his role in the short-term or even mid term. The company runs two other production sites with procurement teams. From the site in Changchun Mrs Zhang Li could be a potential successor in one to two years, but Thomas does not know her well enough.

So, that is the situation in Shanghai. "What standards and frames of reference do I have to work with?" Thomas asks himself. To better prepare, Thomas takes out his copy of the company's people manager handbook and reviews the following figures and definitions.

EXHIBIT A   Annual performance management process (PMP)

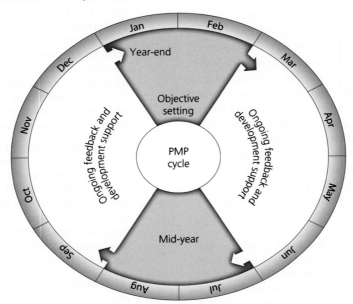

Printed with permission of Bombardier Transportation GmbH (from Talent Handbook)

EXHIBIT B   PMP rating scale

Rating scale	
5 **Significantly exceeds expectations**	Performance and behaviors far exceed expectations. Employee clearly stands out and consistently demonstrates exceptional accomplishments in terms of quality and quantity of work that is easily recognized as truly exceptional by others.
4 **Exceeds expectations**	Performance frequently exceeds expectations. Accomplishments and behaviors are regularly above the expected levels. Employee sustains performance at a level beyond expectations and the quality of work is uniformly high.
3 **Fully meets expectations**	Performance fully meets expectations in terms of quality and quantity of work. Employee consistently demonstrates a solid performance, with thorough and on-time results. Accomplishments and behaviors completely fulfill all expectations.
2 **Partially meets expectations**	Performance partially meets expectations. Employee needs development and performance improvements. Employee generally demonstrates a few expected levels of accomplishments and behaviors, but shows difficulty to fully meet them all.
1 **Does not meet expectations**	Performance, accomplishments, and behaviors are noticeably not aligned to expectations. Performance must improve substantially with an action plan if the employee is to remain in this position.

Printed with permission of Bombardier Transportation GmbH (from Talent Handbook)

EXHIBIT C Feedback rules

- Give it directly and face-to-face
- Criticize action or result **not** the person
- Have evidence to support what you are saying: facts, figures, KPIs – second-hand feedback has second-hand value
- Adapt to the situation: listen to what other person is saying. They may have a perfectly good explanation for things
- Do not give too much information at once
- Use 'I' messages
- Avoid extremes: 'never' or 'always'
- Create the right atmosphere
- Do not get drawn into a discussion
- Use measurable to review performance objectively
- Give examples while for good/improvable performance.

Printed with permission of Bombardier Transportation GmbH (training material for people managers)

EXHIBIT D Employee development by 70:20:10 rule

70%	20%	10%
On-the-job experience	**Personal relationships**	**Training**
◎ Cross-functional projects	◎ Coaching and mentoring	◎ Classroom
◎ On-the-job learning	◎ Learning from peers	◎ Websites
◎ Transfer/rotation	◎ Co-development groups	◎ Articles/books/movies

Printed with permission of Bombardier Transportation GmbH (training material for people managers)

In a moment of unappreciated irony, Thomas reads from the BT handbook's development materials on the topic of succession management:

> Succession management is not just replacement management. Succession management is making provisions for the development, replacement, and strategic application of key people over time. It requires the identification of the organization's values, mission, and strategic plans. It is a proactive approach that ensures continuing leadership by cultivating talent from within the organization through planned development activities.

Thomas himself wrote that into policy statements, in Berlin five years ago. When and how did 'fully meets expectations' become something to cause a loss of face? Is the discontinuity between success in Mr Wei's current job and success in the job Thomas is leaving part of the problem? Does performance in the present get in the way of performance in the future?

EXHIBIT E   On-the-job-learning ideas

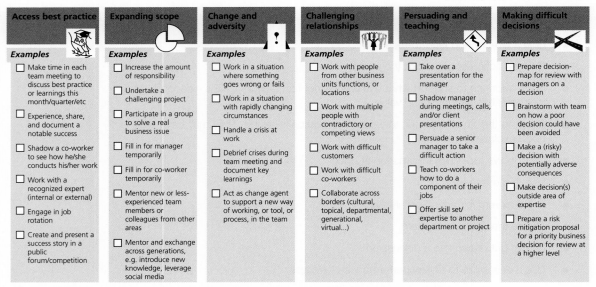

Access best practice	Expanding scope	Change and adversity	Challenging relationships	Persuading and teaching	Making difficult decisions
Examples	**Examples**	**Examples**	**Examples**	**Examples**	**Examples**
☐ Make time in each team meeting to discuss best practice or learnings this month/quarter/etc	☐ Increase the amount of responsibility	☐ Work in a situation where something goes wrong or fails	☐ Work with people from other business units functions, or locations	☐ Take over a presentation for the manager	☐ Prepare decision-map for review with managers on a decision
☐ Experience, share, and document a notable success	☐ Undertake a challenging project	☐ Work in a situation with rapidly changing circumstances	☐ Work with multiple people with contradictory or competing views	☐ Shadow manager during meetings, calls, and/or client presentations	☐ Brainstorm with team on how a poor decision could have been avoided
☐ Shadow a co-worker to see how he/she conducts his/her work	☐ Participate in a group to solve a real business issue	☐ Handle a crisis at work	☐ Work with difficult customers	☐ Persuade a senior manager to take a difficult action	☐ Make a (risky) decision with potentially adverse consequences
☐ Work with a recognized expert (internal or external)	☐ Fill in for manager temporarily	☐ Debrief crises during team meeting and document key learnings	☐ Work with difficult co-workers	☐ Teach co-workers how to do a component of their jobs	☐ Make decision(s) outside area of expertise
☐ Engage in job rotation	☐ Fill in for co-worker temporarily	☐ Act as change agent to support a new way of working, or tool, or process, in the team	☐ Collaborate across borders (cultural, topical, departmental, generational, virtual...)	☐ Offer skill set/ expertise to another department or project	☐ Prepare a risk mitigation proposal for a priority business decision for review at a higher level
☐ Create and present a success story in a public forum/competition	☐ Mentor new or less-experienced team members or colleagues from other areas				
	☐ Mentor and exchange across generations, e.g. introduce new knowledge, leverage social media				

Printed with permission of Bombardier Transportation GmbH (training material for people managers)

Decisions: Past, present and future

The morning has passed very quickly. Thomas sets the documents aside and reviews his decision processes. Strong southeasterly winds have blown in, as predicted, and rain and sleet can be expected to follow. The yellow-gray pollution has noticeably cleared and he can see the top of the China Merchants Tower building out of his window. Increased clarity in the view out of his office window, at least.

He is finding it hard to detach his personal commitment to the local operations over the last two and a half years from the cold mechanics and logical steps of the talent and performance systems. What are the trade-offs between the long-term goal of 'deep roots in local markets' and 'transparent and measurable' business performance processes? If Mr Wei is not ready, is it Thomas' fault? Does Thomas really want to spend another year in Shanghai helping to grow deeper roots? Right on cue the local classic rock station playing in the background starts in with the first few bars of "Should I Stay or Should I Go?" by The Clash.

Questions:

1. What decision about the future would you take if you were Thomas and why?

2. From the company's perspective: which solution brings more benefit to the business in this case? Do you follow the 'local roots in local markets' strategy? Why (not)?

3. How can Thomas prepare the feedback for the performance review meeting with Li Wei? Prepare a red thread of the conversation for Thomas as well as argumentation points for his rating 3. What obstacles do you see from an intercultural perspective?

4. From the perspective of Li Wei: how might he feel as a Chinese person getting a rating of 3?

5. Which learning activities should be part of Li Wei's personal development plan to successfully develop him into a General Manager position? Please prepare one to two development goals with three learning activities per objective using the 70:20:10 rule.

6. Regarding Thomas' succession plan, put yourself in the role of his HR business partner: which ideas would you have to help him to identify a local successor?

Glossary

Achievement culture focuses on status achievement. People are judged based on what they have achieved – in other words, the goals they have fulfilled recently.

Acquisition occurs when one company buys another company with the interest of controlling the activities of the combined operations.

Ad hoc see *Tax, Ad hoc.*

Affective dimension refers to intercultural competence reflecting the emotional attitude towards a foreign culture.

Agents of socialization approach is based on assumptions that appropriate behavior will have been instilled in the local workforce through training programs and hiring practices, and that the multinational's way of operating has been accepted by the local staff in the manner intended. In this way, the multinational's corporate culture will operate as a subtle, informal control mechanism – a substitution of direct supervision.

Artefacts are described as visible organization structures and processes.

Ascriptive culture: the status is ascribed from birth by characteristics such as origin, seniority, and gender.

Assertiveness is the degree to which individuals are assertive, confrontational, and aggressive in their relationship with others.

Asymmetric events have been described as threats that our political, strategic, and military cultures regard as unusual.

Balance Sheet Approach The basic objective is to "keep the expatriate whole" (that is, maintaining relativity to PCN colleagues and compensating for the costs of an international assignment) through maintenance of home-country living standard plus a financial inducement to make the package attractive. This approach links the base salary for expatriates to the salary structure of the relevant home country.

Base salary: in a domestic context, base salary denotes the amount of cash compensation serving as a benchmark for other compensation elements (such as bonuses and benefits). For expatriates, it is the primary component of a package of allowances, many of which are directly related to base salary (e.g. foreign-service premium, cost-of-living allowance, housing allowance) as well as the basis for in-service benefits and pension contributions. The base salary is the foundation block for international compensation whether the employee is a PCN or TCN.

Best practice: a method or technique that has consistently shown results superior to those achieved with other means, and that is used as a benchmark (Businessdictionary.com).

Boundary spanning refers to activities, such as gathering information, that bridge internal and external organizational contexts. Expatriates are considered boundary spanners because they can collect host-country information, act as representatives of their firms in the host country, and influence agents.

Boundaryless careerist is the highly qualified mobile professional who builds his or her career competencies and labor market value through transfers across boundaries.

Bribery involves the payment of agents to do things that are inconsistent with the purpose of their position or office in order to gain an unfair advantage. Bribery can be distinguished from so-called 'gifts' and 'facilitating' or 'grease' payments.

Bureaucratic control system: control of an organization and the individuals that make up the organization through systems of standardized rules, methods, and verification procedures. Bureaucratic control is used to ensure efficient operation of large organizations, where face-to-face communication is not possible or practical and informal methods of enforcing compliance may not be sufficient (Businessdictionary.com).

Centralized . . .

Centralized practice: Management practice in which all or most decision-makers (who have the authority, control, and responsibility for the entire organization) are located in one central office (Businessdictionery.com).

Chaebols: Korean conglomerates.

Change facilitator . . .

Chief Executive Officer or subsidiary manager, who oversees and directs the entire foreign operation.

Cognitive layer relates to culture-specific knowledge.

Collaborator . . .

Collective bargaining: process between an organization's management and a trade union representing its employees, for negotiating wages, working hours, working conditions, and other matters of mutual interest. To the management, this process presents (usually) one set of people to negotiate with; to the employees, it gives greatly enhanced bargaining power. Collective bargaining is the fundamental principle on which the trade union system is based (Businessdictionary.com).

Collectivism, Hofstede study: personal or social orientation that emphasizes the good of the group, community, or society over and above individual gain (Business dictionary.com).

Communication medium: a medium through which a message is transmitted to its intended audience, such as print media or broadcast (electronic) media (Business dictionary.com).

Communitarianism is about the rights of the group or society. It seeks to put the family, group, compan, and country before the individual. It sees individualism as selfish and short-sighted.

Commuter assignments: special arrangements where the employee commutes from the home country on a weekly or bi-weekly basis to the place of work in another country. Cross-border workers or daily commuters are not included. Usually the family of the assignee stays in the home country.

Compensation: sum of direct benefits (such as salary, allowances, bonus, commission) and indirect benefits (such as insurance, pension plans, vacations) that an employee receives from an employer (Businessdictionary .com).

Competency base salary: compensation given on the basis of an employee acquiring a critical skill or knowledge (Businessdictionary.com).

Competency-based assessment . . .

Confucianism dynamics, Hofstede study: this dimension essentially reflects a basic orientation in the life of people, which can be either more long-term or short-term in nature.

Contextual goals attempt to take into consideration factors that result from the situation in which performance occurs.

Contractual assignments are used in situations where employees with specific skills vital to an international project are assigned for a limited duration of six to 12 months.

Corporate culture or organizational culture is the sum total of an organization's past and current assumptions, experiences, philosophy, and values that hold it together, and is expressed in its self-image, inner workings, interactions with the outside world and future expectations. It is based on shared attitudes, beliefs, customs, express or implied contracts, and written and unwritten rules that the organization develops over time and that have worked well enough to be considered valid (Business dictionary.com).

Cost-of-living allowance (COLA), which typically receives the most attention, involves a payment to compensate for differences in expenditures between the home country and the foreign country. COLA payments are intended to compensate for cost differentials between an expatriate's home and host country – for example, the costs of transportation, furniture and appliances, medical expenditures, alcohol and tobacco, automobile maintenance, and domestic help.

Country-of-origin effect refers to the extent to which multinationals are shaped by institutions existing in their country of origin.

Cross-cultural management studies aim to describe and compare the working behavior in various cultures.

Cultural awareness training program seeks to foster an appreciation of the host country's culture so that expatriates can behave accordingly, or at least develop appropriate coping patterns.

Cultural intelligence is a specific form of intelligence focused on capabilities to grasp, reason, and behave effectively in situations characterised by cultural diversity.

Culture consists of "patterned ways of thinking, feeling and reacting, acquired, and transmitted mainly by symbols, constituting the distinctive achievements of human groups […], including their embodiments in artefacts; the essential core of culture consists of traditional […] ideas and especially their attached values" (Kluckhohn and Kroeber, 1952: 181).

Culture shock: a phenomenon experienced by people who move across cultures. The new environment requires many adjustments in a relatively short period of time, challenging people's frames of reference to such an extent that their sense of self, especially in terms of nationality, comes into question. People, in effect, experience a shock reaction to new cultural experiences that cause psychological disorientation because they misunderstand or do not recognize important cues.

Cyber-terrorism: hardware, software, and human systems to deal with hacking, information theft, internal sabotage, the sabotage of software systems, and the development and maintenance of an architecture of back-up systems and multiple independent operations for information systems.

Decentralized practice subsidiaries have decision-making power and are assigned accountability and responsibility for results. They are accompanied by delegations of commensurate authority to individuals or units at all levels of an organization, even those far removed from headquarters or other centers of power (Businessdictionary.com).

Development aims to increase abilities in relation to some future position or job.

Developmental assignments focus on in-country performance and the acquisition of local or regional understanding by the assignee.

Diffuse culture is characterized by: a large private life that includes a relatively large number of people; a small public space that is difficult to enter (e.g. an outsider needs a formal introduction from a mutual friend in order to do business with a particular manager); indirect communication that does not always say what is really meant; and no clear distinction between work and private life.

Direct costs of expat failure include airfares and associated relocation expenses, and salary and training.

The precise amount varies according to the level of the position concerned, country of destination, exchange rates, and whether the 'failed' manager is replaced by another expatriate.

Disaster protocols: planned steps taken to minimize the effects of a disaster and to be able to proceed to business continuity stage (Businessdictionary.com).

Domestic human resource management is involved with employees within only one national boundary.

Education allowances: provision of education allowances for the children of expatriates is frequently an integral part of an international compensation policy. Allowances for education can cover items such as tuition (including language classes), application and enrolment fees, books and supplies, meals, transportation, excursions and extra-curricular activities, parent association fees, school uniforms and, if applicable, room and board.

Emic refers to culture-specific aspects of concepts or behavior.

Emotional culture: in affective cultures, an emotional basis is accepted as a part of business life and emotions are freely expressed across many social contexts.

Equity . . .

Equity mode involves a foreign direct investor's purchase of shares of an enterprise in a country other than its own.

Equity, compensation: the degree to which the actual pay of an employee matches what he or she thinks they deserve. High pay equity means high employee satisfaction with his or her job; low pay equity increases the potential for absenteeism, grievances, strikes, and turnover (Businessdictionary.com).

Ethical absolutist believes that, "when in Rome, one should do what one would do at home, regardless of what the Romans do".

Ethical relativist believes that there are no universal or international rights and wrongs, it all depends on a particular culture's values and beliefs. For the ethical relativist, "when in Rome, one should do as the Romans do".

Ethical universalist believes that there are fundamental principles of right and wrong which transcend cultural boundaries, and that MNEs must adhere to these fundamental principles or global values.

Ethics: the basic concepts and fundamental principles of right human conduct. It includes the study of universal values such as the essential equality of all men and women, human or natural rights, obedience to the law of land, concern for health and safety and also, increasingly, for the natural environment (Businessdictionary.com).

Ethnocentric staffing: key positions in domestic and foreign operations are held by managers from headquarters (PCNs). Subsidiaries are managed by staff from the home country.

Ethnorelativism: an acquired ability to see many values and behaviors as cultural rather than universal. It is characterized by adjustment to foreign cultures and integration.

Etic refers to culture-common aspects.

ETUC: European Trade Union Confederation.

EU: the European Union.

Expatriate is an employee who is working and temporarily residing in a foreign country.

Experiential market knowledge is knowledge gained through experience operating in the chosen market.

Extended international assignment is up to one year. This may involve similar activities as those for short-term assignments.

External control, Concept of nature describes the concept of nature and refers to the extent to which societies try to control nature. These societies believe they can influence their environment and others to achieve their goals.

External recruitment: the assessment of the current available pool of job candidates, other than existing staff, to ascertain if any are sufficiently skilled or qualified to fill and perform existing job vacancies. When a business engages in external recruitment, a headhunter might be used to facilitate the search, contact, and recruitment process (Businessdictionary.com).

Extrinsic rewards are expected by an employee and do not lead to his or her greater satisfaction (Business dictionary.com).

Feedback, in an organizational context, is the information sent to an entity (individual or a group) about its prior behavior so that the entity may adjust its current and future behavior to achieve the desired result (Businessdictionary.com).

Feminine orientation, Hofstede study is based on the assumption that values can be distinguished as more masculine or more feminine. The feminine orientation contains preferences for life quality, modesty, and interpersonal relationships.

Field experience see *Preliminary visit*.

Foreign service inducement: PCNs often receive a salary premium as an inducement to accept a foreign assignment.

Foreign subsidiary is a partially or wholly owned company that is part of a larger corporation with headquarters in another country (Businessdictionary .com).

Functional assignments are described as more enduring assignments with local employees that involve the two-way transfer of existing processes and practices.

Genchi genbutsu stresses that production problems can only be analyzed and solved at the source and not behind a desk.

Gender egalitarianism, GLOBE study is the degree to which a collective minimizes gender inequality.

Geocentric staffing approach: the MNE is taking a global approach to its operations, recognizing that each part (subsidiaries and headquarters) makes a unique contribution with its unique competence. Subsidiaries are usually managed by TCNs.

Global industry is one in which a firm's competitive position in one country is significantly influenced by its position in other countries. Examples include commercial aircraft, semiconductors, and copiers.

Global innovator provides significant knowledge for other units.

Global mindset requires a HR manager to think globally and to formulate and implement HR policies that facilitate the development of globally oriented staff.

Going Rate Approach: the base salary for the international transfer is linked to the salary structure in the host country.

Greenfield is a type of venture where finances are employed to create a new physical facility for a business in a location where no existing facilities are currently present.

Guanxi: dyadic personal relationships between people in China.

Hard goals are objective, quantifiable and can be directly measured – such as ROI, market share, and so on.

Hardship premium compensates for challenging locations.

Heterarchy is a structural form in which a MNC may have a number of different kinds of centers apart from that traditionally referred to as 'headquarters'.

High context communication: in high context cultures a more indirect form of expression is common, where the receiver must decipher the content of the message from its context.

Home leave allowances cover the expense of one or more trips back to the home country each year.

Home-country effect refers to the extent to which management practices in multinational companies' subsidiaries are influenced by the home-country environment.

'Honeymoon' or 'tourist' phase refers to an upswing of mood upon arrival in the assignment country.

Host country is the country in which the MNC is operating and has established a foreign subsidiary.

Host-country effect refers to the extent to which management practices in multinational companies' subsidiaries are impacted by the host-country context.

Host country nationals (HCNs) . . .

Housing allowance: the provision of a housing allowance implies that employees should be entitled to maintain their home-country living standards (or, in some cases, receive accommodation that is equivalent to that provided for similar foreign employees and peers).

Human resource refers to the accumulated stock of knowledge, skills, and abilities that the individuals possess, which the firm has built up over time into an identifiable expertise.

Human resource management refers to those activities undertaken by an organization to effectively utilize its human resources. These activities would include at least the following: HR planning, staffing (recruitment, selection, placement), performance management, training and development, compensation (remuneration) and benefits, and industrial relations.

Humane orientation includes the degree to which a collective encourages and rewards individuals for being fair, altruistic, generous, caring, and kind to others.

Humane orientation, GLOBE study includes "the degree to which a collective encourages and rewards individuals for being fair, altruistic, generous, caring, and kind to others".

ILO: International Labor Organization.

Implementer relies heavily on knowledge from the parent or peer subsidiaries and creates a relatively small amount of knowledge themselves.

In-facility security comprises perimeter security, search protocols into and out of facilities (truck inspections, deliveries, etc.), internal search protocols (lockers, etc.), bomb threat procedures, risk control for violence in the facility and threats to management (including training on warning signs, protection of property and equipment, and safeguarding executives), protection and lighting in parking areas, and the use of cameras in the workplace.

In-group collectivism is the degree to which individuals express pride, loyalty, and cohesiveness in their organizations or families.

In-house security is the prevention of and protection against assault, damage, fire, fraud, invasion of privacy, theft, unlawful entry, and other such occurrences caused by deliberate action.

Index of transnationality is an average of ratios of foreign assets to total assets; foreign sales to total sales; and foreign employment to total employment.

Indirect costs of expat failure or 'invisible costs' are harder to quantify in monetary terms but can prove to be more expensive for firms.

Individualism is about the rights of the individual. It seeks to let each person grow or fail on their own, and sees group focus as denuding the individual of their inalienable rights.

Individualism, Hofstede study describes the extent to which individual initiative and caring for oneself and the nearest relatives is preferred by a society.

Industrial espionage, theft and sabotage – activities to secure internal communications (emails, telephones, etc.), open records protection, employee privacy regulations, clearly defined physical inspections, and search processes.

Industrial theft: criminal act of dishonest assumption of the rights of the true owner of a tangible or intangible property by treating it as one's own, whether or not one is taking it away with the intent of depriving the true owner of it (Businessdictionary.com).

Information speed focuses on whether information flow in groups is high or low during communication.

Innovator . . .

Inpatriate refers to the transfer of subsidiary staff into the parent-country (headquarters) operations.

Institutional collectivism, GLOBE study describes the degree to which organizational and societal institutional practices encourage and reward collective distribution of resources and collective action.

Institutionalism perspective indicates that institutional pressures may be powerful influences on HR practices. Elements which are relevant to HRM are, for example, the characteristics of the education system or the industrial relations system.

Integrated player creates knowledge but at the same time is the recipient of knowledge flows.

Intellectual capital: collective knowledge (whether or not documented) of the individuals in an organization or society. This knowledge can be used to produce wealth, multiply output of physical assets, gain competitive advantage, and/or enhance value of other types of capital (Businessdictionary.com).

Intercultural . . .

Intercultural competence is defined as the ability to function effectively in another culture.

Internal control, Concept of nature describes the concept of nature and refers to the extent to which one accepts they can only control themselves and accepts they have no control over their environment. For example, in the religion of Islam they have a saying: "If it's Allah's will".

Internal recruitment is the assessment of an employer's current staff to ascertain if any current employees are sufficiently skilled or qualified to perform required job vacancies. When a business engages in internal recruitment, a current employee might be reassigned to the new position by giving them either a promotion or an internal transfer (Businessdictionary.com).

International base pay for key managers, regardless of nationality, that is paid in a major reserve currency such as the US dollar or the euro. This system allows MNEs to deal with considerable variations in base salaries for managers.

International cadre usually refers to a group of high-potential employees who have been selected for specialized management training to enable the MNE to continue to expand its international operations.

International human resource management covers all issues related to managing the global workforce and its contribution to firm outcomes and includes comparative analyses of HRM in different countries.

International joint venture is a separate legal organizational entity representing the partial holdings of two or more parent firms, in which the headquarters of at least one is located outside the country of operation of the joint venture. This entity is subject to the joint control of its parent firms, each of which is economically and legally independent of the other.

Internationalization process theory, which is derived from the behavioral model of uncertainty avoidance, suggests that specific features of the owner or founder of an SME have an impact on the internationalization process of this particular enterprise.

Intrinsic rewards are outcomes that give an individual personal satisfaction, such as that derived from a job well done (Businessdictionary.com).

Investment strike refers to the act of some multinationals whereby the multinational refuses to invest any additional funds in a plant, thus ensuring that the plant will become obsolete and economically non-competitive.

Iron rice bowl refers to the guaranteed continuation of employment, along with various welfare and benefits offered to employees, such as accommodation, medical treatment, childcare, and pensions.

Kaizen is the continuous improvement philosophy.

Knowledge, in an organizational context, is the sum of what is known and resides in the intelligence and the competence of people (Businessdictionary.com).

Laissez-faire see *Tax, Laissez-faire*.

Lobbying The act of attempting to influence business and government leaders to create legislation or conduct an activity that will help a particular organization. People who do lobbying are called lobbyists (Businessdictionary.com).

Local innovator subsidiaries engage in the creation of relevant country/region-specific knowledge in all key functional areas because they have complete local responsibility.

Local Plus Approach is one in which expatriate employees are paid according to the prevailing salary levels, structure, and administration guidelines of the host location, plus provided 'expatriate-type' benefits such as assistance with transportation, housing, and dependents' education in recognition of the employee's 'foreign' status.

Local responsiveness is to respect local cultural values, traditions, legislation, or other institutional constraints such as government policy and/or education systems regarding HRM and work practices.

Local staff or host country national (HCN) is an employee who is a citizen of a country in which an organization's branch or plant is located, but the organization is headquartered in another country (uslegal.com).

Long-term international assignment varies from one to five years, involving a clearly defined role in the receiving operation (e.g. a senior management role in a subsidiary). The long-term assignment has also been referred to as a traditional expatriate assignment.

Long-term orientation, Confucianism dynamics is characterized by great endurance and/or persistence in pursuing goals, position of ranking based on status, adaptation of traditions to modern conditions, respect of social and status obligations within certain limits, high savings rates and high investment activity, readiness to subordinate oneself to a purpose, and the feeling of shame.

Low context communication: the players tend to communicate more to the point and verbalize all-important information.

Macro level terrorist threats are threats of a terrorist attack on the global environment.

Masculinity, Hofstede study is based on the assumption that values can be distinguished as more masculine or more feminine. The masculine orientation comprises the pursuit of financial success, heroism, and strong performance approach.

Matrix structure an organizational structure that facilitates the horizontal flow of skills and information. It is used mainly in the management of large projects or product development processes, drawing employees from different functional disciplines for assignment to a team without removing them from their respective positions. Employees in a matrix organization report on day-to-day performance to the project or product manager, whose authority flows sideways (horizontally) across departmental boundaries. They also continue to report on their overall performance to the head of their department, whose authority flows downwards (vertically) within his or her department.

Mental programs . . .

Mentor is usually in a more senior position than the expatriate, from the sending work unit, and often knows the expatriate personally. The rationale behind the use of a mentor is to alleviate the "out-of-sight, out-of-mind" feeling through the provision of information (such as workplace changes) on a regular basis, so that the expatriate is more prepared for conditions faced upon re-entry.

Merger is the result of an agreement between two companies to join their operations together.

Merit base: basing an employee's salary on his or her performance over a predetermined period and according to agreed-upon criteria (Businessdictionary.com).

Micro-level terrorist threats are threats at specific regions, industries, or levels in international value chains.

Monochrome concept of time is dominated by processes where one thing is done after the other.

Multicultural: celebrating human diversity by willingly promoting legal, political, and social recognition of cultural, ethnic, linguistic, and religious differences.

Multidomestic industry is one in which competition in each country is essentially independent of competition in other countries. Traditional examples include retailing, distribution, and insurance.

Neutral culture tends to express little emotion; business is transacted as objectively and functionally as possible.

Non-equity cross-border alliance is an investment vehicle in which profits and other responsibilities are assigned to each party according to a contract.

Non-expatriates are people who travel internationally but are not considered expatriates as they do not relocate to another country. Popular terms for these employees include 'road warriors', 'globetrotters', 'frequent fliers', and 'flexpatriates'.

OECD: the Organization for Economic Cooperation and Development.

Offshoring of labor is work done for a company by people in another country that is typically done at a much cheaper cost (Businessdictionary.com).

Operative is the individual whose assignment is to perform functional job tasks in an existing operational structure, in generally lower-level, supervisory positions.

Organizational culture is defined as the sense of common identity and purpose across the whole organization.

Parent-country nationals (PCN) see *Expatriate*.

Particularism pays more attention to individual cases, deciding what is good and correct depending on relationship and special friendship arrangements.

Partnership role . . .

Pay strategy is defined in terms of a series of interlocking strategic choices on the basis of pay (job vs. skill, performance vs. seniority), unit of aggregation, (paying individuals, groups, organizations, short- vs. long-term orientation to pay), patterns of variation in pay (variability or risk in pay, hierarchical vs. egalitarian pay orientation), and an overall focus on internal equity – as captured by job evaluation systems – as opposed to external equity, as captured by market surveys.

Performance management is a process that enables a company to evaluate and continuously improve individual, unit, and corporate performance against clearly defined, pre-set goals, and targets.

Performance orientation is defined as the degree to which a collective encourages and rewards group members for performance improvement and excellence.

Performance orientation, GLOBE study is defined as "the degree to which a collective encourages and rewards group members for performance improvement and excellence".

Performance-related-pay is a financial reward system for employees where some or all of their monetary compensation is related to how their performance is assessed relative to stated criteria (Businessdictionary.com).

Polycentric staffing approach involves the MNE treating each subsidiary as a distinct national entity with some decision-making autonomy. Subsidiaries are usually managed by local nationals (HCNs), who are seldom promoted to positions at headquarters, and PCNs are rarely transferred to foreign subsidiary operations.

Polychrome concept of time: processes actions occur at the same time.

Power distance, GLOBE study is defined as "the degree to which members of a collective expect power to be distributed equally".

Power distance, Hofstede study represents the scale on which the members of a culture accept that power is not distributed equally in institutions. It expresses the emotional distance between employees and superiors. Power inequality exists in many cultures but may be more or less pronounced from culture to culture.

Pre-departure training is a set of training programmes provided before expatriates depart for their overseas assignment, designed to increase the success of expatriates in their international assignments; training might include cross-cultural and language training, business etiquette, and so on (Referencebusiness.com).

Preliminary visit to the host country is a well-planned visit for the candidate and spouse that provides a preview that allows them to assess their suitability for and interest in the assignment. Such a visit also serves to introduce expatriate candidates to the business context in the host location and helps encourage more informed pre-departure preparation.

Primary terrorist threats are threats at the level of the individual person and firm.

Processes refer to activities that firms use to convert the resources into valuable goods and services.

Psychological contract is the unwritten understandings and informal obligations between an employer and its employees regarding their mutual expectations of how each will perform their respective roles. Within a typical business, the psychological contract might include such things as the levels of employee commitment, job satisfaction, and the quality of working conditions (Businessdictionary.com).

Recruitment is defined as searching for and obtaining potential job candidates in sufficient numbers and of sufficient quality so that the organization can select the most appropriate people to fill its job needs.

Redundancy is the elimination of jobs or job categories caused by downsizing, rightsizing, or outsourcing (Businessdictionary.com).

Regiocentric staffing approach reflects the geographic strategy and structure of the MNE. Like the geocentric approach, it utilizes a wider pool of managers but in a limited way. Staff may move outside their home countries but only within the particular geographic region.

Relocation allowances typically cover items including moving, shipping, and storage charges; temporary living expenses; subsidies regarding appliance or car purchases (or sales); and down-payments or lease-related charges.

Remuneration is the reward for employment in the form of pay, salary, or wage, including allowances, benefits (such as company car, medical plan, pension plan), bonuses, cash incentives, and monetary value of the non-cash incentives (Businessdictionary.com).

Repatriation is the activity of bringing the expatriate back to the home country.

Resources are defined as tangible assets such as money and people, and intangible assets such as brands and relationships.

Reverse diffusion is the transfer of management practices from foreign locations to the headquarters.

Risk management is the identification, analysis, assessment, control and avoidance, minimization, or elimination of unacceptable risks. An organization may use risk assumption, risk avoidance, risk retention, risk transfer, or any other strategy (or combination of strategies) in proper management of future events (Businessdictionary.com).

Role plays involve acting out a role player's actions in a simulated situation such as a training program (Businessdictionary.com).

Rotational assignments: employees commute from the home country to a place of work in another country for a short, set period followed by a break in the home country. The employee's family usually remains in the home country.

Selection is the process of gathering information for the purposes of evaluating and deciding who should be employed in particular jobs.

Selection criteria: list of knowledge, abilities, experience, and skills one must have in order to perform the job successfully.

Self-initiated assignments: while standard expatriations are usually initiated by the organization, self-initiated assignments are initiated by the individual.

Sensitivity training is designed to make people more aware of group dynamics and their own behavior, interpersonal traits, and role within a group (Businessdictionary.com).

Short-term international assignment is up to three months. These are usually for troubleshooting, project supervision, or a stopgap measure until a more permanent arrangement can be found.

Short-term, Confucianism dynamics are characterized by: personal candor and stability, avoiding loss of face, respect of social and status obligations without the consideration of costs, low savings rates and low investment activity, expectations of quick profit, respect for traditions, and greetings, presents, and courtesies based on reciprocity.

Six Sigma quality control was originally developed in 1986 by Motorola, and the business management strategy is now used in many different industries in an effort to improve the quality of products or services produced by the business through the removal of defects and errors. The strategy involves creating groups of people within the business or organization who have expert status in various methods, and then carrying out each project according to a set of steps in an effort to reach specific financial milestones.

Social dumping is the movement of work from one region to another and its effect on employment levels; and the need for trade union solidarity to prevent workers in one region from accepting pay cuts to attract investment at the expense of workers in another region.

Soft goals tend to be relationship- or trait-based, such as leadership style or interpersonal skills.

Software of the mind . . .

Spatial orientation is the focus on the distance between people of various cultures when communicating. Distance that is adequate for members of one culture may feel intrusive for members of another culture.

Specific culture is characterized by: a small private life that is kept private; a large social/public life that is very open to others; extroversion; 'no-nonsense' directness in communications; and a clear distinction between work and personal life.

Spouse assistance helps guard against or offset income lost by an expatriate's spouse as a result of relocating abroad.

Standardization-localization is a system of processes and procedures that operates effectively in multiple countries by exploiting local differences and interdependencies and at the same time sustaining global consistency.

Strategic assignments refer to high-profile activities that focus on developing a balanced global perspective.

Strategy implementer . . .

Strikes are a collective, organized cessation or slowdown of work by employees to force acceptance of their demands by the employer (Businessdictionary.com).

Structure reproducer carries the assignment of building or reproducing in a foreign subsidiary a structure similar to that which he or she knows from another part of the company.

Sub-optimizing is knowingly accepting less than the best possible outcome or output, in order to avoid unintended adverse effects of trying harder (Businessdictionary.com).

Tacit knowledge is an unwritten, unspoken, and hidden vast storehouse of knowledge held by practically every normal human being, based on his or her emotions, experiences, insights, intuition, observations, and internalized information. Tacit knowledge is integral to the entirety of a person's consciousness, is acquired largely through association with other people, and requires joint or shared activities to be imparted from one to another.

Tacitness . . .

Tax equalization firms withhold an amount equal to the home-country tax obligation of the expatriate, and pay all taxes in the host country.

Tax protection: the employee pays up to the amount of taxes he or she would pay on compensation in the home country.

Tax, Ad hoc: each expatriate is handled differently, depending upon the individual package agreed to with the MNE.

Tax, Laissez-faire employees are "on their own" in conforming to host-country and home-country taxation laws and practices.

Technical assignments refer to short-term knowledge transference activities.

The costs of expatriate failure can be both direct and indirect.

Third country nationals (TCNs) . . .

Trade unions are organizations whose membership consists of workers and union leaders, united to protect and promote their common interests. The principal purposes of a labor union are to (1) negotiate wages and working condition terms; (2) regulate relations between workers (its members) and the employer; (3) take collective action to enforce the terms of collective bargaining; (4) raise new demands on behalf of its members; and (5) help settle their grievances.

Traditional expatriate assignment . . .

Training aims to improve employees' current work skills and behavior.

Transnational is an organizational form that is characterized by an interdependence of resources and responsibilities across all business units regardless of national boundaries. The term has also become a descriptor of a particular type of multinational – one that tries to cope with the large flows of components, products, resources, people, and information among its subsidiaries, while simultaneously recognizing distributed specialized resources and capabilities.

Transnational corporate is a commercial enterprise that operates substantial facilities, does business in more than one country, and does not consider any particular country its national home (Businessdictionary.com).

Troubleshooter is the individual who is sent to a foreign subsidiary to analyze and solve a particular operational problem.

Turnover rates are a human resources metric which expresses the number of employees lost through firing, attrition, and other means compared to the total number of employees in the company (Businessdictionary.com).

Uncertainty avoidance, GLOBE study includes "the extent to which a society, organization, or group relies on social norms, rules, and procedures to alleviate unpredictability of future events".

Uncertainty avoidance, Hofstede study represents the extent to which the members of a culture feel threatened by uncertain, ambiguous, and/or unstructured situations and try to avoid them. Cultures with strong uncertainty avoidance are characterized by strict beliefs and behavioral codes and do not tolerate people and ideas that deviate from these. In cultures with weak uncertainty avoidance, the significance of practice exceeds the significance of principles and there is high tolerance for deviations.

UNCTAD: the United Nations Conference on Trade and Development.

Universalism is characterized by the logic: "What is good and right can be defined and always applies".

Values are the ways in which employees think about what they do and why they do it. Values shape employees' priorities and decision-making.

Virtual assignees monitor and evaluate a physically and geographically distant group of employees.

Virtual assignments: where the employee does not relocate to a host location but manages, from home base, various international responsibilities for a part of the organization in another country. In this case, the manager relies heavily on communications technologies such as telephone, email, or video conferences. Visits to the host country are also necessary.

Workplace violence is the expression of physical or verbal force against other people in the workplace. Workplace violence activities range from threats and verbal abuse to actual physical contact and assaults that cause physical harm to other people (Businessdictionary.com).

INDEX